FOUNDATIONS OF NEURAL NETWORKS, FUZZY SYSTEMS, AND KNOWLEDGE ENGINEERING

FOUNDATIONS OF NEURAL NETWORKS, FUZZY SYSTEMS, AND KNOWLEDGE ENGINEERING

Nikola K. Kasabov

A Bradford Book
The MIT Press
Cambridge, Massachusetts
London, England

This book was set in Times Roman by Asco Trade Typesetting Ltd., Hong Kong and was printed and bound in the United States of America.

Library of Congress Cataloging-in-Publication Data

Kasabov, Nikola K.
  Foundations of neural networks, fuzzy systems, and knowledge
engineering / Nikola K. Kasabov.
      p.   cm.
  "A Bradford book."
  Includes bibliographical references and index.
  ISBN 0-262-11212-4 (hc : alk. paper)
  1. Expert systems (Computer science) 2. Neural networks (Computer
science) 3. Fuzzy systems. 4. Artificial intelligence. I. Title.
QA76.76.E95K375   1996
006.3—dc20   95-50054
                                                         CIP

To my mother and the memory of my father,
and to my family, Diana, Kapka, and Assia

Contents

Foreword

We are surprisingly flexible in processing information in the real world. The human brain, consisting of 10^{11} neurons, realizes intelligent information processing based on exact and commonsense reasoning. Scientists have been trying to implement human intelligence in computers in various ways. Artificial intelligence (AI) pursues exact logical reasoning based on symbol manipulation. Fuzzy engineering uses analog values to realize fuzzy but robust and efficient reasoning. They are macroscopic ways to realize human intelligence at the level of symbols and rules. Neural networks are a microscopic approach to the intelligence of the brain in which information is represented by excitation patterns of neurons.

All of these approaches are partially successful in implementing human intelligence, but are still far from the real one. AI uses mathematically rigorous logical reasoning but is not flexible and is difficult to implement. Fuzzy systems provide convenient and flexible methods of reasoning at the sacrifice of depth and exactness. Neural networks use learning and self-organizing ability but are difficult for handling symbolic reasoning. The point is how to design computerized reasoning, taking account of these methods.

This book solves this problem by combining the three techniques to minimize their weaknesses and enhance their strong points. The book begins with an excellent introduction to AI, fuzzy-, and neuroengineering. The author succeeds in explaining the fundamental ideas and practical methods of these techniques by using many familiar examples. The reason for his success is that the book takes a problem-driven approach by presenting problems to be solved and then showing ideas of how to solve them, rather than by following the traditional theorem-proof style. The book provides an understandable approach to knowledge-based systems for problem solving by combining different methods of AI, fuzzy systems, and neural networks.

Shun-ichi Amari
Tokyo University
June 1995

Preface

The symbolic AI systems have been associated in the last decades with two main issues—the representation issue and the processing (reasoning) issue. They have proved effective in handling problems characterized by exact and complete representation. Their reasoning methods are sequential by nature. Typical AI techniques are propositional logic, predicate logic, and production systems.

However, the symbolic AI systems have very little power in dealing with inexact, uncertain, corrupted, imprecise, or ambiguous information. Neural networks and fuzzy systems are different approaches to introducing humanlike reasoning to knowledge-based intelligent systems. They represent different paradigms of information processing, but they have similarities that make their common teaching, reading, and practical use quite natural and logical. Both paradigms have been useful for representing inexact, incomplete, corrupted data, and for approximate reasoning over uncertain knowledge. Fuzzy systems, which are based on Zadeh's fuzzy logic theory, are effective in representing explicit but amgibuous common-sense knowledge, whereas neural networks provide excellent facilities for approximating data, learning knowledge from data, approximate reasoning, and parallel processing. Evidence from research on the brain shows that the way we think is formed by sequential and parallel processes. Knowledge engineering benefits greatly from combining symbolic, neural computation, and fuzzy computation.

Many recent applications of neural networks and fuzzy systems show an increased interest in using either one or both of them in one system. This book represents an engineering approach to both neural networks and fuzzy systems. The main goal of the book is to explain the principles of neural networks and fuzzy systems and to demonstrate how they can be applied to building knowledge-based systems for problem solving. To achieve this goal the three main subjects of the book—knowledge-based systems, fuzzy systems, and neural networks—are described at three levels: a conceptual level; an intermediate, logical level; and a low, generic level in chapters 2, 3, and 4, respectively. This approach makes possible a comparative analysis between the rule-based, the connectionist, and the fuzzy methods for knowledge-engineering.

The same or similar problems are solved by using AI rule-based methods, fuzzy methods, connectionist methods, hybrid AI-connectionist, or hybrid fuzzy-connectionist methods and systems. Production systems are chosen as the most widely used paradigm for knowledge-engineering.

Symbolic AI production systems, fuzzy production systems, connectionist production systems, and hybrid connectionist production systems are discussed, developed, and applied throughout the book. Different methods of using neural networks for knowledge representation and processing are presented and illustrated with real and benchmark problems (see chapter 5). One approach to using neural networks for knowledge engineering is to develop connectionist expert systems which contain their knowledge in trained-in-advance neural networks. The learning ability of neural networks is used here for accumulating knowledge from data even if the knowledge is not explicitly representable. Some learning methods allow the knowledge engineer to extract explicit, exact, or fuzzy rules from a trained neural network. These methods are also discussed in chapter 5. There are methods to incorporate both knowledge acquired from data and explicit heuristic knowledge in a neural network. This approach to expert systems design provides an excellent opportunity to use collected data (existing databases) and prior knowledge (rules) and to integrate them in the same knowledge base, approximating reality.

Another approach to knowledge engineering is using hybrid connectionist systems. They incorporate both connectionist and traditional AI methods for knowledge representation and processing. They are usually hierarchical. At a lower level they use neural networks for rapid recognition, classification, approximation, and learning. The higher level, where the final solution of the problem has to be communicated, usually contains explicit knowledge (see chapter 6). The attempt to use neural networks for structural representation of existing explicit knowledge has led to different connectionist architectures. One of them is connectionist production systems. The fusion between neural networks, fuzzy systems, and symbolic AI methods is called "comprehensive AI." Building comprehensive AI systems is illustrated in chapter 6, using two examples—speech recognition and stock market prediction.

Neural networks and fuzzy systems may manifest a chaotic behavior on the one hand. On the other, they can be used to predict and control chaos. The basics of chaos theory are presented in chapter 7. When would neural networks or fuzzy systems behave chaotically? What is a chaotic neural network? These and other topics are discussed in chapter 7. Chapter 7 also comments briefly on new developments in neural dynamics and fuzzy systems.

This book represents an engineering problem-driven approach to neural networks, fuzzy systems, and expert systems. The main question answered in the book is: If we were given a difficult AI problem, how could we apply neural networks, or fuzzy systems, or a hybrid system to solve the problem? Pattern recognition, speech and image processing, classification, planning, optimization, prediction, control, decision making, and game simulations are among the typical generic AI problems discussed in the book, illustrated with concrete, specific problems.

The biological and psychological plausibility of the connectionist and fuzzy models have not been seriously tackled in this book, though issues like biological neurons, brain structure, humanlike problem solving, and the psychological roots of heuristic problem-solving are given attention.

This book is intended to be used as a textbook for upper undergraduate and postgraduate students from science and engineering, business, art, and medicine, but chapters 1 and 2 and some sections from the other chapters can be used for lower-level undergraduate courses and even for introducing high school students to AI paradigms and knowledge-engineering. The book encompasses my experience in teaching courses in Knowledge Engineering, Neural Networks and Fuzzy Systems, and Intelligent Information Systems. Chapters 5 and 6 include some original work which gives the book a little bit of the flavor of a monograph. But that is what I teach at the postgraduate level.

The material presented in this book is "software independent." Some of the software required for doing the problems, questions, and projects sections, like speech processors, neural network simulators, and fuzzy system simulators, are standard simulators which can be obtained in the public domain or on the software market, for example, the software package MATLAB. A small education software environment and data sets for experimenting with are explained in the appendixes.

I thank my students and associates for the accurately completed assignments and experiments. Some of the results are included in the book as illustrations. I should mention at least the following names: Jay Garden, Max Bailey, Stephen Sinclair, Catherine Watson, Rupert Henderson, Paul Jones, Chris Maffey, Richard Kilgour, Tim Albertson, Grant Holdom, Andrew Gray, Michael Watts, and Jonas Ljungdahl from the University of Otago, Dunedin, New Zealand; Stephan Shishkov, Evgeni Peev, Rumen Trifonov, Daniel Nikovski, Nikolai Nikolaev, Sylvia Petrova, Petar

Kalinkov, and Christo Neshev from the Technical University in Sofia, Bulgaria; and L. Chen and C. Tan, masters students from the University of Essex, England, during the year 1991.

In spite of the numerous experiments applying neural networks and fuzzy systems to knowledge-engineering which I have conducted with the help of students and colleagues over the last 8 years, I would probably not have written this book without the inspiration I received from reading the remarkable monograph of Bart Kosko, *Neural Networks and Fuzzy Systems* (Englewood Cliffs, NJ, Prentice Hall, 1992); nor without the discussions I have with Shun-ichi Amari, Lotfi Zadeh, Teuvo Kohonen, John Taylor, Takeshi Yamakawa, Ron Sun, Anca Ralescu, Kunihiko Fukushima, Jaap van den Herik, Duc Pham, Toshiro Terano, Eli Sanches, Guido Deboeck, Alex Waibel, Nelson Morgan, Y. Takagi, Takeshi Furuhashi, Toshio Fukuda, Rao Vemuri, Janusz Kacprzyk, Igor Aleksander, Philip Treleaven, Masumi Ishikawa, David Aha, Adi Bulsara, Laslo Koczy, Kaoru Hirota, Jim Bezdek, John Andreae, Jim Austin, Lakmi Jain, Tom Gedeon, and many other colleagues and pioneers in the fields of neural networks, fuzzy systems, symbolic AI systems, and nonlinear dynamics. Before I finished the last revision of the manuscript a remarkable book was published by The MIT Press: *The Handbook of Brain Theory and Neural Networks*, edited by Michael Arbib. The handbook can be used for finding more detail on several topics presented and discussed in this book. It took me three years to prepare this book. Despite the many ups and downs encountered during that period I kept believing that it would be a useful book for my students. I thank my colleagues from the Department of Information Science at the University of Otago for their support in establishing the courses for which I prepared this book, especially my colleagues and friends Martin Anderson, Philip Sallis, and Martin Purvis. Martin Anderson carefully read the final version of the book and made many valuable comments and suggestions for improvement. I would like to thank Tico Cohen for his cooperation in the experiments on effluent water flow prediction and sewage process control. I was also encouraged by the help Gaynor Corkery gave me as she proofread the book in its preliminary version in 1994.

And last, but not least, I thank The MIT Press, and especially Harry Stanton for his enthusiastic and professional support throughout the three-year period of manuscript preparation.

FOUNDATIONS OF NEURAL NETWORKS, FUZZY SYSTEMS, AND KNOWLEDGE ENGINEERING

1   The Faculty of Knowledge Engineering and Problem Solving

This chapter is an introduction to AI paradigms, AI problems, and to the basics of neural networks and fuzzy systems. The importance and the need for new methods of knowledge acquisition, knowledge representation, and knowledge processing in a climate of uncertainty is emphasized. The use of fuzzy systems and neural networks as new prospective methods in this respect is briefly outlined from a conceptual point of view. The main generic AI problems are described. Some specific problems, which are used for illustration throughout the book, are also introduced. A heuristic problem-solving approach is discussed and applied to some of them. A general approach to problem solving and knowledge engineering is presented at the end of the chapter and developed further on in the book.

1.1   Introduction to AI Paradigms

Artificial intelligence comprises methods, tools, and systems for solving problems that normally require the intelligence of humans. The term *intelligence* is always defined as the ability to learn effectively, to react adaptively, to make proper decisions, to communicate in language or images in a sophisticated way, and to understand. The main objectives of AI are to develop methods and systems for solving problems, usually solved by the intellectual activity of humans, for example, image recognition, language and speech processing, planning, and prediction, thus enhancing computer information systems; and to develop models which simulate living organisms and the human brain in particular, thus improving our understanding of how the human brain works.

The main AI directions of development are to develop methods and systems for solving AI problems without following the way humans do so, but providing similar results, for example, expert systems; and to develop methods and systems for solving AI problems by modeling the human way of thinking or the way the brain works physically, for example, artificial neural networks.

In general, AI is about modeling human intelligence. There are two main paradigms adopted in AI in order to achieve this: (1) the *symbolic*, and (2) the *subsymbolic*. The first is based on symbol manipulation and the second on neurocomputing.

The *symbolic paradigm* is based on the theory of physical symbolic systems (Newel and Simon 1972). A symbolic system consists of two sets:

(1) a set of elements (or symbols) which can be used to construct more complicated elements or structures; and (2) a set of processes and rules, which, when applied to symbols and structures, produce new structures. The symbols have semantic meanings. They represent concepts or objects. Propositional logic, predicate logic, and the production systems explained in chapter 2 facilitate dealing with symbolic systems. Some of their corresponding AI implementations are the simple rule-based systems, the logic programming and production languages, also discussed in chapter 2. Symbolic AI systems have been applied to natural language processing, expert systems, machine learning, modeling cognitive processes, and others. Unfortunately, they do not perform well in all cases when inexact, missing, or uncertain information is used, when only raw data are available and knowledge acquisition should be performed, or when parallel solutions need to be elaborated. These tasks do not prove to be difficult for humans.

The subsymbolic paradigm (Smolenski 1990) claims that intelligent behavior is performed at a subsymbolic level which is higher than the neuronal level in the brain but different from the symbolic one. Knowledge processing is about changing states of networks constructed of small elements called neurons, replicating the analogy with real neurons. A neuron, or a collection of neurons, can represent a microfeature of a concept or an object. It has been shown that it is possible to design an intelligent system that achieves the proper global behavior even though all the components of the system are simple and operate on purely local information. The subsymbolic paradigm makes possible not only the use of all the significant results in the area of artificial neural networks achieved over the last 20 years in areas like pattern recognition and image and speech processing but also makes possible the use of connectionist models for knowledge processing. The latter is one of the objectives of this book. As the subsymbolic models move closer, though slowly, to the human brain, it is believed that this is the right way to understand and model human intelligence for knowledge engineering.

There are several ways in which the symbolic and subsymbolic models of knowledge processing may interact:

1. They can be developed and used separately and alternatively.

2. Hybrid systems that incorporate both symbolic and subsymbolic systems can be developed.

3. Subsymbolic systems can be used to model pure symbolic systems.

So, there is a third paradigm—a *mixture of symbolic and subsymbolic systems*. We shall see that fuzzy systems can represent symbolic knowledge, but they also use numerical representation similar to the one used in subsymbolic systems.

At the moment it seems that aggregation of symbolic and subsymbolic methods provides in most cases the best possible solutions to complex AI problems.

1.2   Heuristic Problem Solving; Genetic Algorithms

1.2.1   The Fascinating World of Heuristics

Humans use a lot of heuristics in their everyday life to solve various problems, from "simple" ones like recognizing a chair, to more complex problems like driving a jet in a completely new spatial environment. We learn heuristics throughout our life. And that is where computers fail. They cannot learn "commonsense knowledge," at least not as much and as fast as we can. How to represent heuristics in computers is a major problem of AI. Even simple heuristics, which every child can learn quickly, may not be easy to represent in a computer program.

For example, every small child can, after exercising for a little while, balance a pencil upright on the palm or finger. The child learns simple heuristics, for example, if the pencil is moving in one direction, then you move your palm in the same direction, the speed depending on the speed of movement of the pencil. If only two directions, that is, "forward" and "backward" are allowed, then the heuristics are simplified, for example, if the pencil is moving forward, then the palm is moved forward, or if the pencil is moving backward, then the palm is moved backward. The heuristic rules for solving this task are in reality more complex, involving, for example, the speed of movement of the pencil. But they number about a dozen. Is that all we use to do this very complicated task? And is it possible to teach a computer these heuristics? How many heuristic rules do we use when frying eggs, for example? Do we use millions of rules for the number of the different possible situations that may arise are, such as the size of the pan, the size of the eggs, the temperature of the heating element, the preferences of those waiting to eat the eggs, the availability of different ingredients, etc? Or do we use a simple set of heuristic rules, a "can" of rules only? The second suggestion seems to be more realistic as we cannot have billions of rules in our mind to do all the everyday simple and complex tasks. But now the question arises: How can we represent in a computer program this small set of rules for solving a particular problem? Can we represent commonsense skills and build a computer program which balances an inverted pendulum, or balances other objects or processes which need balancing, for example, the temperature and humidity in a room, an airplane when flying or landing?

Take another example—car or truck driving. Anyone who has a driving licence knows how to park a car. He or she applies "commonsense" knowledge, and skill. At any moment the situation is either very different or slightly different from what the person has experienced before. Is it possible to represent the "common sense" of an ordinary driver in a computer and to build a program which automatically parks the car when the parameters describing its position are known?

These examples show the fascinating world of heuristics—their power, their expressiveness, the "mystery" of their interpretation in the human mind, and the challenge for implementing them in computers. Articulating heuristics for solving AI problems is discussed and illustrated later in this chapter, and their computer implementation is given later in the book. Symbolic expert systems, fuzzy systems, neural networks, genetic algorithms, they all ease the efforts of the knowledge engineers to represent and interpret heuristics in computers.

1.2.2   The Philosophy of the Heuristic Problem-Solving Approach

When a problem is defined, it is usually assumed that a set of n independent input variables (attributes) $x_1, x_2, \ldots, x_n$, and a set of m variables of the solution $y_1, y_2, \ldots, y_m$, are defined, for which observations or rules are known. Every possible combination of values for the input variables can be represented as a vector $\mathbf{d} = (a_1, a_2, \ldots, a_n)$ in the domain space D, and every possible value for the set of output variables can be represented as a vector $\mathbf{s} = (b_1, b_2, \ldots, b_m)$ in the solution space S.

An ideal case is when we have a formula that gives the optimal solution for every input vector from the domain space. But this is not the case in reality. The majority of the known AI problems do not have a single formula that can be used.

In general, problem-solving can be viewed as mapping the domain space D into the solution space S. Usually the number of all possible

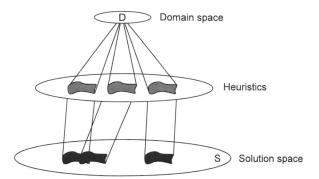

Figure 1.1
Heuristics as a means of obtaining restricted projections from the domain space (*D*) into the solution space (*S*).

solutions is huge, even for simple problems. An exhaustive search in the solution space means testing all the possible vectors in the solution space and then finding the best one. This is unrealistic and some methods for restricting the zones where a solution will be sought have to be found. If we refer to the way people solve problems, we can see that they do not check all the possible solutions yet they are still successful at problem-solving. The reason is that they use past experience and heuristic rules which direct the search into appropriate zones where an acceptable solution to the problem may be found. Heuristics are the means of obtaining restricted projection of the domain space *D* to patches in the solution space *S*, as is graphically represented in figure 1.1.

Heuristic (it is of Greek origin) means discovery. Heuristic methods are based on experience, rational ideas, and rules of thumb. Heuristics are based more on common sense than on mathematics. Heuristics are useful, for example, when the optimal solution needs an exhaustive search that is not realistic in terms of time. In principle, a heuristic does not guarantee the best solution, but a heuristic solution can provide a tremendous short-cut in cost and time.

Many problems do not have an algorithm or formula to find an exact solution. In this case heuristics are the only way. Some examples are diagnosis of automobile problems, medical diagnosis, or creating a plan. All these problems belong to the AI area. When heuristics are used to speed up the search for a solution in the solution space *S*, we can evaluate the "goodness" of every state *s* in *S* by an evaluation function: $h(s) = \text{cost}$

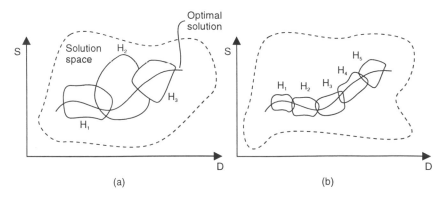

Figure 1.2
(a) Ill-informed and (b) well-informed heuristics. They are represented as "patches" in the problem space. The patches have different forms (usually quadrilateral) depending on the way of representing the heuristics in a computer program.

(s, g), where g is the goal state. A heuristic H1 is "more informed" than a heuristic H2 if the cost of the states obtained by H1 is less than the cost of the states obtained by H2. Ill-informed heuristics require more search and lead to worse solutions, in contrast to well-informed heuristics. Figure 1.2 is a graphical representation of ill-informed heuristics (a), and well-informed heuristics (b), in a hypothetical problem space (D, domain space; S, solution space). Heuristics contain symbols, statements, and concepts, no matter how well defined they are. A general form of a heuristic rule is:

IF ⟨conditions⟩, THEN ⟨conclusions⟩

What heuristic for solving a given problem can we use when, for example, we have past data available only? One possible heuristic is the following:

IF the new input vector $\mathbf{d}'$ is similar to a past data set input vector $\mathbf{d}_i$, THEN assume that the solution $\mathbf{s}'$ for $\mathbf{d}'$ is similar to the solution $\mathbf{s}_i$ for $\mathbf{d}_i$.

Generally speaking, problem knowledge for solving a given problem may consist of heuristic rules or formulas that comprise the *explicit* knowledge, and past-experience data that comprise the *implicit, hidden knowledge*. Knowledge represents links between the domain space and the solution space, the space of the independent variables and the space of the dependent variables.

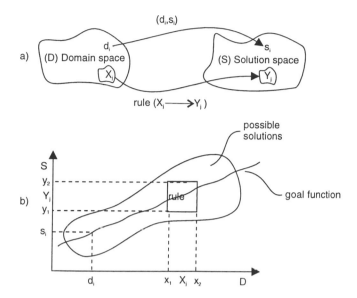

Figure 1.3
The problem knowledge maps the domain space into the solution space and approximates
the objective (goal) function: (a) a general case; (b) a two-dimensional case.

The goal of a problem-solving system is to map the domain space into
the solution space and to find the best possible solution for any input data
from the domain space. The optimal, desired mapping is called *objective* or
goal function. Two types of objective functions can be distinguished: (1)
computable functions, that is, there exists an algorithm or heuristics to
represent them; and (2) *random functions*, where the mapping is random
and noncomputable. We deal in this book with the computable functions.
This class also includes the chaotic functions, even though the latter seem
to manifest random behavior.

Past, historical data can be represented as pairs $(\mathbf{d}_i, \mathbf{s}_i)$ of input-output
vectors, for $i = 1, 2, \ldots, p$. Heuristic rules in a knowledge base can be
represented in the form of: IF Xj, THEN Yj, $j = 1, 2, \ldots, N$ (or, simply
$Xj \rightarrow Yj$), where Xj is a collection of input vectors (a pattern, a "patch"
in the input domain space) and Yj is a collection of output vectors (an
output pattern, a "patch" in the output solution space). Figure 1.3 represents the problem-solving process as mapping the domain space D into the
solution space S.

The heuristic rules should be either articulated or learned by a learning system that uses past data, instances, and examples of successful solutions of the problem. In order to learn heuristics from past data, learning methods are necessary, that is, heuristics which say "how to learn heuristic rules from past data."

The information learned by a learning system may or may not be comprehensible to us. We may need to use both approaches and combine knowledge acquired by humans with that learned by a system. A formula that gives a partial solution to the problem may also be available. This formula should also be incorporated into the knowledge-based system for solving the given problem.

Of course, methods and tools are required to accomplish the problem-solving mapping. The symbolic AI methods, while designed to solve typical AI problems, cannot accomplish this task completely. They do not provide good tools for partial mapping, for learning to approximate the goal function, for adaptive learning when new data are coming through the solution process, for representing uncertain and inexact knowledge. These requirements for solving AI problems are fulfilled by the inherent characteristics of the fuzzy systems and neural networks, especially when applied in combination with the symbolic AI systems. Fuzzy systems are excellent tools for representing heuristic, commonsense rules. Fuzzy inference methods apply these rules to data and infer a solution. Neural networks are very efficient at learning heuristics from data. They are "good problem solvers" when past data are available. Both fuzzy systems and neural networks are universal approximators in a sense, that is, for a given continuous objective function there will be a fuzzy system and a neural network which approximate it to any degree of accuracy. This is discussed in detail in chapters 3 and 4.

Learning from data is a general problem for knowledge-engineering. How can we learn about an unknown objective function $y = F(x)$? Statistical methods require a predefined model of estimation (linear, polynomial, etc.). Learning approximations from raw data is a problem which has been well performed by neural networks. They do not need any predefined function type. They are "model-free" (Kosko 1992). They can learn "what is necessary" to be learned from data, that is, they can learn selectively. They can capture different types of uncertainties, including statistical and probabilistic. It is possible to mix in a hybrid system explicit heuristic rules and past-experience data. These techniques are demonstrated in chapter 6.

A brilliant example of a heuristic approach to solving optimization problems are the genetic algorithms introduced by John Holland in 1975.

1.2.3 Genetic Algorithms

A typical example of a heuristic method for problem solving is the genetic approach used in what is known as genetic algorithms. Genetic algorithms solve complex combinatorial and organizational problems with many variants, by employing analogy with nature's evolution. Genetic algorithms were introduced by John Holland (1975) and further developed by him and other researchers.

Nature's diversity of species is tremendous. How does mankind evolve into the enormous variety of variants—in other words, how does nature solve the optimization problem of perfecting mankind? One answer to this question may be found in Charles Darwin's theory of evolution. The most important terms used in the genetic algorithms are analogous to the terms used to explain the evolutionary processes. They are:

• *Gene*—a basic unit, which controls a property of an individual.

• *Chromosome*—a string of genes; it is used to represent an individual, or a possible solution of a problem in the solution space.

• *Population*—a collection of individuals.

• *Crossover* (*mating*) operation—substrings of different individuals are taken and new strings (offsprings) are produced.

• *Mutation*—random change of a gene in a chromosome.

• *Fitness* (*goodness*) function—a criterion which evaluates each individual.

• *Selection*—a procedure for choosing a part of the population that will continue the process of searching for the best solution, while the other part of the population "dies".

A simple genetic algorithm consists of the steps shown in figure 1.4. Figure 1.5 shows graphically the solution process at consecutive time moments in the solution state space. The solution process over time has been "stretched" in the space.

1. Initialize population of possible solutions

2. WHILE a criterion for termination is not reached DO
     {
          2a. Crossover two specimens ("mother and father") and generate new
             individuals;
          2b. Select the most promising ones, according to a fitness function;
          2c. Development (if at all);
          2d. Possible mutation (rare) }
     }

Figure 1.4
An outline of a genetic algorithm.

There is no need for in-depth problem knowledge when using this method of approaching a complex multioptional optimization problem. What is needed here is merely a "fitness" or "goodness" criterion for the selection of the most promising individuals (they may be partial solutions to the problem). This criterion may require a mutation as well, which could be a heuristic approach of the "trial-and-error" type. This implies keeping (recording) the best solutions at each of the stages.

Genetic algorithms are usually illustrated by game problems. Such is a version of the "mastermind" game, in which one of two players thinks up a number (e.g., 001010) and the other has to find it out with a minimal number of questions. Each question is a hypothesis (solution) to which the first player replies with another number indicating the number of correctly guessed figures. This number is the criterion for the selection of the most promising or prospective variant which will take the second player to eventual success. If there is no improvement after a certain number of steps, this is a hint that a change should be introduced. Such change is called mutation. "When" and "how" to introduce mutation are difficult questions which need more in-depth investigation. An example of solving the "guess the number" game by using a simple genetic algorithm is given in figure 1.6.

In this game success is achieved after 16 questions, which is four times faster than checking all the possible combinations, as there are $2^6 = 64$ possible variants. There is no need for mutation in the above example. If it were needed, it could be introduced by changing a bit (a gene) by random selection. Mutation would have been necessary if, for example,

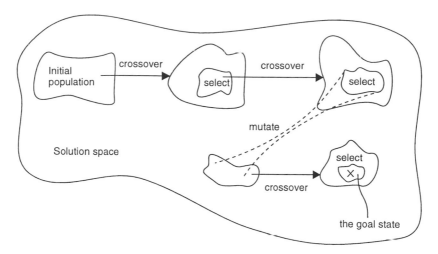

Figure 1.5
A graphical representation of a genetic algorithm.

there was 0 in the third bit of all three initial individuals, because no matter how the most prospective individuals are combined, by copying a precise part of their code we can never change this bit into 1. Mutation takes evolution out of a "dead end."

The example above illustrates the class of simple genetic algorithms introduced by John Holland, they are characterized by the following:

• *Simple, binary genes*, that is, the genes take values of 0 and 1 only.

• *Simple, fixed single-point crossover operation*: The crossover operation is done by choosing a point where a chromosome is divided into two parts swapped with the two parts taken from another individual.

• *Fixed-length encoding*, that is, the chromosomes had fixed length of genes.

Many complex optimization problems find their way to a solution through genetic algorithms. Such problems are, for example, the Traveling Salesman Problem (TSP)—finding the cheapest way to visit *n* towns without visiting a town twice; the Min Cut Problem—cutting a graph with minimum links between the cut parts; adaptive control; applied physics problems; optimization of the parameters of complex computational

```
Second player
Answer (according to the criterion 001010)
Produced variants (individuals)
        A) 010101      1
        B) 111101      1
        C) 011011      4  *
        D) 101100      3  *

Using the criterion, the best ones are chosen - C (mother) and D (father).
        Mating          New variants     Evaluation
        C) 01:1011      E) 01:1100       3
        D) 10:1100      F) 10:1011       4 *
        C) 0110:11      G) 0110:00       4 *
        D) 1011:00      H) 1011:11       3

Selection of F (mother) and G (father)
        Mating          New variants     Evaluation
        F) 1:01011      H) 1:11000       3
        G) 0:11000      I) 0:01011       5 *
        F) 101:011      J) 101:000       4 *
        G) 011:000      K) 011:011       4

Selection of I (mother) and J (father)
        Mating          New variants     Evaluation
        I) 0010:11      L) 0010:00       5
        J) 1010:00      M) 1010:11       4
        I) 00101:1      N) 00101:0       6 (success) * END
        J) 10100:0      O) 10100:1       3
```

Figure 1.6
An example of a genetic algorithm applied to the game "guess the number."

models; optimization of neural network architectures; finding fuzzy rules and membership functions for the fuzzy values, etc.

The main issues in using genetic algorithms are the choice of genetic operations (mating, selection, mutation) and the choice of selection criteria. In the case of the Traveling Salesman the mating operation can be merging different parts of two possible roads (mother and father road) until new usable roads are obtained. The criterion for the choice of the most prospective ones is minimum length (or cost).

Genetic algorithms comprise a great deal of parallelism. Thus, each of the branches of the search tree for best individuals can be utilized in parallel with the others. This allows for an easy realization of the genetic algorithms on parallel architectures.

Genetic algorithms are search heuristics for the "best" instance in the space of all possible instances. Four parameters are important for any genetic algorithm:

1. *The encoding scheme*, that is, how to encode the problem in terms of genetic algorithms—what to choose for genes, how to construct the chromosomes, etc.

2. *The population size*—how many possible solutions should be kept for further development

3. *The crossover operations*—how to combine old individuals and produce new, more prospective ones

4. *The mutation heuristic*—"when" and "how" to apply mutation

In short, the major characteristics of the genetic algorithms are the following:

• They are *heuristic* methods for search and optimization. As opposed to the exhaustive search algorithms, the genetic algorithms do not produce all variants in order to select the best one. Therefore, they may not lead to the perfect solution but to one that is closest to it taking into account the time limits. But nature itself is imperfect too (partly due to the fact that the criteria for perfection keep changing), and what seems to be close to perfection according to one "goodness" criterion may be far from it according to another.

• They are *adaptable*, which means that they have the ability to learn, to accumulate facts and knowledge without having any previous knowledge. They begin only with a "fitness" criterion for selecting and storing individuals (partial solutions) that are "good" and dismissing those that are "not good."

Genetic algorithms can be incorporated in learning modules as a part of an expert system or of other information-processing systems. Genetic algorithms are one paradigm in the area of *evolutionary computation*. *Evolution strategies* and *evolutionary programming* are the other (Fogel, 1995). Evolution strategies are different from the genetic algorithms in several ways: they operate not on chromosomes (binary codes) but on real-valued variables; a population is described by statistical parameters (e.g., mean and standard deviation); new solution is generated by perturbation of the parameters. One application of evolutionary computation is creating distributed AI systems called *artifical life*. They consist of small elementary elements that collectively manifest some repeating patterns of behavior or even a certain level of intelligence.

1.3   Why Expert Systems, Fuzzy Systems, Neural Networks, and Hybrid Systems for Knowledge Engineering and Problem Solving?

The academic research area for developing models, methods, and basic technologies for representing and processing knowledge and for building intelligent knowledge-based systems, is called *knowledge engineering*. This is a part of the AI area, directed more toward applications.

1.3.1   Expert Systems

Expert systems are knowledge-based systems that contain expert knowledge. For example, an expert system for diagnosing car faults has a knowledge base containing rules for checking a car and finding faults in the same way an engineer would do it. An expert system is a program that can provide expertise for solving problems in a defined application area in the way the experts do.

Expert systems have facilities for representing existing expert knowledge, accommodating existing databases, learning and accumulating knowledge during operation, learning new pieces of knowledge from existing databases, making logical inferences, making decisions and giving recommendations, communicating with users in a friendly way (often in a restricted natural language), and explaining their "behaviour" and decisions. The explanation feature often helps users to understand and trust the decisions made by an expert system. Learning in expert systems can be achieved by using machine-learning methods and artificial neural networks.

Expert systems have been used successfully in almost every field of human activity, including engineering, science, medicine, agriculture, manufacturing, education and training, business and finance, and design. By using existing information technologies, expert systems for performing difficult and important tasks can be developed quickly, maintained cheaply, used effectively at many sites, improved easily, and refined during operation to accommodate new situations and facts.

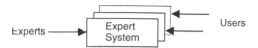

Figure 1.7
The two sides of an expert system.

There are two easily distinguishable sides of an expert system—the expert's side, and the users' side (figure 1.7). Experts transfer their knowledge into the expert system. The users make use of it.

In spite of the fact that many methods for building expert systems have been developed and used so far, the main problems in building expert systems are still there. They are:

1. How to acquire knowledge from experts?

2. How to elicit knowledge from a huge mass of previously collected data?

3. How to represent incomplete, ambiguous, corrupted, or contradictory data and knowledge?

4. How to perform approximate reasoning?

These questions were raised at the very early stage of expert systems research and development. Ad hoc solutions were applied, which led to a massive explosion of many expert systems applied to almost every area of industrial and social activity. But the above questions are still acute. Good candidates for finding solutions to these problems are fuzzy systems and neural networks.

1.3.2 Fuzzy Systems for Knowledge Engineering

One way to represent inexact data and knowledge, closer to humanlike thinking, is to use fuzzy rules instead of exact rules when representing knowledge.

Fuzzy systems are rule-based expert systems based on fuzzy rules and fuzzy inference. Fuzzy rules represent in a straightforward way "commonsense" knowledge and skills, or knowledge that is subjective, ambiguous, vague, or contradictory. This knowledge might have come from many different sources. Commonsense knowledge may have been acquired from long-term experience, from the experience of many people, over many years.

There are many applications of fuzzy logic on the market now. These include control of automatic washing machines, automatic camera focusing, control of transmission systems in new models of cars, automatic landing systems for aircraft, automatic helicopter control, automatic air-conditioning systems, automatic control of cement kilns, automatic control of subways, fuzzy decision making, fuzzy databases, etc. These, and many other industrial applications of fuzzy logic have been developed mainly in Japan, the United States, Germany, and France. They are spreading now all over the world. Many other applications of fuzzy logic in areas like control, decision-making and forecasting, human-computer interaction, medicine, agriculture, environmental pollution, cooperative robots, and so forth are in the research laboratories and are expected to enter the market.

The most distinguishing property of fuzzy logic is that it deals with *fuzzy propositions*, that is, propositions which contain fuzzy variables and fuzzy values, for example, "the temperature is high," "the height is short." The truth values for fuzzy propositions are not TRUE/FALSE only, as is the case in propositional boolean logic, but include all the grayness between two extreme values.

A fuzzy system is defined by three main components:

1. *Fuzzy input and output variables*, defined by their fuzzy values
2. *A set of fuzzy rules*
3. *Fuzzy inference mechanism*

Fuzzy rules deal with fuzzy values as, for example, "high," "cold," "very low," etc. Those fuzzy concepts are usually represented by their membership functions. A *membership function* shows the extent to which a value from a domain (also called universe) is included in a fuzzy concept (see, e.g., figures 3.1 and 3.2).

Case example. The Smoker and the Risk of Cancer Problem   A fuzzy rule defines the degree of risk of cancer depending on the type of smoker (figure 1.8). The problem is how to infer the risk of cancer for another type of smoker, for example, a "moderate smoker," having the above rule only.

In order to solve the above and many other principally similar but much more complex problems, one needs to apply an approximate reasoning method. Fuzzy inference methods based on *fuzzy logic* can be used successfully. Fuzzy inference takes inputs, applies fuzzy rules, and pro-

Rule: IF a person is a "heavy smoker"
         THEN the risk of cancer is "high",

where the two fuzzy concepts "heavy-smoker" and "high" can be represented by their
membership functions, for example:

A fuzzy concept "heavy-smoker":

No.of cigarettes per day	0	2	4	6	8	10
Grade (membership)	0	0.1	0.6	0.8	0.9	1.0

A fuzzy concept: "High risk of cancer"

Level of risk:	1	2	3	4	5
Grade (membership)	0.0	0.2	0.7	0.9	1.0

Figure 1.8
A simple fuzzy rule for the Smoker and the Risk of Cancer case example.

duces outputs. Inputs to a fuzzy system can be either exact, crisp values
(e.g., 7), or fuzzy values (e.g., "moderate"). Output values from a fuzzy
system can be fuzzy, for example, a whole membership function for the
inferred fuzzy value; or exact (crisp), for example, a single value is produced on the output. The process of transforming an output membership
function into a single value is called defuzzification.

The secret for the success of fuzzy systems is that they are easy to
implement, easy to maintain, easy to understand, robust, and cheap. All
the above properties of fuzzy systems and the main techniques of using
them are explained in chapter 3.

1.3.3 Neural Networks for Knowledge Engineering

During its development, expert systems have been moving toward new
methods of knowledge representation and processing that are closer to
humanlike reasoning. They are a priori designed to provide reasoning
similar to that of experts. And a new computational paradigm has already
been established with many applications and developments—artificial
neural networks.

An *artificial neural network* (or simply a neural network) is a biologically inspired computational model that consists of processing elements (neurons) and connections between them, as well as of training and recall algorithms.

The structure of an artificial neuron is defined by inputs, having weights bound to them; an input function, which calculates the aggregated net input signal to a neuron coming from all its inputs; an activation (signal) function, which calculates the activation level of a neuron as a function of its aggregated input signal and (possibly) of its previous state. An output signal equal to the activation value is emitted through the output (the axon) of the neuron. Drawings of real and artificial neurons are given in figures 4.1. and 4.2, respectively. Figures 4.3 and 4.4 represent different activation functions. Figure 4.5 is a graphical representation of a small neural network with four inputs, two intermediate neurons, and one output.

Neural networks are also called *connectionist models* owing to the main role of the connections. The weights bound to them are a result of the training process and represent the "long-term memory" of the model. The main characteristics of a neural network are:

• *Learning*—a network can start with "no knowledge" and can be trained using a given set of data examples, that is, input-output pairs (a supervised training), or only input data (unsupervised training); through learning, the connection weights change in such a way that the network learns to produce desired outputs for known inputs; learning may require repetition.

• *Generalization*—if a new input vector that differs from the known examples is supplied to the network, it produces the best output according to the examples used.

• *Massive potential parallelism*—during the processing of data, many neurons "fire" simultaneously.

• *Robustness*—if some neurons "go wrong," the whole system may still perform well.

• *Partial match* is what is required in many cases as the already known data do not coincide exactly with the new facts

These main characteristics of neural networks make them useful for knowledge engineering. Neural networks can be used for building expert systems. They can be trained by a set of examples (data) and in that way they represent the "hidden" knowledge of an expert system. For example, if we have good clinical records about patients suffering from cancer, we can use the data to train a neural network. The same network can also accommodate expertise provided by experts where the expertise is represented in an explicit form. After that, the network can recognize the health status of a new patient and make recommendations. Neural networks can be used effectively for building user interface to an expert system. There are connectionist models for natural language processing, speech recognition, pattern recognition, image processing, and so forth. The knowledge-engineering applications of neural networks inspire new connectionist models and new hypotheses about cognitive processes in the brain. Neural networks have been applied to almost every application area, where a data set is available and a good solution is sought. Neural networks can cope with noisy data, missing data, imprecise or corrupted data, and still produce a good solution.

1.3.4 Hybrid Systems

These are systems which have rule-based systems, fuzzy systems, neural networks, and other paradigms (genetic algorithms, probabilistic reasoning, etc.) in one. Hybrid systems make use of all their ingredients for solving a given problem, thus bringing the advantages of all the different paradigms together. Hybrid systems are introduced in chapter 6.

1.4   Generic and Specific AI Problems: Pattern Recognition and Classification

1.4.1   An Overview of Generic and Specific AI Problems

Knowledge engineering deals with difficult AI problems. Three main questions must be answered before starting to develop a computer system for solving a problem:

1. What is the *type of the problem*, that is, what kind of a generic problem is it?

2. What is the *domain and the solution space* of the problem and what problem knowledge is available?

3. *Which method* for problem solving should be used?

A *generic problem* (task) is a theoretically defined problem (task) for which methods are developed regardless of the contextual specificity of parameters and variables and their values. The variables used in the specification or a solution of the problem are domain-free.

A *specific problem* is a real problem which has its parameters, values, constraints, and so forth contextually specified by the application area the problem falls into.

In order to solve a specific problem, domain-specific knowledge is required. The problem knowledge could be a set of past data or explicit expert knowledge in the form of heuristic rules, or both. In spite of the fact that specific knowledge in a given area is required, we can use methods applicable for solving the corresponding generic problem, for example, methods for classification, methods for forecasting, etc.

What kind of methods do humans use when solving problems? Can we develop machine methods close to the human ones? Are fuzzy systems and neural networks useful in this respect? Which one to use, or maybe a combination of both? Answering these questions is one of the main objectives of this book.

1.4.2   Pattern Recognition and Classification; Image Processing

Pattern recognition is probably the most used generic AI problem in knowledge engineering. The problem can be formulated as follows: given a set of n known patterns and a new input pattern, the task is to find out which of the known patterns is closest to the new one. This generic problem has many applications, for example, handwritten character recognition, image recognition, speech recognition. Patterns can be: *Spatial*, for example, images, signs, signatures, geographic maps; and *Temporal*, for example, speech, meteorological information, heart beating, brain signals.

The methods used for solving pattern recognition problems vary depending on the type of patterns. Often, temporal patterns are transformed into spatial patterns and methods for spatial pattern recognition are used afterward.

Pattern recognition problems are usually characterized by a large domain space. For example, recognizing handwritten characters is a difficult task because of the variety of styles which are unique for every individual. The task is much more difficult when font-invariant, scale-invariant, shift-invariant, rotation-invariant, or noise-invariant characters should be recognized.

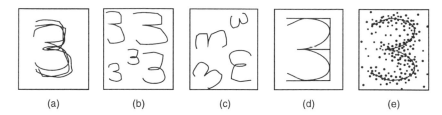

Figure 1.9
A pattern recognition system may allow for different variants of writing the digit 3: (a) centered; (b) scale-invariant and shift-invariant; (c) rotation-invariant; (d) font-invariant; (e) a noisy character.

Case Example: Handwritten Characters Recognition This is a difficult problem because of the variability with which people write characters. This variability is illustrated in figure 1.9. But this is not a difficult problem for humans. So, humanlike problem-solving methods might be applied successfully. This problem is tackled in the book by using fuzzy logic methods in chapter 3 and neural networks in chapters 4 and 5.

A pattern can be represented by a set of features, for example, curves, straight lines, pitch, frequency, color. The domain space of the raw patterns is transformed in the feature space before the patterns are processed. How many features should be used to represent a set of patterns is an issue which needs thorough analysis. Figure 1.10 shows how a defined set of features can be used for representing the letters in the Roman alphabet. But is the set of features used in figure 1.10 enough to discriminate all different characters? And what kind of extra features must be added in order to distinguish *K* from *Y* for example? Features can have different types of values: *Symbolic, qualitative values,* like "black," "curve," etc., and *numerical, quantitative values,* which can be continuous or discrete.

The set of features must satisfy some requirements, for example: *be large enough* to allow unique representation of all the patterns; *not be redundant,* as this may reflect in a poor classification due to considering features that are not important for the object classification; this may introduce noise in the system; and *allow flexibility* in pattern representation and processing depending on the concrete task.

A class of patterns can be represented in two major ways: (1) as a set of pattern *examples*; and (2) as a set of *rules* defining features which the patterns (objects) from a given class must have.

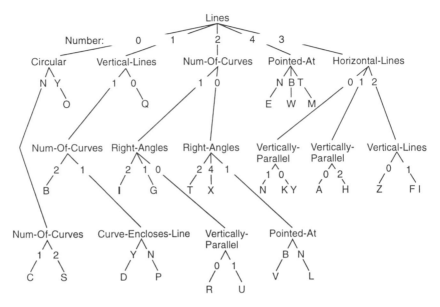

Figure 1.10
Features used to discriminate the letters in the Roman alphabet. *B*, bottom; *T*, top; *Y*, yes;
N, no/non.

The *classification problem*, as a generic one, is to associate an object
with some already existing groups, clusters, or classes of objects. Classification and pattern recognition are always considered as either strongly
related or identical problems.

Classes may be defined by a set of objects, or by a set of rules, which
define, on the basis of some attributes, whether a new object should be
classified into a given class.

Case Example: Iris Classification Problem   A typical example of such a
problem is the Iris Classification Problem. This is based on a data set used
by Fisher (1936) for illustrating discriminant analysis techniques. Afterward, it became a standard benchmark data set for testing different classification methods. The Iris data set contains 150 instances grouped into
three species of the plant genus *Iris—setosa, versicolor, virginica*. Every
instance is represented by four attributes: sepal length (SL), sepal width
(SW), petal length (PL), and petal width (PW), each measured in centimeters. Ten randomly chosen instances from the Iris data set are shown
in the example below. Figure 1.11 shows graphically all the 150 instances
in the Iris data set. The data set is explained in appendix A.

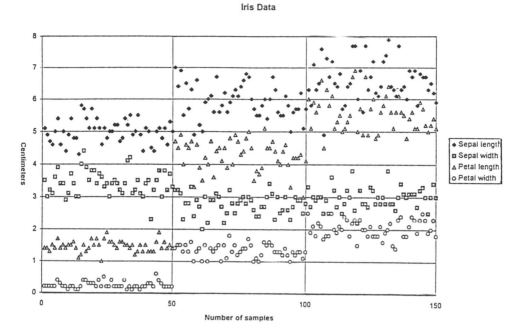

Figure 1.11
Graphical representation of the Iris data set. The first 50 instances belong to class Setosa, the second 50 to class Versicolor, and the last 50 to class Virginica.

No.	SL	SW	PL	PW	Class
1	5.1	3.5	1.4	0.2	Setosa
2	4.7	3.2	1.3	0.2	Setosa
3	5.0	3.6	1.4	0.2	Setosa
4	6.5	2.8	4.6	1.5	Versicolor
5	6.3	3.3	4.7	1.6	Versicolor
6	6.6	2.9	4.6	1.3	Versicolor
7	7.1	3.0	5.9	2.1	Virginica
8	6.5	3.0	5.9	2.2	Virginica
9	6.5	3.2	5.1	2.0	Virginica
10	6.8	3.0	5.5	2.1	Virginica

The problem is to classify a new instance, for example, 5.4, 3.3, 4.7, 2.1, into one of the classes. The Iris Classification Problem is a specific problem which illustrates the generic classification problem. It is used throughout the book as a case example to illustrate different methods of classification.

Different groups of methods can be used for solving classification problems:

• *Statistical methods*, based on evaluating the class to which a new object belongs with the highest probability; Bayesian probabilities are calculated and used for this purpose (see chapter 2 for using probabilities to represent uncertainties).

• *Discriminant analysis techniques*, the most used among them being linear discriminant analysis; this is based on finding linear functions (linear combinations between the features) graphically represented as a line in a two-dimensional space, as a plane in three-dimensional space, or as a "hyperplane" in a more-dimensional space, which clearly distinguishes the different classes (figure 1.12.)

• *Symbolic rule-based methods*, based on using heuristic symbolic rules. A general form of a heuristic rule for classification is as follows:

IF (features), THEN (class)

Symbolic rules usually use intervals. The following rough rules can be articulated after having a quick look at figure 1.11. The rules attempt to discriminate the three classes of Iris:

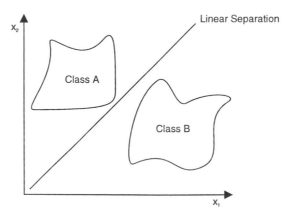

Figure 1.12
Linear separation between two classes A and B in a two-dimensional feature space (x_1 and x_2 are features).

IF PW <0.8, THEN Iris Setosa, else
IF PL >4.8 and PW > 1.5, THEN Iris Virginica,
otherwise, Iris Versicolor.

The question is how good the discrimination is.

• *Fuzzy methods*, based on using fuzzy rules. Fuzzy rules represent classes in fuzzy terms, for example, a rule for classifying new instances of Iris into class Setosa may look like:

IF PL is Small and PW is Small, THEN Setosa

where Small is defined for the two attributes PL and PW separately by two membership functions.

Example   A heuristic fuzzy rule for recognizing the handwritten digit 3 is given below. The features are of the type "the drawing of the digit crosses a zone of the drawing space," "does not cross a zone," or "it does not matter" (figure 1.13). If we divide the drawing space into five horizontal zones as was done in Yamakawa (1990), a heuristic rule to recognize 3 could be written as:

IF (the most upper zone is crossed) and
   (the middle upper zone is uncrossed)
   (the middle zone does not matter)
   (the middle lower zone is uncrossed)
   (the lowest zone is crossed),
THEN (the character is 3)

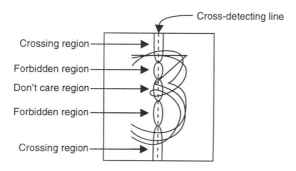

Figure 1.13
Using "crossing zones" as features for pattern recognition. (Redrawn with permission from Yamakawa 1990.)

Fuzzy systems provide simple and effective methods for handwritten character recognition because the characters can be represented by fuzzy features. For example the digit 3 may have a small line in the central area of the drawing space if it is centered. Two fuzzy concepts were used in the last sentence when we described the shape of the digit 3, that is, "small line," and "central area."

• *Neural networks and other machine-learning methods,* based on learning from examples of objects and their respective classes. The task is to build a classification system when a set of patterns (instances) only is available. The machine-learning methods and the methods of neural networks are appropriate for this task. One can also look at the "hidden" knowledge in the data set and try to represent it by explicit heuristic rules learned from the data. Because of the variety of patterns and the difficulties in uttering heuristic rules, pattern recognition is very often based on training a system with patterns. Neural networks are especially suitable for this task.

• *k- Nearest neighbor methods,* based on evaluating the *distance* between a new object and *k*-nearest objects for which the classes they belong to are known. The class that appears most frequently among the *k* neighbors is chosen.

Here the concept of *distance* between objects (patterns) is introduced for the first time. A distance between two patterns $\mathbf{a} = (a_1, a_2, \ldots, a_n)$ and $\mathbf{b} = (b_1, b_2, \ldots, b_n)$ can be measured in different ways, for example,

—*Absolute distance,*

$$D_{ab} = \sum_{i=1}^{n} abs(a_i - b_i)$$

—*Euclidean distance,*

$$E = \sqrt{\sum_{i=1}^{n} (a_i - b_i)^2}$$

—*Various normalized distances,* for example, a distance between a pattern and a center of a class is divided to the radius of the class region (*cluster*).

Based on measured distances between instances (objects) of different classes, areas in the problem space of all instances can be defined. These areas are called *clusters*. *Clustering* is an important procedure which helps

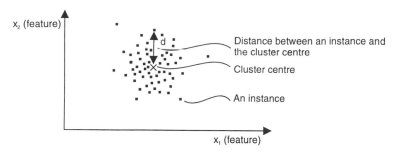

Figure 1.14
A cluster in the problem space.

to understand data. A *center* c_i of a cluster C_i is a point or an instance to which the mean of the distances from each instance in the cluster is minimum (figure 1.14). A cluster C_i can be defined by a characteristic function $M_i: S \rightarrow \{0,1\}$. It defines whether an instance from the whole problem space S belongs (1) or does not belong (0) to the cluster.

If the class labels for the instances are not known, then clustering may be useful for classification purposes. In this case a number of clusters and class centers, which minimize the mean difference between all the instances and these centers, may be defined.

In order to better illustrate the important generic classification problem, another example is used throughout the book.

Case Example: Soil Classification Problem   There are six main types of soil typical for a certain region. Each type of soil is characterized by different ion concentrations, the average being shown in the table 1.1 (Edmeades et al. 1985). The task is to recognize the soil type from a sample of unknown soil after having measured those concentrations. The solution to this problem as a set of production rules is given in chapter 2 and as a neural network, in chapter 5. A small database on the problem is described in appendix F.

Image processing is a part of the generic pattern recognition problem area. The smallest data element from an image is called a *pixel*. Different image processing tasks are *image recognition*, *image compression*, and *image analysis*.

Image recognition associates a new image with an already existing one, or with a class of images. The recognition process is hard, as images are usually blurry, corrupted, noisy. Image compression aims at encoding an

Table 1.1
The soil classification case example: Average concentration of elements in different types of soils

Soil	NH_4^+	NO_2^+	SO_4^{2-}	Ca^{2+}	Mg^{2+}	K^+	Na^+	Cl^-
Egmont YBL	0.39	2.79	0.44	0.82	0.37	1.03	1.72	0.31
Stratford YBL	0.19	1.10	0.50	0.65	0.15	0.45	0.64	0.28
Taupo YBP	0.31	0.64	0.46	0.52	0.19	0.83	0.43	0.14
Tokomaru YGE	0.15	1.09	0.58	0.75	0.29	0.52	0.89	0.26
Matapiro YGE	0.09	0.21	0.45	0.34	0.18	0.24	0.98	0.30
Waikare YBE	0.17	0.86	0.59	1.12	0.17	0.38	0.74	0.25

Adapted from Edmeades et al. (1985).

image with a minimum number of bits per pixel in such a way that a decoding process reconstructs the image to a satisfactory approximation of the original image. The compactness of the compression is measured in number of bits used to encode a pixel of the image. *Feature extraction, segmentation,* and other tasks are part of the image analysis problem area.

Associative memories are often used as a means for pattern storage and recognition. They are devices which can store patterns and recall them from a partial presentation as an input.

1.5   Speech and Language Processing

Speech-processing tasks are among the most difficult AI problems. Basic notions of speech processing are presented here. Different solutions are presented elsewhere in the book.

1.5.1   Introduction to Speech-Processing Tasks

Speech processing includes different technologies and applications. Some of them, according to Morgan and Scofield (1991), are listed below:

• *Speech encoding* aims at voice transmission, speech compression, and secure communications.

• *Speaker separation* aims at extracting speech signals of each of the speakers when multiple talkers are present.

• *Speech enhancement* aims at improving the intelligibility of the speech signals.

• *Speaker identification* aims at "identifying an uncooperative talker in an environment where a large number of talkers may be present."

• *Language identification* aims at discriminating languages.

• *Keyword spotting*, that is, recognizing spoken keywords from a dictionary (for database retrieval, etc).

But the most interesting and most rapidly developing of the speech-processing problems is the *automatic speech recognition (ASR) problem*. It aims at providing enhanced access to machines via voice commands. A voice interface to a computer is related strongly to analysis of the spoken language, concept understanding, intelligent communication systems, and further on, to developing "consciousness" in the machines. These are challenging problems for the AI community. Can neural networks and fuzzy systems help in getting better solution to ASR problems? Yes, they can.

The elaboration of practical systems for speech recognition takes two major trends: (1) recognition of *separately pronounced words* in extended speech; (2) recognition and comprehension of *continuous speech*.

Two approaches are mainly used in ASR: global and analytical. The global approach is based on comparison of the whole word with standard patterns, whereas in the analytical approach a word is broken into segments (subwords, units) on the basis of the phonetic characteristics of the speech signal. In both global and analytical approaches, obtained parametric vectors from the speech signal must be classified. A parametric vector of n elements can be represented as a point in n-dimensional space. This point can be seen as a pattern.

Phonemes are the smallest speech patterns that have linguistic representation in a language. They can be divided into three major conventional groups: vowels (e.g., /e/, /o/, /i/, /I/, /u/), semivowels (e.g., /w/) and consonants (e.g., /n/, /b/, /s/) (see appendix J). Vowels and consonants can be divided into additional subgroups. There are 43 phonemes in the received pronunciation (R.P.) English language, but their number varies slightly among the different dialects (American, Australian, New Zealand, etc.)

Before we discuss connectionist models for speech recognition and fuzzy models for speech and language understanding, a brief introduction to the nature of speech, speech features and transformations, and the technical and social problems that arise when building a speech recognition system, will be presented.

1.5.2   The Nature of Speech

Speech is a sequence of waves which are transmitted over time through a
medium and are characterized by some features, including *intensity* and
frequency. Speech is perceived by the inner ear in humans. It activates
oscillations of small elements in the media of the inner ear, which oscillations are transmitted to a specific part of the brain for further processing.
The biological background of speech recognition is used by many researchers to develop humanlike ASR systems, but other researchers take
other approaches. Speech can be represented on the:

- *Time scale*, which representation is called a waveform representation
- *Frequency scale*, which representation is called a spectrum
- *Both a time and frequency scale*, which is the spectrogram of the speech
signal

The three factors which provide the easiest method of differentiating
speech sounds are the perceptual features of *loudness*, *pitch*, and *quality*.
Loudness is related to the amplitude of the time domain waveform, but it
is more correct to say that it is related to the energy of the sound (also
known as its intensity). The greater the amplitude of the time domain
waveform, the greater the energy of the sound and the louder the sound
appears. *Pitch* is the perceptual correlate of the fundamental frequency of
the vocal vibration of the speaker organ. Figure 1.15(A) represents the
time domain waveform of the word "hello" (articulated by the author).
The *quality of a sound* is the perceptual correlate of its spectral content.
The *formants* of a sound are the frequencies where it has greatest acoustic
energy, as illustrated in figure 1.15(B) for the word "hello." The shape of
the vocal tract determines which frequency components resonate. The
short hand for the first formant is *F1*, for the second, *F2*, etc. The fundamental frequency is usually indicated by F_0. There are four major
formants for the word "hello," well distinguished in figure 1.15(B).

A spectrogram of a speech signal shows how the spectrum of speech
changes over time. The horizontal axis shows time and the vertical axis
shows frequency. The color scale (the gray scale) shows the energy of the
frequency components. The darker the color, the higher the energy of the
component, as shown in figure 1.16. This figure compares the spectra of
a pronounced word by a male speaker and a female speaker. Similarities

a.

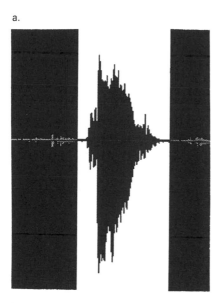

b.

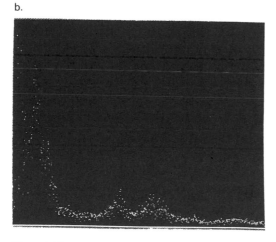

Figure 1.15
The word "hello" pronounced by the author: (A) Its waveform, time is represented on the
x-axis and energy—on the y-axis. (B) Its frequency representation where four major formants can be depicted, the x-axis represents frequencies and the y-axis represents energy of
the signal.

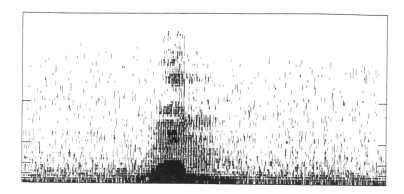

Male Speaker - "one"

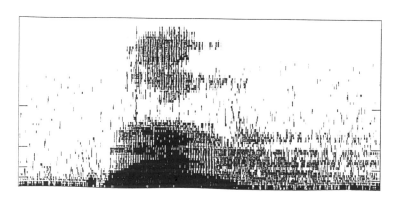

Female Speaker - "one"

Figure 1.16
Spectra of the word "one" pronounced by a male and a female speakers. The second pronounciation has higher energy in higher frequency louds.

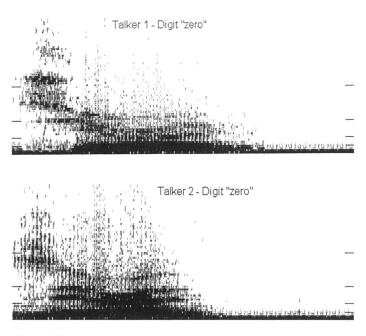

Figure 1.17
Spectra of digits pronounced by a male speaker (*Talker* 1), and the same speaker with a cold (*Talker* 2). The x-axis represents time in milliseconds (0–800); the y-axis represents frequency in kilohertz (0–11).

and differences in pronunciation depending on the health status of the same speaker, are illustrated graphically in figure 1.17.

1.5.3 Variability in Speech

The fundamental difficulty of speech recognition is that the speech signal is highly variable according to the speaker, speaking rate, context, and acoustic conditions. The task is to find which of the variations is relevant to speech recognition (Lee et al., 1993).

There are a great number of factors which cause variability in speech such as the speaker, the context, and the environment. The speech signal is very dependent on the physical characteristics of the vocal tract, which in turn depend on age and gender. The country of the speaker and the region in the country the speaker is from can also affect speech. Different accents of English can mean different acoustic realizations of the same phonemes. If English is the second language of the speaker, there can be an even greater degree of variability in the speech.

The same speaker can show variability in his or her speech, depending on whether it is a formal or informal situation. People speak precisely in formal situations and imprecisely in informal situations because the speaker is more relaxed. The more familiar a speaker is with a computer speech recognition system, the more informal his or her speech becomes, and the more difficult for the speech recognition system to recognize the speech. This could pose problems for speech recognition systems if they could not continually adjust.

Words may be pronounced differently depending on their context. Words are pronounced differently depending on where they lie in a sentence and the degree of stress placed upon them. In addition, the speaking rate can cause variability in speech. The speed of speech varies according to such things as the situation and emotions of the speaker. The duration of sounds in fast speech, however, do not reduce proportionately to their duration in slow speech.

Case Example: Phonemes Recognition   Recognizing phonemes from a spoken language is an important task because if it is done correctly, then it is possible to further recognize the words, the sentences, and the context in the spoken language. But it is an extremely difficult task. And this is because of the various ways people speak. They pronounce vowels and consonants differently depending on the accent, dialect, and the health status of the person (a person with the flu sounds differently). Figure 1.18 shows the difference between some vowels in English pronounced by male speakers in R.P. English, Australian English, and New Zealand English, when the first and the second formants are used as a feature space and averaged values are used. The significant difference between the same vowels pronounced in different dialects (except /I/ for the R.P. and Australian English; they coincide on the diagram) can be noted. Solutions to the problem of phonemes recognition is presented in chapters 5 and 6.

Case Example: Musical Signal Recognition   This is a similar problem to that of speech recognition. The problem is how to recognize individual notes from a sequence of musical signals and how to eventually print them out. There are some differences also. The frequency band used for speech is usually $[0, 10]$ kHz, but for music it is usually $[0, 20]$ kHz. Musical notes are easier to recognize as they are more similar, whatever the instru-

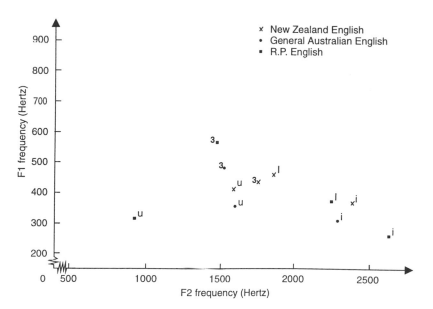

Figure 1.18
The first two formants used to represent the vowels /u/, /I/, /i/ and /ʒ/ pronounced by a male speaker in R.P English, Australian English, and New Zealand English. (Redrawn and adapted with permission from Maclagan 1982.)

ment is used to produce them, than phonemes pronounced by different persons. Still there may be difficulties for a computer system in recognizing a tune produced by one piano when a system is trained on signals produced by another.

A further problem for computer speech recognition is *ambiguity of speech.* This ambiguity is resolved by humans through some higher-level processing. Ambiguity may be caused by:

• *Homophones*—words with different spellings and meanings but that sound the same (e.g., "*to*," "*too*," and "*two*" and "*hear*" and "*here*"). It is necessary to resort to higher levels of linguistic analysis for distinction.

• *Overlapping classes*, as in the example above illustrating overlapping of phonemes pronounced in different dialects of a language.

• *Word boundaries.* By identifying speech through a string of phonemes only, ambiguities will arise, for example, /greiteip/ could be interpreted as "gray tape"or "great ape"; /laithau skipʒ/ could be cither "lighthouse keeper" or "light housekeeper." Once again it is necessary to resort to high-level linguistic analysis to distinguish boundaries.

• *Syntactic ambiguity.* This is the ambiguity of meaning until all the words are grouped into appropriate syntactic units. For example, the phrase "the boy jumped over the stream with the fish" means either the boy with the fish jumped over the stream or the boy jumped over the stream with a fish in it. The correct interpretation requires more contextual information.

The above examples show that the ASR problem is one of the most difficult AI problems. It contains features of other generic problems, like pattern recognition, classification, data rate reduction, and so forth. Once we know how to tackle it, we will have the skills and knowledge to tackle other AI problems of a similar nature.

1.5.4 Factors That Influence the Performance of the ASR Systems

All the speech recognition tasks are constrained in order to be solved. Through placing constraints on the speech recognition system, the complexity of the speech recognition task can be considerably reduced. The complexity is basically affected by:

• *Vocabulary size* (the range of words and phrases the system understands). Many tasks can be performed with a small vocabulary, although ultimately the most useful systems will have a large vocabulary. In general, vocabulary size is as follows:

Small, tens of words.

Medium, hundreds of words.

Large, thousands of words.

Very large, tens of thousands of words.

• *The speaking format of the system*, that is,

Isolated words (phrase) recognition.

Connected word recognition; this uses fluent speech but a highly constrained vocabulary, for example, digit dialing.

Continuous speech recognition.

• *The degree of speaker dependence of the system*, that is, whether it is:

Speaker-dependent (trained to the speech patterns of an individual user).

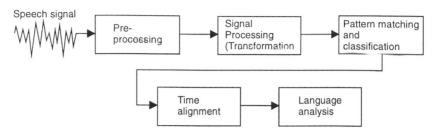

Figure 1.19
Main blocks in a speech recognition system.

Multiple speakers (trained to the speech patterns of a limited group of people).

Speaker-independent (such a system could work reliably with speakers who have never used the system).

• *The constraints of the task*, that is, as the vocabulary size increases, the possible combinations of words to be recognized grows exponentially. Some form of task constraint, such as formal syntax and formal semantics, is required to make the task more manageable.

1.5.5   Building ASR Systems

Figure 1.19 shows a simplified diagram of a computer speech recognition system. It comprises five major blocks:

1. *Preprocessing*—sampling and digitizing the signal.

2. *Signal processing*—transforming the signal taken for a small portion of time into an *n*-dimensional feature vector, where *n* is the number of features used (fast Fourier transform, mel-scaled cepstrum coefficient; see below in this section).

3. *Pattern matching*—matching the feature vector to already existing ones and finding the best match.

4. *Time alignment*—a sequence of vectors recognized over a time are aligned to represent a meaningful linguistic unit (phoneme, word).

5. *Language analysis*—the recognized language units recognized over time are further combined and recognized from the point of view of the syntax, the semantics, and the concepts of the language used in the system.

Here a short explanation of the different phases of the process of speech recognition will be given. Computer speech recognition is performed on digitized signals. Speech, however, is a continuous signal and therefore has to be sampled in both time and amplitude. To ensure that the continuous signal can be reconstructed from the digitized signal, the speech signal has to be band-limited and sampled at the so-called Nyguist sampling frequency or higher. The Nyguist sampling frequency is twice the maximum frequency in the band-limited speech signal.

Digitized speech is not only discrete in the time domain but also in the amplitude domain. The average intensity of speech at conversational level is about 60 dB, increasing to about 75 dB for shouting and decreasing to about 35 to 40 dB for quiet but not whispered speech (silence is taken to be 0 dB). It is important that the amplitude quantization allow for an adequate representation of the dynamic range of speech. Typically, speech is quantized by using 8 or 16 bits.

Speech signals carry a lot of information, most of which is redundant. How to *reduce the rate of data* to be processed and not lose important information? This is the task of the signal-processing phase. For example, to store the information from a sampled speech for 1 second with a 20-kHz sampling rate, using 16 bits, 40,000 bytes of memory are needed. After a signal transformation (spectral analysis), the whole signal may be represented as a 26-element vector, which occupies only 52 bytes. What transformation should be used for a compromise among accuracy, speed, and memory space?

When the speech signal is processed, the processing is performed on sequential segments of the speech signal rather than on the entire signal. The length of the segment is typically between 10 ms and 30 ms; over this period of time the speech signal can be considered stationary. Taking segments of the speech signal is usually done by using a window, thus removing the discontinuities at the edges. The discontinuities, if present, will distort the spectrum of the speech signal.

Different types of *spectral analysis* are used in speech recognition systems (Picone 1993). One of them is the *Digital Filter Banks* model. The filter bank is a crude model of the initial stages of transduction in the human auditory system. The model is based on so-called *critical bands* (Picone 1993). Two attempts to emulate these bands are the Bark and mel scale, with the mel scale being more popular in speech recognition. According to Lee et al. (1993) "[the] mel frequency scale is a psychologically based frequency scale, which is quasi-linear until about 1 kHz and quasi-logarithmic above 1 kHz. The rational for using it [in speech recognition] is because the human ear perceives frequencies on a non-uniform scale." Since the typical human auditory system can obviously distinguish speech sounds, it is desirable to represent spectral features for a speech recognition system on a psychologically based frequency scale. The following formula is used to calculate a pitch in mels:

$$p = c \log_{10}(1 + f/1000)$$

where f is the frequency in hertz, p is the pitch in mels, and $c = 1000/\log_{10} 2$ is a constant.

Another transformation is the *Fourier transform (FT)*. An alternative way of forming a filter bank is through the Fourier transform. The discrete Fourier transform (DFT) calculates frequency components of the speech signal from its waveform, a special, less computationally heavy version of it being the fast FT (FFT). The filter banks are then made up by adding up series of consecutive frequency components which fall within the bandwidth of each filter. The spacing of the filter banks depends on whether a linear, mel, or Bark scale was used.

The formula for the FT and some other transformations used on speech signals are given in fig.1.39 and explained in section 1.10.

Once a parametric representation of speech has been obtained, the next step is to perform recognition on it. This step is called *pattern matching*. There are four major ways to do this: (1) template matching, (2) hidden Markov models, (3) neural networks, and (4) rule-based systems.

For the time-alignment phase different methods can be applied, for example, the Viterby method, dynamic programming, and fuzzy rules; see chapters 5 and 6.

1.5.6   Language Analysis: The Turing Test for AI

Natural language understanding is an extremely complex phenomenon. It involves recognition of sounds, words, and phrases, as well as their combining forms, comprehension, and usage. There are various levels in the process of language analysis:

• *Prosody* deals with rhythm and intonation.

• *Phonetics* deals with the main sound units of speech (phonemes) and their correct combination.

• *Lexicology* deals with the lexical content of language.

• *Semantics* deals with the meaning of words and phrases seen as a function of the meaning of their constituents.

• *Morphology* deals with the semantic components of words (morphemes).

• *Syntax* deals with the rules, which are applied for matching words in order to form sentences.

• *Pragmatics* deals with the modes of use of language and their impact on the listener.

The importance of language understanding in communication between humans and computers was the essence of the *Turing test for AI*. Alan Turing, a British mathematician and computer scientist, introduced a definition of AI. A machine system is considered to posseses AI if, while communicating with a person behind a "bar," the person cannot recognize whether it is a machine or a human. To put it more simply, an AI system is a system that can communicate with humans in their natural language. This test has not been passed by any computer system so far, and it is unlikely to be passed by any machine in the near future.

Computer systems for language understanding require methods which can represent ambiguity, commonsense knowledge, and hierarchical structures. Humans, when communicating with one another, share a lot of commonsense knowledge which is inherited and learned in a natural way. This is a problem for a computer program. Humans use facial expressions, body language, gestures, and eye movements when they communicate. So they communicate in a multimodal manner. Computer systems that analyze speech signals, gestures, and facial expressions when communicating with users are called *multimodal interfaces*.

1.5.7   Intelligent Human-Computer Interfaces

One application of speech recognition and language modeling systems is for building intelligent human computer interfaces (IHCI). A general block diagram of an IHCI is graphically depicted in figure 1.20. The system allows for retrieving information from a database or for connecting the user to other communication ports by using both speech and text. It consists of the following major modules:

• *Speech recognition and language modeling block.* This module is trained on a speech corpus and uses a linguistic knowledge corpus. It recognizes

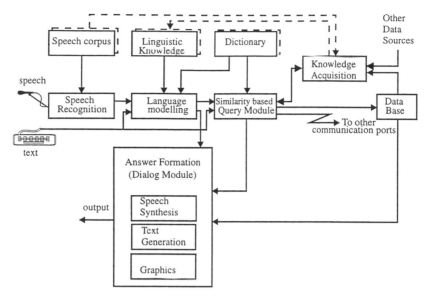

Figure 1.20
A block diagram of an intelligent human computer interface (IHCI).

spoken words, phrases, and sentences from a defined dictionary. The input speech signals are first digitized, transformed into feature vectors, and then used in the speech recognition submodule to match with already known speech patterns and to recognize small speech units, for example, phonemes. The language modeling submodule takes the recognized speech units and combine them into meaningful and relevant words and sentences.

• *Similarity-based query module.* This module does approximate reasoning over user's query and allows for vague, fuzzy queries to be used. For example, the user can ask for a list of patients who have "high blood pressure" when the database contains the blood pressure parameter in a numerical form only. The module performs two levels of matching a query to a database. The first one is exact matching, when the query matches exactly the information in the database. The second one is similarity-based matching, which involves interaction between the user and the system. The module finds language or conceptual similarities based on previous knowledge represented in terms of fuzzy rules. Fuzzy logic can be used for implementing the module as fuzzy systems have proved to be good at representing humanlike reasoning based on similarities.

• *Knowledge acquisition module.* The module is used to extract knowledge from different sources of information, for example, for extracting linguistic rules from linguistic database or extracting trading rules from a stock exchange database.

• *Answer formation module.* This module produces the answer to the user and performs a dialogue at any phase of the information retrieval. It has speech synthesis and text generation submodules.

A small-scale realization of the above general IHCI is presented in chapter 6.

1.6   Prediction

1.6.1   What Is the Problem?

Prediction (forecasting) is the process of generating information for the possible future development of a process from data about its past and its present development. Three different tasks can be distinguished under the generic prediction problem:

1. *Short-term prediction* (which is the restricted and default meaning of the word "prediction").

2. *Modeling*, which is finding global underlying structures, models, and formulas, which can explain the behavior of the process in the long run and can be used for long-term prediction as well as for understanding the past.

3. *Characterization*, which is aimed at finding fundamental properties of the process under consideration, such as degrees of freedom, etc. (Weigend and Gershefeld, 1993).

Prediction is something that is done every day in weather forecasting, agricultural harvest forecasting, commodity market forecasting, and stock and bond market forecasting. Prediction of earthquakes and other disasters, prediction of solar flares, prediction of the ozone layer movement, for example, are of extreme importance. Prediction is a very important generic AI problem. Predicting the future is what everybody wants to be able to do. But how?

If prediction is based on past data, the methods used might differ depending on the type of data available (Weigend and Gershefeld, 1993):

- Natural vs. synthetic
- Stationary vs. nonstationary
- Low-dimensional vs. stochastic
- Clean vs. noisy
- Short-term vs. long-term
- Linear vs. nonlinear
- Scalar vs. vector
- One trial vs. many trials
- Continuous vs. discrete.

Two types of data on which prediction is discussed in this section, are (1) *time-series data*, for example, predicting the stock market, predicting water flow coming to a sewage plant on an hourly basis; predicting gas consumption on a monthly basis; and (2) *static, stationary data*, for example, predicting the outcome of a disease, the effect of a new drug.

Before that, the major difficulties in solving the prediction problem should be mentioned, namely:

- Establishing whether a process is predictable at all
- Establishing the type of data and the process subject to prediction
- Defining the right features for presenting the prediction problem
- Defining how much past data are required for a good prediction
- Defining a methodology to test the accuracy of the prediction

1.6.2   Time-Series Prediction

Prediction of time-series events is called *time-series prediction*. When a prediction is done on the basis of only one independent variable it is called a *univariate prediction*; otherwise it is called a *multivariate prediction*. A general form of a heuristic rule for time-series prediction is:

IF (previous time-moment values for the features from the feature space are d_i), THEN (next time-moment values for the predicted variable(s) will be s_j)

Many techniques available for multivariate time-series analysis assume simple, often linear relationships between the variables. But, in reality,

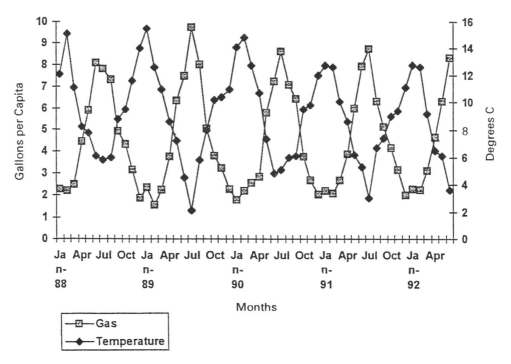

Figure 1.21
The Gas Consumption case example data; the average monthly minimum temperatures and the gas consumption per capita are graphed (see appendix B).

temporal variations in data do not exhibit simple regularities and are difficult to analyze.

In general, the predicted value of a variable in a future time is based on k previous values. In this case k is a lag of the prediction. If we have the values of a variable x for the moments from 1 to t, that is, $x(1)$, $x(2)$, ..., $x(t)$, we may predict $x(t + 1)$, and also the next time interval values $x(t + 2)$, ..., $x(t + m)$. The variable subject to prediction can be different from the past data variables (independent variables).

Case Example: The Gas Consumption Prediction Problem   The problem is to predict the gas consumption per capita for next few months in the town of Hamilton, based on the average minimum temperatures and previous data (Gonzales 1992), as shown graphically in figure 1.21. The whole data set is given in appendix B. A simple prediction system is shown in figure

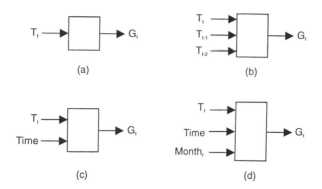

Figure 1.22
Different prediction models for predicting average gas consumption Gt for month t, based on the average minimum temperature T_t, time over a long period, and the month of prediction.

1.22a. It uses an assumption that the gas consumption G_t during the next month (t) can be predicted only on the basis of the prediction for the average minimum temperature T_t during this month. So one input variable is used only—T_t. Figure 1.22b shows another model for solving the same problem, but here two "lags" for the temperature are used, T_{t-1} and T_{t-2}, in addition to the predicted T_t. This scheme assumes longer-term dependence of the next values on the previous, past data. If long-term trends are anticipated (e.g., decreasing consumption because of the global warming effect, or some other reason), then the prediction model should include a long term variable, *Time*, for example, represented in consecutive numbers (months) over a long period as in figure 1.22c. The model in figure 1.22d uses another variable, the calender month of prediction *Month$_t$*, which gives the system an opportunity to learn a dependence between gas consumption and season. The different models shown in figure 1.22 use different feature spaces to deal with the same problem. Which of the prediction models would be better is discussed in chapter 5 where the models are implemented in a connectionist way.

Case Example: The Water Flow to a Sewage Plant Prediction Problem
The problem is as follows: Given a data set for the water flow (in cubic meters) incoming to a sewage plant and the hour and the day it is recorded, predict the water flow at the next hour, as well as the flow over the next several hours (see appendix C). This problem is discussed in chapters 6 and 7.

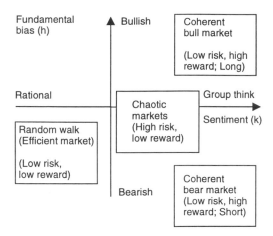

Figure 1.23
Different states of a stock market (Reprinted, with permission, from Financial Analyst
Journal, November/December 1990. Copyright 1990, Association for Investment Manage-
ment and Research, Charlottesville, V.A. All rights reserved).

Case Example: The Stock Market Prediction Problem   A more complex
specific prediction problem is the stock market prediction problem. Is a
stock market predictable at all? According to the *coherent market hypothesis* (see Vaga 1990), a stock market can behave differently, depending on
its state (figure 1.23). Four states are defined on the feature space of
two features only: (1) group sentiment, a measure of whether the level of
"group thinking" is above or below a critical transition threshold; and
(2) fundamental bias, a measure of external preference toward bullish or
bearish sentiment. Only a market that is in a *random walk state* is unpredictable because it fluctuates randomly. A *coherent market* is easily predictable and a *chaotic market* is more or less predictable depending on the
degree of chaos. A chaotic market is defined as a chaotic process, which is
nonlinear, deterministic, strictly nonperiodic but nearly periodic, therefore
predictable over a short term (see chapter 7).

Example   The SE40 stock exchange index data over a period of several
years is given in appendix C.
   There are different theories for predicting the market, one of them being
the *moving averages theory*. The theory says that by computing average values the volatility of the time series is smoothed and the trends
of the market are indicated. A moving average is calculated by using

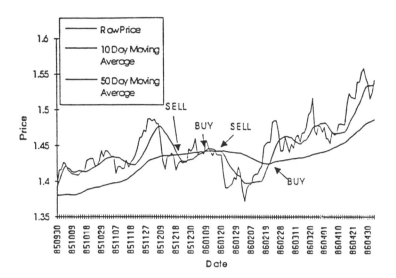

Figure 1.24
The moving averages model of predicting the exchange rate between the U.S. dollar and the British pound (reprinted with permission from Goonatilake and Campbell 1994).

the formula:

$$MA_t = (\sum P_{t-i})/n, \text{ for } i = 1, 2, \ldots, n$$

where n is the number of the days, P_{t-i} is the opening price of the stock on the day $t - i$, and MA_t is the moving average on day t. Two heuristic rules which implement the theory are:

R1: IF the short moving average crosses the long moving average from below, THEN the market is likely to rise (BUY)

R2: IF the short moving average crosses the long moving average from above, THEN the market is likely to fall (SELL)

Example   Figure 1.24 shows an example of using the above decision rules for predicting the US dollar and British pound exchange rate (Goonatilike and Campbell 1994).

1.6.3   Prediction Based on Static Data

Another type of prediction problem is when data are static or when time is not represented as a parameter. These tasks are in general easier to

	Experimental Tumors															Effect on Cancer
	1	2	3	4	5	6	7	8	9	10	11	12	13	14	15	
Drugs	1.0	1.0	0.5	0.5	1.0	0.5	1.0	1.0	0.5	0.5	0.5	1.0	1.0	0.5	0.5	1.0
	1.0	1.0	1.0	1.0	1.0	1.0	1.0	0.0	1.0	0.0	1.0	1.0	1.0	1.0	1.0	1.0
	1.0	1.0	1.0	1.0	0.0	0.0	1.0	1.0	1.0	1.0	1.0	1.0	1.0	1.0	0.0	1.0
	1.0	1.0	0.5	0.0	0.0	0.5	1.0	0.5	0.5	0.5	0.5	1.0	1.0	0.5	0.5	1.0
	1.0	1.0	1.0	0.0	1.0	0.0	1.0	1.0	0.0	1.0	0.0	0.0	1.0	0.0	1.0	1.0
	1.0	1.0	0.0	1.0	0.0	0.5	1.0	1.0	1.0	0.0	0.0	0.0	1.0	1.0	0.5	1.0
	1.0	1.0	1.0	0.5	1.0	0.0	1.0	1.0	0.0	1.0	0.0	0.5	0.5	0.5	0.0	1.0
	0.0	1.0	0.0	1.0	0.0	0.5	0.0	1.0	1.0	0.0	0.0	1.0	0.0	0.5	1.0	1.0
	1.0	1.0	1.0	0.0	0.0	0.0	0.0	0.0	1.0	0.0	0.5	1.0	0.0	0.0	1.0	1.0
	1.0	1.0	1.0	1.0	1.0	0.0	1.0	1.0	1.0	0.0	1.0	0.0	0.0	0.0	1.0	1.0
	1.0	1.0	1.0	0.0	0.0	0.5	0.0	0.0	0.5	0.0	0.5	1.0	1.0	0.0	0.5	1.0
	1.0	0.5	1.0	0.5	0.0	0.0	0.0	0.0	0.5	0.0	1.0	0.5	1.0	0.5	0.5	1.0
	0.0	0.0	1.0	0.0	1.0	0.0	0.5	0.5	0.5	0.0	0.5	1.0	1.0	0.5	0.5	0.0
	1.0	1.0	1.0	0.0	0.5	0.5	0.0	0.5	0.0	0.0	0.0	0.5	0.5	0.5	0.0	0.0
	1.0	0.5	1.0	1.0	0.0	0.0	1.0	1.0	0.0	0.0	0.0	0.0	0.0	1.0	0.0	0.0

Figure 1.25
The effect of 15 drugs on 15 experimental tumors and on a tumor in a patient with breast cancer.

handle because of the missing time variation problem, still subject to having enough representative past data or expertise on the problem.

Case Example   An example of such a problem is predicting the effect of a new chemotherapeutic agent for breast cancer treatment based on the presumed similarity between the tumor and a set of experimental tumors. Figure 1.25 contains the known effect of 15 established drugs on 15 experimental tumors and on a clinical tumor (malignant breast cancer) (Karaivanova et al. 1983). The problem is to find an analogous mapping between the set of 15 experimental tumors and the clinical tumor based on their known reactions to the same 15 drugs. In this way it may be possible to predict the effect of a new drug on the clinical tumor after having tested it on the experimental tumors and knowing the reactions, subject to established similarities between the new drug and those previously used. A solution to this problem is given in chapter 5.

1.6.4   About the Methods for Prediction

Prediction can be carried out based on:

• *Past data*, for example, the Gas Consumption Prediction

• *Heuristic expert rules*, for example, rules which suggest whether to buy or sell depending on the current political situation, economic situation, business growth, exports, and so forth.

• *Both past data and heuristic rules*

Depending on the information used, the following methods have been applied to solving prediction problems:

• *Statistical methods*, based on regression analysis and probability analysis

• *Neural networks*, which perform pattern matching

• *Rule-based systems*, including fuzzy rule-based systems, which represent heuristic expert knowledge; rules might be extracted from past data by using machine-learning techniques

• *Hybrid systems*, which make use of past data and expert rules in one system

The last three methods are demonstrated in chapters 3, 5, 6, and 7. Several time-series data sets for experimenting with are given in appendix C.

1.7   Planning, Monitoring, Diagnosis, and Control

Planning, monitoring, diagnosis and control are three generic AI problems which are based on representing the object (process) under consideration by its state space and transitions between the states. The state space of the object is usually huge, which demands heuristic rules to search in it and to find the desired state (goal, set point, dangerous situation, fault).

1.7.1   Planning

Planning is a very important generic AI problem which is about generating a sequence of actions in order to achieve a given goal when a description of the current situation is available. The main terms used in planning systems are:

• *A set of goals*

• *A set of actions*

• *A set of objects* (*processes*)

• *A set of conditions* for the actions to take place

• *Descriptors* for representing relations between the objects

```
WHILE no termination condition is reached DO
        {
                read data (current situation, goals);
                evaluate the input data;
                generate a plan ;
                execute the plan
        }
```

Figure 1.26
A simple algorithm for a planning program.

Planning is usually realized as an interactive task which has four major phases repeated until the termination condition is reached (figure 1.26). A general heuristic rule for planning is in the form of:

IF (a given situation) and (a defined goal), THEN (a sequence of actions)

Example   A good example of a planning problem is the *Blocks World Problem*. The task is to move blocks ordered in piles (stacks). A simple blocks world of only two blocks (*A* and *B*) is shown in figure 1.27a. When the goal to take block *B* is given, the system should produce a sequence of actions to achieve this goal. If there were three or more blocks, then the goal would have to be represented as a set of subgoals (e.g., to clear the upper and the lower blocks, to move blocks on the floor, etc.).

A planning system can be represented functionally as a graph where the nodes represent situations (states in the state space of all the possible situations) and the arcs represent actions that cause changes in the situations. This is illustrated in figure 1.27b for the above example.

Case Example: The Monkey and Bananas Problem   This is another typical example of a planning problem. It is actually a problem of planning the movement of a robot. This problem has been widely used as a benchmark problem for evaluating different implementations of rule-based production systems. The problem itself is the following: A monkey is in a room containing a couch, blanket, ladder, and a bunch of bananas. The objects are assembled on the floor and the bananas hang from the ceiling. Each object has its coordinates. The aim is to generate the steps the monkey should take to achieve the goal of grasping the bananas (figure 1.28). Here is an exemplary rule for this problem:

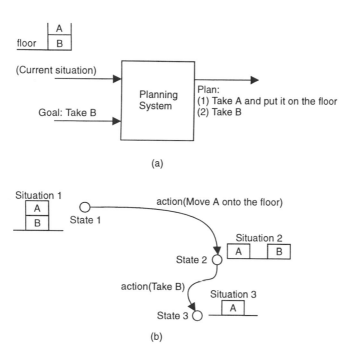

Figure 1.27
A simple Blocks World Problem as a planning problem: (a) the problem's input-output diagram; (b) a functional diagram of the system execution.

IF (monkey is at position x on the floor) and
    (monkey does not hold anything) and
    (bananas are at position y on the ceiling) and
    (ladder is at position z, z being different from x and y),
THEN (monkey walks to position z in order to take the ladder)

1.7.2 Monitoring

Monitoring is a generic task which consists of a continuous recording of the states of a process or object and emitting messages about some extreme cases. Monitoring is the process of interpretation of continuous input information, and recommending intervention if appropriate. It could be, for example, a dangerous situation in a reactor when the alarm signals have to be triggered. Many medical, agricultural, and military systems are of this type. Monitoring is usually accomplished as a loop. A general form of a heuristic rule for monitoring looks like:

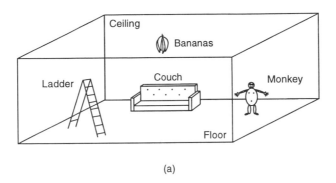

(a)

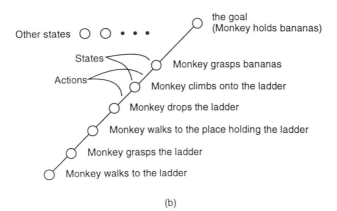

(b)

Figure 1.28
The Monkey and Bananas Problem: (a) a graphical representation of the problem; (b) a possible plan shown as actions changing the states in the states space.

IF (a situation is one of the predefined specific and possibly dangerous situations), THEN (report on the situation and consequences).

Case example: Monitoring of a Car on the Road   A specific simple problem of a monitoring type will be used to illustrate the generic one. The problem is to develop a monitoring system which *monitors a car* and gives a signal to the driver to stop the car when there is dangerous malfunctioning, for example, if the engine overheats or the brakes react slowly. The temperature sensor (gauge) and brakes sensor measure the adequacy of those devices. A real car monitoring problem of assessing when the driver should be alerted to stop the car is complicated and needs a lot of

```
( Rule 1
        IF (* conditions *)
            ( there is an overheating ) OR
            ( the brakes respond slowly when pressed )
        THEN (* conclusions *)
            ( give a message to the driver to stop the car))

( Rule 2
        IF (* conditions *)
            ( the temperature gauge works properly) AND
            ( the temperature is over 120 )
        THEN (* conclusions*)
            (there is an overheating) )
```

Figure 1.29
Two simple rules for the Car Monitoring case example.

checks without any guarantee that there can be a complete solution. Two simple rules of thumb are shown in figure 1.29.

1.7.3 Diagnosis

Diagnosis is another typical generic AI problem. This is the process of finding faults in a system. A simple way to represent a diagnostic system is to use a triple (M, D, R), where M is a set of manifestations, $M = \{m1, m2, \ldots, mk\}$, $D = \{d1, d2, \ldots, dl\}$ is a set of possible faults, and $R = \{r1, r2, \ldots, rn\}$ is a set of diagnostic rules which give the relations between the faults and the symptoms, if known. A set of examples which associate manifestation vectors to faults may also be used.

Considerable research work has been done on automating the fault diagnosis process. Most of the diagnostic procedures fall into two categories: (1) *shallow, or symptom-based diagnostic reasoning*; and (2) *deep or model-based diagnostic reasoning*.

The advantage of shallow or symptom-based reasoning is its efficiency and ease in representing knowledge. The symptom-based fault diagnosis systems can be developed by using rule-based expert systems, by using neural network techniques, or by using fuzzy logic. Two simple diagnostic problems are used as case examples in this book. One of them, the *Smoker and the Risk of Cancer Problem*, was introduced in a previous section. A fuzzy rule and the membership functions that define the fuzzy values are shown in figure 1.8. In general, a heuristic rule for diagnosis looks like:

R1:   IF (m1 is always and m2 is weak and m3 is no and m4 is no)
        THEN (d1 is very strong)

R2:   IF (m1 is no and m2 is always and m3 is weak and m4 is no)
        THEN (d2 very strong)

R3:   IF (m1 is more or less weak and m2 is no and m3 is always and m4 is no)
        THEN (d3 very strong)

R4:   IF (m1 is weak and m2 is more or less weak and m3 is always and m4 is no)
        THEN (d4 is very strong)

Figure 1.30
Diagnostic rules for the Medical Diagnosis case example.

While no termination condition is reached DO
        {
                read the data about the current state of the object;
                evaluate data and infer control actions;
                send control signals to the object
        }

Figure 1.31
An outline of a control loop.

IF (symptoms), THEN (diagnosis)

Case Example: Hypothetical Medical Diagnosis Problem   The second diagnostic case example is adopted from Chen (1988) and modified for the purpose of this book. The example comprises a set $M = \{m1, m2, m3, m4\}$ of four manifestations, a set of four faults (diseases) $D = \{d1, d2, d3, d4\}$, and a set of four medical diagnostic rules $R = \{r1, r2, r3, r4\}$ which represent vague expressions, as given in figure 1.30. A solution to this problem is given in chapter 3.

1.7.4   Control

Control is the process of acquiring information for the current state of an object and emitting control signals to it in order to keep the object in its possible and desired states. A control loop is given in figure 1.31. A general rule for the control problem would be:

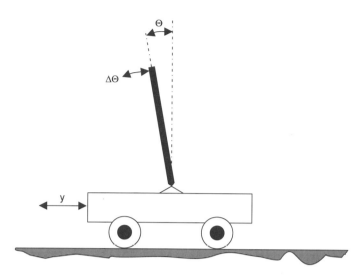

Figure 1.32
The Inverted Pendulum case example—a physical presentation of an experimental system.

IF (the object is in a state $\mathbf{d}_i$), THEN (emit a control signal $\mathbf{s}_j$)

Three groups of methods are mainly used today for solving control problems. These are:

1. *Classic nonlinear control*, based on mathematical formulas to calculate the values for the control variables when the values of the input variables and values for other parameters of the system under control are given

2. *Fuzzy systems*, based on fuzzy rules

3. *Neural networks*, based on training with input-output data collected when the object has been operating properly

Case Example: The Inverted Pendulum Problem   This is a classic control problem used in many experiments, books, and real systems (Yamakawa 1989; Kosko 1992). Figure 1.32 is a graphical representation of the problem. A pendulum is fixed to a cart with two degrees of movement. The cart can move in two directions: forward and backward. The problem is to keep the pendulum standing vertical. To keep the pendulum balanced, a force *y* should be applied to the cart to move forward or backward continuously according to the current state of the pendulum, here represented by two parameters—the current value of the angle Θ of the pendulum with the vertical line and its angular velocity $\Delta\Theta$.

The inverted pendulum problem is solved by using second-order differential equations for calculating the force to be used for moving the cart, when the current angle, the current angular velocity, and the values for the length of the pendulum, its mass, and the resistance of the medium (the air) in which the pendulum is moving are given. Solving a set of differential equations might be too slow for a fast real-type control process. Something more, a slight change in the parameters of the object (say the resistance of the medium increases a little bit) requires a new set of differential equations to be defined. These two major difficulties of using mathematical formulas are overcome in the fuzzy systems for control.

A fuzzy system for controlling the inverted pendulum is much easier to develop (Yamakawa 1989). Articulating fuzzy rules for controlling the inverted pendulum can be done similar to the way the heuristic rules for balancing a pencil on a palm were articulated:

Rule 1: IF the pendulum tilts to the right, THEN move the cart backward

Rule 2: IF the pendulum tilts to the left, THEN move the cart forward

Those two rules are far from being the solution to the problem. It must also be decided how far "backward" and "forward." This depends on the static and dynamic state of the pendulum. The initial heuristics have to be developed further, taking into account the domain values for the angle Θ (between -90 and 90 degrees), the domain values for the angular velocity (the same), and the values for the force applied to the cart. In order to make the above two heuristic rules more precise, the intervals of all three parameters are discretized into five subintervals as follows: (1) positive medium (PM); (2) positive small (PS); (3) zero (ZE); (4) negative small (NS); and (5) negative medium (NM). Having such a quantization, one can articulate more heuristic rules as a development of the initial two. This problem is discussed further in chapter 3, when the fuzziness of the intervals is defined. Some heuristic rules, which refine the rough heuristic rules above, are given in figure 1.33.

Fuzzy systems are *robust*, that is, changing the parameters of the object under control does not necessarily require changing the set of fuzzy rules. This was brilliantly demonstrated by Professor Takeshi Yamakawa. He implemented the above fuzzy rules in hardware and showed that an inverted pendulum can be controlled in this way. Then he put a glass of wine on top of the pendulum. Without changing the set of rules, the pendulum

---

IF Θ is PM AND ΔΘ is ZR, THEN y is PM,

IF Θ is PS AND ΔΘ is PS, THEN y is PS,

IF Θ is PS AND ΔΘ is NS, THEN y is ZR,

IF Θ is NM AND ΔΘ is ZR, THEN y is NM,

IF Θ is NS AND ΔΘ is NS, THEN y is NS,

IF Θ is NS AND ΔΘ is PS, THEN y is ZR,

IF Θ is ZR AND ΔΘ is ZR, THEN y is ZR.

Figure 1.33
Seven heuristic rules for balancing the inverted pendulum. (Adapted with permission from Yamakawa 1989.)

with the glass of wine was balanced. He then replaced the glass of wine with a live mouse which was trying to escape unsuccessfully from the platform on top of the pendulum. The pendulum stayed balanced. But, on the other hand, it is difficult to estimate how much the parameters may change without the need for changing the fuzzy rules. This problem is known as the *stability problem* (see details in L-X Wang 1994). For example, it is difficult to calculate the stability of the inverted pendulum if the mouse is replaced by a small rabbit.

Fuzzy and neural control techniques are used to control the landing of missiles and airplanes, track flying objects, in automatic control of trucks, and so forth (Kosko 1992). The pendulum toy example is actually a serious contribution to the human way of controlling the environment and objects in the universe. Similar problems of keeping objects or processes in balanced states can be found easily in any research and application area (air conditioning, "balancing" blood pressure, controlling heart beat, balancing the profits of a company, etc.)

1.8   Optimization, Decision Making, and Games Playing

These three generic AI problems are similar in the sense that the search for a solution needs to set *a strategy*.

1.8.1   Setting Strategies and Evaluating Complexities

A strategy is usually expressed by a set of heuristic rules. The heuristic rules ease the process of searching for an optimal solution. The process is usually iterative and at one step either the global optimum for the whole problem (state) space is found and the process stops, or a local optimum for a subspace of the state space of the problem is found and the problem continues, if it is possible to improve.

Many simple specific problems which fall in the pools of these generic ones use simple strategies or straightforward heuristics.

The reason for setting a strategy when searching for the solution is to minimize the *complexity* of the system. Complexity is measured by the number of typical operations for reaching a solution. It is usually expressed as a function of the *size of the problem*, which is represented by a typical parameter of the problem that is dominant when evaluating the volume of data required to be processed for finding a solution. For example, for the Traveling Salesman Problem the size is defined by the number of the towns n to visit. The complexity is represented by a function $f(n)$ defining how many operations (summation, comparison, etc.) overall are needed to find a solution to the problem.

Complexity can be represented by the *asymptotic complexity function*, which is the function $f(n)$ when n grows to infinity. Typical values for estimating asymptotic complexity of algorithms are: $\log_2 n$, n, $n \log_2 n$, n^2, polynomial function of n of k degree, etc. Problems for which the complete solution can be reached only by applying an algorithm (method) where asymptotic complexity is an exponential function, are called NP-complete problems (NP stands for nonpolynomial).

So, the difficult AI problems very often are NP-complete because of their huge state space in which finding a solution requires a lot of operations. And that is why good search strategies to search through the solution space are needed!

1.8.2   Optimization

Optimization problems are about finding optimal values for parameters of an object or a system which minimizes an objective (cost) function. There are many methods applicable to optimization problems. From the point of view of the solution achieved, one can distinguish methods that guarantee the *complete optimal solution,* and *heuristic methods,* which do not guarantee an optimal solution, but in most cases give a satisfactory solution for much less complexity.

Heuristic methods may aim at local optimization rather than at global optimization, that is, the algorithm optimizes the solution stepwise, finding the best solution at each small step of the solution process and "hoping" that the global solution, which comprises the local ones, would be satisfactory. A heuristic rule for such a strategy is:

WHILE the final solution is not reached DO
  {IF (next step decision satisfies a local optimum criterion), THEN
    (choose it)}

Case Example: The Traveling Salesman Problem   A graphical representation of an example of the problem when $n = 5$ and for certain traveling costs c_{ij} to travel from town i to town j, is given in figure 1.34. In the general case, there are $(n - 1)! = (n - 1)(n - 2)\dots2.1$ possible paths (this is the solution state space). Choosing the cheapest one is a NP complete optimization problem. A heuristic approach to solving this problem is possible. A heuristic rule to solve the problem is the following:

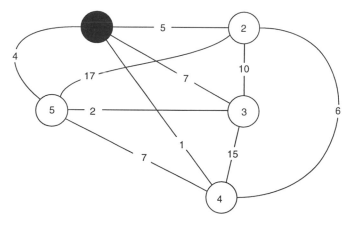

Figure 1.34
A graphical representation of a simple version of The Traveling Salesman Problem (TSP) case example. The nodes of the graph denote towns and the arcs denote connections between the towns weighted by the corresponding traveling costs.

WHILE there are more towns to visit DO
   {IF (j is a town which has not been visited yet) AND
     (the cost from the last visited town to j is the lowest among the
     nonvisited ones),
   THEN (visit town j)}

The asymptotic complexity of this heuristic solution is n^2, while the complete optimal solution achieved through an *exhaustive search* by generating and checking the cost of all the possible paths has a complexity of $n!$. Applying this heuristic to the example given in figure 1.34, a path 1–4–2–3–5–1 with a cost of 23 is found for about 25 operations (comparison and summation), while applying an exhaustive search for finding the optimal path requires about 120 operations and in this case the same path as in the heuristic search is found to be the optimal one.

A brilliant example of a general heuristic optimization method is the genetic algorithms (see section 1.2). They are applicable to probably any optimization problem and it is up to us to compromise between the time for getting a solution (we can stop the algorithm at any step having the partial solution to the problem till that step) and its precision.

Some types of neural networks, for example, the Hopfield network, or more generally, the attractor type of neural networks, are also applicable to optimization problems. A neural network solution to the TSP is given in chapter 5.

1.8.3 Decision Making

Decision-making systems are AI systems which choose one among many variants as a solution to a particular problem. The solution is then recommended to the user. The decision-making systems may contain different subsystems, like systems for classification, optimization, and diagnosis. A general heuristic rule for a generic decision-making problem is:

IF (circumstances), THEN (decisions)

Case Example: The Bank Loan Decision Problem A decision-making system which advises on bank loan applications is considered here as a case example. The purpose of the system is to "decide" whether an applicant for a loan should be given a loan or not. The applicant is represented by three aggregate attributes. The first is called "critical score" (CScore, or simply

Score)—a numerical rating on place of residence, employment, and bank accounts. The second attribute is "critical ratio" (CRatio, or simply Ratio) —the client's profile on loan repayment, mortgage, rent, and other expenses. The third attribute is "critical credit" (CCredit, or simply Credit)— previous loans, credit cards, and the client's credit history in general. The problem has been introduced and used by Lim and Takefuji (1990) for a hardware implementation of a bank loan approval system, FXLoan. This problem is used throughout the book to show the similarity of fuzzy and connectionist reasoning as well as to demonstrate learning fuzzy rules through using neural networks (see chapter 5). The initial heuristic rules for loan approval suggested by the above authors are given here, but the full example is revealed in chapter 3, where the fuzzy concepts "High," "Low," "Good," and "Bad" are defined:

R1: IF CScore is High, and CRatio is Good, and CCredit is Good, THEN Decision is Approve

R2: IF CScore is Low, and CRatio is Bad, or CCredit is Bad, THEN Decision is Disapprove

Decision-making systems can be incorporated in larger decision support systems, where access to a large database would be available, and different subsystems might be included for processing different subtasks.

Case Example: Investment adviser   Another typical decision-making problem is that of investment advising. The problem is to advise a client investing amounts of money either in a bank or in the share market when the following parameters are known: amount of money for investing, risk willing to be taken, period of investment, and income.

Another case example of decision-making problems considered also in this book is *mortgage approval decision making* (see appendix C).

1.8.4   Games Playing

Playing games is an intellectual activity of humans based on the following concepts:

- *Rules of the game*
- *Opponent teams*

- *Playing media, for example, board*
- *Criterion for ending the game* and choosing the winner

Typical examples of games are chess, ticktacktoe, Go.

The difficulties in developing an AI system that plays a game are mainly due to the large problem space of all possible moves and the impossibility of checking or trying all of them in order to choose the optimal one which leads to a win. For example, at a certain stage of the game, all the possible moves in chess from a current position could be about 10^{200}. In order to cut off moves that are not prospective, one has to use some strategic heuristic rules. Some questions which should be answered before we develop a computer game player are:

1. How should the game's rules and the game's media be represented in the system?

2. What heuristic strategy should we use to choose the next move?

3. Can we possibly create a system that will improve its playing with the number of games played?

Choosing the next move should be done in a realistic way (not counting all possible moves if there are many), but, if possible, not sacrificing the final outcome. For choosing the next move, heuristic strategies are used, which evaluate the *goodness* (*fitness*) of prospective moves. A simple general heuristic rule is:

IF (move *j* has highest goodness coefficient), THEN (choose move *j*)

This general rule is used in genetic algorithms (remember the illustrative example in section 1.2 for playing the "mastermind" game with the use of a genetic algorithm). Here, two other games are described, for which systems are developed later on in the book.

Case Example: A Computer System for Playing Ticktacktoe   This is an old game given as an example in many AI books. It is played between two opponents on a flat board marked out with three vertically aligned rows of three equally sized squares. A simple heuristic for playing ticktacktoe is: we choose the position which counts more for us than for our opponent. Every move is assigned a coefficient which estimates the "goodness" or the "fitness" of the move. The move that has the maximum "fitness" is chosen. Here, an example of a fitness (gain) function is given:

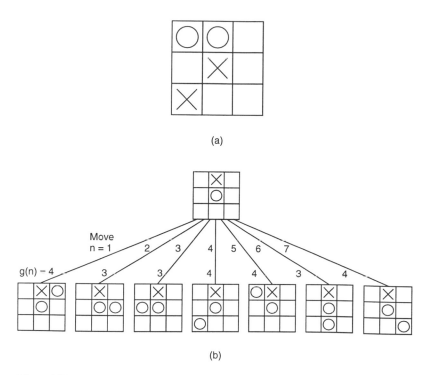

Figure 1.35
(a) The board of the tictactoe (TTT) game case example; (b) an example of implementing a heuristic strategy for choosing the next best move.

$g(n) = W(n) - O(n)$, for all possible moves $n = 1, 2, \ldots, N$.

where $W(n)$ is the number of all possible potential winning positions for "us" if we chose the nth possible move; $O(n)$ is the same for our opponent. Following the strategy set by using the fitness function above, one of the moves 1, 4, 5, or 7 must be chosen in the example shown in figure 1.35, as they have the highest goodness coefficients. But which of them? Of course, the heuristic strategies may be made more sophisticated with a little cost to pay in time. More specific strategic rules to play ticktacktoe are given in figure 1.36.

Go-Moku is a similar game. The game board consists of 19×19 squares. The winner is the player who first puts in a row, in a column, or diagonal five successive pieces. The bigger the game board, the bigger the problem space and the more difficult the task.

IF (a triple is made when putting on a position j)
        THEN (put on a position j) (priority 1)

IF (the opponent can make a triple when putting at a position j)
        THEN (put on a position j) (priority 0.9)

IF (putting on a position j gives us the most possible ways to make triples after the next
    moves and gives our opponent fewer possibilities to make triples)
        THEN (choose j to put on)(priority 0.8)

Figure 1.36
Several specific heuristic strategies for choosing the next move in the tictactoe case example.

Computer games can be realized by using different methods, some of them being:

• Symbolic AI rule-based systems, which realize heuristic strategy rules; heuristic rules make ticktacktoe easily realizable as a symbolic AI rule-based system.

• Fuzzy systems, which realize fuzzy rules for playing the game.

• Neural networks, which are trained with examples of good moves without a need to articulate the fitness function or possible strategies, etc. Neural networks can learn from examples the strategy to play successfully. Connectionist realizations are more difficult, but they highlight new methods for modeling human cognition, especially when the "goodness" function is learned by the system during play with a skilled player or a skilled computer program.

• Genetic algorithms, which do not require heuristic strategies to be articulated in advance, but require a simple selection criterion.

1.8.5 Design

The generic design problem can be formulated as creating objects that satisfy particular requirements following a given set of constraints. This area is still to be developed, as design is one of the most intellect-demanding and imagination-demanding human creative activities. Heuristics are very often used in automatic solving of design problems. This is because the constraints and the goals of the design can often be articulated in a linguistic form. A general heuristic rule for design would be:

IF (constraints Xi) and (goals Yj),
THEN (choose variant Zk with an estimated "goodness" CFk)

1.9   A General Approach to Knowledge Engineering

The main goal of the design of an intelligent system is to represent as adequately as possible the existing problem domain knowledge in order to better approximate the goal function, in most cases not known a priori. Problem solving was represented in section 1.2 as a process of mapping the domain space into the solution space of a problem by using problem knowledge—heuristic rules or data, or both.

Different methods can be used to achieve a solution. Figure 1.37 represents different methods and the relationship between them when used for problem solving. Different *pathways*, which map the domain space to the solution space through the problem knowledge, are shown. If we name a method (shown in a box) with the philosophical term paradigm, then we can distinguish *single-paradigm pathways* and *multiparadigm pathways*, comprising more than one path used in a chain. Depending on the type of the problem and the available problem knowledge, different methods could be recommended for use. Some considerations of when to use each of the methods for knowledge engineering and problem solving are the following:

• *Statistical methods* can be used when statistically representable data are available and the underlying type of goal function is known.

• *Symbolic AI rule-based systems* can be used when the problem knowledge is in the form of well-defined, rigid rules; no adaptation is possible, or at least it is difficult to implement.

• *Fuzzy systems* are applicable when the problem knowledge includes heuristic rules, but they are vague, ill-defined, approximate, possibly contradictory.

• *Neural networks* are applicable when problem knowledge includes data without having any knowledge as to what the type of the goal function might be; they can be used to learn heuristic rules after training with data; they also can be used to implement existing fuzzy or symbolic rules, providing a flexible approximate reasoning mechanism.

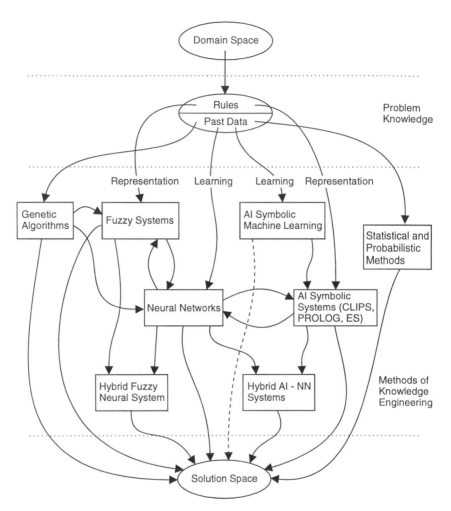

Figure 1.37
Different "pathways" can be used for knowledge engineering and problem solving to map the
domain space into the solution space.

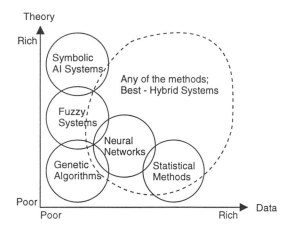

Figure 1.38
Usability of different methods for knowledge-engineering and problem-solving depending on availability of data and expertise (theories) on a problem.

• *Genetic algorithms* require neither data sets nor heuristic rules, but a simple selection criterion to start with; they are very efficient when only a little is known to start with.

Two *generic operations* are shown in figure 1.37 which are used by the methods: *representation*, when heuristic rules are available, and *learning*, when data are available. Different methods facilitate these two operations to a different degree, as shown graphically in figure 1.38. For example, symbolic AI methods are applicable when the problem knowledge is rich in theory and poor in data. Multiparadigm pathways involve more than one paradigm for solving a problem. Typical multiparadigm pathways are explained in chapter 6. Some of them are (see figure 1.37):

• A neural network is used to learn fuzzy rules, which are implemented in a fuzzy inference system.

• Symbolic AI machine-learning method is used and the rules learned are implemented in a symbolic AI reasoning machine.

• Symbolic AI rules are combined with neural networks in a hybrid system.

• Genetic algorithm is used to define values for some learning parameters in a neural network.

• Fuzzy rules are either implemented in a connectionist architecture or combined with neural networks in a hybrid system.

1.10   Problems and Exercises

Part A: Case Example Solution

1. Solving *speech recognition problems* requires adequate transformation techniques to transform the raw speech signal into a set of features. This transformation reduces the data and makes the recognition easier through dealing with smaller amounts of data. In addition to the Fourier transform, the following transformation can be used:

• *Cepstral coefficients*: The *cepstrum* is defined as an aggregated coefficient calculated over logarithm transformation of filtered signals. Some computer speech recognition systems use mel-scaled cepstrum coefficients (MSCC) (Davis and Mermestein 1980). Cepstral parameters are often preferred for speech recognition applications in noisy environments because they have been derived from high-resolution spectral estimators (Picone 1993). One segment of a wave speech signal is represented by a vector of n MSCC.

• *Linear prediction*: The linear prediction model of speech states that each speech sample can be predicted from the sum of weighted past samples of speech. The values of the coefficients are calculated by minimizing the error between the actual speech and the predicted speech.

Figure 1.39 shows the formulas that can be used to achieve the above transformations.

Part B: Practical Tasks

2. Give a definition of *heuristics* for problem-solving. What is "goodness" of a heuristic? What does it mean for a heuristic to be "informed?" Give examples of ill- and well-informed heuristics.

3. What is the difference between past historical data and heuristic rules? What is the difference between a rule and a formula? Give three examples of each for a different generic problem and a different application domain area.

4. Give a general form of a heuristic rule and explain it. Give general forms of heuristic rules for four generic problems and explain each of them.

(1) Discrete Fourier Transform (DFT):

$$S(k) = \sum_{n=0}^{N_s} s(n) e^{-j2\pi kn/N_s} \qquad k=0,1,..N_s-1$$

where $S(k)$ is the kth frequency component, and N_s is the size of the analysis frame.

(2) Cepstrum transformation:

$$c(n) = \frac{1}{N_s} \sum_{k=0}^{N_s-1} \log_{10} |S(k)| e^{j2\pi kn/N_s} \qquad 0 \le n \le N_s-1$$

where $c(n)$ is the cepstrum coefficient and N_s is the number of samples in a frame.

(3) Mel-scaled cepstrum coefficients $(c_m(n))$:

$$c_m(i) = \sum_{k=1}^{N_f} X_K \cos[i(k-\frac{1}{2})\frac{\pi}{N_f}] \qquad i=1,2...M$$

where N_f is the number of mel-scaled filters, X_k, $k=1,2,...N_f$, represents the log-energy output of the kth filter and M is the number of cepstrum coefficients. Cepstral parameters are often preferred for speech recognition applications in noisy environments as they have been derived from high resolution spectral estimators (Picone, 1993).

(4) Linear prediction:

$$s(n) = -\sum_{i=1}^{N_{LP}} a_{LP}(i) s(n-i) + e(n)$$

where $s(n)$ is the current speech sample, N_{LP} is the number of linear predictor coefficients, $a_{LP}(i)$ are the weights of the past speech samples, also known as predictor coefficients, and $e(n)$ is the error of the model. The values of the coefficients are calculated by minimising the error between the actual speech and the predicted speech.

Figure 1.39
Different transformations applicable to speech signals.

5. Give one more example of a specific problem for every generic problem type.

6. Suggest a minimum set of features which can be used to distinguish the two handwritten digits 3 and 5.

7. What is the meaning of *data rate reduction* in speech recognition systems? Give an example.

8. Why are speech signal transformations needed?

9. What are the difficulties in building ASR systems?

10. Is the stock market predictable according to figure 1.23? Explain your arguments.

11. What reasons should one use when choosing the feature space for prediction?

12. Give another example of a specific problem of prediction. Explain all the general issues given in section 1.6.1 for this particular problem.

13. Imagine that two more fuzzy values are defined for the angle and the angular velocity in the Inverted Pendulum control example, which are named positive large and negative large. Add some more fuzzy rules to the set given in figure 1.33 to describe the reaction of the control system if these values happen on the input.

14. Imagine a problem called the *Ball and Beam Problem*. The beam is made to rotate in a vertical plane around the center of rotation. The ball is free to roll along the beam. The task is to articulate an initial set of fuzzy rules for keeping the ball in a balanced position by applying a force to the beam, if the object is represented by four state variables—the distance between the center of the ball and the center of rotation; the change in the distance; the angle between the beam and the horizontal axis; and the change in the angle.

15. An example of an optimization problem is *the Resource Scheduling Problem*. A project consists of a set of activities on a time scale. Every activity has been assigned five parameters: the earliest possible starting day, the earliest possible completion day, the latest possible starting day, the latest possible completion day, and the number of workers involved. The problem is to find the most "leveled" (even) distribution of number of workers until completion of the whole project. Give heuristic rules for solving the problem after introducing reasonable restrictions.

16. *The Resource Assignment Problem* consists of assigning n workers to n jobs in the best (most profitable) way, when given the profit c_{ij} of assigning every worker i to every job j. Give heuristic rules for solving that problem. How can you evaluate the "goodness" of these heuristics?

17. What characteristic of neural networks makes them suitable for solving the specific problems given in this chapter?

18. Explain the difference between the different pathways in figure 1.37.

19. Looking at the data set of water flow into a sewage plant graphed in appendix C and in figure 7.1, try to elaborate rules for predicting the flow depending on the time (the hour) of day.

Part C: A Sample Project on Data Analysis

Topic: Speech Data Analysis

TASKS (see Appendixes G and J)

1. *Speech data collection*: Record three times each the digit words from 0 to 9 spoken by yourself. Save the recorded raw speech files on a disk. Explain in a few sentences what "sampling frequency" is and how it should be chosen for particular recordings. Report the values for the following parameters for one recorded digit from each of the groups: {0, 1, 2, 3}; {4, 5, 6}; {7, 8, 9}:

a. Recording time.

b. Sampling frequency.

c. Number of samples.

d. Size of the raw data (in kilobytes).

Explain the relationship between the recording time, sampling frequency, number of samples, and size of the raw signal.

2. *Speech data display*: Explain in a paragraph the principles of at least three ways of displaying speech data, for example, waveform, spectrum, frequency display. Display the spectra of the digits chosen for analysis.

3. *Speech data grouping—phoneme analysis*: Define by observation the boundary between the following phonemes in the pronounced words: /z/and /e/ in *zero*; /t/ and /u/ in *two*; /f/ and /o/ in *four*; /f/ and /ai/ in *five*; /s/ and /e/ in *seven*; /ei/ and /t/ in *eight*; /n/ and /ai/ in *nine*. Separate the areas of the different phonemes. Explain briefly some general differences

between the spectra of the fricatives you have in your examples (/z/, /f/, /s/, /Θ/) and the vowels (/e/, /u/, /o/, /ai/, etc.). Such differences can be, for example, amplitude in the time domain, energy in the frequency domain, etc.

4. *Variations of speech*

a. Compare the spectra of one digit in its three pronunciations. Explain the difference.

b. Compare the spectra of different appearances of a phoneme in different words, for example, /f/ appears in "five" and "four." Explain the difference (the so-called coarticulation effect).

5. *Speech data transformations*

a. Explain why speech data transformation would be needed.

b. Explain the rationale of the Fourier and the mel-scale transformations.

c. Give an example of two small consecutive segments of a spoken digit where the waveforms look the same (or very similar), but the spectra are very different. Explain why this is happening.

d. Select a vowel segment from the spectrum of speech data and plot the "frequency vs. energy" for this segment. Find and report the frequency with the highest energy.

1.11   Conclusion

The main point of this chapter is to try to answer the following questions:

1. What is knowledge engineering about?

2. What is the "Beauty" of the heuristics?

3. What are the major AI generic problems, for example, pattern recognition, speech recognition and language analysis, prediction, control, decision-making, monitoring, diagnosis, games-playing, design? A particular emphasis is given on the problem of speech recognition.

4. What are the major difficulties in solving these problems and what are the main reasons for bringing the methods of fuzzy systems and neural networks to these areas?

5. How do different methods of knowledge-engineering relate to one another? What major "pathways" can be followed when solving a particular problem?

I hope that after having read this chapter, you will proceed to the next chapters with a clearer idea of why you should read about data analysis, the symbolic AI and probabilistic methods (chapter 2), the methods of fuzzy systems (chapter 3), and the methods of neural networks (chapters 4 and 5); about using hybrids of all the above techniques (chapter 6), and finally, how to make use of chaos (chapter 7).

1.12   Suggested Reading

For the points discussed in this chapter the following references can be recommended for further reading.

Symbolic AI, expert systems—Giarratano and Riley (1989); Pratt (1994); Dean et al. (1995)

Genetic algorithms—Holland (1992); Goldberg (1989); Davis (1991); Michaliewicz (1992); Fogel (1995)

Pattern recognition—Weiss and Kulikowski (1991); Nigrin (1994); Pao (1989); Bezdek and Pal (1992)

Speech and language processing—Morgan and Scofield (1992); Owens (1993); Kasabov and Watson (1994)

Time-series prediction—Weigend and Gershenfeld (1993)

Financial and business prediction—Deboeck (1994); Kaufman (1987); Goonatilake and Kheball (1994)

Control—Werbos (1992); Wang (1994); for a mathematical solution of the Ball and Beam Problem, see Hanser et al. (1992)

Statistical methods—Metcalfe (1994)

Generic and specific AI problems: Schwefel and Manner (1990)

2 Knowledge Engineering and Symbolic Artificial Intelligence

This chapter begins with an explanation of the basic issues in knowledge engineering: representation, inference, learning, generalization, explanation, interaction, validation and adaptation. The methods of knowledge representation and methods of inference are discussed. Two main problems of today's expert systems, the problem of knowledge acquisition and the problem of reasoning in uncertainties (approximate reasoning), are discussed. Probabilistic methods of representing uncertainty, as well as nonprobabilistic ones are introduced. The chapter prepares the reader to look at fuzzy systems and neural networks as prospective "candidates" for solving those problems. It is demonstrated later in the book that the former are very powerful in representing and reasoning with vague heuristic knowledge, while the latter are excellent tools for knowledge acquisition and data-based reasoning.

Production systems are discussed more thoroughly here as they are used as a major AI paradigm implemented as symbolic AI production systems, as fuzzy production systems, as connectionist production systems, and as hybrid connectionist production systems elsewhere in the book.

2.1 Data, Information, and Knowledge: Major Issues in Knowledge Engineering

2.1.1 Data, Information, and Knowledge

What are *data*? What is *information*? What is *knowledge*? Well, data are the "raw material," the "mess of numbers." They could be numbers only, without contextual meaning, for example, 3, 78.5, -20. Data can also be contextually explained, structured, organized in groups and structures. Such data are called information. So, information is any structured data which have contextual meaning, for example, the temperature is 20°C. Knowledge is high-level structured information. Information, in its broad meaning, includes both structured data and knowledge, which is explained below.

Knowledge is "condensed" information. It is a concise presentation of previous experience. It is the "rules of thumb" which we use when we do things. How many rules of thumb do we use in our everyday life? Are there many, or are there only a few, very general ones, which are widely applicable to different problems? Is there anything else we apply in addition to these few rules of thumb, in order to be able to solve millions and millions of very different, or slightly different problems?

2.1.2   Major Issues in Knowledge Engineering

In order to realize the pathways given in figure 1.37, which lead from the domain space D to the solution space S for a given problem and given problem knowledge, eight major issues have been considered. These are: (1) representation, (2) inference, (3) learning, (4) generalization, (5) interaction, (6) explanation, (7) validation, and (8) adaptation. The main characteristics of these issues are discussed briefly in this subsection and thoroughly in the remainder of the chapter.

1. *Representation* is the process of transforming existing problem knowledge to some of the known knowledge-engineering schemes in order to process it by applying knowledge-engineering methods. The result of the representation process is the problem knowledge base in a computer format. Explicitly represented knowledge is called *structured knowledge*.

Some questions to be considered when choosing methods to represent problem knowledge are:

a. *What kind of knowledge is it?* Structured or unstructured? Exact or inexact? Precise or imprecise? Complete or incomplete?

b. *Which method* of representation best suits the way people solve that problem?

c. *Are there alternative methods* for representing the problem knowledge? Which one is the simplest? Using alternative methods for knowledge representation is recommended at the design stage of a knowledge-based system. The one which least "corrupts" the problem knowledge should be chosen.

2. *Inference* is the process of matching current facts from the domain space to the existing knowledge and inferring new facts. An inference process is a chain of matchings. The intermediate results obtained during the inference process are matched against the existing knowledge. The length of the chain is different. It depends on the knowledge base and on the inference method applied.

Fuzzy inference methods assume that all the rules are activated at every cycle and contribute collectively to the solution. It is a parallel one-shot inference, but the inference process can continue as the new inferred results can be fed again as inputs.

In the neural inference models no explicit rules are used. Neural structures are obtained as a result of training with past data. This is not true for the connectionist production systems which can interpret explicit production rules in a connectionist way.

A match can be either exact, with the new facts matching exactly the conditions in the heuristic rules, or partial, when the facts are allowed to partially match the existing knowledge base.

3. *Learning* is the process of obtaining new knowledge. It results in a better reaction to the same inputs at the next session of operation. It means improvement. It is a step toward adaptation. Learning is a major characteristic of intelligent systems. Three major approaches to learning are the following:

a. *Learning through examples.* Examples of the form of $(\mathbf{x}_i, \mathbf{y}_i)$, where $\mathbf{x}_i$ is a vector from the domain space $\mathbf{D}$ and $\mathbf{y}_i$ is a vector from the solution space $\mathbf{S}$, $i = 1, 2, \ldots, n$, are used to train a system about the goal function $F: \mathbf{D} \rightarrow \mathbf{S}$. This type of learning is typical for neural networks. Symbolic AI machine-learning methods based on learning from examples are also very popular.

b. *Learning by being told.* This is a direct or indirect implementation of a set of heuristic rules into a system. For example, the heuristic rules to monitor a car can be directly represented as production rules. Or instructions given to a system in a text form by an instructor (written text, speech, natural language) can be transformed into internally represented machine rules. This kind of "learning" is typical for symbolic AI systems and for fuzzy systems.

c. *Learning by doing.* This way of learning means that the system starts with nil or little knowledge. During its functioning it accumulates valuable experience and profits from it, so it performs better over time. This method of learning is typical for genetic algorithms.

Symbolic methods for machine learning are discussed in this chapter; connectionist methods for learning explicit rules are presented in chapter 5.

4. *Generalization* is the process of matching new, unknown input data with the problem knowledge in order to obtain the best possible solution, or one close to it. Generalization means reacting properly to new situations, for example, recognizing new images, or classifying new objects and situations. Generalization can also be described as a transition from a particular object description to a general concept description. This is a major characteristic of all intelligent systems.

5. *Interaction* means communication between a system on the one hand and the environment or the user on the other hand, in order to solve a given problem. Interaction is important for a system to adapt to a new situation, improve itself, learn. Interaction between systems is a major characteristic of the distributed decision systems, where each module of a system takes part in the problem-solving process and communicates with the other modules. This is the essense of the so-called *agent-based approach*.

6. *Explanation* is a desirable property for many AI systems. It means tracing, in a contextually comprehensible way, the process of inferring the solution, and reporting it. Explanation is easier for the symbolic AI systems when sequential inference takes place. But it is difficult for parallel methods of inference and especially difficult for the massive parallel ones.

7. *Validation* is the process of testing how good the solutions produced by a system are. The results produced by a system are usually compared with the results obtained either by experts or by other systems. Validation is an extremely important part of the process of developing every knowledge-based system. Without comparing the results produced by the system with reality, there is little point in using it.

8. *Adaptation* is the process of changing a system during its operation in a dynamically changing environment. Learning and interaction are elements of this process. Without adaptation there is no intelligence. Adaptive systems are discussed in chapter 7.

2.1.3 Symbolic, Fuzzy, and Neural Systems—Which One Is the Best?

Symbolic AI, fuzzy, and neural systems facilitate differently the realization of the eight major issues of knowledge engineering discussed above. Table 2.1 gives a rough comparison between them.

While the symbolic AI and fuzzy systems facilitate representing structured knowledge, neural networks facilitate using predominantly unstructured knowledge. Inference is exact in the AI symbolic systems and approximate in the other two. Learning is difficult to achieve in the symbolic AI and fuzzy systems, but it is an inherent characteristic of neural networks. Generalization in the symbolic AI systems is not as good as it is in the fuzzy systems and neural networks as the latter can deal with inexact, missing, and corrupted data better. Good explanation is more difficult to achieve in the connectionist systems as knowledge in them, after learning, is distributed among many connections, while symbolic AI

Table 2.1
A comparison of symbolic, fuzzy, and neural systems

Issue	Symbolic	Fuzzy	Neural
Representation	Structured	Structured	Unstructured
Inference	Exact	Approximate	Approximate
Learning	Modest	No	Very good
Generalization	Weak	Very good	Very good
Interaction	Good	Good	Good
Explanation	Very good	Very good	Weak
Validation	Good	Good	Modest
Adaptation	Modest	Modest	Good

and fuzzy systems, if well written, could be self explaining. Of course, building a sophisticated explanation of what is happening in a system while solving a problem requires deep understanding of both the domain problem and the computer reasoning methods used in the system. Good adaptation is achieved in fuzzy neural networks. The above issues are discussed in this book.

2.1.4   Separating Knowledge from Data and from Inference in the Knowledge-Based Systems

There are many reasons for separating data from knowledge, and separating both from the control mechanism in a system. Some of these are the following:

• Data may represent a current situation, for example, the temperature of the cooling system in a car. A characteristic of data is that they may vary frequently.

• Rules are stable, long-term information. Rules do not depend on slight variations in data describing a current situation.

• Separating the control, as an inference procedure applicable to a set of rules and data, provides an opportunity to expand the knowledge when necessary without changing the inference procedure. It also makes the decision process clearer and the process of designing the whole program much easier.

Separating knowledge from data and from the inference means easier modification of each of these components. But they all make one system, so they should fit to one another, be coherent.

In symbolic AI systems explicit knowledge is separated from the representation of the current data and from the inference mechanism. Separating data from knowledge and from control contrasts with standard programming techniques. Imperative computer languages, for example, C, PASCAL, MODULA 2, separate data (variables and constants) from knowledge (procedures), but the control mechanism is still embodied in the procedures. A full separation is achieved in the so-called declarative computer languages, for example, logic programming languages (PROLOG), and production languages (e.g., CLIPS). Both languages require the presence of structured problem knowledge.

In neural networks current data are usually represented by the activation level of neurons and knowledge is distributed among the connection weights. The principle of local processing in neurons means that every neuron is a separate processing element, but the results are obtained by the neural system as a whole. It is difficult to separate data and knowledge in a neural network unless special encoding is used to represent the information.

2.2 Data Analysis, Data Representation, and Data Transformation

We are surrounded by masses of data. Data may be very informative, containing a lot of information about different aspects of the processes. It is up to us to make use of it. Before developing sophisticated methods for problem solving, our first task is to scrutinize the data, look at it from different points of view. In order to do that, it might be necessary to apply certain transformations. This is the topic of this section.

2.2.1 About the Variety of Domain Data

Domain data can be of various types. Some of them are described here:

• *Quantitative vs. qualitative data.* Quantitative data are a collection of numerical values; qualitative data are a collection of symbols, for example, red, small, John Smith. Quantitative data can be either *numerical continuous* or *numerical discrete*.

• *Static vs. dynamic data.* Static data do not change over time; while dynamic data describe the changes in a process over time.

• *Natural vs. synthetic.* Natural data are data collected from a process during its operation; synthetic data are artificially generated according to some laws or rules describing the process.

• *Clean vs. noisy data.* Data obtained without any external disturbance or corruption are called clean; noisy data mean that a small random ingredient is added to the clean data.

2.2.2 Data Representation

It is very important to correctly represent data before they are processed in a computer system. Representation should satisfy some requirements:

• *Adequateness.* Data should be adequately represented in a computer system.

• *Unambiguity.* Different data items should possibly be represented differently before being processed.

• *Simplicity.* Data should be represented in the simplest possible way before being processed.

A tradeoff is sought between the above requirements.

Different representation schemes are known from the area of database systems. For example, an object can be described by a relation and represented as a tuple of the type of ⟨object-attribute-value⟩: ⟨name_of_the_ object attribute$_1$ value$_1$ attribute$_2$ value$_2$ ... attribute$_k$ value$_k$),

Example

(example23 SL = 5.7 SW = 4.4 PL = 1.5 PW = 0.4), or in a shorter form,

example23 = (5.7 4.4 1.5 0.4)

In a general notation, a data set is characterized by an attribute vector $X = (x_1, x_2, \ldots, x_k)$, where x_i is the ith attribute. One data instance is a point (vector) in a k-dimensional attribute space. In the example above, the Iris instances can be represented as points in a four-dimensional space. Same objects can be represented by data points in different dimensional spaces. For example, data may contain information about the class, for example, example23 = (5.7 4.4 1.5 0.4 Setosa), which is the representation of the same instance, but this time in a five-dimensional space.

How many dimensions should a problem space contain in order to adequately represent objects and to achieve satisfactory processing? Should we include the size of the stem for a better classification of new instances of Iris? If we consider, say, 50 attributes for the iris classification problem, would it be more difficult to do the classification because of considering too many unimportant attributes which may simply be noise?

The problem of choosing appropriate dimensionality for solving a given problem is called "the curse of dimensionality." Two classes of data can be distinguished in this respect, namely, *small-dimensional* vs. *large-dimensional data.*

Some objects or processes called fractals can be represented in a space that is composed of fractions of dimensions. A fractal space has noninteger dimensionality, for example, 2.5. A point has a dimensionality of 1, a straight line a dimensionality of 2, but a figure may occupy a small part of an *embedding* two-dimensional space, for example, a curving line around a point, or a spiral with a small radius, etc. One hypothesis about the stock market, called the *fractal market hypothesis*, says that a market is a nonlinear dynamical system with noninteger fractal dimensions (Deboeck, 1994).

Visualizing data may help to chose a good data representation, a proper dimensionality and a proper method for solving the problem. Different way of visualization can be used:

Bar graphs: Figure 2.1 shows the soil case example average data from table 1.1 as bar graphs. The bar "patterns," which represent different classes, seem different, which may be a hint that the chosen eight features should be enough for a good classification.

Scattered points graphs: Figure 2.2 shows a representation of the Iris data in a two-dimensional space of "petal length" and "petal width" attributes. This representation shows that there is overlapping between the classes Virginica and Versicolor and using the two attributes only would not be sufficient for building a classification system. If discretization on the data is required, the graphs from figure 2.2 can help to define in a reasonable way the discretization intervals. One possible discretization is shown in figure 2.3 and commented on in the next section (see figure 1.11).

2.2.3   Data Transformations

Data can be used in a system either as raw data or after some transformations. Why should data be transformed? A data transformation may have the following objectives:

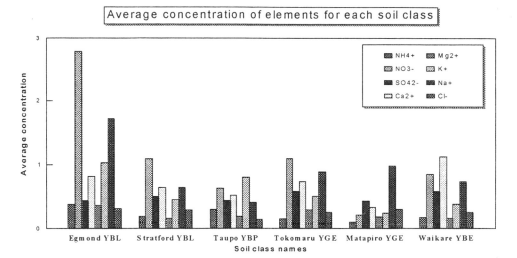

Figure 2.1
Bar graphs representing the data from table 1.1. The difference between the class patterns is noticeable.

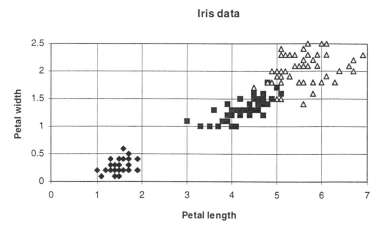

Figure 2.2
Iris data represented in the two-dimensional space of the two variables Petal length and Petal width. Class denotation: Setosa-diamond; Versicolor-square; Virginica-triangle.

4 intervals for the first attribute:[4.00, 4.99], [5.00, 5.99], [6.00, 6.99],
          [7 and above]

3 intervals for the second attribute: [2.00, 2.99],[3.00, 3.99], [4.00, 8.00]

6 intervals for the third attribute: [1.00, 1.99], [2.00, 2.99], [3.00, 3.99],
          [4.00, 4.99], [5.00, 5.99], [6.00, 7.00];

3 intervals for the fourth attribute: [0, 0.99], [1, 1.99], [2, 3].

Figure 2.3
A set of intervals for Iris data discretization.

• *Data rate reduction.* Instead of using all the recorded data, some meaningful features are extracted from it and used further on, for example, Fourier transform on speech data and mel-scale cepstrum coefficients, which may reduce the data rate by several orders of magnitude.

• *Noise suppression.* Raw data may be noisy, a problem that is overcome by using transformed data values.

Different data transformations are possible.

• *Sampling.* This is the process of selecting a subset of the data available. Sampling can be applied to continuous time-series data, for example, speech data are sampled at a frequency of 22 kHz, or to static data in which a subset of the data set is taken for processing purposes.

• *Discretization.* This is the process of representing continuous-value data with the use of subintervals where the real values lie. In figure 2.3 Iris data are discretized such that the first attribute is discretized in four intervals, the second attribute in three intervals, the third attribute in six intervals, and the fourth attribute in three intervals. Having this discretization, the instance (5.3 4.7 1.2 3.0), for example, becomes, after discretization, (2 3 1 3). Instances in a data set may contain attributes with different types of values—numerical, linguistic, and so on. An instance (5.3 male 8.4 high ill), for example, after a discretization becomes (6 2 9 1 1), assuming that the first and the third attributes are discretized into 10 intervals having cardinal numbers as boundaries; the second attribute has two possible values; the fourth one, three; and all the instances are classified into two classes, "ill" or "healthy," where 1 represents "ill" and 0 represents "healthy." Discretization is a kind of approximation. When we discretize we may lose information.

• *Normalization.* Normalization is moving the scale of the raw data into a predefined scale, for example, [0, 1]. Normalization is usually required by most of the connectionist models. Normalization can be:

> *Linear*; a formula which can be used for linear normalization of data in the interval [0, 1] is the following:
>
> $v_{norm} = (v - x_{min})/(x_{max} - x_{min})$,
>
> where v is a current value of the variable x, x_{min} is the minimum value for this variable, and x_{max} is the maximum value for that variable x in the data set.
>
> *Logarithmic,*
>
> *Exponential*, etc.

• *Linear transformations.* These are transformations $F(\mathbf{x})$ of data vectors $\mathbf{x}$ such that F is a linear function of $\mathbf{x}$, for example, $F(x) = 2x + 1$.

• *Nonlinear transformations.* These are transformations $F(\mathbf{x})$ of data vector $\mathbf{x}$ where F is a nonlinear function of $\mathbf{x}$, for example, $F(x) = 1/(1 + e^{-x \cdot c})$, where c is a constant. Other typical nonlinear transformations are:

> *Logarithm function*, for example, $F(x) = \log_{10} x$
>
> *Gaussian function* (used later in the book)

Nonlinear transformations impose a "desirable distortion." For a comparison between a linear transformation ($y = x$) and a nonlinear transformation (gaussian function) on the same two values x_1 and x_2 for the independent variable x, see figure 2.4.

Two special nonlinear transformations are discussed below:

• *Fast Fourier transform (FFT)* is a special nonlinear transformation applied mainly to speech data to transform the signal taken for a small portion of time from the time-scale domain into the frequency-scale domain. The idea is as follows. The signal is assumed to be stationary within a small period of time (say 10 ms) called *window.* After having digitized the signal with, say, 20-kHz sampling rate, we take the raw data values of the energy of the signal falling in a window of 10 ms (in this case 200 points) and calculate the frequency distribution of this portion of the

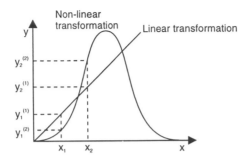

Figure 2.4
Linearly and nonlinearly transformed data.

signal on the frequency scale (usually up to half the sampling rate, this frequency being called the Kotelnikov-Nyquist frequency). The discrete Fourier transform and its variant FFT are transformations used to find the frequency distribution of a signal from its digitized energy values over time for a small window of the signal (see figure 1.39). FFT can be applied not only on speech data but on any time-series data taken from a process, if frequency is considered to be an important characteristic of the process.

• *Wavelet transformation* is another nonlinear transformation. It can represent slight changes of the signal within the chosen window from the time scale (for the FFT it was assumed that the signal does not change or at least does not change significantly within a window). Here, within the window, several transformations are taken from the raw signal by applying *wavelet basis functions* of the form:

$$W_{a,b}(x) = f(ax - b),$$

where: f is a nonlinear function, a is a *scaling parameter*, and b is a *shifting parameter* (varies between 0 and a). So, instead of one transformation, several transformations are applied by using wavelet basis functions Wa, $0, \ldots, Wa, 1, \ldots Wa, 2, \ldots Wa, a$. An example of such set of functions when $f(x) = \cos(\pi x)$ is given in figure 2.5. Wavelet transformations preserve time variations of a signal within a certain time interval.

2.2.4   Data Analysis

Very often, when dealing with a complex task like stock market prediction, it is important to analyze the process by analyzing data available for this process, before any methods for solving the problem are applied.

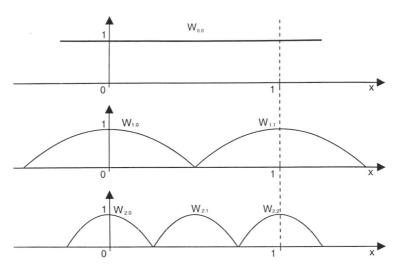

Figure 2.5
Wavelets.

Usually, the results from the analysis suggest the method that will be used later on. Data analysis aims at answering important questions about the process under investigation:

• What are the statistical parameters of the data available for the process —mean, standard deviation, distribution (see below)?

• What is the nature of the process—random, chaotic, periodic, stable, etc.?

• How are the available data distributed in the problem space—clustered into groups, sparse, covering only patches of the problem space and therefore not enough to rely on them fully when solving the problem, uniformly distributed?

• Are there missing data? How much? Is that a critical obstacle which could make the process of solving the problem by using data impossible? What other methods can be used, either by addition to, or substitution of, methods based on data?

• *What features can be extracted from data?*

Three groups of methods for data analysis are outlined below:

1. *Statistical analysis methods* discover the repetitiveness in data based on probability estimation. Simple parameters, like mean, standard deviation,

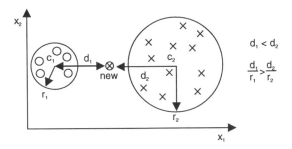

Figure 2.6
Clustering data may help to classify new data.

distribution function, as well as more complex analysis like factor analysis, to weight the importance of different input variables on the values of output variables; regression analysis, to find a formula that approximates data for a given output variable, and so forth, can be used.

2. *Clustering methods* find groups in which data are grouped based on measuring the distance between the data items. Clustering in a two-dimensional space by using two circlelike clusters is illustrated in figure 2.6. The distances between a new data point and the two centers of clusters c_1 and c_2 can be either absolute or normalized values. In the case presented in the figure, the latter is more appropriate for classification purposes.

Let us have a set X of p data items represented in an n-dimensional space. A clustering procedure results in defining k disjoint subsets (clusters), such that every data item (n-dimensional vector) belongs to only one cluster. A cluster membership function M_i is defined for each of the clusters $C_1, C_2, \ldots, C_k$:

$M_i: X \rightarrow \{0, 1\}$,

$M_i(\mathbf{x}) = 1$, if $\mathbf{x} \in Ci$,

       0, otherwise.

where $\mathbf{x}$ is a data instance (vector) from X.

There are various algorithms for clustering, one of them being the *k-means clustering algorithm*. It aims at finding k centers $\{c_1, c_2, \ldots, c_k\}$ in an n-dimensional space, such that the mean of the squares of the distances between each data point $\mathbf{x} \in X$ and the cluster center closest to it is minimized. In chapter 3 a fuzzy clustering algorithm is given, which uses fuzzy borders between the clusters, thus allowing one item to partially belong to more than one cluster.

3. *Methods for feature extraction* transform data into another space, a space of features. We can use different transformation techniques to transform raw data space into a feature space knowing how to calculate the features, for example, FFT points, wavelets, etc. But if there is no formula to calculate features, how are significant features extracted from data and how is the processing done over them? Extracting features is an ability of the human brain for abstraction. But how can computer systems do that? Different methods can be applied, depending on the application area and the generic problem under consideration. For example, in pattern recognition and image processing, specialized methods for extracting lines, curves, edges, and so forth from images or patterns can be applied. Neural networks can also be used for feature extraction.

2.3   Information Structures and Knowledge Representation

This section is a brief introduction to structures in which information and knowledge can be represented. Though the structures are for general use, they are widely used in AI methods and techniques.

2.3.1   What Is an Information Structure?

Information is a collection of structured data. In its broad meaning, it includes knowledge as well as simple meaningful data. But how to represent these structures in a computer in such a way that no significant information is lost, further processing of information is facilitated, representation is adequate to the nature of the data links and relations, and the representation is flexible, allowing expanding of information items, links, and the relations between them?

Representing data and knowledge in structures may, and usually does, influence the functionality of the system as a whole. Data should be handled with care and as much information as possible should be kept throughout the information processing for further use.

An information structure contains information elements and links between them. A structure can represent data and links between them from the solution space S, or from the domain space D of a problem, or from both of them, as they may be considered as a general problem state space

P. Every state in the state space *P* is a data item, but there can be links between the states representing possible transitions between states (all or only some of them might be possible). For the ticktacktoe game, for example, one state makes it possible to go on to other states afterward.

An information structure is a collection of information elements with a defined organization, operations over the elements, and a defined method of access to every element. Structures can be organized as *static* or *dynamic*. Static structures have a fixed number of elements. Dynamic structures do not have a fixed number of elements as the elements are created and deleted during the process of handling the information. Some ways of machine representation and operation over dynamic data structures are more useful than others. They are based on using elements called *pointers*. A pointer is a data element whose content is the location of another element. Sets, stacks, queues, linked lists, trees, and graphs are used as dynamic information structures.

2.3.2   Sets, Stacks, Queues, and Lists

The most common structure in mathematics and computing is the *set*. The set is a generic concept. It is defined as a collection of objects with operations defined over it as shown in figure 2.7. Typical set operations are union, intersection, complement, relative complement, difference, membership, equality, and subsethood.

A *stack* is a collection of ordered elements and two operations which can be performed only over the element that is currently at the "top," that is, to "push" an element on top of the stack, and "pop" an element from the stack. A stack has only one pointer element to point at the top of the stack. Figure 2.8 shows two realizations of a stack. The first is a dynamic stack where the elements do not have fixed positions in a memory space; they are "floating" in this space, their positions being kept in a pointer field of the previous elements of the whole stack. The second is a static realization of a stack, where the stack elements occupy consecutive places in a memory space.

Queues are data structures similar to the stack structure, but here two pointers are used—one for the input, and one for the output element of the structure. In figure 2.9 two realizations of a queue are shown: dynamic and static.

Linked lists are more general structures than stacks or queues. Elements in a list may be linked in different ways (figure 2.10). Typical operations

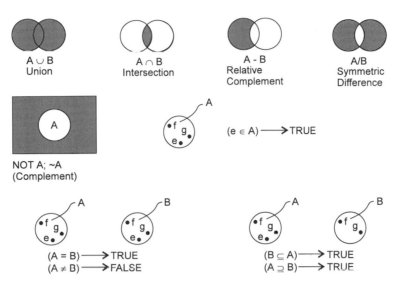

Figure 2.7
Set operations over two sets *A* and *B*.

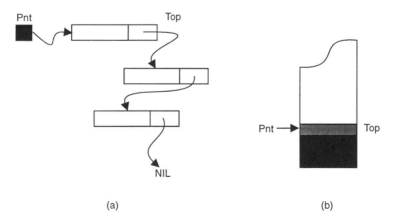

(a)

(b)

Figure 2.8
The stack organization—two possible realizations.

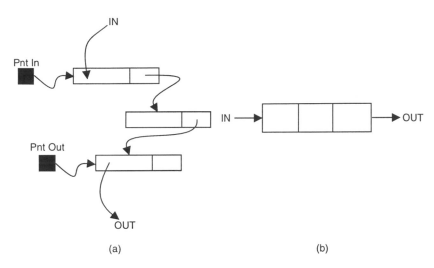

Figure 2.9
Organization in a queue structure: (a) dynamic realization; (b) static realization.

over lists are *insert* an element into a list, *delete* an element from a list, *search* for an element in a list. The first two are illustrated in figure 2.10. The way in which these operations are realized is mainly an efficient use of pointer fields in each of the elements in a list.

2.3.3   Trees and Graphs

Very useful structures used in knowledge engineering are *trees*. They are often used for representing decision charts, classification structures, plans, etc. A tree is a special case of a more general structure called a *directed graph*. A directed graph consists of a finite set of elements called *nodes* or *vertexes*, and a finite set of *directed arcs* that connect pairs of vertexes.

A *tree* is a directed graph in which one of the nodes, called *root*, has no incoming arcs, but from which each node in the tree can be reached by exactly one path. Vertexes that have no outgoing arcs are called *leaves*. Nodes that can be reached directly from a given node using one directed arc are called the *children* of that node, and the node is said to be the *parent*. Examples of using trees for representing problem knowledge are shown in figure 2.11A (a genealogical tree), in (B) (a parsing tree), and in (C) (an algebraic expression tree).

Tree structures are often used for representing the decision process for solving diagnostic, classification, and other generic problems. Figure 1.10

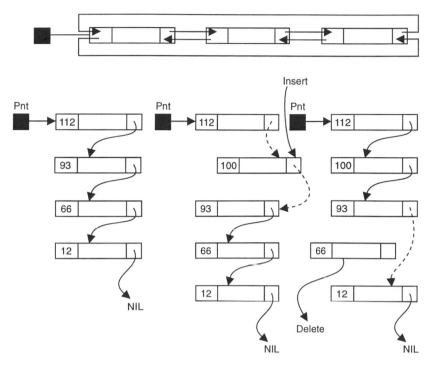

Figure 2.10
Linked lists: a general representation scheme and two operations over elements in a list—
"insert a new element" and "delete an element from a list."

is a good example of that. Such trees are called *decision trees*. If we consider every rule in a knowledge base as an item, then a decision tree links the rules such that if a conclusion in a rule *Ri* appears as a condition in another rule *Rj*, then *Ri* and *Rj* are connected in the tree structure.

Graphs are also often used as data structures. A graph is a set of *nodes* (*vertexes*) and a set of *arcs* connecting the nodes $G = (V, C)$. Figure 2.12(a) shows a simple graph.

If the edges in a graph are directed (arrows), the graph is called a *directed graph*; otherwise it is nondirected. The edges may be weighted, that is, a number is bound to every edge. If we traverse a graph by following edges from one vertex to another, we are following a *path in a graph*. A path is a sequence of contiguous arcs in a graph. Different types of paths may be distinguished in a graph:

a.

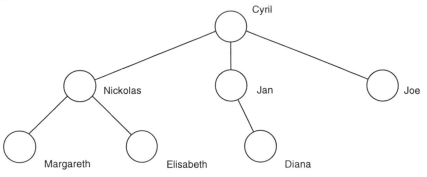

b.

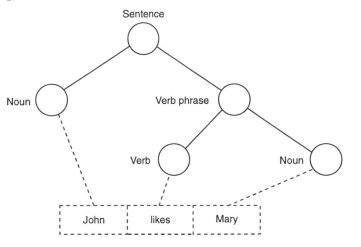

c.

$$(SIN\ x)^2\ +\ (A\ *\ B\ -\ C)$$

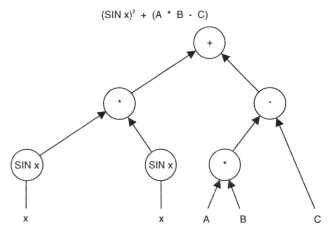

Figure 2.11
(a) A genealogical tree. (B) Parsing tree. (C) Algebraic expression tree.

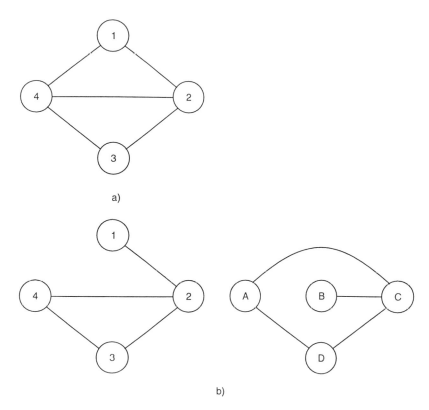

Figure 2.12
(a) A simple graph; (b) isomorphic graphs.

- *A cycle.* The path starts from one node and ends at the same node; a graph containing a cycle is said to be a *cyclic graph*; a graph with no cycles is *acyclic*.

- *A spanning tree.* A subset of edges of a graph that forms a tree (there are no cycles).

- *An Euler path* is a path in which every edge (arc) is traversed exactly once.

- *A Hamiltonian path* is a path in which every vertex (node) is traversed exactly once.

A *fully connected graph* contains a path between every pair of nodes. In a non-fully connected graph there should be at least one pair of nodes with no path between them.

Many interesting and difficult problems for graphs have been explored in the literature and different solutions suggested. Some *generic graph problems* are listed and explained below:

• *The shortest path problem*—to find the shortest path between two arbitrary nodes in a graph.

• *The Traveling Salesman Problem (TSP)*—the problem (introduced in chapter 1) is to find the minimum-cost cycle path starting from an arbitrary node.

• *Check for existence of a path* with a given length K between two arbitrary nodes in a graph.

• *Finding isomorphic graphs.* Structurally identical graphs are called isomorphic. Formally, we define a pair of graphs $G1$ and $G2$ to be isomorphic if there is one-to-one correspondence between the nodes of the graphs, such that if two nodes of one graph are adjacent, then their corresponding nodes in the other graph are adjacent too. An example of two isomorphic graphs is shown in figure 2.12b.

• *Transitive closure.* A graph GT is called a transitive closure of a graph G if for every vertexes X and Y in G such that Y is reachable from X, X and Y are adjacent in GT, that is,

IF Reachable(X, Y in G), THEN Adjacent (X, Y in GT)

• *Graph-coloring problem.* The problem is to "color" the nodes of a graph in such a way that there are no adjacent nodes with the same color.

2.3.4   Frames, Semantic Networks, and Schemata

Frames are structures which represent structured information for standard situations. Frames consist of slots (variables) and fillers (values). The slots represent typical characteristics of objects. With such uniform representation it would be easy to process this information (compare, search, or update). An example of a frame representation is given in figure. 2.13. Slots may represent not only static information but dynamic information as well. For example, a slot may represent a procedure to be processed over data from other slots. Frames are valuable when explicit and exact data and knowledge are available for solving comparatively simple problems.

Semantic networks use directed graphs to represent contextual information. The nodes represent objects and concepts, and the arcs, relations. Typical relations are: is_a; part_of; implies; etc. Semantic networks are

Slots	Filler
age	21
sex	female
name	Judith
occupation	programmer
hobby	swimming

Figure 2.13
Frame representation.

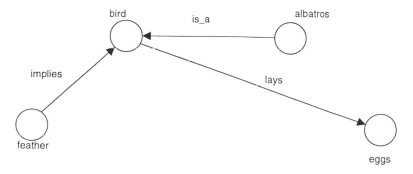

Figure 2.14
A semantic network. The nodes denote features, objects or classes and the arcs the relations between them.

useful for representing either flat, or hierarchical knowledge, but they are static. Updating data by learning and changing knowledge may be difficult to handle. Figure 2.14 shows an example of a simple semantic network where the arcs represent relations and the nodes represent objects.

Schemata are more general structures than a semantic network. They are based on representing knowledge as a stable state of a system consisting of many small elements which interact with one another when the system is moving from one state to another. The state of a system is composed by the states of all these elements. This way of representing knowledge is a distributed one: knowledge is represented as a state of a coalition of elements. It is dynamic as well because a small change in the input values (stimulus) would most probably lead to a new stable coalition—a new state of the whole system. Schemata are a valuable way of representing knowledge currently being explored because of their physiological plausibility.

2.3.5   About the Variety of Problem Knowledge and the Limitations of Current Techniques for Its Representation

Knowledge, as pointed out in chapter 1 and in section 2.1 of this chapter, is the information which represents long-term relationships, that is, ways of doing things, commonsense, ideas, methods, skills, and so forth. Knowledge is "condensed" information, "squashed" information, an extraction, the "essence" of things. A huge amount of knowledge has been accumulated worldwide during the conscious existence of humanity. This knowledge is changing all the time. How to make use of existing knowledge in a computer program? How to represent it in such a way that we keep the richness and the depth of the knowledge and also make it reasonable to use? To what extent do we compromise with these controversial requirements? Different categories of problem knowledge can be distinguished:

• *Global vs. local knowledge.* Knowledge can be global, for example, the knowledge that human beings have learned throughout their evolution, or local, for example, a rule on how to react to traffic lights.

• *Shallow vs. deep knowledge.* Knowledge can be shallow, for example, based on stimulus-reaction associations, or deep, for example, encapsulating complex models for explanation and analysis.

• *Explicit vs. implicit knowledge.* Knowledge can be explicit, for example, structured, or implicit, for example, unstructured, hidden, buried in data.

• *Complete vs. incomplete knowledge.* Knowledge is complete if it ensures a solution to the problem in all cases or situations, or incomplete if it has a restricted applicability.

• *Exact vs. inexact knowledge.* Knowledge is considered to be exact if it can be used and an exact solution to the problem is produced when exact input data are supplied, or inexact, uncertain, when it produces an approximate solution when exact or inexact data are supplied.

• *Hierarchical vs. flat knowledge.* Knowledge is hierarchical when some pieces of knowledge apply over others, or flat when all the knowledge is applicable at the same level. Hierarchical knowledge contains *meta-knowledge*, knowledge applicable over knowledge, for example, "We know what we do not know."

We have discussed different methods to structurally represent domain information and problem knowledge. But knowledge engineering requires mathematical models and theories to represent and do reasoning over knowledge in a consistent way. Such theories are the logic systems. Three of them are presented in the next sections, namely: (1) *propositional logic*, (2) *predicate logic*, and (3) *fuzzy logic*. Each uses different kinds of *rules* of the form of:

IF A, THEN B, or shortly: $A \rightarrow B$, where A is an antecedent (conditions), and B a consequent (conclusions, actions), and each uses different *methods for reasoning* (inference method).

Whatever method for representing problem knowledge is used in a computer system, it is usually a way of simplifying the problem to make it reasonable to handle. There is no universal method that can handle the variety of problem knowledge in the way humans do.

One problem should be mentioned when discussing the issue of knowledge representation. This is the so-called *frame problem*. What should we keep unchanged in the representation when the situation has changed? What should we update in the computer? How can the system know what has changed without checking all the data? For example, imagine that we have a computer system which maintains data about a house and monitors whether there is a possibility for a dangerous situation to occur (fire, burglary, earthquake, etc.). In order to monitor the house, the system keeps information about the location and many other properties and parameters of all the objects in the house. A camera takes pictures and the information in the computer is updated regularly, subject to an event which may happen. Suddenly, a glass drops on the floor in the kitchen. The global situation in the house has changed. Which data should be updated? To update all the data in the system may block the computer for days so that it is unable to react to new changes which might occur after this event and which might be really dangerous. Obviously, relationships between objects must be introduced in the computer system. But how many? This example illustrates the so-called frame problem.

2.4   Methods for Symbol Manipulation and Inference: Inference as Matching; Inference as a Search

Inference is the process of acquiring new facts when interpreting existing knowledge with current data. The whole process of inferring new facts and their manipulation is called reasoning. Inference in an AI system is what corresponds to the control process in conventional computer programs and what corresponds to the process of "thinking" in the human brain (both analogies are extremely slight and vague). An inference process has many aspects, some of which are discussed in this section. It is differently realized in different logic systems and AI methods.

2.4.1   Inference as a Process of Matching and Generalization

Suppose the knowledge base contains input-output associations (rules, data pairs) $R_j = (X_j, Y_j), j = 1, 2, \ldots, n$. The problem is to find a solution for a new input vector $\mathbf{x}_i^*$. This vector is mapped to the solution space S through a chain of rules until a solution $\mathbf{y}_i^*$ in the solution space S is found. Figure 2.15 illustrates this process. The solution is found after firing three rules in a chain. The first two infer partial solutions which are used as input data for the next rules in the chain. In some cases, in the fuzzy rule-based systems, for example, the solution is a single parallel match of the new facts with all the rules. Partial solutions, obtained by individual rules, are combined in order to achieve the final solution. The inference process can be considered as a *trace of states* in the problem space, every state representing a closer approximation to the solution. The trace can be used for explaining the solution process later on. The trace itself may

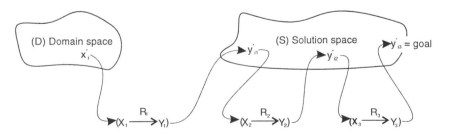

Figure 2.15
Inference as a chain of matches.

represent a solution to the problem. For example, a spoken word can be recognized as a sequence of phonemes on a phoneme map (the solution space).

The matching process can be either *exact*, or *partial*. Exact matching means that the matching facts coincide exactly with the condition elements in the left-hand side of the rules. For example, if the fact is x_i^*, there has to be a rule $x_j \rightarrow y_j$, such that $x_j = x_i^*$. Exact matching is typical for symbolic AI systems.

A partial match does not require equality between facts and the left-hand side of a rule. In this case an approximation or closeness is enough. But how approximately and how closely should a fact match a rule in order to fire that rule? This point has to be determined by the method used for approximate reasoning. Partial match is typical for fuzzy systems and for neural network models.

A generalization process can be represented as a chain of stepwise generalizations (see figure 2.15). At every step in the chain of inference, a generalization may be made.

2.4.2 Inference as a Search and Constraint Satisfaction

Generally speaking, inference is a process of searching for the solution in the solution space. The solution space for real problems is usually huge and contains states which have to be checked through as intermediate solutions to the problem. A search through the problem state space has to be performed in order to find out which state should be checked for a possible solution, or which rule should be applied to the new facts.

If the problem state space is not structured, that is, if there is no structure that represents relations between the states in the space, then a random search may be used and the *generate and test* strategy applied. A state is generated randomly, and a criterion for "fitness" (a function, a heuristic, etc.) is applied to evaluate how good the generated state is as a possible solution. To avoid generating all the possible states in the state space, a heuristic is required.

A simple strategy for search in the state space is the *exhaustive search*— trying all the possible states, either sequentially or in parallel, and then making a conclusion about the best one. This search is not practical because it requires an unrealistic number of operations, even for a problem of small size.

An inference can be considered as a process of searching for a state which optimizes a goal function. In this case, gradient-descent, or hill-climbing methods can be applied. Such methods are often used in neural networks.

When the problem space is structured, for example, in a tree, then the most favored searching strategies are "breadth first search"—testing first all the states which are at a certain level in the tree and then going to search among their "children," and "depth first search"—searching for the leftmost leaf of the tree first and then for the next one. Figures 2.16A and B illustrates the two search strategies in a tree structure. The numbers assigned to the nodes of the trees represent the order in which the nodes are checked (visited). Each of the two search techniques has its extreme case in the exhaustive search when all the nodes (points) of the decision space are checked before the final decision is found.

If constraints are given which the solution must satisfy, then the search problem can be represented as a *constraint satisfaction problem*. It can be formulated as follows. Given a set Y of variables $\{y_1, y_2, \ldots, y_m\}$ each variable y_i ranging over a domain Si, and a set of constraints $C_1, \ldots, C_l$, each constraint C_j representing relations between variables in a subset of Y, to find tuples $(s_1, s_2, \ldots, s_m)$ of values for the variables $(y_1, y_2, \ldots, y_m)$ such that all the constraints are satisfied. It might happen that this problem does not have a solution. If this is the case, i.e., one cannot satisfy the entire set of constraints, one has to "weaken" the constraints to find a solution. This process is called *constraint relaxation*. It is now an approximate solution that is sought rather than an exact solution. Both fuzzy systems and neural networks can be successfully used for finding approximate solutions.

2.4.3   Forward and Backward Chaining

An inference process is a chain of matchings. Two mechanisms to organize these matchings are called *forward chaining inference* and *backward chaining inference*. There is another mechanism, which uses both in a predefined order.

A *forward chaining procedure* applies all the facts that are available at a given moment to all the rules to infer all the possible conclusions.

Example   An example of a forward chaining inference is given in figure 2.17A where the car monitoring rule base is represented as a decision tree

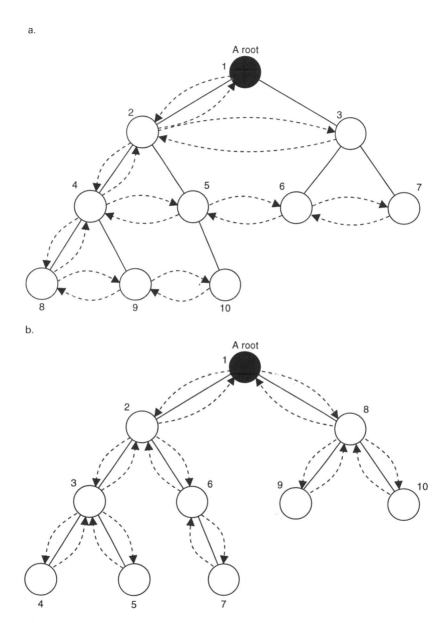

Figure 2.16
Searching in a tree structure: (A) Breadth first search. (b) Depth first search.

a.

Fact: temperature = 130   Fact: gauge - OK

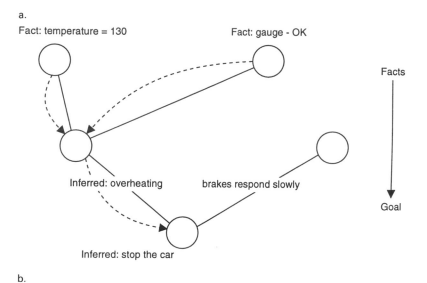

Facts

Inferred: overheating   brakes respond slowly

Goal

Inferred: stop the car

b.

Goal

stop the car

Subgoal

Goal

there is overheating

the brakes respond slowly

the gauge
works properly

the temperature
is over 120

Facts

Concrete facts
for the moment: yes   yes(128)   no

Figure 2.17
(A) Forward chaining inference over the Car Monitoring decision tree. (B) Backward chaining inference.

(see the problem description in chapter 1). Forward chaining inference starts with data. It is *data-driven*. This mechanism is implemented in the production languages. Simple neural networks and fuzzy systems can also realize this type of reasoning because they require data to be supplied to the inputs in order to start reasoning.

In the backward chaining inference, which is a *goal-driven inference*, the inference process starts after a goal is identified. Then a search for a rule which has this goal in its antecedent part is performed, and then data (facts) which satisfy all the conditions for this rule are sought in the database. The process is recursive, that is, a condition in a rule may be a conclusion in another rule (other rules). The process of searching for facts goes backward.

Example   The same problem is used in figure 2.17B to demonstrate backward chaining reasoning methods. Backward chaining may imply *backtracking*, that is, if the goal is not satisfied with the first checked fact, then other conditions and facts are checked (if more are available). This mechanism is implemented in the AI logic programming languages.

2.4.4   The Variety of Reasoning Methods and The Role of Variables

Various types of reasoning methods can be used for knowledge engineering. Some of them are listed below:

• *Monotonic vs. non-monotonic reasoning.* An inference process is *monotonic* when every new fact contributes to an increase in present knowledge. It is *non-monotonic* when knowledge may decrease in "volume" as new facts are entered into the system. In the latter case, some facts that have been previously inferred based on the previous set of facts might need to be revised and retracted as being no longer valid.

• *Exact vs. approximate reasoning.* A reasoning process is *exact* if it produces exact solutions when current data are supplied; it is *approximate* if it ends up with an approximate solution or a degree of approximation attached to the inferred solution. An example of an exact solution is classification of an Iris exemplar to the class Setosa if two possibilities are given—yes or no. But if the classification procedure produces a confidence factor, say 0.93, to which the new exemplar belongs to Setosa, 0.01 for the class Virginica, and 0.203 for the class Versicolor, respectively, this is an approximate reasoning procedure.

• *Iteration vs. recursion.* In an iterative process of searching for a solution, a rule (set of rules) is applied over input data many times, each time producing a better approximation to the solution; *recursion* is represented by a rule(s) or function that is defined by the same function but for different values of its variables. A recursive function is, for example, the factorial function:

Factorial$(n) = n! = n.$Factorial$(n - 1) = \ldots = n.(n - 1)\ldots2.1$

The problem of finding a path of a length of K between two arbitrary nodes X and Y in a graph can be represented as a recursive problem, as shown below:

IF there exists a node Z, such that X and Z are adjacent, AND there is a path $(Z, Y, K - 1)$ between Z and Y with a length of $K - 1$, THEN there is a path (X, Y, K) between X and Y with a length of K

Recursion is a way to express a solution to a problem over the whole problem state space as a sequence of solutions to the same problem on *subspaces* of the space. The same function, procedure, or rule represents a general solution to the problem as well as a local one. Recursion operates in two ways: (1) a backward way, which is the top-down way of consecutive moves from the general space to local subspace until the smallest possible element from the space is reached and the rule is evaluated; and (2) a consecutive forward propagation of the results obtained as local solutions to a wider subspace until the global solution is reached. This is illustrated in figure 2.18 by a procedure for calculating the factorial function.

Fuzzy recursive rules and systems are discussed in chapter 7.

Variables play a significant role in the process of inference. Unfortunately, the mechanism of brain "variables" is completely unknown. That is probably why variables are such a big problem to implement in connectionist systems. A variable x is an entity to which any value from its domain (range) can be bound. *Variable binding* is a dynamic process. A value is either temporarily or constantly bound to a variable during the operation of a system. Variables ensure a dynamic way of information updating. Many explicit rules use variables to express validity for different values which can satisfy the condition elements, for example:

IF [Temperature] > 120, THEN there is overheating

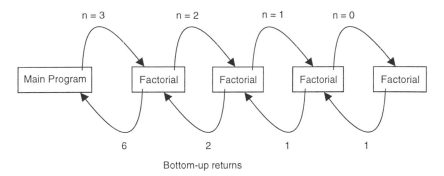

Figure 2.18
A recursive solution for the factorial function $f(n) = n!$ The figure represents a recursive execution of the function for $n = 3$. The recursive process, which takes place in time, is here represented in space.

In the above rule [Temperature] is a variable and can be bound to any value for the cooling temperature of the car. Variable binding is done through searching in the variable domain space—the space of all the possible values for the variables in the system. There are some solutions to this NP complete problem. For example, a so-called RETE algorithm is used in the production languages. It makes possible an efficient variable binding without checking all the possible values of all the variables in the production rules each time a matching process between the facts and the rules in the system is performed.

Different types of variables are facilitated in the different logic systems and AI models and languages: no variables at all (propositional logic); local (within a rule or a function) or global (valid for the whole program); and variables that can be bound to single values, or bound to a whole multivalued fact or list of values, etc.

Symbolic AI systems are very good at representing variables, but not very efficient in variable binding. Variables can be used in fuzzy systems. Representing variables in the contemporary connectionist models is possible, though extremely difficult.

One interesting issue to be raised here is the difference between *learning through reasoning* and *learning about reasoning*. Through reasoning, new facts and rules can be obtained by the system. Whether a system can learn to do reasoning is a completely different question and much more difficult to answer. How do humans learn to reason? Do we learn how to reason from books and theories, or it is genetically embodied in our brain? How do we know about logic? Is logic a theory or it is simply "common sense" which we use in our everyday decision-making? Before we discuss logic systems, we shall have a look at simple, but universal computational mechanisms.

2.4.5 Turing Machines

The *Turing machine*, created by Alan Turing (1936), is a simple universal model for symbol manipulation. It is a device comprising indefinitely extendable tape, each discrete position of which can take one symbol from a predefined alphabet. Simple operations of reading a symbol from the tape, writing a symbol on the current position of the tape, moving the tape, are used. This simple model was proved to be universal in that it can be used for realizing any computation based on a finite and explicit set of rules if a suitable program to control the device is provided.

2.4.6 Finite State Automatons; Cellular Automatons

Simple symbol manipulation can be performed in a finite state automaton, the latter being a computational model represented by a set X of input states, set Y of output states, set Q of internal states, and two functions, f_1 and f_2:

$f_1: X \times Q \to Q$, i.e.: $(\mathbf{x}, \mathbf{q}(t)) \to \mathbf{q}(t+1)$,

$f_2: X \times Q \to Y$, i.e.: $(\mathbf{x}, \mathbf{q}(t)) \to \mathbf{y}(t+1)$,

where $\mathbf{x} \in X$, $\mathbf{q} \in Q$, $\mathbf{y} \in Y$, and t and $(t+1)$ represent two consecutive time moments.

A simple automaton is illustrated in figure 2.19(A) (the tables defining the transfer function f_1 and the output function f_2); (B), a graphical representation of the transfer function, and (C), a block diagram of a possible realization of the automaton. This simple automaton can produce sequences of symbols of the two-element alphabet when sequences of inputs are fed into it. For example, if the state q_1 denotes the letter A and the state q_2 denotes the letter B, then the sequence $ABBA$ of internal states will be produced by the automaton when an input sequence of $x_2 x_1 x_2$ is fed into it and the automaton is in an initial state q_1. If the automaton was in an initial state q_2, then for the same conditions as above, the sequence $BAAB$ would be produced.

f_1		
$X(t)$	$Q(t)$	$Q(t+1)$
x_1	q_1	q_1
x_1	q_2	q_2
x_2	q_1	q_2
x_2	q_2	q_1

f_2		
$X(t)$	$Q(t)$	$Y(t+1)$
x_1	q_1	y_2
x_1	q_2	y_1
x_2	q_1	y_1
x_2	q_2	y_1

(a)

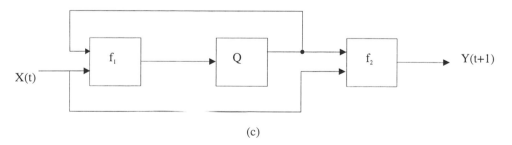

(b)

(c)

Figure 2.19
Simple finite state automaton: (a) the transition and the output functions defined as tables; (b) directed graph representing the transition function; (c) a structural realization.

The applicability of the finite state automata theory to processes modeling and to building information-processing machines has been widely explored, not to mention that it is one of the basic theories of present-day computers. A finite automaton can be realized as a production system, as a neural network structure built on simple McCulloch-Pitts neurons, on a recurrent neural network structure.

Except for the deterministic finite automatons illustrated above, probability finite automatons and fuzzy finite automatons can be used for approximate reasoning rather than for exact symbol manipulation.

A *cellular automaton* is a set of regularly connected simple finite automatons. The simple automatons communicate and compute when solving a single global task. Cellular automatons may be able to grow, shrink, and reproduce, thus providing a flexible environment for computations with arbitrary complexity. This area is of growing interest because of the possibility of implementing cellular automatons in a neural network environment.

2.5 Propositional Logic

A logic system consists of four parts:

1. *An alphabet*—a set of basic symbols from which more complex sentences (constructions) are made.

2. *Syntax*—a set of rules or operators for constructing sentences (expressions) or alternatively more complex structures from the alphabet elements. These structures are syntactically correct sentences.

3. *Semantics*—for defining the meaning of the constructions in the logic system.

4. *Laws of inference*—a set of rules or laws for constructing semantically equivalent but syntactically different sentences; this set of laws is also called a set of inference rules.

Propositional logic dates back to Aristotle. There are three types of symbols in propositional logic: (1) *Propositional symbols* (*the alphabet*), (2) *Connective symbols*, and (3) *Symbols denoting the meaning of the sentences*.

There are rules in propositional logic to construct syntactically correct sentences (called well-formed formulas) and rules to evaluate the semantics of the sentences.

A propositional symbol represents a statement about the world, for example, "The temperature is over 120." The semantic meaning of a propositional symbol is expressed by two possible semantical symbols—*true* or *false*. Statements or propositions can be either true or untrue (false), nothing in between.

Propositional logic has the following syntactic connective symbols for constructing more complex propositions from simple ones:

∧ *AND, conjunction*

∨ *OR, disjunction*

¬ *NOT, negation*

→ *implication*

= *equality*

The semantics of the compound structures (sentences, expressions) are defined by the truth table given in figure 2.20.

Example Given that the propositions $P =$ "Temperature is high" and $Q =$ "Humidity is high" are true, a compound proposition "P AND Q" is inferred to be true as well as the proposition "P OR Q."

Propositional logic has rules or laws for defining semantic equivalence of syntactically correct structures. These rules make the process of inference in the space of propositions possible. These rules give the truth values for some propositions when the truth values for other propositions are known. All the laws of inference can be proved for correctness using the truth table method, that is, by obtaining the truth table for the left and right sides of the equation and then comparing them.

P	Q	P∧Q	P∨Q	P⇒Q	P=Q	¬P	¬Q
T	T	T	T	T	T	F	F
T	F	F	T	F	F	F	T
F	T	F	T	T	F	T	F
F	F	F	F	T	T	T	T

Figure 2.20
The truth-table of the basic connectives in propositional logic.

Some laws of inference are given below. The most popular laws of inference in propositional logic are called *modus ponens* ("mood that affirms") and *modus tollens* ("mood that denies"). The rules are expressed as follows:

Modus ponens: $P \rightarrow Q$, and P $\therefore$ Q

Modus tollens: $P \rightarrow Q$, and $\neg Q$ $\therefore$ $\neg P$

Modus ponens and modus tollens are widely used in fuzzy logic in the form of *generalized modus ponens* and *generalized modus tollens*.

Two other important inference rules are the *laws of De Morgan*:

$\neg(P \wedge Q)$ $\therefore$ $\neg P \vee \neg Q$

$\neg(P \vee Q)$ $\therefore$ $\neg P \wedge \neg Q$

The following two rules, the "chain rule," or *law of syllogism*, and the *law of contrapositive*, are valid not only for propositional logic but as we shall see in chapter 3, they are also valid for some of the inference methods in fuzzy logic:

Law of syllogism: $P \rightarrow Q$, and $Q \rightarrow R$ $\therefore$ $P \rightarrow R$

Law of contrapositive: $P \rightarrow Q$ $\therefore$ $\neg Q \rightarrow \neg P$ (*Modus Tollens*)

Some simple inference laws, which are obvious to the reader, are also valid in propositional logic:

Double negation: $\neg(\neg P)$ $\therefore$ P

Disjunctive inference: $P \vee Q$, and $\neg P$ $\therefore$ Q $P \vee Q$, and $\neg Q$ $\therefore$ P

Propositional logic is a useful way of representing a simple knowledge base consisting of propositions and logical connectives between them. The major problem is that propositional logic can only deal with complete statements. That is, it cannot examine the internal structure of the statement. A classic example given in all the AI books is the following:

Example   The following inference is not possible in propositional logic:

All humans are mortal.
Socrates is a human.
Therefore, Socrates is mortal.

Propositional logic cannot even prove the validity of a simple syllogism such as that above. With the use of propositional logic we can construct rules like this:

IF (the temperature is above 120), THEN (there is overheating),

where the left-hand and the right-hand sides of the rule contain propositions which can be only true or false. Variables cannot be used. A proposition is an unbreakable symbol element. Only an exact match is possible, that is, two propositions match if they are syntactically equivalent.

Propositional logic has been used in some simple expert systems for representing propositional rules.

Example: The Car Monitoring Problem. In propositional logic, this problem can be represented as follows:

Rule 1: (there is overheating) ∨ (the brakes react slowly) → (stop the car)

Rule 2: (the cooling temperature is over 120) ∧
(the gauge works properly) → (there is overheating)

2.6   Predicate Logic: PROLOG

2.6.1   Predicate Logic

The following types of symbols are allowed in predicate logic:

• *Constant symbols* are symbols, expressions, or entities which do not change during execution. Constant symbols are the "true" and "false" symbols, for example, used to represent the truth of the expressions.

• *Variable symbols* are symbols which represent entities that can change during execution.

• *Function symbols* represent functions which process input values for a predefined list of parameters associated with the function, and obtain resulting values. The number of parameters in a function is called *arity.*

Constant symbols, variable symbols, and function symbols are called "terms."

• *Predicate symbols* represent predicates which are true/false-type relations between objects. Objects are represented by constant symbols. The number of arguments attached to a predicate define the arity of the predicate. For example, "father (person, person)" is a predicate of arity 2, and "father (John, William)" is a constant predicate.

• *Connective symbols* are the same as those which are valid for propositional logic, that is, conjunction, disjunction, negation, implication, equivalence. They are defined by the same truth table as given for propositional logic.

• *Quantifiers* are valid for variable symbols—an *existential quantifier* ($\exists$), which means "there exists at least one value for x from its domain," and a *universal quantifier* ($\forall$), which means "for all x in its domain." For example, the Socrates syllogism can be expressed in predicate logic by two predicates, a universal quantifier, and an implication, as follows:

$\forall x$, Human(x) $\rightarrow$ Mortal(x).

Human(Socrates)

Sentences can be created in predicate logic with the use of connectives and the allowed symbols. The truth of the sentences is calculated on the basis of the truth tables of the connectives. Well-formed expressions, sentences, and formulas in predicate logic are all the syntactically correct sentences. If a set of sentences in predicate logic is matched by a domain D, which means that every variable is assigned a value and every predicate is assigned a truth value, this is called *interpretation*.

First-order logic allows quantified variables to refer to objects and not to predicates or functions. This is not a limit for higher-order predicate logic.

In order to apply an inference to a set of predicate expressions, the system should be able to determine when two expressions match each other. The process of matching is called *unification*. In order to allow more freedom for matching and not restricting the variable domains, the existential quantifier has been eliminated by a so-called skolemization process. A skolem function replaces the existential quantifier $\exists$ by a function which is returning a single value:

$\forall X$, human(X) $\rightarrow$ $\exists Y$, mother (Y, X), can be skolemized as follows:

$\forall X$, human(X) $\rightarrow$ mother $(f(X), X)$, where f is a skolem function

2.6.2   Programming in Logic: PROLOG

In PROLOG, a quantifier-free, so-called Horn-clausal notation is adopted, which can adequately represent a first-order predicate logic system. The Socrates syllogism is represented in PROLOG as follows:

mortal(X):-human(X)
human(Socrates)

A rule $(A1, A2, \ldots, An) \rightarrow B$ in a *Horn-clausal* form has the following form:

$B: -A1, A2, \ldots, An$

which means that the goal B is true if all the subgoals $A1, A2, \ldots, An$ are also true, where $B, A1, A2, \ldots, AN$ are correct predicate expressions.

A fact is represented as a literal clause with a right side being the constant "true." So the clause representing a fact is always true:

human (Socrates):-true

or shortly

human (Socrates)

Knowledge is represented in PROLOG as a set of clauses which have one conclusion (left side) and premises (right side of the clause). The character "," may be used in clauses to denote an "AND" connective, ";" to denote an "OR" connective, and "⌐" for a "NOT" connective. A backward chaining inference engine is implicitly built in. A program in PROLOG consists of clauses and facts. It is of a declarative, rather than of a procedural type. The engine starts when a goal is given. A goal can only be a predicate used in the program. A block diagram of a PROLOG program is given in figure 2.21.

An example program, *searching for a family relationship*, written in Turbo PROLOG, is given in figure 2.22. An AND-OR tree, which represents the relations between the rules from the example above, is shown in figure 2.23. The matching operation during the inference process is called "unification." That is, it matches predicates, variables, and facts between the clauses in the process of finding facts which prove the goal and the subsequent subgoals (figure 2.24). This is how variable binding is done in PROLOG. A sample dialogue between user and the program for searching for family relationship is given below:

Goal?- grandfather(John, Jilly).
yes
Goal?- grandmother(Helen, X).
2 solutions
X = Andy X = Tom
Goal?- grandmother(X, Y), $X = Y$.
fail

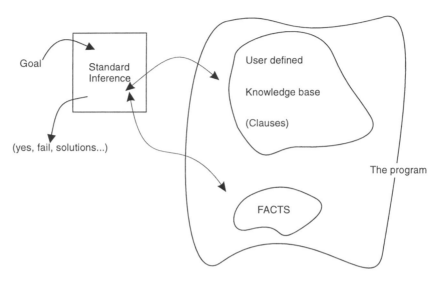

Figure 2.21
A block diagram of a PROLOG program.

(* A Turbo PROLOG program "Searching for a Family Relationship" *)
(* defining the objects in the domain ..: *)
domain
 name=*symbol*
(* defining the relations between the objects..:*)
predicates
 father(name,name)
 mother(name,name)
 parent(name,name)
 grandfather(name,name)
 grandmother(name,name)
clauses
 (*facts - defining the existing initial facts...:*)
 father(John,Mary).
 father(Jack, Andy).
 father(Jack,Tom).
 mother(Helen,Jack).
 mother(Mary,Jilly).
 grandfather(Barry,Jim).
 (* rules - defining the knowledge base of rules..:*)
 grandfather(X,Y):- father(X,Z), parent(Z,Y).
 grandmother(X,Y):- mother(X,Z), parent(Z,Y).
 parent(X,Y):-mother(X,Y).
 parent(X,Y):-father(X,Y).

Figure 2.22
A PROLOG program—searching for a relationship problem.

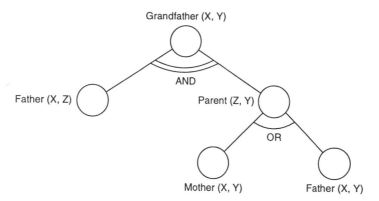

Figure 2.23
AND-OR tree of the exemplar PROLOG program.

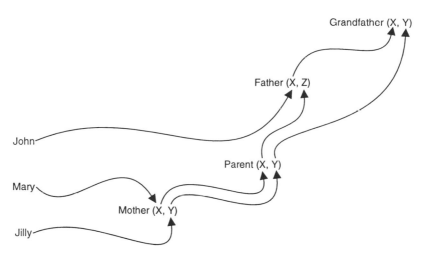

Figure 2.24
Unification in PROLOG exemplified on the family relationship example.

Natural language structures can be easily represented in predicate logic. A parsing tree for simple sentences was given in figure 2.11(B). The following expressions in PROLOG define parsing of simple sentences written in English:

sentence = sentence(noun, verb-phrase) (*a compound object*)

noun = noun(word) (*a noun is a simple word*)

verb-phrase = verb-phrase (verb, noun); verb (word) (*a verb-phrase is either a verb or a verb plus noun*)

verb = verb (word)

word = symbol

One of the limitations of first-order logic, and of PROLOG languages in particular, is that this mechanism can be used only for exact matching and exact reasoning over symbolic representations. But how many real-life and engineering problems are similar to those of finding exact family relations? We may know for sure that John is the father of William but we may not be so sure about the effect of virus V or machine fault F. These limitations are overcome in the connectionist and fuzzy reasoning systems, and in the hybrid connectionist-logic programming systems. Overall, logic programming systems are based on a rigid theory and have potential for further development by implementing higher-order predicate logic and mixing with fuzzy logic and connectionist systems.

2.7 Production Systems

2.7.1 The Production Systems Paradigm

Productions, from a terminological point of view, are known as *transformation rules* which are applied for obtaining one sequence of characters from another, for example:

$ACDE \rightarrow F$

the patient has a fever → take an aspirin

A new development in the production systems idea was achieved after the introduction of Markov rules which define priorities for sequential application of productions in order to obtain desired transformations. Productions are also used as a theoretical basis for developing compilers and other transformation systems.

A lot of the old ideas about productions are adopted in today's production systems which are the most common languages, methods, and formal systems for representing and processing of knowledge in expert systems and in AI systems in general.

A production rule has two sides: a *left-hand side*, which expresses the conditions or the premises, and a *right-hand side*, which defines what kind of actions are to be performed when the conditions are satisfied.

Example

```
(production example
; condition elements
(there is an overheating) or
(the brakes respond slowly)
⇒; action
(give a message to the driver to stop the car))
```

Inference over production rules is based on the modus ponens law. A production system consist of three main parts:

1. A list of facts, considered *a working memory* (the facts being called *working memory elements*); the working memory represents the short-term memory of the system.

2. A set of productions, considered the *production memory*; this is the long-term memory of the system.

3. *An inference engine*, which is usually a forward chaining one; this is the reasoning procedure, the control mechanism.

Here, the three parts of a production system are explained in more details.

The *facts* are represented within the framework defined by the user templates, for example:

$$(\langle \text{object or relation} \rangle \langle \text{attribute}_1 \rangle \langle \text{attribute}_2 \rangle \dots \langle \text{attribute}_k \rangle)$$

The templates for representing facts and their corresponding facts for the Family Relationship and the Car Monitoring problems are shown below:

Example 1

(is_a ⟨relationship⟩ ⟨name1⟩ ⟨name2⟩)—a template
(is_a father John Mary)—a fact

Example 2

(⟨car_par⟩ ⟨parameter⟩ ⟨value⟩)—a template
(car_par temperature 135)—a fact
(⟨car_status⟩ ⟨system⟩ functioning ⟨status⟩)—a template
(car_status brakes functioning slowly)—a fact
(car_status cooling functioning overheating)—a fact
(car_status gauge functioning OK)—a fact

Productions can have expressions as condition elements in their left-hand sides. If facts from the working memory match all the expressions in the left-hand side of a production, the production is called "to be satisfied" at the current matching phase.

Condition elements can be a negation of a fact (means absence of this fact); expressions with variables or *wild cards*; a wild card is a variable which can be satisfied by any value; and predicates, for example, temperature > 120.

The right-hand side of a production contains actions which manipulate facts in the working memory (assert, retract, etc.) or perform interaction with the environment. These commands for CLIPS, a typical production language, are given in appendix D. *CLIPS* (*C l*anguage *i*nterpreter of *p*roduction *s*ystems) was developed by NASA (Giarratano and Riley 1989).

The *inference engine* of a production system performs a forward inference in the following way:

1. *Matches* all the facts from the working memory into the left-hand sides of all the productions and defines which of them are satisfied. Every combination of facts which satisfies a production is called *instantiation*. All the production rules which are satisfied by the current match form *a conflict set*, also called *Agenda*.

2. *Selects* one rule from the Agenda using selection strategies. Some of the selection strategies used in production systems are the following:

a. *Recency*. The rule matched by the most recent facts is selected.

b. *Specificity.* The rules with more condition elements have higher priority; this restricts the matching as those rules are supposed to be matched by fewer instantiations.

c. *Refraction.* Once a rule is activated (fired) for a particular instantiation, it will not be fired again for the same instantiation; the refraction period for some systems can be controlled, that is, productions can be suspended for firing with the same instantiations for some cycles or "forever."

d. *Salience.* A priority number can be assigned to every rule and this will be the first criterion for selecting a rule from the Agenda.

e. *Random selection.* A rule is selected randomly from the Agenda.

3. *Executes* the selected rule (or rules, depending on the realization of the production system) performing the specified actions.

The inference engine works repetitively until there are no productions in the Agenda, or it is compulsorily stopped. Figure 2.25 represents the three phases of the inference engine and the data structures used in a production system.

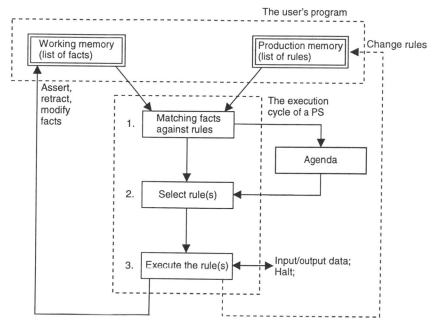

Figure 2.25
A production system (PS) cycle.

```
; fact template
;(account <number> <money> <holder>)

(deffacts initiallist
        (account 1234 45.67 smith)
        (account 3421 0.0 feldman)
        (account 3333 0.0 grisman))

(defrule printt
        (account ?num ?money&:(= ?money 0.0) ?name)
    =>
        (printout t "clear account " ?num " " ?name crlf ))
```

Figure 2.26
An example of a production rule for searching and processing a database (fact base).

2.7.2 How to Program in Production Rules

Here some techniques for programming simple tasks in production rules are given.

• *Searching through databases.* The match operation of the inference process can be used for searching through a database.

Example An example of searching through bank records for accounts with 0.0 money in them is given in figure 2.26. The symbols preceded by "?" in the rules represent variables. The rule will fire until there are no facts in the working memory that satisfy this rule.

• *Programming logical inferences.* The inference process in a production language is data-driven. It begins with entering data. Then data match rules, a rule fires and possibly changes the working memory, then again facts match rules, and so on. It is in contrast to the inference process in PROLOG-like languages which is a goal-driven backward-chaining inference mechanism with backtracking.

Example In order to compare both languages, a program written in a production language for the Family Relationship Problem is given in figure 2.27. It can be easily compared with the program written in PROLOG (see section 2.6) and similarities and differences between both paradigms and languages picked up.

```
;;; a CLIPS program Searching For Relationships
;;; the following template for representing facts is used:
;;; (is_a <relationship> <name> <name>)

deffacts initial_facts
        (is_a father John Mary)
        (is_a father Jack Andy)
        (is_a father Jack Tom)
        (is_a mother Helen Jack)
        (is_a mother Mary Jilly)
        (is_a grandfather Barry Jim))

;;; the following rules define how a relationship can be inferred
;;; from facts

(defrule grandfather
        (is_a father ?name1 ?name2)
        (is_a parent ?name2 ?name3)
    =>
        (assert (is_a grandfather ?name1 ?name3)))

(defrule grandmother
        (is_a mother ?name1 ?name2)
        (is_a parent ?name2 ?name3)
    =>
        (assert (is_a grandmother ?name1 ?name3)))

(defrule parent
        (or (is_a mother ?name1 ?name2)
            (is_a father ?name1 ?name2))
    =>
        (assert (is_a parent ?name1 ?name2)))
```

Figure 2.27
A program written in a production language for the family relationship problem.

• *Expressing the concept of "doesn't matter." Wild cards* represent variables which can be bound to any value from the fact memory, that is, the value in that field "doesn't matter." The rule in the example below will cause printing out all the names of the persons from the fact base who are grandfathers without taking into account who the grandchildren are.

```
(defrule grandfather-print
   (is_a grandfather ?name ?)
  =>(printout t ?name))
```

• *Maintaining dynamic information structures.* Retracting facts from the working memory, when they will no longer be used in the program execution, is necessary not only for saving memory space but sometimes for the correct functioning of a production system. A rule which retracts all the processed facts is given as an example:

(defrule print-all-facts
    ?f ← (is_a ?relation ?name1 ?name2)
    ⇒(printout *t* ?name1 "is a" ?relation ?name2) (retract ?f))

Thus the working memory in a production system is a dynamic memory structure, that is, elements are asserted when necessary and retracted after use.

• *Using two types of variables.* Two types of variables can be used in production systems. The first is a variable for representing attribute values. The second is a variable for representing a whole fact from the working memory. In the example above two types of variables were used, "?relation," which takes values from the facts, and "?f," which takes as a value a whole fact. These two types of variables are an interesting property of production languages.

• *Using logic expressions as condition elements in production rules.* For the condition elements in the left-hand sides of the productions, the propositional logic connectives are allowed, that is, *AND*(&), *OR*(|) and *NOT*— (~).

Examples

(person ?name ? brown|black);
(person ?name1 ?eyes&blue|green ?hair& ~ black);
(and (or (person ?name has_a fever)
        (person ?name has_a cough));
(not (person ?name has-a high-temperature)))

• *Functions and expressions* are allowed in production languages but they are represented in different ways. For example CLIPS language allows representing functions only in a prefix form, for example, (+2 3).

2.7.3   Exact Matching and Generalization in Production Systems: Production Systems for Problem-Solving

Production languages have been widely used for problem-solving and knowledge-engineering. There are reasons for this, two of them being the following:

1. Production systems are a *universal computational mechanism*, that is, every algorithm or set of heuristic rules can be represented as a production system.

2. *Production systems are universal function approximators*, that is, any function can be approximated to any degree of accuracy by a set of rules if the number of the rules is unlimited. In figure 1.3, one rule is shown, that is, IF x is in the interval $[x_1, x_2]$, THEN y is in the interval $[y_1, y_2]$, which covers part of the goal function. To cover the whole function more rules are needed. These rules are *interval rules*. In the extreme case the number of rules can be as many as the points describing the goal function, which for continuous functions is unlimited. The rules then have the form of: *IF x is x_j, THEN y is y_j*, for $j = 1, 2, \ldots$. Using an unlimited number of rules is not possible, and using a small number of rules may cause too big an error of approximation.

Here examples of solving some of the generic problems introduced in chapter 1 are given. These solutions are compared with possible solutions using fuzzy models and neural network models later in the book.

Symbolic AI production systems are very efficient when used for symbolic representation, for example, attribute color: values red, green, yellow; attribute sex: values male, female. Matching between facts and rules is *exact*. But numerical attributes can also be used. In this case intervals for the numerical values are defined in order to achieve generalization.

Some examples of using production systems for problem solving are given below, but the full solutions are explained in section 2.12.

Example   A production system which recognizes musical signals based on the energy of the signal in 10 different frequency bands, for example, 0–1000 Hz, 1000–2000 Hz, … has rules which define intervals for those values:

IF (average energy in the first frequency band is between 40 and 44 dB) and (average energy in the third frequency band is between 0 and 5), THEN (the musical signal is EaboveMidC)

Example   After discretizing the average values for the ion concentration for the class Egmont_Ybl (0.39 2.79 0.44 0.82 0.37 1.03 1.72 0.31) where the attribute values correspond to the attributes described for this problem in chapter (table 1.1), the class template will look like (3 27 4 8 3 10 17 3). A classification rule for classifying soil in class Egmont_Ybl could be written as: IF (3 27 4 8 3 10 17 3), THEN (Soil class is Egmont_Ybl). An important task here is to properly choose the discretization intervals.

Production systems can be used for solving pattern recognition, classification, monitoring, planning, and decision-making problems. Note that the use of intervals facilitates partial match, but at the same time introducing intervals may cause imprecision in the solution process. For example, what will happen if the average power of a musical signal for the first frequency band is not 40, but 39.999, and the average power of the third interval is 3? Will this signal be classified into EaboveMidC? According to the above rule, no. This simple example illustrates the imprecision of the interval approach and the lack of a smooth grayness at the border of the intervals. The drawback of *crisp borders* between intervals is overcome in fuzzy systems and neural networks. The examples below illustrate this.

Recognition and classification problems are implemented easily in production languages when heuristic rules are available in the problem knowledge. The rules are of the form "IF (a set of features), THEN (class)." The templates and only two rules for classification of animals (a well-explored AI example) are given in figure 2.28.

Games modeling is usually done in AI production languages by using heuristic rules. This can be illustrated by a program given in (Giarratano and Riley, 1989). In the program, production rules are used to generate a move according to the current situation. First, the situation is recognized; second, a move is performed. The heuristics used for the game could be *well-informed* or *ill-informed*, could cover the whole problem state space, or could cover only a small part, etc. The success of the production program depends on how good the heuristics are (see chapter 1).

More examples of solving problems by using production languages are given in section 2.12. Each example takes a different approach to solving the problem, and the problems are the case examples introduced in chapter 1.

2.7.4   Advantages and Limitations of Production Systems

The advantages of using productions for representing structured knowledge (in the form of rules) are the following:

• Production systems are universal computational mechanisms and universal function approximators.

```
; fact templates
; (animal is_a <class>)
; (animal has < attributevalue>)
; (animal does <action>)

(defrule mammal
        (or  (animal has hair)
             (animal does gives_milk))
     =>
        (assert (animal is_a mammal)))

(defrule ungulate
        (or  (animal is_a mammal)
             (animal does chews_the_cud))
     =>
        (assert (animal is_a ungulate)))
```

Figure 2.28
The fact templates and two rules from a program for classification of animals according to
their features.

• They are very often *close to how humans articulate their knowledge*; this
might be an explanation of why production systems have been used widely
for cognitive modeling.

• *Readability*. It is easy to understand what a production rule represents
as knowledge.

• *Explanation power*. When a production has been executed, it leaves a
clear trace and an explanation can be easily provided.

• *Expressiveness*. Sometimes only one production is enough to express the
solution of a whole problem (see the Soil Classification Program in section
2.12).

• *Modularity*. Every production is a separate piece or module of knowledge; knowledge can be easily added or deleted; it may contain local
variables; the production rules do communicate with one another, but
only through the facts in the working memory, and not directly.

The principal limitations of the production systems from the knowledge-
engineering point of view are the same as the limitations of first-order
logic. They are not efficient for approximate reasoning and they are
sequential.

Simple production systems have been implemented as neural networks (see chapters 5 and 6). The approximate reasoning and partial match achieved there are principally different from those achieved by interval match after data discretization in the symbolic production systems.

2.8 Expert Systems

After the introduction to expert systems in chapter 1, here are more details on the subject.

2.8.1 An Expert System's Architecture

Expert systems are knowledge-based systems that provide expertise, similar to that of experts in a restricted application area. An expert system consists of the following main blocks: knowledge base, database, inference engine, explanation module, user interface, and knowledge acquisition module (see figure 2.29), as explained below:

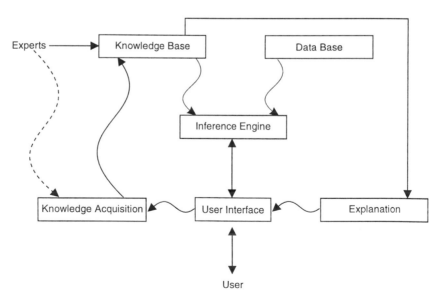

Figure 2.29
An expert system architecture.

• The *knowledge base* module is where the problem knowledge resides. It may be a production memory in production languages; it may be a neural network that has been trained with past data in the connectionist expert systems; it may be a set of fuzzy rules in a fuzzy system.

• The *database* module contains current facts or past data. It is the working memory in the production languages. In some architectures this module, containing past data, can be used as a source of knowledge in addition to the knowledge base.

• The *inference engine* is a program that controls the functioning of the whole system. It contains an inference mechanism, either forward chaining, or backward chaining, or a combination of them.

• An *explanation module* is a module that traces the execution of the expert system and accumulates information about the course of the reasoning process; it then transfers this information to the user. An expert system should be able to explain its behavior, for example, *WHY* it is checking a condition element in a rule, or *HOW* it has inferred some conclusion. Usually, the WHY explanation is done by showing to the user what is expected to be proved or disproved after having received information about a particular condition. The HOW explanation aims at showing all the facts and inferred conclusions during the whole inference process that support the final decision.

Example A possible HOW and WHY explanation for the Car Monitoring case example is shown graphically in figure 2.30.

• The *user interface* module's role is to communicate with the environment, to interact with the user in a friendly, yet sophisticated way. Natural language and speech processing may be used for communication with users.

• The *knowledge acquisition module* is designed to accumulate knowledge to build up the knowledge base.

2.8.2   Expert Systems Design

An expert systems design is very much a heuristic process although some global phases have been shared among expert systems designers. At each stage of the design process, some points should be discussed and made clear. Some possible questions, which need to be answered at different stages of an expert systems design, are given below as examples of the variety of problems.

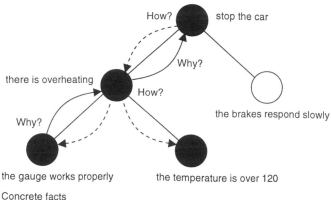

Figure 2.30
HOW and WHY explanation for the Car Monitoring production system.

1. *Stage 1—identification of the problem*

• What class of problems will the expert system be expected to solve?

• How can these problems be defined?

2. *Stage 2—conceptualization*

• What is given and what should be inferred?

• What types of data and knowledge are available? Is there a need for knowledge acquisition?

3. *Stage 3—formalization.* Here all the eight major issues from section 2.1.2 should be discussed, for example:

• Are data and knowledge sparse and insufficient, or plentiful and redundant? Is there a need to deal with uncertainty?

• Are data and knowledge reliable, accurate and precise, or unreliable, inaccurate, and imprecise? Are they consistent and complete?

• What kind of explanation is needed?

4. *Stage 4—realization*

• What methods and tools are appropriate for representing data and knowledge—data based systems, symbolic AI methods, fuzzy systems, neural networks, etc.? Is there a need for a hybrid system?

• Extendability, friendliness, reliability, robustness of the realization.

5. *Experiments and validation of the results*

• How to evaluate the system and its error?

• How to validate the results—compare experimental results with the results obtained by experts; compare results with the results obtained by other methods, etc?

In order to speed up the design process, *expert system shells* have been developed. They have the architecture of an expert system, but are "empty" of knowledge. The problem knowledge is supposed to be entered in the empty knowledge-based modules of the shell.

2.8.3   The Knowledge Acquisition Problem

The most difficult part of creating an expert system is knowledge acquisition. Knowledge may be elicited from an expert or experts, data and examples, literature, etc. Knowledge can be either stored or learned. Learning can be performed in either of two ways: (1) in advance (past data are used; this is the case in learning by example or from experience); (2) during the functioning of the expert system (adaptive learning, learning by doing).

There are many reasons why knowledge acquisition should be difficult to implement in a computer program; some of them are discussed in section 2.11. Neural networks have proved to be one of the most promising paradigms for learning knowledge from examples. A section in chapter 5 is entirely devoted to learning explicit knowledge from raw data.

2.8.4   Difficulties with Symbolic AI Languages for Expert Systems

Knowledge-engineering, when using symbolic AI systems, has some difficulties in:

• Representing both exact and inexact knowledge.

• Knowledge formalization. What is the connective between the condition elements in a rule? Is it AND or OR or something else?

• Representing both explicit and implicit knowledge.

• Dealing with exact and inexact data (facts).

• Partial matching.

• Adaptive behaviour.

• Parallelism.

These principal limitations of symbolic AI languages can be overcome by using fuzzy systems and neural networks, as well as by using hybrid systems, which incorporate both symbolic AI and connectionist methods for knowledge representation and processing.

Before we discuss them, we will have a look at the sources of uncertainty in domain data and problem knowledge, and at some of the existing methods for handling these uncertainties.

2.9   Uncertainties in Knowledge-Based Systems: Probabilistic Methods

There are many ways to represent and process uncertain knowledge and inexact data. One of them—fuzzy sets and fuzzy logic—is presented in chapter 3. But the most used so far is the classic probabilistic way discussed briefly here.

2.9.1   Uncertainties in Data and Knowledge

Representing existing uncertainties in data and knowledge is a major problem in knowledge engineering. How to infer a decision in the presence of inexact, incomplete, corrupted data and uncertain knowledge? Ambiguity is something that should not be underestimated when creating a knowledge-based system. The opposite is true. Ambiguity should be analyzed and treated properly in order to increase the validity of the inferred results. Sources of uncertainties and errors may be grouped into the categories *objective uncertainty* and *subjective uncertainty*.

The objective uncertainties are mainly due to incomplete data and uncertain evidence. The subjective ones are due to not well-known domain or unknown relations, functions, dependencies, etc. Uncertainty can be a characteristic of data or of the problem knowledge, or of both. Error in data can be due to acquisition of incorrect data, lack of precision and accuracy, or noise. Noise may be present in the environment, and instead of having a value of 1.2345 for a given attribute, we acquire a value of 1.2346, for example. Uncertain data can be represented by using fuzzy terms or intervals. For example the cost between town A and town B in the TSP could be "about fifteen," or "between ten and twenty." The approximateness can be represented by fuzzy quantifiers, for example, "very much," "more or less," etc., or fuzzy qualifiers, which express the belief in the statement, for example, "very probable," "less probable," etc.

Uncertainty in data may also mean uncertainty relating to the presence of an event, or uncertainty of the appearance of the event. The former is treated by the fuzzy theory which "says" that an event or a concept is present to some degree, say 0.7. Other types of uncertainties are treated by the probability theory, which "says" that an event will happen with some probability of, say, 0.8.

Some main questions about uncertainty in data we should be clear about are:

- Is a fact uncertain because of some "noise?"
- Is a fact uncertain because it has not happened yet?
- Is a fact uncertain because it is present but only partially present?

Representing uncertainty in problem knowledge by using knowledge-engineering schemes is a more complex problem than representing uncertainties in data. There are different types of errors resulting from incomplete and uncertain knowledge: semantic, casual, systematic, logical. *Semantic errors* are due to the possibility of interpreting incomplete and uncertain knowledge in variable ways. *Casual errors* are due to variations in the cases which have to be treated by the same rules. *Systematic* or *logical error* is due to the inappropriateness of the scheme used for representing problem knowledge. An error may be derived either from individual rules or from rules interaction. The task of the knowledge engineer is to remove or minimize this error, if possible. The errors that emerge as a result of the interaction of rules can be caused by the incompatibility of some rules.

Most symbolic AI systems require a coherent knowledge base. That is, knowledge free of missing or superfluous rules, or rules that contradict one another to the point of total incompatibility. This is not a problem for fuzzy systems and neural networks, as they can accommodate ambiguous and contradictory data and rules. Some typical cases of uncertainty represented in rules are the following:

- Uncertain condition part C in a rule IF C, THEN A.

- Uncertain condition element Ci in the condition part of a rule IF $C1$, $C2, \ldots, Ck$, THEN A.

• Uncertain action (consequent) part in a rule; even if we assume that C is 100% matched by the existing facts, the conclusion A is a priori— not 100% sure but 75%; this type of uncertainty is represented mainly by the so-called confidence factors (CF) and the rule has the form of

IF C, THEN A (0.75).

• Different degrees of importance for the antecedent elements; $C2$, for example, may be twice as important as $C3$, and $C1$ and $C3$ may be of equal importance. The rule will be:

IF $C1(1)$ and $C2(2)$ and $C3(1)$, THEN A (CF).

• A noise tolerance of the rule, that is, a rule IF C, THEN A may react to small changes in the fact space, or it may be resistant to small changes and react only if substantial evidence of facts is present; a rule can be represented in the form of IF C (noise tolerance = 0.6), THEN A.

• A sensitivity of a rule to relevant facts, that is, a rule IF C, THEN A may be more sensitive to a higher degree of the presence of the relevant condition C facts, or the rule can be equally sensitive whatever the presence of a fact is—100% or 50%, etc.

Uncertainties in knowledge may be captured only approximately, but that could be sufficient. It is sometimes even preferable not to represent everything exactly, in order to make a good generalization.

Ambiguity in a rule base exists when there are at least two rules which infer different conclusions but have identical condition parts:

$R1$: IF C, THEN A

$R2$: IF C, THEN B

Different ways to deal with ambiguities are:

• To assign coefficients of uncertainty to the condition elements, which will make a difference during the matching process if the present fact C' is not certain

• To assign confidence factors to the action part of the rules

• To use fuzzy rules when more than one rule can be activated simultaneously and every one will contribute to the final solution, even in a case when the rules are contradictory. In this case a trade-off will be found, e.g., a trade-off between A and B is appropriate.

2.9.2 Defining Probabilities

Generally speaking, there are two major approaches to processing uncertain knowledge: (1) *probabilistic* and (2) *nonprobabilistic*. The formal theory of probability relies on the following three axioms:

AXIOM 1 $0 \leq p(E) \leq 1$

The axiom defines the probability $p(E)$ of an event E as a real number in the closed interval $[0, 1]$. A probability $p(E) = 1$ indicates a certain event, and $p(E) = 0$ indicates an impossible event.

AXIOM 2 $\Sigma p(E_i) = 1$, $E_1 \cup E_2 \cup \ldots \cup E_k = U$, U—problem space (universum)

The axiom reads that the sum of the probabilities of all mutually exclusive (disjoint) events fully covering the problem space U is 1. The following is a corollary:

$$p(E) + p(\neg E) = 1$$

where $\neg E$ is the complement of the event E. The corollary shows that the sum of the probability of an event occurring and the probability that it will not occur is 1. This is the probability version of the excluded middle law known from Aristotelian logic and pointed out in section 2.5. An object or an event either exists or does not exist, either happens or does not happen, there is nothing in between. This law is broken in the nonprobabilistic theories and in the fuzzy theory in particular.

AXIOM 3 $p(E_1 \vee E_2) = p(E_1) + p(E_2)$, where $E1$ and $E2$ are mutually exclusive events.

This axiom indicates that if the events $E1$ and $E2$ cannot occur simultaneously, the probability of one or the other happening (disjunction) is the sum of their probabilities.

There are three main approaches to defining probabilities represented by the three schools in probability theory:

1. Classic probability:

$$p(E) = w/n,$$

where w is the number of occurrences of the event E for a total of n possible appearances. Laplace defines the probability as a ratio between the number of equally possible cases when an event has occurred to the number of all the possible cases. The classic approach to probabilities uses the principle of indifference, that is, if we do not have reasons to assume the opposite, we should judge the alternatives equally probable. The classic definition of probability assumes that probability exists objectively. It led some scientists to the deterministic theory which claims that the future is as predictable as the past.

2. *Posterior, experimental, frequency probability*:

$p(E) = \lim f(E)/n$, when $n \to \infty$,

where $f(E)$ is the frequency of appearance of event E among a sequence of repetitive experiments. It is a characteristic of recurrent, experiment-based events. It is valid, if we have sufficient reason to believe, that the probability will tend to a fixed number when the number of experiments tend to infinity. Two main issues are to be discussed. How can we be 100% sure about the tendency of the events? And how many experiments will be enough to adequately approximate the probability?

3. *Subjective probability*. In contrast to the classic and experimental probabilities, subjective probability deals with events which are not recurrent and cannot be estimated through previous experiments. It is rather a belief, view, and estimation of experts, in the form of probability. For example observing dice we can articulate a subjective probability of 1/6 about the event that any of the numbers between 1 and 6 happens. Subjective probabilities are beliefs that meet the three probability axioms. There is rationalism, pragmatism, heuristics in their statements. The subjective probability theory does not deny the existence of objective probabilities. The subjectivist only claims that the estimation of objective probability has to be considered, but a pragmatic evaluation is the way the probability theory has to be applied to real problem-solving.

Probability characteristics can be learned from data sets by using standard statistical methods. Some of these characteristics are revised here:

• For a random scalar variable x, defined in a domain Ux, a *probability density function* is a function such as $P(x): Ux \to [0, 1]$. Typical distribution functions used in practice are *uniform distribution, gaussian distribution (bell-like), an exponential distribution, trapezoidal,* and *triangular* (figure 2.31). As we shall see, they look very much like membership functions of fuzzy sets, but they have a completely different meaning.

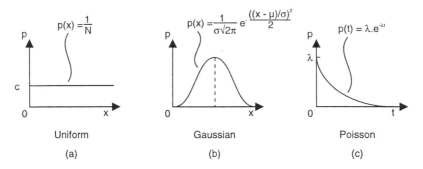

Figure 2.31
Different probability distribution functions: (a) Uniform: N represents all discrete units in the domain of the random variable x; (b) gaussian: μ is the mean and σ is the standard deviation; (c) Poisson: λ is a rate parameter, t is time.

- For a discrete random variable x, which takes values $u_1, u_2, \ldots, u_k$ the *mean* is calculated as

$$M(x) = \Sigma u_i \cdot p(u_i)$$

- The *mathematical expectation* $E(x)$ of a random continuous variable x is measured by the formula:

$$E(x) = \int u \cdot p(u), \text{ for all values } u \text{ from } Ux$$

- *A variance $V(x)$, or a standard deviation σ, of a random scalar variable is measured by*

$$V(x) = E((x - M(x))$$

- For two uncorrelated random variables x and y the following is valid:

$$E(x, y) = E(x) \cdot E(y)$$

- When considering two random variables x and y, a *correlation* and a *covariance* can be calculated as follows:

$$\text{Corr}(x, y) = E(x, y)$$

$$\text{Cov}(x, y) = E[(x - M(x)), (y - M(y))] = E(x, y) - M(x) \cdot M(y)$$

- For a random vector $\mathbf{x} = (x_1, x_2, \ldots, x_k)$ the probability distribution function is a surface in a k-dimensional space. The correlation $\text{Corr}(\mathbf{x}, \mathbf{y})$ and the covariance $\text{Cov}(\mathbf{x}, \mathbf{y})$ of two random vectors $\mathbf{x}$ and $\mathbf{y}$ are calculated as inner products:

$Corr(\mathbf{x}, \mathbf{y}) = E(\mathbf{x} \cdot \mathbf{y}^T)$, where $\mathbf{y}^T$ is the transposed vector of $\mathbf{y}$

$Cov(x, y) = E((\mathbf{x} - M(\mathbf{x}), \mathbf{y} - M(\mathbf{y})))$

• If two random vector variables $\mathbf{x}$ and $\mathbf{y}$ are independent, their joint density function $P(\mathbf{x}, \mathbf{y})$ is represented as:

$P(\mathbf{x}, \mathbf{y}) = P(\mathbf{x}) \cdot P(\mathbf{y})$

2.9.3 The Probabilistic Approach to Representing and Processing of Uncertainty: Bayesian Probabilities, Probability Automatons, Markov Models

In a rule *IF C, THEN A*, the "appearance" of *A* is conditional, depending on the condition element *C*. Here *conditional probabilities* can be used to represent uncertainty denoted as $p(A/C)$. The probability $p(A/C)$ defines the probability of the event *A* to occur, given that the event *C* has occurred. It is given by the formula:

$p(A/C) = p(A \wedge C)/p(C)$

where $p(A \wedge C)$ denotes the probability of both events to happen (conjuction).

For example, in medical diagnosis, the most probable causes of a disease must be detected from a set of symptoms. The *conditional probability* of nonrecurring events is interpreted as a degree of certainty (the expert's belief) that hypothesis *A* is true when condition *C* is given. The following formula, which represents the conditional probability between two events *C* and *A*, is known as the *Bayes's theorem*:

$p(A/C) = p(C/A) \cdot p(A)/p(C)$

If instead of one event *C* there is a set of events $C1, C2, \ldots, Ck$, which form the condition part in a rule *IF C1, C2, ..., Ck, THEN A*, a probability $p(C1, C2, \ldots, Ck)$ has to be evaluated instead of $p(C)$ in the above formula.

Using the Bayes's theorem involves difficulties, mainly concerning the evaluation of the prior probabilities $p(A)$, $p(C)$, $p(C/A)$. In practice (e.g., in statistical pattern recognition), the latter is assumed to be of a gaussian type. Bayes's theorem is applicable if the condition *C* consists of condition elements $C1, C2, \ldots, Ck$, that are independent (which may not be the case). Bayes's theorem does not consider the connectives between the condition elements. Are these elements connected by "AND" or by "OR" or by any other connective? Some ad hoc methods are applied to calculate the cumulative probability of the whole condition element. For "AND" connectives a MIN operation is used, and for "OR" connective, a MAX operation (Giarratano and Riley 1989). In practice, we may have many rules which infer different conclusions if a certain condition is true, that is, *IF C, THEN Ai* $(i = 1, 2, \ldots, n)$. In this case Bayes's theorem fails, as it assumes than the conclusions are mutually exclusive in principle. For example, if a patient has a high temperature, the most probable diagnosis may be flu, but meningitis is also possible.

In brief, probabilistic methods imply estimation of a *posterior probability* for a certain conclusion in a rule to be accepted as correct, given the probabilities for the condition elements in the rule.

Probability (or *stochastic*) *automatons* are finite automatons, the transitions of which are defined as probabilities. The same example of a finite automaton as given in fig. 2.19, but this time as a probability automaton, is represented graphically in figure 2.32.

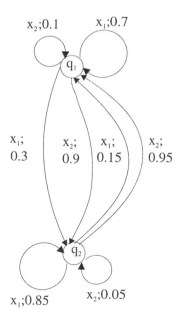

Figure 2.32
Directed graph representing the transition function of a simple probability automaton.

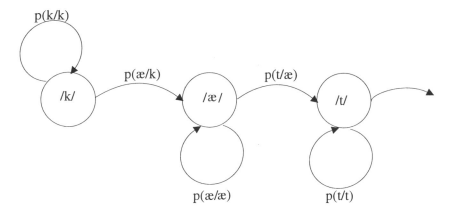

Figure 2.33
A simple Markov model for recognizing the word "cat." The conditional probabilities attached to the arcs represent the chances for the transitions to happen.

Markov models and their variant *hidden Markov models* are stochastic finite automatons with some restrictions imposed on them (Rabiner 1989). They are called "hidden" because stochastically defined transitions are not possible to observe in advance. Figure 2.33 shows a hidden Markov model of the pronunciation of the word "cat" as a sequence of the phonemes /k/, /æ/, /t/ and probabilities attached to the transition from one phoneme to another. This is a "left-to-right" model. The flow of information and activation goes in one direction without feedbacks.

2.10   Nonprobabilistic Methods for Dealing with Uncertainties

Probabilities have some limitations. One is that they cannot represent ignorance. An event has to be either "present" or "not present" at every moment. If we don't know anything about the event we will have difficulty using probabilities. Some theories have extended the probability theory to overcome this limitation. Such theories are, for example, the Dempster-Shafer theory, certainty factors, and possibility theory. Some of them do not provide operational definitions for the new probability terms, that is, the definition does not necessarily state the way to find out the values for the parameters of uncertainty. But some axioms are given with formulas for calculating how to operate with a set of data or rules with parameters of uncertainty assigned to them.

2.10.1   The Dempster-Shafer Theory: Credibility and Plausibility

Dempster (1967) and Shafer (1976) introduced a measure called *mass m(E)*, or a *basic probability assignment (bpa)*, associated with every event E or set of events, $\{E2, E3\}$ for example, which is a subset of the domain space U of all the possible events. The idea is that a probability of an event E can be either concentrated in one element (as it is in probability theory), or it can be a distributed mass among some items—subsets of U where E appears as a member. We can have a solution of a problem, for example, in the following form:

$$m(\{E2\}) = 0.7, \, m(\{E2, E3\}) = 0.1$$

The main idea is to represent the uncertainties of an event E not as a single probability $p(E)$, but as an interval of lower probability and a higher probability. The following *axioms* are held for the Dempster-Shafer theory:

A1. $0 \le m(E) \le 1$, and E is called a *focal point* in U if $m(E) > 0$

A2. $\Sigma m(E) = 1$, for each subset E of U

Defining the term *mass* allows us to determine the *credibility Cr(E)* (the lower possible probability) and the *plausibility Pl(E)* (the higher possible probability). A probability of any set E of events, subset of U, is represented as a probability interval $[Cr(E), Pl(E)]$. When dealing with single element sets E, the intervals are reduced to the probability $p(E) = Cr(E) = Pl(E)$. So this theory is an extension of the probability theory. The measure of credibility $Cr(E)$ is based on the mass m:

A3. $Cr(E) = \Sigma m(C)$, C entails E, that is, $C \subseteq E$

A measure of *plausibility Pl(E)* is introduced as:

A4. $Pl(E) = 1 - Cr(\neg E) = \Sigma m(C)$, C does not entail $\neg E$.

It has been proved as a corollary that

$$\forall E \subseteq U, \, Cr(E) + Cr(\neg E) \le 1; \, Pl(E) + Pl(\neg E) \ge 1$$

The mass $m(U)$ of the whole domain gives the level of the total ignorance about the whole domain knowledge. In case of complete ignorance about a focal point E, we will have $Cr(E) = Cr(\neg E) = 0$, and $Pl(E) = Pl(\neg E) = 1$. It is also true that: $\forall E \subseteq U, \, Cr(E) \le Pl(E)$.

Using uncertainty parameters for inference over rules means propagation of uncertainties along the inference chain. It also means combining uncertainties when two rules contribute to the certainty of the same fact. The combination rule suggested by Dempster and Shafer is simple. If the intersection of two focal points $A1$ and $A2$ is a nonempty set $A3$, then

$$m(A3) = m(A1) \cdot m(A2)$$

Let us consider two rules of the form of:

Rule 1: IF C, THEN $A1$ $(CF1)$

Rule 2: IF P, THEN $A2$ $(CF2)$,

where $A1$, $A2 \subseteq U$. $CF1$ and $CF2$ mean certainty of the conclusions $A1$ and $A2$ respectively. It can be either a prior probability or a subjective certainty. For $A3 = A1 \cap A2$, we have $m(A3) = m(A1) \cdot m(A2) = Cr(C) \cdot CF1 \cdot Cr(P) \cdot CF2$. If $A3$ takes part in other rules as a condition, then $Cr(A3)$ can be calculated based on axiom 3 above. An interval $[Cr(A3), Pl(A3)]$ can be defined as well.

Example   The credibility Cr and the plausibility Pl of a set $E = \{C2, C3\}$ are calculated as given below when the mass probabilities of the other focal points in $U = \{C1, C2, C3\}$ are known: $m(C1) = 0.2$; $m(C2) = 0.5$; $m(C3) = 0.1$; $m(C1, C2, C3) = 0.1$; $m(C2, C3) = 0.1$

$$Cr(E) = 0.5 + 0.1 + 0.1 = 0.7;$$

$$Pl(E) = 1 - Cr(\neg E) = 1 - Cr(C1)$$

$$= 1 - 0.2 = 0.8$$

2.10.2   Measure of Belief and Measure of Disbelief: Certainty Factors

Another approach, introduced in the early expert systems, for example, MYCIN (see Giarratano and Riley, 1989) to overcome the limitation of the probability theory concerning the excluded middle, is called *certainty factors*. A *measure of belief* $MB(A, C)$ that if the event C happens the event A will happen too, and a *measure of disbelief* $MD(A, C) = MB(\neg A, C)$, have been introduced. A certainty factor then is calculated as:

$$CF(A, C) = MB(A, C) - MD(A, C), \text{ or}$$

$$CF(A, C) = (MB - MD)/(1 - \min\{MB, MD\})$$

The following formulas have been suggested and used in MYCIN to calculate the measures of belief and disbelief:

$MB(A, C) = 1$, if $p(A) = 1$, or

$MB(A, C) = (\mathrm{MAX}\{p(A|C), p(A)\} - p(A))/(1 - p(A))$, otherwise

$MD(A, C) = 1$, if $p(A) = 0$, or

$MD(A, C) = (\mathrm{MIN}\{p(A|C), p(A)\} - p(A))/p(A)$, otherwise

Certainty factors are numbers between -1 and 1. A certainty factor $CF(A, C) = +1$ means a proven true hypothesis A, while $CF(A, C) = -1$ means a proven untrue hypothesis A, when C is present. $CF(A, C) = 0$ denotes lack of a proof for the hypothesis A. It is true for the certainty factors, that $CF(A, C) + CF(\neg A, C) = 0$, but $MB(A, C) + MD(A, C)$ is not necessarily equal to 1.

There are ways to combine certainty factors from many condition elements in the condition part of a rule. Support for an inferred fact may be obtained from different rules and an integrated certainty of the fact has to be estimated. Let us discuss this having the two rules below as an example:

$R1$: IF C, THEN A $(CFr1)$

$R2$: IF P, THEN A $(CFr2)$

An event C', which is supposed to match to some extent the condition C in the first rule, may happen with a certainty of $CF(C')$. The conditional certainty factor of the antecedent C will be $CF(C, C') = CF(C')$. The certainty factors inferred by the two rules for the action part A will be:

$CF1 = CF(A, C) = CF(C, C') \cdot CFr1; CF2 = CF(A, P) = CF(P, P') \cdot CFr2$

Aggregating two certainty factors $CF1$ and $CF2$ inferred for one and the same fact A into one certainty factor $CF(A)$ can be done by using different aggregating formulas:

MAX formula, that is, $CF(A) = \max\{CF1, CF2\}$;

The formula suggested by Shortliffe:

$CF(A) = CF1 + CF2(1 - CF1)$, if $CF1$ and $CF2 > 0$;

$CF(A) = (CF1 + CF2)/(1 - \mathrm{MIN}\{|CF1|, |CF2|\})$, if $CF1$ or $CF2 < 0$;

$CF(A) = (CF1 + CF2)/(1 + CF1)$, if $CF1$ and $CF2 < 0$

Example

$$CF(C, C') = 0.5; \ CFr1 = 0.6; \ CF(P, P') = 0.4; \ CFr2 = 0.8;$$

$$CF(A) = 0.3 + 0.32 \cdot (1 - 0.3) = 0.524.$$

The combined $CF(A)$ is greater than any of those inferred by the individual rules. This is logical as we have two sources ($R1$ and $R2$) that infer A.

When the condition part consists of more than one condition element, e.g., $C = C1$ AND $C2$ AND ... AND Ck, the combined condition part certainty factor is usually calculated as a minimum of the certainty factors of all the condition elements:

$$CF(C, C') = \min\{CF(C1, C1'), \ldots, CF(Ck, Ck')\}$$

When the OR connective is used in the antecedent part of a rule, the maximum certainty factor of a condition element is taken. The formula above is heuristic. It does not follow from the main axioms for the certainty factors. Another limitation to applying certainty factors for approximate reasoning is that the precision of the certainties propagated through a chain of rules decreases rapidly with the length of the chain.

2.10.3 Possibility and Necessity

As a general concept to represent a measure of uncertainty of a event (or a set) E, Zadeh, Sugeno, Dubois and Prade, and others (see Dubois and Prade, 1988) developed a so-called *confidence parameter*—$g(E)$: $0 \leq g(E) \leq 1$, $E \subseteq U$, where E is an event from a domain U of all possible events. When an event is sure, it implies $g(E) = 1$. The implication in the other way is not necessarily true, for example, if $g(E) = 1$ it does not mean that E is a sure event. If an event is impossible, it implies $g(E) = 0$, but not the other way around.

Possibility is the degree to which an expert considers a hypothesis H to be feasible or simply possible. A possibility of an event A and the possibility of its complement event $\neg A$ are weakly connected, in contrast to their probabilities. Possibility is nonstatistical, while probability is statistical. Possibility is capacity or capability. It refers to allowed values, rather than to frequencies.

Example The possibility that soccer team A will win against team B is 0.8, but the possibility that it won't win is 0.4.

Example   The possibility of getting 2 after having thrown a die could be 1, but the probability ideally is 1/6.

The following *axioms* are valid for the confidence parameter g:

A1. g is monotonic with respect to inclusion, that is,

$$E1 \subseteq E2 \Rightarrow g(E1) \leq g(E2),$$

A2. $\forall A, B \subseteq U, g(A \cup B) \geq \max(g(a), g(b))$

A3. $\forall A, B \subseteq D, g(A \cap B) \leq \min(g(A), g(B))$

There is a measure for the confidence parameters of A and B that makes the axiom 2 an equality, and this measure is called *possibility*:

$$\forall A, B \subseteq U, \Pi(A \cup B) = max(\Pi(A), \Pi(B))$$

A function Π takes values in $[0, 1]$ and is defined as follows:

$\Pi(A) = 1$, if $A \cap E \neq \varnothing$ and the event $E \subseteq U$ is considered to be sure; $\Pi(A) = 0$ otherwise.

An event A and its complement $\neg A$ are *weakly connected*:

$$MAX\{\Pi(A), \Pi(\neg A)\} = 1$$

There is also a measure N that makes axiom 3 an equality, which is called *necessity*:

$$\forall A, B \subseteq U, N(A \cap B) = \min(N(A), N(B))$$

The function $U \rightarrow [0, 1]$, such that $E \rightarrow \Pi(E)$, is called a *possibility distribution function*. The following formulas are true for the above-defined terms (see also Neapolitan, 1989):

A4. $\Pi(A) = 1 - N(\neg A)$

A5. $\min(N(A), N(\neg A)) = 0$

A6. $\forall A \subseteq U, \Pi(A) \geq N(A)$

A7. $N(A) > 0 \Rightarrow \Pi(A) = 1$

A8. $\Pi(A) < 1 \Rightarrow N(A) = 0$

A9. $\Pi(A) + \Pi(\neg A) \geq 1$

A10. $N(A) + N(\neg A) \leq 1$

It can be shown that credibility Cr is equivalent to necessity N and plausibility Pl to possibility Π if and only if the focal elements, defined in the Dempster-Shafer theory, form a nested sequence of sets (Dubois and Prade 1988). And something more, if the focal elements are elementary, then $\forall A$, $Cr(A) = Pl(A) = p(A)$. A possibility distribution function can be induced from fuzzy membership function. From a given fuzzy set A, a possibility function can be obtained provided the fuzzy set is normalized, that is, $\exists u \in U$, $\mu_A(u) = 1$, where μ_A is the membership function of A.

2.11   Machine-Learning Methods for Knowledge Engineering

2.11.1   Issues in Machine Learning

Machine-learning methods are computer methods for accumulating, changing, and updating knowledge in an AI computer system. Some major issues which concern the process of learning knowledge in general are:

• What can a system learn objectively from a set of data? The point is that if data do not contain enough information a system cannot "learn" much from it.

• What should a system learn? In order to solve a particular problem, a system has to learn specific features, dependencies, and so forth, relevant to the solution, but not learn everything, or even in the worst scenario, irrelevant features only.

• How to test how well the system has learned appropriate knowledge? Testing the learning process is usually done through measuring the learning error. The main approaches are:

Partitioning of data. A part of the data, say 70%, is used for training and the other part for testing; more sophisticated methods for partitioning are discussed in chapter 5.

The leaving-one-out method means that we train n times the system with $(n - 1)$ examples and check the system's reaction to the left-out example. After doing this n times we can calculate the correct answer of the system as the ratio between the number of correctly processed examples and the number n of all the examples.

Methods of learning exact and fuzzy rules through neural networks is a new area and a very promising one (see chapter 5).

2.11.2   Inductive Learning: Learning from Examples

These methods assume that a set of examples or instances is known. The instances are either of the form of (x_i, y_i), where $x_i \in D$ is a state of the domain space D and $y_i \in S$ is a state of the solution space S, or in the form of (x_i), $i = 1, 2, \ldots, n$, where no output vectors are specified. The task is to create a system which can learn the input-output associations $\{(x, y)\}$ or to learn inherent characteristics of the data $\{x\}$. The first case will be referred to as *supervised learning*, where the solution y_i (a class label) for every input vector x_i is provided. The examples will be called "labeled" examples. The second case will be referred to as *unsupervised learning*, that is, the system will learn some characteristics, features, clusters, concepts, etc. from unlabeled examples.

Example   A classic example of an inductive learning task adopted from psychology is given in figure 2.34A (also used in (Pratt, 1994)). The task is to observe the five examples classified into two classes A and B and learn common rules for placing examples into one of these groups. Figure 2.34B gives a truth table type of representation of this problem and figure 2.35 gives a boolean map for the same example. The following boolean rules can be articulated from this map: class $A = \neg t$; class $B = t$. These boolean rules can be used to classify unknown examples. Other techniques may also be used for learning the common rules and for generalization. Some of them allow using non-boolean variables, for example, continuous values variables.

Inductive decision trees and the ID3 algorithm   How to discriminate the classes, what formula, or rule, or structure should be used for generalizing new examples? A technique called *inductive decision tree* "observes" the examples and builds a binary tree which can *discriminate* all the classes. The process of building the tree is based on recursive choosing of a node, an attribute, or any of its value, which divides the whole set of examples into two groups.

Example   Figure 2.36 shows a decision tree for classifying the objects from figure 2.34(A) into the two classes A and B. The paths in the tree can be represented as rules (also shown on fig. 2.36).

An inductive decision tree for classifying the Iris data examples is given in Barndorff-Nielsen et al. (1993). This tree can classify all the 50 examples of Setosa correctly, 49 of the examples of Virginica, and 47 of the examples

a.

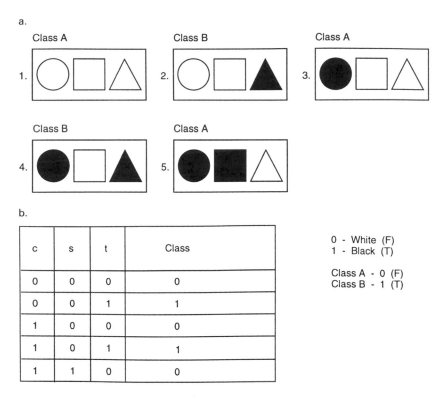

b.

c	s	t	Class
0	0	0	0
0	0	1	1
1	0	0	0
1	0	1	1
1	1	0	0

0 - White (F)
1 - Black (T)

Class A - 0 (F)
Class B - 1 (T)

Figure 2.34
Psychology example for inductive learning (adapted from Pratt 1994): (A) the objects and their classes are given. (B) the task represented as a truth-table.

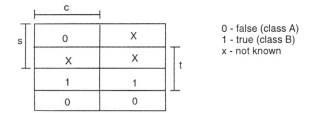

0 - false (class A)
1 - true (class B)
x - not known

Figure 2.35
Inductive learning from boolean examples by using boolean table of Carno—the example from fig. 2.34(B).

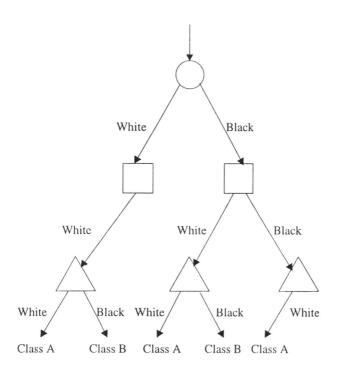

If △ is White THEN Class A
If △ is Black THEN Class B

Figure 2.36
Decision-classification tree for the psychology example. The decision tree is also represented
as a set of rules.

of Versicolor. In order to improve the classification, a further refinement
of the values at the leaves must be done.

The question is how to choose the attributes and their values when
splitting the data? One possibility is to evaluate each "split candidate test"
a in respect of a desired property *C* and choose the one with a highest
information gain or minimal *lack of information*. Measuring the information gain and the lack of information can be done in different ways. One
of them is by using the formulas (see also (Pratt, 1994)):

$\inf(C, a) = -p \cdot \log_2 p - (1 - p) \cdot \log_2(1 - p)$, *p*—proportion of examples
which pass test *a* (experimental probability).

$\inf(C, \neg a) = -q \cdot \log_2 q - (1 - q) \cdot \log_2(1 - q)$, q—proportion of examples which fail to pass a

$\mathrm{INF}(C, a) = p \cdot \inf(C, a) + (1 - p) \cdot \inf(C, \neg a)$—lack of information.

At any step of deciding which test to allocate to a node, starting from the root of the decision tree, the test a with a minimal lack of information is chosen.

A well-known symbolic AI method for inductive learning of a decision tree from a set of symbolic examples is ID3 (Quinlan 1986). This method induces an "optimal" decision tree for classification problems from a set of labeled examples. Optimal here means that if a new example is to be classified, the system follows the decision tree and checks the fewest features of the example in order to classify it into one of the known classes (predefined labels given in the examples).

The decision trees learned can be translated into a form of IF-THEN rules or formulas. It is a compromise between the precisely learned examples and the generalization ability of a tree. A decision tree can be pruned to some depth which may accelerate the decision process but may lead to an increase in the error. Learning from examples can be:

• *Incremental.* Every new example contributes to the knowledge learned by the system from the previous examples. The system does not count all the previous examples again.

• *"One-shot" learning.* The system observes all the examples only once and extracts some features from the set.

Neural networks are very powerful techniques for learning from examples. They can be used for learning unstructured knowledge. Knowledge is captured in a neural network but it cannot be articulated explicitly. Learning structured knowledge can also be done in neural networks, but the rules in that case have to be formulated after analysis of a trained neural network. The rules can be fuzzy or exact. Different types of inexactness and uncertainty can also be extracted.

Learning in a system cannot be discussed separately from its generalization ability. For example, can the rules learned from figure 2.36 be used to place the case given in figure 2.37 into the most appropriate class from the two given in figure 2.34(A)? Here it is necessary to apply reasoning by analogy. This is natural for humans, but difficult to implement in a computer program.

Figure 2.37
A different case from that given in figure 2.34(A) to be classified in the most appropriate class there.

2.11.3   Other Methods of Machine Learning

• *Learning by doing, learning by observation and discovery.* The system starts without knowledge or with very little knowledge: for example, a "goodness" criterion. The goodness criterion may not be introduced to the system a priori. It can be learned from the reaction of the user or the environment. Gradually, the system accumulates correct solutions and learns how to react properly. A simple case is *rote learning,* that is, memorizing previous solutions and using one of them for new data. Genetic algorithms are another example. These methods can be implemented either as symbolic AI systems, where exact knowledge can be learned, or as neural networks, where approximate knowledge can be learned without any previous knowledge being provided. The latter include unsupervised learning in some neural network types.

• *Learning by being told, learning from advice.* This is simply the process whereby a system obtains knowledge in some form and transforms it to its internal form in order to use it effectively. Little learning is involved in these methods. It is more a kind of interpreting and a molding of given knowledge into well-known schemes. The method is a typical symbolic AI method.

• *Learning by analogy.* This is the case whereby a system learns how to solve a problem on the basis of previous solutions of analogous problems, or on the basis of previous solutions of the same problem but in a different domain. Learning by analogy has been explored through symbolic AI methods, but because it involves measuring similarities and approximate reasoning, this approach has not gone far. There is plenty of potential for using neural networks and fuzzy systems.

• *Case-based learning* is based on using a set of exemplars. The system stores only a selected set of examples (exemplars) and uses them for finding the best match between a new example and the exemplars in order to generalize, that is, to classify the new example. Here exemplars (not rules) are learned and stored in a system. Classification of a new instance in exemplar-based learning approaches is based on nearest-neighbor matching against those instances or exemplars already stored in the memory. Different criteria are used to measure the distance between the stored representations and a new instance. An exemplar-based method of learning, called template-based method, is given in the next subsection as an example of AI-symbolic methods and also as a basis for comparing different approaches to learning the same problem, in this case the problem of classifying Iris plants when the Iris data set is given as a set of examples.

2.11.4   A Template Case-Based Method for Learning and Classification (Optional)

A method for exemplar-based learning and classification is presented here. The learning method assumes a set of examples. The following main steps are performed:

1. *Discretization of the data.* Discretizing intervals chosen on the basis of statistical characteristics can be used. For the Iris data set the discretization interval scheme given in section 2.2.2 is used here. After discretizing an instance from the raw data set, it becomes a case, or a template.

2. *A set of representative templates (SRT)* with an associated probability coefficient (PC) indicating the number of instances associated with the same representative template (RT) is learned from the discretized data. A representative template RT for a class C is a template which represents some of the instances which belong to class C. An example of a representative template is (5 2 9 1 1 23) where the first four numbers are attribute-interval values, the fifth is the class number, and the sixth is called the probability coefficient, the number of all the instances from class 1, represented by this RT.

3. *A global probability vector (GPV)* for the whole data set is calculated. The GPV consists of the global probabilities of all the different attribute-interval values over the entire data set.

The result of learning is a set of representative templates and the GPV. This approach is implemented as "supervised" and "unsupervised" learning, as they are called here. The first assumes labels attached to the instances; the second one does not assume or does not take into account

Instances					Discretised Instances					Representative Templates (RT)					
A1	A2	A3	A4	Class	A1	A2	A3	A4	Class	A1	A2	A3	A4	Class	PC
5.1	3.5	1.4	0.2	Set.	2	2	1	1	1	2	2	1	1	1	2
4.7	3.2	1.3	0.2	Set.	1	2	1	1	1	1	2	1	1	1	1
5.0	3.6	1.4	0.2	Set.	2	2	1	1	1	-					
6.5	2.8	4.6	1.5	Vers.	3	1	4	2	2	3	1	4	2	2	2
6.3	3.3	4.7	1.6	Vers.	3	2	4	2	2	3	2	4	2	2	1
6.6	2.9	4.6	1.3	Vers.	3	1	4	2	2	-					
7.1	3.0	5.9	2.1	Virg.	4	2	5	3	3	4	2	5	3	3	1
6.5	3.0	5.9	2.2	Virg.	3	2	5	3	3	3	2	5	3	3	3
6.5	3.2	5.1	2.0	Virg.	3	2	5	3	3	-					
6.8	3.0	5.5	2.1	Virg.	3	2	5	3	3	-					

Figure 2.38
A small subset of 10 instances from the Iris data set, their discretized interval representation according to the intervals given in figure 2.3, and a set of representative templates (RT) obtained through a supervised template-based learning algorithm.

class labels. After learning representative templates, a generalization procedure which classifies a new example into one of the classes known or extracted from unlabeled data is applied.

Example A small subset of 10 instances taken from the Iris data set is used to illustrate the above algorithm. The same data are used with the "unsupervised" learning algorithm yet to be given. Figure 2.38 shows the raw data, the discretized data, and the SRT obtained by the supervised learning algorithm.

The classification algorithm classifies a new instance (denoted here as NEW) into one of the possible classes. The classification procedure developed here is based on a nearest-neighbor match of the new instance template (Tnew) and the SRT.

In the classification process, if there is an exact match between Tnew and RT, the probability coefficients PCi of each of the matched RTs belonging to the same class are summed and normalized. The class that has the highest sum is the winner if a single classification result is required.

Otherwise a classification set with certainty degrees is created based on the normalized sums for all the classes. If Tnew does not match exactly any of the RTs, then the most typical attribute for the entire data set is turned into a wild card ("?") and the matching procedure continues with the rest of the attributes. The logic is that the most typical attribute value is assumed to appear in the majority of instances regardless of their class; therefore it cannot help in distinguishing between classes when classifying a new instance. So the most typical attribute for the whole data set is sacrificed in order to achieve a partial matching. To sacrifice a whole attribute may not be a good idea in many cases and it has been avoided in fuzzy and neural systems.

Using the SRT obtained in the example above, we can demonstrate how we would attempt to classify a new instance of the Iris data into one of the classes—Setosa, Versicolor, or Virginica. If the new instance is (4.4 2.9 1.4 0.2), then its template (Tnew) after discretization is (1 1 1 1 ?). The corresponding probabilities for each attribute, stored in the GPV, are (.1 .2 .3 .3). The first step fails to find an exact match. The next step replaces the most typical attribute value by a wild card ("?") which yields the template (1 1 1 ? ?). However there are still no matching templates. The next step is to turn the next most typical attribute (in this case the third attribute) into a wild card, but again there are no matching templates. As the general probabilities of PL = 1 and PW = 1 are the same (0.3), the first template was chosen arbitrarily over the second. But as we shall see later, this choice may turn to be important and ambiguity in such cases can be met by applying a classification with certainty degrees. Only on the third partial-matching cycle, when the second attribute is turned into a "?," a matching RT is found. The matching RT is (1 2 1 1 1 1), which belongs to class1. The classification for this example would be (class1/1, class2/0, class3/0).

In the case of Tnew = (3 2 4 3), the template (3 2 4 ?) matches class2's RT with a PC = 1 and the template (3 2 ? 3) matches class3's RT with a PC = 3. The resulting classification set is (class1/0, class2/0.25, class3/0.75).

Here "unsupervised" learning is performed on a data set when the instances do not contain any information on the classes (labels) to which they belong. In some cases the target number of classes (Ncl) may be given explicitly. If Ncl is not known, all the different representative templates are given a different class number and the corresponding PCs are created. If a given number (Ncl) of classes is required, then the procedure described below can be applied.

Using the same data set as above, but without class information in the examples, the data set is discretized and a set of representative templates SRT1 is created. The RTs are associated with (numerical) class labels based on the order in which they are derived. When the number of required classes is not known, SRT1 becomes SRT and is used for classification. If the number of classes required is provided (e.g., Ncl = 3), then the procedure is as follows:

1. Derive the Ncl class centers, a class center being an RT with the highest probability coefficient, PC, that is, representing most of the examples. In this case three centers, $C1 = (2\ 2\ 1\ 1)$, $C2 = (3\ 1\ 4\ 2)$, and $C3 = (3\ 2\ 5\ 3)$, are chosen from the RTs in SRT1. Their corresponding probability vectors are (.2 .8 .3 .3), (.6 .2 .3 .3) and (.6 .8 .4 .4).

2. Match $C1$, $C2$, and $C3$ against SRT1. All RTs are matched using the wild-carding of attributes, based on typicality, and associated with one of the classes. Figure 2.39 illustrates an implementation of the unsupervised learning algorithm to the data set above when the number of classes is given (Ncl = 3).

The extracted RTs during the so-called supervised and unsupervised learning can be represented by interval production rules, which written in the CLIPS syntax look like the rules shown in figure 2.40. The representative templates can also be used for articulating fuzzy rules, as shown in chapter 3. The confidence factors attached to the rules are calculated on the basis of the probabilities of an instance from a defined class to be represented by the rule.

2.12 Problems and Exercises

Part A: Case Example Solutions

1. *The Soil Classification Example.* The soil class templates are represented as facts (figure 2.41). The same problem, that is, the lack of a smooth match between facts and conditions in the rules, as pointed out in section 2.7.3 for the Musical Recognition Problem, will appear here because of the principle of exact match "(fact-template) → (class template)" used.

Discretized Instance				SRT1						SRT					
A1	A2	A3	A4	A1	A2	A3	A4	Class	PC	A1	A2	A3	A4	Class	PC
2	2	1	1	2	2	1	1	1	2	2	2	1	1	1	2
1	2	1	1	1	2	1	1	2	1	1	2	1	1	1	1
2	2	1	1	3	1	4	2	3	2	3	1	4	2	2	2
3	1	4	2	3	2	4	2	4	1	3	2	4	2	2	1
3	2	4	2	3	2	5	3	5	1	4	2	5	3	3	1
3	1	4	2	4	2	5	3	6	3	3	2	5	3	3	3
4	2	5	3												
3	2	5	3												
3	2	5	3												
3	2	5	3												

Figure 2.39
An illustration of the "unsupervised" template-based learning algorithm applied to the small subset of 10 discretized Iris instances from figure 2.37. The set SRT1 contains all the six different (class) templates. If the number of classes is a priori given, for example, Ncl = 3, then these six representative templates are labeled with three labels only, thus producing a set SRT and probability coefficients for each of the representative templates.

2. Production systems are very useful for solving monitoring and diagnostic problems. Figure 2.42 shows a production system for solving the Car Monitoring Problem. In order to have a real monitoring system, the working memory should be fed with new facts from the car sensors every few seconds, for example.

3. *Musical signals recognition* production system (or converting sounds-into-notes program). Figure 2.43A shows graphically a musical signal represented as a fact and figure 2.43B shows two production rules for recognition of two notes. Intervals are used for representing typical values for the energy of the signal in the 10 frequency bands between 0 and 10,000 Hz. A real application would require either more bands or at least a higher value for the highest frequency to be considered. The borders of the intervals are either communicated by experts or articulated after analyzing samples of known signals. In both of the two cases, the interval values are

```
(defrule Setosa1
        (SL is_in 2 SW is_in 2 PL is_in 1 PW is_in 1)
        =>
        (assert (class setosa 0.66)))

(defrule Setosa2
        (SL is_in 1 SW is_in 2 PL is_in 1 PW is_in 1)
        =>
        (assert (class setosa 0.33)))

(defrule Versicolor1
        (SL is_in 3 SW is_in 1 PL is_in 4 PW is_in 2)
        =>
        (assert(class versicolor 0.66)))

(defrule Versicolor2
        (SL is_in 3 SW is_in 2 PL is_in 4 PW is_in 2)
        =>
        (assert (class versicolor 0.33)))

(defrule Virginica1
        (PL is_in 4 PW is_in 2 SL is_in 5 SW is_in 3)
        =>
        (assert (class virginica 0.25)))

(defrule Virginica2
        (SL is_in 3 SW is_in 2 PL is_in 5 PW is_in 3)
        =>
        (assert (class virginica 0.75)))
```

Figure 2.40
Rules extracted from the representative templates in figure 2.38 for the Iris classification.

not precise. On the other hand, they impose crisp borderlines between classes. This contradiction may result in a not very good generalization.

4. An example of a decision-making problem (briefly discussed in chapter 1) was the Investment Advisor Problem. The same approach, as used in the program above, is used here, that is, an attribute-value interval quantization in the condition elements of the rules. Figure 2.44 shows two rules for investment advising. Again, the same problem, that is, "lack of plausible partial match," may be experienced.

5. Planning systems are usually goal-driven. Using the built-in selection strategies appropriately, one can develop a goal-driven system within the data-driven inference mechanism of a production language. A typical

```
(deffacts KNOWN_SOILS
        (SOIL EGMONT_YBL 3 27 4 8 3 10 17 3)
        (SOIL STRATFORD_YBL 1 11 5 6 1 4 6 2)
        (SOIL TAUPO_YBP 3 6 4 5 1 8 4 1)
        (SOIL TOKOMARU_YGE 1 10 5 7 2 5 8 2)
        (SOIL MATAPIRO_YGE 0 2 4 3 1 2 9 3)
        (SOIL WAIKARE_YBE 1 8 5 11 1 3 7 2))

(defrule identify_soil_type
        (nhi ?nhi)  (noi ?noi)   (soi ?soi)  (cai ?cai)  (mgi ?mgi)  (ki ?ki)  (nai ?nai)
          (cli ?cli)
        (SOIL ?sname ?nh&:(= ?nh ?nhi) ?no&:(= ?no ?noi) ?so&:(= ?so ?soi)
        ?ca&:(= ?ca ?cai) ?mg&:(= ?mg ?mgi) ?k&:(= ?k ?ki) ?na&:(= ?na ?nai)
        ?cl&:(= ?cl ?cli) )
     =>
        (printout t "The type of soil indicated by these element amounts is ")
        (printout t ?sname crlf))
```

Figure 2.41
A simple production system for solving the Soil Classification case problem.

```
; A program to monitor a car
; Templates for representing the facts
; (car_param parameter_name value)
; (car_status system functioning status)

; Initial facts
(deffacts initial_facts
        (car_param temperature 130)
        (car_status brakes functioning OK)
        (car_status gauge functioning OK))

; Rules
(defrule stop_the_car
          ( or  (car_status cooling functioning overheating)
                (car_status brakes functioning slowly))
      =>
          (printout t "Stop the car " crlf ))

(defrule overheating
          (car_status gauge functioning OK)
          (car_param temperature ?temp &: ( > ?temp 120 ))
      =>
          (printout t " There is an overheating" crlf )
          (assert (car_status cooling functioning overheating)))
```

Figure 2.42
A production system for solving the Car Monitoring case problem.

a.

FACT Template

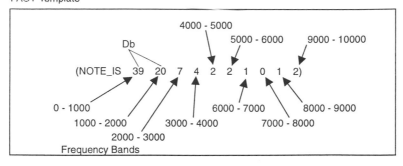

b.

```
; Template for representing the facts
; (Note_Is <param1> <param2> <param3> ....... <param10>)


; Rules

(defrule CaboveMidC
        (Note_Is ?param1&:(>= ?param1 45)& ?param1&:(<= ?param1 50) $?)
    =>
        (printout t crlf "The note is C above Middle C!" crlf))

(defrule BaboveMidC
        (Note_Is ?param1&:(>= ?param1 30)& ?param1&:(<= ?param1 34) ?
        ?param3&:(>= ?param3 0)& ?param3&:(<= ?param3 10) $?)
    =>
        (printout t crlf "The note is B above Middle C!" crlf))
```

Figure 2.43
(A) A template of a musical signal. (B) A single production rule for recognizing a note.

```
; Template for holding information about clients.
; (client <fname> <lname> <amount> <risk> <period> <income>)

(defrule SmAv/Low/ShLg
         (client ?fname ?lname ?amount&:(> ?amount 0)
                 &?amount&:(< ?amount 100000)
         ?risk&low|LOW ?period ?income)
    =>
         (printout t "?fname " As you are looking for a return with the minimum
                 amount of risk on your money it would be best to put your money in a
                 fixed term deposit with a bank. This will provide you with a secure
                 investment and also allow for a return on your money."))

(defrule Med/Lng/Low
         (client ?fname ?lname ?amount&:(> ?amount 0)
                 &?amount&:(< ?amount 100000)
         ?risk&medium|MEDIUM ?period&:(> ?period 24)
                 ?income&:(<= ?income 35000))
    =>
         (printout t " ?fname  " Invest around 30% of your money in shares. It
                 would be wise to invest the remainder with a bank as on your income
                 you really cannot afford to open yourself up to too much risk"))
```

Figure 2.44
Two production rules as part of a solution to the Investment Adviser case example problem.

characteristic of planning systems is that they are sequential because a plan is a sequence of actions. Production systems are also sequential, that is, a single production is executed at every cycle. Therefore production systems may be good AI mechanisms for solving planning problems. The fact templates, an initial state, and some rules of a production system for the Monkey and Bananas Problem, are given in figure 2.45.

Part B: Practical Tasks and Questions

6. Explain how you recognize a cup. Can you formulate the rules? Give examples of three cups described in a set of features you think are important for the process of recognition.

7. Explain the eight main issues in knowledge engineering. Compare symbolic AI systems, fuzzy systems, and neural networks for knowledge engineering (see table 1.1).

8. What is discretization and what is normalization? Give examples.

```
;A template for representing facts that contain information about the monkey.
;        (monkey <location>
;               <ontopof>
;               <holding>)

;A template for representing facts that contain information about the objects.
;        (object <name>
;               <location>
;               <ontopof>
;               <weight>)

;A template for representing monkey's goals.
;        (goalisto <action>
;               <<arguments>>)

;Initial state
(deffacts initialstate
        (monkey t57 floor blank)
        (object ladder t64 floor light)
        (object bananas t49 ceiling light)
        (goalisto hold bananas))

(defrule grabobject
        ?f1 <(goalisto hold ?obj)
        ?f2 <(object ?obj ?place ?on light)
        ?f3 <(monkey ?place ?on blank)
        =>
        (printout t "Monkey grabs the " ?obj crlf)
        (retract ?f1 ?f2 ?f3)
        (assert (object ?place held light))
        (assert (monkey ?place ?on ?obj)))

(defrule holdobjecttomove
        (goalisto move ?obj ?place)
        (object ?obj ~?place ? light)
        (monkey ? ? ~?obj)
        (not (goalisto hold ?obj))
        =>
        (assert (goalisto holds ?obj)))
```

Figure 2.45
Part of a program for the Monkey and Bananas Problem written in CLIPS.

9. What is the principle difference between FFT and wavelet transformation?

10. Why may data analysis be important?

11. Describe five symbolic AI methods for knowledge representation. Give examples.

12. What are modus ponens, modus tollens, forward chaining and backward chaining? What is the relationship between them? Do they relate to partial matching, or not?

13. What are the main types of symbol expressions used in predicate logic? Give examples of every one. Write a clause for recognizing a handwritten character 3.

14. Explain the main phases of the inference engine in a production system. Write down a production for recognizing a handwritten character 3.

15. What is a variable as a general term? How many types of variables are allowed in the production language CLIPS? Give examples. What kind of variables are allowed in PROLOG? How do they get bound to values?

16. Explain the matching process in CLIPS and in PROLOG. Give one example and explain how this example is executed in the both systems.

17. Explain how production languages can be used for solving the following generic AI problems introduced in chapter 1: classification; planning; decision making.

18. Give at least three points for discussion at each steps in developing an expert system.

19. Explain the ways data (facts) are represented in CLIPS and in PROLOG.

20. What is the difference between probability, credibility, plausibility, belief, disbelief, certainty factor, fuzzy membership function, possibility, necessity with respect to representing a set A and its complementary set $\neg A$?

21. Give the main axioms for defining each of the following: probability $p(A)$, mass parameter $m(A)$, certainty factor $CF(A, C)$, fuzzy set A, confidence measure $g(A)$.

22. Outline three main methods for machine-learning.

23. Write a set of production rules for the game ticktacktoe. Be sure that the rules "cover" the whole domain space; otherwise the program may fail to make a move if some situations are present on the board.

24. Write in CLIPS a heuristic rule for the Traveling Salesman Problem.

25. Create fact templates and a set of production rules for solving the assignment problem (explained in chapter 1).

26. Create fact templates and write a set of production rules for the Resource Scheduling Problem explained in chapter 1.

27. Compare the partial interval match used in 2.11.4 and the exact interval match in the Soil Classification Problem example given in 2.12, part A. What is the difference?

28. How can a partial match be realized in PROLOG?

Part C: Project Specification

Topic: Developing a Small Rule-Based Production System

1. Choose a problem to solve as a production rule-based system. Explain the problem. You may use one of the problem domains listed below.

2. Develop a set of rules for solving the problem using the "matching facts against rules" principle. Represent facts as templates.

3. Develop a production system. Write the program (normally between 10 and 30 productions).

4. Make experiments with your production system for different data inputs. Validate the results. What extension of the program can be done in the future?

Note. A list of problems from different application domains:

1. Printed characters recognition

2. Handwritten digits or character recognition

3. Objects recognition and classification: plants, earth samples, weather patterns, blood samples under a microscope

4. Speech recognition—a small subset of phonemes recognition

5. Musical notes recognition

6. Planning robot navigation

7. Device (plant) monitoring

8. Medical diagnosis

9. Technical diagnosis

10. Prediction of possible failure of a device

11. Prediction of disasters (storms, earthquakes, floods, etc.)

12. Stock market prediction (see appendix C)

13. Control of manufacturing processes

14. Resource scheduling

15. Game simulation—playing ticktacktoe

16. Game simulation—playing Go-Moku (see chapter 1).

17. Decision-making—investment adviser

18. Mortgage approval (see appendix C)

2.13   Conclusion

This chapter was a brief presentation of symbolic AI methods for knowledge-engineering. But it also made the bridge to the fuzzy and neural network models. The main issues in knowledge-engineering, which are data and knowledge representation and inference, are also the main issues in using fuzzy systems and neural networks. The short presentation of propositional and predicate logic is used later to refer to and make comparisons between the fuzzy, connectionist, and the symbolic AI inference methods. The detailed presentation of production systems and its realization aim at deeper understanding of the principles in order to use them for practical applications as well as to implement them (or their modifications) in fuzzy and connectionist environments.

2.14   Suggested Reading

The following texts are recommended for further reading on general or specific topics:

Statistical methods for data analysis—Weiss and Kulikowski (1991); Barndoff-Nielsen et al. (1993)

Clustering algorithms—Hartigan (1975); Stolcke (1992)

Introduction to AI and expert systems—Pratt (1994); Robinson (1988); Ralston (1988); Schalkoff (1990); Dean et al. (1995); Luger and Stubblefield (1989)

AI logic systems—Doyle (1979)

Principles of expert systems—Giarratano and Riley (1989); Feigenbaum (1989)

Introduction to AI, expert systems, and CLIPS language—Giarratano and Riley (1989)

CLIPS user's guide—Giarratano (1989)

Probability methods for approximate reasoning—Neapolitan (1989); Kanal and Lemmer (1986)

Nonprobability methods for approximate reasoning—Dempster (1967); Shafer (1976); Dubois and Prade (1980, 1988); Whalen and Schott (1985); Yager and Zadeh (1992)

Machine-learning methods—Bratko and Lavrac (1987); Quinlan (1986); Clark (1989); Thornton (1992); Tsypkin (1973); Elliot and Scott (1991); Fisher (1936); Aha et al. (1991)

Methods for knowledge acquisition for expert systems—Hart (1992)

Template-based method for learning representative templates (section 2.11)—Kasabov and Clarke (1995)

Early expert systems—Waterman and Hayes-Roth (1978); Feigenbaum (1989)

3 From Fuzzy Sets to Fuzzy Systems

In chapter 1 a short introduction to *fuzzy sets* was given. This chapter continues to present some basic notions about fuzzy sets, but it also introduces the process of designing real fuzzy systems for solving generic and specific problems. Different methods of fuzzy reasoning are discussed and illustrated. The process of a fuzzy system design is described as a process of articulating commonsense knowledge by using linguistically plausible terms, creating fuzzy rules and numerically defined membership functions for them, and applying a fuzzy inference method.

3.1 Fuzzy Sets and Fuzzy Operations

3.1.1 Fuzzy Sets

The notion of a fuzzy set was introduced first by Lotfi Zadeh in 1965, who later developed many of the methods of *fuzzy logic* based on this simple notion. It took a couple of decades for the rationale of fuzzy sets to be understood and applied by other scientists.

The traditional way of representing elements u of a set A is through the *characteristic function*:

$\mu_A(u) = 1$, if u is an element of the set A, and

$\mu_A(u) = 0$, if u is not an element of the set A,

that is, an object either belongs or does not belong to a given set.

In fuzzy sets an object can belong to a set partially. The degree of membership is defined through a generalized characteristic function called *membership function*:

$\mu_A(u): U \rightarrow [0, 1]$

where U is called the *universe*, and A is a *fuzzy subset* of U.

The values of the membership function are real numbers in the interval $[0, 1]$, where 0 means that the object is not a member of the set and 1 means that it belongs entirely. Each value of the function is called a membership degree. One way of defining a membership function is through an analog function. Figure 3.1 shows three membership functions representing three fuzzy sets labeled as "short," "medium," and "tall," all of them being fuzzy values of a variable "height." As we can see, the value 170 cm belongs to the fuzzy set "medium" to a degree of 0.2 and at the same time to the set "tall" to a degree of 0.7.

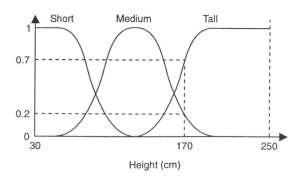

Figure 3.1
Membership functions representing three fuzzy sets for the variable "height."

If the universe is *discrete*, a membership function can be defined by a finite set in the following way:

$$A = \mu(u_1)/u_1 + \mu(u_2)/u_2 + \cdots + \mu(u_n)/u_n,$$

or simply

$$A = \sum \mu_i/u_i,$$

where the symbol / separates the membership degrees $\mu(u_i)$ from the elements of the universe $u_i \in U$, and + stands for union. In a simpler form, a fuzzy set is represented as a sequence of membership degree/value pairs: (0/150, 0.3/160, 0.68/170, 0.9/180, 1/190, 1/250).

Venn diagrams, which were used in chapter 2 for graphical representation of ordinary sets, are not appropriate for representing fuzzy sets. The principle difference between an ordinary, *crisp set* and a fuzzy set is illustrated by the graphical representation shown in figure 3.2. Crisp sets use "clear cut" on the boundaries. Fuzzy sets use grades. The membership degree to which two values, for example, 14.999 and 15.001, belong to the fuzzy set "medium" are very close to each other, which represents their closeness in the universe, but because of the crisp border between the crisp sets "cool" and "medium," the two values are associated with different crisp sets.

Some basic notions of fuzzy sets are defined below:

• A *support* of a fuzzy set A is the subset of the universe U, each element of which has a membership degree to A different from zero (figure 3.3):

$$\text{supp}(A) = \{u | u \in U, \mu_A(u) > 0\}$$

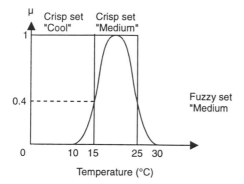

Figure 3.2
Representing crisp and fuzzy sets as subsets of a domain (universe) U.

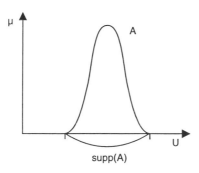

Figure 3.3
Support of a fuzzy set A.

For example, the support of the fuzzy set "medium temperature" is the interval $(10, 30)$ on the Celsius scale. A fuzzy set A can be formulated entirely by its support, that is:

$$A = \{\mu_A(u)/u | u \in \text{supp}(A)\}$$

• *Cardinality* of an ordinary, crisp set is defined as the number of the elements in the set, but *cardinality* of a fuzzy set $M(A)$ is defined as follows:

$$M(A) = \sum \mu_A(u), \quad u \in U$$

• *Power set* of A is called the set of all fuzzy subsets of A.

• A fuzzy set A is called a *normal fuzzy set* if its membership function has a grade of 1 at least for one value from the universe U.

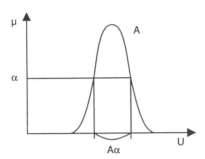

Figure 3.4
I-cut of a fuzzy set.

• Every fuzzy set A can be represented by its α-*cut*, which can be defined as *weak* or *strong* (figure 3.4). The α-*cut* of a fuzzy set A is a subset A_α of the universe U which consists of values that belong to the fuzzy set A with a membership degree greater (weak cut), or greater or equal (strong cut) than a given value $\alpha \in [0, 1]$.

• An interesting property of fuzzy sets, introduced by Kosko (1992), was called *subsethood*. It measures not the degree to which a fuzzy set belongs to the universe, but the other way round, the degree to which the whole universe U belongs to any of its fuzzy subsets. Thus, everything is subjective and depends on the viewpoint.

Fuzzy set theory can be considered as an extension of ordinary set theory. Operations similar to the well-known ordinary set operations have been introduced for fuzzy sets, as shown in the next section.

3.1.2   Operations with Fuzzy Sets

Ordinary (crisp) sets are a special case of fuzzy sets, when two membership degrees only, 0 and 1, are used, and crisp borders between the sets are defined. All definitions, proofs, and theorems that apply to fuzzy sets must also be valid in the case when the fuzziness becomes zero, that is, when the fuzzy set turns into an ordinary one.

We shall now look at some fuzzy operators. An analog-function representation of membership functions is used in figure 3.5 to represent some operations with fuzzy sets. The following operations over two fuzzy sets A and B defined over the same universe U are the most common in fuzzy theory:

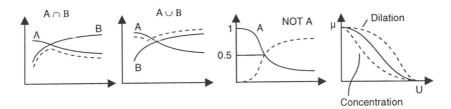

Figure 3.5
Five operations with two fuzzy sets A and B approximately represented in a graphical form.

- *Union, $A \cup B$*:

$$\mu_{A \cup B}(u) = \mu_A(u) \vee \mu_B(u), \quad \text{for all } u \text{ from } U, \text{ where } \vee \text{ means MAX}$$

- *Intersection, $A \cap B$*:

$$\mu_{A \cap B}(u) = \mu_A(u) \wedge \mu_B(u), \quad \text{for all } u \text{ from } U, \text{ where } \wedge \text{ means MIN; the}$$
De Morgan's laws are valid for intersection and union.

- *Equality, $A = B$*:

$$\mu_A(u) = \mu_B(u), \quad \text{for all } u \text{ from } U$$

- *Set complement, $not A$, $\neg A$*:

$$\mu_{not A}(u) = 1 - \mu_A(u), \quad \text{for all } u \text{ from } U$$

- *Concentration, $CON(A)$*:

$$\mu_{CON(A)}(u) = (\mu_A(u))^2, \quad \text{for all } u \text{ from } U; \text{ this operation is used as a}$$
linguistic modifier *"very"*

- *Dilation, $DIL(A)$*:

$$\mu_{DIL(A)}(u) = (\mu_A(u))^{0.5}, \quad \text{for all } u \text{ from } U; \text{ this operation is used as a}$$
linguistic modifier *"more or less."*

- *Subset, $A \subseteq B$*:

$$\mu_A(u) \leq \mu_B(u), \quad \text{for all } u \text{ from } U$$

- *Algebraic product, $A \cdot B$*:

$$\mu_{AB}(u) = \mu_A(u) \cdot \mu_B(u), \quad \text{for all } u \text{ from } U$$

- *Bounded sum*:

$$\max\{1, \mu_A(u) + \mu_B(u)\}, \quad \text{for all } u \text{ from } U$$

- *Bounded difference, $A \mid - \mid B$*:

$$\mu_{A \mid - \mid B}(u) = \min\{0, \mu_A(u) - \mu_B(u)\}, \quad \text{for all } u \text{ from } U$$

- *Bounded product*:

$\max\{0, \mu_A(u) + \mu_B(u) - 1\}$,   for all u from U

- *Normalization NORM(A)*:

$\mu_{NORM(A)}(u) = \mu_A(u)/\text{MAX}\{\mu_A(u)\}$,   for all u from U

- *Algebraic sum*:

$\mu_{A+B}(u) = \mu_A(u) + \mu_B(u)$,   for all u from U; the De Morgan laws are valid for the algebraic sum and difference.

The operations over fuzzy sets have some *properties*, for example, they are *associative*, *commutative*, and *distributive*, that is,

Associative: $(a * b) * c = a * (b * c)$

Commutative: $a * b = b * a$ (not valid for the bounded difference)

Distributive: $a * (b \circ c) = (a \circ b) * (a \circ c)$

where $*$ and $\circ$ denote any operations from those listed above.

An interesting and most distinguishing property for fuzzy sets, when compared with ordinary sets, is that fuzzy sets break the law of the *excluded middle* and the *law of contradiction*, so the following may be true:

$A \cup \neg A \neq U$

$A \cap \neg A \neq \varnothing$

So the union of a fuzzy set A and its complement $\neg A$ should not necessarily give the whole universe U. And the intersection between the two is not necessarily equal to the empty set.

Measuring the *ambiguity* (the *fuzziness*) of a fuzzy set is an interesting issue. Kosko (1986) suggested that the fuzziness of a fuzzy set is measured by its *entropy*:

$E(A) = M(A \cap \neg A)/M(A \cup \neg A)$

where M denotes the cardinality. The greater the entropy, the greater the fuzziness. Crisp sets have an entropy of 0. This simple definition opens the doors for applying fuzzy sets to real problems as it is well known that an entropy of 0 is rather too idealistic a case. Another formula for measuring the entropy of a fuzzy set A is:

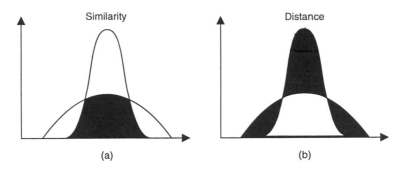

Figure 3.6
Showing graphically one way of measuring similarity and distance between fuzzy sets (a) and (b). The black area represents quantitatively the measure.

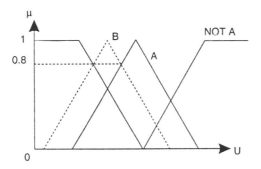

Figure 3.7
A graphical representation of calculating the similarity S between two fuzzy sets B and A based on possibility P and necessity N measures (see the formulas in the text).

$$E(A) = -k \sum \{\mu_A(u_i) \cdot \log \mu_A(u_i) + \mu_{\neg A}(u_i) \cdot \log \mu_{\neg A}(u_i)\}, \quad \text{for all } u \in U.$$

where: $k > 0$ is a constant.

Different metric parameters have been introduced to measure *similarity* and *distance* between fuzzy sets. One graphical approach is shown in figure 3.6. Similarity S between two fuzzy sets A and B (which is also a measure of how much B *matches* A) can be measured by calculating *possibilities* P and *necessities* N as shown below and illustrated in figure 3.7 (see chapter 2 for the definitions of possibility and necessity):

$$S = P(A/B), \quad \text{if } N(A/B) > 0.5$$

$$S = (N(A/B)) + 0.5) * P(A/B), \quad \text{otherwise}$$

where $P(A/B) = \max\{\min\{\mu_A(u), \mu_B(u)\}\}$, for all $u \in U$; $N(A/B) = 1 - P(\neg A/B)$ (see chapter 2). The above formula seems complicated, but it is really simple to implement, as illustrated in figure 3.7. For the example there $N(A/B) = 0.2$, and $S = (0.2 + 0.5) \cdot 0.8 = 0.56$. The above method is widely used in fuzzy expert systems for calculating the degree to which an observation (B) matches a condition element (A) in a fuzzy rule.

3.1.3   Geometrical Representation of Fuzzy Sets

A geometrical interpretation of fuzzy sets as middle points in a hypercube is introduced by Kosko in his monograph *Neural Networks and Fuzzy Systems* (1992). The fuzzy power set of the universe $U = \{u_1, u_2, \ldots, u_n\}$ is an n-dimensional hypercube in this representation. This idea is illustrated in figure 3.8, where the concept of "heavy smoker," being defined as $(0/0, 0.8/6, 1/10)$, is shown for the case example of the Smoker and the Risk

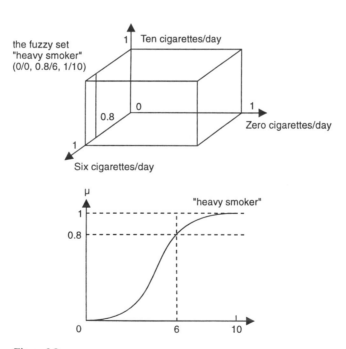

Figure 3.8
A geometrical representation of the concept of "heavy smoker" from the Smoker and the Risk of Cancer case example as a point in a (three-dimensional) cube and as a (two-dimensional) membership function.

of Cancer. A small discrete universe $U = \{0, 6, 10\}$ of the number of cigarettes a person may smoke a day on average has been used. Any crisp subset of U is represented by a vertex on a coordinate axis. A fuzzy subset of U is represented by a point in three-dimensional space. The more fuzzy a fuzzy set is, the deeper inside the cube is its corresponding point. The fuzziest subset, the set with the highest entropy, is the center point. This is the set defined as (0.5/0, 0.5/6, 0.5/10).

3.2 Fuzziness and Probability; Conceptualizing in Fuzzy Terms; The Extension Principle

Let us suppose that a particular problem is not well defined, the existing knowledge is vague, and so forth. How to represent the problem in fuzzy terms? Should we use probability representation or a fuzzy representation? But first, what is the difference between them?

3.2.1 Fuzziness and Probability

In probability theory an event $u \in U$ either happens or not and its probability $p(u)$ represents the chance for the event to happen, that is, the chances that a random variable x takes a value u. A probability $p(u)$ can be represented by the ratio between the number of experiments of a series when u happens and the total number of experiments (see chapter 2). For example, the probability that it will rain on August 22 is 0.73, because 73 out of 100 days on this date were recorded for the last 100 years as rainy days. The probability density function $P(x)$ gives the probability of each of the possible values of a random variable x (events $u \in U$). But August 22 comes and it is not quite clear whether it is "rainy" or not. The notion of rainy can be represented as a fuzzy set A on the universe of the rainfall and represented by its membership function μ_A. In general, a membership coefficient $\mu_A(u)$ measures the grade to which an event u, which has already happened, is a member of the concept labeled as A. The membership function represents the degree to which the total set U (every element from U) is contained in the subset A. For example, August 22 was a rainy day to a degree of 0.6. So the probability density function $P(x)$ is a completely different concept from the membership function of a fuzzy set A. Another example, given below, is a classic example—throwing a dice. Figure 3.9 shows in tabular and graphical form the probability density

Dice			1	2	3	4	5	6
Probablity density function			$\frac{1}{6}$	$\frac{1}{6}$	$\frac{1}{6}$	$\frac{1}{6}$	$\frac{1}{6}$	$\frac{1}{6}$
μ_A small number			1	0.5	0	0	0	0

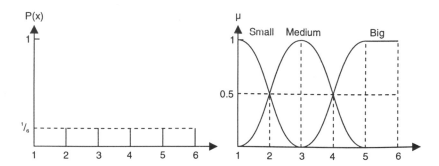

Figure 3.9
Probability density function for throwing dice and the membership functions of the concepts "Small," "Medium," "Big."

function of the random number achieved after each throw, and the membership function that the number is "small."

In the above example two events can be distinguished—a crisp event, achieving a number of 2, and a fuzzy event, achieving a "small" number. One can calculate the probability for a crisp event, $p(x = 2) = 1/6$, but it is also possible to calculate the probability $p(A)$ of a fuzzy event, the probability that a small number will be achieved, $p(x = $ "small").

In general, a probability of a fuzzy event is calculated as:

$p(A) = \sum \mu_A(u)/n,$ for uniformly distributed variable x having n discrete values, and

$p(A) = \sum \mu_A(u) \cdot p(x = u),$ for the general case.

Example   For the membership functions shown in figure 3.9, we calculate:

$p(x = $ "*small*"$) = 1.5/6; \quad p(x = $ "*medium*"$) = 2/6; \quad p(x = $ "*big*"$) = 2.5/6$

Probabilities of fuzzy events have same properties as probabilities of crisp events. For example, if A and B are two fuzzy events, then the following is held:

(1)   if $A \subseteq B$, $p(A) \le p(B)$

(2) $p(\neg A) = 1 - p(A)$

(3) $p(A \cup B) = p(A) + p(B) - p(A \cap B)$

Is it true that probabilities are only "about future events" and "fuzziness" is only "about something that has happened?" Definitely not. A conditional probability for a crisp event may represent the probability of an event happening at moment t based on the probabilities of events which have happened at moments $(t - 1)$ and $(t - 2)$ and the events that will (or have) happen(ed) at the next moments, $(t + 1)$ and $(t + 2)$, for example. This is the philosophy behind the time-delay networks and the so-called delayed decision making approach. The idea is to wait until future events happen and decide what has happened at a previous moment in time. For example, the probability that a phoneme is pronounced at the moment t depends on the probability of some other phonemes being pronounced at the moments $(t - 1)$, $(t - 2)$ and also pronounced next at moments $(t + 1)$ and $(t + 2)$. The reason is that when a person talks he or she has in mind the whole word or a whole sentence before starting to articulate the sounds.

The conditional probability of fuzzy events is defined in the same way as the conditional probability of crisp events. For example, $p(A/B)$ denotes the conditional probability for the fuzzy event A to happen if the fuzzy event B has happened. So fuzziness can also be used to represent future events either by calculating the probability for the fuzzy events or by applying existing knowledge, for example, "tomorrow's value for the stock index will be *high*, if today's value is *moderate*, and yesterday's value was *low*."

By analogy to calculating the entropy of fuzzy sets, we can calculate the *probabilistic entropy* of a fuzzy set:

$$E^p(A) = -\sum (\mu_A(u) \cdot p(u) \cdot \log p(u)),$$

and also the *entropy for the occurrence* of the fuzzy event A:

$$E(A) = -p(A) \cdot \log p(A) - p(\neg A) \cdot \log p(\neg A)$$

Probabilities can be attached to fuzzy terms. And fuzzy terms can be attached to probabilities too. In fact every probability p can be considered as "about p" as in reality future events never happen exactly as defined by their probability to happen. For example, the probability of having a rainy day tomorrow might have been calculated very precisely to be 0.70135. But a fuzzy number "about 0.7" may better represent the chances of having a rainy day tomorrow. *Fuzzy probability* theory is discussed in D. Ralescu (1995).

The life-and-death phenomenon might be an example is worth investigating from the point of view of probability, fuzziness, probability for fuzzy events, and entropy of occurrence. For example, there is a probability that every single person will die at a certain time, but when this moment comes, there is a state of the brain which is between the two states.

3.2.2   Conceptualizing in Fuzzy Terms

One of the most important steps toward using fuzzy logic and fuzzy systems for problem-solving is representing the problem in fuzzy terms. This process is called *conceptualization in fuzzy terms*. We often use linguistic terms in the process of identification and specification of a problem, or in the process of articulating heuristic rules. If we look at the case examples in chapter 1 and at the heuristic rules there, we will note the use of the following linguistic terms: *higher, lower, very strong, slowly, much dependent* and *less dependent, high, low, good, bad*, and many others. All of these are fuzzy concepts representable as fuzzy sets.

We shall use the term *linguistic variable* to denote a variable which takes fuzzy values and has a linguistic meaning. A linguistic variable is "velocity" if it takes as values: "low," "moderate," or "high," for example. A linguistic variable is the variable "Score" if it takes the values "high" and "low." Linguistic values, also called *fuzzy labels*, fuzzy predicates or fuzzy concepts, have semantic meaning and can be expressed numerically by their membership functions. For example a fuzzy variable "Score" may have as a universe all the numbers between 150 and 200. Linguistic variables can be *Quantitative*, for example, "temperature" (low, high); time (early, late); spatial location (around the corner); or *Qualitative*, for example, "truth," "certainty," "belief." The process of representing a linguistic variable into a set of linguistic values is called *fuzzy quantization*.

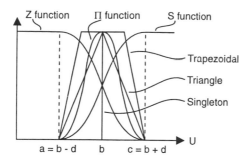

Figure 3.10
Standard types of membership functions: Z function; π function; S function; trapezoidal function; triangle function; singleton.

In many cases a linguistic variable can be quantized into some linguistic labels that can be represented by standard functional representations. Standard types of fuzzy membership functions are given graphically in figure 3.10. The following are the most favored in fuzzy expert systems design:

- *Single-valued*, or *singleton*, for example, $u = b$, where b is a scalar value.
- *Triangular*: $\mu(u) = 1 - |u - b|/|b - a|$; if triangular membership functions μ_i, $i = 1, 2, \ldots, l$, which represent a fuzzy variable, are uniformly distributed over the universe U, then this representation has the following interesting property:

$$\sum_{(i)} \mu_i(u) = 1 \qquad \text{for any } u \in U$$

and for each value u from the universe U at most two membership degrees to which u belongs to all membership functions μ_i, $i = 1, 2, \ldots, l$, are not equal to zero. Examples of such representation are given in figures 3.11(A) and (B) where the Iris attributes and class variables are fuzzy-quantized by using $l = 3$ fuzzy labels and $l = 5$ fuzzy labels respectively.

- *Trapezoidal*
- *S-function* (*sigmoid function*):

$S(u) = 0, \qquad u \leq a,$

$S(u) = 2((u - a)/(c - a))^2, \qquad a < u \leq b,$

$S(u) = 1 - 2((u - a)/(c - a))^2, \qquad b < u \leq c,$

$S(u) = 1, \qquad u > c.$

• *Z function*:

$Z(u) = 1 - S(u)$

• $\prod$ *function* (*bell function*):

$\prod(u) = S(u),\qquad u \le b$ (here b is used instead of c used above)

$\prod(u) = Z(u),\qquad u > b.$

Two parameters must be defined for the quantization procedure: (1) the number of fuzzy labels, and (2) the form of the membership functions for each of the fuzzy labels.

Choosing the number and the form of all the fuzzy labels that represent a fuzzy variable is a crucial point for a fuzzy system. Are "Low" and "High" fuzzy labels sufficient to represent the fuzzy variable "Score," or do we need a third one, say "Medium," or are even more fuzzy labels needed? How do we place the standard labels on the universe U if this information is not provided by an expert? To answer the latter, Kosko (1992) uses a heuristic rule to choose how much the neighboring labels should overlap, which is about 25%. But this is very much a subjective choice.

If we have defined the fuzzy-quantizing labels, for example, "small," "medium," or "large," we can represent any particular data item as a set of membership degrees to the fuzzy labels. Do we lose information when representing raw data through fuzzy labels? Fuzzy discretization does not lead to loss of information if the fuzzy labels are correctly chosen (this is not the case with interval discretization). This can be experimented on figure 3.11 with the Iris case example. An attribute-value is uniquely represented by the membership coefficients obtained from the membership functions for the fuzzy labels. This process is called fuzzification, or fuzzifying.

Fuzzy values defined by standard membership functions have some useful properties when used in fuzzy rules, for example, the rules approximate the goal function as explained further on. Choosing a standard type of membership function, when not given or known a priori, resembles choosing the gaussian probability distribution for the conditional probability in the Bayes's theorem.

A good example of fuzzy-quantizing of a quantitative variable is the representation of natural or real number variables as *fuzzy numbers*. A fuzzy number represents the approximateness of a natural (real) number, for example, "about 600," represented graphically in figure 3.12. Fuzzy

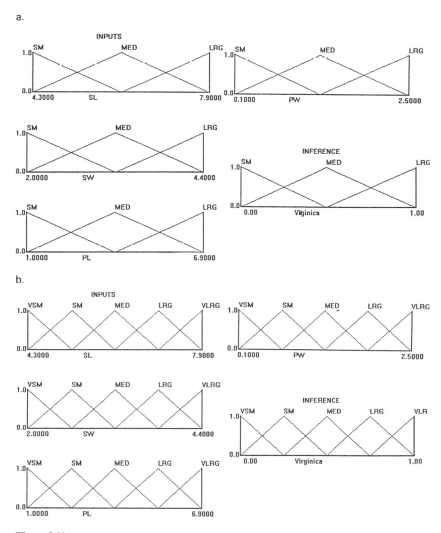

Figure 3.11
Fuzzy predicates (labels) defined as triangular, uniformly distributed membership functions for the Iris data attributes and classes. (A) Three labels used. (B) Five labels used.

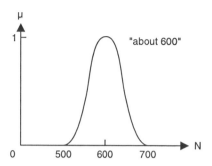

Figure 3.12
One representation for the fuzzy number "about 600."

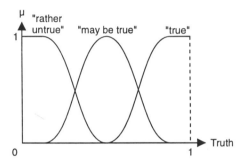

Figure 3.13
Representing truthfulness (certainty) of events as fuzzy sets over the [0, 1] domain.

numbers can be manipulated in fuzzy theory as they are represented by fuzzy sets. *Operations over fuzzy numbers*, such as addition, subtraction, etc., are also possible. Some of them are similar to the operations with exact numbers. For example, if A and B are fuzzy numbers defined by their membership functions μ_A and μ_B respectively, then their sum is simply defined by:

$$\mu_C = \mu_A + \mu_B, \qquad \text{where } + \text{ is an algebraic summation.}$$

Fuzzy quantization is possible not only on numerical variables but also on qualitative variables like "truthfulness of events." *Fuzzy qualifiers* give a fuzzy evaluation of the truthfulness of an event. Typical fuzzy qualifiers are "very true," "more or less true," and "not true," Fuzzy qualifiers can be represented on the scale of truthfulness by fuzzy membership functions, as shown in figure 3.13.

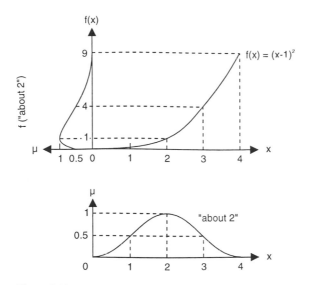

Figure 3.14
An illustration of the extension principle in fuzzy theory: an example of transforming a fuzzy set "x is about 2" into a fuzzy set "f (x is about 2)" for $f(x) = (x - 1)^2 x \in [1, 4]$.

The classic certainty factors used in MYCIN and in many other expert systems may be represented as single-value membership functions over the universe of all possible certainties between 0 and 1.

3.2.3 The Extension Principle

A useful principle, called the *extension principle*, defines how any single real value, or function, or set, can be represented by a corresponding fuzzy membership function, that is, how it can be fuzzified. If we have a function $f: X \to Y$ between two crisp sets X and Y, and we know the membership function μ_A of a subset $A \subseteq X$, we can obtain the fuzzy representation of $f(A)$ in Y through the following formula:

$$\mu_{f(A)}(f(x)) = \mu_A(x)$$

Example   Given $f(x) = (x - 1)^2$ and the fuzzy set $A =$ "about 2" = (0.5/1, 1/2, 0.5/3, 0/4) as shown in figure 3.14, the membership function of the fuzzy set f ("about 2") can be calculated as shown in the same figure for $x \in [1, 4]$.

The extension principle allows for fuzzy quantization and makes possible many fuzzy logic applications. For example, if we have a set of patients

X checked for risk of cancer and classified into risk groups which form a set Y, we have a function $f: X \to Y$. Applying the extension principle we can obtain the membership function for the risk of cancer of different fuzzy subsets $A \subseteq X$, for example, "hard smokers," "overweight people," etc.

3.3 Fuzzy Relations and Fuzzy Implications; Fuzzy Propositions and Fuzzy Logic

Fuzzy logic is an excellent tool for implementing commonsense knowledge, vague knowledge in a computer program, and performing reasoning over them. Fuzzy logic is based on fuzzy relations and fuzzy propositions, the latter being defined on the basis of fuzzy sets.

3.3.1 Fuzzy Relations, Fuzzy Implications, Fuzzy Composition

Fuzzy relations make it possible to represent ambiguous relationships like "the grades of the third- and second-year classes are similar," or "team A performed slightly better than team B," or "the more fat you eat, the higher the risk of heart attack." Fuzzy relations link two fuzzy sets in a predefined manner.

If A is a fuzzy set defined over a universe U, and B is a fuzzy set defined over a universe V, then a *fuzzy relation* $R(A, B)$ is any fuzzy set defined on the cross-product universe $U \times V = \{(u,v)/u \in U, v \in V\}$. A fuzzy relation is characterized by its membership function

$$\mu_{R(u,v)}: U \times V \to [0,1]$$

Example A direct product of A and B may be defined as: $\mu_{A \times B} = \mu_A(u) \wedge \mu_B(v)$.

A very important fuzzy relation is the *fuzzy implication*, denoted as $A \to B$. In fuzzy logic there are different ways to define an implication, which is in contrast to propositional logic where the implication is defined by a single truth-table. There are 15 different implications studied by Mizumoto and Zimmermann (1982). Some of them are shown in figure 3.15. The first two implications from figure 3.15 were introduced by Zadeh (1971), the third one, Rc, was introduced by Mamdani (1977). The rest of the implications were experimented on by Mizumoto and Zimmermann. The different implications can be used for building different inference methods, as is shown in the next section.

Table. Implication relations R: A->B over the universe U x V, u ∈ U, v ∈ V.

Ra	$1 \wedge (1 - u + v)$
Rm	$(u \wedge v) \vee (1 - u)$
Rc	$u \wedge v$
Rb	$(1 - u) \vee v$
Rs	$u \to v = 1$, if $u <= v$,
	s 0, if $u > v$
Rg	$u \to v = 1$, if $u <= v$,
	g v, if $u > v$
Rgs	$[u \to v] \wedge [(1 - u) \to (1 - v)]$
	g s
Rgg	$[u \to v] \wedge [(1 - u) \to (1 - v)]$
	g g
Rsg	$[u \to v] \wedge [(1 - u) \to (1 - v)]$
	s g
Rss	$[u \to v] \wedge [(1 - u) \to (1 - v)]$
	s s

Figure 3.15
Several useful fuzzy implications. The following short denotations are used: u instead of $\mu_A(u)$; v instead of $\mu_B(v)$; "$\wedge$" is minimum; "$\vee$" is maximum; "$+$" is algebraic summation; "$-$" is algebraic substraction.

A fuzzy relation can be represented by a matrix or a fuzzy graph. The Rc implication relation "heavy smoker" → "high risk of cancer" is represented in a matrix form in figure 3.16.

A *composition relation* or simply *composition* of fuzzy relations $R1(A, B)$ and $R2(B, C)$ is a relation $R(A, C)$ obtained after applying relations $R1$ and $R2$ one after another.

A typical composition is the MAX-MIN composition (Zadeh 1965):

$$R(A, C): \mu_{R(a,c)} = \vee \{\mu_{R1}(a, b) \wedge \mu_{R2}(b, c)\},$$

where $\vee$ denotes MAX and $\wedge$ denotes MIN, $a \in A$, $b \in B$, $c \in C$.

Figure 3.17 shows the MAX-MIN composition applied over the membership function of "moderate smoker" and the implication Rc "heavy smoker → high risk." The inferred fuzzy set is the membership function representing the risk of cancer for the class of "moderate smokers." Two other composition operators have been successfully applied to fuzzy reasoning, the three composition operators being shown in figure 3.18. A composition and an implication make possible fuzzy inference, as they are the "ingredients" of the so-called compositional inference law: given

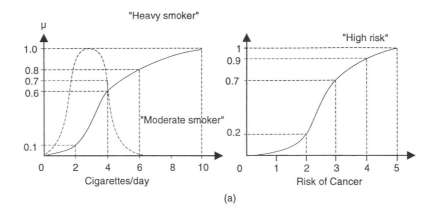

Figure 3.16
(a) Membership functions for fuzzy sets for the Smoker and the Risk of Cancer case example.
(b) The Rc implication relation: "heavy smoker →high risk of cancer" in a matrix form.

an implication $R: A \rightarrow B$, and a composition $\circ$, a fuzzy value B' can be inferred when a fuzzy value A' is known:

$$B' = A' \circ R$$

3.3.2   Properties of Fuzzy Relations

Fuzzy relations have different properties. Let R represent a relation on the cross-product universe $U \times V$. Then the following properties may be held for R (Terano et al. 1992):

(1)   *Reflexiveness*: $\mu_R(u, u) = 1$

(2)   *Irreflexiveness*: $\mu_R(u, u) = 0$

min{"Mod_Sm",(Heavy_Sm" $\rightarrow$ "High_Risk")}

"Mod_Sm"	Cigarettes	Risk	1	2	3	4	5
0 | 0		0	0.0	0.0	0.0	0.0	0.0
2 | 0.7		2	0.0	0.1	0.1	0.1	0.1
4 | 0.7		4	0.0	0.2	0.6	0.6	0.6
6 | 0		6	0.0	0.0	0.0	0.0	0.0
10 | 0		10	0.0	0.0	0.0	0.0	0.0
		Max	0.0	0.2	0.6	0.6	0.6

Figure 3.17
MAX-MIN composition applied over the fuzzy set "moderate smoker" and the Rc implication "heavy smoker → high risk of cancer" from figure 3.16 for the Smoker and the Risk of Cancer case example.

(3)   *Symmetry*: $\mu_R(u, v) = \mu_R(v, u)$

(4)   *Transitivity*: $\vee_v \{\mu_R(u, v) \wedge \mu_R(v, p)\} \leq \mu_R(u, p)$, for each $v \in V$

Based on the above properties, some other relations are defined in (Terano et al. 1992):

• *Similarity relation*, for which reflexiveness, symmetry, and transitivity are held

• *Resemblance relation*, for which reflexiveness and symmetry are held

Different combinations of an implication and a composition can be compared based on different inference *properties*, for example, whether they satisfy or not two of the inference rules of propositional logic, *syllogism* and *contrapositive*:

$A \rightarrow B$ *and* $B \rightarrow C \therefore A \rightarrow C$ (syllogism)

$A \rightarrow B \therefore \neg B \rightarrow \neg A$ (contrapositive)

The following implications satisfy these two laws, when a MAX-MIN composition is used (Mitzumoto and Zimmerman 1982): Syllogism—*Rc*, *Rs*, *Rg*, *Rgs*, *Rgg*, *Rsg*, *Rss*; Contrapositive—*Ra*, *Rb*, *Rs*, *Rss*. This gives some hint to how different implications can be used for inference. In

Max-min $b' = \vee (a' \wedge (a\text{->}b))$
Max- θ $b' = \vee (0 \vee (a' + (a\text{->}b) - 1))$
Max- λ $b' = \vee a'$,   if (a->b) = 1,
                  (a->b),   if a'= 1,
                  0,   if a' < 1 and (a->b) < 1

Figure 3.18
Fuzzy compositions; here $(a \rightarrow b)$ denotes membership degrees of the values from the cross-product $U \times V$; $\wedge$ denotes minimum, and $\vee$ denotes maximum; b', a' are membership degrees of corresponding values from U and V; $+$ is algebraic summation; $-$ is algebraic subtraction.

order to achieve a fuzzy inference that satisfies predefined laws, we have to choose not only which implication to use but also which composition. If, for example, the laws of syllogism and contrapositive have to be satisfied for a given application and they are not satisfied for a preliminary chosen implication and a composition, then another composition may be tried.

3.3.3 Fuzzy Graphs

Fuzzy graphs are graphs which have membership degrees attached to their edges. A fuzzy graph may be used to represent a fuzzy relation. This is another application of the information structure *graph* (see chapter 2).

3.3.4 Fuzzy Propositions and Fuzzy Logic

The biggest restriction in classic propositional and predicate logic is the fact that the propositions can have their truth-values as either True or False. This restriction has its assets as well as its drawbacks. The main asset is that the decision obtained is exact and precise. The main drawback, however, is that it cannot reflect the enormous diversity of the real world, which is analog and not digital. The truth value of a proposition in classic logic *cannot be unknown*, for example.

In order to overcome this limitation of classic logic, multivalued logic has been developed. The truth of a proposition is represented by a set T of n possible truth-values, when n-valued logic is considered. For the three-valued logic, $T = \{0, 0.5, 1\}$. There are a huge number of theories, formulated on the basis of the multivalued nature of truth. Fuzzy logic can be considered an extension of the multivalued logic developed by Lukasiewicz

AND: $\mu_{A \text{ and } B} = \mu_A \wedge \mu_B$
OR: $\mu_{A \text{ or } B} = \mu_A \vee \mu_B$
  NOT: $\mu_{\neg A} = 1 - \mu_A$

Figure 3.19
Fuzzy logic connectives AND, OR, NOT illustrated over two fuzzy propositions A and B.
"$\wedge$" denotes min; "$\vee$" denotes max; and "$-$" denotes algebraic substraction.

in 1930. The main operators in Lukasiewicz multivalued logic for calculating the truth-value of complex propositions having the truth-values for elementary ones are as follows:

$$\neg A = 1 - A; \quad A \wedge B = \min\{A, B\}; \quad A \vee B = \max\{A, B\};$$

$$A \rightarrow B = \min\{1, 1 + A - B\}$$

Fuzzy logic operates with *fuzzy propositions*, *fuzzy connectives*, and *fuzzy rules* (or *laws*) *of inference*.

Fuzzy propositions are propositions which contain fuzzy variables with their fuzzy values. The truth value of a fuzzy proposition "X is A" is given by the membership function μ_A.

Examples   A person is a "heavy smoker." The temperature is "high." The speed is "moderate."

Fuzzy propositions are no more true or false only, but they have grayness of truth defined by the fuzzy values in them. In propositional logic every proposition is either true or false, nothing in between. The fuzzy connectives are the same as in propositional logic, but here applied differently (figure 3.19). The truth-values of the complex propositions are defined by the fuzzy membership function calculated by using MIN and MAX operations and complement. Operations over membership functions were discussed when fuzzy sets were introduced. So fuzzy logic operations are based on operations over fuzzy sets.

Fuzzy propositions may include *modifiers*, also called *hedges*. The general form of a fuzzy proposition with a modifier is X *is mA*. The negation "not" can be viewed as a *modifier*. Other modifiers are *very A*, denoted as A^2 (concentration); *more or less A*, denoted as $A^{1/2}$ (dilation). Their corresponding membership functions are shown in figure 3.5.

The most used *laws of inference* in fuzzy logic are given for two fuzzy propositions A and B:

- *Generalized modus ponens*:

$A \rightarrow B$ and $A' \therefore B'$,   where $B' = A' \circ (A \rightarrow B)$

- *Generalized modus tolens* (law of the contrapositive):

$A \rightarrow B$ and $B' \therefore A'$,   where $A' = (A \rightarrow B) \circ B'$

- *Transitive law* (law of syllogism):

$A \rightarrow B$ and $B \rightarrow C \therefore A \rightarrow C$

- *DeMorgan's laws*:

$$\neg(A \wedge B) = \neg A \vee \neg B$$
$$\neg(A \vee B) = \neg A \wedge \neg B$$

Other laws for fuzzy inference are given in Yager and Zadeh (1992).

A combination of an implication operator and a composition operator is the key to realizing a proper fuzzy inference mechanism. For example, it can be easily shown that if we use Ra and MAX-MIN composition, the *exact modus ponens law* (when $A' = A$, then $B' = B$) is not satisfied, that is, the inferred value (membership function) is not μ_B, but for example, $(1 + \mu_B)/2$. When any of the other composition operators are applied, the modus ponens law is satisfied. In order to realise a humanlike fuzzy reasoning, we may want that the system not only satisfies the exact modus ponens law, but should infer "Very B" if "Very A" is the input, "More or less B," if the input is "More or less A," etc. A thorough investigation of the properties of different implication relations has been done by Mizumoto and Zimmermann (1982). Figure 3.20 shows for which of the implications the following laws of inference are held: $A \rightarrow B$, modus ponens, very $A \rightarrow$ very B; very $A \rightarrow B$; more or less $A \rightarrow$ more or less B; more or less $A \rightarrow B$; not $A \rightarrow$ unknown; not $A \rightarrow$ not B; not $B \rightarrow$ not A (modus tolens); not very $B \rightarrow$ not very A; not more or less $B \rightarrow$ not more or less A; $B \rightarrow$ unknown; $B \rightarrow A$.

Why are the above properties so important? Suppose we had a rule "IF an apple is red, THEN the apple is ripe." Depending on the chosen implication and its properties, different conclusions can be inferred for one and the same input, for example, "the apple is very red," "the apple is more or less red," etc. As we could see, some of the implications do not obey the strict modus ponens law, so even if we had an input "the apple is red" there will be another value inferred for the ripeness and not the value "ripe," whatever the fuzzy definition of this concept is.

Law Law A -> B New	Inferred	Ra	Rm	Rc	Rb	Rs	Rg	Rgs	Rgg	Rsg	Rss
		\multicolumn{10}{l}{Implication Relation}
A	B (ModPon)	-	-	+	-	+	+	+	+	+	+
very A	very B	-	-	-	-	+	-	-	-	+	+
very A	B	-	-	+	-	-	+	+	+	-	-
more or less A	more or less B	-	-	-	-	+	+	+	+	+	+
more or less A	B	-	-	+	-	-	-	-	-	-	-
not A	unknown	+	+	-	+	+	+	+	+	+	+
not A	not B	-	-	-	-	-	-	+	+	+	+
not B	not A (modus tollens)	-	-	-	-	+	-	-	-	+	+
not very B	not very A	-	-	-	-	+	-	-	-	+	+
not more or less B	not more or less A	-	-	-	-	+	-	-	-	+	+
B	unknown	+	-	-	+	+	+	-	-	-	-
B	A	-	-	+	-	-	-	+	-	-	+

Figure 3.20
Implications which satisfy (+) or do not satisfy (−) the laws of inference in fuzzy logic. (From Mizumoto and Zimmermann 1982.)

Fuzzy logic is the theoretical basis for the fuzzy rule–based systems and fuzzy reasoning methods described in the next section.

3.4   Fuzzy Rules, Fuzzy Inference Methods, Fuzzification and Defuzzification

A fuzzy system consists of three parts: (1) fuzzy input and output variables and their fuzzy values; (2) fuzzy rules; (3) fuzzy inference methods, which may include fuzzification and defuzzification. The first part was discussed in the previous section. The last two are discussed here.

3.4.1   Fuzzy Rules

Several types of fuzzy rules have been used for fuzzy knowledge engineering so far:

Zadeh-Mamdani's fuzzy rules:

IF x is A, THEN y is B,

where (x is A) and (y is B) are two fuzzy propositions; x and y are fuzzy variables defined over universes of discourse U and V respectively; and A and B are fuzzy sets defined by their fuzzy membership functions μ_A: $U \rightarrow [0, 1]$ and μ_B: $V \rightarrow [0, 1]$. A generalized form of the fuzzy rule is the following:

IF x_1 is A1 AND x_2 is A2 AND ... AND x_k is Ak, THEN y is B,

where $x_1, x_2, \ldots, x_k, y$ are fuzzy variables (attributes) over different universes of discourse $Ux_1, Ux_2, \ldots, Ux_k, Uy$ and $A1, A2, \ldots, Ak, B$ are their possible fuzzy values over the same universes. A set of fuzzy rules has the following form:

Rule 1: *IF x_1 is A1, 1 AND x_2 is A2, 1 AND ... AND x_k is Ak, 1, THEN y is B1, ELSE*

Rule 2: *IF x_1 is A1, 2 AND x_2 is A2, 2 AND ... AND x_k is Ak, 2, THEN y is B2, ELSE*

...

Rule n: *IF x_1 is A1, n AND x_2 is A2, n AND ... AND x_k is Ak, n, THEN y is Bn*

Example: The Bank Loan Case Decision Problem   This is represented here as a set of two fuzzy rules:

Rule 1: IF (CScore is high) and (CRatio is good_cr) and (CCredit is good_cc), then (Decision is approve) else

Rule 2: IF (CScore is low) and (CRatio is bad_cr) or (CCredit is bad_cc), then (Decision is disapprove)

The universes of all four fuzzy variables as well as the fuzzy values "high score," "low score," "good_cc," "bad_cc," "good_cr," "bad_cr," "approve," and "disapprove" are shown in figure 3.21. This example is used as an experimental case study on which different inference methods are illustrated further on. The example consists of two fuzzy rules. Two fuzzy values (fuzzy sets) defined by their membership functions for each of the three fuzzy input variables take part in the rules. During the fuzzy

Cscore	150	155	160	165	170	175	180	185	190	195	200
high	0	0	0	0	0	0	.2	.7	1	1	1
low	1	1	.8	.5	.2	0	0	0	0	0	0

Ccredit	0	1	2	3	4	5	6	7	8	9	10
good_cc	1	1	1	.7	3	0	0	0	0	0	0
bad_cc	0	0	0	0	0	0	.3	.7	1	1	1

Cratio	.1	.3	.4	.41	.42	.43	.44	.45	.5	.7	1
good_cr	1	1	.7	.3	0	0	0	0	0	0	0
bad_cr	0	0	0	0	0	0	0 .	.3	.7	1	1
Decision	0	1	2	3	4	5	6	7	8	9	10·
approve	0	0	0	0	0	0	.3	.7	1	1	1
disapprove	1	1	1	.7	.3	0	0	0	0	0	0

Figure 3.21
Fuzzy sets definitions for the the Bank Loan Decision Problem. Adapted from Lim and Takefuji, 1990 (Copyright © IEEE 90).

system design, more precise fuzzy quantization of the fuzzy variables and more rules may be required for a better inference.

In general, every rule that has two condition elements in its antecedent part connected by an OR connective can be represented by two rules, for example, the rule *IF x_1 is A1 or x_2 is A2, THEN y is B* is logically equivalent to the following two rules: *IF x_1 is A1, THEN y is B and IF x_2 is A2, THEN y is B*. This property is used in some fuzzy system realizations, which do not facilitate OR connectives.

• *Fuzzy rules with confidence degrees*: Apart from the simple form of Zadeh-Mamdani's fuzzy rules described above, fuzzy rules having coefficients of uncertainty have often been used in practice. A fuzzy rule that contains a confidence factor of the validity of the conclusion has the form of: *if x is A, then y is B (with a CF)*.

Example

IF (current economic situation is good) and
(current political situation is good) and
(the predicted value for tomorrow is up),
THEN (action—buy) ($CF = 0.9$)

Fuzzy facts may have certainty factors attached to them, which show how certain is the fact. For example, a fuzzy set for the variable "current economic situation" can be assigned a certainty factor $CF = 0.8$. Fuzzy sets and certainty factors are processed differently, as shown in the next section.

• *Takagi-Sugeno's fuzzy rules*: Another type of fuzzy rule was introduced by Takagi and Sugeno (1985). A function is used in the consequent part:

Rule i: IF x is Ai and y is Bi, THEN z is $f_i(x, y)$

If the function is linear, the rule takes the following form:

Rule i: IF x_1 is A1, i and x_2 is A2, i and ... x_m is Am, i, THEN $z = C_{0,i} + C_{1,i} \cdot x_1 + \cdots + C_{m,i} \cdot x_m$

Example   IF x is A and y is B, THEN $z = 5x - 2y + 3$.
These kind of fuzzy rules are very useful especially for function approximation.

• *Gradual fuzzy rules*: These are rules of the Zadeh-Mamdani type, but instead of using fuzzy values for the fuzzy variables in the rule, they use fuzzy representation of gradual properties, for example, "the more a tomato is red, the more it is ripe." By using gradual rules, one can reduce significantly the overall number of rules still covering the whole input space. These kind of rules are very useful for modeling social, political, and economic systems.

Example   The higher the FF (federal funds), the higher the U.S. short-term interest rate.

• *Generalized production rules* with degrees of importance, noise tolerance, and sensitivity factors. Very often the condition elements (the fuzzy propositions) in the antecedent part of the rule are not equally important for the rule to infer an output value. For example, one symptom might be five times more important than another, but the latter still has to be considered for tuning the diagnosis decision. Relative coefficients of importance DIi of the condition elements in the antecedents, *noise tolerance* (NT) coefficients and *sensitivity factor* (SF) coefficient, have been introduced in the generalized production rules in addition to the confidence factors (CF) already discussed (Kasabov and Shishkov 1993, Kasabov 1994).

IF $C1(DI1)$ and $C2(DI2)$ and... $Cn(DIn)$, THEN $A1, A2, ..., Ak$
(NT, SF, CF)

where the condition elements Ci are either fuzzy or exact propositions of the form (x *is* A) and the actions Aj are either *insert* or *delete* fuzzy or exact facts.

Example   IF $M1$ is High (2) and $M2$ is Medium (5) and $M3$ is High (1), THEN $D1$ is High and $D2$ is No (0.7, 1, 0.9), where $M1$, $M2$ and $M3$ are manifestations, and $D1$ and $D2$ are diagnoses.

• *Generalized production rules with variables* (Kasabov 1994). This is an option in the generalized production rules described above, where a fuzzy proposition can have a variable in the place of the fuzzy value.

Example   The following rule shows that whatever the index values for today and yesterday are, the former being twice as important as the latter, the same value will keep tomorrow with a certainty of 0.8. The variable is represented by the letter V and its possible values (not shown here) could be "low," "medium," "high." For example, IF (the index yesterday is V) ($DI = 1$) and (the index today is V) ($DI = 2$), THEN (the index tomorrow will be V) ($CF = 0.8$).

More about the last two types of fuzzy rules is given in chapter 6.

- *Recurrent fuzzy rules* (see chapter 7).

3.4.2   Fuzzy Inference Methods

In chapter 2 the inference process was described as a process of *matching*. This is matching in a wider sense, that is, matching a domain space with a solution space. It is a matching in a narrower sense too, that is, matching a new fact, for example X', with a set of rules Ri ($i = 1, 2, \ldots, n$) and inferring a solution Y', the whole inference process being a *chain* of such matches. We saw that matching in the symbolic *AI* systems (e.g., production systems) is an *exact matching*. In the case of the modus ponens law, for instance, if we have $X \rightarrow Y$, and X is present, exactly Y will be inferred. But in fuzzy representation we may not have exact values for the input variables. Some fuzzy input value X' is supplied instead. What, then, will the inferred result for Y' be? If X' and X are similar, will Y and Y' be similar as well, and how much similar? In a special case, if $X' = X$, will $Y' = Y$? These questions relate to fuzzy inference and are discussed here.

We refer here to *fuzzy inference* as an inference method that uses fuzzy implication relations, fuzzy composition operators, and an operator to link the fuzzy rules. The inference process results in inferring new facts based on the fuzzy rules and the input information supplied.

Different reasoning strategies over fuzzy rules are possible. Most of them use either the *generalized modus ponens rule* or the *generalized modus tolens inference rule* (see above). The generalized modus ponens inference law applied over a simple fuzzy rule can be expressed as follows: (*IF x is A, THEN y is B*) and (*x is A'*), then (*y is B'*) should be inferred. The compositional rule of inference, discussed in section 3.2, is one way to implement the generalized modus ponens law:

$$B' = A' \circ (A \rightarrow B) = A' \circ Rab,$$

where $\circ$ is a *compositional operator*, and Rab is a fuzzy relational matrix representing the *implication relation* between the fuzzy concepts A and B.

A fuzzy inference method combines the results Bi' for the output fuzzy variable y inferred by all the fuzzy rules for a given set of input facts. In a fuzzy production system, which performs cycles of inference, all the fuzzy rules are fired at every cycle and they all contribute to the final result. Some of the main *else-links* between fuzzy rules are:

• *OR-link*: The results obtained by the different rules are "OR-ed" in a monotonic fashion, so the more that is inferred by any of the rules, the higher the resulting degree of the membership function for B'. MAX operation is applied to achieve this operation.

• *AND-link*: The final result is obtained after a MIN operation over the corresponding values of the inferred by all the rules or fuzzy membership functions.

• *Truth qualification-link*: A coefficient Ti' is calculated for the inferred fuzzy set Bi' by every rule Ri. The result obtained by a rule Rj with the maximum coefficient is taken as a final result:

$$Tj = \text{MAX}\{Ti\}, \qquad i = 1, 2, \ldots, n$$
$$Ti = \sum \mu_{B_i'}(v) / \sum \mu_B(v), \qquad \text{for all } v \in V$$

• *Additive link*: The fuzzy results Bi' inferred by the rules Ri are added after being multiplied to weighting coefficients:

$$\mu_{B'} = \sum \mu_{Bi'} \cdot w_i, \qquad \text{for } i = 1, 2, \ldots, n$$

The selection of the "else-link" depends on the context in which the rules are written.

We have described so far a fuzzy inference method as a triple $Fi = (I, C, L)$, where I is an implication relation, C is one of the possible composition operators, and L is one of the possible "else-links." The general inference method discussed above is applicable not only when the number of condition elements in the antecedent part of the fuzzy rules is one (as in the examples above), but in the general case too:

Rule i: IF x_1 is A1i and x_2 is A2i ... and x_k is Aki,
THEN y is Bi ($i = 1, \ldots, n$)

In this case the *decompositional inference* (also called the *decompositional rule of inference*) can be applied. It is based on the assumption that a rule of k condition elements is decomposed into k implications $Aji \to Bi$ (*for $j = 1, 2, \ldots, k$*). Each implication is used separately to infer a value for Bi' by applying the compositional rule $Bi' = Aji' \circ (Aji \to Bi)$, (*for $j = 1, 2, \ldots, k$*). The values Bi' are aggregated by one of the aggregation operators

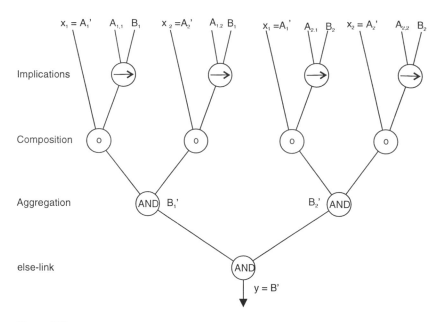

Figure 3.22
The inference tree for the decompositional inference strategy over two fuzzy rules. Adapted from Lim and Takefuji, 1990. (Copyright © IEEE 90).

(usually AND, OR). The decompositional fuzzy inference method is illustrated in figure 3.22 on the set of the following two rules:

Rule 1: *IF x_1 is A1, 1 and x_2 is A1, 2 THEN y is B1*

Rule 2: *IF x_1 is A2, 1 and x_2 is A2, 2 THEN y is B2*

Before applying the fuzzy rules for an inference procedure, input values for the input variables must be entered. The input values entered and the output values produced can be of two types: (1) *fuzzy values*, and (2) *real values*. The latter case is explained in the next section. The former is illustrated here.

Example: The Bank Loan Case   The two rules for solving the problem and the membership functions of fuzzy values were given above. A bank loan applicant can be represented either by three membership functions for the three fuzzy input variables Cscore, Cratio, and Ccredit, or by three real numbers, Cscore, Cratio, and Ccredit, which are exact and nonfuzzy

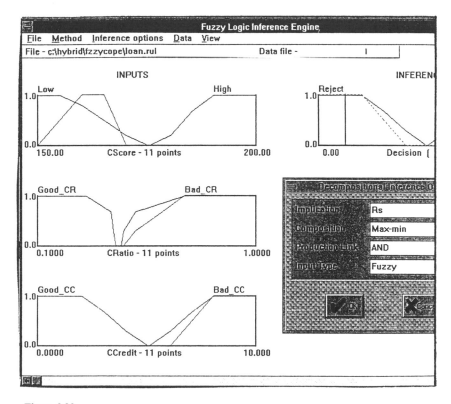

Figure 3.23
The inferred fuzzy value for "Decision" for a particular application for the Bank Loan Decision system. Decompositional inference rule is used with Rs implication, MAX-MIN composition, and AND-link between the rules.

input values. The latter case is shown in the next section. The inferred fuzzy value for the output variable Decision when *Rs* implication, MAX-MIN composition, and AND-link between the rules are used for a set of input fuzzy values describing an applicant for a loan (or a group of applicants) is graphically shown in figure 3.23 as produced in a fuzzy inference system.

Having in mind the variety of different possible combinations between implications, compositions, and link operators, the difficulties in choosing the appropriate inference strategy for a given task, especially in a changing environment, are unavoidable. Of course, some of the combinations are not applicable according to the context of the fuzzy rules. It has been

```
Case 1:
Cscore=  0 0 0 0 0 0 0 .2 .8 1     Cratio=   1 1 .6 .2 0 0 0 0 0 0
Ccredit= 0 1 1 .7 .3 0 0 0 0 0 0

Case 2:
Cscore=  .9 .7 .5 .3 0 0 0 0 0 0     Cratio=   0 0 0 0 0 0 0 .3 .5 .7 .9
Ccredit= 0 0 0 0 0 0 0 .3 .5 .7 .9

Case 3:
Cscore=  0 0 0 0 0 0 0 .4 .6 .8     Cratio=   0 0 0 0 0 0 0 .4 .6 .8
Ccredit= 1 1 1 .8 .6 .4 0 0 0 0 0
```

Figure 3.24
Three fuzzy input cases for testing the Bank Loan Decision fuzzy system.

	Decision vector-Case_1	Decision vector-Case_2	Decision vector-Case_3
Rc	0 0 0 0 0 0 0 0 0 0 0	0 0 0 0 0 0 0 0 0 0 0	0 0 0 0 0 0 0 0 0 0 0
Rs	0 0 0 0 0 0 0 .2 1 1 1	.9 .9 .9 .3 0 0 0 0 0 0 0	0 0 0 0 0 0 0 .4 1 1 1
Rg	0 0 0 0 0 0 .3 .7 1 1 1	.9 .9 .9 .7 .3 0 0 0 0 0 0	0 0 0 0 0 0 .3 .7 1 1 1
Rgs	0 0 0 0 0 0 .3 .7 1 1 1	.9 .9 .9 .7 .3 0 0 0 0 0 0	0 0 0 0 0 0 0 0 0 0 0
Rgg	0 0 0 0 0 0 .3 .7 1 1 1	.9 .9 .9 .7 .3 0 0 0 0 0 0	0 0 0 0 0 0 .3 .3 0 0 0
Rsg	0 0 0 0 0 0 0 .2 1 1 1	.9 .9 .9 .3 0 0 0 0 0 0 0	0 0 0 0 0 0 0 .3 0 0 0
Rss	0 0 0 0 0 0 0 .2 1 1 1	.9 .9 .9 .3 0 0 0 0 0 0 0	0 0 0 0 0 0 0 0 0 0 0

Figure 3.25
The inferred decision membership functions for the three input cases from figure 3.24 when
different implication operators are applied.

suggested by several authors that the AND else-link be used for fuzzy
production systems. Lim and Takefuji (1990) considered *Rc*, *Rsg*, *Rgg*,
Rgs, and *Rss* as reasonably suitable implication operators for fuzzy production systems. They use Rsg, MAX-MIN composition, and AND-link
in their hardware implementation, while in Togai and Watanabe's hardware implementation of a fuzzy inference engine (Togai and Watanabe
1986) *Rc* was assumed. It has been suggested in some research papers that
the MAX-MIN composition operator is quite satisfactory for fuzzy production systems. The use of different implications with the MAX-MIN
composition operator and the AND-link is illustrated over a set of input
data for three cases shown in figure 3.24. The resulting decision fuzzy sets
(decision vectors) obtained by using different implication operators are
shown in figure 3.25. Analysis of the results shows that *Rc* does not infer
appropriate results for case 1 and case 2; *Rs* and *Rg* do not work properly

for case 3; the remaining four implication operators, *Rgs*, *Rgg*, *Rsg*, and *Rss*, perform reasonably well, but preference may be given to *Rss* or *Rgs* which infer most accurately what is supposed to be inferred according to the fuzzy rules. This is not surprising because they satisfy the most important properties for a fuzzy production system inference (laws), as shown in figure 3.20.

3.4.3 Fuzzification, Rule Evaluation, Defuzzification

When the input data are crisp and the output values are expected to be crisp too, then the "fuzzification, rule evaluation, defuzzification" inference method is applied over fuzzy rules of the type of *IF x_1 is A1 and x_2 is A2, THEN y is B.*

Fuzzification is the process of finding the membership degrees $\mu_{A1}(x_1')$ and $\mu_{A2}(x_2')$ to which input data x_1' and x_2' belong to the fuzzy sets A1 and A2 in the antecedent part of a fuzzy rule. *Singleton* fuzzification is used in the example shown in figure 3.27. Through fuzzification the degrees to which input data match the condition elements in a rule are calculated. When fuzzy input data are used, such a degree can be represented by the similarity between the input membership function and the condition element as discussed in section 3.1.2. A similarity measure is a single number.

Rule evaluation takes place after the fuzzification procedure. It deals with single values of membership degrees $\mu_{A1}(x_1')$ and $\mu_{A2}(x_2')$ and produces output membership function B'. There are two major methods which can be applied to the rule above:

• *Min inference*:

$$B' = B \cdot \min\{\mu_{A1}(x_1'), \mu_{A2}(x_2')\}$$

• *Product inference*:

$$B' = B \cdot \mu_{A1}(x_1') \cdot \mu_{A2}(x_2')$$

where $\cdot$ denotes algebraic multiplication.

In general aggregation operators must be used within a fuzzy rule with more than one condition elements to aggregate the matching results of new facts across the condition elements. Two general extensions of the operators AND and OR, called *T*-norms and *T*-conorms, were introduced by Dubois and Prade (1985).

A *T-norm* is a binary mapping $T: [0, 1] \times [0, 1] \rightarrow [0, 1]$, which has the following properties: commutativity, associativity, monotonicity. A boundary condition is held: $T(a, 1) = a$. The following T-norm operators have been used in practice: $T(a, b) = \min\{a, b\}$; $T(a, b) = a * b$ (product); $T(a, b) = \max\{0, a + b - 1\}$.

A *T-conorm* $S(a, b)$ differs from a T-norm in that it has the property of $S(a, 0) = 0$ instead of the boundary property of the T-norms. Widely used T-conorms are $S(a, b) = \max\{a, b\}$; $S(a, b) = a + b - a \cdot b$; $S(a, b) = \min\{1, a + b\}$.

If more fuzzy rules are activated simultaneously, for example:

Rule 1: *IF x_1 is $A1, 1$ and x_2 is $A1, 2$, THEN y is $B1$, and*

Rule 2: *IF x_1 is $A2, 1$ and x_2 is $A2, 2$, THEN y is $B2$,*

the inferred fuzzy sets $B1'$ and $B2'$ can be added algebraically after being multiplied to a weighting factor (additive system), or MAX-values of the corresponding membership degrees $B1'(v)$ and $B2'(v)$, for $v \in V$ are taken.

Defuzzification is the process of calculating a single-output numerical value for a fuzzy output variable on the basis of the inferred resulting membership function for this variable. Two methods for defuzzification are widely used:

1. *The center-of-gravity method (COG)*. This method finds the geometrical centre y' in the universe V of an output variable y, which center "balances" the inferred membership function B' as a fuzzy value for y. The following formula is used:

$$y' = \sum \mu_{B'}(v) \cdot v / \sum \mu_{B'}(v)$$

2. *The mean-of-maxima method (MOM)*. This method finds the value y' for the output variable y which has maximum membership degree according to the fuzzy membership function B'; if there is more than one value which has maximum degree, then the mean of them is taken as shown in figure 3.26.

Example: The Bank Loan Case   Inference with crisp input and crisp output data is shown in figure 3.27 as produced in the same fuzzy inference software system as in fig. 3.23 COG defuzzification is used.

3.4.4   Inference over Fuzzy Rules with Confidence Factors

When the fuzzy rules and the fuzzy facts have confidence factors attached to them, then in addition to the fuzzy inference done by using one of the methods described above, confidence factors for the resulting fuzzy facts are calculated.

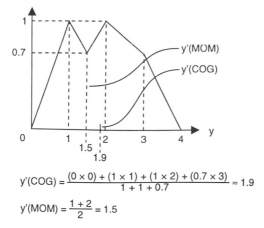

$$y'(\text{COG}) = \frac{(0 \times 0) + (1 \times 1) + (1 \times 2) + (0.7 \times 3)}{1 + 1 + 0.7} \approx 1.9$$

$$y'(\text{MOM}) = \frac{1 + 2}{2} = 1.5$$

Figure 3.26
Methods of defuzzification: the center-of-gravity method (COG), and the mean-of-maxima method (MOM) applied over the same membership function for a fuzzy output variable y. They calculate different crisp output values.

Example   Given a fuzzy rule:

IF (current economic situation is good) and
(current political situation is good) and
(the predicted value for tomorrow is up),
THEN (action is buy) (CFrule = 0.9),

which has a fuzzy output "buy" defined by a membership function and the following fuzzy input facts:

(current economic situation is $A1'$) $(CF = 0.9)$
(current political situation is $A2'$) $(CF = 0.8)$
(the predicted value for tomorrow is $A3'$) $(CF = 0.7)$,

then the fuzzy value for the output variable "action" will be inferred and a certainty factor CFres for it will be calculated as follows:

$$\text{CFres} = \text{CFrule} \cdot \min\{CF_{A1'}, CF_{A2'}, CF_{A3'}\} = 0.9 \cdot 0.7 = 0.63.$$

If the consequent part of the rule did not have a fuzzy, but a crisp output variable (buy—yes/no), then the certainty factor for it will be calculated without a fuzzy inference to be performed, but the similarity between the corresponding input facts $A1'$, $A2'$, and $A3'$ and the antecedent condition

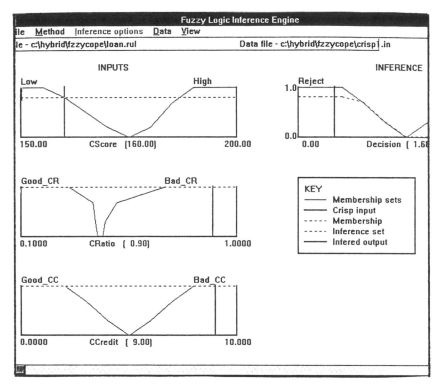

Figure 3.27
An illustration of "crisp input data, rules evaluation, deffuzification" inference for a particular crisp input data for the Bank Loan Decision system. A segment from the window of a fuzzy logic inference tool that was used for this problem is shown.

elements $A1$, $A2$, $A3$ evaluated, say $S1$, $S2$, $S3$ (based on the similarity measure described earlier). Then a certainty factor for the crisp fact "buy" is calculated if the value "yes" for it is inferred:

$$CFres = CFrule \cdot \min\{CF_{A1} \cdot S1, CF_{A2} \cdot S2, CF_{A3} \cdot S3\}$$

3.4.5   Other Methods for Fuzzy Inference: General Comments

Different inference methods may produce different results on the same rule base.

There are other methods for fuzzy inference than those discussed above. Some of them are specifically applied to fuzzy control systems, even though being more general (Tereno et al. 1992). There are methods for reasoning over fuzzy rules which are implemented in connectionist architectures (Kasabov, 1994). Fuzzy inference methods are sometimes called methods for approximate reasoning, which represents their inherent property for approximate reasoning and for dealing with uncertainties. Generally speaking fuzzy inference is based on the following: (1) evaluating the degrees to which input data match all condition elements in a rule; (2) aggregating these degrees over all condition elements in the antecedent part of the rule; (3) evaluating the rules and producing output fuzzy values; (4) aggregating all the produced for one output variable output values; and (5) producing final output values across all the rules.

Fuzzy finite automatons provide another paradigm for fuzzy inference. These are finite automatons which can simultaneously be in several states to a certain degree.

Which fuzzy inference method to choose for a particular application is a question to be decided by the knowledge engineer but usually only a few well-explored and established methods are used.

3.5   Fuzzy Systems as Universal Approximators: Interpolation of Fuzzy Rules

In chapter 1 a problem-solving process was represented as mapping the domain space into the solution space through existing problem knowledge. The mapping aims at achieving a goal function, which represents the desired solution for given input data. The desired solutions can be defined either as a set of "input-output" data pairs (x_i, y_i), or by expert knowledge. The former task relates to the task of *interpolation*. Interpolation aims at finding a function $y = f(x)$, such that it approximates to a certain level of accuracy all the data (x_i, y_i). The function f is then used to calculate the output value y' for a new input x' possibly not in the data set. Finding a function f is a task for the regression analysis. But can we use a fuzzy system to approximate the data?

Can fuzzy systems be used to achieve arbitrary complex mapping, that is, can fuzzy systems approximate any goal function? If they can, how can it be done? These two questions are discussed in this section.

3.5.1   Fuzzy Systems are Universal Approximators

We describe a family of systems as *universal function approximators* if for any function there exists a system from this family that approximates it to any degree of accuracy.

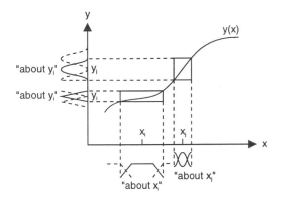

Figure 3.28
A fuzzy rule IF *xi*, THEN *yi* covers a segment of the goal function $y(x)$ bounded in a "quadrangular patch" of the problem space. The figure illustrates the statement that by using triangular-, trapezoidal-, or π-shaped membership functions for the fuzzy quantization labels, any goal functions $y(x)$ can be approximated to any degree of accuracy through their segmentwise approximation.

A fuzzy rule *IF* **x** *is "about* $\mathbf{x}_i$*", THEN* **y** *is "about* $\mathbf{y}_i$*"*, covers a "patch" in the problem space. After fuzzification and defuzzification, the fuzzy rule approximates a segment of a function $\mathbf{y}(\mathbf{x})$. Two examples, one for bell-shape membership functions and one for trapezoidal and triangular membership functions, are shown in figure 3.28. We discussed crisp and interval rules in chapter 2 and their characteristic of being universal approximators when the number of rules is unlimited. By analogy to the example given in Yamakawa (1993), it is shown in figure 3.29 that a set of crisp rules can cover a set of discrete points from a given function $y(x) = (x - 1)^2$, and interval rules can cover the function in a stepwise manner. If the number of the intervals is small, the approximation is very rough. We can also see from the figure that if the number of the rules increases infinitely, a system of exact rules can approximate this and any other function. Unfortunately, a large number of rules are required to achieve a good generalization, which makes this approach impractical. But a small set of fuzzy rules, with carefully chosen membership functions of the fuzzy terms, can approximate the function. As we shall see, fuzzy systems are universal approximators.

THEOREM (Kosko 1992)   An additive fuzzy system uniformly approximates a function $f: x \to y$, if the domain of x is compact (closed and bounded) and f is continuous. The proof of the theorem is given in the reference above.

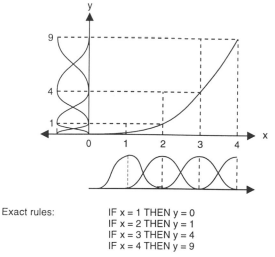

Exact rules:

IF x = 1 THEN y = 0
IF x = 2 THEN y = 1
IF x = 3 THEN y = 4
IF x = 4 THEN y = 9

Interval rules:

IF x ≤ 1 THEN y = 0
IF 1 < x ≤ 2 THEN y = 1
IF 2 < x ≤ 3 THEN y = 4
IF 3 < x ≤ 4 THEN y = 9

Fuzzy rules:

IF x is "about 1" THEN y is "about 0"
IF x is "about 2" THEN y is "about 1"
IF x is "about 3" THEN y is "about 4"
IF x is "about 4" THEN y is "about 9"

Figure 3.29
Approximating a function $y = f(x) = (x - 1)^2$, $x \in [1, 4]$, by a set of crisp rules, a set of interval rules, and a set of fuzzy rules. The four exact rules cover only four points. The interval rules approximate the function very roughly as a step function. The four fuzzy rules approximate the function precisely.

THEOREM (Wang, 1994)   For any given real continuous function f on a compact set $U \subseteq \mathbb{R}^n$ and arbitrary $\acute{\varepsilon}$, there exists a fuzzy logic system F with a COG deffuzifier, with a product inference, singleton fuzzifier, and gaussian membership functions ($\prod$ functions) such that

$$|F(x) - f(x)| < \acute{\varepsilon},$$

The above result can be extended to discrete functions as well.

Similar theorems can be proved for other types of fuzzy inference and other membership functions (triangular, trapezoidal). The above theorems justify the application of fuzzy logic systems to almost any nonlinear modeling problems. They are existence theorems, that is, they proof that there exists a system, but they do not say how to find the system.

3.5.2   Fuzzy Rules Interpolation: Inference with Gradual Rules

In figure 3.28 two fuzzy rules are graphically shown. They are obviously not sufficient to cover the whole goal function. Suppose there are no more rules. Such a set of rules is called a *sparse rule base*. A procedure, called *rule interpolation*, should be applied if we want to obtain an output value of y for any of the input values for x.

Example   The two rules:

IF a tomato is red, THEN the tomato is ripe, and
IF a tomato is green, THEN the tomato is unripe

are not enough to infer a conclusion if the observation does not overlap with any of the antecedent condition elements, for example, "a tomato is yellow."

The other extreme task is that we have a large number of rules, a so called dense rule base, which covers the goal function with redundant overlapping. How to find the minimal set of rules that is still sufficient for an approximate reconstruction of the dense rule base?

Different techniques can be applied to ensure that the inference process will cover the whole problem space. One of them is using gradual rules, introduced by Dubois and Prade (see Yager and Zadeh 1992). *Gradual rules*, described briefly in a previous section, refer to gradual properties, for example, "the more x is A, the more y is B," or "the more x is similar to A, the more y is similar to B." In order to use gradual fuzzy rules, the fuzzy variables have to be of a gradual type (a natural full ordering exists), for example, spatial position, speed, velocity, acceleration.

The results of an inference with a gradual rule "the more x is A, the more y is B" for an input value x' is not fuzzy, but imprecise; it is an interval $y' = B_\alpha$ (which is the α-cut of B), where $\alpha = \mu_A(x')$ (figure 3.30).

3.6   Fuzzy Information Retrieval and Fuzzy Databases

Databases have been well developed and established so far. The current database systems are very efficient when storing and retrieving exact information. But when information for one attribute is fuzzy, vague or missing, the whole data item (record) is usually not stored and information is lost. So there is an obvious need for methods and tools which facilitate (1)

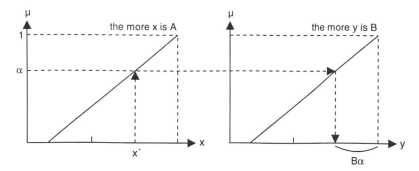

Figure 3.30
Inference with a gradual rule "the more x is A, the more y is B" for a particular crisp value x' for the input variable x. The result is imprecise; this is the α-cut interval B_α.

fuzzy data to be stored and retrieved, and (2) better use of existing information through fuzzy interface for retrieving it. These two requirements can be achieved by using fuzzy information retrieval methods and fuzzy databases, the latter method currently in its infancy.

3.6.1   Fuzzy Information Retrieval

Information retrieval is considered here as a process of retrieving relevant information from an information storage, for example, retrieving relevant documents by specifying keywords when all the documents are stored and for each document a list of keywords is known.

The standard approach is to compare literally keywords, and if a document contains, say, 50% of the keywords specified in the query, it is retrieved. The problem with this approach is that if the keywords are spelled differently or substituted by similar ones, it does not work, as it does not have information about the *conceptual similarity*, or *conceptual distance*, between different keywords as has the librarian, who has read these documents. For example, if x is a specified keyword, and a and b are two keywords, then using conceptual distances $d(x, a)$ and $d(x, b)$ makes possible a comparison between them, for example, $d(x, a) > d(x, b)$. The conceptual distance is also called *conceptual affinity*.

By using conceptual distance the keyword space can be structured in a priori knowledge space where a search will be performed. One way to measure the affinity is based on the simultaneous appearance, or frequency $f(a, b)$, of two keywords a and b appearing in one document. Any query, based on a specified keyword x, can be represented as a fuzzy set A

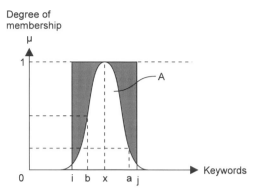

Figure 3.31
Defining a query by a keyword x as a fuzzy set A over the domain of a structured and quantized one-dimensional keyword space. The difference between A and a crisp subset defined for all the keywords between i and j is represented by the shaded area. The degree to which keywords b and a belong to the concept A are also shown.

over this space as a universe. An example is given in figure 3.31. The universe is quantized into a one-dimensional, structured keyword space. The difference and similarity between all the documents which have all the keywords between i and j in them and the query fuzzy set can be measured as a measure of similarity and distance between two fuzzy sets. The search can be done in an interactive mode, when the system asks questions whether the keyword j, for example, should be included or not, thus giving the user a chance to refine the membership function of the fuzzy set for the query. The above-described approach is based on representing ambiguity of documents by a structured feature space of keywords. After having searched in this space and having resolved ambiguities of the query, then the actual search in the document space is performed for retrieving the relevant documents.

3.6.2   Fuzzy Interfaces to Standard Databases

We consider here standard *relational databases*. The information in a relational database is structured in *relations*. A relation is a named tuple of n attributes $(x_1, x_2, \ldots, x_n)$, each of them x_i having its own domain Di $(i = 1, 2, \ldots, n)$. The queries to such databases, facilitated by standard database systems, include giving a particular value for an attribute, giving an interval, or ignoring an attribute. But if the query values do not match exactly what is in the data base, the answer will be an empty set.

A *fuzzy query interface* allows giving fuzzy terms as values for the attributes, which values are not stored in the standard database.

Example   A fuzzy query: Find the towns in the country which have "high" average temperature in August and have "big" or "medium"-sized hotels. In general, a query can be formulated in fuzzy terms and for any of the attributes a fuzzy proposition formed: x_i *is* A_{ij}. Fuzzy queries are possible to ordinary databases if the fuzzy predicates used in the queries are represented in advance by their membership functions. The search through a standard database is also modified according to the requirements of fuzzy logic theory. An example is given below.

Example   Here is a segment of an ordinary database, "Employees":

Name	Age	Salary	Experience (yrs)
Brown	56	80,000	10
Long	44	56,000	20
Smith	28	40,000	2
Patrick	37	50,000	19

Let us assume that the following concepts (predicates) of the attributes "age," "experience," and "salary" are defined by membership functions, as shown in figure 3.32(A): age—"young," "middle-aged," "mature"; experience—"little," "moderate," "good"; salary—"low," "about average," "high." Let us now assume the following query: "Give me the names of the employees who are 'middle-aged' AND have 'good experience' AND have 'average salary'". In order to answer such a query, all the attribute-values for age, experience, and salary are fuzzified with the use of the defined membership functions. MIN operation is applied over the membership degrees of a particular data item. The results for Long is MIN $\{0.9, 0.95, 0.8\} = 0.8$, and for Patrick is MIN $\{0.85, 0.89, 0.87\} = 0.85$. Figure 3.32B shows an exampler distribution of the degrees to which all elements from a database match a fuzzy query.

A fuzzy query to a standard database resembles matching a fuzzy rule against crisp data, which is opposite to the fuzzy inference methods in fuzzy systems. Finding the data items which best match the "rule of query" might be computationally expensive; therefore special methods should be applied to speed up this process (see Bosc and Kacprzyk 1995).

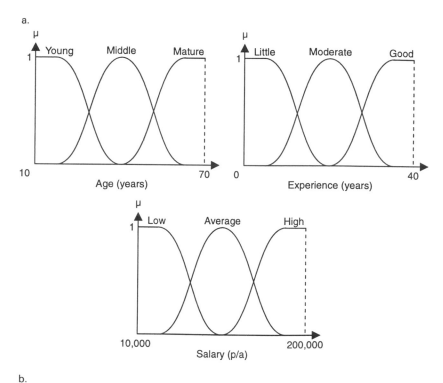

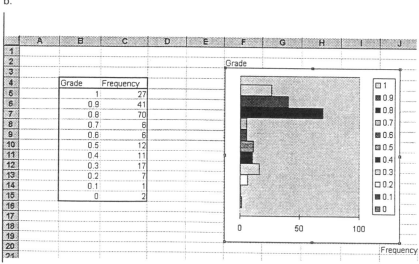

Figure 3.32
Defining fuzzy concepts for performing fuzzy queries to an ordinary database "Employees"
given in the text; (B) Distribution diagram of the degrees to which all the elements from a
standard database match a fuzzy query.

Name	Age	Salary	Experience
Brown	56	80,000	10
Long	(55,56)	average	good
Smith	young	(30,000 - 70,000)p	(2,3)p
Patrick	(middle, young)p	(high, average)p	unknown

Figure 3.33
A small fuzzy database which illustrates the use of possibility distribution functions as values in a database on the example of the database "Employees" given in the text.

3.6.3   Fuzzy Databases

Another approach to realizing fuzzy information retrieval is to build *fuzzy databases*, that is, databases which contain fuzzy information. There are different approaches toward creating fuzzy databases:

• The fuzzy database is an *extension to a relational database*. The membership degrees to which the data elements belong to the fuzzy concepts defined for every attribute are added to the database.

Example   An extended relation with fuzzy terms for the database used in the previous example will look like: ("name"; "age"—young, middle-aged, mature; "experience"—little, moderate, good; "salary"—low, about_average, high).

Such fuzzy databases can be searched through quickly and efficiently, but they are appropriate when the fuzzy concepts used do not change frequently, as this requires change of the whole database.

• *Possibility-distribution relational databases*—facilitate entering fuzzy information when creating the database and processing it, and when searching through the database. The domains Di for the attributes x_i include fuzzy information represented by membership functions, as well as exact information. A membership function is used to represent a *possibility-distribution function*, for example: age $= (55, 56)$poss, that is, for the attribute age two values are equally possible; or age $= (0.9/55, 0.7/56)$poss, but the first is more likely.

Example   In figure 3.33, a simple fuzzy database is given, similar to the relational database from the previous example. The values in some slots are not exact values, but possibility distributions instead.

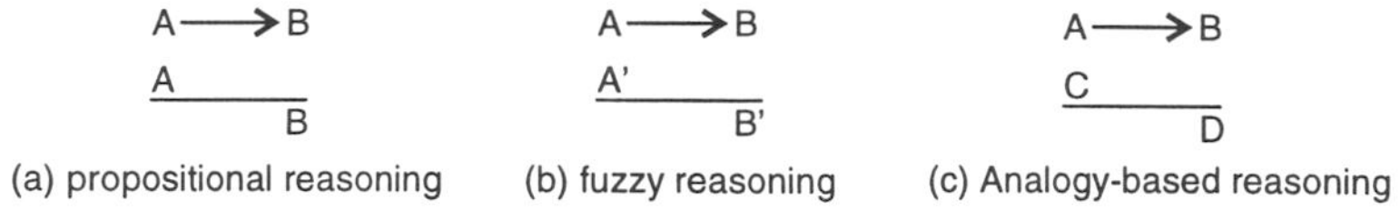

$$A \longrightarrow B$$
$$\frac{A}{B} \qquad \frac{A'}{B'} \qquad \frac{C}{D}$$

(a) propositional reasoning   (b) fuzzy reasoning   (c) Analogy-based reasoning

Figure 3.34
Propositional-, fuzzy-, and analogy-based reasoning are represented by different inference laws.

• *Modular fuzzy databases* (Zemankova and Kandel 1984) consist of three parts: (1) the value database, which is the same as the possibility-distribution relational databases presented above; (2) the explanation database, which contains the definition of the fuzzy terms, and is subject to update depending on the particular applications; and (3) conversion rules for processing modifiers and qualifiers.

• *Fuzzy object-oriented databases,* in which fuzzy properties are allowed to be defined for objects in the database.

3.6.4   Conceptual Information Retrieval Through Natural Language Interfaces

Such interfaces facilitate communication between users and systems in a natural language allowing for fuzziness and imprecision. The natural language query is transferred into a semantic representation and reasoning is performed based on similarity between concepts. A non-fuzzy logic reasoning, fuzzy reasoning, as well as some other types of reasoning, for example, *analogy-based fuzzy reasoning*, can be applied. The difference between the last and the first two is depicted in figure 3.34. In analogy-based reasoning an analogy between the concept C given for a query and the concept A in the antecedent of the rule is found, and a new concept, D, is inferred as a result.

Example (Ozawa and Yamada 1994)   Suppose a database contains information about available apartments for rent, having an attribute "floor size." An exact query to such a database will look like: "an apartment in which floor size is between 50 and 100 square meters." A fuzzy query will look like: "an apartment in which floor size is big." Conceptual query will look like: "an apartment for a big family."

In 1978, Zadeh developed a language called PRUF (possibility relational universal fuzzy) to evaluate possibilities related to natural language semantics (Zadeh 1978b). The aim of the theory is to estimate a fuzzy quantifier Q', if a proposition "QA is F" is known and the query is formed as "$Q'A$ is mF."

Example   Known fact: "Most foreigners are tall." Conceptual query: "How many foreigners are very tall?," where Q = most, A = foreigners, F = tall, m = very, and Q' is sought (e.g., could be "few").

The research on fuzzy information retrieval, natural language interfaces with fuzziness, and fuzzy databases is still finding its way. A large contribution is expected from this area to the development of intelligent human-computer interfaces.

3.7   Fuzzy Expert Systems

Fuzzy expert systems emerged as a result of applying fuzzy theory to building expert systems.

3.7.1   General Characteristics of Fuzzy Expert Systems

A *fuzzy expert system* is defined in the same way as an ordinary expert system, but here methods of fuzzy logic are applied. Fuzzy expert systems use fuzzy data, fuzzy rules, and fuzzy inference, in addition to the standard ones implemented in the ordinary expert systems. A block diagram of a fuzzy expert system is shown in figure 3.35.

The *fuzzy rules and the membership functions* make up the system knowledge base. In general, different types of fuzzy rules can be used in a fuzzy expert system. Some systems use production rules extended with fuzzy variables and confidence factors. In addition to exact productions, fuzzy productions can be handled as well, so different types of production rules can be processed depending on the type of the antecedent and the consequent part in the rule: crisp → crisp (CF); crisp → fuzzy (CF); fuzzy → crisp (CF); fuzzy → fuzzy (CF). These types of production rules are facilitated in FuzzyCLIPS (NRC Canada 1994).

Data can be exact or fuzzy. The *database* which the fuzzy inference machine refers to can contain exact data or fuzzy data with certainty factors attached to them, for example, (economic_situation good CF = 0.95).

A *fuzzy inference machine* is built on the theoretical basis of fuzzy inference methods. A fuzzy inference machine, which activates all the satisfied rules at every cycle, is different from the sequential inference in symbolic systems, but the control and search mechanisms implemented in the latter can be used successfully during the fuzzy reasoning process. A

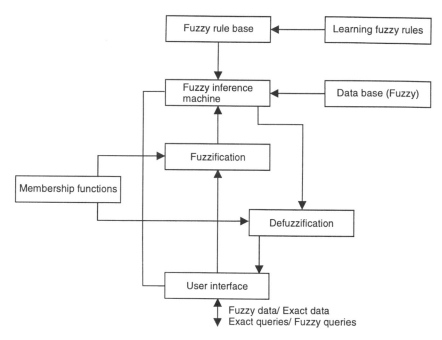

Figure 3.35
A block diagram of a fuzzy expert system.

significant characteristic of fuzzy expert systems is the realization of partial match between exact or fuzzy facts (observations, input data) and
fuzzy condition elements in the antecedents of the rules. A measure of the
degree of matching is calculated for every case, that is, (fuzzy fact—fuzzy
condition); (crisp fact—fuzzy condition); (fuzzy fact—exact condition);
(crisp fact—exact condition). A rule is fired only if the matching degree of
the left-hand side of the rule is greater than a predefined threshold.

Fuzzification and *defuzzification* may be used in a fuzzy expert system
depending on the type of inference machine implemented in the system.

The *interface unit* of the fuzzy expert system communicates with the user
or the environment, or both, for collecting input data and reporting output results. Fuzzy queries might be possible when the user inputs information in fuzzy terms, for example, high temperature, severe headaches,
devastating hurricane, etc.

An *explanation module* explains the way the expert system is functioning
during the inference process, or explains how the final solution has been

reached. HOW and WHY explanations are appropriate to use. The system may use fuzzy terms for explanation as well as exact terms and values.

A module for *learning fuzzy rules* is usually optional. Learning fuzzy rules can take place either before the inference machine starts the reasoning process, or during the fuzzy inference process. In the former case the learning module can be built on the basis of AI machine-learning methods (see further in this section) or neural networks (see chapter 5). Fuzzy neural networks can be used to implement the latter, (see chapters 6 and 7).

3.7.2   Fuzzy Systems Design

The following are the main phases of a fuzzy system design:

1. Identifying the problem and choosing the type of fuzzy system which best suits the problem requirements. A modular system can be designed consisting of several fuzzy modules linked together. A modular approach, if applicable, may greatly simplify the design of the whole system, dramatically reduce its complexity, and make it more comprehensible.

2. Defining the input and output variables, their fuzzy values, and their membership functions.

3. Articulating the set of heuristic fuzzy rules.

4. Choosing the fuzzy inference method, fuzzification, and defuzzification methods if necessary; some experiments may be necessary until a proper inference method is chosen.

5. Experimenting with the fuzzy system prototype; drawing the goal function between input and output fuzzy variables; changing membership functions and fuzzy rules if necessary; tuning the fuzzy system; validation of the results.

The main problem in building fuzzy expert systems is that of articulating the heuristic fuzzy rules and membership functions for the fuzzy terms. Here are some methods for obtaining fuzzy rules:

• The first is to *interview an expert*. Sometimes, communication between expert and interviewer can be difficult owing to a lack of common understanding. The shape of membership functions, the number of labels, and so forth should be defined by the expert. However, sometimes the human expert is unfamiliar with fuzzy sets or fuzzy logic and the knowledge engineer is unfamiliar with the domain area.

• The second approach, as formulated by Yamakawa (1993), is to imagine (in the designer's own mind) physical behaviour of the real system and think about the physical meaning in natural and technical languages. The system designer has to be particularly experienced with the system in order to imagine its behaviour. There is no need to explain the behaviour with mathematical equations, typically differential equations. In some cases, the designer has to assign by imagination and intuition, the consequences of the fuzzy rules which usually appear on the grid of the rule map.

• The third approach is to use the methods of machine-learning, neural networks, and genetic algorithms to learn fuzzy rules from data and to learn membership functions if they are not given in advance. Connectionist methods for learning fuzzy rules from data are introduced in chapter 5.

Another problem may arise when designing a fuzzy expert system that has its fuzzy rules already articulated, namely, the choice of inference method. For any particular fuzzy production system, several possible inference methods have to be considered before implementing one of them. In order to facilitate the choice of an appropriate inference method from among a set of possible ones, *fuzzy expert system shells* have been developed and put into practice. Choosing the inference method depends also on the type of fuzzy rules used.

3.7.3   Clustering-Based Methods for Learning Fuzzy Rules from Data

Here, two nonconnectionist methods for generating fuzzy rules from numerical data are explained. The methods are illustrated on the Iris data set.

Many methods for extracting fuzzy rules from data are based on clustering of data into groups (clusters). Algorithms for fuzzy clustering are discussed in the next section. These groups can later be assigned labels. Fuzzy labels and membership functions can be defined for different subdomains of the problem space. The two methods presented below use different approaches. The first method uses fuzzy quantization (or fuzzification) only for the purpose of inference over already extracted rules. This means that the rules may not change after having changed the membership functions. The second method uses fuzzification during the rules extraction and the extracted rules are dependent on the chosen membership functions.

Method 1

In section 2.11 a case-based method for learning representative templates from numerical data was presented and illustrated with the Iris data set. Here, the method is extended to a simple method for extracting fuzzy rules. The following steps are taken:

Step 1 The attributes are discretized into intervals, for example, the four Iris attributes, that is, petal length, petal width, sepal length, and sepal width, are discretized in the example given there into 4, 3, 6, and 3 intervals respectively. The whole data set is then represented by a set of representative templates, which is a sort of clustering. For example, a representative template given in figure 2.38 is ($SL = 2$ $SW = 2$ $PL = 1$ $PW = 1$ Class = 1 Frequency_coefficient = 2).

Step 2 The discretization intervals are represented as fuzzy intervals and membership functions are attached to them, as illustrated in figure 3.11. The intervals are labeled, for example, SM (or S), MED (or CE), LRG (or B). For the discretization used in the example of figure 2.38, these labels will read as follows: sepal length—$S2$, $S1$, CE, B; sepal width—S, CE, B; petal length—$S3$, $S2$, $S1$, CE, $B1$, $B2$; petal width—S, CE, B. The fuzzy membership functions are defined as follows: triangular functions are used for intermediate intervals and trapezoidal membership functions are used for the end intervals; the center of a triangular membership function is placed at the center of the interval and the other two vertexes at the middle points of the neighboring intervals.

Step 3 A representative template is directly expressible as a fuzzy rule if the intervals are substituted by their fuzzy labels and the probability strength is used as a relative class rule strength (confidence factor), for example:

IF (SL is $S1$) AND (SW is CE) AND (PL is $S3$) AND (PW is S),
THEN (Class is Setosa) (rule_strength is 2/3).

A set of numerical data can be represented in a supervised mode (class labels are provided), or in an unsupervised mode (no class labels are attached to data) as a set of representative templates, therefore as a set of fuzzy rules.

Step 4 Inference over the set of fuzzy rules with fuzzification and defuzzification is performed. The accuracy of approximation depends on the discretization process. Using more intervals results in better approximation in general, but using too many of them slows down the learning and inference processes.

Method 2

A similar method for learning fuzzy rules from numerical data is presented in L.-X. Wang (1994). It differs from the above mainly in the following steps:

Step 1   Data are first fuzzy-quantized and the membership functions are defined.

Step 2   All the data examples are fuzzified, for example, the instance $(SL = 5.1, SW = 3.5, PL = 1.4, PW = 0.2, \text{Class} = \text{Setosa})$ is fuzzified as follows: $SL = 5.1$ belongs to $S2$ to a degree of 0.3 and to $S1$ to a degree of 0.7; $SW = 3.5$ belongs to CE to a degree of 0.6 and to B to a degree of 0.4; $PL = 1.4$ belongs to $SE3$ to a degree of 0.55 and to $S2$ to a degree of 0.45; $PW = 0.2$ belongs to S with a degree of 1.0. The classes can also be fuzzy-quantized by using certainty degrees if such information is available.

Step 3   Each instance is represented by one fuzzy rule, where the fuzzy label to which an attribute-value belongs to the highest degree is taken. A degree for each of the rules is calculated by multiplying the membership degrees of the condition elements by one another, by the membership degrees of the antecedent, and also by a confidence factor for the validity of the data in that instance. We shall assume a membership degree to which the instances belong to classes to be 1.0, and the confidence factor for each of the examples to be equal to 0.95, that is, the data are sufficiently reliable. The above example generates the following rule:

Rule: IF (SL is $S1$) AND (SW is CE) AND (PL is $SE3$) AND (PW is S), THEN (Class is Setosa) with a degree of confidence 0.22, calculated as: $0.7 \times 0.6 \times 0.55 \times 1 \times 1 \times 0.95 = 0.22$.

Step 4   The obtained fuzzy rules are aggregated and ambiguity in rules is sorted out by using the principle of the greater confidence factor, that is, if two rules have the same antecedents but a different consequent, the one with the higher confidence factor is left.

Step 5   A product fuzzy inference is used for the set of extracted fuzzy rules that is based on a multiplication operator between the degrees of membership to which a new instance belongs to the antecedent membership functions and the centroid defuzzification method (see section 3.4.3).

The method described above and illustrated with the Iris data set is generally applicable to any numerical data. It is especially effective when applied to learning fuzzy rules from chaotic time-series data and for approximating these data.

The methods based on clustering bear the *curse of dimensionality* burden, that is, the number of rules increases exponentially with the number of variables and number of fuzzy labels used. To resolve this problem, scatter (and not uniform) partitioning may be used when the whole problem space is not necessarily uniformly covered. Dynamic partitioning may also be used when the partitioning is not fixed in advance, but it changes iteratively with the change of the extracted rules until a satisfactory set of rules is found.

3.7.4   Learning Fuzzy Rules Through Genetic Algorithms

Genetic algorithms can be used for learning fuzzy rules from data as they can optimize the number of fuzzy labels to be used, the number of condition elements in a rule, and the total number of fuzzy rules subject to some constraints set in advance. The goodness criterion can be either a numerical assessment of testing the set of rules over a part of the data set (Lim et al. 1995) or an analytical goal function (Furuhashi et al. 1994).

A chromosome is defined as a set of rules, the genes being defined differently (condition elements, membership functions, action elements, certainty factors).

3.7.5   Fuzzy Expert System Shells

A *fuzzy expert system shell* is a tool which facilitates building and experimenting with fuzzy expert systems. It facilitates building the main modules in a fuzzy expert system. Examples of such shells are TIL Shell (1993), FuzzyCLIPS (1994), FLIE (fuzzy logic inference engine) which is part of a hybrid system FuzzyCOPE (Kasabov 1995b). Some of the built-in functions for dealing with fuzzy rules and fuzzy inference in FuzzyCLIPS are shown in appendix E. Functions of FLIE are given in appendix H.

Fuzzy system shells facilitate experimenting with different inference methods, different types of rules, and different membership functions, until the best fuzzy system is designed. Figure 3.36 shows the code of a fuzzy

```
MEMBERSHIPS INPUT
CScore:{150,155,160,165,170,175,180,185,190,195,200}
  > High:        {0, 0, 0, 0, 0, 0, 0.2, 0.7, 1, 1, 1}
  > Low:         {1, 1, 0.8, 0.5, 0.2, 0, 0, 0, 0 ,0 ,0}

INPUT CRatio:{0.1,0.3,0.4,0.41,0.42,0.43,0.44,0.45,0.5,0.7,1.0}
  > Good_CR:     {1 ,1 , 0.7, 0.3, 0 ,0, 0, 0, 0, 0, 0}
  > Bad_CR:      {0, 0, 0, 0, 0, 0, 0, 0.3, 0.7, 1, 1}

INPUT CCredit: {0,1,2,3,4,5,6,7,8,9,10}
  > Good_CC:     {1, 1, 1, 0.7, 0.3, 0, 0, 0, 0, 0, 0}
  > Bad_CC:      {0, 0, 0, 0, 0, 0, 0.3, 0.7, 1, 1, 1}

OUTPUT Decision: {0,1,2,3,4,5,6,7,8,9,10}
  > Approve:     {0, 0, 0, 0, 0, 0, 0.3, 0.7, 1, 1, 1}
  > Reject:      {1, 1, 1, 0.7, 0.3, 0, 0, 0, 0, 0, 0}

RULES
if  <CScore is High> and  <CRatio is Good_CR> and  <CCredit is Good_CC>
          then  <Decision is Approve>
else
if  <CScore is Low>  and  <CRatio is Bad_CR> or  <CCredit is Bad_CC>
          then   <Decision is Reject>
```

Figure 3.36
The code of a fuzzy system for the Bank Loan Decision Problem prepared in the syntax of a
fuzzy logic shell.

system for the Bank Loan case example written in the syntax of the shell
FLIE and figure 3.37 shows a view of the shell. After having designed the
fuzzy system, it can be compiled and linked with other programs. The
fuzzy rule base is in a simple text format, thus portable and able to run on
different platforms. A fuzzy inference can be activated as an external program from another program as shown below.

Example   A function call: (dcmfuzzy "loan.rul" $?x 1 2 1), will activate
a function for a decompositional inference over fuzzy rules, in the file
"loan.rul," when an implication operator numbered as 1 in a list of possible operators for use, composition operator numbered by 2, and else-link
operator numbered by 1, will be used.

Example   A section of a program for predicting the stock market index
written in FuzzyCLIPS is given in figure 3.46 and explained in 3.12.

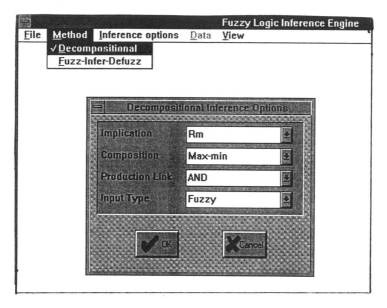

Figure 3.37
A view of the menu of a fuzzy logic shell, FLIE (see appendix H). Different inference methods
can be selected in order to tune the fuzzy inference to the domain problem.

3.8   Pattern Recognition and Classification, Fuzzy Clustering, Image and Speech Processing

3.8.1   Pattern Recognition and Classification

Pattern recognition tasks ideally suit fuzzy theory, as patterns are very
often inexact, ambiguous, or corrupted. In the Handwritten Characters
Recognition case example, described in chapter 1, the patterns to be recognized are not well defined and are ambiguous in many cases. Fuzzy rules
for handwritten character recognition are given in Yamakawa (1990). The
recognition of the handwritten digit 3 is based on the fuzzy rule given in
chapter 1, but in addition to that, membership functions are defined and a
fuzzy inference is applied.

Pattern recognition and *classification* are usually considered as very
similar tasks as discussed in chapter 1. Classes can be described by *fuzzy
classification rules*, for example, the example above, or *a set of examples*

(data points in the problem space) from which fuzzy classification rules are extracted.

Fuzzy rules can be used for classification purposes when the objects to be classified are noisy, corrupted, blurry, etc. Fuzzy rules can cope with those ambiguities. This is the case with the Blood Cells Classification Problem, the solution to which is shown in section 3.12. Fuzzy classification of Iris plants by using rules extracted from data is discussed in chapter 5.

Fuzzy systems, as we have already discussed, are *robust*. Contradictory fuzzy rules can be accommodated in one system, the tradeoff being achieved through the inference mechanism. This characteristic of fuzzy systems is very important for their applications in solving classification problems.

Classification problems, when data examples labeled with class labels are available, have been successfully solved by classic statistical methods, especially when the data set is unambiguous and dense. If the data set is *sparse* in the problem state space, the problem is rather difficult. A simple example of 19 data instances, which belong to two classes, is shown in figure 3.38. The instances are represented by two attributes $A1$ and $A2$ discretized with three fuzzy labels—"Small," "Medium," and "Large." The following fuzzy rules can be articulated after an analysis of the data distribution. The confidence factors represent the percentage of instances of a given class which fall in a particular "patch" of the problem space:

Rule 1: IF $A1$ is M and $A2$ is S, THEN Class1 ($CF = 1$)

Rule 2: IF $A1$ is L and $A2$ is S, THEN Class1 ($CF = 0.45$)

Rule 3: IF $A1$ is L and $A2$ is S, THEN Class2 ($CF = 0.55$)

Rule 4: IF $A1$ is L and $A2$ is M, THEN Class2 ($CF = 0.75$)

Rule 5: IF $A1$ is L and $A2$ is M, THEN Class1 ($CF = 0.25$)

The above set of rules is ambiguous and contradictory. Rules 2 and 3 have the same antecedents, but different consequences, which is also true for rules 4 and 5. This situation is impossible for a symbolic production system to cope with. A fuzzy production system can infer a proper classification, as for every input data vector all rules may fire to some degree and all of them contribute to the final solution to different degrees. The

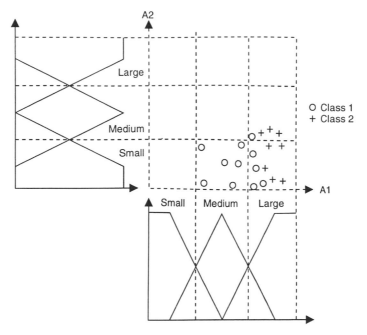

Figure 3.38
A two-dimensional feature space representation of a data set of 19 points which belong to two classes.

points at the border between the two classes should be correctly classified by the fuzzy rules as they take support not only from one of the contradictory rules but from a rule that has lateral fuzzy labels with it.

When the data examples are not labeled with the class or pattern labels, that is, when the classes they belong to are not known, then different clustering techniques can be applied to find the groups, the *clusters*, in which data examples are grouped. The clusters show the typical patterns, the similarity, and the ambiguity in the data set. In addition to the exact clustering (see chapter 1), fuzzy clustering can be applied too.

3.8.2 Fuzzy Clustering

Fuzzy clustering is a procedure of clustering data into possibly overlapping clusters, such that each of the data examples may belong to each of the clusters to a certain degree. The procedure aims at finding the cluster centers Vi ($i = 1, 2, \ldots, c$) and the cluster membership functions μ_i

which define to what degree each of the n examples belong to the ith cluster. The number of clusters c is either defined a priori (supervised type of clustering) or chosen by the clustering procedure (unsupervised type of clustering). The result of a clustering procedure can be represented as a fuzzy relation $\mu_{i,k}$, such that:

(1) $\sum_{i=1}^{c} \mu_{i,k} = 1$, for each $k = 1, 2, \ldots, n$; (the total membership of an instance k to all the clusters equals 1)

(2) $\sum_{k=1}^{n} \mu_{i,k} > 0$, for each $i = 1, 2, \ldots, c$ (there are no empty clusters)

A widely used algorithm for fuzzy clustering is the *C-means algorithm* suggested by J. Bezdek (see 1992 and 1987). Its simplified version is given in figure 3.39. A validity criterion for measuring how well a set of fuzzy clusters represents a data set can be applied. One criterion is that a function $S(c)$ reaches local minimum:

$$S(c) = \sum_{(i)} \sum_{(k)} (\mu_{i,k})^2 [(x_k - Vi)^2 - (Vi - Mx)^2]$$

1. Initialise c fuzzy cluster centers V_1, V_2,..., V_c arbitrarily and calculate the membership   degrees $\mu_{i,k}$, i=1,2,...,c, k=1,2,...,n such that the general conditions are met.

2. Calculate the next values for cluster centres:
$$V_i = (\sum_{k=1}^{} (\mu_{i,k})^2 . x_k) / (\sum_{k=1}^{} (\mu_{i,k})^2), \text{ for } i=1,2,...,c$$

3. Update the fuzzy degree of membership:
$$\mu_{i,k} = \frac{1}{[\sum_{j=1}^{c} \frac{d_{i,k}}{d_{j,k}}]}, \text{ for } d_{i,k} > 0, \forall i,k$$

where: $d_{i,k} = (x_k - V_i)^2$, $d_{j,k} = (x_k - V_j)^2$ (Euclidean distance)

4. If the currently calculated values V_i for the cluster centers are not different from the values calculated at the previous step (subject to a small error ε), then stop.

Figure 3.39
An outline of the C-means fuzzy clustering algorithm.

where Mx is the average of x. If the number of clusters is not defined, then the clustering procedure should be applied until a local minimum of $S(c)$ is found, which means that c is the optimal number of clusters. One of the advantages of the C-mean fuzzy clustering algorithm is that it always converges to a strict local minimum. A possible deficiency is that the shape of the clusters is ellipsoid, which may not be the most suitable form for a particular data set.

Fuzzy clustering is an important data analysis technique. It helps to understand better the ambiguity in data. It can be used to direct the way other techniques for information processing are used afterward. For example, the structure of a neural network to be used for learning from a data set can be defined to a great extent after knowing the optimal number of fuzzy clusters.

3.8.3   Image Recognition

Image recognition is an area where fuzzy representation and fuzzy reasoning can be successfully applied, mainly for two reasons: (1) *ambiguity* in the images to be recognized; and (2) the need for *fast processing*, that is, complicated formulas may not be applicable for a real-time recognition; in this case a fuzzy system may be more convenient.

Different approaches are possible depending on the image recognition tasks, two of them being (1) *objects recognition*, that is, recognizing shape, distance, and location of objects; and (2) *texture analysis*, for example, an image X of size $m \times n$ pixels can be represented as a set of fuzzy sets and membership degrees to which pixels belong to the fuzzy concepts, such as "brightness," "darkness," "edginess," "smoothness."

Fuzzy methods can be used at two levels of image recognition and image processing: (1) *low-level image processing*, tasks to be performed at this level being image segmentation, boundary detection, image enhancement, and clustering; and (2) *high-level image understanding*, which process ends up with a symbolic description of the image.

Example   The problem is to identify the expression of a face from a photograph. First, linguistic fuzzy features like "big eyes," "small nose," "round mouth" are extracted from a photograph of a face. In order to extract features, some facial characteristic points are detected. According to these features another categorization can be made which defines the expression of the face, for example, "happy," "surprised," "normal," based on fuzzy rules. An experimental system was published in Ralescu and Hartani (1995).

3.8.4   Speech and Music Signals Recognition

The main difficulties in speech recognition were discussed in chapter 1. The extreme complexity of this task due to different levels and sources of ambiguities were pointed out.

Fuzzy systems can be applied at different levels of the speech recognition process, that is, at a low or pattern-matching level, at a higher or language analysis level, and at the highest level, concept understanding, subject to the rules available. Articulating rules for speech and language processing is a difficult task, even though there is a huge amount of literature on the subject. How to bring this knowledge to the computers through the methods of fuzzy logic is a challenging task.

Fuzzy rules can be automatically extracted from data mapped into a feature space. Figure 1.18, for example, shows a mapping of spoken phoneme signals into the two-dimensional space of the first formant frequency $F1$ and the second formant frequency $F2$. The intervals of these frequencies can be represented by fuzzy labels in a similar manner, as shown in figure 3.38 for a classification problem. If five labels are used to label consecutive intervals—VS, S, M, L, VL—then fuzzy rules can be articulated, such as:

IF $F1$ is S and $F2$ is L, THEN it is very likely that the pronounced phoneme is either /I/ in the R.P. English or /I/ in the general Australian English

IF $F1$ is M and $F2$ is M, THEN it is very likely that the pronounced phoneme is /I/ in New Zealand English

In spite of the existing ambiguity between different phonemes in the different English languages, a system of fuzzy rules can deal with the problem. Such fuzzy rules can be extracted from samples of spoken phonemes by using neural networks.

The problem of musical signals recognition is by nature similar to the problem of speech recognition. One solution to a simple problem is given in section 3.12.

3.9   Fuzzy Systems for Prediction

Complex prediction tasks, such as the Stock Market Prediction Problem, are characterized by *time variability* and *ambiguous information*, as was discussed in chapter 1. They can be solved by using different techniques, or a combination of them, as, for example, fuzzy rules, neural network, and genetic algorithms. The use of fuzzy systems is discussed here. More examples are given in chapters 5, 6 and 7.

3.9.1   Fuzzy Rules for Solving Complex Prediction Tasks

In complex prediction tasks the next values (events) to be predicted depend on many variables, usually of different types. These tasks are usually solved in two stages: (1) *state recognition,* and (2) *scenario evaluation.*

For the state recognition stage, time-series data may be used, while the scenario evaluation stage requires expert knowledge. If we take the Stock Market Prediction example, during the first stage parameters such as volatility and trends can be evaluated. At the next stage, fuzzy rules can be applied for suggesting an investment decision (very short term, medium short, medium long, long, etc.).

Time-series prediction fuzzy rules can be learned from data. Suppose a time series of index prices, taken for a certain period of days, is mapped into a two-dimensional space: today's price, yesterday's price. The data can be visualized in a similar way, as the data in fig 3.38. Fuzzy rules, such as:

IF (today's price was medium) AND (yesterday's price was low),
THEN (tomorrow's price will be up) (0.8)

can be extracted by using different techniques. Extracting fuzzy rules for chaotic time-series prediction is illustrated in chapter 7. Higher-level rules, such as:

IF (current economic situation is good) and
    (current political situation is good) and
    (the predicted value for tomorrow is up),
THEN (action—buy) ($CF = 0.9$)

can be applied afterward.

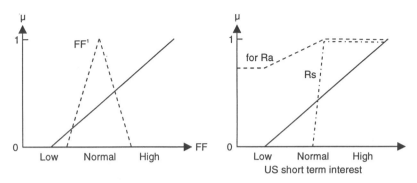

Figure 3.40
Inferencing over a gradual rule "the higher the FF, the higher the U.S. short-term interest" with the use of two implications Ra and Rs; the membership functions in the rule are drawn as a solid line; the current value for the FF denoted as FF' is drawn as a dotted line; the inferred function for the "US short-term interest" by applying Ra is drawn as a dashed line and for Rs as a dotted-dashed line. The Rs implication is more suitable than Ra. (Adapted with permission from Katoh et al, 1992).

3.9.2   Using Gradual Rules

Very often economic, social, or psychological behavior can be represented by gradual fuzzy rules because of the gradual properties of the processes under consideration.

Example (Katoh et al. 1992)   The gradual fuzzy rule is: "the higher the *FF* rate, the higher the U.S.-short-term interest rate". When the membership function for the state of the *FF* rate is known, a membership function for the output variable can be inferred. In a previous section one way of inferencing over gradual rules was shown. Here, two different implications *Ra* and *Rs* are applied to inferring the fuzzy output membership function for the "U.S. short-term interest rate" when the membership function FF^1 for the current value of the input variable "federal funds" (*FF*) is known (see figure 3.40). The *Rs* implication gives better results according to the experts' expectations.

3.10   Control, Monitoring, Diagnosis, and Planning

3.10.1   Fuzzy Control

Fuzzy control systems were one of the first industrial fuzzy systems. The first system was designed and implemented by Mamdany for cement kiln

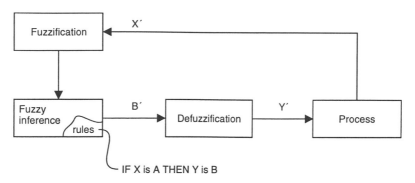

Figure 3.41
A block diagram of a fuzzy control system.

control in the United Kingdom in the early 1970s. Since then many fuzzy control systems have been developed, for example, subway control, washing machines, camera focusing, automatic transmission control, rice cookers, dishwashers, and many other engineering applications. Intelligent robotics is an area where fuzzy control systems will be used in the future.

By *fuzzy control*, an application of fuzzy logic to control problems is meant. Fuzzy control is different from standard control, mainly in three respects: (1) the use of *linguistically described concepts*, rather than formulas; (2) the use of *commonsense knowledge*, rather than mathematical knowledge; and (3) the use of *methods of fuzzy logic*.

Ordinary controllers usually represent a system's uncertainty by a probability distribution. Probability models describe the system's behavior with the use of first-order and second-order statistics—means and covariances. Mathematical models of control systems facilitate a mean-square-error (MSE) analysis of the system's behavior. In case of many variables, it is extremely difficult to accurately articulate such mathematical models. They also require a lot of computations, which might be difficult to perform in real time. Fuzzy control systems consist of fuzzy rules and an inference machine which includes fuzzification and defuzzification. The system works in a cycle, as shown graphically in figure 3.41. The case example of the Inverted Pendulum Problem is discussed below. The problem was described in chapter 1, where heuristic rules for its possible solution were articulated and shown in figure 1.33. After fuzzy quantization of the two input parameters angle Θ and angular velocity

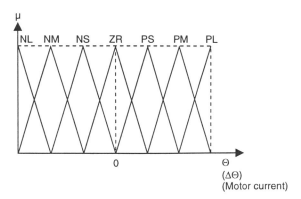

Figure 3.42
A set of fuzzy rules and membership functions for the Inverted Pendulum case problem.
(Adapted with permission from Yamakawa 1989.)

$\Delta\Theta$, and the output parameter, the force applied to the cart, by using seven fuzzy labels (*PL* and *NL* are added to the fuzzy terms used in chapter 1), seven rules were set experimentally by Professor Yamakawa (1989). They are shown in the form of a *rule map* in figure 3.42 along with the membership functions of the fuzzy labels.

By using the same approach, much more complex tasks can be solved. For complex control tasks, a modular system, which comprises two or more simple control systems, can be designed as demonstrated in an example solved in section 3.12.

In the fuzzy control systems the control algorithm is described by fuzzy words and not analytically. Therefore it is difficult to evaluate the stability of the model, that is, how stable the system will be if some parameters of the objects change, for example, the length of the pendulum, the weight of the mouse put on top of a pendulum, and so forth. This problem has been thoroughly investigated by Li-Xin Wang (1994).

In adaptive fuzzy control systems the set of fuzzy rules dynamically change according to the changes in the process or object under control (see Brown and Harris 1994, Wang 1994).

3.10.2   Monitoring

Fuzzy theory is useful for creating monitoring systems when the parameters and the conditions to be monitored can be expressed in fuzzy linguistic terms. The simple problem of monitoring a car, described in chapter 1 and realized as an exact production system in chapter 2, is presented in section 3.12 as a fuzzy rule–based system.

Using fuzzy rules makes the system more sensitive to the borderline values for the parameters. Monitoring of a process that is described by a large number of parameters can be handled in a similar way.

3.10.3   Diagnosis

Diagnosis is a generic problem suitable for solving by the methods of fuzzy logic. This is because of ambiguity in the diagnostic process. The latter may have many causes; for example, the earlier we try to diagnose an abnormality, the more ambiguous the indicators are; the difference between the normal and abnormal state might be slight.

Fuzzy diagnostic systems can contain fuzzy rules of two different forms:

1. *IF disorders* (x), *THEN symptoms* (y); in this case x is sought from the set of equations: $y = x \circ R$, where R is the set of relations between the disorders and the symptoms and "$\circ$" denotes a composition operator; this is the inverse problem of the fuzzy inference composition rule and more difficult to solve.

2. *IF symptoms* (x), *THEN disorders* (y); in this case y is sought from the fuzzy compositional equation $y = x \circ R$.

More sophisticated fuzzy diagnostic systems use fuzzy concepts for representing not only static symptoms but their dynamic properties too, for example, "tendency"—"increasing," "decreasing," "not changing," etc.

In some fuzzy medical diagnostic systems patients are allowed to answer in fuzzy terms, for example, the question "Do you feel fatigue?" could be answered by using the fuzzy concepts "seldom," "sometimes," "always." There answers can be processed further as fuzzy input values.

3.10.4   Planning

Planning in uncertain and ambiguous conditions is also a problem, too difficult to be tackled by the traditional symbolic AI methods. Take the Monkey and Bananas case example. When the exact positioning of all the objects and exact goals are known, there is no problem. But suppose we do not have the exact positioning of the monkey and instead of the exact position, for example (5,8), we know that the monkey is "near" the couch, the ladder is "at about the most distant corner from the monkey," and bananas are on the ceiling "somewhere in the middle." The goal can be "monkey to grasp bananas." A plan in this case can be generated by using a set of fuzzy rules and a fuzzy inference machine to perform the reasoning process.

Complex planning problems can be solved in stages, for example, first stage, recognition of the situation; second stage, generation of a plan; third stage, execution of the plan. For each of the stages fuzzy rules may be used and combined with other techniques used for other stages.

3.11   Optimization and Decision Making

These two generic problems are about finding an optimal option among a set of options. This process is difficult to model when the decision is required to be "humanlike," especially in a group decision-making process.

3.11.1   Optimization

Optimization problems sometimes do not have well-defined parameters and values. Finding an optimal solution in this case is extremely difficult. For example, the cost from one town to another for the TSP case example might not be a single value, but an interval or a fuzzy number, say, about 600. A fuzzy solution to this problem when inexact costs are provided instead of exact values is presented in Dubois and Prade (1988).

3.11.2   Decision Making

Fuzzy logic, when applied to decision-making problems, provides formal methodology for problem solving, and human consistency. These are important general characteristics of fuzzy decision making systems. Such systems should have the following functionality:

- Explain the solution to the user
- Keep a rigorous and "fair" way of reasoning;
- Accommodate subjective knowledge
- Account for "grayness" in the solution process, when, for example, it is impossible to draw a rigid border between "bad" and "good."

Fuzzy logic can either be used instead of, or in addition to, probability theory. For example, suppose we have the probability distribution for the monthly sales of item x over a certain period of time. The distribution can be used to estimate the probability $p(x_i)$ that a certain amount of this item will be sold next month. But to make a decision on what should be produced next month, it is necessary to know whether the predicted through probability $p(x_i)$ sell of x is "good" or "bad," or "OK," from the point of view of the profit of the company. So we have to define the fuzzy concepts of "good" and "bad" for this particular company.

Solving decision-making problems by using fuzzy systems was illustrated in previous sections of this chapter with the Bank Loan case example. Similar decision-making tasks are investment advising, mortgage approval, insurance risk evaluation, house pricing, selecting the best candidate for a job, assessing complex projects, assessing student papers, assessing the risk of failure of a company, and many others.

3.11.3   Group Decision Making

Fuzzy reasoning particularly suits modeling a *group decision-making* process. The following terms relate to this task:

- A group of individuals (*experts*): $x_1, x_2, \ldots, x_p$
- A set of *options*: $s_1, s_2, \ldots, s_n$
- *Parameters* describing the experts' opinions and preferences

And the task is to find the option s_i on which there is a consensus among the experts. Two approaches to using fuzzy logic for this problem are:

1. *Using linguistic quantified propositions of the form of* QB*x are* F. For example, Q denotes "most"; B denotes "important"; x denotes "expert"; F denotes "convinced." Each of the fuzzy terms can be represented by a membership function on the universe X representing the degree to which each expert $x \in X$ "belongs" to the fuzzy set. A value $\mu_F(x_i)$ denotes how much convinced expert x_i is with regard to the option under discussion for consensus. The final truth-value of the proposition "most important experts are convinced" is calculated as:

$$t = \sum_{i=1}^{p} (\mu_B(x_i) \wedge \mu_F(x_i))/(\sum \mu_B(x_i))$$

2. *Using fuzzy preference relations.* In this case a fuzzy relation $Rk{:}SxS \rightarrow [0,1]$ represents the preference $r_{i,j}^{(k)}$ of the expert x_k between each of the pairs $(s_{i\_}s_j)$ of options for decision. One way to process these fuzzy preference relations to achieve the final preference relation R over all the experts before finding the optimal solution from it is given below:

$$R(i,j) = (\sum q_{i,j}^{(k)})/p,$$

where $\quad q_{i,j}^{(k)} = 1, \quad$ if $r_{i,j}^{(k)} > 0.5$

$$0, \quad \text{if } r_{i,j}^{(k)} \Leftarrow 0.5$$

Fuzzy methods for modeling group decision-making is an area of growing interest.

3.12   Problems and Exercises

Part A: Case Example Solutions

1. *Blood Cell Classification case example.* Experts are very good at classifying blood cells by looking at a blood sample through a microscope. But when they try to explain how they do the classification, they usually come up with a set of ill-defined, incomplete rules. A set of such rules is given as an illustration in figure 3.43. The rules, though, are not difficult to implement as a fuzzy system. The five features—nucleus exists, segmented or granular cell, darkness of the nucleus, size of the nucleus, and size of granules—are used as input variables in the realization described here. Fuzzy values are defined for the input fuzzy variables, for example: "yes," "maybe," "no." The output variables are the blood cell classes. Their fuzzy values are defined as certainty degrees for the object to be classified in the

class "yes," "likely," "possibly," "maybe," and "not." Membership functions of singleton type for representing those fuzzy values are shown on the screenshot in figure 3.44. The three membership functions for representing the fuzzy variable nucleus-exists and the fuzzification result for a particular input data, as well as the classification result, are graphically and numerically presented there.

2. *Recognition of musical notes.* A partial solution to the problem with the use of exact production rules was shown in chapter 2. Instead of the intervals used there for representing variations of the energy of the signal in different frequency bands, fuzzy quantization can be applied and fuzzy rules can be articulated based on the exact interval rules (figure 3.45).

3. *Decision-making on stock market trading.* Figure 3.46 shows a part of a program written in FuzzyCLIPS for decision-making on future investments. Three fuzzy input variables are used (economic situation, political situation, trend of the predicted value) for which fuzzy values are defined by using standard membership functions. The FuzzyCLIPS functions are explained in appendix E. Extended program is given in appendix I.

4. *Control of a two-stage inverted pendulum* (figure 3.47). Fuzzy Controller 1 (which is similar to the one described in a previous section) takes data from the upper stage of the two-stage pendulum. It has two inputs—angle $A2$ and angular velocity $V2$. The output of it called "Stage 1" is used as an input variable to Fuzzy Controller 2, which takes two more parameters—angle $A1$ and angular velocity $V1$ from the lower stage—and actually controls the current to the motor by producing an output value for the control variable "Motor." For each output value of the variable "Stage 1," a separate rule map is used to represent the rules for Fuzzy Controller 2. The rule map for Stage $1 = ZR$ is given in figure 3.48 with the rule map of the rules for Fuzzy Controller 1. In case of stage $1 = ZR$ the two maps are identical, but not in the other cases.

5. Fuzzy system for the *Car Monitoring Problem.* Figure 3.49 shows a fuzzy quantization of the parameters of the task. The parameter "brakes' response" is represented here on the universe of time with three linguistic labels—"quick," "normal," and "slow." The state of the cooling system is represented by three linguistic fuzzy values—"underheating," "normal," and "overheating." The status of the temperature gauge is represented by two labels—"OK" and "damaged"—on the universe of grades of sensitivity of the gauge. The variable "temperature" is represented by the labels

RULE 1:
IF Nucleus might exist and cell might be segmented and granular and Nucleus is dark,
    THEN the cell is unlikely to be an Erythrocyte and the cell is possibly a
        Lymphocyte.
RULE 2:
IF Nucleus might exist and cell might be segmented and granular and Nucleus is light
    THEN the cell is unlikely to be an Erythrocyte and the cell is unlikely to be a
        Lymphocyte.
RULE 3:
IF Nucleus might exist and cell is not segmented and granular and Nucleus is light,
    THEN the cell maybe an Erythrocyte and the cell is unlikely to be a Lymphocyte
        and the cell is likely to be a Monocyte.

RULE 4:
IF Nucleus might exist and cell is not segmented and granular and Nucleus is dark,
    THEN the cell is unlikely to be an Erythrocyte and the cell is unlikely to be a
        Monocyte and the cell is likely to be a Lymphocyte.

RULE 5:
IF Nucleus exists and the cell might be segmented and granular and the nucleus is
        light
    THEN the cell is likely to be a Monocyte.

RULE 6:
IF Nucleus exists and the cell might be segmented and granular and the Nucleus is dark
    THEN the cell is likely to be a Lymphocyte.

RULE 7:
IF Nucleus exists and the cell is not segmented and granular and the Nucleus is dark
    THEN the cell is a Lymphocyte.

RULE 8:
IF Nucleus exists and the cell is not segmented and granular and the Nucleus is light
    THEN the cell is a Monocyte.

RULE 9:
IF Nucleus is large and granules are large and Nucleus is medium dark
    THEN the cell is likely to be a Basophil.

RULE 10:
IF Nucleus is large and granules are large and Nucleus is light
    THEN the cell is Basophil.

RULE 11:
IF Nucleus is large and granules are medium and Nucleus is light
    THEN the cell is likely to be a Basophil.

Figure 3.43
A set of expert fuzzy rules for the Blood Cell Classification Problem.

RULE 12:
IF Nucleus is large and granules are medium and Nucleus is medium dark
        THEN the cell is possibly a Basophil.

RULE 13:
IF Nucleus is medium and granules are large and nucleus is medium dark
        THEN the cell is possibly a Basophil and the cell is possibly a Eosinophil.

RULE 14:
IF Nucleus is medium and granules are large and Nucleus is light
        THEN the cell is a Basophil.

RULE 15:
IF Nucleus is medium and granules are large and Nucleus is light
        THEN the cell is likely to be a Basophil.

RULE 16:
IF Nucleus is medium and granules are medium and Nucleus is dark
        THEN the cell is likely to be an Eosinophil.

RULE 17:
IF Nucleus is medium and granules are large and Nucleus is medium dark
        THEN the cell is likely to be a Basophil and the cell is likely to be an Eosinophil.

RULE 18:
IF Nucleus is medium and granules are medium and Nucleus is dark
        THEN the cell is possibly an Eosinophil and the cell is maybe a Neutrophil.

RULE 19:
IF Nucleus is small and granules are large and Nucleus is dark
        THEN the cell is an Eosinophil.

RULE 20:
IF Nucleus is small and granules are large and Nucleus is medium darkness
        THEN the cell is likely to be an Eosinophil.

RULE 21:
IF Nucleus is small and granules are medium and Nucleus is medium dark
        THEN the cell is likely to be an Eosinophil and the cell is likely to be a Neutrophil.

RULE 22:
IF Nucleus is small and granules are medium and Nucleus is medium dark
        THEN the cell is possibly an Eosinophil and the cell is may be a Neutrophil.

Figure 3.43 (continued)

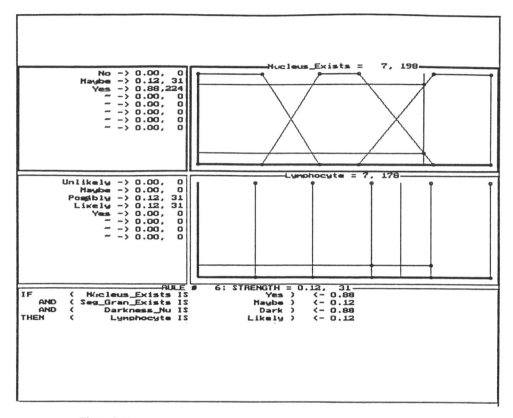

Figure 3.44
Membership functions of one input fuzzy variable (Nucleus_Exists) and of one output variable (Lymphocyte) and a graphical representation of an inference for a particular input data for the Blood Cells Classification problem. The input and output values are on a grade of 0 to 10. The particular sample has been classified to class Lymphocyte to a degree of 7. The second numbers on the figure are internal representation (from 0 to 255).

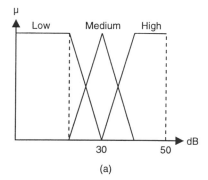

(a)

IF 0-1000 is Medium AND
  1000-2000 is Medium AND
  2000-3000 is Low THEN
       the note is Middle C

IF 0-1000 is High AND
  1000-2000 is Medium AND
  2000-3000 is Low THEN
       the note is D above Middle C

IF 0-1000 is High AND
  1000-2000 is Low AND
  2000-3000 is Low THEN
       the note is E above Middle C

IF 0-1000 is Medium AND
  1000-2000 is Medium AND
  2000-3000 is Medium THEN
       the note is F above Middle C

IF 0-1000 is Low AND
  100-2000 is Medium AND
  2000-3000 is Medium AND
  3000-4000 is Low THEN
       the note is G above Middle C

IF 0-1000 is Low AND
  1000-2000 is Medium AND
  2000-3000 is Medium AND
  3000-4000 is Medium THEN
       the note is A above Middle C

IF 0-1000 is Low AND
  1000-2000 is Medium AND
  2000-3000 is Low THEN
       the note is B above Middle C

IF 0-1000 is High AND
  1000-2000 is High AND
  2000-3000 is High THEN
       the note is C above Middle C

(b)

Figure 3.45
(a) Membership functions for the Musical Recognition Problem; (b) some fuzzy rules for classification of a musical signal.

;;; **A part of a FuzzyCLIPS program for stock market prediction**

;; a single rule for decision making - a fuzzy value is inferred by it:
(defrule hybrid_system_step3
  (declare (CF 0.9))
  ?step3 <- (step3)
  (political_climate good)
  (economic_climate good)
  (predicted_value up)
  =>
  (assert (shares buy) CF 0.9)
  (assert (end_run))
  (retract ?step3))

;; a single rule for defuzzification and final decision making:
(defrule final
  (end_run)
  ?f<- (shares ?)
=>
  (printout t crlf " THE DECISION OBTAINED BY THE SYSTEM IS: " crlf (get-fs
?f) crlf " with a degree of certainty of:" (get-cf ?f) crlf "On the scale of 0 - 9 levels,
where 0 means definitely "sell", 5 means - "hold", and 9 means definitely "buy", the
suggested action is " (moment-defuzzify ?f))

Figure 3.46
A part of a program written in FuzzyCLIPS for decision-making on future investment in the
stock market.

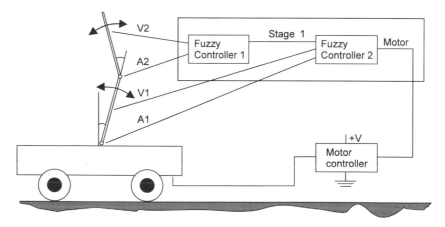

Figure 3.47
A sketch of the two-stages Inverted Pendulum Problem.

Controller One (Output: Stage 1)

Angle 2	Velocity 2				
	NL	NM	ZR	PM	PL
NL	NL	NL	NL	NM	NS
NM	NL	NL	NM	NS	PS
NS	NL	NM	NS	PS	PM
PS	NM	NS	PS	PM	PL
PM	NS	PS	PM	PL	PL
PL	PS	PM	PL	PL	PL

Controller Two (Output: Motor)
Stage 1 = ZR Zero

Angle 1	Velocity 1				
	NL	NM	ZR	PM	PL
NL	NL	NL	NL	NM	NS
NM	NL	NL	NM	NS	PS
NS	NL	NM	NS	PS	PM
PS	NM	NS	PS	PM	PL
PM	NS	PS	PM	PL	PL
PL	PS	PM	PL	PL	PL

Figure 3.48
Two maps of fuzzy rules for the two-stages Inverted Pendulum Problem. The map for controller one and one map only of fuzzy rules for the controller two are shown.

"low," "normal," and "high." The conclusion "stop the car," can be represented as a single-valued membership function representing the certainty of the advice. A chain fuzzy inference is performed in this case. When the system is realized by the use of the centroid defuzzification inference method, even slight matching of the conditions in the fuzzy rules by the current status of the car will cause a message to be communicated to the driver. The fuzzy rules are:

Rule 1: IF Brakes'_response is Slow, THEN Message is Stop_the_car

Rule 2: IF Cooling_status is Overheating, THEN Message is Stop_the_car

Rule 3: IF Temperature is High and Gauge_status is OK, THEN Cooling_status is Overheating

6. A fuzzy diagnostic system for the *Medical Diagnosis* case example described in chapter 1 is explained here. The rules vaguely articulated there are now presented in a more precise form as fuzzy rules, shown in figure 3.50. $M1$, $M2$, $M3$, and $M4$ are manifestations (symptoms), defined with their linguistic values, and $D1$, $D2$, $D3$, and $D4$ are disorders, defined with linguistically represented confidence factors $CF1$, $CF2$, $CF3$, and $CF4$. In the same figure, another representation of the same rules after substituting the fuzzy quantifiers with its corresponding typical numerical values, as given in Chen (1988), is shown. A table of corresponding fuzzy linguistic

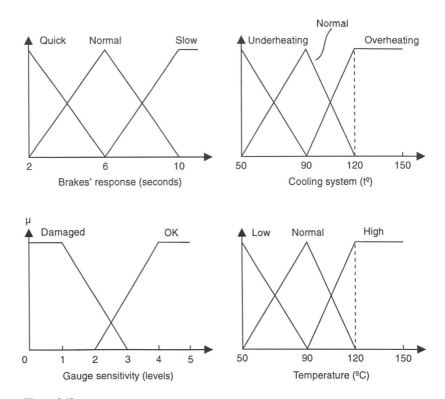

Figure 3.49
Membership functions of linguistic values for the Car Monitoring Problem.

labels, numerical intervals, and typical single values for the frequency of appearance and strength of symptoms is given in figure 3.51.

7. *The Investment Adviser Problem.* Here, a solution to this problem is presented. It can be compared with its solution as a production system (see chapter 2). A set of fuzzy rules for solving the problem are shown in figure 3.52. Standard triangular membership functions are specified for the fuzzy values. The system is written in the syntax of FLIE (see appendix H).

Part B: Practical Tasks and Questions

8. Why do fuzzy sets break the law of the excluded middle?

9. What is the main difference between propositional and fuzzy logic?

10. What major fuzzy inference methods can you outline?

Fuzzy rules:
Rule 1:IF(M1 is Always AND M2 is Weak AND M3 is No AND M4 is No)
        THEN D is D1 (CF is very strong);

Rule 2:IF (M1 is No AND M2 is Always AND M3 is Weak AND M4 is No)
        THEN D is D2 (CF is very strong);

Rule 3:IF(M1 is More_or_less_weak AND M2 is No AND M3 is Always AND M4 is No)
        THEN D is D3 (CF is very strong);

Rule 4:IF(M1 is Weak AND M2 is More_or_less_weak AND M3 is Always
        AND M4 is No)
        THEN D is D4 (CF is very strong); .

Use of typical values instead of fuzzy values:
Rule 1: IF (M1=1.0, M2=0.2, M3=0.0, M4=0.0) THEN D1 (CF=0.99);

Rule 2: IF (M1=0.0, M2=1.0, M3=0.2, M4=0.0) THEN D2 (CF=0.99);

Rule 3: IF (M1=0.3, M2=0.0, M3=1.0, M4=0.0) THEN D3 (CF=0.99);

Rule 4: I F (M1 =0.2, M2=0.3, M3=1.0 , M4=0.0) THEN D4 (CF=0.99);

Figure 3.50
Two sets of similar rules for the Medical Diagnosis Problem.

Fuzzy label	Numerical interval	Typical value
Always	[1.00, 1.00]	1.0
Very strong	[0.95, 0.99]	0.99
Strong	[0.80, 0.94]	0.9
More or less strong	[0.65, 0.79]	0.7
Medium	[0.45, 0.64]	0.5
More or less weak	[0.30, 0.44]	0.3
Weak	[0.10, 0.29]	0.2
Very weak	[0.01, 0.09]	0.05
No	[0.00, 0.00]	0.0

Figure 3.51
Corresponding linguistic values, numerical intervals, and typical exact values for representing frequency of appearance and strength of symptoms.

MEMBERSHIPS
  INPUT amount:{0, 10, 25, 40, 55, 70, 100}
    > very_small:{ 1, 1, 0, 0, 0, 0, 0}
    > small: { 0, 0, 1, 0, 0, 0, 0}
    > average: { 0, 0, 0, 1, 0, 0, 0}
    > large: { 0, 0, 0, 0, 1, 0, 0}
    > very_large:{ 0, 0, 0, 0, 0, 1, 1}
  INPUT risk:{0, 0.1, 25, 40, 55, 70, 100}
    > no: { 1, 0, 0, 0, 0, 0, 0}
    > very_low: { 1, 1, 0, 0, 0, 0, 0}
    > low: { 0, 0, 1, 0, 0, 0, 0}
    > medium: { 0, 0, 0, 1, 0, 0, 0}
    > high: { 0, 0, 0, 0, 1, 0, 0}
    > very_high:{ 0, 0, 0, 0, 0, 1, 1}
  INPUT period: { 0, 5, 12, 24, 36, 48, 60}
    > short: { 1, 1, 0.6, 0, 0, 0, 0}
    > medium: { 0, 0, 0, 1, 1, 0, 0}
    > long: { 0, 0, 0, 0, 0, 1, 1}
  INPUT income: { 0, 10, 15, 25, 36, 40, 46, 64, 67, 100}
    > poor: { 1, 1, 0.8, 0.1, 0, 0, 0, 0, 0, 0}
    > good: { 0, 0, 0, 0, 1, 1, 1, 0, 0, 0}
    > excellent: { 0, 0, 0, 0, 0, 0, 0.2, 0.9, 1, 1}
  OUTPUT investment: { 0, 20, 40, 60, 80, 100 }
    > none: { 1, 0, 0, 0, 0, 0 }
    > very_small: { 0, 1, 0, 0, 0, 0 }
    > small: { 0, 0, 1, 0, 0, 0 }
    > average: { 0, 0, 0, 1, 0, 0 }
    > large: { 0, 0, 0, 0, 1, 0 }
    > all: { 0, 0, 0, 0, 0, 1 }
RULES
if <amount is average> and <risk is high> and <period is short> and <income is good>
    then <investment is very_small>
else
if <amount is small> and <risk is no> and <period is short> and <income is poor>
    then <investment is all>
else
if <amount is small> and <risk is high> and <period is medium> and <income is good>
    then <investment is very_small>
else
if <amount is average> and <risk is high> and <period is long> and <income is good>
    then <investment is none>
else
if <amount is very_large> and <risk is no> and <period is medium> and <income is excellent>
    then <investment is all>
else
if <amount is average> and <risk is high> and <period is short> and <income is poor>
    then <investment is small>

Figure 3.52
A fuzzy system for solving the Investment Adviser Problem written in the syntax of FLIE (see chapter 6 and appendix H). The membership functions are chosen as triangular, defined by their centers and uniformly distributed over the whole universe. The output variable represents how much should be invested in bank. The rest is meant to be invested in shares.

11. From figure 1.18, write fuzzy rules for recognizing the vowels /u/, /i/ and /3/ in the R.P., New Zealand, and Australian English languages, similar to the rules given in section 3.8.4.

12. By using the fuzzy rule from chapter 1 for recognizing the handwritten digit 3 as an example, develop a set of fuzzy rules for recognizing and classifying all the digits in a handwritten form. How many fuzzy input variables will be needed?

13. Develop a set of fuzzy rules for a hypothetical air-conditioning control, where input variables are "temperature" and "humidity" and output variables are "openness of the cooling valve" and "openness of the heating valve."

14. Articulate gradual fuzzy rules for solving the air-conditioning problem and show an example of how the system works.

15. Define membership functions and articulate fuzzy rules for solving the Monkey and Bananas Problem, as explained in section 3.10.

16. Develop a set of fuzzy rules for solving the TSP case problem when inexact values for traveling costs are given, as explained in section 3.11.

17. What is the stability problem in fuzzy control systems?

18. Develop a fuzzy system and make experiments for the Ball and the Beam Problem explained in chapter 1 (section 1.12).

Part C: Project Specification

Topic: A fuzzy System Development

Choose one of the problems listed below or a problem of your own. Develop a fuzzy system to solve the chosen problem following the requirements below:

1. Specify and identify the problem. Why is the problem suitable for using a fuzzy system?

2. Define the input and output variables for the fuzzy system. Define the membership functions of the fuzzy values for every input and every output variable. Explain the physical meaning of the membership functions.

3. Develop a set of rules for solving the problem. Explain the meaning of the rules.

4. Make experiments of fuzzy inference over different input data and validate the results. If necessary, change the rules or membership functions, or both.

5. Draw a function between an input variable and an output variable when the rest of the input variables have fixed values. Explain the meaning of the function.

A list of suggested problems for the fuzzy system project

1. Automatic truck control [see Kosko (1992) for the specification of the problem]

2. Target-tracking system [see Kosko (1992) for the specification of the problem]

3. Pattern recognition: handwritten characters recognition

4. Pattern recognition-musical signals recognition

5. Recognition of three English vowels

6. Control: washing machine control, when two input variables, for example, "degree of dirtiness" and "type of dirt," and one output variable, for example, "washing time," are used (see Aptronix 1993)

7. Control, air-conditioning control (see Aptronix Inc. 1993)

8. Control, camera-focusing control (see Aptronix Inc. 1993)

9. Control, airplane landing control (Terano et al. 1992; Yamakawa 1992)

10. Decision-making, bank loan approval case example

11. Decision-making, investment adviser

12. Diagnosis, medical diagnosis case example

13. Diagnosis, the Smoker and the Risk of Cancer case example

14. Monitoring, The Car Monitoring case example

15. Optimization, the TSP, when inexact constraints are given, for example, the cost from town A to town B is "about 50"

16. Planning, the Monkey and Bananas Problem, if parameters are not exactly specified, for example, monkey is "near" the ladder which is to the "left" of the bananas

3.13 Conclusions

Some of the main characteristics of the fuzzy systems are:

• Fuzzy concepts have to have linguistic meaning; they need to be articulated.

- Membership functions are numerical representations of the linguistic concepts; they can be built either through learning from data, or through experts' opinion, or through both.

- Fuzzy rules can represent vague, ambiguous or contradictory knowledge.

- Fuzzy systems are robust; even if some rules are removed from the rule map, the system could still work properly; fuzzy systems are also robust toward changing conditions in the environment.

- Fuzzy systems are simple to build, easy to realize, easy to explain.

These characteristics of fuzzy systems make them suitable for solving practically all the generic problems in knowledge-engineering.

3.14 Suggested Readings

Further reading recommended on specific topics are:

Theory of fuzzy sets and fuzzy logic—Zadeh (1984); Terano et al. (1992); Dubois and Prade (1988); Sugeno (1974); Kosko (1992, 1987); Mizumoto and Zimmermann (1982)

General fuzzy system applications—Yamakawa (1990, 1992, 1994); Terano et al. (1992); Yager and Zadeh (1992); Aptronix (1993)

Fuzzy systems for pattern recognition—Bezdek and Pal (1992)

Fuzzy systems for control—Sugeno (1985); Yamakawa (1989); Wang (1994); Aptronix Inc. (1994); Brown and Harris (1994)

Fuzzy systems for financial prediction and decision-making—Deboeck (1994); Zimmermann (1987)

Fuzzy information retrieval and fuzzy databases—Terano et al. (1992); Gupta and Sanches (1982); Ozawa and Yamada (1994); Zemankova-Leech and Kandel (1984); Bosc and Kacprzyk (1995)

Fuzzy systems for image analysis—Ralescu and Hartani (1995); Hirota (1984); Zahzah et al. (1992)

Hardware implementation of fuzzy systems; fuzzy chips—Yamakawa (1987, 1988, 1993); Lim and Takefuji (1990); Hirota (1995)

Fuzzy expert systems: Kandel (1991); TIL Shell (1993)

4 Neural Networks: Theoretical and Computational Models

Artificial neural networks realize the *subsymbolic* paradigm of representing and processing of information. The area of science that deals with methods and systems for information processing using neural networks is called *neurocomputation*. In this chapter, the basic principles of artificial neural networks are explained and illustrated. The chapter gives a background for going from neurons to models and systems, some of which are presented here from an engineering point of view. The material is meant to be sufficient for developing connectionist models and systems for problem-solving and knowledge-engineering, which is the topic of chapters 5, 6, and 7.

4.1   Real and Artificial Neurons

An *artificial neural network* (or simply a *neural network*) is a biologically inspired computational model which consists of processing elements (called neurons) and connections between them with coefficients (weights) bound to the connections, which constitute the neuronal structure, and training and recall algorithms attached to the structure. Neural networks are called *connectionist models* because of the main role of the connections in them. The connection weights are the "memory" of the system.

Even though neural networks have similarities to the human brain, they are not meant to model it. They are meant to be useful models for problem-solving and knowledge-engineering in a "humanlike" way. The human brain is much more complex and unfortunately, many of its cognitive functions are still not well known. But the more we learn about the human brain, the better computational models are developed and put to practical use. Therefore, it pays to have a look at the main characteristics of the human brain from the information-processing point of view and understand to what extent they have been realized in artificial neural networks.

This section emphasizes the main characteristics of real and artificial neural networks, namely:

- Learning and adaptation
- Generalization
- Massive parallelism
- Robustness

- Associative storage of information
- Spatiotemporal information processing

The next subsection is far from being a detailed and precise presentation of the organization and functions of the human brain. It is only a brief introduction to its main characteristics which nonbiologists might find useful for understanding artificial neural networks and some of the trends in their development. But the question, how much should an artificial computational model be biologically plausible in order to be useful for engineering, is beyond the scope of this chapter.

4.1.1 Biological Neurons

At least three levels can be distinguished in the human brain from the point of view of the information processing performed in it: (1) the *structural level*: neurons, regions of neurons, and the connections between them; (2) the *physiological level*: the way the brain processes information as chemical and physical reactions and transmission of substances; and (3) the *cognitive level*: the way humans think.

Three points are briefly discussed here: (1) the brain's structure and organization, (2) the brain as a communication system which is massively parallel and robust, and (3) the major information-processing functions and characteristics of the brain: learning, recall and generalization, associative storage, chaotic behavior.

Let us look at *brain organization* first. The human brain contains about 10^{11} neurons participating in perhaps 10^{15} interconnections over transmission paths. Each of these paths could be a meter long or more. Neurons share many characteristics with the other cells in the body, but they have unique capabilities for receiving, processing, and transmitting electrochemical signals over the neural pathways that make up the brain's communication system. Figure 4.1 shows the structure of a typical *biological neuron*. The neurons are composed of a *cellular body*, also called the *soma*, and its one or several branches. According to the traditional definition, the branches conducting information into a cell (*stimulus*) are called *dendrites*, and the branch that conducts information out of the cell (*reaction*) is called an *axon*. An activation of a neuron, called an *action potential*, is transmitted to other neurons through its axon at the first instance. A signal (*spike*) emitted from a neuron is characterized by *frequency*, *duration*, and *amplitude*.

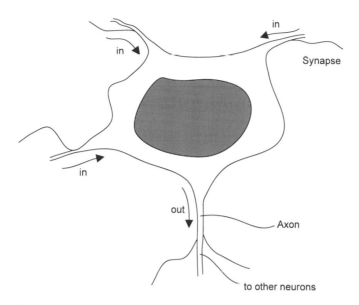

Figure 4.1
A structure of a typical biological neuron. It has many inputs (in) and one output (out). The connections between neurons are realized in the synapses.

The interaction between neurons takes place at strictly determined points of contact called *synapses*. In the region of the synapses, the neurons almost "touch" each other; however, there always remains a tiny cleft between them. In a synapse, two parts can be distinguished: (1) a *presynaptic membrane*, belonging to the transmitting neuron, and (2) a *postsynaptic membrane*, which belongs to the receiving neuron. An impulse emitted from a transmitting neuron and fed to a presynaptic part of a synapse induces a release of a *transmitter*. The transmitter carries a substance known as a *mediator*. As the transmitter passes across the cleft, it takes the mediator to the postsynaptic part. There, under its influence, the permeability of the membrane of the receiving neuron changes proportionally to the *algebraic sum* of the potentials received in all postsynaptic parts of this neuron. If the result surpasses a *threshold value* established beforehand, the neuron in its turn takes on the function of transmitting an action potential. The electric potential on the two sides of the membrane is called the *membrane potential*. The membrane potential is formed by the diffusion of electrically charged particles. All cells contain a solution rich in potassium salts. At rest, the cellular membrane is 50 to 100 times more permeable to K^+ ions than to Na^+ ions. Chloride ions (Cl^-) are also of great importance in the process of information processing in the brain. The structure of the membrane is such that its permeability to ions changes under the influence of the mediators. When the postsynaptic part of the synapse receives mediators, the membrane potential shifts toward a positive end, because now the membrane is more permeable to Na^+ than to K^+, and there is more of it outside rather than inside the neuron. In other words, the action potential represents a change of the membrane potential in a positive direction. In general, an activation of a neuron is proportional to the difference between its current potential and the resting potential.

The brain consists of different types of neurons. They differ in shape (pyramidal, granular, basket, etc.) and in their specialized functions. There is a correlation between the function of a cell and its shape; for example, pyramidal cells are excitatory and basket cells are inhibitory. In terms of variety, over 50 kinds of functionally different neurons are found in the cerebellum (one of the major parts of the brain). This fact may influence the creation of heterogeneous neuronal computational models which consist of different types of specialized artificial neurons.

The human brain is a complicated communication system. This system transmits messages as electric impulses, which seem always the same, recurring in monotonous succession. A single nerve impulse carries very little information; therefore, processing of complex information is only possible by the interaction of groups of many neurons and nerve fibers, which are enormous in number and size. The total length of all neural branchings inside the human body comes to about 10^{14} m. The presence of such a high number of links determines a high level of *massive parallelism*, which is specific to the brain mechanisms. Indeed, while each neuron reacts to outside *stimuli* relatively slowly (the reaction of a neuron takes about 200 ms), the human brain as a whole is capable of solving complex problems in a comparatively short time—parts of a second or several seconds.

The brain's ability to analyze complex problems and to react adequately to unfamiliar situations is due to its heuristic faculty of taking decisions on the basis of previously stored knowledge and its ability to adapt to new situations. The human brain has the ability to *learn* and to *generalize*. The information we accumulate as a result of our learning is stored in the *synapses* in the form of concentrated chemical substances.

The brain receives information through its receptors which are connected by dendrites to neurons of the respective part of the cortex (the part of the brain which receives signals from the human sensors). So two of the major processes which occur in the brain from the information-processing point of view are learning and recall (generalization).

Learning is achieved in the brain through the process of chemical change in synaptic connections. There is a hypothesis which says that the synaptic connections are set genetically in natal life and subsequent development (learning) is due to interactions between the external environment and the genetic program during postnatal life. Synapses either stabilize or degenerate. The learning process in the brain is a complex mixture of innate constraints and acquired experience. But learning is not only a process of "filtering" sensory inputs. "Brains actively seek sensory stimuli as raw material from which to create perceptual patterns and replace stimulus-induced activity" (Freeman and Skarda 1985). Brains are goal seekers. A brain activity pattern is a drive toward a goal (Freeman 1991). The activity patterns are *spatial* and *temporal* and large patterns of activity are self-organized.

The *recall process* activates a collection of neurons in time. Some experimental results on the hippocampus (a major part of the brain) of rats show that the mean activity of all 330,000 neurons upon a given stimulus is 0.001, that is, only 330 neurons on average are activated at one time. The distribution of the activated neurons over the time scale is not random. Neurons activate one another locally as the neurons are mainly connected on a neighboring basis (the probability of two neurons being connected decreases exponentially with the distance between them). The connectivity for the CA3 region of the hippocampus in the human brain is about 4% (Rolls and Treves 1993) and every neuron produces from zero to 50 spikes per second depending on its state of activity.

The recall process in the brain is characterized by *generalization*, that is, similar stimuli recall similar patterns of activity. The brain can react to an unseen stimulus in the "best" possible way according to previously learned patterns. The "distance" between a learned pattern and a newly recalled pattern defines the level of generalization.

The human brain stores patterns of information in an associative mode, that is, as an associative memory. *Associative memory* is characterized in general by its ability to store patterns, to recall these patterns when only parts of them are given as inputs, for example, part of a face we have seen before, or the tail of a rat. The patterns can be corrupted, for example, an airplane in foggy weather. It has been proved experimentally (Rolls and Treves 1993) that part of a region of the human brain called CA3 works as an associative storage and another part (which consists of "mossy" fiber connections) is nonassociative. The number of patterns which can be associatively stored can be calculated by the use of the formula

$$P\max = c \cdot k/(a \cdot \ln(1/a)),$$

where a is the coefficient representing the *sparseness* of the connections between the neurons, c is the number of connections which connect one neuron to another, and k is a constant whose typical value is 0.2 to 0.3. It has been estimated that at any given moment about 36,000 patterns can be stored in the CA3 region, but not all of them are "lifetime" patterns. Patterns evolve for a certain period of time and have a certain spatial structure, that is, the memorized patterns are *spatiotemporal patterns*.

The question of how information is stored in the brain relates to the dilemma of *local vs. distributed representation*. There is biological evidence that the brain contains parts, areas, and even single neurons that react to specific stimuli or are responsible for particular functions. A neuron, or group of neurons, which represent a certain concept in the brain, is referred to as a *grandmother cell*. At the same time, there is evidence that the activity of the brain is a collective activity of many neurons working together toward particular patterns, features, functions, tasks, and goals.

Study of the olfactory lobe gives evidence that the chaotic behavior of the brain is a global property (Freeman 1987). A *chaotic* process is, in general, not strictly repetitive. It does not repeat exactly the same patterns of behavior, but still certain similarities of patterns can be found over periods of time, not necessarily having the same duration. A chaotic process may be an oscillation between several states, called attractors, which oscillation is not strictly regular. A common oscillation in cortical potential over an entire array of neurons has been recorded (Rolls and Treves 1993). Elements of chaotic behavior in local neurons have also been seen. Chaos theory and its application to neural computing is discussed in chapter 7.

It is beyond the current level of existing knowledge and technology to simulate a human brain in a computer. Such a goal will be difficult to realize for many years to come, if ever, but useful computational models and systems can be developed based on the principles and characteristics

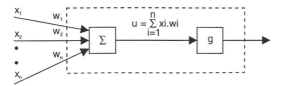

Figure 4.2
A model of an artificial neuron.

observed in the human brain. The collective efforts of neuroscientists, biologists, and physiologists, computer and information scientists, mathematicians, physicists, chemists, and others have led to new explanations of brain processes and new neuronal computational models that modify the existing ones. Some simple artificial neuronal models are discussed later in this chapter.

4.1.2 Artificial Neurons

The first mathematical model of a neuron was proposed by McCulloch and Pitts in 1943. It was a binary device using binary inputs, binary output, and a fixed activation threshold. In general, a model of an artificial neuron is based on the following parameters which describe a neuron (see figure 4.2):

• *Input connections* (or inputs): $x_1, x_2, \ldots, x_n$. There are weights bound to the input connections: $w_1, w_2, \ldots, w_n$; one input to the neuron, called a *bias*, has a constant value of 1 and is usually represented as a separate input, say x_0, but for simplicity it is treated here just as an input, clamped to a constant value.

• *Input function f*, calculates the aggregated *net input signal* to the neuron $u = f(\mathbf{x}, \mathbf{w})$, where $\mathbf{x}$ and $\mathbf{w}$ are the input and weight vectors correspondingly; f is usually the summation function: $u = \sum_{i=1,n} x_i \cdot w_i$.

• *An activation (signal)* function s calculates the activation level of the neuron $a = s(u)$.

• *An output function* calculates the output signal value emitted through the output (the axon) of the neuron: $o = g(a)$; the output signal is usually assumed to be equal to the activation level of the neuron, that is, $o = a$.

According to the type of values which each of the above parameters can take, different types of neurons have been used so far. The input and

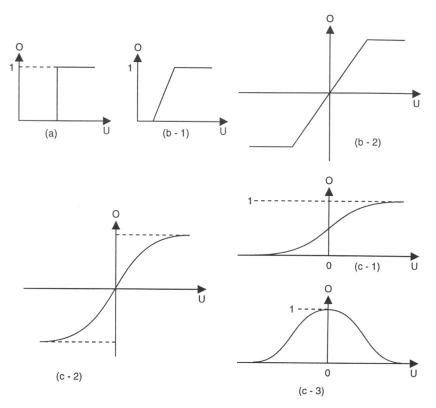

Figure 4.3

The most used activation functions: (a) hard-limited threshold; (b) linear threshold: if the input is above a certain threshold, the output becomes saturated (to a value of 1); there are different variants of this function depending on the range of the neuronal output values shown in (b-1) and (b-2); (c) sigmoid function: logistic function (c-1); bipolar logistic function (c-2); (c-3) gaussian (bell shape) function.

output values of a neuron can be binary, $\{0, 1\}$; bivalent, $\{-1, 1\}$; continuous, $[0, 1]$; or discrete numbers in a defined interval.

The most used activation functions are shown in figure 4.3. They are:

1. *The hard-limited threshold function.* If net input value u to the neuron is above a certain threshold, the neuron becomes active (activation value of 1); otherwise it stays inactive (activation value of 0) (figure 4.3[a]).

2. *The linear threshold function.* The activation value increases linearly with the increase of the net input signal u, but after a certain threshold, the

output becomes saturated (to a value of 1, say); there are different variants of this function depending on the range of neuronal output values (figure 4.3[b-1] and [b-2]).

3. *The sigmoid function.* This is any S-shaped nonlinear transformation function $g(u)$ that is characterized by the following:

a. Bounded, that is, its values are restricted between two boundaries, for example, $[0, 1]$, $[-1, 1]$.

b. Monotonically increasing, that is, the value $g(u)$ never decreases when u increases.

c. Continuous and smooth, therefore differentiable everywhere in its domain. Different types of sigmoid functions have been used in practice. Most of them are The *logistic function*: $a = 1/(1 + e^{-u})$, where e is a constant, the base of natural logarithm (e, sometimes written as *exp*, is actually the limit of the n-square of $(1 + 1/n)$ when n approaches infinity) (figure 4.3[c-1]). In a more general form, the logistic function can be written as:

$a = 1/(1 + e^{-c \cdot u})$, where c is a constant.

The reason why the logistic function has been used as a neuronal activation function is that many algorithms for performing learning in neural networks use the derivative of the activation function, and the logistic function has a simple derivative, $\partial g/\partial u = a(1 - a)$. Alternatives to the logistic function as *S*-functions are the *bipolar logistic*: $h(u) = (1 - e^{-u})/(1 + e^{-u}) = 2 \cdot g(u) - 1$; this function has a range of $[-1, 1]$ (figure 4.3 [c-2]) and *hyperbolic tangent*: $\tanh(u) = (e^u - e^{-u})/(e^u + e^{-u})$.

4. *Gaussian (bell shape) function* (figure 4.3[c-3]).

An output signal from a neuron can be represented by a single static potential, or by a pulse, which either occurs (coded as 1) or does not occur (coded as 0) (see figure 4.4).

In addition to the types of the neurons described above, many other types have been developed and used: the RAM-based neuron, fuzzy neuron, oscillatory neuron, chaotic neuron, and wavelet neuron. They are presented later in this book. Which one is the most biologically plausible is difficult to say, but all of them have proved to be very useful for building artificial neural networks for engineering applications. We shall use the types of neurons described above later in the book, except when another type is explicitly defined.

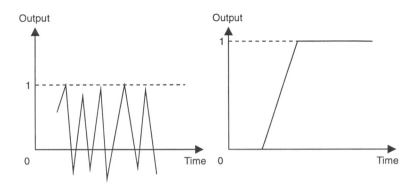

Figure 4.4
Pulse and potential encoding of an output signal of a neuron.

4.1.3   From Neurons to Systems; What Is Learning and What Is Generalization in Artificial Neural Networks?

Although a single neuron can perform certain simple information-processing functions, the power of neural computation comes from connecting neurons in networks. Developments in this area have been exciting, with periods of success and failure, promises and expectations, and periods of rapid development.

One way to understand the ideas behind the process of developing more and more complex artificial neural networks as computational models that comprise small processing elements (neurons) is to look at the history of this process.

Donald Hebb, in his psychological study published in 1949, pointed out the importance of the connections between synapses to the process of learning. Rosenblatt (1958) described the first operational model of a neural network, putting together the ideas of Hebb, McCulloch, and Pitts. His perceptron was inspired by studies of the visual system. In 1969 Minsky and Papert demonstrated the theoretical limits of the perceptron. Many researchers then abandoned neural networks and started to develop symbolic AI methods and systems. New connectionist models, among them the associative memories (Amari 1977; Hopfield 1982), the multilayer perceptron and backpropagation learning algorithm (Rumelhart et al. 1986b; see also Werbos, 1990; and Amari 1967), the adaptive resonance theory (ART) (Carpenter and Grossberg 1987a,b), self-organizing networks (Kohonen 1982), and others, were developed later, which brought

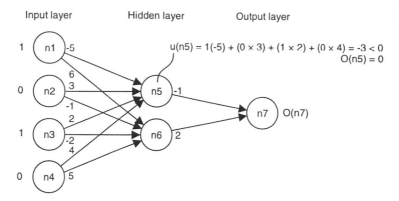

Figure 4.5
A simple neural network with four input nodes, two intermediate nodes, and one output node. The connection weights are shown, presumably a result of training. The activation value of node *n5* is shown too.

researchers back to the subsymbolic paradigm. Now, many more types of neural networks have been designed and used. The bidirectional associative memory (Kosko 1988), radial basis functions (Moody and Parken 1989), probabilistic RAM neural networks (Taylor and Mannion 1989; Aleksander, 1989), fuzzy neurons and fuzzy neural networks (Yamakawa 1990; Furuhashi et al. 1993), and oscillatory neurons and oscillatory neural networks (Freeman 1991; Kaneko 1990; Borisyuk, 1991), are only a small number of the neural network models developed, not to mention their enormous areas of application.

An *artificial neural network* (or simply *neural network*) is a computational model defined by four parameters:

1. *Type of neurons* (also called *nodes*, as a neural network resembles a graph)

2. *Connectionist architecture*—the organization of the connections between neurons

3. *Learning algorithm*

4. *Recall algorithm*

A simple neural network is shown in figure 4.5. It contains four input nodes, two intermediate, and one output node. The weights bound to the connections are achieved as a result of a training procedure with the use of a learning (training) algorithm. A new example, for example, (1 0 1 0), will drive the network to an output signal 1 when a threshold activation function is used with a threshold value of 0.

The functioning of a neural network, when an input vector $\mathbf{x}$ is supplied, can be viewed as a *mapping function F*: $X \rightarrow Y$, where X is the input state space (domain) and Y is the output state space (range) of the network. The network simply maps input vectors $\mathbf{x} \in X$ into output vectors $\mathbf{y} \in Y$ through the "filter" of the weights, that is, $\mathbf{y} = F(\mathbf{x}) = s(W, \mathbf{x})$, where W is the connection weight matrix. The functioning of a network is usually based on vector-matrix real-number calculations. The weight matrix represents the "knowledge", the *long-term memory*, of the system, while the activation of the neurons represents the current state, the *short-term memory*.

Types of artificial neurons were discussed in the previous subsection, but the type of connections between neurons in a neural network defines its topology. Neurons in a neural network can be *fully connected*, that is, every neuron is connected to every other one, or *partially connected*, for example, only connections between neurons in different *layers* are allowed, or in general not all the possible connections between all the neurons of the neural network are present.

Two major connectionist architectures can be distinguished according to the number of input and output sets of neurons and the layers of neurons used (see figure 4.6): (1) *autoassociative*, that is, input neurons are

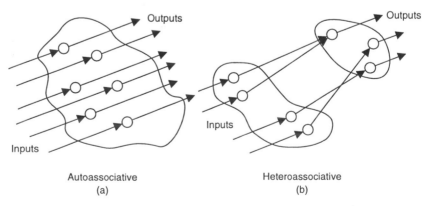

Autoassociative
(a)

Heteroassociative
(b)

Figure 4.6
Autoassociative and heteroassociative types of neural networks.

the output neurons too; the Hopfield network is an autoassociative type of network; and (2) *heteroassociative*, that is, there are separate sets of input neurons and output neurons; examples are the perceptron and the multilayer perceptron (MLP), the Kohonen network, etc.

According to the absence or presence of feedback connections in a network, two types of architectures are distinguished:

1. *Feedforward architecture.* There are no connections back from the output to the input neurons; the network does not keep a memory of its previous output values and the activation states of its neurons; the perceptron-like networks are feedforward types.

2. *Feedback architecture.* There are connections from output to input neurons; such a network keeps a memory of its previous states, and the next state depends not only on the input signals but on the previous states of the network; the Hopfield network is of this type.

The most attractive characteristic of neural networks is their ability to learn. Learning makes possible modification of behavior in response to the environment. A neural network is trained so that application of a set X of input vectors produces the desired (or at least a consistent) set of output vectors Y, or the network learns about internal characteristics and structures of data from a set X. The set X used for training a network is called a *training set*. The elements $\mathbf{x}$ of this set X are called *training examples*. The training process is reflected in changing the connection weights of the network. During training, the network weights should gradually converge to values such that each input vector $\mathbf{x}$ from the set training data causes a desired output vector $\mathbf{y}$ produced by the network. Learning occurs if after supplying a training example, a change in at least one synaptic weight takes place.

The learning ability of a neural network is achieved through applying a *learning (training) algorithm*. Training algorithms are mainly classified into three groups:

1. *Supervised.* The training examples comprise input vectors $\mathbf{x}$ and the desired output vectors $\mathbf{y}$. Training is performed until the neural network "learns" to associate each input vector $\mathbf{x}$ to its corresponding and desired output vector $\mathbf{y}$; for example, a neural network can learn to *approximate a function* $y = f(\mathbf{x})$ represented by a set of training examples $(\mathbf{x}, y)$. It encodes the examples in its internal structure.

2. *Unsupervised*. Only input vectors **x** are supplied; the neural network learns some internal features of the whole set of all the input vectors presented to it.

3. *Reinforcement learning*, sometimes called *reward-penalty learning*, is a combination of the above two paradigms; it is based on presenting input vector **x** to a neural network and looking at the output vector calculated by the network. If it is considered "good," then a "reward" is given to the network in the sense that the existing connection weights are increased; otherwise the network is "punished," the connection weights, being considered as "not appropriately set," decrease. Thus reinforcement learning is *learning with a critic*, as opposed to *learning with a teacher*.

Learning is not an individual ability of a single neuron. It is a collective process of the whole neural network and a result of a training procedure. The connection weight matrix W has its meaning as a global pattern. It represents "knowledge" in its entirety. We do not know exactly how learning is achieved in the human brain. But learning (supervised or unsupervised) can be achieved in an artificial neural network. And there are some *genetic laws* of learning which have been discovered and implemented.

The most favored learning law in contemporary connectionist models is the *Hebbian learning law*. The idea of this generic learning principle is that a synapse connecting two neurons i and j increases its strength w_{ij} if the two neurons i and j are repeatedly *simultaneously activated* by input stimuli. The synaptic weight change Δw_{ij} is then calculated as a function of the product of the two activation values a_i and a_j of the neurons i and j:

$$\Delta w_{ij} = c \cdot a_i \cdot a_j$$

Other laws of learning are discussed in the following sections. Some learning methods include *forgetting*. This is the case when, for example, calculating the aggregation input signal u_i to a neuron i coming from neurons j ($j = 1, 2, \ldots, n$), connected to the neuron i, is done by using the so-called additive model:

$$u_i(t + 1) = -d_i \cdot u_i(t) + \sum o_j(t) \cdot w_{ji} + I_i(t + 1),$$

where u_i is the aggregated (net) input signal to the ith neuron; o_j is the output signal of the jth neuron connected to the ith; t and $(t + 1)$ are discrete time intervals; I_i is an external input signal to the ith neuron; and d_i is a decay coefficient. The decay coefficient represents the process of forgetting.

When a forgetting ingredient is included in the Hebbian learning law, it becomes the following:

$$w_{ij}(t + 1) = -d \cdot w_{ij}(t) + c \cdot a_i \cdot a_j$$

Other *learning-with-forgetting* formulas for calculating weight changes during learning have been developed, for example:

$$\Delta w'_{ij}(t) = \Delta w_{ij}(t) - a \cdot \text{sgn}\{w_{ij}(t)\},$$

where a is a small "forgetting" coefficient, and $\text{sgn}\{w_{ij}(t)\}$ is the sign of the weight. Learning with forgetting causes the unnecessary connections to fade away and a skeleton network to emerge after learning, which may result in better generalization (Ishikawa 1995).

The general process of learning in a neural network is described by a characteristic called *convergence*. The network reacts better and better to the same training example **x**, the more it is introduced to it through training, eventually ending up with the desired output **y**. After the network has stopped learning the training examples, the synaptic weights do not change any more, that is, $\Delta w_{ij} = 0$, for every connection (i, j) in the network when training examples from the training set are further presented. The network can stop learning for two reasons: (1) the network has learned the training examples, and (2) the network has become saturated. *Grossbergs saturation theorem* states that large input signals saturate a neuron when it is sensitive to small input signals, but if it is sensitive to large input signals, small signals are ignored as noise.

Small random values introduced as *noise* during a learning process tend to increase the robustness of the performance of the neural network. In this case the Hebbian learning law will take the form of:

$$\Delta w_{ij} = c \cdot a_i \cdot a_j + n,$$

where n is a noise signal.

When noise is presented during learning, the neural network reaches a convergence when weights change within the magnitude of the noise (*stochastic equilibrium*):

$$\Delta w_{ij} \leq n$$

The state of convergence may also be reached in a so-called oscillatory mode, that is, the synaptic weights oscillate between two or more states.

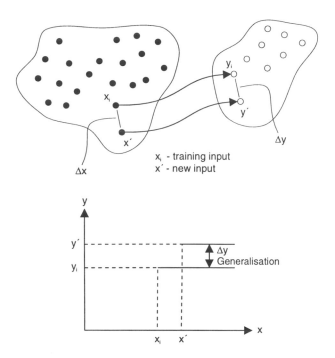

Figure 4.7
The generalization principle illustrated as a mapping of the domain to the solution space for a new input x'. The figure below illustrates the case for one-dimensional domain space and one-dimensional solution space.

The other general characteristic of artificial neural networks, similar to the ability of the human brain, is *generalization*. This happens when, after having trained a neural network, a new input vector $\mathbf{x}'$ is presented to the network and a *recall procedure* is activated. The network would produce an output $\mathbf{y}'$ which is similar to the output $\mathbf{y}_i$ from the training examples, if $\mathbf{x}'$ is similar to the input vector $\mathbf{x}_i$. The general principle is that *similar stimuli cause similar reactions*. Figure 4.7 shows graphically how a neural network generalizes to a new input. Generalization may take several iterations of calculating consecutive states of the network, which is the case for the recurrent networks. Eventually, the network goes into a state of *equilibrium*, when the network does not change its state during the next iterations, that is, it "freezes" into this state. This phenomenon is seen in the Hopfield network. It is analogous to the process of trying to associate a face with one seen in the past, in order to remember where we have seen the person who said "hello" to us at a party.

4.2   Supervised Learning in Neural Networks: Perceptrons and Multilayer Perceptrons

Learning is a major functional characteristic of artificial neural networks. We shall start discussing different ways of implementing learning in neural networks by introducing the most popular and simple learning method—supervised learning—when the data set for training contains information for the desired results (outputs, class labels, reaction) in the same way we have been given explicit answers by our teachers.

4.2.1   Supervised Learning in Neural Networks

Supervised learning is a process of approximating a set of "labeled" data, that is, each datum (which is a data point in the input-output problem space) contains values for attributes (features, independent variables) labeled by the desired value(s) for the dependant variables, for example, the set of Iris examples, each labeled by the class label.

Supervised learning can be viewed as approximating a mapping between a domain and a solution space of a problem: $X \to Y$, when samples (examples) of (input vector, output vector) pairs $(\mathbf{x}, \mathbf{y})$ are known, $\mathbf{x} \in X$, $\mathbf{y} \in Y$, $\mathbf{x} = (x_1, x_2, \ldots, x_n)$, $\mathbf{y} = (y_1, y_2, \ldots, y_m)$. How to achieve an approximation F' of labeled data by using a neural network such that it can generalize on new inputs $\mathbf{x}$ is the problem supervised learning is concerned with. Supervised learning in neural networks is usually performed in the following sequence:

1. Set an appropriate structure of a neural network, having, for example, $(n + 1)$ input neurons (n for the input variables and 1 for the bias, x_0) and m output neurons and set initial values of the connection weights of the network.

2. Supply an input vector $\mathbf{x}$ from the set of the training examples X to the network.

3. Calculate the output vector $\mathbf{o}$ as produced by the neural network.

4. Compare the desired output vector $\mathbf{y}$ (answer, from the training data) and the output vector $\mathbf{o}$ produced by the network; if possible, evaluate the error.

5. Correct the connection weights in such a way that the next time $\mathbf{x}$ is presented to the network, the produced output $\mathbf{o}$ becomes closer to the desired output $\mathbf{y}$.

6. If necessary, repeat steps 2 to 5 until the network reaches a convergence state.

Evaluating an error of approximation can be done in many ways, the most used being *instantaneous error*:

$Err = (\mathbf{o} - \mathbf{y})$, or $Err = |\mathbf{o} - \mathbf{y}|$;

mean-square error (*MSE*):

$Err = (\mathbf{o} - \mathbf{y})^2/2$;

a total MSE sums the error over all individual examples and all the output neurons in the network:

$$Err = \left(\sum_{k=1}^{p} \sum_{j=1}^{m} (o_j^{(k)} - y_j^{(k)})^2 \right) \Big/ p \cdot m$$

where: $o_j^{(k)}$ is the output value of the jth output of the network when the kth training example is presented; $y_j^{(k)}$ is the desired result (the desired output) for the jth output (jth independent variable) for the kth training example; p is the number of training examples in the training data; and m is the dimension of the output space (the number of independent variables equal to the number of the output neurons in the neural network); and *root-mean-square error* (*RMS*), the root of the MSE.

Depending on how an error is calculated, two types of error can be evaluated for a neural network. The first, called *apparent error*, estimates how well a trained network approximates the training examples. The second, called *test error*, estimates how good a trained network can generalize, that is, react to new input vectors. For evaluating a test error we obviously have to know the desired results for the test examples.

Supervised learning is a very useful learning paradigm for solving problems like classification, or for learning a certain prescribed behavior, when the classes, labels, or desired behavior patterns are known. Supervised learning can be used for learning "microrules" of stimulus-reaction type, element-class type, source-destination type, etc.

The above general algorithm for supervised learning in a neural network has different implementations, mainly distinguished by the way the connection weights are changed through training. Some of the algorithms are discussed in this section—perceptron learning (Rosenblatt 1958); ADALINE (Widrow and Hoff 1960); the backpropagation algorithm

(Rumelhart et al. 1986b; and others); and (learning vector quantization) LVQ1,2,3 algorithms (Kohonen 1990).

Supervised learning uses as much of the information and knowledge as given in the data, but it is considered by many authors not to be plausible at a low, synaptic level. It is obviously plausible at a psychological level because people do learn by being supervised in one way or another, as well as through their own experience (which sometimes can be painful).

4.2.2 The Perceptron

One of the first models which made use of the McCulloch and Pitts (1943) model of a neuron was a neural network called the *perceptron* (Rosenblatt 1958). The aim of the experiment was to model visual perception phenomena. The neurons used in the perceptron have a simple summation input function and a hard-limited threshold activation function or linear threshold activation function. The input values are in general real numbers and the outputs are binary.

The connection structure of the perceptron is feedforward and three-layered. The first layer is a buffer, where sensory data are stored. The elements of the first layer are connected either fully or arbitrarily to elements of a second layer, called the "feature layer." Each neuron from this layer combines information coming from different sensory elements and represents a possible feature. The neurons from this layer are connected fully to output neurons from an output layer called the "perceptron layer." The weights between the buffer and the feature layer are fixed; that is why usually only the two layers are presented graphically. This is also the reason why perceptrons are sometimes called "single-layer networks." Figure 4.8 is an illustration of a simple perceptron with two elements in the feature layer and one perceptron element in the output layer. The bias (x_0) is also shown.

A learning (training) algorithm for a perceptron is given in figure 4.9. A perceptron learns only when it misclassifies an input vector from the training examples. Then it changes the weights in such a way that if the desired output value is 1 and the value produced by the network is 0, the weights of this output neuron increase and vice versa. If the produced output value $o_j^{(k)}$ equals the desired output value $y_j^{(k)}$ for a training example $(\mathbf{x}, \mathbf{y})^{(k)}$, then the weights w_{ij} (for $i = 0, 1, \ldots, n$) do not change.

Widrow and Hoff (1960) proposed another formula for calculating the output error during training: $Err_j = y_j - \sum w_{ij} x_i$. This learning rule was used in a neural machine called ADALINE (*ada*ptive *linea*r neuron).

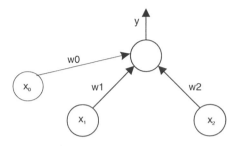

Figure 4.8
A simple two-input, one-output perceptron and a bias.

P1.   Set a (n+1)-input, m-output perceptron. Randomize all network weights w_{ij}, i=0,1,2,..n, j=1,2,...,m, to small numbers.

P2.   Apply an input feature vector x and calculate the net input signal u_j to each output perceptron neuron j using the standard formula:
$u_j = \Sigma (x_i . w_{ij})$, for i = 0,1,2,...,n, for j = 1,2,...,m, where x_0=1 is the bias.

P3.   Apply a hard-limited threshold activation function to the net input signals as follows:
$o_j = 1$ if $u_j >$ threshold, oj = 0 otherwise,
(Applying linear thresholding function is also possible).

P4.   Compute the error for each neuron by subtracting the actual output from the target output: $Err_j = y_j - o_j$

P5.   Modify each weight w_{ij} by calculating its next value $w_{ij}(t+1)$ from the previous one $w_{ij}(t)$ and from the evaluated error Err_j:
$w_{ij}(t+1) = w_{ij}(t) + \alpha x_i . Err_j$,
where: α is a learning coefficient - a number between 0 and 1;

P6.   Repeat steps P2 through P5 until the error vector Err is sufficiently low, i.e. the perceptron goes into a convergence.

Figure 4.9
The learning algorithm for a perceptron neural network. The perceptron learns when it misclassifies a training example.

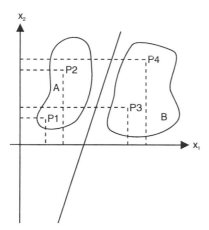

Figure 4.10
Linearly separable classes A and B represented by two points each in a two-dimensional
space (x_1, x_2). Such classes can be learned by a perceptron network.

The recall procedure of the perceptron simply calculates the outputs for
a given input vector using the summation thresholding formulas given in
figure 4.9.

An example of using a perceptron for recognizing points on the two-
dimensional plane (x_1, x_2) where two possible areas (classes) A and B are
distinguished is given in figure 4.10. If there are sufficient examples the
perceptron can learn to approximate the training examples and converge
after a number of training cycles (epochs). It will correctly recognize a new
input vector whether it lies in the class B or class A area.

Minsky and Papert (1969) discovered a very severe limitation of perceptrons, that is, they can be trained to recognize only *linearly separable
classes*. Examples of classes which are linearly separable lie on one side
only of a hyperplane that separates the classes. If the input space is two-
dimensional, the hyperplane degenerates into a line. Considering a two-
input, one-output perceptron, the line that separates the two classes is
analytically represented by the following equation:

$$x_1 \cdot w_1 + x_2 \cdot w_2 + w_0 = 0,$$

where w_0 is the weight that connects the bias to the output neuron. If the
examples are not linearly separable, the perceptron fails to converge. A
classic example of a classification problem with nonlinearly separable

classes is the *exclusive OR problem* (also known as the *XOR problem*) presented in the following table:

(Point)	$x1$	$x2$	y	(Class)
$p1$	0	0	0	A
$p2$	1	0	1	B
$p3$	0	1	1	B
$p4$	1	1	0	A

A more general example, which the perceptron cannot solve, is the parity function given in the following table, where $n = 3$:

$x1$	$x2$	$x3$	f
0	0	0	1
0	0	1	0
0	1	0	0
0	1	1	1
1	0	0	0
1	0	1	1
1	1	0	1
1	1	1	0

Perceptrons are still used for solving problems because of their very simple architecture and the unconditional convergence when linearly separable classes are considered. They are excellent linear discriminators.

A perceptron with a nonlinear logistic activation function can learn a logistic linear regression function from data, that is, $f = g(\sum w_{ij} x_i + x_0)$. This function does not account for interactions between the independent variables x_i, but is useful for statistical analysis of data. Interaction between the input variables can be learned in multilayer perceptrons (MLP), thus showing what the degree of interaction is between the variables and how important it is for approximating the goal function.

4.2.3   Multilayer Perceptrons and the Backpropagation Algorithm

To overcome the linear separability limitation of the perceptrons, MLPs were introduced. An MLP consists of an input layer, at least one interme-

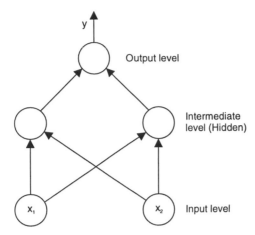

Figure 4.11
An MLP for solving the XOR problem. It has one intermediate layer.

diate or "hidden" layer, and one output layer, the neurons from each layer being fully connected (in some particular applications, partially connected) to the neurons from the next layer. An example of a multilayered network for solving the XOR problem is given in figure 4.11.

The MLPs were put into practice only when learning algorithms were developed for them, one of them being the so-called *backpropagation algorithm* (Werbos 1990; Rumelhart et al. 1986b; among others). The full name of the algorithm is the *error backpropagation algorithm*.

The neurons in the MLP have continuous value inputs and outputs, summation input function, and nonlinear activation function. A *gradient descent rule* may be used for finding optimal connection weights w_{ij} which minimize a global error E. A change of a weight Δw_{ij} at a cycle $(t + 1)$ is in the direction of the negative gradient of the error E:

$$\Delta w_{ij}(t + 1) = -lrate\ (\partial E/\partial w_{ij}(t)),$$

where *lrate* is *learning rate*. The gradient rule ensures that after a number of cycles, the error E will reach a minimum value, or the lowest "plateau," if the error E is represented as a surface in the weights' vector space. A global error for all the training examples can be calculated as follows:

$$E = \sum_{(p)} \sum_{(j)} Err_j^{(p)},$$

where the error for an example (p) $Err_j^{(p)}$ can be calculated, for example, as an MSE: $Err_j(p) = (y_j^{(p)} - o_j^{(p)})^2/2$.

Amari, in 1967, suggested that a gradient descent algorithm can be used for training MLP, but propagating the error backward and adjusting the connection weights was suggested later.

The gradient descent rule for changing a connection weight between neuron i and neuron j can be expressed by the *delta rule*:

$$\Delta w_{ij}(t + 1) = l_{rate} \cdot Err_j \cdot o_i,$$

or alternatively by the *generalized delta rule*:

$$\Delta w_{ij}(t + 1) = lrate \cdot Err_j \cdot g'(u_j) \cdot o_i,$$

where Err_j is the error between the desired output value y_j and the value o_j produced by the neuron j which can be simply expressed as $Err_j = |y_j - o_j|$. The value $g'(u_j)$ is the derivative $\partial g/\partial u$ of the activation function g to the net input u, for a particular value of u_j; and o_i is the output value for the neuron i. When the activation function g is the logistic function, the derivative $g'(u_j)$ is expressed as $o_j \cdot (1 - o_j)$. The formula above is simplified as follows:

$$\Delta w_{ij}(t + 1) = lrate \cdot Err_j \cdot o_j \cdot (1 - o_j) \cdot o_i,$$

At every learning cycle (a cycle, also called iteration or epoch, can be defined as the process of propagating through the network one or several of the training examples and calculating the error E for them) the training algorithm consists of two passes: (1) a *forward pass*, when inputs are supplied and propagated through the intermediate layers to the output layer; and (2) a *backward pass*, when an error is calculated at the outputs and propagated backward for calculating the weights' changes. This is the major feature of this algorithm illustrated in figure 4.12. During the backward pass, an error Err_i for an intermediate node i is calculated by multiplying the errors Err_j of all the neurons j to which the neuron i is connected by the corresponding weights w_{ij}. This error is then used backward to adjust the weights of the neurons k from a previous layer, connected to the neuron i. The training procedure is repeated for many epochs with the same training examples until the global error E is sufficiently small.

Calculating the error and changing the connection weights can be done either in a batch mode (an aggregating or average error is calculated for all or some training examples), or in an individual mode (the error is calculated and weights are changed after every training example).

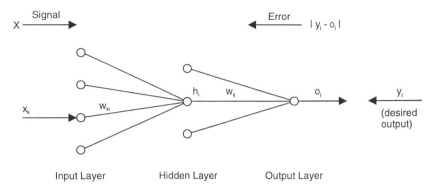

Figure 4.12
A schematic representation of learning in an MLP. The signal is propagated forward and the error backward.

Each connection weight might have its individual learning rate (*delta-bar-delta rule*) (Jacobs 1988). If the weight changes alternate in sign the learning rate should be decreased. If the weight change is stable, the learning rate should increase. Several problems are encountered when using the backpropagation algorithm:

• If the *learning rate* (also denoted in many references by η) is chosen too high (e.g., 0.9) the weights oscillate with a large amplitude; a small learning rate causes a very slow convergence. It has been found that the optimal learning rate is inversely proportional to the number of hidden nodes. In Eaton and Oliver (1992) the following formula for calculating the learning rate has been suggested:

$$\eta = 1.5/(sqrt(\sum p_i^2)),$$

where p_i is the number of all the instances which belong to an output class *i*. One way to accelerate learning when η is chosen small and to prevent oscillation of weights when η is big is to introduce a parameter called *momentum* (also denoted in the literature by α). This parameter brings inertia to the next change $\Delta w_{ij}(t + 1)$ of the weight w_{ij} depending on the direction of its previous change $\Delta w_{ij}(t)$. A modified backpropagation algorithm which uses *momentum* α is given in figure 4.13. The formula used for calculating weight changes is:

$$\Delta w_{ij}(t + 1) = lrate \cdot Err_j \cdot o_j \cdot (1 - o_j) \cdot o_i + \alpha \cdot \Delta w_{ij}(t)$$

Forward pass:

BF1.   Apply an input vector **x** and its corresponding output vector **y** (the desired output).

BF2.   Propagate forward the input signals through all the neurons in all the layers and calculate the output signals.

BF3.   Calculate the Err_j for every output neuron j as for example:
$Err_j = y_j - o_j$, where y_j is the jth element of the desired output vector **y**.

Backward pass:

BB1.   Adjust the weights between the intermediate neurons i and output neurons j according to the calculated error:
$\Delta w_{ij}(t+1) = \text{lrate}. \, o_j(1 - o_j). \, Err_j. \, o_i + \text{momentum}. \, \Delta w_{ij}(t)$

BB2.   Calculate the error Err_i for neurons i in the intermediate layer:
$Err_i = \sum Err_j. \, w_{ij}$

BB3.   Propagate the error back to the neurons k of lower level:
$\Delta w_{ki}(t+1) = \text{lrate}.o_i(1 - o_i). \, Err_i.x_k + \text{momentum}. \, \Delta w_{ki}(t)$

Figure 4.13
A modified backpropagation algorithm, where momentum is used.

· As discussed above, the backpropagation algorithm is a *gradient descent algorithm*. The problem with backpropagation, as with many other gradient descent algorithms, is that it can stop learning at a local minimum instead at the global minimum. This problem is called the *local minima problem*. In order to overcome this problem, some practical recommendations are suggested: randomize the initial weights with small numbers in an interval $[-1/n, 1/n]$, where n is the number of the neuronal inputs; use another formula for calculating the output error; introduce "noise."

Learning with the presence of noise may help overcome the local minima problem. Noise can be introduced in the training patterns, synaptic weights, and output values. In this case the error is calculated as:

$$Err_j = (y_j - (o_j + I_n))^2, \quad \text{or} \quad Err_j = (y_j - o_j)^2 + \sigma_n^2,$$

where σ_n is the variance of the external noise I_n.

· The backpropagation algorithm is very time-consuming. Various modifications to it try to improve its performance.

• Training with a backpropagation algorithm may result in a phenomenon called *overfitting*, or *overtraining*, as explained in 4.2.4.

• There are problems in choosing the optimal number of hidden layers
and hidden nodes (see section 4.2.5).

The backpropagation algorithm has many modifications and improvements, which are difficult to follow and present here. They differ in the
following points: error calculation, activation function, the weights updating formula, number of epochs for updating the weights, and other
parameters.

4.2.4 MLPs as Universal Approximators

Regardless of the training algorithm used for an MLP, there are some
common features of MLP architectures. Some of them are:

• MLPs are *universal approximators*.

THEOREM (Hornik et al. 1989; Cybenko 1989; Funahashi 1989; others).
An MLP with one hidden layer can approximate any continuous function
to any desired accuracy, subject to a sufficient number of hidden nodes.

The proof of this fundamental theorem is based on the *Kolmogorov theorem* (1957), which states that any real-valued continuous function f defined on an n-dimensional cube can be represented as a sum of functions
which have their arguments as sums of single-variable continuous functions. In a more precise form, it is as follows:

$$f(x_1, x_2, \ldots, x_n) = \sum_{k=1, 2n+1} g_k \left(\sum_{i=1, n} \eta_{k,i}(x_i) \right)$$

where: g_k and $\eta_{k,i}$ are continuous functions.

Thus, for any continuous function, there exists an MLP which can
approximate it to a desired degree of accuracy if the continuous increasing
functions are chosen to be, for example, the sigmoid functions. Unfortunately, this statement does not suggest how to construct the MLP, what
number of layers and neurons in the layers can be used. The theorem
supports the prove of the existence of such an MLP. As a corollary, any
boolean function of n boolean variables can be approximated by an MLP.

An easy proof can be shown by using 2^n hidden nodes, but the optimal number of these nodes is difficult to obtain.

Example   A 1-6-1 MLP can learn to approximate the sine function after being trained with enough data.

• *MLP are multivariate nonlinear regression models*. A three-layer MLP, for example, with n inputs, h intermediate nodes, and one output, approximates a set of training data according to the formula:

$$f = s\left(\sum_{i=1,h} o_i \cdot w_i + w_0\right),$$

where s is a sigmoid function; $o_i = s(\sum_{k=1,n} x_k \cdot w_{ki} + w_{0i})$ is the output value of the ith intermediate node; w_i and w_{ki} are the connection weights from the second and the first connection layers correspondingly; and w_0: are bias weights. This formula represents interactions between variables in contrast to the single-layer perceptron, which can be viewed as a linear regression model.

• *MLPs can learn conditional probabilities*. We shall consider here MLPs without feedback connections, or the so-called memoryless MLPs. Such MLPs can learn the conditional probability density function $p(\mathbf{y}|\mathbf{x})$ between the output vectors $\mathbf{y}$ when input vectors $\mathbf{x}$ are presented (see section 5.5.2).

4.2.5   Problems and Features of the MLPs

MLPs are probably the most used neural network models so far. However there are several problems when using them. Some of these problems, with their possible solutions, are presented below.

• The question of *how to choose the number of neurons* in the intermediate layer and the more general question, how to chose the structure of the MLP, are difficult. If the training data set is clustered in groups with similar features, the number of these groups can be used to chose the number of hidden neurons. In the other extreme case, when the training data are sparse and do not contain any common features, then the number of connections might need to be close to the number of training examples in order for the network to reach a convergence. There are many suggestions about how to choose the number h of the hidden neurons in an MLP. For example, the minimum number should be $h \geq (p-1)/(n+2)$, where p is the number of training examples and n is the number of inputs of the network. The more hidden nodes in a network, the more characteristics of the training data it will capture, but the more time-consuming the learning procedure will be.

Another heuristic for choosing the number of hidden nodes is that the number of hidden nodes is equal to the optimal number of fuzzy clusters (see chapter 3). This statement has been proved experimentally. Choosing the number of hidden layers is also a difficult task. Many problems require more than one hidden layer for a better solution.

In order to find the best neural network model, Ishikawa and Moriyama (1995) use structural learning with forgetting, so during training pruning of the connections with small weights is performed. After training, only the connections that contribute to the task are left, thus defining a skeleton of the neural network model.

• Neurons from an *intermediate level in an MLP capture relations* between the input data vectors. When solving the parity problem, for example, the activation of the intermediate neurons reflect the number of 1's in the input vector. The hidden neurons specialize during training to react to certain features in the training data, which features might not be known in advance. The intermediate layer learns and captures structures, clusters, "patches," and rules in the training data.

• *Catastrophic forgetting* is a phenomenon which represents the ability of a network to forget what it has learned from previous examples when they are no longer presented to it, but other examples are presented instead. This is due to a change in the weights according to the newly presented examples, if the past examples are no longer presented for training (or refreshing, retraining). In order to avoid this phenomenon, alternative training might be performed, that is, alternative training with new data and with old data. This is illustrated with an example of alternative training of a network with two sets of examples A and B (figure 4.14). When the network was started to be trained for a second time with the first set A, after being trained with A and then with set B, the initial error was higher than it was at the end of the first training cycle with A. There are methods for training with new data. For example, after several new examples are presented to the network, several old ones, chosen possibly randomly from the past examples, are presented too (rehearsal procedure). The

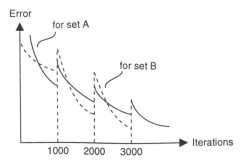

Figure 4.14
An example of alternative training of a network with two sets of examples A and B. When the network was started to be trained for a second time with the first set A, after being trained with A and then with set B, the initial error was higher than it was at the end of the first training cycle with A.

problem arises when the old examples are no longer available. Then pseudoexamples may be used to keep the weights as close to the previous ones as possible. Such pseudoexamples can be generated during training rather than kept in a table. Adaptive training is discussed in chapter 7.

• *Learning hints* in an MLP: In addition to the data set used for training, we can train the network with some existing hints about the unknown function. Prior knowledge (hints) can be introduced as a new set of examples, which the network learns alternatively to the training data set until the error for both training data sets (or more, if more than one hint is available) is sufficiently small. Except by generating new data, which represent a hint (*a soft way* for accommodating the hint), we can use an explicit, *hard way* for introducing the hint to the network by setting an extra connection between the nodes. For example, if we know that the attribute "character of the applicant" is the most important attribute for deciding on his or her loan application, we introduce an extra connection between the node which represents the attribute "character" and the output node "decision" (figure 4.15). We can also add some more data examples to the training data set, all of them having "character" = 1 (good) and "decision" = 1 (approve). The values of the other input attributes have to be consistent too. Hints can be presented in the form of rules. Rules map patches from the domain space into patches of the solution space. Here, in order to train a network to learn rules, there has to be a fair amount of data points taken from these patches and added to the training data set.

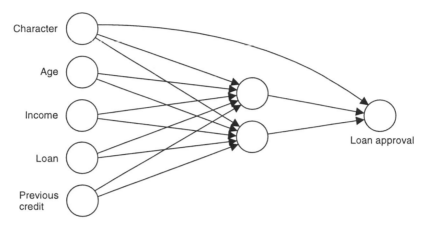

Figure 4.15
A "hard" way of introducing "hints" to a neural network. The attribute "character" of the applicants is known to be the most important attribute for deciding on their loan application. An extra connection between the node which represents the attribute "character" and the output node "decision" is introduced.

• *Overfitting* is a phenomenon which indicates that the neural network has too closely approximated, learned, the data examples, which may contain noise. In such a case the network can not generalize well on new examples (figure 4.16). There are some ways to overcome this problem: *early stopping* of the training process: while the training error is calculated, the test error over test data is calculated also; the process of training stops when the test error is minimal; *Using less hidden nodes*; more hidden nodes lead to too good an approximation;

• How to choose the number of training examples to present to a chosen network architecture if we want the network to approximate a known function? The same problem can be formulated as follows: Given any probability distribution function and a fixed neural network architecture, how many randomly chosen training examples are necessary for its correct approximation? The answer involves the use of the *VC dimension* (*V*apnic-Chervonenkis dimension), a quantitative measure of the set of functions that a neural network can compute. More precisely, the VC dimension of a class {F} of {0, 1} valued functions is the size of the largest set of points that functions in {F} can classify arbitrarily, that is, for all possible desired classifications of the points, there is a function $F \in \{F\}$

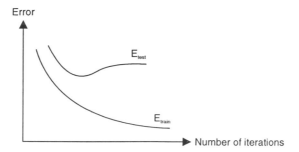

Figure 4.16
The "overtraining" phenomenon. After a certain number of training cycles, the test error E_{test} begins to increase, while the training error E_{train} is continuing to decrease. The process of training should stop at that point.

that classifies each point in the appropriate way. The following formula holds for a neural network:

VC dimension $< 2|W|\log_2$ e.N,

where $|W|$ is the number of connection weights, and N is the number of neurons in the network.

$|W|\log N$ training examples provide enough information for correct learning of a probability distribution function.

For a three-layered feedforward network with n_1, n_2, n_3 number of neurons in the corresponding layers, the following holds:

VC dim $\geq n_1 \cdot n_2 + n_2(n_3 - 1)/2 + 1 \approx \xi|W|$,

where ξ is a constant.

The above formula represents in a precise form something which may not be obvious to a newcomer to the field of neural networks. Roughly speaking, the learning and generalization ability of a network in respect to the size of the training data set is defined by the size of the connection weight space.

In order to overcome some of the problems with MLPs, other neural network models have been developed. Some of them are discussed in the following sections.

4.3   Radial Basis Functions, Time-Delay Neural Networks, Recurrent Networks

The MLP networks with training algorithms, were a giant step forward. They influenced ´very much the development of new models of neural

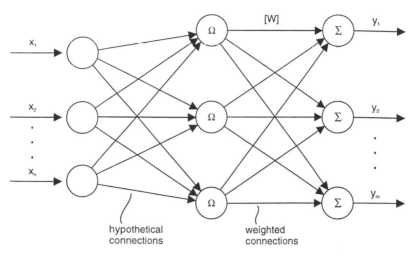

Figure 4.17
A radial basis functions network (RBFN).

networks, which borrowed some ideas from them, but which also generated new ideas. Three of these models are presented in this section.

4.3.1   Radial Basis Function Networks

Radial basis function networks (RBFNs) have been proposed and used by some authors (Moody and Darken 1989; Renals and Rohwer 1989; others). A general architecture of the RBFN is given in figure 4.17. An RBFN consists of three layers. The first layer consists of n inputs. They are fully connected to the neurons in the second layer. A hidden node has a radial basis function (RBF) as an activation function. The RBF is a radially symmetric function (e.g., gaussian, bell-like, Π function):

$$f(x) = \exp[-(x - M)^2/2\sigma^2],$$

where M and σ are two parameters meaning the mean and the standard deviation of the input variable x. For a particular intermediate node i, its RBFi is centered at a cluster center c_i in the n-dimensional input space. The cluster center c_i is represented by the vector $(w_{1i}, \ldots, w_{ni})$ of connection weights between the n input nodes and the hidden node i. The standard deviation for this cluster defines the range for the RBFi. The RBF is nonmonotonic, in contrast to the sigmoid function. The second layer is connected to the output layer. The output nodes perform a simple summation function with a linear threshold activation function. Training of an RBFN consists of two phases: (1) adjusting the RBF of the hidden neurons by applying a statistical clustering method; this represents an unsupervised learning phase; (2) applying gradient descent (e.g., the back-propagation algorithm) or a linear regression algorithm for adjusting the second layer of connections; this is a supervised learning phase. During training, the following parameters of the RBFN are adjusted:

• The n-dimensional position of the centers c_i of the RBFi. This can be achieved by using the k-means clustering algorithm (see chapter 2); the algorithm finds k (number of hidden nodes) cluster centers which mini-mize the average distance between the training examples and the nearest centers.

• The *deviation scaling parameter* σ_i for every RBFi; it is defined by using average distance to the nearest m-cluster centers:

$$\sigma_i = \left(\left(\sum_{p=1,m} abs(c_i - c_{ip}) \right) \Big/ m \right)^{1/2},$$

where c_{ip} is the center of the pth cluster near to the cluster i.

• The weights of the second layer connections.

The recall procedure finds through the functions RBFi how close an input vector $\mathbf{x}'$ is to the centers c_i and then propagates these values to the output layer.

The following advantages of the RBFN over the MLP with the back-propagation algorithm have been experimentally and theoretically proved:

• Training in RBFNs is an order of magnitude faster than training of a comparably sized feedforward network with the backpropagation algorithm.

• A better generalization is achieved in RBFNs.

• RBFNs have very fast convergence properties compared with the con-ventional multilayer networks with sigmoid transfer functions, since any function can be approximated by a linear combination of locally tuned factorizable basis functions.

• There is no local minima problem.

• The RBF model can be interpreted as a fuzzy connectionist model, as the RBFs can be considered as membership functions.

• The hidden layer has a much clearer interpretation than the MLP with the backpropagation algorithm. It is easier to explain what an RBF network has learned than its counterpart MLP with the backpropagation algorithm

There are also disadvantages to using the RBFN, one of them being finding the appropriate number of hidden nodes. Unsupervised learning might be necessary to apply first and find out the number of clusters. The number of hidden nodes is then set to be equal to this number. Too many, or too few, hidden nodes will prevent RBFN from properly approximating the data.

4.3.2   Time-Delay Neural Networks

Time-delay neural networks (TDNNs) are modifications of the MLP which use delay elements to feed input data through (figure 4.18a). The input layer is a *shift register* with delay elements. The shift register is used to keep several old values in a buffer. Then all values, old and new, are fed as input values for further processing in the network.

TDNNs have been developed to facilitate learning time sequences, where the next value of the sequence is correlated with its previous values. Standard MLP training algorithms (e.g., the backpropagation algorithm) can be applied.

The output layer can represent different concepts:

• Next values of the time sequence; this mode is called *sequence reproduction*

• The type (class) of the fed sequence; this task is called *sequence recognition*

• New patterns, belonging to another time sequence; this task is called *temporal association*

TDNNs transform time patterns into spatial patterns. In this transformation several problems arise:

• Does synchronization of the data shift in the input layer correspond to the real-time occurrence of events?

• The number of delay elements is set in advance, which may not represent the existing time correlation in the sequence. A dynamical adjustment may be needed.

TDNNs have been used intensively for speech recognition, as discussed in chapter 5, and for other time sequence–related tasks.

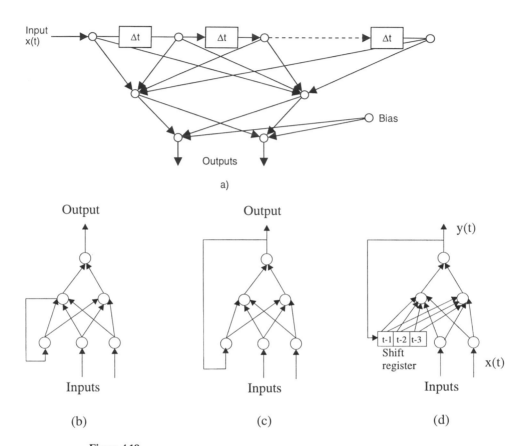

Figure 4.18
(a) Time-delay neural network (TDNN). (b–d) Recurrent neural network architectures:
(b) with feedback connections from hidden nodes; (c) with feedback connections from
output nodes; (d) buffered feedback connections.

4.3.3   Recurrent Neural Networks

Recurrent networks have feedback connections from neurons in one layer
to neurons in a previous layer. Different modifications of such networks
have been developed and explored. A typical recurrent network has concepts bound to the nodes whose output values feed back as inputs to the
network. So the next state of a network depends not only on the connection weights and the currently presented input signals but also on the
previous states of the network. The network leaves a trace of its behavior;
the network keeps a memory of its previous states.

Depending on the architecture of the feedback connections, there are two general models of recurrent networks: (1) *partially recurrent*, and (2) *fully recurrent*. The neural networks of the first type have carefully selected specific feedback connections which are meaningful. They represent (possibly time-) dependence between concepts represented in the network. Feedback connections to the input layer can be established from hidden nodes (Elman 1990); figure 4.18b); and output nodes (Jordan 1986; figure 4.18c).

The weights assigned to the feedback connections may not be adjustable (e.g., may be they set to a value of 1). In this case a standard MLP training algorithm (e.g., the backpropagation algorithm) can be used to adjust the feedforward connection weights. In addition to the feedback connections, which make possible use of a previous-time moment output value for calculating the next one, a buffer of output values for more than one step back in time can be used as an additional input buffer. Such recurrent networks are called *buffered networks* (Elman 1990; see figure 4.18d).

It was shown that a recurrent network which keeps a track of its *k*-previous states can be represented as unfolded MLP with *k* layers of connections. Such networks were called *backpropagation through time* (Rumelhart et al. 1986b, Werbos 1990). The idea is to duplicate the nodes in space in order to achieve time-dependence.

In fully recurrent networks any node may be connected to any other. This is the case with the Hopfield network, presented in a later section.

Recurrent neural networks can model a *finite state automaton* (see chapter 2).

Difficult questions to deal with, when using recurrent networks, are:

• Synchronization is required in order to achieve proper timing when propagating the signals through the network.

• It is difficult to express in a linguistic form or in a formula the time-dependence learned in a recurrent network after training, that is, the balance which the network has achieved between forgetting previous states and remembering new ones. How much "back in time" can a recurrent network keep track of?

• Recurrent networks may manifest chaotic behavior, and therefore learning might be difficult.

Recurrent networks suit time-series prediction problems, speech recognition problems, and many others, where in order to recognize a current state previous states have to be considered. For example, in language understanding and speech processing the semantic meaning of a word is recognized after taking into account the previously recognized words and possibly some of the following words.

Example   Two different meanings of the word "bank" are illustrated in the following sentences: "My bank account was empty" and "We went to the river bank." In order to recognize the meaning of "bank," we need to take into account the meaning of adjoining words which can be eventually done in a recurrent network.

4.4   Neural Network Models for Unsupervised Learning: Adaptive Resonance Theory

Unsupervised learning is considered to be more psychologically plausible, possibly because humans tend to learn more about nature and life through their own experience, rather than by listening to a teacher. For example, imagine that there is nobody to tell us which instance to classify into which class, that is, what we should derive. The patterns in this case are not labeled with class-labels.

There is evidence that unsupervised learning is plausible from a biological point of view too, that is, the way neurons change their connection weights, but we shall look at this paradigm here from an engineering point of view.

4.4.1   Unsupervised Learning in Neural Networks

Two principle learning rules are implemented in the contemporary unsupervised learning algorithms for neural networks: (1) *noncompetitive learning*, that is, many neurons may be activated at a time; and (2) *competitive learning*, that is, the neurons compete and after that, only one is activated at one time, e.g. only one wins after the competition. This principle is also called "winner takes all."

Most of today's training algorithms are influenced by the concept introduced by Donald O. Hebb (1949) (see 4.13). Hebb proposed a model for unsupervised learning in which the synaptic strength (weight) is increased if both the source and destination neurons are simultaneously activated. It is expressed as:

$$w_{ij}(t + 1) = w_{ij}(t) + c \cdot o_i \cdot o_j,$$

where $w_{ij}(t)$ is the weight of the connection between the ith and jth neuron at the moment t, and o_i and o_j are the output signals of neurons i and j at the same moment t. The weight $w_{ij}(t + 1)$ is the adjusted weight at the next moment $(t + 1)$. This principle was used in supervised learning, but then we knew the desired outputs. Here, the outputs are as they are produced by the network only. Different modifications of this rule have been suggested, for example: the *differential Hebbian learning law* (Kosko 1988(A)):

$$w_{ij}(t + 1) = w_{ij}(t) + c \cdot o_i \cdot o_j + \Delta o_i \cdot \Delta o_j$$

The differential Hebbian law introduces the first derivatives of the activation signals to the Hebbian law.

• *Grossberg's competitive law* (Grossberg 1982), expressed as:

$$\Delta w_{ij} = c \cdot o_j \cdot (o_i \cdot w_{ij}),$$

• The *differential competitive learning law* (Kosko 1990):

$$\Delta w_{ij} = c \cdot \Delta o_j (o_i - w_{ij})$$

The differential competitive learning law introduces the first derivative of neuronal output values to the competitive learning law.

• *Adaptive vector quantization* (Kohonen 1982, 1990); the learning law in a vector form is:

$$\mathbf{w}_j(t + 1) = \mathbf{w}_j(t) + c \cdot (\mathbf{x}(t) - \mathbf{w}_j(t))$$

where c is a learning rate, $\mathbf{x}(t)$ is the input vector at moment t, and $\mathbf{w}_j$ is the vector of the weights from the input neurons to the neuron j.

Unsupervised learning is also applicable when noise is present. For example, the *random signal Hebbian law* looks like:

$$w_{ij}(t + 1) = w_{ij} + c \cdot o_i o_j + n_{ij},$$

where n_{ij} is a noise introduced to the connection i-j.

In the major *competitive learning* models, the neural networks are organized in layers. There are excitatory connections between neurons from different layers, and inhibitory connections between neurons in one layer. The neurons in the output layer compete, each one inhibiting the others with its current activation level. *The winner takes all* in the end, that is, the neuron that gets the highest activation level is activated. Then a "reward" follows; this neuron strengthens its weights according to the input pattern and possibly suppresses the other neurons' weights.

Unsupervised learning is applicable for conceptualization, that is, discovering and creating new concepts and categories from data examples. Unsupervised learning in neural networks can be used to learn structures, similarities, and relations.

Another major application for unsupervised learning networks is *vector quantization*. N-dimensional data vectors are represented as k-dimensional, when $k < n$. This is important for signal compression (images, speech, etc.), clustering, reducing dimensionality, etc.

In the following subsections we discuss the competitive learning algorithm based on adaptive resonance theory (ART), developed by Carpenter and Grossberg (1987a,b) and the self-organizing maps (SOMs), developed by Teuvo Kohonen (1982, 1984, 1990).

4.4.2   Adaptive Resonance Theory

Adaptive resonance theory makes use of two terms used in the study of brain behavior: (1) *stability* and (2) *plasticity*. The *stability/plasticity dilemma* is the ability of a system to preserve the balance between retaining previously learned patterns and learning new patterns. Two layers of neurons are used to realize the idea: (1) a "top" layer, an output, concept layer, and (2) a "bottom" layer, an input, feature layer. Two sets of weights between the neurons in the two layers are used. The top-down weights represent learned patterns, expectations. The bottom-up weights represent a scheme for new inputs to be accommodated in the network.

Patterns, associated to an output node j, are collectively represented by the weight vector of this node $\mathbf{t}_j$ (top-down weight vector). The reaction of the node j to a particular new input vector is defined by another weight vector $\mathbf{b}_j$ (bottom-up weight). The key element in Grossberg's realization of the stability/plasticity dilemma is the control of the partial match between new feature vectors and ones already learned, which is achieved by using a parameter called *vigilance* or the *vigilance factor*. Vigilance controls the degree of mismatch between the new patterns and the learned (stored) patterns that the system can tolerate.

Figure 4.19a shows a diagram of a simple ART1 (binary inputs only are allowed) architecture. It consists of two sets of neurons: n input (feature) neurons (first layer) and m output neurons (second layer). The bottom-up connections b_{ij} from each input i to every output j and the top-down

a.

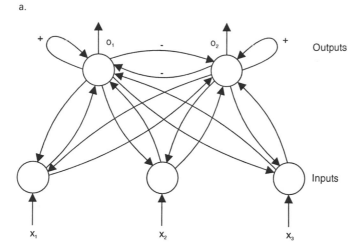

b.

A1.   Weight coefficients are initialized:
        $t_{ij}(0):=1$, $b_{ij}:=1/(1+n)$, for each $i=1,2,..,n$; $j=1,2,...,m$

A2.   A coefficient of similarity r, a so-called vigilance factor, is defined, $0<=r<=1$.
        The greater the value of r, the more similar the patterns ought to be in order to
        activate the same output neuron representing a category, a class, or a concept.

A3.   WHILE (there are input vectors) DO
        (a) a new input vector $\mathbf{x}(t)$ is fed at moment t, $\mathbf{x} = (x_1, x_2,...,x_n)(t)$
        (b) the outputs are calculated:

        $o_j:=\Sigma b_{ij}(t).x_i(t)$, for $j=1,2,..., m$
        (c) an output o_j* with the highest value is defined;
        (d) the similarity of the pattern associated to j* (if there is such a pattern) to
            the input pattern is defined:

        IF (number of "1"s in the intersection of the vector $\mathbf{x}(t)$ and $t_i*(t)$) divided to
        the number of "1"s in $\mathbf{x}(t)$ is greater than the vigilance r) THEN GO TO (f)

        ELSE
        (e) the output j* is abandoned and the procedure returns to (b) in order to
            calculate another output to be associated with $\mathbf{x}(t)$;
        (f) the pattern $\mathbf{x}(t)$ is associated with the vector $t_i*(t)$, therefore the pattern
            $t_j*(t)$ is changed using its intersection with $\mathbf{x}(t)$:
        $t_{ij}*(t+1):=t_{ij}*(t).x_i(t)$, for $i = 1,2,...,n$
        (g) the weights b_{ij} are changed:
        $b_{ij}*(t+1):=b_{ij}*(t) + t_j*(t).x_i/(0.5 + \Sigma t_{ij}*(t).x_i(t))$

Figure 4.19
(A) A schematic diagram of a three-input, two-output ART network. (B) A realization of an
ART1 algorithm.

connections t_{ji} from the outputs back to the inputs are shown in the figure. Each of the output neurons has a strong excitatory connection to itself and a strong inhibitory connection to each of the other output neurons.

The ART1 learning algorithm is given in figure 4.19b. It consists of two major phases. The first presents the input pattern and calculates the activation values of the output neurons. The winning neuron is defined. The second phase calculates the mismatch between the input pattern and the pattern currently associated with the winning neuron. If the mismatch is below a threshold (*vigilance parameter*), this pattern is updated to accommodate the new one. But if the mismatch is above the threshold, the procedure continues for finding either another output neuron or a new one, as the input pattern has to be associated with a new-concept, new-output neuron.

An example of applying the algorithm, where a network learns to categorize sequentially fed patterns, is presented in figure 4.20. The network associates the first pattern with the first output neuron, the second pattern with the first output neuron again, and the third input pattern with the

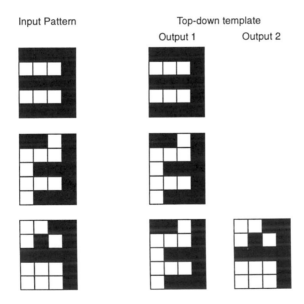

Figure 4.20
Associating groups (concepts, classes) to input patterns in ART1. The three presented patterns are grouped in two groups. An ART1 network with 20 input nodes and 10 output nodes is used.

second output neuron. Every time the network associates a new input pattern with an old one, it changes the old one accordingly. For binary inputs, the simple operation of binary intersection is used.

The ART neural networks are ideal for conceptualization, clustering, and discovering existing types and number of classes in a database. Categorization between different unknown, but existing categories in a set of examples can be successfully achieved. A crucial parameter in the algorithm is the vigilance factor. If it is high, for example, 0.95, only small differences between patterns that will be categorized in one category and assigned to one output neuron will be tolerated. In its extreme value of 1, each of the output neurons will learn to represent a different input pattern, whatever the difference between patterns. If the vigilance factor is small, then slightly different patterns will be grouped in one output group and bound to one output neuron. The top-down weights, which represent the patterns bound to an output neuron, may change dramatically after associating a new pattern with an already existing category.

ART1 was further developed into ART2 (continuous values for the inputs) and ART3 (Carpenter and Grossberg, 1990). The ART3 model is closer to the synaptic processes in real neurons. Algorithms for supervised learning in ART3 architecture have also been developed

Fuzzy ARTMAP is an extension of ART1 when input nodes represent not "yes/no" features but degrees of membership, to which the input data belong to features, for example, a set of features (sweet, fruity, smooth, sharp, sourish) used to categorize wines based on their taste. A particular sample of wine can be represented as an input vector consisting of membership degrees, for example, (0.7, 0.3, 0.9, 0.2, 0.5). The fuzzy ARTMAP allows for continuous values in the interval of [0, 1] for the inputs and the top-down weights. It uses fuzzy operators MIN and MAX to calculate intersection and union between the fuzzy input patterns $\mathbf{x}$ and the continuous-value weight vectors $\mathbf{t}$.

4.5   Kohonen Self-Organizing Topological Maps

One of the most used neural network models, used mainly for vector quantization and data analysis but also applicable to almost all the tasks where neural networks have been tried successfully, is the *self-organizing map* introduced and developed by Teuvo Kohonen (1982, 1990, 1993).

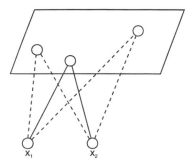

Figure 4.21
A part of a Kohonen SOM with two inputs x1 and x2 and a two-dimensional output map.

Some theoretical background of this type of network is given in this section, and more applications are presented in chapter 5. Practical applications of the SOM neural networks occur in the following problem areas: speech recognition, industrial automatic design of digital systems, and optimization, among others (Kohonen 1990).

4.5.1   The Philosophy of the Kohonen Network

Self-organizing topological or feature maps became popular because they tend to be very powerful at solving problems based on *vector quantization*. A SOM consists of two layers, an input layer and an output layer, called a feature map, which represent the output vectors of the output space (figure 4.21). The weights of the connections of an output neuron j to all the n input neurons, form a vector $\mathbf{w}_j$ in an n-dimensional space. The input values may be continuous or discrete, but the output values are binary only. The main ideas of SOM are as follows:

• Output neurons specialize during the training or recall procedure (both may not be distinguished here) to react to input vectors of some groups (clusters) and to represent typical features shared by the input vectors. This characteristic of the SOM tends to be biologically plausible as there is evidence to show that the brain is organized into regions that correspond to different sensory stimuli. There is also evidence for linguistic units being locatable within the human brain. A SOM is able to extract abstract information from multidimensional primary signals and to represent it as a location, in one-, two-, three-, etc. dimensional space (Kohonen 1990).

• The neurons in the output layer are competitive. Lateral interaction between neighboring neurons is introduced in such a way that a neuron has a strong excitatory connection to itself and fewer excitatory connections to its neighboring neurons within a certain radius; beyond this area, a neuron either inhibits the activation of the other neurons by inhibitory connections, or does not influence it. One possible rule is the so-called *Mexican hat* rule. In general, this is "the winner-takes-all" scheme, where only one neuron is the winner after an input vector has been fed in and a competition between the output neurons has taken place. The winning neuron represents the class, the label, and the feature to which the input vector belongs.

• The SOM transforms or preserves the similarity between input vectors from the input space into topological closeness of neurons in the output space represented as a topological map. Similar input vectors are represented by near points (neurons) in the output space. The distance between the neurons in the output layer matters, as this is a significant property of the network.

There are two possibilities for using the SOM. The first is to use it for the unsupervised mode only, where the labels and classes that the input vectors belong to are unknown. A second option is when SOM is used for unsupervised training followed by a supervised training. LVQ (learning vector quantization) algorithms (Kohonen 1990) have been developed for this purpose. In the LVQ algorithms, after an initial unsupervised learning is performed in a SOM, the output neurons are calibrated, labelled for the known classes, and a supervised learning is performed which refines the map according to what is known about the output classes, regions, groups, and labels. The two possibilities are presented and discussed in the next subsections.

4.5.2   Unsupervised Self-Organizing Feature Maps

The unsupervised algorithm for training a SOM, proposed by Teuvo Kohonen, is outlined in figure 4.22. After each input pattern is presented, the winner is found and the connection weights in its neighbourhood area Nt increase, while the connection weights outside the area are kept as they are. α is a learning parameter. It is recommended that the training time moments t (cycles) are more than 500 times the output neurons. If the training set contains fewer instances than this number, then the whole training set is fed again and again into the network.

K0.   Assign small random numbers to the initial weight vectors wj(t=0), for every
       neuron j from the output map.

K1.   Apply an input vector **x** at the consecutive time moment t.

K2.   Calculate the distance d_j (in n-dimensional space) between x and the weight
       vectors wj(t) of each neuron j. In Euclidean space this is calculated as follows:
       d_j= sqrt(($\Sigma((x_i - w_{ij})^2$)))

K3.   The neuron k which is closest to x is declared the winner. It becomes a centre of a
       neighbourhood area Nt.

K4.   Change all the weight vectors within the neighbourhood area:
       $w_j(t+1) = w_j(t) + \alpha.(x - w_i(t))$, if j $\in$ Nt,
       $w_j(t+1) = w_j(t)$, if j is not from the area Nt of neighbours.

All of the steps from K1 to K4 are repeated for all the training instances. Nt and α
decrease in time. The same training procedure is repeated again with the same training
instances until convergence.

Figure 4.22
A realization of the Kohonen SOM training algorithm.

SOMs learn statistical features. The synaptic weight vectors tend to approximate the density function of the input vectors in an orderly fashion (Kohonen 1990). Synaptic vectors w_j converge exponentially to centers of groups of patterns and the whole map represents to a certain degree the probability distribution of the input data. This property of the SOM is illustrated by a simple example of a two-input, 20 × 20-output SOM. The input vectors are generated randomly with a uniform probability distribution function as points in a two-dimensional plane, having values in the interval [0, 1]. Figure 4.23 represents graphically the change in weights after some learning cycles. The first box is a two-dimensional representation of the data. The other boxes represent SOM weights also in a two-dimensional space. The lines connect neighboring neurons, and the position of a neuron in the two-dimensional graph represents the value of its weight vector. Gradually the output neurons become self-organized and represent a uniform distribution of input vectors in the input space. The time (in cycles) is given in each box as well. If the input data have a well-defined probability density function, then the weight vectors of the output neurons try to imitate it, regardless of how complex it is. The

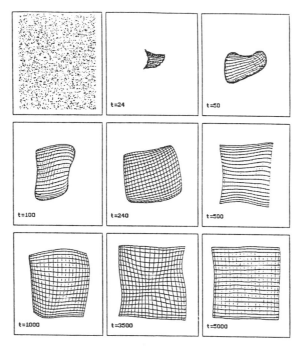

Figure 4.23
Uniformly randomly distributed two-dimensional vectors are learned by a two-dimensional SOM after 5000 iterations. The first image represents the raw data and the next represent the weight vectors of the SOM for each of eight consecutive steps (following the experiments presented in Kohonen (1990)).

weight vectors are also called *reference vectors* or reference codebook vectors, and the whole weight vector space is called a *reference codebook*. Figure 4.24 shows the adaptation of the same network to the generated input vectors in $\mathbb{R}^2$ when the latter are not uniformly distributed but have a gaussian distribution of a star type. Figure 4.25 shows the adaptation of a SOM to a distribution in $\mathbb{R}^2$ achieved with the use of fractal data.

The SOM is very similar to an elastic net which covers the input vector's space.

4.5.3   Learning Vector Quantization Algorithms for Supervised Learning

The problem of distinguishing input vectors that "fall" in the bordering area between two output neurons and the necessity for using known labels of the neurons for better topological mapping of the input vectors into the

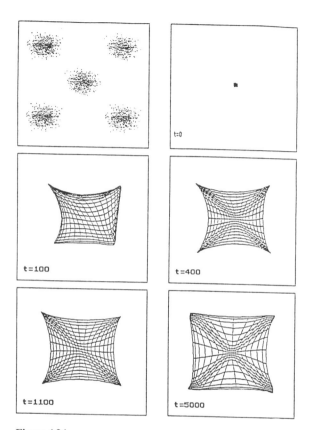

Figure 4.24
Learning gaussian distributed random vectors by a two-dimensional SOM.

output space have led to the development of *learning vector quantization* (*LVQ*) *algorithms* LVQ1, LVQ2, and LVQ3 (Kohonen 1990).

LVQ1 Algorithm   In LVQ1 several codebook vectors are assigned to each class, and each is labeled with the corresponding class symbol (label). Initial values of the codebook vectors are learned by the SOM algorithm. The output neurons are then labeled according to the classes. Then a correction of the weights with the use of the known labels is performed by applying the following formulas to update the weights vectors:

$\mathbf{w}_j(t + 1) = \mathbf{w}_j(t) + \alpha(t)(\mathbf{x}(t) - \mathbf{w}_j(t))$, if $\mathbf{x}$ is classified by the network correctly in class c_j represented by the jth neuron

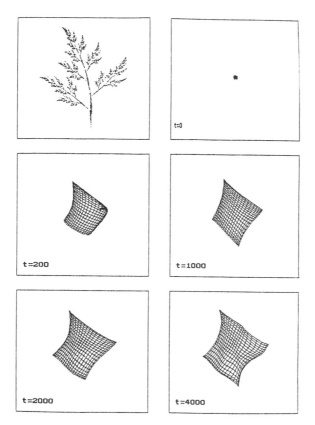

Figure 4.25
Learning fractal data in a two-dimensional SOM.

$\mathbf{w}_j(t + 1) = \mathbf{w}_j(t) - \alpha(t)(\mathbf{x}(t) - \mathbf{w}_j(t))$, if $\mathbf{x}$ has been wrongly associated by the network with class-neuron j

$\mathbf{w}_i(t + 1) = \mathbf{w}_i(t)$, for all i different form j

$\alpha(t)$ is a scalar gain factor which decreases monotonically in time.

LVQ2 Algorithm   In the LVQ2 algorithm, a further tuning of the weights of the immediate neighbors to the winning neuron, after a presentation of an input vector, is done. If, for example, c_i is the class of the winning neuron, but $\mathbf{x}$ belongs to the class c_j of its neighbor j, the following formulas are applied to calculate the new weight vectors for neurons i and j (figure 4.26):

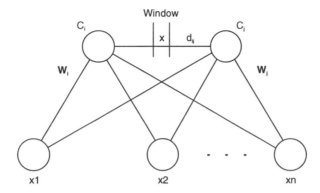

Figure 4.26
The LVQ algorithms use "windows" between nodes C_i and C_j (their weight vectors in the weight space). If the input vector x "falls" in the window between the two classes (nodes), the weights are adjusted depending on the known information about the desired label of that vector.

$$\mathbf{w}_i(t + 1) = \mathbf{w}_i(t) - \alpha(t)(\mathbf{x}(t) - \mathbf{w}_i(t)), \quad \text{or}$$

$$\mathbf{w}_j(t + 1) = \mathbf{w}_j(t) + \alpha(t)(\mathbf{x}(t) - \mathbf{w}_j(t)), \quad \text{or}$$

$$\mathbf{w}_k(t + 1) = \mathbf{w}_k(t), \text{ for the rest of the neurons } k$$

LVQ3 Algorithm   In the LVQ3 algorithm a window between the lateral output neurons i and j is considered. When the input vector $\mathbf{x}$ falls out of the window, it is the LVQ2 algorithm which determines one of the i or j neurons to be a winner and updates the new codebook vectors. But if the input vector $\mathbf{x}$ falls in the window, then other formulas are applied:

$\mathbf{w}_i(t + 1) = \mathbf{w}_i(t) - \alpha(t)(\mathbf{x}(t) - \mathbf{w}_i(t))$, if $\mathbf{x}$ falls in the "window"
and $\mathbf{x}$ belongs to class c_j

$\mathbf{w}_j(t + 1) = \mathbf{w}_j(t) + \alpha(t)(\mathbf{x}(t) - \mathbf{w}_j(t))$, for $k \in \{i, j\}$, if $\mathbf{x}$ falls in the "window"
and $\mathbf{x}$ belongs to class c_j

$\mathbf{w}_k(t + 1) = \mathbf{w}_k(t) + \alpha(t)(\mathbf{x}(t) - \mathbf{w}_k(t))$, for $k \in \{i, j\}$, if $\mathbf{x}$ falls in the window
and i and j represent the same class

4.6   Neural Networks as Associative Memories

4.6.1   Learning Pattern Associations

Pattern association is the process of memorizing input-output patterns in a heteroassociative network architecture, or input patterns only in an

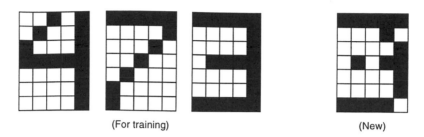

(For training)   (New)

Figure 4.27
The pattern association task, illustrated with three class patterns and a new one, corrupted, which has to be associated to one from the class patterns that is most similar.

autoassociative network, in order to recall the patterns when a new input pattern is presented. It is not required that the new input pattern be exactly the same as one that is memorized. It can be different, but similar to it. Three exemplar patterns are shown in figure 4.27. After memorizing them in a system, a new pattern is presented, a corrupted variant of the pattern 3. An associative memory system should associate this pattern with one of the memorized patterns. This is a task for an autoassociative network architecture.

Autoassociative neuronal architectures can be realized either by feed-forward, or feedback networks. Hopfield networks and Boltzman machines are two examples of autoassociative networks. Other types of pattern associators are the heteroassociative network architectures. One of them is the bidirectional associative memory (BAM) (Kosko 1988). All the above-mentioned neural networks are discussed below.

4.6.2   The Hopfield Network

Hopfield networks, named after their inventor John Hopfield (1982), are fully connected feedback networks (figure 4.28). The neurons in Hopfield networks are characterized by the following: binary or bivalent input signals, binary or bivalent output signals, simple summation function, and hard-limited threshold activation function. There are alternative variants of realizations of a Hopfield network. Every neuron $j, j = 1, 2, \ldots, n$ in the network is connected back to every other one, except itself. Input patterns x_j are supplied to the external inputs I_j and cause activation of the external outputs. The response of such a network, when an input vector is supplied during the recall procedure, is dynamic, that is, after supplying the new input pattern, the network calculates the outputs and then feeds them

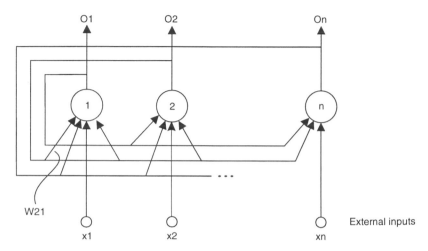

Figure 4.28
Hopfield autoassociative neural network.

back to the neurons; new output values are then calculated, and so on, until an equilibrium is reached. An *equilibrium* is considered to be the state of the system when the output signals do not change for two consecutive cycles, or change within a small constant. The weights in a Hopfield network are *symmetrical* for reasons of stability in reaching equilibrium, that is, $w_{ij} = w_{ji}$. The network is of an *additive type*, that is,

$$u_j = \sum_{(i)} (w_{ij} \cdot o_i) + I_j, \qquad (i \text{ not equal to } j),$$

where $o_j = 1$ if $u_j > \Theta_j$ (threshold for the jth neuron); $o_j = 0$ if $u_j < \Theta_j$; and o_j is unchanged if $u_j = \Theta_j$.

The training procedure for a Hopfield network is reduced to a simple calculation of the weights w_{ij} on the basis of the training examples with the use of the formula:

$$w_{ij} = \left(\sum_{p=1,m} (2 \cdot x_i^{(p)} - 1) \cdot (2 \cdot x_j^{(p)} - 1) \right)$$

where the summation is held for all the training patterns $\mathbf{x}^{(p)}$, $x_i^{(p)}$ is the ith binary value of the input pattern p; and the expressions in parentheses can be only 1 or 0 according to the value of the input pattern.

An interesting characteristic of the weights w_{ij} is that they measure the correlation between the frequencies of firing of neurons i and j over the full

H1.	Apply new input pattern $\mathbf{x}^{\text{new}}$
H2.	Assign initial values $o_j(0)$ to the outputs of the neurons j, j = 1,2,...n, to be the corresponding input values: $o_j(0) = x_j^{\text{new}}$
H3.	Calculate the next output value $o_j(t+1)$ as follows: $o_j(t+1) = s(u_j(t+1))$, where s is the thresholding activation function and $u_j(t+1)$ is calculated as a sum.
H4.	Repeat step for t=1,2,3,.... until all the outputs no longer change their values for at least two consecutive cycles (moments t and t+1). Such a state of the network is called a stable state. The network reaches an equilibrium.

Figure 4.29
Recall procedure for the Hopfield network.

set of examples. It is a variant of the Hebbian learning law, that is, the connection weights increase if two adjacent nodes fire simultaneously.

The recall process is executed as shown in figure 4.29. It can be organized in the following modes:

• *Asynchronous updating*: Each neuron may change its state at a random moment with respect to the others.

• *Synchronous updating*: All neurons change their states simultaneously at a given moment.

• *Sequential updating*: Only one neuron changes its state at any moment; thus all neurons change their states, but sequentially.

A few more words about the network's equilibrium: Borrowing from thermodynamics, Hopfield defined a parameter E called the *energy of the network*, which is a dynamical parameter and which can be calculated at any moment t as:

$$E(t) = -1/2 \sum_{i=1,n} \sum_{j=1,n} (w_{ij}(t) \cdot o_j(t) \cdot o_j(t)), \qquad (i \text{ not equal to } j)$$

The change in E based on a change in a single output value Δo_i, can be expressed as

$$\Delta E = -1/2 \cdot \Delta o_i \cdot \sum_{(j=1,n)} (w_{ij} \cdot o_j), \qquad (i \text{ not equal to } j)$$

This is a steadily decreasing function as the network evolves. During the recall procedure, the network continues to calculate output values until it

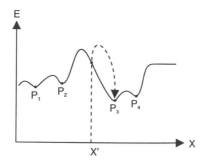

Figure 4.30
When a new input pattern X' is presented the network relaxes in an equilibrium state, a
"basin of attraction" where the energy E is minimum, thus associating the new pattern with
a class pattern P_3.

reaches a minimum of the energy function E, which is an equilibrium state.
The energy E can be represented as a surface in n-dimensional space. The
equilibrium in a trained Hopfield network can be explained by the *attractor principle*. During training, the network "sets" some *basins of attraction*
which are stable states for the network corresponding to the training
patterns (figure 4.30). When a new vector $\mathbf{x}'$ is supplied for a recall, the
network will eventually rest after some cycles in an attractor, thus associating the new vector with one of the known patterns (attractors). In the
extreme case, the number of basins of attraction is equal to the number m
of training patterns. During the recall procedure, when a new input pattern is applied, the network tries to relax into the nearest basin of attraction, thus finding the right pattern to associate the new one with. The
recall process is a process of relaxation.

There are some *limitations* to using the Hopfield network:

• *Memory capacity*. The number m of training patterns should be about
the number of neurons n, or less (according to Hopfield, it should be
less than $0.15 \cdot n$; according to some new results, $m \leq 0.5\, n/\log n$). This
means that the memorizing capacity of a Hopfield network is severely
limited. Catastrophic "forgetting" may occur if we try to memorize more
patterns than the network is supposed to handle. In this case the network may forget all the patterns that it has previously learned; an increase
in capacity can be achieved by introducing a bias to the neurons during
training and recall, and by introducing noise in the patterns (Burkitt
1993):

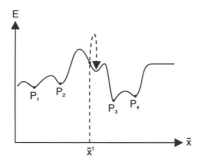

Figure 4.31
A network may relax into a "spurious" state, which phenomenon is called the local minima problem.

$$w_{ij} = \sum_{p=1,m} (x_i^{(p)} - a)(x_j^{(p)} - a),$$

where a is a bias and $0 < a < 1$.

One solution to this problem, when the patterns are sparse in the input space, is suggested by Amari (1989). The memory capacity achieved there is approximately $n^2/\log n^2$ if the density d_n of the domain data tends to 0, that is, $\lim d_n \to 0$ for $n \to \infty$.

Another solution to the problem has been achieved by using couple oscillatory neurons (see chapter 7).

• *Discrepancy limitation.* The new pattern to be recognized as one of the training patterns should not differ from any training pattern by more than about 25%.

• *Orthogonality between patterns.* The more orthogonal (dissimilar) the training patterns, the better the recognition.

• *Spurious states of attraction.* Sometimes the network learns some patterns (creates basins of attraction) called *spurious states*, which are not presented in the set of training patterns. An example of such a state is shown in figure 4.31. In order to overcome this limitation, Hopfield et al. (1983) introduced a "little bit of unlearning" for every learning pattern:

$$\Delta w_{ij} = -\alpha x_i^{(p)} \cdot x_j^{(p)}, \text{ for the } p\text{th pattern } \mathbf{x}^{(p)}$$

Spurious states may be useful, if the Hopfield network is used for partial matching and approximate reasoning (see NPS chapter 6). The input values are between 0 and 1 and represent the certainty of the facts or fuzzy membership degrees.

• *Weight symmetry.* The weight matrix has to be symmetrical in order for the network to reach an equilibrium. The symmetrical synaptic weights are not at all biologically plausible, but they are a useful limitation here.

• *Local minima problem.* A major disadvantage of the Hopfield network is that it can rest in a *local minimum* state instead of a global minimum energy state, thus associating a new input pattern with a spurious state (see figure 4.31).

Hopfield networks are useful for many applications, including pattern recognition, finite state automaton realization, and implementation of AI-reasoning machines.

4.6.3   Boltzmann Machines

In order to overcome the local minima problem, a model based on using a variable called *temperature* was developed. The activation value of a neuron is calculated as a statistical probability:

$o_i = 1$, with a probability $p_i = 1/(1 + e^{-u_i T})$

$o_i = 0$, with a probability $(1 - p_i)$,

where u_i is the net input to the ith neuron, calculated as in the Hopfield network. This model is called a *Boltzmann machine* after its resemblance to processes in thermodynamics. During the recall process the temperature T decreases, which is similar to the process of annealing in metallurgy. The physical meaning is that by changing the temperature T we "shake" the neural network "box" and if it has happened that it has rested at a wrong local minimum attractor, it will "jump out" and continue to "move" until its eventual relaxation at a global minimum attractor (which represents a correct pattern).

4.6.4   Kosko's Bidirectional Associative Memories

A *bidirectional associative memory* (Kosko 1988B) is a heteroassociative memory. It can memorize pattern associations of the type $(\mathbf{a}^{(p)}, \mathbf{b}^{(p)})$ where $\mathbf{a}^{(p)}$ is an *n*-dimensional vector (pattern) and $\mathbf{b}^{(p)}$ is its corresponding *m*-dimensional pattern (figure 4.32).

The neurons are of the same type as in the Hopfield network—either bivalent or binary inputs and outputs. A threshold activation function is

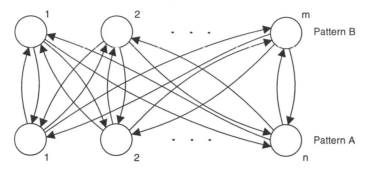

Figure 4.32
Kosko's bidirectional associative memory associates pattern A with pattern B in both directions.

used. The training process of a BAM is simply calculating the weights with the use of the formula

$$w_{ij} = w_{ji} = \sum_{k=1,p} \sum_{i-1,n} \sum_{j-1,m} (a_i^{(k)} \cdot b_j^{(k)}).$$

A recall in both directions is possible, that is, either $\mathbf{a}^{(p)}$ or $\mathbf{b}^{(p)}$ or both, complete or corrupted, can be used to recall corresponding associated patterns. An example of two patterns A and B associated through a BAM network and some recall exercises are shown in figure 4.33.

A severe limitation of BAM is its small capacity, which is less than the minimum number between n and m. In order to overcome this limitation, BAM systems consisting of many BAM modules, BAM_1, BAM_2, ..., BAM_k, have been developed (Simpson 1990). Every association $(\mathbf{a}, \mathbf{b})$ is tried to be memorized in a BAM module. If it is not possible to memorize it in the BAM_j module for example, then it is tried in the next one—the BAM_{j+1} module, and so on, until all the pattern associations are memorized successfully. BAM networks have been applied to pattern recognition.

4.7   On the Variety of Neural Network Models

There is a tremendous variety of neural network models. Some are variants or improvements of the types already presented—MLP, ART, SOM, associative memories. Other connectionist models emerge and evolve with the development of knowledge about the way real neurons work. Neural network models may differ in the following points:

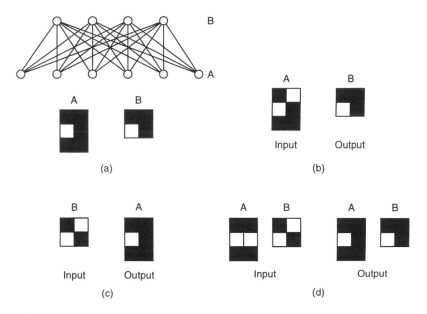

Figure 4.33
An example of associating two patterns A and B in a 6-4 BAM and different recall experiments.

• The type of neurons used, and type of calculations.

• The mathematical model used for representing and processing of information in the network (algebraic, statistical, fuzzy, etc.). This includes methods of training and recall, convergence and equilibrium properties, etc.

• The class of problems they are designed to solve (classification, optimization, pattern association, etc.).

A neural network model may be a *hybrid* between two connectionist models, for example, a model implementing competitive learning and a model for supervised learning.

It is difficult to present all the existing models here. It is also outside the scope of this book. But some derivatives of the above models and some new theoretical models will be presented.

4.7.1   Hamming Networks

The *Hamming network* performs the task of pattern association, or classification, based on measuring the Hamming distance. The network is a

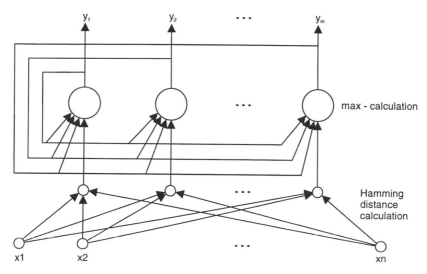

Figure 4.34
A Hamming associative neural network.

pattern associator of *n*-dimensional binary vectors labeled with *m*-class labels (*m*-class patterns). A new vector $\mathbf{x}'$ is associated with class pattern $\mathbf{x}_i$ with the minimum Hamming distance, a Hamming distance being the number of different bits in the two patterns. The Hamming network is similar to the Hopfield network, but it has two layers of connections (figure 4.34). The first layer contains connections between all the *n* inputs, and all the *m* outputs. The second layer is a fully connected recurrent network with *m* neurons (similar to the Hopfield network). All nodes use linear threshold activation functions. The first layer of connections is finding the difference between the number *n* and the Hamming distance between the input pattern $\mathbf{x}'$ and each of the *m*-class patterns used to calculate the connection weights in advance. The second layer of connections is calculating the maximum of these values for finding the best-matched-class pattern $\mathbf{x}_i$. Using a Hamming network has several advantages: it requires fewer connections than the Hopfield network, and it implements the "optimum minimum error classifier when bit errors are random and independent" (Lippman 1987), that is, the network always converges and finds the output node with the maximum value.

4.7.2   Brain-State-in-a-Box

The *brain-state-in-a-Box* network (BSB) was developed by James Anderson. It is an autoassociative network, similar to the Hopfield network. The architecture of the BSB is characterized by the following:

- It is a recurrent, but not fully connected network.
- A connection from a neuron's output to its input is allowed.
- The interconnection weights are generally nonsymmetrical.

In a BSB each class pattern can be viewed as a corner of an *n*-dimensional hypercube, thus the network is forced to converge at the nearest corner during the recall procedure. The states of the network are restricted so as not to go beyond the *n*-dimensional hyperbox, where the name of the network came from. When a next state $\mathbf{x}(t + 1)$ is calculated based on the stimulus $\mathbf{x}(0)$ (the new input pattern) and the previous state $\mathbf{x}(t)$, the following formula is used, which limits the new state to be inside of the box:

$$\mathbf{x}(t + 1) = LIMIT \cdot (a \cdot W \cdot \mathbf{x}(t) + b \cdot \mathbf{x}(t) + c \cdot \mathbf{x}(0)),$$

where $LIMIT$ is a parameter which limits the activation values to be in a range, typically $[-1.5, 1.5]$; a, b, and c are constants; and W is the weight matrix.

The recall procedure of the BSB has several advantages, one being that it always converges, avoiding the local minima problem, as the BSB does not have spurious states.

4.7.3   Counterpropagation Networks

Counterpropagation networks, developed by Hecht–Nielsen (1987, 1988) are a hybrid between two well-known connectionist models—competitive learning (performed by a first layer of connections) and supervised learning (performed by a following layer of connections) (figure 4.35). In this respect they are similar to the RBF networks. The idea behind this architecture is that competitive learning, which is fast, will cluster the input space, assigning one intermediate node to each group. After that, supervised learning is performed, but only on a single layer. The intermediate layer is of the "winner-takes-all" type. The major advantages of such a network are that (1) training is much faster than training a three-layer MLP with the backpropagation algorithm, and (2) the hidden nodes have meanings associated with them.

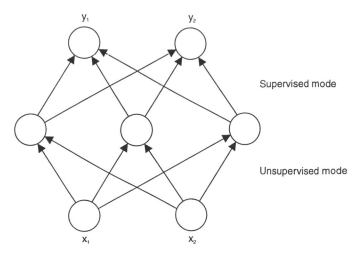

Figure 4.35
Counterpropagation neural network.

Applications of such networks have been developed for data compression, pattern classification, and statistical analysis.

4.7.4 RAM-Based Neurons and Networks, Weightless Networks

The strong development of digital electronic circuits and boolean algebra were influential in the development of connectionist models based on the idea of *random-access memory* (*RAM*). RAM is a device in which binary information can be stored and retrieved, each of the information elements (called words) having its own directly addressable space. The addresses are binary vectors. If n address lines are used, 2^n addressable elements can be stored and retrieved, each consisting of m bits. Figure 4.36 shows a RAM-based structure and its representation as a neural network, where n-inputs, one-output RAM elements are used.

Using such a simple structure, different models have been developed and put into practice. They differ in their training algorithms, and application-oriented characteristics.

Using the above idea, so-called weightless neural networks were developed by Igor Aleksander (1989). The connections between neurons do not have real weights; they are binary, $\{0, 1\}$, that is, a connection either exists or does not exist.

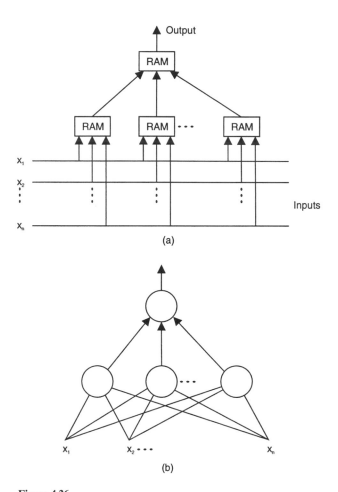

Figure 4.36
(a) A structure of RAM elements can realize any boolean function of n variables. (b) A weightless neural network, that is, there are connections but there are no weights associated with them.

Probabilistic RAM (*pRAM*) models, developed by John Taylor and his group, use a probability parameter for an output of a RAM-neuron to become 1. These probabilities are learned during training and used during recall. For example, if an input vector 1100011 is supplied at the input of a pRAM, an output of 1 is generated with a probability of 0.7, learned during the training phase. A random number generator is used to generate signals (1's) with a given probability. Different reinforcement learning algorithms have been developed for the pRAM models (Glarkson et al. 1992).

4.7.5   Information Geometry of Neural Networks

Studying the geometry of a family of networks means to geometrically represent mutual relations between individual neural networks. A family of networks forms a geometrical manifold which can be studied when trying to find the best neural network model for a particular task (Amari, 1977, 1985, 1990, 1993). Information geometry is applicable to manifolds (families) of different types of neural networks such as MLP, Hopfield and Boltzmann machines, and mixtures of models.

4.7.6   Neural Networks and Statistical Methods

Neural networks learn from data. But what kind of *statistics* can they learn? We summarize here some already-discussed properties of neural networks to learn statistical properties. We also introduce a new property of neural networks, which is that they can learn *principal components* similar to the way it is done through *principal component analysis* techniques. The following is a short list of some statistical properties of neural networks:

• A perceptron and an MLP with a hard-limited threshold activation function can be used as a *discriminating technique.*

• An MLP with a nonlinear activation function can be used for *function approximation* similar to *statistical regression*; but the neural networks are model-free, that is, they do not require that the type of the regression be defined in advance.

• MLP neural networks can learn posterior probabilities that do not strictly follow the probability axioms (see chapter 5);

• SOMs can learn the *probability distribution function* of the input space.

• MLPs can learn *principal components*. This feature is explained below.

Principal component analysis is a technique to economically encode a distribution of input patterns. It finds a fixed number of principal components (*eigenvectors*) with the highest *eigenvalues* of the correlation matrix of the data that describe the distribution of the patterns. If we represent each of the m training patterns as an n-element vector $\mathbf{x}_i$ in the input space, and create the covariance matrix $\mathbf{A}(\mathbf{x}_i\mathbf{x}_i^T)$ of all the patterns, then finding eigenvectors means representing the data in a compact form. Eigenvectors $\mathbf{x}'$ are defined as k-dimensional vectors which multiplied by $\mathbf{A}$ do not change their direction in the space, the result being equivalent to multiplying them with scalars, that is, $\mathbf{A} \cdot \mathbf{x}' = \lambda \cdot \mathbf{x}'$. The scalars λ are called eigenvalues. Eigenvalues measure how much variance of the data set the eigenvectors account for. The larger the eigenvalues, the better the eigenvectors represent the data set. The principal components are the vectors that minimize the mean square error between the actual points in the data set and the points described by a smaller number of components.

There is a similarity between the covariance matrix and the matrix of connection weights in an autoassociative neural network. It was shown by several authors that a hidden node in a three-layer MLP learns one principal component if the MLP is trained in the autoassociative mode, that is, if the input patterns are used as output patterns too. In this case the activation values of the hidden nodes represent in a condensed form the input vectors. That was the idea behind using neural networks for compression of data (speech, images).

4.8   Fuzzy Neurons and Fuzzy Neural Networks

The neural network models presented so far use variants of McCulloch and Pitt's neuron to build a network. New types of neurons have been introduced which use fuzzy membership functions as activation functions or as functions attached to their connections. One of them is the so-called fuzzy neuron (Yamakawa 1990). *Fuzzy neural networks*, neural networks built on fuzzy neurons or on standard neurons but dealing with fuzzy data, have also been introduced and applied successfully. In fuzzy neural networks, connectionist and fuzzy paradigms are mixed at a low level, both paradigms are strongly blended, and there is a mutual penetration. Fuzzy neurons and fuzzy neural networks are explained in the following subsections.

4.8.1 Fuzzy Neurons

A fuzzy neuron has the following features, which distinguish it from the ordinary McCulloch and Pitt's types of neurons:

- The inputs to the neuron $x_1, x_2, \ldots, x_n$ represent fuzzy labels of the fuzzy input variables.

- The weights w_i are replaced by functions μ_i which are the membership functions of the fuzzy labels x_i $(i = 1, 2, \ldots, n)$.

- Excitatory connections are represented by MIN operation, and inhibitory connections by fuzzy logic complements followed by MIN operation.

- A threshold level is not assigned.

In the fuzzy neuron there is no learning. The membership functions attached to the synaptic connections do not change. The fuzzy neuron has been successfully used for handwritten character recognition.

The *Neo-fuzzy neuron* (Yamakawa et al. 1992(A)) is a further development of the fuzzy neuron. A block diagram of a neo-fuzzy neuron with a detailed diagram of its nodes and the membership functions attached to the connections is given in figure 4.37. The features of the neo-fuzzy neuron are:

- The inputs $x_1, x_2, \ldots, x_n$ represent fuzzy variables.

- Each fuzzy segment x_{ij} attached to each of the fuzzy variables x_i, $i = 1$, m; $j = 1$, n are represented as connections between the input i and the output.

- In addition to the membership function μ_{ij}, which is bound to the input segment x_{ij}, weights w_{ij} are also assigned, subject to a training procedure.

- The segments x_{i1}, x_{i2}, $\ldots$, x_{il} have standard triangular membership functions; thus an input activates only two membership functions simultaneously; the sum of the degree to which an input value x_i' belongs to any two neighboring membership functions $\mu_{ik}(x_i')$ and $\mu_{i,k+1}(x_i')$ is always equal to 1. Thus the COG defuzzification does not use a division and the output of the neuron can be represented by the following simple equation:

$$f_i(x_i') = \mu_{ik}(x_i') \cdot w_{ik} + \mu_{i,k+1}(x_i') \cdot w_{i,k+1}.$$

Such a neuron can realize inference over a fuzzy rule.

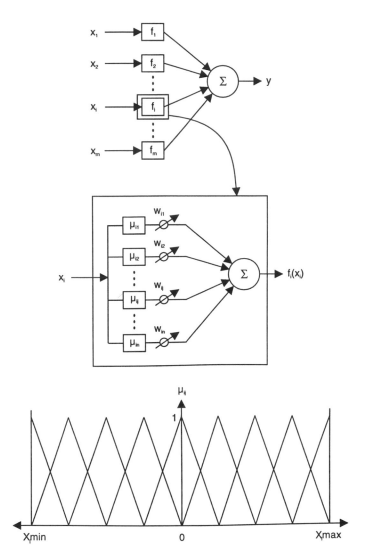

Figure 4.37
Yamakawa's neo-fuzzy neuron. Each of the m functions f_i $(i = 1, 2, \ldots, m)$ bound to each of the m inputs x_i are represented by $n = 9$ fuzzy membership functions T_{ij}, standard triangular ones uniformly distributed over the universe Ux_i, as well as by corresponding weights w_{ij} which are subject to change during training. (Adapted with permission from (Yamakawa et al. 1992a.))

There are some training algorithms applicable to the neo-fuzzy neuron. One of them is called *incremental updating* (stepwise training). If the neo-fuzzy neuron is to learn to associate an input pattern $\mathbf{x}^{(k)} = (x_1^k, x_2^k, \ldots, x_m^k)$ with an output value $y^{(k)}$, then the change of weights should be calculated as follows:

$$\Delta w_{ij} = -\alpha(y^k - d^k)\mu_{ij}(x_i^k), \qquad \text{for } i = 1, 2, \ldots, n \text{ and } j = 1, 2, \ldots, 1,$$

where α is a learning factor; y^k is the actual output from the neuron, and d^k is the desired output for the input pattern $\mathbf{x}^k$. All weights are initially assigned to zero. It has been proved that the neo-fuzzy neuron guarantees global minimum in the error-weight space. In addition to this property, experiments show that learning is faster by about 10^5 times and the accuracy achieved is better than in a three-layer feedforward network with the backpropagation algorithm.

Fuzzy neurons have been applied to prediction and classification problems.

4.8.2 Fuzzy Neural Networks

Similar to the way the fuzzy neuron and the neo-fuzzy neuron were created, different types of fuzzy neural networks have been developed and applied to different tasks. A *fuzzy neural network* (FNN) is a connectionist model for fuzzy rules implementation and inference. There is a great variety of architectures and functionalities of FNN. The FNNs developed so far differ mainly in the following parameters:

• *Type of fuzzy rules* implemented; this affects the connectionist structure used.

• *Type of inference* method implemented; this affects the selection of different neural network parameters and neuronal functions, such as summation, activation, and output function. It also influences the way the connection weights are initialized before training, and interpreted after training.

• *Mode of operation*: we consider here three major modes of operation by:

1. *Fixed mode*, "fixed membership functions–fixed set of rules," that is, a fixed set of rules is inserted in a network, the network performs inference, but does not change its weights. It cannot learn and adapt. A representative of this type of system is NPS (see chapter 6).

2. *Learning mode*, that is, a neural network is structurally defined to capture knowledge in a certain format, for example, some type of fuzzy rules. The network architecture is randomly initialized and trained with a set of data. Rules are then extracted from the structured network. The rules can be interpreted either in the same network structure or by using other inference methods.

3. *Adaptation mode.* A neural network is structurally set according to a set of existing rules, "hints," heuristics. The network is then trained with new data and updated rules are extracted from its structure. Two cases can be distinguished here: (1) *fixed membership functions–adaptable rules* and (2) *adaptable membership functions–adaptable rules.* The *catastrophic forgetting* phenomenon must be investigated in these cases, that is, how much the network forgets about previous data after having learned from completely new data without rehearsing the old ones.

To summarize the above, FNNs have two major aspects:

1. *Structural.* A set of rules is used to define the initial structure of a neural network; two types of neural networks have been mainly used so far: (a) multilayer perceptrons (MLPs), and (b) radial-basis functions networks.

2. *Functional, parametric.* After having defined the structure of a neural network and possibly having trained it with data, some parameters can be observed that would explain the inference which the network performs. Those parameters can be used to derive a (fuzzy) rule-based system represented in linguistic terms.

FuNN is an model of an FNN. It facilitates learning from data, fuzzy rules extraction, and approximate reasoning. FuNN uses an MLP network and a backpropagation training algorithm. It is an adaptable FNN as the membership functions of the fuzzy predicates, as well as the fuzzy rules inserted before training (adaptation), may adapt and change according to the training data. The general architecture of FuNN consists of five following layers (figure 4.38). In the *input layer*—a node represents an input variable. In the *condition elements layer*—each node represents a fuzzy predicate of an input variable. The activation values of the nodes represent the membership degrees of the input variables. Different summation function s_C, activation function a_C, and output function o_C can be used for the neurons of this layer.

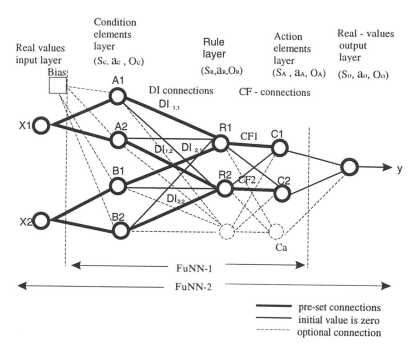

Figure 4.38
General architecture of FuNN (fuzzy neural network).

In the *Rule layer* each node represents either an existing rule, or a rule anticipated after training. When FuNN is used to implement an initial set of fuzzy rules, the connections between the condition elements layer and the rule layers are set according to normalized degrees of importance attached to the antecedent elements in the corresponding rules. If degrees of importance are not attached to the condition elements of a rule Ri, then the connection weights w_{ij} to a rule node R_i are uniformly calculated for each connection as

$$w_{ij} = Net_i/n,$$

where n is the number of condition elements in the rule R_i, and Net_i is a constant defining what the net input to neuron R_i should be in order to fire the rule. The stronger the rule is as a piece of domain knowledge, the higher Net_i should be, which means a higher contribution of this rule to the output value. For a weak rule R_i, Net_i might take a value of 1, and for a strong rule Net_i might need to be 5, provided a logistic activation function is used. The other connection weights are initialized to zero. The following characteristics of this layer define the inference method performed by the FuNN: summation function s_R, activation function a_R, neuronal output function o_R Additional rule nodes may be preset with zero connection weights. This may give the structure more flexibility to adjust initial rules and antecedent elements in them and to possibly capture new rules. The way the connection weights are interpreted here is used in a rules extraction algorithm REFuNN.

In the *Action elements layer* each node represents one fuzzy predicate (label) in the "action" (consequent) elements of the rules. The connections between the rule nodes and the action nodes are set as normalized confidence factors (CFs) of the rules. The rest of the connections are set to zero. Again, three functions are defined for these nodes, (a) summation function s_A, (b) activation function a_A, and (c) output function o_A. Additional nodes may be used to capture additional action (conclusion) predicates during training (adaptation).

The *output variable layer* represents the output variables of the system. It is defined by the three functions: summation s_O, activation a_O, and output o_O. Figure 4.38 depicts a FuNN for the following two rules:

R_1: *IF x_1 is $A_1(DI_{1,1})$ and x_2 is $B_1(DI_{2,1})$, THEN y is $C_1(CF_1)$*

R_2: *IF x_1 is $A_2(DI_{1,2})$ and x_2 is $B_2(DI_{2,2})$, THEN y is $C_2(CF_2)$*

An algorithm REFuNN for rules extraction from a trained FuNN is presented in chapter 5. The algorithm uses three layers from the FuNN architecture shown in figure 4.38 (FuNN-1), as the fuzzy predicates and membership functions are predefined. Fuzzification and defuzzification are supposed to be done outside the structure.

Figure 4.39 shows a simpler version of FuNN consisting of four layers. The output membership functions C1 and C2 are singletons attached to the connection weigths of the last layer.

4.9 Hierarchical and Modular Connectionist Systems

The flexibility of intelligence comes from the enormous number of different information-processing rules, modules, and the levels of operation of such modules. Hierarchical models are biologically and psychologically

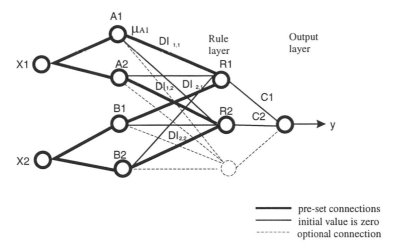

Figure 4.39
A simplified version of a FuNN fuzzy neural network.

plausible. Some possibilities for a connectionist realization of such models is discussed in this section.

Modular systems are systems consisting of several modules linked together for solving a given problem. Representing a system for solving a problem as a modular system may be justified for the following reasons:

• The whole task may be represented as a collection of simpler subtasks, each being solved in one submodel of the whole system, so each module solves a different part of the whole problem, for example, one module is used for feature extraction, and another for pattern classification (which is usually the case in speech recognition systems).

• Different modules may provide alternative solutions, the final one being the best of them or a combination of them; different modules may imitate different experts on the same problem, the final solution being a weighted compromise between the outputs from the modules.

Different modules in a multimodular system may specialize during training to give a good approximation of the solution for a subspace of the whole problem space. They become *local experts*. Another network (a gating network) aggregates the solutions produced by the different modules into a final solution (Jordan and Jacobs 1994). For example, a network that learns the function $f = abs(x)$ can consist of two modules, one to produce the result $f = x$ if $x > 0$, and another to learn the function $f = x$ if $x \leq 0$. A *hierarchy* of simple local experts and gating networks can be built, such that a multimodular network can be used as a local expert at a higher level of the decision structure.

If each of the modules in a modular system is realized in a connectionist way, the system is called a *connectionist modular system*. A connectionist modular system can be *flat*, if all the modules have the same priority for information processing; or *hierarchical*, if some modules have higher priority than other modules in the system. According to the types of neural networks used in a modular neural network, the latter can be classified as *homogeneous*, that is, all the neural networks are of the same type; or *heterogenous*, that is, different types of neural networks are used in one system; this is the case in the example below.

According to the type of connectivity between neural networks in modular neural network systems, the latter can be classified as *fully connected*, where every neural network is connected to every other one by at least one link, or *partially connected*, where only selected neural networks are linked together.

According to the way the neural networks in a modular system are used for solving a task, there are three types of operating modes in a system:

1. *Sequential mode*. Neural networks are used sequentially when different subtasks of the global task are performed; different neural networks are trained either separately or in conjunction with one another.

2. *Parallel mode*. All neural networks work in parallel, either on alternative solutions of one subtask, after which a final solution is worked out based on a given criterion, or on different subtasks if the problem allows a parallel solution.

3. *Mixed mode*. Both of the above modes are implemented in one modular system.

Modular and hierarchical multinetwork systems have been used for:

- Robot control;
- Time-series forecasting (Kohers, 1992);
- Classification of remotely sensed satellite images;
- Geometrical transformation and theorem-proving (Ishikawa, 1992);

• General classification and pattern recognition (Fogelman et al., 1993);

• Planning and predicting of movement of temporospatial objects (Kasabov and Trifonov, 1993)

Sometimes it is possible to solve a problem either by using a single neural network or by using several smaller neural networks. Which way to go? The answer to this question depends very much on the type of task. Modular networks should be used when the task can be adequately represented in a modular or hierarchical way, and when using a single network is unacceptably time- and space-consuming. For more details see the next section.

4.10   Problems

Part A: Case Example Solutions

1. *Using MLP and the Kohonen network for the Bank Loan approval case example.* A two-level hierarchical, modular neural network for solving the Bank Loan case example is shown in figure 4.40. The lower-level network is an MLP using the backpropagation type of training. When

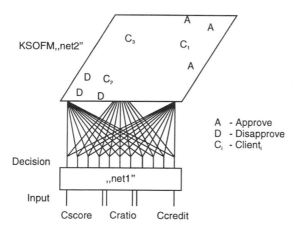

Figure 4.40
Two-layer multimodular network architecture for the Bank Loan Decision Problem. The first layer is an MLP network which produces the output fuzzy vector for the fuzzy variable "Decision." The second layer is an SOM which performs a two-dimensional vector quantization of the decision vectors. The three cases discussed in chapter 3 are presented on the map as points C_1, C_2, C_3. The two parts are trained separately with training data.

recalled with new input data, this network produces the membership function for the decision output variable. The output vector is then fed into a Kohonen SOM network which has quantized the decision space into two topologically distinguished spaces—"approved" and "disapproved." This is an effective way of representing a solution, as it also explains graphically WHY new applications should be approved or disapproved or why the decision is undefined (this is the area between the two clear areas on the SOM). The two parts are trained separately with existing (or generated) data.

2. *Multimodular MLP network for object movement prediction.* A single MLP and a three-modular MLP were trained and tested on the same training data. A comparison between using a single 20-30-40 MLP network and using three smaller MLP networks (figure 4.41A) for

a.

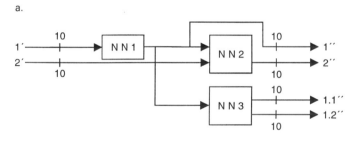

b.

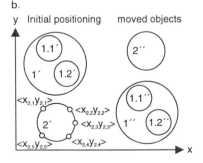

Figure 4.41
(A) A hierarchical neural network architecture consisting of three neural networks, 20 inputs, and 40 outputs. (B) A graphical representation of a task of learning a movement of two objects (denoted as 1 and 2; object 1 has two sub-objects 1.1 and 1.2) from one position (1′ and 2′) to another (1″ and 2″), for which task the modular neural network from (A) is used. Each object or subject is represented by 5 geometrical points in the plain, therefore, by 10 variables.

training with a set of training examples for movement of spatial objects (figure 4.41B) is given in figure 4.42, where the number of neurons (*Nneurons*), number of connection weights (*Nweights*), number of training operations (*Tlearn*), and number of recall operations (*Twork*) are shown for the single neural network (*NNs*) and for the hierarchical, modular network (*NNmod*). The latter consists of three modules: *NNm1*, *NNm2*, and *NNm3*. The figures show that multimodular neural network architecture may have more neurons in total, but a fewer number of connections, thus takes less time for training and less time for recall.

Part B: Practical Tasks and Questions

3. What are the main physical and functional similarities between real and artificial neurons, between real and artificial neural networks?

4. What is the main difference between supervised and unsupervised learning? What does competitive learning mean?

5. What is the essence of the Hebbian learning law?

6. Explain the meaning of the following concepts:

    a. Autoassociative and heteroassociative networks

    b. Autoassociative and heteroassociative memory

    c. Universal function approximator

    d. The winner-takes-all rule

    e. Lateral inhibition;

Architecture	Nepochs	Error	Nweights	Nneurons	Tlearn	Twork
NNs 20:30:40	239	0.0001	1800	70	877130	1870
NNm1 10:10:10	517	0.0001	200	20	217140	220
NNm2 20:15:10	433	0.0001	450	25	227325	475
NNm3 10:15:20	440	0.0001	450	35	235400	485
NNmod (overall)		0.0001	1100	80	679965	1180

Figure 4.42
Comparison between time and space parameters of a single network NNs and the multimodular network NNmod from figure 4.41 for solving the same problem with 20 input variables and 40 output variables.

    f. Feedforward and feedback connections, recurrent networks

    g. Self-organization

    h. Vector quantization

    i. Vigilance factor in ART

    j. Learning rate in the backpropagation algorithm

    k. Gain factor in SOM

    l. Overfitting (overlearning)

    m. Linear separability

    n. Sigmoid function

    o. Radial-basis function

    p. Logistic function

    q. Mean-square error (MSE) and root-mean-square (RMS)

    r. Euclidean distance

    s. Generalization

    t. Massive parallelism in the functioning of the real and artificial neural networks

    u. Gradient-descent optimization algorithm

    v. Momentum in a gradient-descent optimization algorithm

    w. Convergence

    x. Equilibrium

    y. Local minima problem

    z. Capacity of a neural network used as associative memory

7. Explain the meaning of the following concepts:

    a. Castrophic forgetting

    b. Rehearsal in a neural network as a measure against catastrophic forgetting

    c. Deviation scaling parameter in RBF networks

    d. Shift register in a time-delay neural networks

    e. Finite state automatons and their relation to recurrent networks

    f. Hebbian learning law, in case of unsupevised learning

    g. Stability and plasticity in ART neural networks

    h. Codebook vectors in SOM

     i. Attractor point in Hopfield networks

     j. Temperature parameter and annealing in Boltzman pattern associator neural networks

     k. Learning with forgetting

8. What is the difference between ART and BAM networks?

9. What are the main drawbacks of the following neural networks?

     a. Perceptron

     b. MLP with a backpropagation algorithm

     c. Kohonen SOM

     d. Kohonen LVQ

     e. Hopfield network

     f. BAM

     g. ART

10. Why have LVQ1, LVQ2, and LVQ3 been developed and why have they become widely used? How do they differ from SOM?

11. Give an example of bidirectional pattern association with a possible use of BAM.

12. Change the vigilance factor of ART1 to 0.0 and try the examples given in figure 4.20. What will happen then? What will happen if the vigilance factor is 1.0?

13. Run a backpropagation simulator and train an MLP neural network with two randomly selected training subsets A and B from the Iris data set (see appendix A). Observe the change in the training error after each 500 training epochs of alternative training with A and B of the same network. How does the training error decrease?

Part C: Project Specification

Exploratory Analysis of Different Connectionist Models

1. Choose your exploratory data set that contains data and labels of the class elements (see appendixes).

2. Train an MLP neural network with the backpropagation algorithm, using 75% of the data examples for training and the remaining 25% for testing.

a. Explore the correlation between the learning rate and momentum and the speed of training when a training error of 0.001 is chosen to stop the training process. For example, use different values such as:

    i.   Learning rate 0.1, momentum 0.5

    ii. Learning rate 0.5, momentum 0.5

    iii. Learning rate 0.5, momentum 0.9

    iv. Learning rate 0.5, momentum 0.1

    Which values for the learning rate and momentum do you think are the best for your neural network?

b. Explore the influence of the number of hidden nodes and number of layers on the training and test error and on the time for training

3. Train a Kohonen two-dimensional SOM and label it. Use 75% of the data for training and the same data for labeling. Test the SOM with the remaining 25% of the data.

a. Explore the dependence between the classification error and the size of the map; use, for example, 5×5, 10×10, 20×20 SOMs.

b. Explore the influence of the gain factor and the number of training epochs on the time for training.

c. Would the classification error improve if the LVQ algorithm were used?

4. Train an MLP of type FuNN-1 (figure 4.38) after applying fuzzy quantization over the input and output variables. Test the network on the same data as in (2) and (3). Use the backpropagation algorithm.

5. Compare the results obtained by using different connectionist models on the same data set. Which model is the best one for your task?

4.11 Conclusion

Different connectionist models are introduced in this chapter. They are characterized by the types of neurons used, the organization of their connectionist structure, and methods for learning and recall. For this reason, they have different properties which can be used for solving different problems. But all of them are characterized by some common characteristics: learning, generalization, robustness, and massive parallelism.

One of the structural characteristics of the connectionist models makes them very attractive for *hardware realization*, namely, their massive parallelism. A hardware realization of an artificial neural network makes possible building machines that will be faster than the human brain at solving difficult problems.

Some of the numerous applications of the different connectionist models presented in this chapter are discussed in chapter 5. They make these models extremely useful for solving problems and for knowledge-engineering regardless of how much they contribute to our understanding of how the real brain works.

4.12   Suggested Reading

The following references are given for further reading on specified subjects:

Computational models of the brain—Arbib (1987, 1995); Churchland and Sejnowski (1992); Amit (1989); Anderson (1983a,b); Stillings et al. (1995); McShane (1991)

Brief overall presentation on the major neural network models—Arbib (1995); Rumelhart and McClelland (1986); Lippman (1987)

Detailed presentation on the major connectionist models and their applications—Hertz et al. (1991); Zurada (1992)

Algorithms and programs for implementing the major connectionis models—Freeman and Skapura (1992)

Easy-to-read introduction to some basic principles of neural networks—Smith (1993); Davalo and Naim (1991); Anderson (1995)

Fuzzy neurons and fuzzy neural networks: Yamakawa et al. (1992a); Yamakawa (1994), Gupta (1992); Furuhashi et al. (1993); Kasabov (1995c, 1996); Khan (1993); Hashiyama et al. (1993)

This chapter has two major objectives, namely, to present (1) approaches to using neural networks for problem solving and knowledge engineering, and (2) applications of neural networks for solving generic problems.

The main idea behind using neural networks for problem solving is their ability to learn from "past" data and to generalize when responding to new input data. But there are other approaches to using neural networks, such as analyzing neural networks and extracting rules, and explicit knowledge, and inserting rules into connectionist architectures for the purpose of approximate reasoning.

This chapter also presents applications of connectionist systems for solving typical problems such as pattern recognition and classification, speech and language processing, time-series and analogy-based prediction, diagnosis, decision making, control, optimization, and game playing.

5.1 Neural Networks as a Problem-Solving Paradigm

Any of the generic problems discussed in chapter 1 can be solved with the use of neural networks, but how? What is it that makes neural networks such a powerful problem-solving tool?

5.1.1 The Paradigm

The generic characteristics of neural networks, discussed in chapter 4, make possible their use for:

- *Function approximation*, when a set of data is presented
- *Pattern association*
- *Data clustering, categorization, and conceptualization*
- *Learning statistical parameters*
- *Accumulating knowledge through training*
- *"Extracting" knowledge* through analysis of the connection weights
- *Inserting knowledge* in a neural network structure for the purpose of approximate reasoning

Neural network models provide massive parallelism, robustness, and approximate reasoning, which are important for dealing with uncertain, inexact, and ambiguous data, with ill-defined problems and sparse data sets. All the above-mentioned points are discussed here. The problem-solving process, when using neural networks, comprises two phases (figure

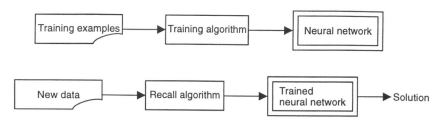

Figure 5.1
Neural networks as a problem-solving paradigm.

5.1): (1) the *training phase*, when training examples are used for training a neural network, or rules are inserted in its structure; and (2) the *recall phase*, when new data are fed into the already trained network and a recall algorithm is used to calculate the results.

Following the representation of the problem-solving process as mapping the domain space into the solution space through problem knowledge, given in chapter 1, this process can be viewed here as mapping the problem domain space into an input state space of a neural network; mapping the solution space into an output space of the neural network; and mapping the problem knowledge (past data and rules) into the synaptic space of all the connection weights of a neural network (or collection of networks); the synaptic connection weights accommodate the problem knowledge (figure 5.2).

There are some general steps to follow when using neural networks as a problem-solving paradigm:

1. Problem identification. What is the generic problem and what kind of knowledge is available?

2. Choosing an appropriate neural network model for solving the problem.

3. Preparing data for training the network, which process may include statistical analysis, discretization, and normalization.

4. Training a neural network, if data for training are available. This step may include creating a learning environment in which neural networks are "pupils."

5. Testing the generalization ability of the trained neural network and validating the results. Different approaches can be used, as discussed below.

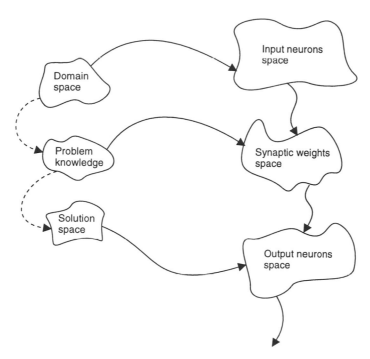

Figure 5.2
Solving problems with neural networks as mapping.

6. Optimizing the architecture, if necessary, which may require a repetition of some of the above steps until satisfactory validation results are obtained. Special strategies to improve the neural network performance may be needed.

The following subsections discuss the implementation of these steps.

5.1.2   Problem Identification and Choosing the Neural Network Model

Before starting to develop a solution to a given problem, questions must be answered. What is the point of using a neural network for solving that specific problem? Why should a neural network be used? What are the benefits of using a network? The generic properties of different neural network types, and connectionist models in general, must be known to answer this question. What properties are going to be useful for solving the problem?

Problem identification also includes analysis of the existing problem knowledge. The problem knowledge may contain data and rules. If data are available, the *independent variables* (the *input variables*) should be clearly distinguished from the *dependent variables* (the *output variables*) in order to choose a proper neural network architecture and a learning method. These variables can be discrete, continuous, linguistic, boolean, etc. In some cases, only input variables are present. In this case, unsupervised learning algorithms and appropriate neural networks can be used to cluster, to conceptualize, and to recognize patterns in the domain data.

If rules are available in the problem knowledge, they can be implemented in an appropriate neural network structure. Especially suitable for connectionist implementation are fuzzy rules. If both rules and data are available, then hybrid systems, which incorporate both neural networks and symbolic AI techniques, can be used, or a neural network can be trained by using both data and rules, the latter being treated as hints or input-output associations.

Choosing the neural network model depends on the type of problem knowledge and on the context of the problem to be solved.

5.1.3 Encoding the Information

Neural networks consist of inputs, outputs, neurons, connections, and so forth. How should existing knowledge and information about the problem be encoded to solve the problem with a neural network? Two possible ways of representing knowledge in neural networks are (1) *local representation*, where every neuron represents one concept or one variable, etc., and (2) *distributed representation*, where a concept or a value for a variable is represented by the collective activation of a group of neurons.

Each way has alternatives. For example, we can represent an output variable that has the context of "percentage" as one neuron (activation values from 0 to 1, a value of 0.01 corresponding to 1%, etc.). Another possible neuronal encoding may use 10 neurons for a "thermometer" encoding (the first neuron represents percentage from 0% to 10%, the second, from 10% to 20%, etc., 100% being represented by the activation of all the output neurons).

When MLP with logistic activation function is used, the output (target) values o are usually chosen in the interval $[0.1, 0.9]$ rather then in $[0.0, 1.0]$ as the derivative of the logistic function which is $o(1-o)$ has a value of 0.0 for $o = 0.0$ and $o = 1.0$.

Output activation values can be interpreted differently, depending on the context of the problem, either as a kind of probability for an event to happen, or as a kind of certainty, confidence, or degree of an event that has happened but only in part, or simply as a value of an output variable.

Encoding the input information is sometimes difficult. This can be caused by problems such as missing values for some of the variables, and unknown dependencies between the problem variables and difficulties in choosing the appropriate set of features. This is the problem with the feature space. Should it be large, or can a better solution be achieved if a smaller number of input variables are used, thereby achieving a smaller problem space?

There are some approaches to solving the first problem. For example, the data instances (training examples) with missing information can be omitted if there are enough other examples. But a better solution may be obtained if the missing values are substituted by the mean value for the corresponding variable over the whole data set.

The second problem seems to be more difficult. Too many variables require much space and time (for training) and may be the cause of a degraded solution due to the introduction of noise through redundant variables and their (possibly) numerous values. Too small a number of variables may not carry sufficient information for solving the problem.

One possible solution to this problem is to analyze the *sensitivity* (S_i) of the neural network to individual variables, say x_i. In this case all the values for x_i in the training data set are substituted with the mean value $\mathbf{M}x_i$ for x_i, and for each individual example $j = 1, 2, \ldots, p$, the error $E(M(x_i))$ is compared to the error $E(x_{ij})$ when x_i is used with its real value x_{ij}:

$$S_i = \sum (E(x_{ij}) - E(M(x_i)))/p$$

Variables with small sensitivity are deleted from the data set, which will increase the speed of training and reduce the size of the network.

Some techniques are often used when preparing data for training a neural network, one of them being *normalization*. The neuronal input signals may be normalized into the same scope, usually in the interval of $[0, 1]$, or $[-1, 1]$. This makes all the neuronal inputs of equal importance. Normalization can be:

• *Linear*, with the use of the formula:

$$x_{ij,\,\mathrm{norm}} = (x_{ij} - x_{i,\,\mathrm{min}})/(x_{i,\,\mathrm{max}} - x_{i,\,\mathrm{min}}),$$

where x_{ij} is a real value, $x_{ij,\,norm}$ is a normalized value, and $x_{i,\,min}$ and $x_{i,\,max}$ are, respectively, the minimum and the maximum values for the variable x_i.

• *Logarithmic normalization*, where logarithms of the values for the variable x_i are used instead of using the real values from the data. This is necessary if the domain of a variable is very broad, for example, winning cash from a lotto competition can be between \$1 and \$1 million; a person's income or a company's weekly profit can be any value between \$0 and, say, \$10,000. There is also evidence (see Cornsweet 1970) that logarithmic scaling is used in biological systems. This also affects the information processing in neural networks, e.g.: $\log x_1 + \log x_2 = \log(x_1 \cdot x_2)$.

Transforming the output-values of the neural network back to real attribute-values, requires the application of an inverse formula, which for the case of linear normalization is:

$$y_{ij} = y_{i,\,min} + (y_{i,\,max} - y_{i,\,min})(o_i - o_{i,\,min})/(o_{i,\,max} - o_{i,\,min}),$$

where o_i is the value of the output from a neuron that represents the output variable y_i, and $o_{i,\,min}$ and $o_{i,\,max}$ are the minimum and maximum output values for the neuron.

Actually, input data to a neural network represent values of a set of features. What features to use depends on the task and the goals. One possibility is to use fuzzy representation (transformation) or real data as input features of neural networks. Using fuzzified data for training neural networks has the following advantages:

• Faster training and better generalization.

• Easier rules extraction and network interpretation.

• Fuzzy labels are extra information (knowledge), which may lead to a better solution.

• It is easy to adjust fuzzy labels according to new situations, thus making the whole system adaptable to new circumstances. For example, 30 years ago, a weakly wage of \$400 was considered to be "good", now it is "low." So, using "old" data is still possible but appropriately labelled.

5.1.4   Training Neural Networks and Validating the Results

Training a neural network requires answering the following two groups of questions, which have specific answers depending on the task and the type of the network used. The first group of questions relates to the design of a learning environment where neural networks are "artificial pupils" that are expected to learn something. The following questions should be discussed here:

• What features should neural networks learn?

• What learning strategies to apply, for example: learning simple features first; dividing the whole task into smaller sub-tasks and training the system on each of the sub-tasks individually, etc.?

• Preparing data for training according to the set strategies; Use of real and synthetic data, etc.

The answers of the above questions may require bringing to this field knowledge from educational psychology, design and engineering, mathematics, and cognitive science.

The second group of questions relates to technical issues, such as:

• What are the neural network architecture and the training algorithm which best suit the task?

• How to initialize the network before starting the training procedure?

• How long to train the network (how many epochs, cycles, iterations, should the training take)? When to stop training?

• How to calculate the training error?

• What training error can assure a good generalization? How to evaluate the generalization ability of the network and its validation?

• How to recognize the convergence?

• How to choose the training parameters, for example, the learning rate, momentum, etc., depending not only on the training algorithm used but also on the training data?

The problem of choosing the best neural network type and architecture and a corresponding training algorithm is discussed briefly later in this section, but it is a heuristic process based on analysis on the available neural network techniques and the requirements of the problem.

Initialization of a neural network means setting the connection weights to some initial values before starting the training algorithm. The initial set of weighs brings the initial error E_0 of the network over the training data to a certain point in the error surface in the weight space. This starting point is important because sometimes, depending on the algorithm, the network goes to the nearest local minimum to this point instead of going to the desired global minimum. Small random numbers set as initial weights usually improve the training results. But there are other algorithms for initialization, which make use of available information, fuzzy rules, which are extracted from the data set can be used to set the initial weight matrix W_0 to a point in a region possibly near to where the global minimum is expected to be (Kasabov 1996).

Two types of error can be calculated in general: (1) when training and (2) when using a network. The error calculated on the basis of the reaction of the neural network to the data used for its training is called *apparent error* or *training error*. It is usually calculated as a mean-square error (see chapter 4). It is important to achieve a small (e.g., 0.001) apparent error, but the network may overlearn data, that is, it may be bound too strongly to the training data and therefore perform an inaccurate generalization.

The *test (validation) error* is calculated when, after having a network trained with a set of training data, another set (test, validation, cross-validation), for which the results are also known, is applied for a recall procedure. The test error (E_{test}) can be calculated differently, two formulas being

$$E_{\text{test}} = \sum_{j=1,m} \sum_{p=1,N \text{ test}} (o_{jp} - y_{jp})^2 / N_{\text{test}},$$

where o_{jp} is the jth output value for the pth testing example, y_{jp} is the desired output for the pth testing example, and N_{test} is the number of test examples, and

$$E_{\text{test}} = N_{\text{correct}} / N_{\text{test}},$$

where N_{correct} is the number of correctly processed test examples and N_{test} is the total number of test examples.

Some schemes to conduct *validation* are as follows:

• *Divide the whole data set into two disjoint sets, training and test*, the first being, for example, 75%, and the second being 25%. This approach is applicable when there are enough data examples. The problem of which data to use for training and which for validation can be solved by random selection, or by applying some specific selection criteria imposed by the nature of the problem. If there are not enough data, this method is not very appropriate. It is always tempting to use the whole data set of N

examples for training, but the problem then arises of how to then validate the results.

• Use the *leave-one-out method*: One example $\mathbf{x}^{(p)}$ is left for validation, and the remaining $(N-1)$ examples are used for training. This is repeated N times, when N different neural networks are trained and then tested with the one left out example. The average of all the validation errors is then calculated:

$$E_{\text{test}} = \sum_{p=1,N} E_{\text{test}}(\mathbf{x}^{(p)})/N$$

This method may be very time-consuming for a big training set.

• *Fold cross-validation*: Here, all the N data examples from a data set D, are used for training and the trained network is then used as an initial set W_0 of weights for validation. The validation is done by dividing the whole data set randomly into several disjoint subsets, D_j $(j = 1, 2, \ldots, k)$, where k is a small number, usually $k = 5$, $k = 10$. Then the network W_0 is trained k times with each of the data sets D/D_j and validated with D_j, the error being $E_{\text{test}}(D_j)$ The total validation error is calculated as an average value of all the errors $E_{\text{test}}(D_j)$, for $j = 1, 2, \ldots, k$ (Geisser 1975).

5.1.5   The Problem of Choosing the "Best" Neural Network Model

Neural networks are universal function approximators. They are "model-free estimators" (Kosko 1992) in the sense that the type of function is not required to be known in order for the function to be approximated. One difficulty, though, is how to chose the best neural network architecture, that is, the neural network model with the smallest approximation error. When a multilayer perceptrons (MLPs) are used, this is the problem (already discussed in chapter 4) of finding the optimal number of hidden nodes. In addition to the heuristics given there, some other techniques are applicable, such as:

• *Growing neural networks*. Training starts with a small number of hidden nodes and, subject to the error calculated, the number of the hidden nodes may increase during the training procedure.

• *Pruning*. This technique is based on gradually removing from the network the weak connections (which have weights around 0) and the neurons connected by them during the training procedure. After removing redundant connections and nodes, the whole network continues to be trained and the rest of the connections "take the functions which the pruned ones might have been doing." Pruning may be implemented through learning-with-forgetting methods, when the weak connections gradually fade away and eventually get pruned (Ishikawa 1995).

Growing and pruning are also applicable to input neurons, thus making the whole neural network dynamically changing according to the existing information in the data set.

5.2   Connectionist Expert Systems

In chapters 2 and 3 we presented block diagrams of a symbolic AI expert system and a fuzzy expert system. Here we introduce *connectionist expert systems*. These are expert systems as previously defined, which have their knowledge base represented in a connectionist structure. The neural network properties of learning and generalization, adaptability, robustness, associative storage of information, massive parallelism, and other characteristics make them a very powerful paradigm for building knowledge-based expert systems.

5.2.1   Architectures and Approaches to Building Connectionist Expert Systems

A general architecture of a connectionist expert system (CES) is given in figure 5.3. It is distinguished from the symbolic AI and fuzzy expert systems in the way problem knowledge is used. Here problem knowledge need not only be a set of heuristic rules but can also be given as a set of past experience examples, for example, case studies of how a physician has previously treated patients. A CES may contain the following modules:

• A *connectionist knowledge-based module*, represented (either partially or fully) as a connectionist architecture. Four different approaches to its building are:

1. Past, historical data are used to train a network. After training, the network contains the system's knowledge.

2. Existing problem knowledge, for example, rules, is implemented in a neural network. One way to do this is to represent the rules in the form of a set of training examples and train a neural network with these examples using standard training algorithms, as presented in chapter 4. The rules are considered as input-output associations to be learned by a neural network.

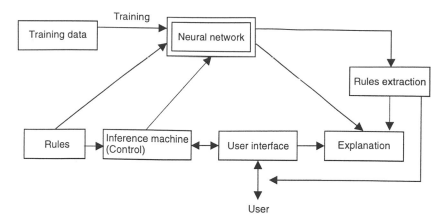

Figure 5.3
Connectionist expert system.

3. Existing problem knowledge, for example, rules, is used to prewire (to calculate the connection weights) a network structure instead of training it. This is the case of inserting explicit knowledge in a neural network structure. Such systems, one of them being the class of connectionist production systems, are discussed later in this chapter.

4. All of the above methods are used for building the system. For example, the neural network is prewired according to an existing (initial) set of rules and then trained with data—either past data or current data accumulated when the system is running.

Apart from the above approaches it is possible to combine knowledge represented in a symbolic or fuzzy form with knowledge represented in a connectionist form. Such systems are called hybrid systems and are discussed in chapter 6.

• A *connectionist inference control module*, which controls the information flow between all the modules and initiates inference over the connectionist knowledge base. A connectionist inference is characterized by some desirable features, one of them being approximate reasoning, that is, if the new input data do not match exactly the previous examples or the conditions in the problem knowledge rules, a solution close to an optimal one is found. Approximate reasoning in connectionist systems is possible because of their faculty for generalization. Different methods for approximate reasoning in connectionist systems have been developed, depending on the task and on the neural network architecture used. Some of them are discussed below. Connectionist systems can realize different reasoning strategies and methods, including fuzzy reasoning methods, finite automata reasoning, and exact symbolic AI reasoning.

• *Rules extraction module*, which analyzes the connectionist knowledge base and produces the underlying rules that are inherent, or "buried," in the data. Methods for rules extraction are presented later.

• *Explanation module*, to explain to the user the behavior of the system when reasoning over particular input data.

• *User interface module*, which "communicates" with the user or with the environment. As a user interface, a spoken or natural language interface can be used, developed on the basis of using neural networks or other techniques.

Different techniques for building connectionist systems for problem-solving and connectionist expert systems in particular, and their applications for solving generic and specific AI problems, are given in the remainder of this chapter. The first two approaches to building a connectionist knowledge-based module are explained in the next two subsections.

5.2.2   Building Connectionist Knowledge Bases from Past Data

When problem knowledge is represented by a set of past data, a neural network can be used and trained with the data. The network should then be treated as a connectionist knowledge base. The data used can be exact or fuzzy or a combination of both.

Example   To illustrate training a neural network with exact data and with fuzzy data, we use data for bank loan applicants. Instead of having fuzzy rules, as was the case in chapter 3, we have a set of examples of loan applications and their degree of approval, each of the examples consisting of three input variables (CScore, CCredit, CRatio) and one output variable—the decision level (DL).

a. Using exact training data an MLP neural network, with 3 input neurons, 11 intermediate nodes, and 1 output neuron, to be trained with the use of the backpropagation algorithm, is shown in figure 5.4. The number of hidden nodes is assigned to be equal to the number of supposed

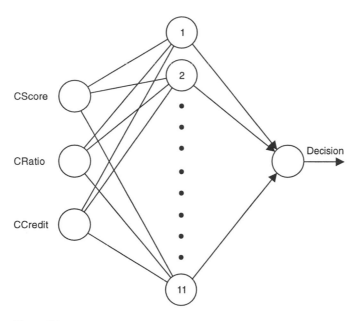

Figure 5.4
A neural network for training with the exact data for the Bank Loan Decision problem.

different groups of applicants. Such a relatively large number of hidden nodes would facilitate effective training on a very large data set. Testing the validity of the neural network after training can be done with an use of a test set.

b. Using fuzzy input data: The three exact input variables above are fuzzy-quantized into six fuzzy values using the fuzzy membership functions given in chapter 3; the output value is represented by two fuzzy numbers, corresponding to the two membership functions of the fuzzy output labels "approve" and "disapprove" (figure 5.5). Figure 5.6 shows the results for three test data examples. The results for the first and for the second application cases are as expected. The network does not infer any particular decision for the third application case, which is also correct. The neural network's "answer" is "don't know." The neural network "cannot suggest" anything about this application.

Some advantages to using this approach to building connectionist knowledge bases are easy and fast knowledge base development, no need for interviewing experts, etc.; easy accommodation of new case examples

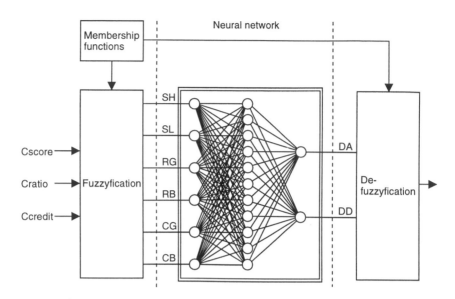

Figure 5.5
A neural network for training a connectionist system for the Bank Loan Decision problem with fuzzified data.

Appl	CScore	SH	SL	Cratio	RG	RB	CCredit	CG	CB	DA	DD	DL
1	190	0.7	0	0.4	0.7	0	3	0.7	0	1	0	10
2	160	0	0.8	0.5	0	0.7	7	0	0.7	0	1	0
3	190	0.7	0	0.5	0	0.7	3	0.7	0	0.5	0.5	5

Figure 5.6
Testing the neural network from figure 5.5 with three test cases. Here, SH, SL, RE, RB, CE, CB denote the membership degrees to which the input data belong to the input fuzzy values, and DA and DD are the inferred degrees for Decision Approve and Decision Disapprove, DL is the level of approval after defuzzification.

as they come through further experience; and good approximate reasoning facilities; new cases are judged on the basis of the closest past cases.

There are also disadvantages to this approach, namely, it is difficult to understand and explain the solution; therefore there is a need for neural network analysis and explicit knowledge extraction for justification and explanation.

5.2.3   Neural Networks Can Memorize and Approximate Fuzzy Rules

When problem knowledge includes explicit (fuzzy) rules, a connectionist system can be trained with them, as with input-output associations where the input patterns are the antecedent parts of the rules and the output patterns are the consequent parts. A fuzzy association $A \to B$ where A and B are fuzzy values, defined, for example, by their membership functions, can be memorized in an n-input, m-output neural network, where n is the cardinality of the universe Ux, m is the cardinality of the universe Uy, and x and y are fuzzy variables with corresponding fuzzy values A and B (Kosko 1992).

This is the basis for using connectionist architectures for reasoning over fuzzy rules of the type *IF x is A, THEN y is B*. An MLP neural network can be trained with a set of fuzzy rules. The rules are treated as input-output training examples. When a new fuzzy set A' is supplied as a fuzzy input, the network will produce an output vector that is the desired fuzzy output B'. The generalized modus ponens law can be realized in a connectionist way. The following inference laws can also be satisfied by the same neural network, subject to a small error: $A \to B$ (modus ponens); Very $A \to$ Very B; More-or-less $A \to$ More-or-less B.

A method for implementing multiantecedent fuzzy rules on a single neural network is introduced in Kosko (1992) and Kasabov (1993a). The dimension of the input vector is the sum of the used discrete representation for the cardinality of the universes of all the fuzzy input variables. The dimension of the output vector is the sum of the corresponding discrete cardinality of all universes of the output fuzzy variables in the fuzzy rules. The fuzzy rules are assumed to have the same input and output variables but different combinations of their fuzzy values. If OR connectives are used in a rule, it may require that more training examples are generated based on combinations between antecedent parts of the rules. This approach is illustrated in figure 5.7 on the set of the two fuzzy rules

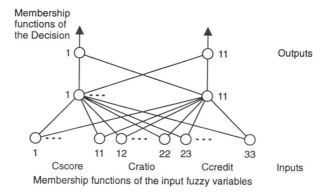

Figure 5.7
33-11-11 neural network for the Bank Loan Decision Problem.

Case   Fuzzy decision

1   0 0 0 0 0 0 .2 .6 1 1 1
2   1 1 1 .7 .3 0 0 0 0 0 0
3   .6 .5 .6 .1 0 0 0 .1 .4 .4 .4

Figure 5.8
Fuzzy decision for three test cases for loan approval, obtained by using an MLP neural network.

for the Bank Loan Decision problem. The MLP consists of 33 input nodes, 11 intermediate nodes, and 11 output nodes. The inferred bank loan fuzzy decision values for the same three bank loan applicants as used in the example above, but here represented as fuzzy input values, are given as fuzzy membership functions in figure 5.8. The experiments show that the decisions inferred by the neural network for the three representative cases defined as fuzzy sets are correct. The ambiguity in the third solution vector clearly suggests 'not known decision' case.

A chain of neural networks can be designed if the fuzzy rules base consists of chains of fuzzy rules, for example:

Rule 1: IF X is A and Y is B, THEN Z is C

Rule 2: IF Z is C, THEN P is D

Using a chain of neural networks is a multimodular realization of the law of inference called "syllogism". A chain of neural networks is the simplest possible multineural network architecture that can realize simple time and space hierarchies in the solution process.

Some advantages when using the discussed here approach to building connectionist knowledge bases are: a possible mixture of rules and data examples, if available, in one system, and fast realization on specialized hardware.

Possible disadvantages of the approach may be poor generalization, if the number of the rules is small and the problem space large, because one rule is treated as one example, and inference results then may be difficult to explain.

5.3 Connectionist Models for Knowledge Acquisition: One Rule Is Worth a Thousand Data Examples

Indeed, a rule, being a "patch" in the problem state space, may cover thousands of data examples. But the number of the examples covered by a rule is not the most important point here.

We have already shown that neural networks can learn from data. But can we use what has been learned by them to improve our understanding of the problems? Can we learn from what a network has? One way to do this is to try to extract explicit knowledge, (e.g., rules) from a trained network. A module for analyzing a connectionist knowledge base and extracting explicit knowledge may be crucial for putting a connectionist expert system in practice, as many decision-making systems are not acceptable if they cannot explain their behavior and "reveal" the knowledge and the reasoning used in solving problems. The rationale of the problem of knowledge acquisition is presented first.

5.3.1 Why Acquisition of Knowledge from Data Is Important

The traditional approach to building knowledge-based systems is to use rules articulated by experts and to build an expert system. If only this approach is used, some problems arise:

• Experts develop their own internal representation of reality, which is only one aspect of the whole process; a data set may contain much more than that.

• Rules valid in one framework may not be valid in another, so it is desirable to be able to extract, to learn rules regularly and easily from fresh, new data.

• Experts may not be aware of the underlying rules in existing data.

• It takes time for experts to learn rules from experience, which rules may reside peacefully in data and may have been deeply buried there.

• It is extremely difficult to articulate, maintain, update, and implement a huge number of rules.

• The path from the expert to the machine is very noisy, that is, information can be easily lost or corrupted.

One alternative to the standard approach is to build automatic learning machines which learn explicit rules from data, if enough data are available. Rules extracted from data can be subsequently used for the purpose of reasoning, explanation, understanding problems, and trying alternative techniques for solving problems, for example, fuzzy inference machines and AI rule-based techniques.

Neural networks are appropriate candidates for the task of knowledge acquisition from data because of the following:

• Neural networks can learn from past data and generalize over new data.

• Neural networks can learn to approximate a function from a table of input-output data.

• Neural networks can learn features from data.

• Neural networks can learn to distinguish groups, categories in which elements are grouped, either in a supervised or unsupervised mode.

• Neural networks can learn probabilities and statistical distribution from data.

• Rules are associations between groups ("clusters" and "patches") from the domain space and "patches" from the solution space. Neural networks trained with data learn these associations.

The problem is how to extract the knowledge that a neural network has accumulated during training, that is, how to open the "black box" and see the rules there.

There are different methods that can be applied for rules extraction from neural network architectures. They can be classified in two major groups: (1) destructive learning, that is, learning by pruning the neural network architecture during training; (2) nondestructive learning of rules.

Learned (or articulated) initial set of rules can be used to "prewire" a neural network before consecutive training with real data for the purpose of better generalization. Two ways of achieving this task are (1) setting only selected connections in a fuzzy neural network, and (2) weights initialization of a fully connected neural network before training. The above groups of methods are presented in the following subsections.

Extracting rules from data may subsequently mean loss of information. The way knowledge is extracted restricts aspects of that knowledge and directs and biases the knowledge acquisition process. A data set may contain much more than is extracted from it, for example, many more interdependencies between attributes, many more relations, many more inference paths. Neural networks are only one technique. Other techniques may be used alternatively or additionally, for example, genetic algorithms.

5.3.2 Destructive Learning of Rules in Neural Networks: Learning Through Forgetting and Pruning

Destructive learning is a technique that destroys the initial neural network architecture for the purpose of better learning. One method in this class is *structural learning with forgetting* (Ishikawa 1995; Ishikawa and Moriyama 1995), described below. The method is based on the following assumptions:

• Training of a neural network starts with all the connections present.

• A standard algorithm for training is used, but the weights "forget" a little bit when they change (see the "learning-with-forgetting" rule in chapter 4).

• After a certain number of cycles, the connections, which have small weights (around 0), are deleted from the structure (pruned).

• Training continues until convergence.

• The trained network consists of connections only, which represent underlining rules in data between the input variables and the output variables.

Forgetting can be selective, that is, only certain connections with small weights forget.

Some advantages of using this approach are that better generalization can be achieved when compared with that of a fully connected trained neural network, and training is faster because unnecessary connections are deleted.

A definite drawback of the method is that the neural network structure is destroyed after training; it may not be possible to accommodate new data, significantly different from the data already used.

5.3.3 Using Competitive Learning Neural Networks for Rules Extraction

Clusters in the input-output problem space represent "patches" of data, which can be represented as rules. Neurons in competitive learning neural networks learn to represent centers of clusters. A weight vector $\mathbf{w}_j$ may be viewed as a geometrical center of a cluster of data.

The above characteristic of competitive learning neural networks can be used for the purpose of rules extraction, and finding fuzzy rules in particular (Kosko 1992). Figure 5.9 shows a two-dimensional input-output space for learning rules of the form of IF X is A, THEN Y is B, where A and B can be defined either as intervals for extracting interval rules or as fuzzy

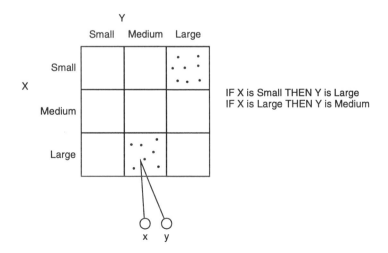

Figure 5.9
A two-dimensional input-output space for learning rules. A fuzzy rule represents a quadruple "patch" from the space with which points of data have been associated.

labels for extracting fuzzy rules. This clustering can be achieved in a competitive learning neural network. The main requirement of learning rules through clustering in competitive learning algorithms is that the training data set should include a significant number of samples. There are some characteristics of this type of learning rules:

• The set of extracted rules may only partially cover the whole input-output space.

• If fuzzy quantization of the input and the output variables is used, then the set of fuzzy rules may overlap, that is, one input data vector may be covered by several fuzzy rules.

• The number of rules can be controlled by a threshold of significance, being proportional to the number of data elements in a cluster, so only significant rules may be extracted.

Figure 5.10 shows a three-dimensional space for learning rules for the Inverted Pendulum case example.

Example Fuzzy rules extracted from Water Flow to a Sewage Plant data (see appendix C) are given in figure 5.11A. The rules have two input variables: the day, a holiday or workday and time of the day, and one output variable: the water flow. The number of rules extracted can be controlled by a threshold which defines how many data points at minimum have to be associated with a "patch" so that this "patch" is represented as a rule. The rules extracted may be approximate and further

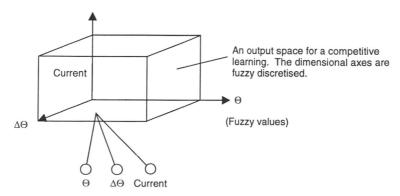

Figure 5.10
A three-dimensional space for learning rules for the Inverted Pendulum case example.

a.

RULE TGRule0:
  IF (Day IS Hol) AND (Time IS Very_early_morning) THEN Flow = Medium
RULE TGRule1:
  IF (Day IS Hol) AND (Time IS Early_morning) THEN Flow = Quite_big_actually
RULE TGRule2:
  IF (Day IS Hol) AND (Time IS Late_morning) THEN Flow = Quite_big_actually
RULE TGRule3:
  IF (Day IS Hol) AND (Time IS Afternoon) THEN Flow = HIGH
RULE TGRule4:
  IF (Day IS Hol) AND (Time IS Evening) THEN Flow = HIGH
RULE TGRule5:
  IF (Day IS Hol) AND (Time IS Night) THEN Flow = Quite_big_actually
RULE TGRule6:
  IF (Day IS Weekday) AND (Time IS Very_early_morning)
  THEN Flow= Quite_big_actually
RULE TGRule7:
  IF (Day IS Weekday) AND (Time IS Early_morning)
  THEN Flow = Quite_big_actually
RULE TGRule8:
  IF (Day IS Weekday) AND (Time IS Late_morning) THEN Flow = HIGH
RULE TGRule9:
  IF (Day IS Weekday) AND (Time IS Afternoon) THEN Flow = Medium
RULE TGRule10:
  IF (Day IS Weekday) AND (Time IS Evening) THEN Flow = Medium
RULE TGRule11:
  IF (Day IS Weekday) AND (Time IS Night) THEN Flow = Medium

b.

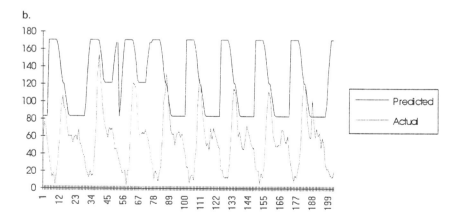

Figure 5.11
(a) Fuzzy rules extracted through differential competitive learning implemented in a tool (TIL Shell, 1993) for the water flow prediction (see appendix C). (B) The rules are applied for predicting new values through max-min compositional inference.

refinement may be needed. This is illustrated in figure 5.11B, where the extracted rules have been applied through a MAX-MIN compositional fuzzy inference method for predicting the next-hour water flow for a set of test data for 199 hours ahead. The prediction is too rough, even though the tendency and the peaks in the next-hour water flow have been predicted. Because there are no rules for the "Low" value of the water flow, the flow predicted by using the rules is much higher than the actual. After a rough set of fuzzy rules is extracted, further refinement of these rules may be achieved by.

• Using more fuzzy labels to quantize the input and output variables

• Using another inference method one more suitable for the actual application task

• Using a more precise form of rules by adding coefficients of importance and other parameters for representing the uncertainty in the data set

• Inserting the initial rules into a connectionist structure, with further training and consecutive (refined) rules extraction (Okada et al. 1992; Kasabov 1996).

The approach presented here uses real data for training a competitive learning neural network. Fuzzy rules were then extracted based on fuzzy quantization. But a neural network can also be trained with fuzzified data, which is the case in the method presented in the next subsection.

5.3.4   Neural Networks for Learning Fuzzy Rules with Degrees of Importance and Certainty Factors: The REFuNN Algorithm

An algorithm called REFuNN (*r*ules *e*xtraction from a *fu*zzy *n*eural *n*etwork) is presented here. The REFuNN algorithm, first published in Kasabov (1993b) and further refined in Kasabov (1995c), is a simple connectionist method for extracting weighted fuzzy rules and simple fuzzy rules in the form of:

Rulei: IF x_1 is $A_{1i}(DI_{1i})$ and x_2 is $A_{2i}(DI_{2i})$ and ... and x_k is $A_{ki}(DI_{ki})$, THEN y is B_i (CF_i)

where A_{ji}, B_i $(i = 1, 2, \ldots, n; j = 1, 2, \ldots, k)$ are fuzzy values (labels) defined by their membership functions, DI_{ji} are relative degrees of importance attached to the condition elements in the rules, and CFi is a confidence factor attached to the rule.

The method is based on training an MLP architecture with fuzzified data. The REFuNN algorithm, outlined below, is based on the following principles:

1. Simple operations are used and a low computational cost is achieved.

2. Hidden nodes in an MLP can learn features, rules, and groups in the training data.

3. Fuzzy quantization of the input and the output variables is done in advance; the granularity of the fuzzy representation (the number of fuzzy labels used) defines in the end the "fineness" and quality of the extracted rules. Standard, uniformly distributed triangular membership functions can be used for both fuzzy input and fuzzy output labels.

4. Automatically extracted rules may need additional manipulation depending on the reasoning method applied afterward.

The REFuNN Algorithm

Step 1. Initialization of an FuNN   A fully connected MLP neural network is constructed as shown in figure 5.12 where an exemplary structure for the Bank Loan case example is also shown. This FuNN is a part of the fuzzy neural network architecture shown in figure 4.38 (see the explanation in chapter 4). The functional parameters of the rule layer and the output fuzzy predicates layer can be set as follows: summation input function; sigmoid activation function; direct output function.

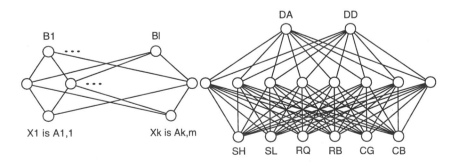

Figure 5.12
A general architecture of a network for learning fuzzy rules and a particular architecture for the Bank Loan Decision Problem. Each of the fuzzy input variables is discretized, the last one, x_k, being discretized into m labels. The output variable has l fuzzy labels.

Step 2. Training the FuNN A supervised training algorithm is performed for training the network with fuzzified data until convergence. A backpropagation training algorithm can be used. A part of the trained FuNN with data generated for the Bank Loan case example is shown in figure 5.13. Stepwise training and zeroing can also be applied.

Step 3. Extracting an initial set of weighted rules A set of rules $\{r_j\}$ is extracted from the trained network as follows. All the connections to an output neuron B_j that contribute significantly to its possible activation (their values, after adding the bias connection weight if such is used, are over a defined threshold Th_a) are picked up and their corresponding hidden nodes R_j, which represent a combination of fuzzy input labels, are analyzed further on. Only condition element nodes that support activating the chosen hidden node R_j will be used in the antecedent part of a rule r_j (the connection weights are above a threshold Th_c). The weights of the connections between the condition-element neurons and the rule nodes are taken as initial relative degrees of importance of the antecedent fuzzy propositions. The weights of the connections between a rule node R_j and an output node B_j define the initial value for the certainty degree CF_j. The threshold Th_c can be calculated by using the formula:

$$Th_c = Net_{max}/k,$$

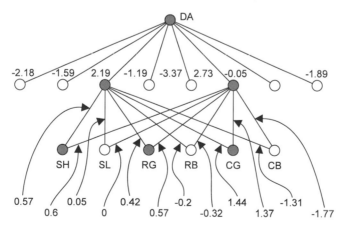

Figure 5.13
A part of the trained network for learning fuzzy rules from data about the Bank Loan Decision Problem.

r1: [SH(0.6) & RG(0.57) & CG(1.37)] (2.73) -> DA;

r2: [SH(0.57)& RG(0.42) & CG(1.44)] (2.19) -> DA.

r3: [SL(1.47) RB(1.54) CB(2.60)] (3.28) -> DD;

r4: [SL(1.39) RB(1.05) CB(1.71)] (2.25) -> DD;

r5: [SL(1.18) RB(0.9) CB(1.9)] (1.89) -> DD;

r6: [SL(0.95) RB(0.85) CB(1.45)] (1.54) -> DD;

r7: [SL(0.65) RB(0.63) CB(1.17)] (1.29) -> DD.

Figure 5.14
Initial set of fuzzy rules extracted from an MLP trained with fuzzified data for the Bank Loan
Decision Problem.

where Net_{max} is the desired value for the net input to a rule neuron to fire
the corresponding rule, and k is the number of the input variables. Figure
5.14 shows a set of initial set of weighted rules extracted for the Bank Loan
example.

Step 4. Extracting simple fuzzy rules from the set of weighted rules The
threshold Th_c. used in step 3 was defined such that all the condition
elements in a rule should *collectively* trigger the activation of this rule.
This is analogous to an AND connective. The number of fuzzy predicates
allowed to be represented in the antecedent part of a rule is not more than
the number of input variables (one fuzzy predicate per variable at most).
The initial set of weighted rules can be converted into a set of *simple fuzzy
rules* by simply removing the weights from the condition elements. Some
antecedent elements, however, can trigger the rules without support from
the test of the condition elements, that is, their degrees of importance
$DI_{ij} = w_{ij}$ (connection weights) are higher than a chosen threshold, for
example, $Th_{OR} = Net_{max}$. Such condition elements form separate rules,
which transformation is analogous to a decomposition of a rule with OR
connectives into rules with AND connectives only.

Example   If there is an initial weighted rule

IF x_1 is A (8.3) and x_2 is B (1.2), THEN y is C, and a threshold of $Th_{OR} = 5.0$ is chosen, then two separate simple fuzzy rules will be formed:

IF x_1 is A and x_2 is B THEN y is C
IF x_1 is A, THEN y is C.

The AND and OR connectives used here are vague, weak, and loosely defined. An AND connective should rather be expressed as a "mutual support" between variables or as *synergism*.

Step 5. Aggregating the initial weighted rules   All the initial weighted rules $\{r_{i1}, r_{i2} \ldots\}$ that have the same condition elements and the same consequent elements, subject only to different degrees of importance, are aggregated into one rule. The relative degrees of importance DI_{ij} are calculated for every condition element A_{ij} of a rule R_i as a normalized sum of the initial degrees of importance of the corresponding antecedent elements in the initial rules r_{ij}. The following two rules R1 and R2 were obtained by aggregating the initial rules from figure 5.14:

R1: $SH(1.2)$ AND $RG(1)$ AND $CG(2.5) \rightarrow DA$

R2: $SL(1.1)$ AND $RB(1)$ AND $CB(1.8) \rightarrow DD$

An additional option in REFuNN is learning NOT connectives in the rules. In this case negative weights whose absolute values are above the set thresholds Th_c and Th_a are considered and the input labels corresponding to the connected nodes are included in the formed simple fuzzy rules with a NOT connective in front. This algorithm is illustrated on the Iris data set in section 5.11 of this chapter.

Other algorithms for fuzzy rules extraction from a trained fuzzy neural network can be found in d'Alche-Buc et al. (1992); Yi and Oh (1992); Mukaidono and Yamaoka (1992); and Hayashi (1991).

5.3.4   Tuning Fuzzy Rules and Membership Functions in Fuzzy Neural Networks

One of the main problems in building fuzzy systems is the problem of defining fuzzy membership functions for the fuzzy-quantizing concepts (fuzzy sets) in addition to the problem of defining fuzzy rules. Fuzzy neural networks (FNNs) can be used for this purpose. An FNN is set according to an initial set of fuzzy rules and initially defined membership functions, as explained in chapter 4. After training with data, more precise fuzzy rules can be extracted from the FNN and more precise membership functions, both of which reflect the information contained in the training data used. The FNN tunes the membership functions in the antecedents of the rules and identifies the fuzzy rules by adjusting the connection weights. Figure 5.15A and B shows an FNN and the 10 rules about *bond rating* implemented in the structure of the FNN (Okada et al. 1992). After training, the membership functions change (see figure 5.15C) and so do the weighting coefficients for the fuzzy rules. As well as being useful for tuning and extracting fuzzy rules and membership functions, the FNN provides better results. The FNN is in this case faster than an MLP when training, and more accurate when tested. A bell-shape membership function for the label "Medium" is realized in figure 5.15A by adding two sigmoids multiplied to 1 and -1 correspondingly.

The connection weights between the input layer and the second layer, which are subject to change during training, represent the sigmoid parameters. The connection weights between the rule neurons and the consequent fuzzy labels nodes represent the weighting (confidence) of the rules. The sixth, seventh, and eighth layers realize COG defuzzification. That could be done in a simpler connectionist structure (see Neo-Fuzzy Neuron, chapter 4) if uniformly distributed triangular membership functions were assumed for the output variable.

5.3.5 Using an Initial Set of Rules for Initialization of Connection Weights Before Training

A set of existing or initial fuzzy rules extracted from a data set can be used for achieving better generalization in an MLP neural network, still keeping all the connections in it for possible further use. Initial rules can be used for defining the number of hidden nodes and for calculating the initial values for the connection weights. If n rules of the form of the ones used in the REFuNN algorithm (see above) are known, then a three-layer MLP can be initialized as follows: $w_{ij} = DI_{ij}/\sum_{(i)} D_{ij}$, if the fuzzy label A_{ij} takes part in the rule Rj, or $w_{ij} = 0$ otherwise, for the connections between the input nodes i ($i = 1, 2, \ldots, k$) and hidden nodes j ($j = 1, 2, \ldots, n$), and $w_{jl} = CD_j$, ($j = 1, 2, \ldots, n$) for the connections between hidden nodes j ($j = 1, 2, \ldots, n$) and output nodes l. Initialization by using fuzzy rules brings the starting weight vector W_0 of the network into a region where the convergence state is anticipated, thus resulting in faster convergence and better generalization (Kasabov 1996). It is not required here that the neural network be set with a few connections only, as is the case with the FNN (Okada et al. 1992). Here, all the connections are kept during the initialization, but some of them, which represent initial rules, have values different from zero. Training and zeroing techniques may be applied.

We have discussed so far fuzzy rules insertion and implementation into connectionist structures, fuzzy neural networks. But what about symbolic rules, i.e. propositional rules, production rules, predicate clauses, etc.? These are discussed in the next section and in chapter 6.

5.4 Symbolic Rules Insertion in Neural Networks: Connectionist Production Systems

Building a connectionist rule base is possible not only by training a neural network with a set of data examples but by inserting existing rules into a neural network structure (see 5.2). Using connectionist representation of problem knowledge has all the advantages of the connectionist systems. It therefore deserves attention. This problem was discussed for fuzzy rules and fuzzy neural networks. Here it is discussed for rigid, symbolic rules.

5.4.1 Representing Symbolic Knowledge as Neural Networks—Why and How?

The standard neural network models have been developed for solving problems based on learning from examples. They have been inspired by the physiology of the human brain and what is known of its structure and organization.

On the other hand, there are many methods for representing and processing explicit knowledge that are claimed to be psychologically plausible. The gap between the physiological processes in the brain and the cognitive processes is still not understood. But from an engineering point of view, it is possible to design artificial neurons and neural networks that are dedicated to representing and processing existing structured knowledge. This approach brings the advantages of connectionism, that is, learning, generalization, robustness, massive parallelism, etc., to the elegant and beautiful methods for symbolic processing, logical inferences, and goal-driven reasoning.

How can both paradigms be blended at a low, neuronal level? How can structured knowledge be built up in a neuron and in a neural network, and a *connectionist rule-based system* realized?

a.

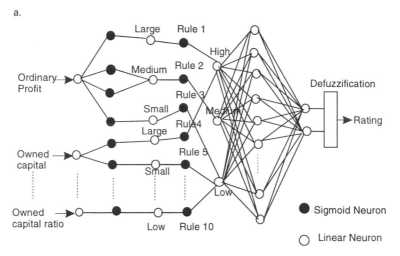

b.

	Basic Rules
Rule 1	Rating is high if ordinary profit is large
Rule 2	Rating is medium if ordinary profit is medium
Rule 3	Rating is low is ordinary profit is small

	Auxilitary Rules
Rule 4	Rating is high if owned capital is large
Rule 5	Rating is low if owned capital is small
Rule 6	Rating is high if interest covarage ratio is high
Rule 7	Rating is low if interest covarage ratio is low
Rule 8	Rating is high if long-term loan ratio is low
Rule 9	Rating is low if long-term loan ratio is high
Rule 10	Rating is low if owned capital ratio is low

Figure 5.15
Implementing 10 rules for bond rating as a fuzzy neural network (FNN). (Adapted with permission from Okada et al. 1992.) (A) The structure of the FNN defined and initialized according to the initial set of fuzzy rules. (B) The initial set of fuzzy rules for bond rating. (C) The initial and modified membership functions after training.

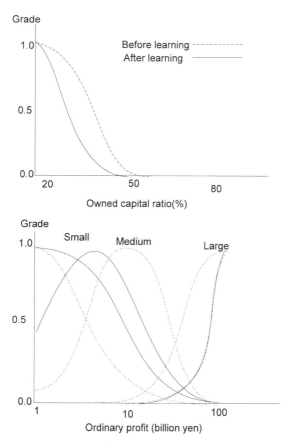

Figure 5.15 (continued)

Representing symbolic knowledge, for example, production rules, predicates and clauses, frames, etc., in a neural network structure requires appropriate structuring of the neural network and special methods.

A neural network that has been built to represent structured knowledge may have connections that are *fixed*, that is, the network cannot learn and "improve" its knowledge; and *adaptable*, that is, the network can learn in addition to its previously inserted structured knowledge; it can adjust, improve, and modify it in a similar way to the FNN (see figure 5.15).

Once rules are represented in a neural network, the type of inference has to be defined. A great advantage to using neural networks for

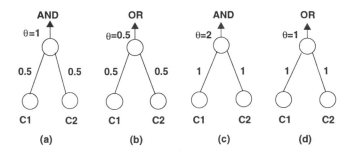

Figure 5.16
A simple binary neuron which realizes AND and OR propositional rules in different ways.

implementing rule-based systems is their capacity for approximate reasoning. It is true only if the neurons used in the network allow for grades. If, for example, they are binary, only exact reasoning would be possible.

5.4.2   Neurons and Neural Networks that Represent Simple Symbolic Rules

A boolean propositional rule of the form of

IF x_1 and x_2 and ... x_n, THEN y,

where x_i $(i = 1, 2, ..., n)$ and y are boolean propositions, can be represented in a binary input–binary output neuron which has a simple summation input function and an activation thresholding function (a threshold of θ) (figure 5.16a and c). Similarly, the boolean propositional rule:

IF x_1 or x_2 or ... or x_n THEN y

will be realized in a similar binary neuron but with different connection weights and thresholds [figure 5.16(b) and (d)]. The neurons cannot learn. These two simple neurons can be used for building neural networks that represent a whole set of rules, but which are not adaptable. A network that represents a set of simple propositions is shown in figure 5.17 (Botha et al. 1988).

Propositional rules that are constructed of more terms in their antecedent parts can also be realized in a similar way. A general scheme of a connectionist system that realizes more complex rules is given in figure 5.18.

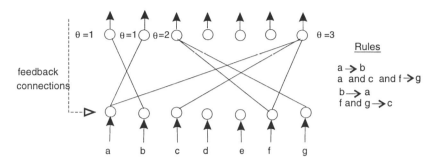

Figure 5.17
A network that realizes a set of simple propositions. A feedback may be used for a chain inference. For each connection a weight of 1 is assumed (Botha et al. 1988.)

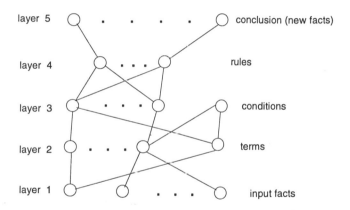

Figure 5.18
A general scheme of a connectionist system for realizing a set of production rules. Each layer realizes one stage of the inference process over production rules.

Symbolic rules that contain different types of uncertainties can also be realized in a connectionist structure. These include *rules where uncertainty is expressed by probabilities*; in this case a neural network is set in such a way that it calculates conditional probabilities; and *rules with confidence factors*, that is,

IF x_1 is A_1 and x_2 is A_2 and ... x_n is A_n, THEN B (CF)

can be realized either by: (1) inserting the rule into the connections of n-input, one output neuron, or (2) applying a training procedure to a neuron with training examples, whose input and output values represent certainties for the existing facts to match the condition elements and confidence for the inferred conclusion.

Example   By applying the second approach from above the rule "IF (high temperature) and (headache), THEN (flu) (CF = 0.7)" can be realized by a single two-input, one-output, continuous-value neuron trained with the training example: 1,1, 0.7. The neuron will make a correct inference and calculate the certainty of the flu transpiring if the two input parameters had different certainties from 1 for a new case, say (high temperature = 0.7) and (headache = 0.9).

Realizing more than one rule in a single neuron of the perceptron type may not be appropriate, having in mind the restrictions of perceptrons pointed out by Minski and Papert (1969). The system described in Fu (1989) represents MYCIN-like symbolic rules. Their certainty factors are bound to the connections in the neural network as initial weights. The weights may be adjusted further by using the backpropagation algorithm.

5.4.3   Connectionist Production Systems: Representing Variables

Production systems that consist of productions of the form IF *C*, THEN *A*, where *C* is a set of conditions and *A* a set of actions, are good as models of cognition as well as practical tools for knowledge engineering, as we have already discussed. A connectionist realization of production systems is an important issue because it can bring all the benefits of the connectionist approach to AI systems and symbolic computation. In connectionist production systems, the following features are achievable:

- Massive parallelism
- Partial match
- Reasoning with inexact, missing, or corrupted data
- Graceful degradation of the system
- Fault tolerance
- Learning and adaptation.

These characteristics would help in overcoming the two major concerns of present-day expert systems: (1) approximate reasoning and (2) knowledge acquisition.

A few connectionist production models and systems have been developed so far. They concentrate on solving some of the basic problems of realizing classic production systems: representing rules and data, chain reasoning, and variable binding.

One of the main problems in the connectionist realization of production systems is the problem of representing variables and variable binding. The variables used in an antecedent part of a production rule should be bound to allowed values. The following example is an illustration of a production with variables:

(deffrule "a rule_from_the_monkey_and_bananas_example"
  (object ladder at ?x on ?)
  (object banana at ?x on ceiling)
  ?monkey ← (monkey on ladder holds nil)
⇒
  (retract ?monkey)
  (assert (monkey on ladder holds bananas)))

This production is satisfied when the variable ?x in the first two condition elements is bound. A distributed representation for solving the variable binding problem has been used in a model of a connectionist production system called DCPS, developed by Touretzky and Hinton (1988). It assumes a fixed number of two condition elements in each production rule and one variable at most, for example:

$$(=x\ A\ B)\ \&\ (=x\ C\ D) \rightarrow +(=x\ E\ F) + (P\ D\ Q) - (=x\ S\ T)$$

The two possible actions in the right-hand side of a production are insert a fact ($+$) and delete a fact ($-$). DCPS uses distributed representation to realize the variable binding and store facts in its working memory. Two gates open at different times, to enable the two phases of the execution cycle: "recognize" and "act."

The system TPPS (Dolan and Smolensky, 1989) has the same limitations as DCPS, but it utilizes a tensor product representation which makes the process of computing the weights easier. In chapter 6 another connectionist architecture, called NPS, is presented in more detail.

5.5 Connectionist Systems for Pattern Recognition and Classification; Image Processing

Having introduced some general approaches to using neural networks for problem solving and knowledge engineering, we can go on to discuss applications of neural networks to solving generic AI problems. This section discusses using connectionist models for pattern recognition. Along with specific techniques for applying standard connectionist models, new models are introduced as well. These are the *leaky integrator*, a type of neuron for representing time patterns, and the *cognitron* and *neocognitron*, for vision.

5.5.1   Representing Spatial and Temporal Patterns in Neural Networks

Representing *space* and *time* is an important issue in knowledge engineering. How can these concepts be represented in a connectionist system? Space can be represented in a neural network by:

• Using neurons that take spatial coordinates as input or output values. Fuzzy terms for representing location, such as "above," "near," and "in the middle" can also be used. An example of representing spatial objects in a neural network was shown in chapter 4.

• Using topological neural networks, which have distance defined between the neurons and can represent spatial patterns by their activations. Such a neural network is the SOM; it is a vector quantizer, which preserves the topology of the input patterns by representing one pattern as one neuron in the topological output map.

Representing time in a neural network can be achieved by:

• Transforming time patterns into spatial patterns.

• Using a "hidden" concept, an inner concept, in the training examples.

• Using an explicit concept, a separate neuron or group of neurons in the neural network, takes time-moments as values.

Different connectionist models for representing "time" and the way they encode time are explained below (figure 5.19):

1. Feedforward networks may encode consecutive moments of time as input-output pairs.

2. Multilag prediction networks encode time in the input vector as well as in the case of (1).

3. Recurrent networks, in addition to (1) and (2), also encode time in the feedback connection.

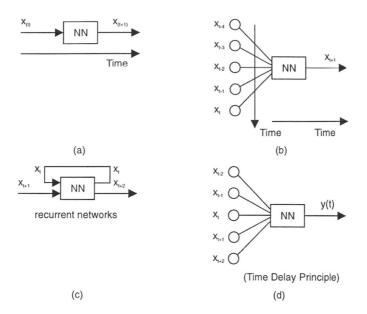

Figure 5.19
Different models for representing "time" in a neural network: (a) feedforward networks encode consecutive moments of time in the input-output pairs; (b) multilag prediction networks encode time in the input vector as well as in the case of (a); (c) recurrent networks, in addition to (a) and (b) methods, also encode time in the feedback connection; (d) time-delay networks encode time in a similar way as (b) but some lags of input values from the past as well as from the future are used to calculate the output value.

4. Time-delay networks encode time in a similar way as (2) but some lags of input values from the past as well as from the future are used to calculate the output value.

An interesting type of a neuron, which can be successfully used for representing temporal patterns, is the *leaky integrator* (figure 5.20a). The neuron has a binary input, a real-valued output, and a feedback connection. The output (activation) function is expressed as:

$y(t + 1) = x(t)$, if x is present, or

$y(t + 1) = f(y(t))$, if x is not present,

where the feedback function is usually an exponential decay. So, when an input impulse is present (i.e., $x = 1$), the output repeats it ($y = 1$). When the input signal is not present, the output value decreases over time, but a

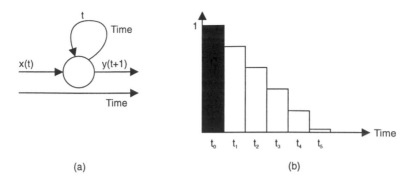

(a)   (b)

Figure 5.20
The leaky integrator neuron: (a) a general model, where the feedback function is usually an exponential decay; (b) when the input signal is not present, the output value decreases over time.

"track" of the last input signal is kept at least for some time intervals (figure 5.20b). The neuron "remembers" an event x for some time, but "forgets" about it in the distant future.

A collection of leaky integrators can be used, each representing one event happening over time, but all of them able to represent complex temporal patterns of time correlation between events. If another neural network, for example, ART, is linked to the set of leaky integrators, it can learn *dynamic categories*, which are defined by time correlation between the events.

5.5.2   Pattern Recognition and Classification

Both supervised and unsupervised learning in neural networks have been used for pattern recognition and classification. The steps to follow when creating a connectionist model for solving the problem are to define (1) the set of features to be used as input variables, and (2) the neural network structure and the learning and validation methods.

A crucial point in using neural networks for pattern recognition is choosing the set of features $X = \{x_1, x_2, \ldots, x_n\}$ which should represent unambiguously all the patterns from a given set $P = \{p_1, p_2, \ldots, p_m\}$. In a simple case, the task of character recognition, some methods use the values of the pixel from a grid where the pattern is projected. Other methods use other features: lines, curves, the angle which a drawing hand makes with the horizontal axis, picked up at some points etc. Some preprocessing operations may be needed to make the recognition scale-invariant, translation-invariant, and rotation-invariant. Preprocessing is a crucial task in pattern recognition. For the task of recognizing ambiguous, noisy, and ill-defined patterns, it is not recommended that primary signal elements be used, such as temporal samples of speech, waveforms, or the pixel of an image, etc.

Figure 5.21A shows an MLP neural network trained to recognize hand-written characters. The inputs represents pixels and the outputs the classes they belong to. After training the network with the training examples from figure 5.21B, centered as in figure 5.21A for learning rate 0.1, momentum 0.5, and number of iterations 50,000, the training MSE became 0.000023.

Instead of using pixels as features, the patterns can be represented by fewer features. A set of features could be a set of $(Nc + Nr)$ features, where Nc is the number of the columns in the grid and Nr is the number of rows. A value for the feature Ni for a given pattern is the number of cells in the ith row (column) crossed by the pattern. Figure 5.22 shows an MLP trained with the backpropagation algorithm for recognizing 10 digits in this way.

A system that recognizes ZIP codes was developed with the use of a five-layered MLP and the backpropagation algorithm (Le Cun et al. 1990). It was implemented on an electronic chip. The learning set consists of 7291 handwritten digits and 2549 printed digits in 35 different fonts.

Other application areas for connectionist handwritten character recognition are banking, fraud detection, automated cartography, automatic data entry, and so forth.

SOM and LVQ algorithms have been successfully applied to pattern recognition tasks. The training algorithm places similar input patterns into topologically close neurons on the output map. An example for recognizing four classes of patterns (letters) is shown in figure 5.23. The new pattern is classified (topologically placed) in the region of A's. These networks have been used successfully for phoneme recognition, as discussed later in this chapter.

When compared with statistical methods, connectionist methods for pattern recognition and classification have several advantages when:

• A large number of attributes (features) describe the input data and the interdependencies between them are not known.

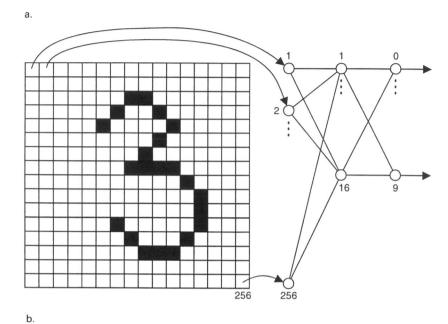

a.

b.

Figure 5.21
(A) A neural network for Handwritten Characters Recognition. (B) The set of training examples (patterns) for the Handwritten Characters Recognition Problem.

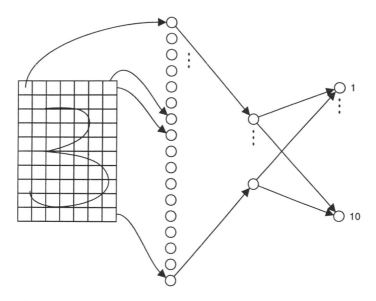

Figure 5.22
An MLP network with the backpropagation algorithm for recognizing 10 digits by representing them with 17 features (7 columns plus 10 rows).

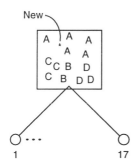

Figure 5.23
A Kohonen SOM for recognizing handwritten letters, each represented as a 17-element feature vector. The new input is likely to be the letter A.

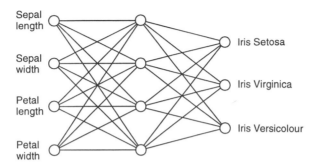

Figure 5.24
An MLP with the backpropagation algorithm for classification of Iris instances.

- Irrelevant, contradictory, or ambiguous instances are present in the data set.
- Noise is present in the input data.
- Underlying distributions are unknown.

Two specific classification problems from chapter 1 are solved here using neural networks.

Example 1: The Iris Classification Problem   An MLP with the backpropagation algorithm (figure 5.24) is trained with the Iris data set and then used to classify new Iris instances into the three classes: Setosa, Versicolor, Virginica. The unknown goal function between the input space of all the Iris plants and the output space of the three classes has been implicitly approximated by the networks. For the network of figure 5.24, a set of 120 randomly chosen instances was used for training, and a set of 30 instances for testing. The MLP, after having been trained to an MSE of 0.0001, classified all the test examples correctly.

A SOM was set and trained with the same Iris data (figure 5.25). A small-sized SOM (e.g., 10×10) would not be enough to obtain a good classification. The problem is simplified in figure 5.25. The neuron denoted by the asterisk was activated by an instance which belongs to the Versicolor class and by an instance which belongs to the class Virginica. This ambiguity can be avoided by using a larger SOM (e.g., 20×20) or by using LVQ algorithms for supervised classification.

A solution to the same problem using a fuzzy neural network is shown in section 5.11.

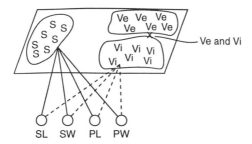

Figure 5.25
Learning Iris classes through SOM and LVQ algorithms. LVQ algorithms can deal better
with the ambiguity in classifying new instances (a new instance activates the neuron denoted
by the asterisk).

Example 2: The Soil Classification Problem   A MLP was set for eight
input variables, six intermediate nodes, and six output variables (classes)
and trained with 72 training examples, 12 for each type of soil (see appendix D). Figure 5.26 shows the training error for 10,100,500, 1000, and 1500
training epochs. A set of six new samples of soil (one for each class) was
used for testing (figure 5.27a). Figures 5.27b through e show the test results
of the network after having been trained for 10, 100, 500, and 1000 epochs
respectively. It can be seen that even after the first 500 epochs of training,
the network generalizes very well on the test set.

In the above two examples of using neural networks for classification
some conditions were satisfied:

1. There is an output neuron bound to each of the classes.

2. A class pattern is encoded in "1 out of *N*" mode, that is, only one 1 is
present in a class pattern for training.

3. The training examples were sufficient.

4. The hidden nodes in the MLP were sufficient to approximate the
underlying mapping function.

When the above conditions are met in an MLP classifier, then its outputs
express the *posterior class probabilities*. This is an important characteristic
of the connectionist classifiers.

Connectionist methods are widely applied nowadays for classifying satellite images and creating maps of regions, for example, corn, tussocks,
bare ground, woods, etc.

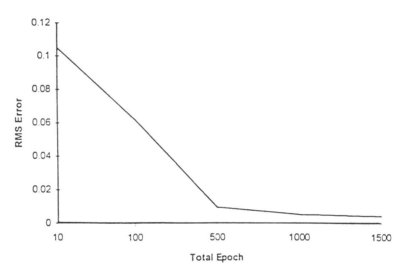

Figure 5.26
The RMS training error for an MLP neural network trained with the data for the Soil Classification Problem.

5.5.3 Neural Networks for Vision

Specialized neural network architectures called *cognitron* and *neocognitron*, developed by K. Fukushima, have been used for recognizing connected characters (Fukushima 1993). The cognitron architectures use specialized units which recognize small parts of the image, for example, a corner element. The results from all units are aggregated and the entire object is reconstructed in the last layer.

5.5.4 Image Processing

Three main tasks in image processing, where connectionist methods can be successfully applied, were discussed and illustrated in chapter 1: (1) image compression and restoration, (2) feature extraction, and (3) image classification. Bart Kosko (1992) shows that competitive learning techniques lead to similar, even slightly better, *image compression* when compared with mathematical transformations. A satisfactory restoration was achieved when the 256×256 black-and-white image was compressed and represented by 0.5 bit/pixel. Modified SOM can also be used for image compression. Other connectionist methods for image compression use MLP with the backpropagation algorithm. The ability of the hidden layer to capture unique representation of the input vectors is exploited here. The hidden layer does the compression. The hidden layer in this case performs a *principal component analysis* (Gallinary et al. 1990). An MLP with n inputs and n outputs is trained with the same patterns for inputs and outputs, where n is the dimension of the input vectors. Restoration of an image is done after transmitting the activation values of the neurons in the hidden layer. Figure 5.28 shows a small simplified network of 256 inputs, 16 hidden nodes, and 256 outputs. The compression here is 0.5 bit/pixel, when one byte is assumed to represent the activation level of a hidden neuron. Better quality of the restored images can be achieved with the use of larger networks, and possibly, structured multinetwork systems, where one neural network is used for compression of only a portion of the original image.

Another well-explored problem in image processing is *features extraction*. Features, such as contours, lines, curves, corners, junctions, roofs, ramps, and so on, can be extracted from an original image. For many image-processing systems these features are enough to classify the image or to apply successfully other processing methods. Connectionist models can be used for different types of feature extraction, such as those that are *region-based*, where areas of images with homogeneous properties are found in terms of boundaries; *edge-based*, where the local discontinuities are detected first and then curves are formed; and *pixel-based*, which classify pixels based on gray levels.

5.6   Connectionist Systems for Speech Processing

Speech processing, and speech recognition in particular, is one challenging problem where neural networks have a lot to offer. The problems of speech processing and speech recognition were discussed broadly in chapter 1. Neural networks have been widely used for solving many tasks and subtasks of speech processing.

5.6.1   Speech Synthesis: NETtalk

One of the first neural network applications of speech processing was NETtalk, developed by Sejnowski and Rosenberg (1987). This is an MLP

a.

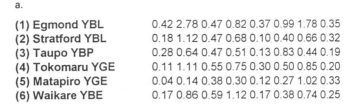

(1)	Egmond YBL	0.42 2.78 0.47 0.82 0.37 0.99 1.78 0.35
(2)	Stratford YBL	0.18 1.12 0.47 0.68 0.10 0.40 0.66 0.32
(3)	Taupo YBP	0.28 0.64 0.47 0.51 0.13 0.83 0.44 0.19
(4)	Tokomaru YGE	0.11 1.11 0.55 0.75 0.30 0.50 0.85 0.20
(5)	Matapiro YGE	0.04 0.14 0.38 0.30 0.12 0.27 1.02 0.33
(6)	Waikare YBE	0.17 0.86 0.59 1.12 0.17 0.38 0.74 0.25

b.

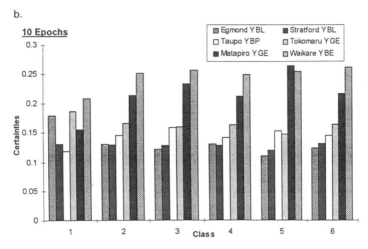

c.

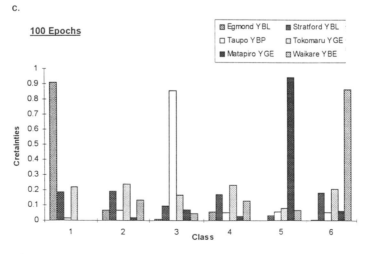

Figure 5.27
(a) Six test examples to test the neural network trained with the soil data. The activation values of the six output neurons are captured in bar graphs after (b) 10, (c) 100, (d) 500, and (e) 1000 epochs of training the network.

d.

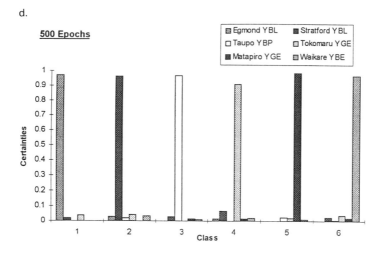

e.

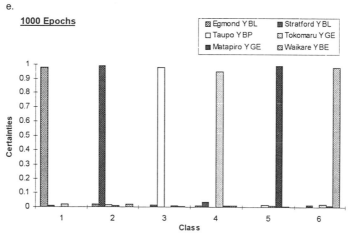

Figure 5.27 (continued)

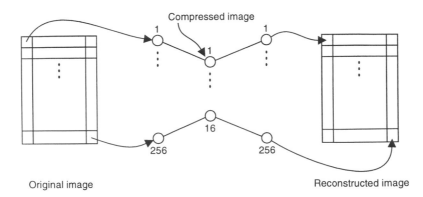

Figure 5.28
A multilayer perceptron for compression of a 256-cell image into a 16-cell image.

trained with a backpropagation algorithm to pronounce an English text. The input of the network consists of seven input modules, one for a letter, each consisting of 29 input nodes (26 for the letters in the alphabet plus three for punctuation), 80 hidden nodes, and 26 output nodes, encoding phonemes. The input text to the network "slides" from left to right as in a window. The desired output is the phoneme that corresponds to the letter at the center of the window. The outputs are connected to a speech generator for the recognized phonemes. The network is trained on 1024 words from English phoneme source. The accuracy after only 50 epochs was 95%. When tested, an accuracy of 78% was achieved.

5.6.2 Speech Recognition

The phases in a speech recognition process were discussed in chapter 1. Neural networks can be used for pattern matching, as well as for the language analysis phase. Here we discuss the former.

The signal processing may be performed in a standard way: a digitizing frequency of 22,050 Hz, a 256-point FFT, and 26 mel-scale cepstrum coefficients obtained for each segment of 11.6 ms of the speech signal. The time segments overlap on 50%. Some of the most commonly used connectionist models for speech recognition are MLP, SOM, time-delay networks, and recurrent networks. These models are discussed and illustrated below. Their use depends on the type of the recognition performed, for example, whole word recognition, or subwords recognition, for example, phoneme recognition.

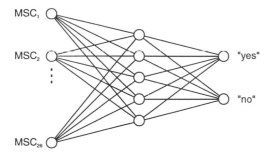

Figure 5.29
"Yes"/"no" words recognition by an MLP neural network. The input vectors are 26 mel-scale cepstrum coefficients (MSCCs).

5.6.3   Using MLP for Speech Recognition

Figure 5.29 shows a "yes"/"no" whole-word recognition MLP. It has 26 input nodes for the 26 mel-scale coefficients, which in this case are averaged over several segments, to cover the whole words. The two words' speech signals are transformed into 26-element vectors. Samples of "yes"/"no" spoken words are collected from different speakers—male, female, various age groups, etc. The network is trained and then tested on newly pronounced "yes"/"no" words. If the test words are pronounced by one of the speakers whose spoken words were used for training, and the system recognizes them, then the system is said to be of a *multiple-speaker* type. If the system recognizes a new speaker, then the system is called *speaker-independent*.

Phoneme recognition is a difficult problem because of the variation in the pronunciation of phonemes, the time alignment problem (the phonemes are not pronounced in isolation), and because of what is called the *coarticulation effect*, that is, the frequency characteristics of an allophonic realization of the same phoneme may differ depending on the context of the phoneme in different spoken words (see chapter 1).

There are two approaches to using MLP for the task of phoneme recognition: (1) using one, big MLP, which has as its outputs all the possible phonemes, and (2) using many small networks, specialized to recognize from one to a small group of phonemes (e.g., vowels, consonants, fricatives, plosives, etc.). A multimodular neural network architecture for recognizing several phonemes—/w/, / ∧ /, /n/, /silence/—is shown in figure 5.30(A). One 78-10-1 MLP network is trained for each of the

a.

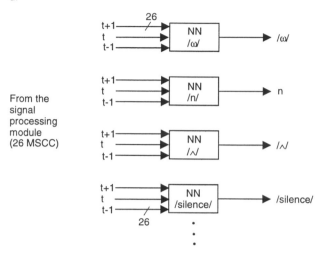

From the
signal
processing
module
(26 MSCC)

b.

"ONE" Male speaker Original Network

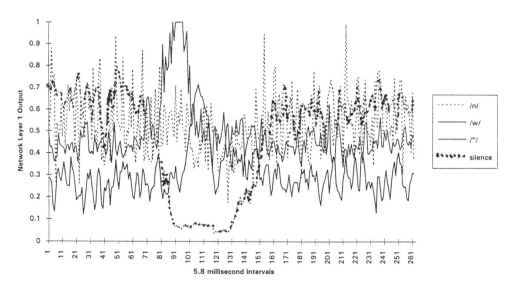

Figure 5.30
(A) Multimodular MLP network for phoneme recognition. (B) The activation values of four
neural network phoneme units for the phonemes /w/, / ∧ /, /n/ and /silence/ when a new
signal is fed over time. (C) The output values of the same neural networks after additional
training. (D) The output values after averaging.

c.

"ONE" Male Speaker, extra training

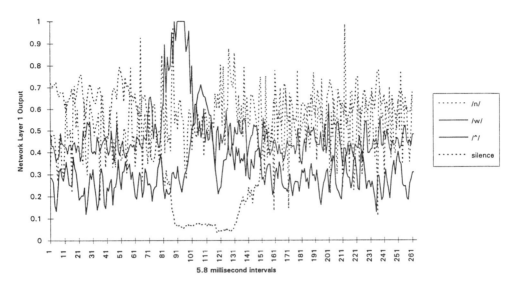

d.

"ONE" Male Speaker , Averaged output, extra training

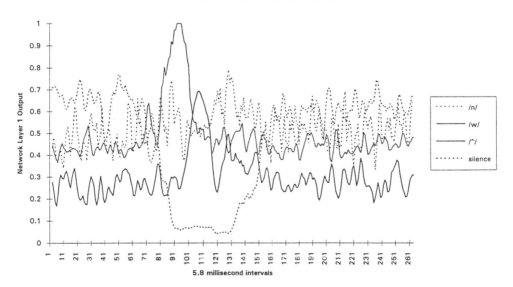

Figure 5.30 (continued)

phonemes. The outputs of these networks need to be monitored, the winner being chosen (and labeled by the corresponding phoneme class label) for any time segment of 11.6 ms. The time sequence of labels, for example, /wwwnww ∧ ∧ ∧ snnsnn/, then may be translated into a corresponding word, for example, "one." An example of solving a phoneme recognition task is given in section 5.11. Using multimodular structure of specialized neural network units allows for experimenting with different *learning strategies*, which were discussed in section 5.1.4. Two of them are illustrated here:

1. *Additional training/adjustment of individual modules* (e.g. neural network units);

2. *Using 3-frames moving average of recognized speech signals.*

These strategies are illustrated here on a small experimental system in which 21 units are trained with same training data for the 21 phonemes from the digits (silence is included), but each training set for an individual neural network unit has different output labels corresponding to the respective phoneme class as shown in figure 5.30A. Speech data from six male and five female speakers was used for training. The activation values of four neural network units when test data of spoken word "one" is fed at the input, are shown on the Y-axis of figure 5.30b. On the X-axis the 5.8 ms time intervals are shown. The phonemes /w/, / ∧ /, /n/ are supposed to be recognized in certain time intervals; for example, the phoneme /n/ should ideally be recognized between the 115 and the 133 time intervals. Before and after the recognition of the phonemes /w/, / ∧ /, and /n/, "silence" should be ideally recognized, that is, the output value from the "silence phoneme unit" should be the highest one. As can be seen from figure 5.30b, the recognition of the phonemes /w/ and / ∧ / is good, but the /n/-phoneme network reacts falsely to /silence/. This ambiguity may be suppressed in following modules of a speech recognition system, but it will be better if it can be resolved at this stage and not passed to the next stages.

It can be seen from figure 5.30b that there are a lot of peak activation values of the /n/ unit instead of the /silence/ unit. Smother output values can be achieved by using averaging techniques. It is obvious from figure 5.30b that the /w/ and / ∧ / units ("pupils") react appropriately, but the /n/ unit needs more training in order to suppress its false positive reaction to silence. The original /n/ unit from figure 5.30b is now trained with a new data set which has all the previous examples, but the examples of silence (negative examples) were doubled. The /n/ network was additionally trained for small number of epochs. Figure 5.30c shows the activation of the same units to the same input data as in figure 5.30b. The true-positive activation of /n/ has increased and now the time interval between 115 and 133 is recognized as a realization of /n/. Still there are some false positive activation peaks of the /n/ unit to /silence/ signals. They are suppressed by averaging the outputs over three consecutive time intervals as shown in figure 5.30d.

An inherent limitation of MLP networks for computer speech recognition is that they cannot implicitly account for variations of speech in time.

5.6.4   Using SOM for Phoneme Recognition

The feature vectors obtained after signal processing e.g. the mel-scale cepstrum coefficients vectors, can be used as training examples for training a SOM. Vectors representing allophonic realizations of the same phoneme are taken from different windows (frames) over one signal sample and from different signals, that is, different realizations of this phoneme. After enough training, every phoneme is represented on the SOM by the activation of some output nodes. One node fires when an input vector representing a segment of the allophonic realization of this phoneme is fed into the network. The outputs, which react to the same phoneme pronounced differently, are positioned closely. The outputs that react to similar phonemes are positioned in proximity on the map. This is due to the ability of the SOM to activate topologically close output neurons when similar input vectors are presented.

This approach has been used and phonemic maps have been created for Finnish (Kohonen, 1990) (figure 5.31), Japanese, English, Bulgarian (Kasabov and Peev 1994) (figure 5.32), and other languages. Figure 5.33A is a two-dimensional drawing of the coordinates of the neurons in a SOM that was labeled with eight phonemes in English selected from digits pronounced by a small group of speakers. Figure 5.33B shows how allophonic segments of phonemes were segmented for training the SOM. It is clear from this drawing that the phonemes are well distinguished, and there are areas where the network cannot produce any meaningful classification.

Instead of having a large, and therefore slow-to-process single SOM, hierarchical models of SOMs can be used. A model published in (Kasabov

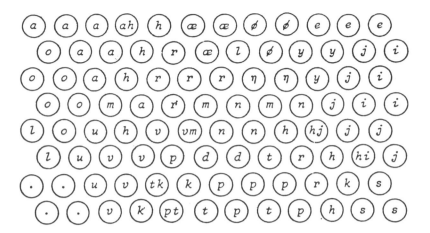

Figure 5.31
SOM of the phonemes in Finish language. (Reprinted with permission from Kohonen 1990, Copyright IEEE@90.)

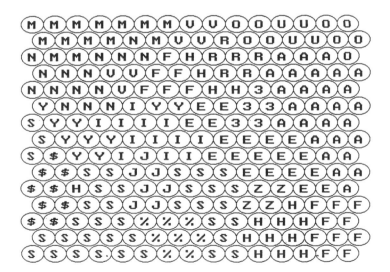

Figure 5.32
SOM of six vowel and ten consonant phonemes in the Bulgarian language. The symbols used to denote phonemes have similar sounds as English, except "%" which denotes the sound "st," as in "Stuttgart," "$" which denotes the sound "sh" as in "shift" and "3" which denotes a similar sound as the beginning of "zip" (From Kasabov and Peev 1994).

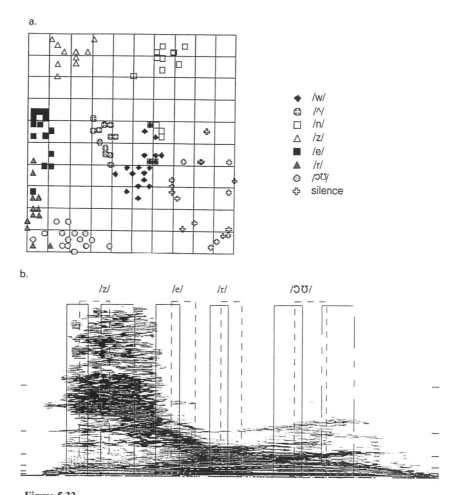

Figure 5.33
SOM of several phonemes in the English language. (From Kasabov et al, 1994). (A) The coordinates of the neurons from a SOM labeled with corresponding phoneme labels. (B) The way the speech samples were segmented for training the SOM.

and Peev 1994) uses one 4×4 SOM at the first level and sixteen 4×4 KSOMs at the second level. Every SOM at the second level is activated when a corresponding neuron from the first level becomes active. The asymptotic computational complexity of the recognition of the two-level hierarchical model is $O(2 \cdot n \cdot m)$ where n is the number of inputs and m is the size of a single SOM. This is much less than the computational complexity $O(n \cdot m^2)$ of a single SOM with a size of m^2 ($m = 16$). For a general r-level hierarchical model, the complexity is $O(r \cdot n \cdot m)$. The first-level SOM is trained to recognize four classes of phonemes: a pause, a vocalized phoneme, a nonvocalized phoneme, and a fricative segment. The network is trained with three features of the speech signal: (1) the mean value of the energy of the time-scale signal within the segment; (2) the number of the crossings of zero for the time-scale signal; and (3) the mean value of the local extremes of the amplitude of the signal on the time scale.

5.6.5 Time-Delay Neural Networks for Speech Recognition

Time-delay neural networks (TDNNs) capture temporal speech information. Time-delay input frames allow the weights in the initial layers to account for time variations in speech (Waibel et al. 1989a). Like the MLP, they are feedforward networks. Figure 5.34 shows a general TDNN scheme for the phoneme classification task. TDNNs are good at recognition of subword units from continuous speech. For the recognition of continuous speech, a higher-level parsing framework is required in addition.

It was discovered (see Waibel et al. 1989b) that a single monolithic TDNN was impractical for recognizing all the phonemes in Japanese. It was then suggested that a modular TDNN be used.

5.6.6 Recurrent Neural Networks for Speech Recognition

Recurrent neural networks, like the TDNNs, account for temporal variations in speech. A feedback loop connects the output nodes to the input nodes which makes them capable of encoding and recognizing sequential speech structures.

Figure 5.35 is an example of using a recurrent network for phoneme recognition. The previously recognized phoneme (or segment of a phoneme) is used at the next cycle, which helps the recognition process. The network can learn temporal dependencies from the speech sequences used for training.

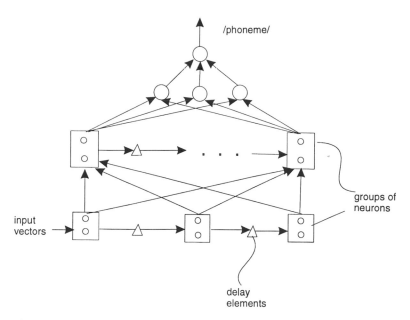

Figure 5.34
A TDNN for phoneme recognition. Each group of neurons has as many neurons as the number of the elements in the input vector representing a segment of the speech signal, for example, the number of the mel-scale cepstrum coefficients. The delay elements ensure that the network learns time-dependencies between the segments within a phoneme.

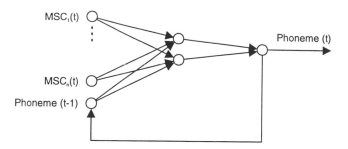

Figure 5.35
An example of using a recurrent neural network for phoneme recognition.

The recurrent networks are good for recognition of short isolated speech units. Owing to their structure they include some kind of time-warping effect. For continuous speech recognition, however, the recurrent neural networks must be used within some hybrid system.

5.6.7   Extracting Speech and Language Rules from Data

Extracting explicit knowledge, rules, from speech and language data is an important task for the following reasons:

• Speech is an ambiguous sequence of sounds. This ambiguity cannot be handled at the pattern-matching phase only. It also has to be dealt with at a higher knowledge-based level. The solution to the problem of building a continuous-speech, speaker-independent, unlimited-vocabulary speech recognition system is more likely to be found in a hybrid system, which combines data and knowledge processing; rules and data processing should reside in one system.

• There is plenty of speech and language repository corpus data, which are easily obtainable and may be very useful.

• Articulating speech and language rules is an extremely difficult task for linguists.

That is why a knowledge acquisition module is included in the general architecture of an intelligent human-computer interface (see figure 1.20).

Mitra and Pal (1995) used fuzzy rules to represent vowel phonemes. An example of such a rule is given below:

IF F_1 is very low and F_2 is very low,
   THEN the vowel is very likely to be /u/,

where F_1 and F_2 are the first and the second formants respectively.

An example of using fuzzy linguistic rules (either extracted from data, or articulated by experts) in a hybrid system is given in chapter 6.

5.7   Connectionist Systems for Prediction

Prediction, as discussed in chapter 1, is a difficult problem, when either chaotic time series are involved or the available static data are sparse. Prediction can be viewed as (temporal) pattern recognition task, for which purpose neural networks suit very well.

5.7.1   Time-Series Prediction with Neural Networks

In reality, temporal variations in time-series data do not exhibit simple regularities and are difficult to analyze. The connectionist approach has proved so far to be applicable to some difficult cases of multivariate time-series analysis.

In general, the predicted value of a variable x at a future time is based on k previous values. In this case, k is a *lag of the prediction*. If we have the values of the variable x for the moments from 1 to t, that is, $x(1), x(2), \ldots,$ $x(t)$, we can try to predict $x(t + 1)$, and also future values $x(t + 2), \ldots,$ $x(t + m)$, which is *univariate prediction*. *Multivariate prediction* uses more variables rather than x only. Figure 5.36 shows neural network structures for univariate and multivariate prediction.

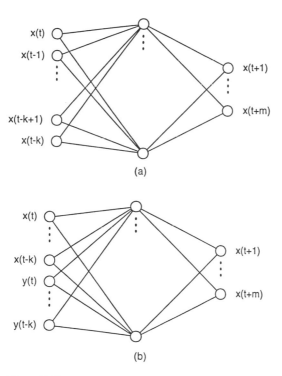

Figure 5.36
(a) Connectionist univariate time-series prediction; (b) connectionist multivariate (two) time-series prediction.

The variable subject to prediction (dependent variable) can be different from the past data variables (independent variables), but both are on the time scale. A case problem of one independent variable (the average monthly minimum temperature) and one dependent variable (gas consumption per capita was presented in chapter 1 and called the Gas Consumption Prediction Problem. This example is used for illustrating different connectionist models for time-series prediction and comparing the results with statistical regression analysis.

Example 1: The Gas Consumption Prediction Problem   Four experiments with different MLP neural network architectures are presented here on the gas consumption time series (see figure 1.21). They realize the four general solutions to the problem as given in figure 1.22. As the past data set consists of 55 records, 48 of them (the years 1988–1991) have been used for training. The seven records for 1992 (January–July) are used for testing. The results obtained by the four neural network architectures are compared with similar experiments using the statistical regression technique (Gonzales 1992).

a. The first neural network architecture does a static prediction, that is, gas consumption is related only to the corresponding monthly temperature, without introducing time lags (figure 5.37). After 10,000 epochs of

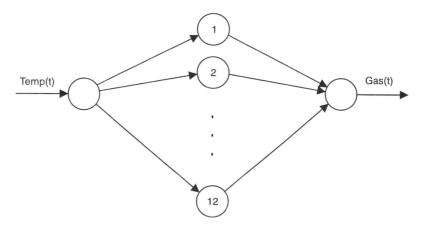

Figure 5.37
A simple neural network for the Gas Consumption Prediction Problem. One input variable is used: the average monthly temperature forecast Temp(t) for predicting the gas consumption Gas(t).

training the network, for learning rate 0.1 and momentum 0.3, the calculated root mean-square training error (RMSE) was 0.0957 and the test error per example was 0.0122. The regression analysis done over the same data set produces a regression function Gas = 10.5 − 0.660 Temp, which explains 87.1% of the data variation.

b. The second neural network architecture (figure 5.38), has an input lag of 2 months, that is, gas consumption for the present month is assumed to depend not only on the average temperature for the month but also on the average temperatures of the preceding 2 months. The achieved training and test error per example were, respectively, 0.0795 and 0.0083.

c. In a third experiment, time was represented as an input variable (figure 5.39). Time is presented as consecutive numbers (indices) of the months. Such a feature can help the network capture trends in gas consumption over time: for example, the decrease in gas consumption year after year. The obtained training and test error per example are 0.0772 and 0.0063. Through a regression technique, the following regression function was found: Gas = 11.3 − 0.681 Temp − 0.0207 Time, which explains 89.1% of the variation in the data.

d. The last experiment was performed when, in addition to the time trend used in the previous experiment, monthly (seasonal) trends were introduced by adding 11 new inputs, each representing the month of the prediction

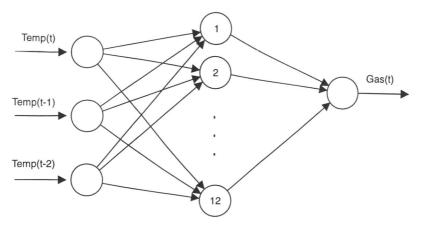

Figure 5.38
A second connectionist model for the Gas Consumption Prediction Problem. Two time lags are introduced here.

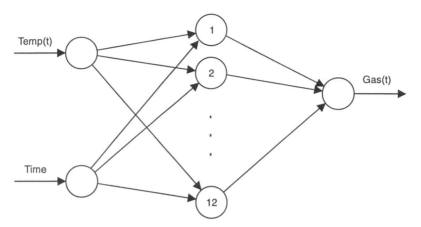

Figure 5.39
A third connectionist model for the Gas Consumption Prediction Problem.

(the 12th month is assumed by default if no others are given). The network architecture is shown in figure 5.40. After 30,000 epochs, the total training and test errors were 0.00366 and 0.01066. When a regression technique was used, the following regression function was obtained: Gas = 5.93 − 0.299 Temp − 0.00895 Time + 0.523. Jan + 0.424 Feb + 0.191 Mar + 0.797 Apr + 2.47 May + 3.60 Jun + 3.98 Jul + 3.30 Aug + 1.98 Sep + 1.22 Oct + 0.492 Nov. The percentage of variation in gas consumption explained by this regression model is 97.4%.

A crucial point for a prediction system, as can be seen from the experiments above, is the set of independent variables (features). The problem above was not difficult because about 90% of the gas consumption was explained by the temperature as a single parameter. If we assume that the price of gas varies over time, we have to include "price" as an independent variable also. The prediction would then become more difficult if a new non-gas heating system was introduced into the subject town.

Connectionist methods for time-series prediction have the following advantages over statistical methods:

• There is no need to know the type of regression function; an assumption of a linear function may lead to a wrong prediction; the ability of the networks to approximate any continuous function represented by a data set is the key to their success in this case.

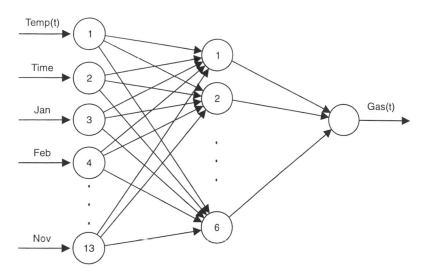

Figure 5.40
A network architecture for the Gas Consumption Prediction Problem with "time trends" and "seasonal trends" introduced as input variables.

- Neural network models are more robust than regression models.

- Neural networks are easier to experiment with.

Example 2: The Stock Market Prediction Problem   (See appendix C for a description of the SE40 stock index data.) Figure 5.41 shows two possible models for the SE40 prediction—(a) an MLP and (b) a recurrent neural network, both using one *time lag* of data. Several different MLP architectures were trained with 1358 data examples and tested with 379 data points. The results for different number of hidden nodes (HD) over the test data are similar (figure 5.41c). Other models were also tested. The network with four input variables, namely Time, SE40(t), the 5-day moving average, Avg(5), and the mean across all the previous examples, Avg(All), gave the best test result.

5.7.2   Rules Extraction from Time-Series Data

Extracting rules from time-series data may have a significant contribution to make to understanding time-series processes. Again, the selection of appropriate features is crucial. For example, the stock market SE40 data (see appendix C) can be used to extract fuzzy rules for calculating the next

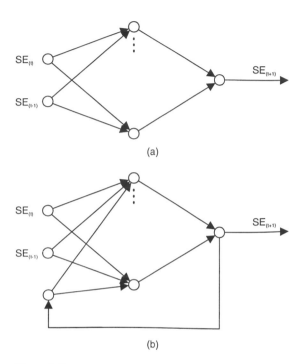

(a)

(b)

Figure 5.41
Stock exchange market SE40 prediction with a feedforward MLP neural network and a recurrent neural network structures using one time lag: testing the two models for different numbers of hidden nodes (HD).

value of the index from its two previous values. The rules can be in the form of:

IF $SE(t)$ is A and $SE(t-1)$ is B, THEN $SE(t+1)$ is C

where A, B, and C are fuzzy values (e.g., small, medium, high). A differential competitive learning (DCL) algorithm may be used with fuzzy labels defined as triangular membership functions for the fuzzy values "small," "medium," "high".

Extracting rules from time-series data may not make any sense if the time series is random, but if it is not the rules represent an approximation of the underlying rules in the data. If the input-output space is not properly selected, it becomes very difficult to extract meaningful rules from it. According to the results from Example 2 in the previous subsection it will be more appropriate if rules are extracted from the neural network

c.

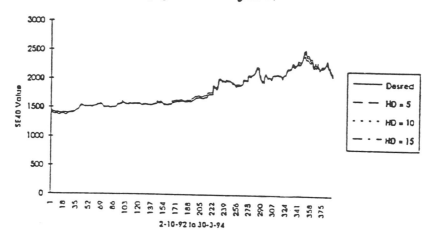

Figure 5.41 (continued)

trained with the four input attributes as described there. A rules extraction module is included in the hybrid system for stock trading given in chapter 6.

5.7.3 Analogy-Based Prediction

Analogy-based prediction is considered here as predicting the behavior of one set of objects $Q = \{Q_1, Q_2, \ldots, Q_n\}$ when stimulus S_j ($j = 1, 2, \ldots, s$) is applied to them, on the basis of the behavior of another set of objects $P = \{P_1, P_2, \ldots, P_m\}$ which have similarities with the first set when the same or similar stimuli are applied.

The main idea of using neural networks for discovering analogies is that similar stimuli will activate corresponding (analogical) neurons to a similar degree of activation. This idea has been employed to discover structural similarity, semantic similarity, and pragmatic centrality.

A connectionist model for a functional analogy-based prediction is introduced here. The ⟨input-output⟩ pairs for training such a network are $\langle \{(P_i)_j\} - \{(Q_l)\}_j \rangle$, where $i = 1, 2, \ldots, m; l = 1, 2, \ldots, n; j = 1, 2, \ldots, s$. The network is used to learn the analogy between two sets of objects on the basis of their behavior (reaction) to the same stimuli. The learned analogy is then used to predict the reaction of the objects Ql ($l = 1, 2, \ldots, n$) to an unseen stimulus S' when the reaction of the first set of objects Pi ($i = 1, 2, \ldots, m$) to the same stimulus is known.

Example: The problem of predicting the effect of a new drug on breast cancer The problem as explained in chapter 1, is to find an analogical mapping between the set of 15 experimentally induced tumors and a clinical tumor, based on their known reactions to the same drugs, so that we are able to predict the effect of a new drug on the clinical tumor after having studied the experimental tumors. The solution is based on the presumed similarity between this tumor and a set of experimental tumors. A set of 15 chemotherapeutic agents was used for training (see figure 1.25) and a set of 11 for testing the prediction. An MLP with 15 input nodes, 3 intermediate nodes, and 1 output node was trained for 10,000 epochs with the use of a backpropagation algorithm (figure 5.42). The predicted effect for the 11 test drugs on the clinical tumor was exactly the same as the clinical data suggested except test case No. 4 (figure 5.43). The learned analogy between experimental tumors and a clinical tumor is a deep analogy. Its explanation lies in the transformation (mapping) of

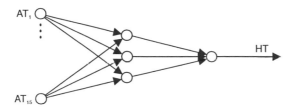

Figure 5.42
A neural network for learning analogy between 15 experimental tumors AT_1 to AT_{15} and a clinical tumor HT.

Test cases															
1	1.0	0.5	0.5	1.0	1.0	1.0	0.0	0.5	1.0	1.0	0.5	0.5	1.0	0.5	1.0
	Expected Output: 1.0										Actual Output: 0.99994				
2	1.0	0.0	0.5	1.0	1.0	0.5	1.0	0.5	0.5	1.0	0.5	0.5	0.0	0.5	0.5
	Expected Output: 1.0										Actual Output: 0.99992				
3	1.0	0.5	1.0	0.5	0.0	0.5	1.0	1.0	0.5	0.0	0.5	1.0	1.0	0.5	0.5
	Expected Output: 1.0										Actual Output: 0.96514				
4	0.0	0.0	1.0	1.0	0.5	1.0	1.0	1.0	0.5	0.0	0.5	0.5	1.0	0.5	0.5
	Expected Output: 1.0										Actual Output: 0.05302				
5	1.0	1.0	1.0	0.0	0.0	0.5	0.0	1.0	0.5	0.5	0.5	1.0	1.0	1.0	0.0
	Expected Output: 1.0										Actual Output: 0.67285				
6	1.0	1.0	1.0	1.0	0.0	0.0	1.0	0.0	0.0	1.0	1.0	0.0	1.0	1.0	1.0
	Expected Output: 1.0										Actual Output: 0.99994				
7	1.0	1.0	0.5	0.0	0.0	0.5	1.0	0.5	0.5	0.5	0.5	0.0	1.0	0.5	0.5
	Expected Output: 1.0										Actual Output: 0.99993				
8	0.0	0.0	0.5	0.0	0.0	0.0	1.0	1.0	1.0	0.5	0.5	1.0	0.0	0.5	1.0
	Expected Output: 1.0										Actual Output: 0.99924				
9	0.0	1.0	0.5	0.0	0.0	0.5	1.0	0.5	0.5	1.0	0.5	0.5	0.0	0.5	0.5
	Expected Output: 1.0										Actual Output: 0.99992				
10	1.0	1.0	0.0	0.5	0.0	0.0	1.0	1.0	0.0	0.0	0.0	1.0	1.0	0.5	0.0
	Expected Output: 1.0										Actual Output: 0.99761				
11	0.0	0.5	0.5	0.0	0.0	0.5	1.0	0.5	0.5	0.0	0.5	0.5	0.0	1.0	0.5
	Expected Output: 0.0										Actual Output: 0.03627				

Figure 5.43
Testing results for the neural network for predicting the effect of a new drug on malignant breast cancer. Eleven test examples are used. If a threshold of 0.65 is chosen to decide on an active neuron, the effect of all the new drugs tested, except one (no. 4), are correctly predicted.

structural, chemical, and biochemical similarities between the medicines used and also similarities between experimental reactions and the reaction of a clinical tumor. Obviously the neural network model from figure 5.42 needs more tuning, explanation and validation before used in practice.

5.7.3   Other Neural Network Techniques for Prediction

Many other connectionist models, in addition to the ones described, above, are applicable to the prediction task, for example, neo-fuzzy neurons can be used for predicting chaotic time series (Yamakawa et al., 1992a); unsupervised learning and categorization can be applied to predicting series of events.

5.8   Connectionist Systems for Monitoring, Control, Diagnosis, and Planning

5.8.1   Monitoring

Monitoring problems may be solved by using a simple neural network model or a hierarchical and modular neural network model.

In the former case, the input nodes take data for the current situation. The output activation signals represent values for the monitored parameters. The network has to be trained with enough examples of the monitoring process. Such a task could be the monitoring of a car for which a simple neural network can be trained subject to enough data available for the input parameters—the cooling temperature, status of the gauge, status of the brakes—and for the output variable level of risk for the driver.

In the latter case, layers of neural networks may need to be used, each performing a different task. For example, bedside critical care monitoring of patients in intensive care may require a complex neural network to recognize dynamic states of several events occurring over a short or long period of time and predicting a dangerous state, such as heart failure, etc. Snapshots are not enough in this case. They contain local information only. It is necessary to observe two or more successive snapshots in their order of occurrence. In this case, two connectionist modules are required: (1) short-term memory, to represent temporal information; (2) a categorization unit, to recognize and categorize dynamic temporal patterns of events which may happen in the future.

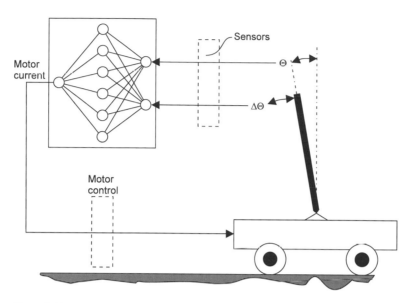

Figure 5.44
A connectionist architecture for the problem of balancing an inverted pendulum.

5.8.2 Control

Control is similar to the monitoring task, as described in chapter 1, but here signals that change the status of the object (the process) under control are to be emitted. Figure 5.44 gives the structure of an MLP network for the *Inverted Pendulum Problem*. The network is trained in a supervised manner by a sufficient number of input-output pairs of data. The network will perform the control task as well as the fuzzy control system did, as both of them gently approximate the same control (goal) function when it is not known in advance. Both control systems are robust. The difficulties in articulating the membership functions for the fuzzy sets in the fuzzy control rules may give a superiority to hybrid fuzzy connectionist models. A crucial point in building connectionist systems for control is time synchronization. The control process is not only about mapping input vectors to output vectors but about mapping them on the time scale. Time is presented either implicitly or explicitly (Werbos 1992).

5.8.3 Connectionist Systems for Diagnosis

Diagnostic systems can be realized in neural networks in which the symptoms are represented by input nodes and the set of diseases by output

Symptoms
(manifestations)   Diagnosis

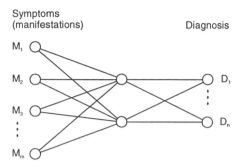

Figure 5.45
A connectionist diagnostic system.

nodes (figure 5.45). The input nodes take input data, which, depending on
the type of the symptoms, can be:

- Real values (possibly normalized)
- True/false values
- Certainty degrees of the presence of symptoms
- Fuzzy values, like "pulse rate high"

On the output nodes, the network can produce, depending on the context of the disease, different values to indicate a diagnosis:

- Real values for output variables
- Probability of a disease occurring
- Certainty or fuzzy membership degrees for a disease that has occurred

A connectionist diagnostic system can evaluate for a given input vector
of values for the symptoms the degree of certainty of not only one but a
number of diseases that may occur simultaneously. This makes a dramatic
difference when comparing the connectionist with Bayesian approaches to
approximate reasoning.

The usual way to develop connectionist diagnostic systems is to train
a network with a set of past data recorded through experience. Neural
networks can also be trained with a set of rules.

Example   The Medical Diagnosis Problem A set of rules, presented in
chapter 1, is realized here as a connectionist system. The symptoms take

Case	Manifestations				Neural network				MFCGdiagnosis			
No.	m1	m2	m3	m4	d1	d2	d3	d4	d1	d2	d3	d4
1.	0.9	.0 0	0.0	0.2	0.883	0.06	0.156	0.302	0.856	0.0	0.243	0.368
2.	0.0	0.9	0.3	0.1	0.069	0.846	0.152	0.224	0.171	0.893	0.270	0.368
3.	0.2	0.3	0.8	0.7	0.045	0.110	0.708	0.648	0.204	0.293	0.669	0.579

Figure 5.46
Comparative analysis of the use of four small neural networks, each trained with diagnostic rules, and a fuzzy inference method over the same three test cases.

part in the rules with their typical values which represent degrees of occurrence of the symptom, rather than with fuzzy values, for example, "weak," "more or less strong," "very strong," etc. (see figure 3.51):

Rule 1: IF $M1 = 1$ and $M2 = 0.2$ and $M3 = 0$ and $M4 = 0$,
    THEN $D1$ ($CF = 0.99$)

Rule 2: IF $M1 = 0$ and $M2 = 1$ and $M3 = 0.1$ and $M4 = 0$,
    THEN $D2$ ($CF = 0.97$)

Rule 3: IF $M1 = 0.3$ and $M2 = 0$ and $M3 = 1$ and $M4 = 0$,
    THEN $D3$ ($CF = 0.98$)

Rule 4: IF $M1 = 0.2$ and $M2 = 0.2$ and $M3 = 0$ and $M4 = 0.9$,
    THEN $D4$ ($CF = 0.96$)

Those rules have been used in Chen (1988) for illustrating a new method (MFCG) for fuzzy reasoning. Here the backpropagation algorithm was applied to train four networks (units, "pupils"), each having four inputs, two hidden nodes, and one output, each trained with four training examples, the corresponding rules in a numerical form encoded differently for the different diagnostic units. The certainty degree of the four possible diagnoses for three new input vectors when using neural networks and when using the MFCG method are given in figure 5.46 for comparison. A better discrimination is achieved in the neural network solution.

In this example we trained a neural network with rules. Why not training it with examples? Suppose we have many examples which are in the "patch" of a rule R and we train the network with them. The network will learn the center of the cluster, which is represented exactly by R. So if we have the rules, they can be used as examples of centers, and we train a network with them. If we do not have those centers, we let the network learn them from the examples available, which might be sparse in a certain area (patch) of the problem space. The neural network approach allows for using both data and expert rules in one system.

5.8.4 Planning

Planning usually consists of two main phases: (1) situation recognition and plan reminding, and (2) plan execution and manipulation.

The former is automatic and "subconscious." After inputting a set of goals, context, constraints, and the current status, a network can relax in a stable coalition of neurons which constitutes a plan. The latter phase is sequential and "conscious." It can be realized by symbolic AI methods. Planning is a suitable task mainly for hybrid connectionist AI systems and for connectionist production systems, when neural networks can be used to recognize the current situation and a goal-driven, logic inference is activated.

5.9 Connectionist Systems for Optimization and Decision Making

5.9.1 Optimization

Neural networks have proved to be efficient at solving some optimization problems. Optimization problems are about finding a minimum of a goal function. A neural network, for example, the Hopfield network, can be represented by an energy function which tends to its minimum during convergence. Now, the problem of using a neural network for solving an optimization task is how to represent the optimization goal function as an energy function of a network.

As an example, a solution to the *Traveling Salesman Problem* (*TSP*) is given here. One connectionist solution of the TSP was suggested by Hopfield and Tank (1985). They represented the problem as an N^2-dimensional Hopfield network. The rows represent N towns, and the columns the position of the town in the route.

Example

Towns	Position				
	1	2	3	4	5
P	0	0	1	0	0
Q	1	0	0	0	0
R	0	0	0	0	1
S	0	1	0	0	0
T	0	0	0	1	0

The boolean matrix shows a possible tour, where 1 denotes an activation of the corresponding neuron. The path in the example is $Q\ S\ P\ T\ R$. There are some constraints to be satisfied by the system when using such a representation: only one 1 in every row; only one 1 in every column; only N 1's in the whole matrix; the shortest path (a minimum sum of the distances Dxy).

The constraints are fulfilled respectively by the following optimization functions (Hopfield and Tank 1985; see also Davalo and Naim 1991):

$$C1 = \sum_x \sum_i \sum_{j, j \neq i} M_{x,i} \cdot M_{x,j}$$

$$C2 = \sum_i \sum_x \sum_{y, y \neq x} M_{xi} \cdot M_{yj}$$

$$C3 = \left(\sum_x \sum_i M_{xi} - N\right)^2$$

$$C4 = \sum \sum \sum d_{xy} \cdot M_{xi} \cdot (M_{y,i+1} + M_{y,i-1}),$$

where M_{xi} denotes the value of the xth row and ith column (town x being at the ith position in the matrix M of the towns and positions; x and y denote towns; i and j denote positions; d_{xy} is the distance between x and y; and xi is town x placed on the ith position in the tour. The four constraint terms can be aggregated in a global optimization goal function:

$$F = -aC_1 - bC_2 - cC_3 - dC_4$$

where a, b, c and d are constants. F takes a minimum value when all the terms are at minimum values. Each of the four terms in the above optimization function has its minimum value when a corresponding constraint is satisfied. If we make the energy function E of a Hopfield network equal to the optimization function F above, the following formulas can be derived for calculating the weights of the network:

$$E = -1/2 \sum\sum\sum w_{ij} M_{x,i} M_{y,j} = F;$$

$$w_{ij} = -a\Delta_{x,y}(1 - \Delta_{i,j}) - b\Delta_{i,j}(1 - \Delta_{x,y}) - c - dd_{x,y}(\Delta_{j,i+1} - \Delta_{j,i-1})$$

The symbol Δ_{ij} is the *Cronecker function*, $\Delta_{ij} = 1$, if $i = j$, otherwise $\Delta_{ij} = 0$. There are some other connectionist methods for solving the TSP, for example, with the use of SOM (Angeniol et al. 1988).

Other optimization problems, like the shortest path problem, dynamic programming problems, the transitive closure problem, the assignment problem, and so on, have also been solved using connectionist models (Lam and Su 1992).

5.9.2   Decision Making

The decision-making tasks are usually characterized by a tremendous variety of data and available knowledge, different requirements and constraints, and a dynamically changing environment, which make the use of neural networks quite appropriate. For example, a decision-making system might require taking into account exact data, fuzzy data, and fuzzy rules and membership functions.

Different problems have been discussed so far and connectionist models for their decision making presented, for example, bank loan applications approval, bond rating, and stock market decision making. Decision-making may require good explanatory facilities, for which purpose rules extraction from data might be a useful technique. SOM can well be used for visualization of a decision and placing it in regions of similar cases. An example of using SOM for the Bank Loan Decision Problem is shown in figure 5.47. The applicants $C1$, $C2$, and $C3$ are "placed" by the network in the areas of "approve," "disapprove," and "not known," respectively. These are the same three cases used in chapter 2 (to illustrate fuzzy inference) and in the beginning of this chapter (to illustrate using a neural network for problem-solving through training).

As another example, a neural can be used to evaluate the possible ranking of a new model of car on the market. The decision is based on training a neural network with ranking data for different models of cars represented by a set of attributes (price, fuel consumption, maintenance, etc.). The system evaluates the ranking if a set of values for the input variables of a new model is entered.

The idea of ranking a new model can also be used in the area of design. Which variant to choose when designing an object can be evaluated on the

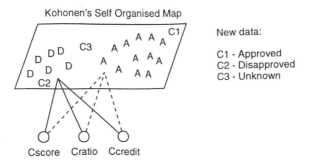

Figure 5.47
A Kohonen SOM for the Bank Loan approval case example.

basis of a set of training examples and a set of constraints introduced to an appropriate neural network architecture. Constraints can be implemented as a second level of knowledge, "above" the network. Fletcher and Goss (1993) used a neural network for predicting bankruptcy of large companies. The evaluation is based on three ratio parameters and training data for 18 "failed" and 18 "nonfailed" real companies. There are many more applications of neural networks for decision-making. References to some of these can be found in Zahedi (1993) and Davalo and Naim (1991).

5.10   Connectionist Systems for Modeling Strategic Games

Symbolic AI systems have proved to be efficient in cognitive modeling and modeling of intelligent games in particular. It has been a long time since computers started to play chess. Production systems, and symbolic AI systems in general, implement the rules of the game that work out the future consequences of a move. Many moves ahead can be simulated, their consequences evaluated, and, the most prospective move chosen. Can neural networks contribute anything to this paradigm of games simulation?

5.10.1   Game Playing as Pattern Recognition

The way of playing games by revealing consequences through applying logic and heuristic rules is only one approach to game playing. Another approach, mainly applicable to simple board games, is to learn how to react to certain patterns on the board. Such a stimulus-reaction approach can be represented by associations in the form of:

IF $\langle$pattern $i\rangle$, THEN $\langle$move $j\rangle$

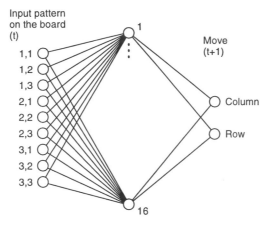

Figure 5.48
A feedforward neural network for training with examples of playing ticktacktoe.

This strategy does not require the program (the computer system) to know many concepts, like rows, columns, etc. The program can learn how to react to certain patterns. This is exactly what neural networks can do. This approach is implemented by setting a proper neural network architecture and training the network with associations of the type:

$$\langle \text{input pattern} \rangle \rightarrow \langle \text{output move} \rangle$$

that is, it is trained with "good" moves; "bad examples" or examples of "what not to do" should not necessarily be used in this approach as they may be too many.

Example: Playing Ticktacktoe by MLP   Figure 5.48 shows a feedforward neural network for training with good examples for playing ticktacktoe. A disadvantage to this approach is that for bigger game boards and games that are not as simple, many examples of good moves are required, which may be impossible to supply.

5.10.2   Hierarchical Multimodular Network Architectures for Playing Games

This approach is based on building different layers of neural networks that perform different consecutive tasks in the process of finding the best next move, for example, layer 1, an input layer, receives data from the board; layer 2, an intermediate layer of receptor neurons, recognizes pat-

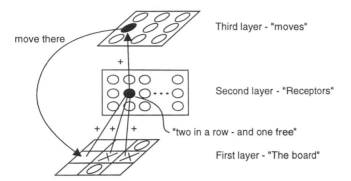

move there

Third layer - "moves"

Second layer - "Receptors"

"two in a row - and one free"

First layer - "The board"

Figure 5.49
A neural network with predefined connections for modeling ticktacktoe game.

terns, features, and situations on the game board; and layer 3, an output layer of effector neurons, selects the best next move.

The patterns on the board are detected, and appropriate neurons in the intermediate layer are activated accordingly. This requires prewired connections. The weights are preset and no training is required. A connectionist model of this type was presented in Rumelhart et al. (1986a). The idea is illustrated in figure 5.49 for ticktacktoe. Having established the links between the neurons from different layers in the network, the system will "play," performing the algorithm given in figure 5.50.

The representation of game strategies in the suggested connectionist model is carried into effect in the following way. The operator, creating or perfecting the network, defines the most important configurations (characteristics) generated in the game process. The presence or absence of one such characteristic determines the need for performing, or refraining from performing, certain moves. For every major characteristic of the game a neural element is constructed in the second layer of the network, sensitive to the appearance (or absence) of the respective configuration characteristic on the game board. If we consider that the appearance of a certain configuration on the board implies a responsive move, we have to connect the neuron from the second layer corresponding to this configuration to the effector from the third layer corresponding to the move, with a positive link. If it is required that the absence of a certain characteristic implies a certain move (or moves), a neuron is introduced at the second layer which is activated by the absence of that characteristic and is similarly connected to the respective effectors with positive links. When certain moves become

1. The network is initialised - all the neurons are set in non-active state.

2. The current position on the playing board is fed to the layer 1 of the network.

3. The receptor neurons at layer 2, acknowledging a presence of a certain pattern on the input layer, move into an active state, i.e.:
    the activation levels a_i of the neurons i at the second layer, for all i, are calculated by using the additive law, for example: if a neuron from the second layer recognises a situation which is "victory" for one of the opponents, or a "draw", an appropriate signal/message/ is produced and the algorithm jumps to the END.

4. The activation value for every neuron j from the third level is calculated; each neuron of the third layer sums up the products of the second layer neurons connected to it and the weights of the respective links.

5. The effector neuron with the biggest activation value is found and announced as a winner (becomes active); if there is more than one effectors with equally large activations, one of them is chosen as winner by random selection.

6. The move for which the winning effector is responsible, is announced as a move of the network.

7. Repet the steps from Step 1.

Figure 5.50
An algorithm for playing the game by the hierarchical multimodular neural network of figure 5.49.

undesirable owing to the presence or absence of a certain configuration, their corresponding effector elements are connected to the neuron responsible for detecting this particular configuration, with a negative link.

5.10.3   Building Adaptable Connectionist Models for Game Playing

There is a third way to build connectionist systems to learn how to play a game. One of them is based on the following assumptions:

1. The system starts playing with a good player ("expert") without any preknowledge.

2. While playing, the system records all the moves.

3. The system is told when the game is over and who the winner is.

4. The system analyzes the game, punishing itself for bad moves and rewarding itself for good moves (good moves may be considered those

generated by the expert or by the winner). An expert could be a human, a computer program, or another, "more experienced" neural network.

A connectionist system that has learned to play GO-Moku was described in Freisleben (1995). A feedforward neural network without predefined weights, but with predefined connections (the network is not fully connected), was trained. During play it evaluates every square for every move and the neuron (the square) that receives the highest activation level is the winner. During the learning session (when the network analyzes its moves, comparing them to the expert's moves) the network corrects its weights. The network can start playing even without any preliminary set connections. In this case it can learn any board game that is played between two opponents.

These connectionist models for game simulation are good exercises for developing cognitive models that simulate human behavior. They are becoming useful for building intelligent robots.

5.11 Problems

Part A: Case Example Solutions

1. *Phoneme recognition experiment.* The task is to build a small modular neural network for recognizing several English phonemes and to test it with new speakers. The multi-modular neural network structure of figure 5.30(A) is used, that is, one phoneme is recognized by one neural network. We shall call them the *phoneme neural networks.* The phoneme neural networks were trained for 200 epochs, with segmented and transformed into 26 mel-scale cepstrum coefficient (MSCCs) speech, produced by five male speakers of New Zealand English. Each MSCC vector represents one frame (12 ms). A graphical representation of 19 vectors of 26 MSCCs for a produced phoneme $/n/$ is given in figure 5.51. The neural networks were tested on new speech samples produced by a New Zealand speaker and by a Swedish student (Jonas Ljungdahl) who spoke English. Figure 5.52 shows the output values of the trained networks for the phonemes $/f/$ and $/ai/$ when tested with the word "five" pronounced by the New Zealand speaker, and figure 5.53 shows the same networks when tested by the Swedish student. Figure 5.54 is a multiple graph showing the activation of the phoneme networks $/f/$, $/ai/$ and $/n/$ when the word "five" was pronounced by the Swedish student.

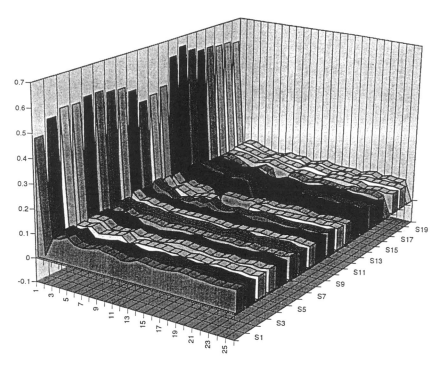

Figure 5.51
A three-dimensional graphical representation of 19 consecutuve vectors of 26 MSCC each,
for a realized phoneme /n/.

It can be seen that a small erroneous activation of the phoneme /n/
neural network appears, but it does not influence the final recognition
results. The false positive activation of /n/ is not so strong as it was in
figure 5.30(B). So, this time the "pupil" /n/ does not need additional
training.

2. *Iris classification through fuzzy neural networks, fuzzy rules extraction,
   and fuzzy inference with the extracted rules.* By using the REFuNN
   algorithm several sets of fuzzy rules were extracted from the Iris data
   set (see appendix A and figures 1.11 and 2.2) (Kasabov 1995c). First,
   three fuzzy predicates, small (*Sm*), medium (*Med*), and large (*Lrg*), were
   used to represent each of the four input attributes and each of the three
   output variables, the latter representing possibilities for a data example
   to be classified into one of the three classes as shown in figure 3.11(A).
   A FuNN structure having 12 input nodes, 6 intermediate nodes, and 9

digit five, phoneme recognition/f/

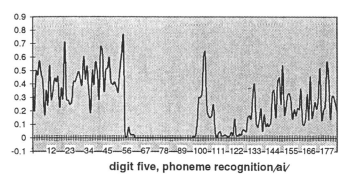

digit five, phoneme recognition/ai/

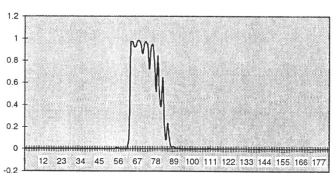

Figure 5.52
Output values of the trained networks for the phonemes /f/ and /ai/ when tested with the word "five" pronounced by a New Zealand speaker.

output nodes was trained with fuzzified Iris training data for 1000 training cycles, a learning rate of 0.1 and momentum of 0.3 until an RMS error of 0.023. Fuzzy rules were then extracted. Figure 5.55 shows the set of initial weighted rules, the sets of simple rules for each of the classes, and a set of rules which has the last two input variables only. It can be seen from the list of extracted rules that the most important for the classification task attributes are petal length and petal width. Several experiments with 30 test examples were conducted and the results are shown in figure 5.56, which is the "confusion" table of the desired classification (left column) and the classification produced by the network (top row). All the test examples were classified correctly by the fuzzy neural network (a). When the extracted simple fuzzy rules

digit five, phoneme recognition/f/

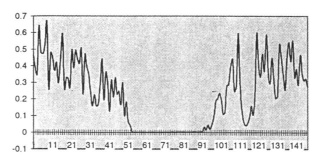

digit five, phoneme recognition/ai/

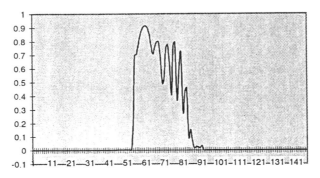

Figure 5.53
Output values of the trained networks for the phonemes /f/ and /ai/ when tested with the word "five" pronounced by the Swedish speaker.

were tested with the MAX-MIN composition fuzzy inference method (see chapter 3) for classification, one example of Virginica was classified incorrectly and two received ambiguous classifications (b). But when only the rules for the last two attributes were used, the classification deteriorated (c).

Another set of rules was extracted when five membership functions were used for the input and output variables shown in figure 3.11B. An MLP having the structure of a 20-10-15 FuNN was trained with fuzzified training data for 1000 cycles, with the same learning rate and momentum values as above. An RMS error of 0.014 was achieved this time. In this case the fuzzy neural network and the MAX-MIN compo-

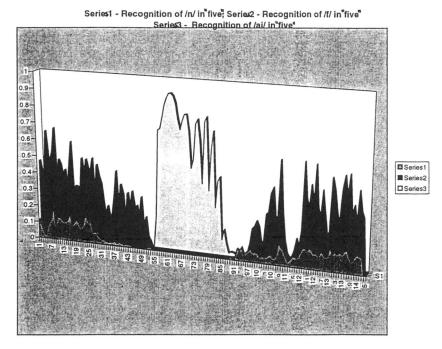

Figure 5.54
Multiple graph showing the activation of the phoneme networks /f/, /ai/ and /n/, when tested with the word "five" pronounced by the Swedish student. A small false positive activation of the phoneme /n/ neural network can be noticed, but it is not going to influence the final recognition results.

sition fuzzy inference method over the simple fuzzy rules achieved a 100% correct classification. It can be seen that when simple rules are used, a better classification is obtained for the rules having five membership functions. This can be explained as follows: the loss of information when "cutting off some weights" for the purpose of simple rules extraction needs to be compensated by a higher granularity in the fuzzy representation.

Part B: Practical Tasks and Questions

3. Explain the main ideas of:

   a. Learning fuzzy rules through supervised learning in an MLP.

   b. Learning fuzzy rules through clustering.

Extracted Iris classification rules for 3 membership functions and thresholds Th$_a$=Th$_c$= 2.0

(a) Weighted Rules:

if <SL is Sm 2.5> and <SW is Sm 4.2>and<PL is Lrg 8.8> and <PW is Lrg 10.8> then <Set is Sm   4.7> if <PL is Med 3> and <PW is Med 3.5> then <Set is Sm 2.2>

if <PL is Sm 2.2> and <PW is Sm 2.21> then <Set is Lrg 2.2>

if <PL is Sm 2.3> and <PW is Sm 2.4> then <Versi is Sm 4.9>

if <SL is Sm 2.5> and <SW is Sm 4.2> and <PL is Lrg 8.8> and <PW is Lrg 10.8> then <Versi is Sm   7.8>

if <PL is Sm 2.2> and <PW is Sm 2.2> then <Versi is Sm 4.9>

if <PL is Med 3> and <PW is Med 3.5> then <Versi is Lrg 3>

if <PL is Med 3> and <PW is Med 3> then <Virgi is Sm   3.8>

if <SL is Sm 2.5> and <SW is Sm 4.2>and<PL is Lrg 8.8> and <PW is Lrg 10.8> then <Virgi is Lrg   8.3>

(b) Simple rules for Th$_{\cdot OR}$ =5.0

RULES for Setosa

if <SL is Sm> and <SW is Sm> and <PL is Lrg>and<PW is Lrg> then <Set is Sm>

if <PL is Lrg> then <Set is Sm>

if <PW is Lrg> then <Set is Sm)

if <PL is Med> and <PW is Med> then <Set is Sm>

if <PL is Sm> and <PW is Sm> then <Set is Lrg>

RULES for Versicolor

if <PL is Sm> and <PW is Sm> then <Versi is Sm>

if <SL is Sm> and <SW is Sm> and <PL is Lrg>and<PW is Lrg> then <Versi is Sm>

if <PL is Med> and <PW is Med> then <Versi is Lrg>

if <PL is Lrg> then <Versi is Sm>

if <PW is Lrg> then <Versi is Sm>

RULES for Virginica

if <PL is Med> and <PW is Med> then <Virgi is Sm>

if <SL is Sm> and <SW is Sm> and <PL is Lrg>and<PW is Lrg> then <Virgi is Lrg>

if <PL is Lrg> then <Virgi is Lrg>

if <PW is Lrg> then <Virgi is Lrg>

(c) Sub-set of rules with two attributes only - petal length and petal width

if <PL is Lrg> then <Set is Sm>

if <PW is Lrg> then <Set is Sm)

if <PL is Med> and <PW is Med> then <Set is Sm>

if <PL is Sm> and <PW is Sm> then <Set is Lrg>

if <PL is Sm> and <PW is Sm> then <Versi is Sm>

if <PL is Med> and <PW is Med> then <Versi is Lrg>

if <PL is Lrg> then <Versi is Sm>

if <PW is Lrg> then <Versi is Sm>

if <PL is Med> and <PW is Med> then <Virgi is Sm>

if <PL is Lrg> then <Virgi is Lrg>

if <PW is Lrg> then <Virgi is Lrg>

Denotation: SL- sepal length; SW - sepal width; PL - petal length; PW - petal width; Set - Setosa; Versi - Versicolor; Virgi - Virginica; Sm- small; Med - medium; Lrg - large.

Figure 5.55

The set of initial weighted rules, the set of simple rules for each of the classes and a set of rules which have the last two input variables only, extracted from a fuzzy neural network trained with the Iris data set when the REFuNN algorithm is used for three membership functions to fuzzy quantize the input and the output variables (see figure 3.11).

	Setosa	Versicolor	Virginica
Setosa	10		
Versicolor		10	
Virginica			10

(a)

	Setosa	Versicolor	Virginica
Setosa	10		
Versicolor		10	
Virginica		1 (2)	7 (2)

(b)

	Setosa	Versicolor	Virginica
Setosa	10		
Versicolor		10	
Virginica		2 (1)	7 (1)

(c)

Figure 5.56
Test results with 30 test examples from Iris data set presented in the form of "confusion tables" of the desired (left column) and the produced (the top row) classification. (A) All the test examples are classified correctly by the fuzzy neural network. (B) The extracted simple fuzzy rules are tested with the compositional MAX-MIN fuzzy inference method. (C) The rules for the last two attributes only are used with the compositional MAX-MIN fuzzy inference method.

4. With the use of the fuzzy rules for *The Smoker and the Risk of Cancer Problem* and the membership functions given in chapter 3, generate a set of 100 data examples for the "number of cigarettes per day–risk of cancer" input-output relation. On this data set, train an MLP and use the REFuNN method to extract simple fuzzy rules. Compare the learned fuzzy rules with the initial fuzzy rules. How can you explain the difference?

5. On the topic of using neural network for prediction (forecasting):

   a. Explain what the forecasting problem is about.

   b. Explain briefly the main principles and possible schemes of applying neural networks for time-series forecasting.

c. Outline the main steps of using a neural network for forecasting on an example problem.

6. On the topic of using MLP with the backpropagation algorithm for the task of phoneme recognition:

a. Create a speech data set of all the digits spoken by four female and four male speakers between 20 and 50 years old, each of whom has an academic education and all of whom belong to the same ethnic group; use 22,050-Hz digitizing frequency.

b. Segment small segments from the wave signals to represent the different allophonic realizations of the phonemes; use 26 MSCCs as a set of features.

c. Create a multi-modular MLP neural network similar to the one shown in figure 5.30(A), and train it with the backpropagation algorithm on the prepared training sets as explained in 5.10 and in the case study above.

d. Make experiments for phoneme recognition for a multiple speaker mode, and a speaker-independent mode. Which mode gives better classification results?

7. Phoneme recognition with the use of SOM:

a. With the use of the training data set created in (6), train a SOM. Calibrate it and explain the resulting topological phonemic map (see, for example, figure 5.33A).

b. Make experiments for phoneme recognition with the trained network and define the accuracy of recognition. Use the same test set as in (6).

8. Comparative study: Imagine a problem that requires recognition of the following handwritten letters: *A*, *E*, *O*, *I*, and *U*. Choose ONE of the options (a), (b), or (c) for solving this problem:

a. Define a set of features and represent each of the qualified letters in it. Write production rules for the recognition task.

b. Give an outline of a fuzzy system for recognizing the qualified letters.

c. Give an outline of a neural network solution to the problem.

d. Compare the above three approaches to solving the specified problem.

Part C: Project Specification

Topic: Problem-Solving and Rules Extraction with Neural Networks

Solve a chosen problem by training an appropriate model of a neural network or a combination of several models. Extract rules from the neural network. Follow the steps:

a. Explain *WHAT* is the chosen problem.

b. Explain *WHY* a neural network should be used for its solution.

c. Explain *HOW* you are going to solve the problem.

d. For the chosen task create a data set that has a set of input and a set of output variables.

e. Create an appropriate neural network structure.

f. Prepare data sets for training and for validation (choose an appropriate method for validation).

g. Train the model; evaluate the training error.

h. Validate the network.

i. Analyze the internal structure of the neural network (the weights), the dependencies between the input and output variables.

j. Use one of the methods for extracting rules from a trained neural network.

k. After having analyzed the extracted rules, can you suggest alternative solutions to the same problem?

Use one of the following problems for the project:

1. Iris Classification (see appendix A)

2. The Smoker and the Risk of Cancer

3. Gas Consumption Prediction (see appendix B)

4. Handwritten Characters Recognition

5. Bank Loan Decision

6. Inverted Pendulum

7. Medical Diagnosis

8. Mortgage approval (see appendix C)

9. Traveling Salesman

10. Resource Scheduling

11. Unemployment prediction (see appendix C)

12. Musical signals-to-notes transformation

13. Playing ticktacktoe

14. Predicting beer sales (see appendix C)

15. Stock Market Prediction (see appendix C)

16. Water Flow to a Sewage Plant Prediction (see appendix C)

5.12   Conclusions

The applications of neural networks to solving knowledge-engineering problems are numerous. All of them are based on the abilities of neural networks to learn from past data or rules, and to generalize over new, previously "unseen" input data. Neural networks provide a smooth approximation of a goal function which maps the domain space into the solution space. Neural networks facilitate approximate mapping, which means that they can handle approximate data, unknown or missing data, and corrupted data. The outputs may have different contextual meaning, that is, probabilities, certainties, real values, symbolic concepts, categories, etc.

Using neural networks for learning explicit knowledge has been presented. The use of neural networks for knowledge acquisition is becoming an important issue because neural networks can learn rules with uncertainties, which are objectively represented in a data set. So it is up to us to extract as much information and knowledge from data as possible, the ultimate goal being to extract and make use of ALL the existing knowledge in data, which goal is not achievable at present, if ever.

5.13   Suggested Readings

For further reading on specific topics, see the following references:

General readings on connectionist models and applications—Arbib (1995); Kosko (1992); Gallant (1993); Zurada (1992); Hertz et al. (1991); Davalo and Naim (1991)

Connectionist models for learning from hints—Abu-Mostafa (1993, 1995)

Differential competitive methods for clustering and learning fuzzy rules—Kosko (1992)

Learning fuzzy rules through neural networks—d'Alche-Buc et al. (1992); Yi and Oh (1992); Mukaidono and Yamaoka (1992); Hayashi (1992); Binaghi (1992); Limkens and Nie (1992); Kasabov (1995c)

Connectionist symbol processing and connectionist production systems—J. Hinton (1990); Shavlik (1994); Gallant (1993); Touretzy and Hinton (1988); Dolan and Smolensky (1989); Kasabov and Shishkov (1993); Fodor and Pylyshyn (1988)

Neural networks for pattern recognition—Pao (1989); Nigrin (1994); Bezdek and Pal (1992)

Various applications of neural networks—D. Touretzky (1989); Yamakawa (1994)

Variable binding in connectionist rule-based systems—Ajjanagadde and Shastri (1991); Shastri (1988, 1991); Sun (1992); Kasabov and Shishkov (1993)

Neural networks for prediction—Deboeck (1994); Chakraborty et al. (1992); Hoptroff (1993); Jia and Chua (1993); Schoenenburg (1990)

Neural networks for diagnosis—Hoskins and Himmelbaum (1990); Peng and Reggia (1989)

Neural networks for signal and speech processing—Kosko (1991); Morgan and Scofield (1991); Waibel et al. (1989a,b); Lippman (1989)

6 Hybrid Symbolic, Fuzzy, and Connectionist Systems: Toward Comprehensive Artificial Intelligence

Hybrid systems mix different methods of knowledge engineering and make them "work together" to achieve a better solution to a problem, compared to using a single method for the same problem.

This chapter shows that standard AI methods, fuzzy system methods, and the methods of neural networks complement one another according to the properties they possess. Different hybrid models are introduced and illustrated by solving generic problems, such as speech recognition and decision making.

6.1 The Hybrid Systems Paradigm

Here, three points are discussed: (1) the need for hybrid systems; (2) why it is useful to mix symbolic AI systems, fuzzy systems, and neural networks; and (3) generic hybrid models.

6.1.1 Hybrid Systems: Why?

There are at least two main reasons for using hybrid systems for problem solving and knowledge engineering: (1) Some requirements for solution of a problem may not be possible to meet by using a single method (see the eight issues of knowledge engineering discussed in chapter 2); (2) there exist models for AI problem solving that cannot be implemented by using a single method, or they would be implemented better if more than one method were used.

Problem-solving requirements for knowledge representation and processing when solving difficult AI problems are growing with technological and social development. Some of these requirements, from the knowledge-engineering point of view, are:

- Representing exact and inexact knowledge in one system
- Representing explicit and implicit knowledge
- Learning knowledge from data
- Approximate reasoning and partial match between data and knowledge to find the best possible solution in a new situation
- Adaptive behavior according to changes in the environment
- Fault tolerance, robustness
- Modularity, expansibility, hierarchy; building *multimodular, multiparadigm* systems

- Accommodating both commonsense knowledge and past-experience data
- Good explanation
- Trying *alternative solutions*

All or some of the above requirements may need to be considered when looking for a method to solve a problem, and there is no single method so far which can satisfy all of them. Knowledge engineering has been around for decades. Many models for solving generic problems have been developed, some of them multimodular, hierarchical. One general hierarchical model for problem solving is the *two-level hierarchical model* for knowledge representation and processing (Kasabov 1990). The first (low) level communicates with the environment, recognizes images and more complex situations, learns new knowledge in a stimulus-reaction way, and so forth, but the final solution is communicated at a higher level, which performs "deliberate thinking," planning, and symbol processing. The low level is fast, flexible, adaptable, and subconscious. The high level is slow, serial, and conscious. The low level operates mainly with numbers. The high level is mainly symbolic. It operates with objects, relations, concepts, rules, premises, hypotheses, plans, strategies, classes, etc. Both levels communicate either in a loosely coupled way (only one bottom-up way), or in a tightly coupled way (intensive communication in both bottom-up and top-down ways) until the final solution is reached (figure 6.1).

Each of the two main levels of the general two-level model can consist of more sublevels. This is illustrated in figure 6.2 where two examples of the general model are shown. They represent two different modes of functioning:

1. *The feedforward mode.* The low level passes information to the higher level, but does not receive feedback. In figure 6.2(a), the low level consists of three submodules (preprocessing, feature extraction, pattern matching), and the higher level consists of one submodule only; such a structure is suitable for realizing speech recognition systems, pattern recognition, decision-making, and many other generic problems.

2. *The recurrent mode,* where the two levels communicate before the final solution is made by the system (figure 6.2b); this structure can also be used for the speech recognition task and for solving other generic problems.

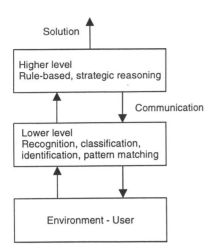

Figure 6.1
A two-level model of knowledge representation and processing. (From Kasabov 1990.)

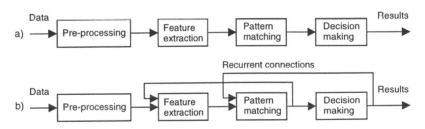

Figure 6.2
Examples of multimodular, multiparadigm systems: (a) feedforward structure; (b) feedback structure.

It will be advantageous if different methods for implementing the different levels and sublevels of the models above are available for use in one system. This will make it possible to find the best solution to the whole problem, based on the possible use of already existing optimal solutions for the different subtasks. A hybrid system may be the best solution to the problem. For example, neural networks may be used for pattern matching, when frequency feature vectors have to be classified into phoneme classes, but fuzzy rules may be the most appropriate to use for words, sentence, and language recognition and context understanding. For the latter subtask, there may also be symbolic AI and connectionist solutions available.

On the other hand, looking for a hybrid solution to the problem, requires from the knowledge engineer:

- Knowledge and skills about different paradigms and methods
- Investigation and comparison of alternative solutions
- Suitable software environment and simulation equipment

Developing such environments requires analysis of the suitability of combining different paradigms and methods. This is the topic of the next subsection.

6.1.2 Symbolic AI Systems, Fuzzy Systems, and Neural Networks Overlap and Complement One Another

Among the methods used for knowledge-engineering so far are the *symbolic AI methods*, the *fuzzy logic methods*, and the *methods of neural networks*. In order to better understand why these paradigms should be combined when solving problems, we must look again to their strengths and limitations as presented in chapters 2, 3, 4, and 5. Each of the paradigms has a contribution to make to the ultimate solution of a problem, as is pointed out below:

Symbolic AI systems can contribute with:

- Rigid theory for symbol manipulation; theorem proving
- Rigorous exact reasoning mechanisms, including chain reasoning and different reasoning strategies
- Universal computational models (e.g., the production systems)

Fuzzy systems can contribute with:

- Well-developed fuzzy logic theory
- Humanlike reasoning mechanisms; using linguistic terms
- Accommodating commonsense knowledge, ambiguous knowledge, imprecise but rational knowledge
- Universal approximation techniques
- Robustness, fault tolerance
- Low cost of development and maintenance
- Low computational cost

Neural networks can contribute with:

- Learning from data
- Modeling empirical behavior of humans
- Universal approximation techniques
- Good generalization
- Methods for extracting knowledge from data
- Methods for data analysis
- Associative memories and pattern-matching techniques
- Massive parallelism
- Robustness

We showed that the three paradigms are applicable to solving the same problems, for example, function approximation and diagnosis. They may provide similar or equivalent solutions, that is, they "overlap" as problem-solving techniques (figure 6.3.).

We can also view these three groups of methods as complementary for three reasons: (1) They facilitate dealing with different kinds of knowledge representation, different inference, different accuracy and fault tolerance, etc. (2) Each of them may be superior to the others when solving a concrete subtask of a problem; for example, the symbolic approach and the connectionist approach have demonstrated strengths in solving different tasks. The former has been successful in high-level cognitive tasks, whereas the latter is more successful in low-level perceptual and learning tasks. (3) One method may be applied to improve the performance of another, as shown graphically in figure 6.4, for example:

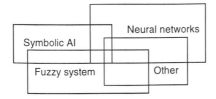

Figure 6.3
Different paradigms and methods overlap as problem-solving and knowledge-engineering techniques.

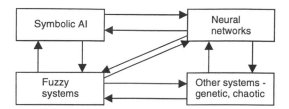

Figure 6.4
Different paradigms and methods complement one another.

- Fuzzy rules can be used to "prewire" a neural network structure for faster training and better generalization.
- Fuzzy rules can be used for initialization of connection weights.
- Neural networks can be used for learning fuzzy rules.
- Neural networks can be used to refine fuzzy rules and membership functions.
- Genetic algorithms can be used to learn fuzzy rules from data and membership functions.
- Genetic algorithms can be used to adjust the connection weights during training, instead of a gradient-descent algorithm.
- Neural networks and fuzzy systems can be used as parts of a symbolic reasoning machine.

The area of integrating ordinary, symbolic, neural networks, fuzzy systems, and other AI techniques (genetic algorithms, evolutionary programming, etc.) is called here *comprehensive artificial intelligence*. Comprehensive AI deals with hierarchical, multiparadigm systems. Building comprehensive AI is possible by integrating different AI methods as shown in the remainder of this chapter. Comprehensive AI is a more general area than the area of *soft computing*. The latter integrates fuzzy logic, neural networks, genetic algorithms, and probabilistic reasoning.

6.1.3 How to Combine Different Paradigms in One System

A hybrid system is a *mixture of paradigms* in the philosophical sense. In a technical sense, it is a mixture of methods and tools used in one system. There are three major modes of functioning in which different knowledge-engineering paradigms can be coupled:

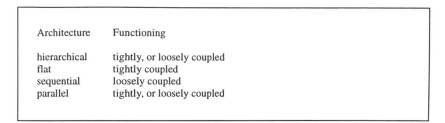

Figure 6.5
Some structural and functional models of hybrid systems.

1. *Loosely coupled*: Different paradigms are applied separately, either in parallel, or, more typically, in a sequence, on different subtasks of the problem. For example, a neural network can be used for feature extraction and rule extraction, and a rule-based system for inference.

2. *Tightly coupled*: The paradigms are used in different subsystems, which work in a close "collaboration" to reach the solution; they communicate intensively and possibly frequently.

3. *Blended at a low structural and functional level.* Paradigms are mixed at a very low level so that they are not separable from a structural and functional point of view. For example, a neuron may have an activation function that is a membership function of a fuzzy set. Both paradigms are embodied structurally into "one body" and are functionally indistinguishable. Examples of such systems are fuzzy neural networks and connectionist production systems. The former were discussed in chapter 4, and the latter in part in chapter 5. A concrete connectionist production system, the neural production system (NPS), is introduced in this chapter.

Loosely and tightly coupled systems are multimodular. The modules can be organized in different architectures: hierarchical vs. flat; sequential vs. parallel; or a combination of the above.

Different combinations between architectures and modes of functioning are possible in a hybrid system, as illustrated in figure 6.5. For example, in a sequential hybrid system a connectionist system may be used for preprocessing or initial processing of raw data, and a symbolic rule-based system used to suggest a solution. An example of a sequential, loosely coupled model is given below.

Example SCRuFFY (signals, connections and rules, fun for everyone) (Hendler and Dickens 1991) was developed for the purpose of classifying signals. A sensor signal feeds through a digital signal-processing program which converts it into a vector of discrete values. An MLP was trained with set of known signals to perform the signal classification task. After training, the neural network is ready to receive a new signal, classify it, and pass on the result for signal-to-symbol conversion. After that a rule-based inference machine does the symbol-processing task to make a recommendation on possible actions.

An example of a flat and tightly coupled architectural model is given below.

Example LIFIA HS (Giacommeti et al. 1992) is a one-level hybrid system composed of two processing modules: (1) a logic module (LM) and (2) a connectionist module (CM). The LM is a standard expert system using IF-THEN rules. It performs both forward and backward chaining inference. The CM combines two neural classifiers, Ns and Nd, linked by an associative network Nsd. When a situation is presented to the hybrid system, it activates first the CM, which proposes an intuitive decision. This decision is sent to an interaction administrator which asks the LM to prove it by backward chaining. If LM proves the intuitive decision of the CM, then the decision is explained. If LM does not have enough information to prove the CM's decision, it communicates with the user and collects more facts. The CM is then activated again for a new decision-making cycle. If no more information is available and still the CM and the LM "do not agree upon the decision," then a forward chaining inference is run in the LM, the LM infers a decision, and the CM is "asked" whether it will agree with this decision. In this way, after repetitive communication, the system produces a solution that is proved by both LM and CM. During functioning of the whole hybrid system, the CM can continually acquire new knowledge, which is then transferred to the LM.

Loosely and tightly coupled hybrid systems, in their structural varieties, can be realized if the following steps are taken:

1. The whole task is first structured into modules connected with one another, for example, an output from one module is an input to another. Recurrent connections are allowed.

2. The input variables and the output variables for each of the modules are defined.

3. The solution procedure for each of the modules is defined as a symbolic AI solution (e.g., production rules), as a neural network, to be trained with data, as a set of fuzzy rules with an inference mechanism, or by using some other method.

4. The whole system is assembled in a way to be controlled by either a *global control* (external control), or by the *flow of data* (internal, self-control).

The next two sections present techniques of coupling neural networks with symbolic production rules and logic programming clauses, respectively. Section 6.4 introduces a methodology for building hybrid systems with the use of the three paradigms, as well as an illustrative software environment that can be used for this purpose. Sections 6.6 and 6.7 illustrate the methodology by building hybrid systems for solving two generic AI problems.

6.2   Hybrid Connectionist Production Systems

The topic of this section is mixing one of the symbolic AI paradigms—the production systems—with neural networks. The presented material is based on one methodology only. The same idea is used in section 6.3 for mixing neural networks and clauses in logic programming environments, and also in the hybrid fuzzy connectionist production systems (see section 6.4). Other methodologies are referenced in section 6.10.

6.2.1   Incorporating Neural Networks into Production Rules

The idea of two-level knowledge processing, discussed in the previous section, is implemented here by using a standard production system for higher-level processing and neural networks for low-level processing.

The main idea of incorporating neural networks into a production rule is to activate the networks as actions in the right-hand side of the production. Facts from the working memory are passed as input vectors to the neural networks. The output vectors, produced by the neural networks, are considered new facts. They may be either asserted in the working memory and possibly affect other productions during a next match-select-act cycle of the production system, or they can be used in the current production by activating other actions (figure 6.6A). The following example illustrates how neural networks are incorporated into productions.

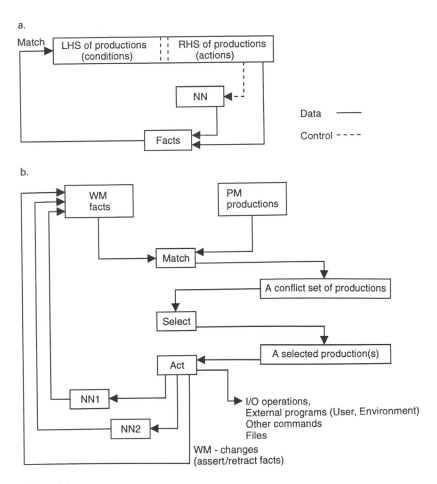

Figure 6.6
(A) Incorporating a neural network into a production rule as an action. (B) The execution cycle of a hybrid connectionist production system with neural networks participating in it. (From Kasabov 1993a).

Example   The problem is to classify a new object into defined categories, and to make a decision how to react to it—to "greet" or "destroy" it. We assume that there are plenty of examples available about different objects which can be used to train a neural network to do the classification task. The final decision will be taken as a conclusion in a production rule (higher-level processing). The following three rules realize the whole task. A neural network is called for the classification task:

(Rule 1 "classify"
 IF (the goal is to classify a new object O) AND
   (data about the object O is available in the working memory),
  THEN (activate a trained neural network NN to classify the object O)
   (assert the classification result into the working memory))
(Rule 2 "destroy"
 IF (the object O is classified as "an enemy"),
  THEN (send a message and "destroy" the object O))
(Rule 3 "greet"
 IF (the object O is classified as a "friend"),
  THEN (send a message and "greet" the object O)

The first rule in the example above activates an already trained network for rapid recognition of a new object O supplying the data about the object from the working memory to a trained neural network as an input vector. It saves the result from the connectionist classification (the network outputs) back into the working memory. The second and third rules are to make the decision.

In this way, productions in a production system may deal with incomplete data and perform approximate reasoning, in this case a best-fit classification.

Neural networks can accumulate knowledge during operation. A neural network, for example, can be trained during execution of the production system. A rule that illustrates training a network as an action in a production and consequent use of the trained network to recognize an object are shown in the next example.

Example

(Rule "train_and_activate"
 IF (the goal G is to classify a new object O) AND
   (data about the object O is available) AND
   (there is no rule or neural network to perform the goal G),

THEN (train a network NN with existing data to perform the task G—
in this case classification)
(activate the trained network NN with data about the new object O)
(put the classification results for the object O into the working
memory))

The above rule illustrates a learning activity in an adaptive production
system, which is a difficult task for symbolic production systems in general.

6.2.2   Building Hybrid Connectionist Production Systems

Using the above-described method of incorporating neural networks into
production rules, where data communication between productions and
neural networks take place through the working memory, makes it possible to use the execution cycle of the production system as a control cycle
for the whole hybrid connectionist production system. Figure 6.6B is a
block diagram of the execution cycle of a hybrid system. The overall
control is done with the use of production rules. Through production rules
different modules can be chained in a sequence, one module using the
output from another, the whole chain solving one task. The inference is
controlled through the production system's inference engine.

Loosely and tightly coupled hybrid connectionist production systems,
in their structural varieties, can be realized in the above connectionist
production system environment. To achieve this, the steps given in the
previous section should be taken with respect to the specificity of the
production systems and connectionist paradigms. The solution procedure
for each of the modules is defined either as a set of production rules, or as
a neural network, to be trained with data. The whole system is assembled
in a way to be controlled by the inference engine of the production
system, taking into account inference strategies, priorities and other
requirements.

By mixing the symbolic production systems paradigm with the connectionist paradigm, each is enriched with the advantages of the other. To
summarize, a connectionist production system can perform:

• Chain reasoning

• Approximate reasoning

• Fast computations

- Learning during execution
- Dealing both with data and rules as problem knowledge

6.3   Hybrid Connectionist Logic Programming Systems

In the same way neural networks were incorporated into production rules, here they are incorporated into clauses, thus enhancing the logic programming systems. One method is presented here.

6.3.1   Incorporating Neural Networks into a Clause

A logic program is a declaration of objects, predicates, and clauses dealing with them. A standard backward chaining with backtracking inference mechanism is applied.

A neural network is considered an object in a logic programming environment, with three predicates defined over it. Such predicates, for example, are the following:

• *create_net* (Net_file, NumInp, NumHidd, NumOut) creates and initializes a three-layer MLP network with the given values for the self-explaining parameters.

• *train_net* (Net_file, Exmp_file, NEpochs, Lrate, Weights_file) trains a network with the given parameters; the initial network is taken from a file "Net_file" and the resulting one after training, in the file "Weights_file"; the training examples are taken from a file "Exmp_file"; the rest of the parameters specify training parameters, in this case parameters for training an MLP with the backpropagation algorithm.

• *recall_net* (Net_file, Inp_vec, Out_vec) activates a network "Net_file" with an input vector Inp_vec; the result produced by the network is returned as a vector Out_vec.

Example 1   This is the same example as in 6.2.1. The predicate "data" checks whether for an object X, a data vector Y exists:

destroy(X):- classify(X,enemy).
classify(X,Z):- data(X,Y), recall_net(Net_file, Y, Z).

A neural network can be trained while a clause is being executed. This is illustrated by the next example:

Example 2

classify (X,Z):- data(X,Y), recall_net(Net_file, Y, Z).
classify (X,Z):-
    data (X,Y),
    create_net (Net_file, NumInp, NumHidd, NumOut),
    train_net (Net_file, Exmp_file, NEpochs, Lrate, Net_file),
    recall_net (Net_file, Y, Z).

The communication between the symbolic logic part and neural networks is achieved by using *shared variables* within a clause. The input and output vectors are represented as lists.

More than one neural network can be activated within one clause. For example, suppose that a SOM was trained in advance to quantize *n*-dimensional vectors into two-dimensional ones, and to display them in such a way as to assist the user making a final decision on loan applications.

Example 3   A clause in a connectionist logic programming system, which calls in a sequential mode the two neural networks, one of MLP type—net1, and the other of a SOM type—net2 for the Bank Loan Decision Problem, is given below (see figure 4.40):

fxloan (Cscore, Cratio, Ccredit):-
    append (Cscore, Cratio, Ccredit, InputV),
    recall_net (net1, InputV, Decision1),
    recall_SOM (net2, Decision1, Decision2).

6.3.2   Building Hybrid Connectionist Logic Programming Systems

Building a whole system is possible by using the built-in inference mechanism in a logic programming environment. This process is illustrated by the problem of medical diagnosis presented in chapter 1 and solved in chapters 3 and 5. Here, one network is trained for each of the four possible disorders, as explained in chapter 5.

Example   The Medical Diagnosis Problem. The following program controls the reasoning process and ends up with a diagnostic solution:

diag(X,Y):- recall_net (net1, X, Diag1),
    recall_net (net2, X, Diag2),
    recall_net (net3, X, Diag3),

recall_net (net4, X, Diag4),
append (Diag1, Diag2, Diag3, Diag4, Y).

where X is the input vector of the manifestation values.

In such a way, reasoning with inexact data is possible. For example, if the following goal is given to the hybrid connectionist logic programming system:

goal:- diag([0.9, 0.0, 0.0, 0.2], Y),

the following solution will be produced:

Y = [0.883, 0.06, 0.156, 0.302].

To summarize, incorporating neural networks into logic programming systems brings new power to the classic logic programming paradigm with respect to two new characteristics: (1) approximate reasoning, and (2) learning.

6.4   Hybrid Fuzzy Connectionist Production AI Systems

Here, the idea of incorporating neural networks into production rules (see section 6.2) is used for building comprehensive AI systems. Fuzzy inference modules are incorporated into production rules in a similar way. An environment for building comprehensive AI systems is presented here and illustrated in the following sections.

6.4.1   Building Comprehensive AI Systems

Building comprehensive AI systems requires *methodologies for mixing different paradigms*; and *software environments* that facilitate these methodologies. These two requirements are discussed in this and the next subsection.

A *methodology for building comprehensive AI systems* should include means for:

• Building complex multimodular and hierarchical hybrid systems

• Experimenting with different combinations of methods (symbolic AI, fuzzy logic methods, connectionist) for solving a given problem before choosing the best model

• Improving the human's understanding of the problem under consideration through extracting, refining, and interpreting explicit knowledge (e.g., fuzzy rules).

• Mixing explicit expert knowledge, raw data, and extracted knowledge from data when creating a system

• Tuning and revising existing or extracted knowledge

• Data analysis: clustering, feature extraction, principal component analysis, etc.

• Data transformations: FFT, mel-scale cepstrum transformations, wavelet transformations, etc.

• Knowledge-processing that meets all the current knowledge engineering requirements, as listed in section 6.1.

• Automation of the decision process on choosing the best model

An exemplar software environment for building comprehensive AI systems is presented next.

6.4.2   Hybrid Fuzzy Connectionist Production Systems Environments

Using hybrid fuzzy connectionist production systems environments is only one possibility for building comprehensive AI systems, as discussed above. They include:

• Production rules and forward chaining reasoning

• Fuzzy rules and different methods of fuzzy reasoning, when fuzzy variables and fuzzy membership functions are defined in advance

• Different types of neural networks

• Different methods for rules extraction

• Methods for data analysis

The idea of building such environments is illustrated with a concrete environment called *FuzzyCOPE* (Kasabov 1995b). FuzzyCOPE is a software environment that has five main modules (figure 6.7). Relevant modules are compatible from the point of view of linking output from one module as input to another. This is also shown in the figure. The modules are explained below:

The FuzzyCOPE production system module is an extension of Fuzzy-CLIPS (presented briefly in chapter 3; see also appendix E) with functions to call fuzzy inference methods, rules extraction methods, and neural networks and data-processing methods, all of them being available for experimenting with in the corresponding modules of the environment. A user

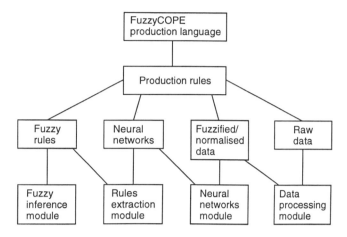

Figure 6.7
Block diagram of FuzzyCOPE—a hybrid fuzzy connectionist production systems environment.

program can be written in the FuzzyCOPE production language and compiled to executable code. A list of built-in functions in FuzzyCOPE to facilitate the above is given in appendix H.

The fuzzy inference module offers different fuzzy inference methods for experimenting with, while tuning the fuzzy reasoning over a set of fuzzy rules. The compositional inference methods, as well as the decompositional method for reasoning with fuzzy inputs and fuzzy outputs, are implemented. This module processes a set of fuzzy rules either designed by the user or by the expert, or automatically extracted from raw or preprocessed data in the rules extraction module.

The neural networks simulation module contains several neural network simulators which can be initialized, trained with raw or fuzzified data, and tested either as separate modules, or as a part of production rules written and executed at the higher level. The fuzzification of the raw data may be done in the data-processing module. The output from this module can be used as input to the rules extraction module.

The data processing module does operations over raw data, like fuzzification, normalization, clusterization. The output of this module can be used as input to the neural network module.

The rules extraction module includes several connectionist methods for rules extraction from raw or fuzzified data. One of them is for extracting a set of rough rules when the membership functions for the fuzzy predicates are chosen of a standard triangular type. The method is based on a standard feedforward neural network architecture and the backpropagation algorithm. The neural network structures are initialized, trained, and tested either in the neural network module or directly in the production system at the higher level, where the neural network functions are called as actions in the production rules.

With the use of the above explained modules and functions, different techniques of building hybrid systems are possible as discussed and illustrated below:

• Calling functions from production rules for operations facilitated in the neural networks module, fuzzy systems module, data analysis module, and rules extraction module. For example, the following function will perform a decompositional inference over fuzzy input "inp" for a set of rules which are in the file "loan.rul," when implication 3, composition 1, and else-link 3 are used:

(dcmfuzzy "loan.rul" inp 3 1 3)

The following function will perform a fuzzification-evaluation-defuzzification inference over crisp input values "inp" for a rule base "pendulum.rul":

(fidfuzzy "pendulum.rul" inp)

• Having available different decompositional inference methods in the fuzzy inference module, the question which one to choose for a particular application is quite reasonable. The answer depends on the inference laws we want our system to obey. Different inference methods satisfy different laws of logical inference. As fuzzy inference functions are available either for direct use from the fuzzy inference module, or can be called from higher-level production rules, the selection and execution of the most suitable fuzzy inference method can be done automatically by interpreting the following production rules:

Rule 1:
IF (a set of fuzzy rules "fuzz1.rul" is available) AND
   (there is a fuzzy inference method fi which has not been tested),
THEN (run the fuzzy inference method fi over the set of fuzzy rules
"fuzz1.rul" for a set of test data "test.dat")
   (save the method fi as f_best if it produces better results than the
   methods tested before)

Rule 2:

IF (a set of fuzzy rules "fuzz1.rul" is available) AND
  (new input data "new.dat" is available),

THEN (run the fuzzy inference method f_best on "fuzz1.rul" for
  "new.dat")
  (assert the results in the working memory)

• The whole process of initialisation, training, and recalling neural networks can be controlled from a higher level of production rules. This option is illustrated in figure 6.8A and B on the Iris Classification Problem.

• Different transformations over raw data, like fuzzification, normalization, and clusterization may be crucial for the accuracy of the final results. They can be dynamically controlled and executed from a higher level, as illustrated in the example below.

Example Calling data fuzzification function for a stock index data set "stock.dat":

(fuzzify "stock.dat" "stock.fuz" 3),

where the value 3 for the third parameter stands for the number of fuzzy labels used for the input and output variables. Standard triangular membership functions are used.

• Rules extraction from data can also be controlled from higher level, as shown below for the stock index data set.

Example Calling rules extraction function for the stock index data set. The prediction neural network model from figure 5.41(A) is used.

```
; training a network and analyzing the network
(fuzzify "stock.dat" "stock.fuz" 3)
(newbp "stock-net.wgt" 6 6 3)
(trainbp "stock_net.wgt" "stock.fuz" 10000 0.5 0.01 0.05))
(extract "stock_net.wgt" "stock.rul" 1 1)
```

• The process of the whole system design can be optimized and automated through interpreting a set of production rules. After having represented the problem solution as a multimodular structure as explained earlier, for each of the modules different alternative solutions can be tried until the optimal one is found. Different techniques can be experimented with—symbolic rules, fuzzy inference, neural network techniques,

a.

```
( defrule IrisBPNet
; initialization of a neural network for iris classification
          (initialize iris)
     =>
          (bind $?m (newbp "a:\\iris.wgt" 4 4 3) )
          (printout t "Status (1 is success) = " $?m crlf ))

( defrule TrainIrisBP; training a neural network for iris classification
          (training iris epochs ?x)
     =>
          (bind $?m (trainbp "a:\\iris.wgt" "a:\\iris.dat  ?x  0.5  0.01 0.05) )
          (printout t "Training error = " $?m crlf ))

(defrule RecallIrisBP
          (recall iris)
     =>
          (bind $?in 4.9 3.1 1.5 0.1 ) ; new instance to be classified
          (bind $?m (recallbp "a\\iris.wgt" $?in) )
          (printout t "Output activations are " $?m crlf ))
```

Figure 6.8
Initialization, training, and recalling an MLP with the backpropagation algorithm as function calls from production rules in FuzzyCOPE for the problem of Iris Classification. (B) A hybrid system for fuzzifying the Iris data, initializing and training a fuzzy neural network, extracting fuzzy rules, and running fuzzy inference over the extracted rules.

and combinations of these; rules extraction and refinement; and many others.

Example

Rule 1:
IF (past data "data.dat" is available),
THEN (train a neural network "net1.net" with data "data.dat" for a low-level processing)
   (fuzzify data from "data.dat" into "data2.dat" by using special membership functions defined by experts)
   (train a neural network "net2.net" with data "data2.dat" for rules extraction)
   (extract fuzzy rules "fuzz2.rul" for higher level processing from the network "net2.net")

b.

;; A program in FuzzyCOPE for training a fuzzy neural network,
;; for fuzzy rules extraction and approximate reasoning with new data

```
( defrule initialisation_of_a_FuNN(fuzzy_neural_network)
  (start)
=>
  ( bind $?status (newbp "iris.wgt" 12 6 9) )
  ( assert (FuNNexists) ))
( defrule fuzzify_Iris_data
  (start)
=>
  ( bind $?status (fuzzify "iris.trn" "iris-fz.trn" 3))
  ( assert (DataFuzzified)))
( defrule Training_FuNN
  (FuNNexists)
  (DataFuzzified)
=>
  ( bind $?error (trainbp "iris.wgt" "iris-fz.trn" 1000 0.1 0.3 0.001))
  ( assert (FuNNtrained)))
( defrule Fuzzy_rules-extraction_from_FuNN
  (FuNNtrained)
=>
  ( bind $?status (extract "iris.wgt" "iris-fz.rul" 2 2.0))
;; (defrule input-new-data ;this rule is only commented here
;; this rule reads input data for a new instance and asserts
;; a fact (F $?new_iris) in the working memory

(defrule reasoning_in_FuNN
    (F $?new_iris)
=>
    (bind $?results1 (recallbp "iris.wgt" $?new_iris))
    (printout t $?results1))

;;;; separation of the set of fuzzy rules "iris-fz.rul" into three sets of
;;;; rules - "iris_se.rul", "iris_ve.rul" and "iris_vi.rul" has to be done
;;;; before the following rule is fired

(defrule a_fuzzy_inference_method_for_approximate_reasoning
    (F $?new_iris)
=>
    (bind ?se (fidfuzzy "c:iris_se.rul" $?new_iris ))
    (bind ?ve (fidfuzzy "c:iris_ve.rul" $?new_iris ))
    (bind ?vi (fidfuzzy "c:iris_vi.rul" $?new_iris ))
    (bind $?results2 ?se ?ve ?vi) (printout t $?results2 crlf))
```

Figure 6.8 (continued)

• Controlling the execution process of a hybrid system by calling different modules and then combining the partial solutions to produce the final one.

Example

Rule:
IF (a neural network "net1.net" for low-level processing has been trained) AND
(a fuzzy rule system "fuzz1.rul" for higher-level processing is available) AND
(higher-level processing fuzzy rules "fuzz2.rul" are available),
THEN (read new input data "inp")
(recall the network net1 with the input data "inp"; bind the resulting vector to "res1")
(run a fuzzy inference method over fuzzy rules "fuzz1.rul" for input vector res1; bind the resulting vector in "res2")
(run a fuzzy inference method over fuzzy rules "fuzz2.rul" for input vector res1; bind the resulting vector in "res3")
(find the trade-off between "res2" and "res3" and bind it to "res4")
(assert "res2", "res3" and "res4" into the working memory for further analysis)

Two examples of building comprehensive AI systems are given in sections 6.6 and 6.7.

6.5   ("Pure") Connectionist Production Systems: The NPS Architecture (Optional)

The major principles of connectionist production systems (CPS) were explained in chapter 5. They are connectionist systems "prewired" according to a set of production rules, that is, the connection weights are precalculated. CPS are hybrid systems—a mixture between the symbolic production systems paradigm and the connectionist paradigm, where both paradigms are "blended at a low level, at a structural and functional level" (this is the third type of hybrid systems according to the classification given at the beginning of this chapter). Some CPS are very appropriate for realizing fuzzy rules, in addition to their ability for realizing symbolic production rules. Such a CPS is the neural production system (NPS) described in this section (Kasabov and Shishkov 1993).

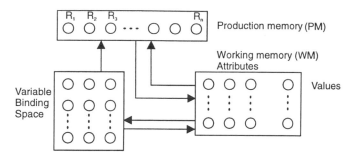

Figure 6.9
Block diagram of the NPS architecture.

6.5.1   The NPS Architecture

An NPS is a "pure" connectionist system. A concrete NPS system is constructed for each defined set of production rules. An NPS consists of three neural subnetworks (figure 6.9): (1) production memory (PM); (2) working memory (WM); and (3) variable binding space (VBS).

The PM contains r neurons, where $r = r_1 + r_2$ is the total number of rules (productions), r_1 the number of productions with variables, and r_2 the number of productions without variables. Only one variable is allowed in a rule.

All the facts held in the WM have the form of $\langle$attribute-value$\rangle$ pairs. WM is a matrix of $v \times a$ neurons, where a is the number of attributes and v is the number of their possible values. Each neuron in the WM corresponds to one fact, either boolean, or fuzzy proposition.

VBS is a matrix of $v \times r_1$ neurons. Each column of this matrix corresponds to one production with a variable, and each row to one of v possible values of the variables. The PM and the VBS form one attractor neural network and the WM provides the external inputs to its neurons.

The inference cycle of an NPS is similar to the cycle of the classic symbolic production systems (recognize-act), but it is implemented in a connectionist way. Here, the match and select parts of the "recognize" phase are mixed, which is different when compared with the symbolic production systems. The act phase consists of updating the WM after opening two gates, one from the PM and another from the VBS.

Simple propositional "true/false" rules can be realized as an NPS system:

R_i: IF $C1$ AND $C2$... and Cn THEN $A1, A2, \ldots, Am$,

where $Ci, i = 1, 2, \ldots, n$, are "true/false" condition elements and $Aj, j = 1,$
$2, \ldots, m$, are actions of the form of "assert"/"retract" a proposition in the
working memory.

For these kinds of simple production rules, the connection weights of
the attractor network can be calculated in such a way that each rule is
considered to be a "pattern," a stable attractor. During the match phase,
when the facts in the WM match the production memory, the PM network goes into an equilibrium state after several iterations, which state is
an attractor representing one rule. Then the activated rule (a neuron in the
PM) updates the WM according to its consequent part (asserts or deletes
propositions). The propositions (the facts) are represented by activation
values of 0 and 1 of the neurons in the WM.

The PM always converges into a stable state representing a rule when
input values are supplied to exactly match the condition elements in the
rule. NPS can realize any production system that consists of propositional
rules. The inference results are equivalent to those, produced by the built-
in inference in a production language (e.g., CLIPS).

The existence of a huge amount of spurious states in attractor neural
networks, which may cause a *local minima problem*, can be used for
approximate reasoning when the facts can have any truth value between
0 and 1; therefore the condition elements in a rule are partially matched.
In this case, the attractor PM network will relax in a spurious state, which
means that more than one rule may get activated to a certain degree. The
WM then can be updated either by the rule with the highest level of
activation (*sequential updating*), or by all the rules, which level of activation is above a threshold (*parallel updating*).

Using *partial match* for approximate reasoning in an NPS is a very
strong point, which makes an NPS applicable to solving difficult AI problems. This is actually the focus of the material presented in this section.

In general, production rules to be realized in an NPS can have the
following form:

R_i: IF $C_{i1}(DI_{i1})$ & $C_{i2}(DI_{i2})$ & ... & $C_{ik}(DI_{ik})$,

THEN $A_{i1}, A_{i2}, \ldots, A_{il}$ $(\Theta_i, P_i, \beta_i, CD_i)$,

where C_{ij} are condition elements of the form of ⟨attribute-value⟩ pairs
representing boolean or fuzzy propositions of the type "⟨attribute⟩ is

⟨value⟩," or their negation; DI_{ij} is a *relative degree of importance* of the ij-th condition element C_{ij}; and A_{ij} is one of the actions *insert* or *delete* a fact in the WM. Four inference control coefficients $(\Theta_i, P_i, \beta_i, CD_i)$ may be attached to every production. Θ_i is a threshold which determines the *noise tolerance*. The lower the value of Θ_i, the greater the noise tolerance, but at the same time, the greater the possibility of erroneous activation of the rule. P_i is a *data sensitivity* factor which controls the sensitivity of the rule R_i toward the presence of relevant facts. Θ_i and P_i control the partial match in NPS. β_i is a *reactiveness factor* for the rule R_i. It regulates the activation of the rule R_i depending on how much it is matched by the current facts in the working memory. It is an important element in conflict resolution when only one rule has to be chosen and updated. The fourth coefficient, CD_i, is the *certainty degree* (confidence factor) of the rule, representing the uncertainty in the conclusions when the condition elements in the rule are fully matched by the current facts.

The number of conditions and actions in a production rule R_i is arbitrary and each condition element C_{ij} and action A_{ij} may or may not have a variable (denoted by x) in the place of the value. The relative degrees of importance are used in NPS to regulate the partial match and the approximate reasoning. The proper use of DIs may prevent the rules from firing when the most important facts are not known. The lack of evidence about an unimportant fact for a particular rule should not stop its firing. All the facts of a production system are held in the WM subnetwork.

NPS has two modes of representing facts in the production rules and in the WM, respectively (1) without negated condition elements, and (2) with negated condition elements. In the first mode, the facts are represented in the WM with a truth (certainty) degree between 0 and I_e (I_e is a constant parameter of NPS with a default value of 1) representing how certain the presence of the fact is at the moment. In the second mode, the facts are represented in the WM by certainty degrees in the interval $[-I_e, I_e]$. A negative evidence for the fact is represented by a negative number and a positive evidence by a positive number. An unknown fact (the case "don't know") is represented by a certainty degree of 0.

The NPS model is designed to facilitate partial match and to be used afterward for approximate reasoning. In this context, the inference control coefficients are plausible from an engineering point of view. The noise tolerance shows how much a production will be resistant to the presence of limited evidence of facts, that is, should it be activated or will it be assumed that this little evidence for the facts might be a noise? The data sensitivity factor represents the dynamics of the relations between the facts and the rules. The certainty degrees CD define the relations between the activation level of the productions and the final certainty degrees of the inferred facts.

In an NPS, there are values for the parameters Θ_i, P_i, β_i, and CD_i attached by default, if they are not declared explicitly in the rules. It is also possible to declare global values for all inference control coefficients in a PS. The example below gives an idea of the syntax of NPS and the partial match provided.

Example

Productions:

$Ax\ Bx - CA\ CB \rightarrow Dx\ AB\ (0.5,1,1,1)$;
$AB - CA \rightarrow -CC\ (0.5,1,1,1)$;

Facts:

$AA = 1;\ BA = 1;\ CA = -0.8$;

Let us follow the inference according to a simulation performed in an NPS simulator. The facts partially match the rules, but the support for the first one is stronger. The neuron in the PM corresponding to the first rule will fire with an activation of 0.6. The variable x will be bound to the value A, and two new facts, DA and AB, will be added to the WM with certainty degrees of 0.6. In the next cycle, the second rule will fire (the refractoriness of the neurons in PM will prevent the first rule from firing again). The final result is the fact CC with a certainty degree of -0.9.

Another example will illustrate the use of relative degrees of importance, DI_{ij}, attached to the condition elements of the rules.

Example

Productions:

$Ax(9)\ Bx(1) \rightarrow CC - Ax;\ BA \rightarrow CC;\ Cx - Dx \rightarrow CA$;

Facts:

$AB = 0.8;\ BB = 0.3$;

In this example, only the first rule is matched by the content of the WM. As the contribution of the first condition element Ax to firing the rule is 90% (very high), the limited information for the second condition element may not prevent the rule from firing. After the first inference cycle, this rule will fire with a certainty degree of 0.7 and x will be bound to the value B with the same certainty degree. If we exchange the degrees of importance of the conditions in the first production, it will not fire because the evidence for the more important fact (BB in this case) is very low.

The "act" phase is done in an NPS after the match-select phase. Then a "gate" from the PM to the WM and a "gate" from the VBS to the WM open and allow updating the WM nodes. The weights of the connections from the PM and the VBS to the WM represent the actions in the right-hand side of the rules and have the following values: CD_i (assert), $-CD_i$ (delete), where CD_i is the certainty degree of the ith production. The neurons in the WM use the following activation functions:

$$u_{ijnew} = d. \, o_{ijold} + I_{ij}$$

$$o_{ijnew} = \begin{array}{l} I_e, \text{if } u_{ijnew} > I_e \\ u_{ijnew}, \text{if } -I_e \leq u_{ijnew} \leq I_e \\ -I_e, \text{if } u_{ijnew} < -I_e \end{array}$$

where $0 \leq d \leq 1$ is a decay factor for the WM; o_{ijold} is the output signal of the ijth neuron in the WM calculated at its last updating cycle, o_{ijnew} being its new updated value; and I_{ij} is the aggregated signal from the VBS and the PM to the ijth neuron in the WM. I_{ij} is not equal to 0 only if the ijth neuron in the WM is connected to the winner in the PM and possibly to the winner in the VBS.

In general, a new state of a neuron in the WM depends on its previous state, and on the input signal from the PM and the VBS. The decay factor d is used to implement forgetting in the WM.

A truth-value (certainty degree) of a fact in the WM can be changed (increased or decreased) after every "recognize-act" cycle, thus making the whole inference process *nonmonotonic*.

6.5.2   Partial Natch in NPS

A *partial match* is defined here as a process of matching the uncertain, inexact, and missing facts from the WM with the production rules. The main problem is to decide when the facts sufficiently match a rule in order to determine whether the rule is ready to be activated, and what level of activation it should receive. This problem is solved in NPS at three stages of matching: (1) partial match for binding variables; (2) partial match of the whole left-hand side of the rules; and (3) calculation of the activation level of the matched productions (including the already bound variables).

We should note that these three stages of matching are accomplished concurrently, as a process of relaxation in the attractor network, formed by the two subspaces—the PM and the VBS. This separation is to facilitate the explanation only. Otherwise the PM and VBS form a single network. Every neuron is connected to every other. The weights bound to the connections are calculated in such a way that every neuron from the PM has excitatory connections to itself and to the neurons in the VBS, which represent possible binding of its variable and inhibitory connections to all the rest of the neurons. Every neuron from the VBS has excitatory connections to itself and to the corresponding neuron in the PM which represents the rules where the variable appears, and inhibitory connections to the rest of the neurons.

In order to achieve the mechanism of partial match, the two coefficients Θ_i (noise tolerance) and P_i (sensitivity factor) bound to a production R_i, and the two coefficients noise tolerance Θ_{VBS} and sensitivity P_{VBS} (global for all neurons in the VBS) are used. The degree of importance DI_{ij}, attached to a condition element C_{ij} in R_i, is also used for the purpose of partial match. Connectionist realization of the three stages of partial match is described below.

In order to realize the first two stages of the partial match, the WM's contribution S (called support) to every neuron in the PM and in the VBS is calculated after every WM update. There is a connection from a neuron k in the WM to a neuron i in the PM, with a strength of $w_{ik} = \pm DI_{ik}/\sum_{j=1,m}(DI_{ij})$ if the first neuron k represents a pair which takes part as a condition element in the rule R_i, represented by the second neuron i, DI_{ik} being the relative degree of importance of this pair within the rule. $\sum DI_{ij}$ (for $j = 1, 2, \ldots, m$) is the sum of the degrees of importance for all the condition elements in the production R_i.

There is a connection from a neuron k in the WM, representing an attribute-value pair, to a neuron corresponding to a value j from column i in the VBS, if the rule R_i contains the pair in its LHS. This is to ensure a consistent variable binding. The weights of the connections from the WM to the VBS have the following values: $w_{jik} = +DI_{ik}/\sum_l(DI_{il})$, where $\sum_l(DI_{il})$ is the sum of the degrees of importance of the condition elements with a variable in the ith production R_i, and DI_{ik} is the degree of importance of the condition element with a variable matched by a fact, represented by the kth neuron in the WM. The sign of the weights is negative if the kth condition element has a negation.

There is a connection from every neuron p in the ith column of the VBS to the neuron R_i in the PM with a weight of $w_{ip} = \sum_l(DI_{il})/\sum_m(DI_{im})$, where the sums $\sum_l$ and $\sum_m$ have the same meaning as above. The formulas for calculating the support from the neurons k in the WM to a neuron in the VBS ($Svbs_{ji}$), to a neuron in the PM representing a rule with a variable (Srv_i), and to a neuron in the PM representing a rule without a variable (Sr_i), are as follows:

$$Svbs_{ji} = \sum_k(w_{jik}V_k), (Svbs_{\max} = I_e),$$

$$Srv_i = \sum_k(w_{ik}V_k) + V_p w_{ip}, (Srv_{\max} = I_e),$$

$$V_p = \max_j\{Svbs_{ji}\}$$

$$Sr_i = \sum_k(w_{ik}V_k), (Sr_{\max} = I_e),$$

where the sums $\sum_k$ above are over the neurons k in the WM which support the corresponding neurons in the PM and in the VBS, V_k being their output values, V_p the output value of the winning neuron p in the VBS representing the binding of the variable in the rule R_i, and w_{ip} being the weight of the connection from this neuron to the neuron R_i in the PM.

In order to control the calculation of the activation levels of the matched productions (third stage of the partial match), the support S_i from the WM to the neuron i in the PM, or in the VBS, is filtered as follows:

$$I_i = I_e((S_i - \Theta_i)/(I_e - \Theta_i))^{P_i}, \text{ if } S_i \geq \Theta_i, i = 1, \ldots, n, \text{ or it is 0, otherwise.}$$

where I_i is the net input to the ith neuron in the PM, or in the VBS; I_e is the maximum activation level of the neurons in the WM (1 by default); Θ_i is the noise tolerance of the ith neuron (i.e., the noise tolerance of the rule R_i, or a global value for all the neurons); and P_i is the sensitivity of the ith neuron toward the supporting facts in the WM. The above formula was selected empirically after experiments to find out a way to effectively control the partial match in NPS.

The filters allow a fine-tuning of the influence of the facts from the WM to the firing of the rules. The filters have the following characteristics:

If $S_i = I_e$, then $I_i = I_e$ (maximum support)

If $S_i \leq \Theta_i$, then $I_i = 0$ (lack of support)

If $\Theta_i = 0$ and $P_i = 1$, then $I_i = S_i$ (the filter is omitted)

If $P_i = 0$, the filter works like a threshold element

This formula is simple, effective, and comprehensive. The introduction of a filter between the current data and the knowledge, captured in a connectionist structure, is a way of representing *meta*knowledge. The filter controls how the neuronal "knowledge" should be used when data are present, and to what extent. This is an example of how we can introduce psychologically plausible parameters to a connectionist PS at a low, neuronal level.

The partial match between the facts in the WM and the rules in the PM is due to the activation values of the nodes in the WM, the degrees of importance of the condition elements, and the two coefficients Θ_i and P_i. Θ_i is a threshold that is used to restrain the input from the WM to the neurons in the PM and the VBS assuming that it is a "noise". It separates "noise" from the relevant information. This coefficient determines the noise tolerance of the neurons and thus the extent of the partial match. P_i regulates the sensitivity of a rule R_i, or of a variable binding, toward the presence of relevant facts. If P_i increases, the sensitivity decreases, and it is more difficult to activate the rule R_i even if the support from the WM is above the noise tolerance threshold Θ_i. Θ_i and P_i can be used to control the process of the partial match at the level of the whole knowledge base (by their default values), as well as at the level of each particular rule (see the examples below). Two cases of filtering are represented graphically in figure 6.10.

The partial match can be tuned to specific requirements by tuning the values of the noise tolerance parameters Θ and the sensitivity factors P as global values (valid for all productions and variable bindings), as well as by setting individual values for every production.

An important element of every production system is the way a rule is chosen for firing among the other satisfied rules if a sequential mode of updating the WM is used. The partial match explained in the previous

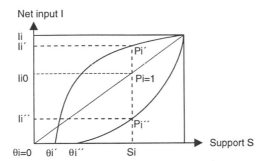

Figure 6.10
Different noise tolerance θ_i and sensitivity factor P_i define different values for the net input I_i to a rule-neuron R_i for a same data support S_i from the current facts in the working memory and the variable binding space.

section makes the realization even more difficult, as the term "satisfied" means here "partially satisfied." But how "partially" should a rule be satisfied in order to be chosen for execution? (This does not impose a problem in the parallel mode of realization, when all the rules satisfied above a given threshold fire and update the WM in parallel.)

Different *conflict resolution criteria* are realized in NPS as follows:

• *Refractoriness.* All the neurons in the PM and in the VBS are refractory —once fired, they may not fire again during the next inference cycles. The period of prohibition can be different for each group of neurons. This prohibition may not extend indefinitely. The prohibition is controlled by four time-delay parameters, implemented through inhibitory weights from a special highly activated neuron to the rest of the neurons in the PM and in the VB.

• *Priorities among the rules.* They can be imposed in two ways. The first is to use suitable values for the two partial match control coefficients Θ (noise tolerance) and P (sensitivity). In this case different rules having the same support S from the WM receive different external input signals after the filter. If the support S is less than some critical value S_c, then the first rule will have greater priority; if the support S is above S_c, than the other rule will win. This method of assigning dynamic priorities is a side effect of the connectionist realization of the partial match in NPS. It does not work if the rules receive the maximum support I_e. These dynamic priorities represent a feature not seen in existing symbolic production systems. Another way to realize priorities—this time, explicit priorities—is to use the third inference control coefficient possibly attached to every rule R_i, the reactiveness factor β_i. As the connections between the neurons in the PM are inhibitory, the "fastest" neuron (rule) would suppress the others and would win (attain the highest activation value). By assigning different values for the reactiveness of the productions, we can better differentiate the productions as different knowledge modules.

6.5.3 Approximate Reasoning in NPS

We consider approximate reasoning in NPS as a process of inferring new facts and achieving conclusions when inexact facts and uncertain rules are present. The process of approximate reasoning in an NPS can be described as matching facts represented by their truth degrees against antecedents of rules. Then the truth values (certainty degrees) of the new facts (conclusions) are computed. This is repeated as a chain of inferring new facts, matching the newly inferred facts (and the old facts of course) to the productions again, and so forth. The reasoning process is nonmonotonic; processing of new facts may decrease the certainty degree of an already inferred fact. The main idea of controlling the approximate reasoning in an NPS is that by tuning the inference control parameters we can adjust the reasoning process for a particular production system to the requirements of the experts. Approximate reasoning in an NPS is a consequence of its partial match. For example, by using the noise tolerance coefficients Θ_i, an NPS can separate facts that are relevant to the decision process from irrelevant facts. Rules with different sensitivity coefficients P_i react differently to the same set of relevant facts.

An NPS can work with missing data. One rule may fire even when some facts are not known. By adjusting the degrees of importance DI_{ij} we declare that some condition elements are more important than others and rules can fire if only the important supporting facts are known.

Adjustment of the inference control parameters facilitates the process of choosing an appropriate inference for a particular production system.

Example A simple diagnostic production system with four manifestations, $M1$ through $M4$, three rules R1, R2, and R3, and three diagnoses $D1$, $D2$, and $D3$ is represented in an NPS as follows:

R1: $M1(10)\ M2(2) \rightarrow D1\ (0.4, 0.8, 1.0, 0.9)$;

R2: $M2(8)\ M3(7) \rightarrow D2\ (0.2, 0.3, 2.0, 1.0)$;

R3: $M3(10)-M4(8) \rightarrow D3\ (0.7, 1.5, 0.8, 0.6)$;

Rule R2 is the most sensitive one to the facts, rule R1 is less sensitive, and R3 is least sensitive. The same distinctions apply to the reactiveness and certainty degrees of the productions. The noise tolerance threshold Θ_3 of the third rule is highest, which means that this rule needs more strong evidence to be activated. The final values for these coefficients are to be set after experiments with real data and consultations with experts who are supposed to evaluate the correctness of the inference process. The attached inference coefficients are used to represent uncertainties based either on a statistical or on a heuristic evaluation. They can also be adjusted during the experiments.

For a concrete set of manifestation values, $M1 = 0.8$, $M2 = 0.3$, $M3 = 0.5$, $M4 = -0.9$, and for an output threshold of the PM 0.15, the inferred diagnoses are $D1 = 0.9$, $D2 = 1.0$, $D3 = 0.0$. It could be seen that even having the strongest evidence for its supporting facts $M3$ and $M4$, the third rule fails to infer anything. This is due to its low noise tolerance (high value of Θ_3) and low sensitivity (high value of P_3). The second production is very sensitive (low value of P_2) and has a high noise tolerance (low value of Θ_2), so it reaches its diagnosis with the highest certainty degree. The first rule reaches a high certainty degree because its most important manifestation $M1$ ($DI_{11} = 10 > DI_{12} = 2$) is strongly supported by the fact $M1 = 0.8$ in the WM.

The simple diagnostic rules may be extended to fuzzy diagnostic rules, when the manifestations and the diagnoses are given linguistic values, for example:

If $M1$ is Strong and $M2$ is More-Or-Less-Small, Then $D1$ is Medium

Implementing fuzzy production systems in an NPS is discussed in the next subsection.

6.5.4   NPS for Knowledge-Engineering

Fuzzy production systems have already been implemented in this book with the use of fuzzy logic inference techniques, with the use of multilayer perceptrons and the backpropagation learning algorithm, and with some other inference techniques. The use of an NPS for approximate reasoning over fuzzy productions is illustrated here by the simple Bank Loan problem. The main idea of realizing fuzzy production systems as an NPS is that activation values of nodes in the WM contextually represent membership degrees when dealing with fuzzy variables.

```
/*This is The Bank Loan Example written in NPS syntax*/

Network Additive;
Parameters {dVmin = 0.001
 /* this is the minimum difference of an output activation of a neuron in the attractor PM
network for achieving an equilibrium state*/

Vrmin=0.3
/* The output threshold of the neurons in the PM*/ }

Rules {
/* Rule 1: If Score is High & Ratio is Good & Credit is Good  Then Decision is Approve
   Rule 2: If Score is Low & Ratio is Bad
         Then Decision is Disapprove
   Rule 3: If Credit is Bad Then Decision is Disapprove */

   SH RG CG→ DA;
   SL RB →DD;
   CB → DD; }

WM {
/* Initial facts for the current application*/

   SH = 0.7;  SL = 0.0;  // Score  = 190
   RG = 0.7;  RB = 0.0;  // Credit =  3
   CG = 0.7;  CB = 0.0;  // Ratio  = .4 }
```

Figure 6.11
The Bank Loan Decision fuzzy rules implemented in an NPS.

Example   The Bank Loan fuzzy rules are implemented in an NPS, as shown in figure 6.11. New input values (e.g., Score = 190, Ratio = 0.4, Credit = 3) must be fuzzified first and then used as activation values for the neurons in the WM. After a run of the NPS, new facts about the decision are inferred. The latter can be applied over the Decision Approve and Decision Disapprove fuzzy membership functions, and the final value for the Decision variable obtained after deffuzification.

A realization of a fuzzy production system using an NPS assumes that fuzzification and defuzzification are done as preprocessing and postprocessing.

By adjusting different values for the inference control parameters attached to an NPS realization, different approximate reasoning methods can be realized (Kasabov 1994, 1996).

6.6   Hybrid Systems for Speech Recognition and Language Processing

6.6.1   Hybrid Systems for Speech Recognition: What to Combine?

The speech recognition process is representable as a two-level hierarchical process, consisting of a low-level—subwords recognition, for example, phoneme recognition, and a high-level—words, sentences, contextual information recognition, language analysis; each of the levels being representable in a recursive manner as many other levels of processing. For example, subwords recognition may include feature extraction; allophonic segments classification; and grouping the recognized segments over time into subwords (time-alignment problem). Different combinations of techniques for low-level and higher-level processing have been explored so far, with one of the most used techniques being:

• *Template matching and dynamic time warping* for low-level processing. Speech recognition using template-matching involves comparing an unclassified input pattern to a dictionary of patterns (templates) and deciding which pattern in the dictionary the input pattern is closest to. Distance measures are used to decide the best match. Before the matching is done it is necessary to perform some time alignment between the input pattern and each reference template. Owing to the variability of speech there will be local and global variations in the time scale of two spoken examples of the same word, regardless of whether the two examples were uttered by the same speaker or not. An effective technique utilized in computer speech recognition for time-aligning two patterns is a nonlinear time-normalizing technique, dynamic time warping. Speech recognition systems based on dynamic time warping have been used successfully for isolated word recognition. Usually the vocabulary is medium-sized or less (i.e., < 100 words) because the dictionary of reference templates takes up a lot of storage space. Dynamic time-warping systems are also usually speaker-dependent. For speaker-independent systems reference templates have to be collected from a large number of people; these are then clustered to form a representative pattern for each recognition unit (Owens 1993). Speech recognition systems utilizing dynamic time warping have also been used for connected speech recognition and recognizing strings of words such as a series of digits (e.g., a telephone number).

A limitation of dynamic time warping, when the recognition units are words, is that its time-aligning capabilities can lead to confusion between words when the principle distinguishing factor is the duration of a vowel, for example, "league" and "leek". A further limitation is the large memory required for a speaker-independent, large-vocabulary speech recognition system.

• *Hidden Markov models* for low-level and higher-level processing. Like dynamic time warping, they can account for the variations of speech in time. While dynamic time warping is a template-matching technique, hidden Markov models are statistical modeling techniques. A set of training speech data is used to generate a probabilistic model (see chapter 2 and figure 2.33). This training can be time-consuming and requires large amounts of memory. However, once trained, the hidden Markov model is fast and requires little memory. The hidden Markov model represents a process with a finite set of states. The states cannot be observed, they are hidden. Each state contains statistical probabilities and functions that perform pattern-matching and time-normalization. The structures of hidden Markov models fall into three major categories: (1) unconstrained; (2) constrained serial; and (3) constrained parallel.

The constrained serial and constrained parallel models are used for isolated word recognition. They allow for temporal variation because they "move from left to right." Once a state is passed in the constrained serial and constrained parallel models, it cannot be revisited later on. The states in a hidden Markov model are not necessarily physically related to any single observable phenomenon. The limitations of the hidden Markov models are (Lippman 1989): poor low-level modeling of speech (at the acoustic-phonetic level), which leads to confusions between acoustically similar words; and poor high-level modeling of speech (semantic modeling), which restricts systems to simple situations where finite state or probabilistic grammars are acceptable. It is difficult to model linguistic rules directly.

• *Neural networks* for each of the phases at the low-level and higher-level processing. This was discussed in chapter 5.

• *Symbolic AI rule-based systems* for higher-level processing (discussed in chapter 2).

• *Fuzzy systems*, mainly for higher-level processing (discussed in chapter 3).

Combinations of the above techniques lead to more powerful systems. For example, a simple speech recognition system may consist of a low-

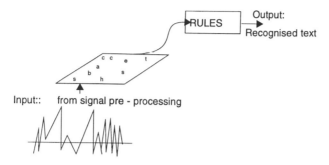

Figure 6.12
A hybrid system for speech recognition. The phoneme recognition task is performed at a low level and is realized as an SOM. The higher level performs a text recognition task and is realized as a rule-based system.

level SOM for phoneme segments classification and a higher-level, rule-based system (figure 6.12.). Before using rules (or instead of using rules) a method for time alignment may be applied to the sequence of segment labels recognized at consecutive time intervals by the SOM (Kasabov et al. 1993).

A more comprehensive hybrid connectionist fuzzy model is presented in the next subsection.

6.6.2   A Hybrid Connectionist Fuzzy Logic Model for Speech Recognition and Language Understanding

The model described here is based on the assumption that the whole process of speech recognition and language analysis is an integrated continuous process and the border between the two is not well defined. Where does the speech recognition process end and where does the language analysis process really begin? Are they not two overlapping processes?

This process can be viewed in two dimensions—time and type of knowledge applied in order to recognize and understand a spoken sequence, where the speech recognition and language analysis phases overlap in both dimensions. For example, correctly recognizing a spoken phoneme may require understanding the context of the whole word, and also some words pronounced before and after it. Figure 6.13 represents the applicability of neural networks and fuzzy systems to solving different subtasks from the speech recognition and language understanding processes

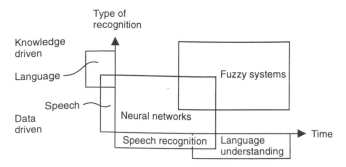

Figure 6.13
The use of neural networks and fuzzy systems for different types of processing during speech recognition and language understanding processes. As both processes overlap over the time scale and over the "type of recognition" scale (the scale between data driven and knowledge-driven recognition) so do the applicability of the two paradigms.

represented in the two dimensions: "time" and "type of recognition." As both processes overlap over the "time" scale and over the "type of recognition" scale (the range between data-driven and knowledge-driven recognition) so does the applicability of the two paradigms.

Based on the general architecture of an intelligent human computer interface given in figure 1.20 and on the applicability of neural networks and fuzzy systems to different phases of this task, a multimodular hybrid model for speech recognition and language modeling can be developed, as shown in figure 6.14. It has the following main modules:

• *Preprocessing module.* This performs nonlinear transformations over the raw speech signal and extracts features. Different standard transformations could be applied.

• *A neural network module for low-level, phoneme recognition.* This can be a single neural network or a multinetwork structure of many specialized neural networks for recognizing patterns of sub-units, for example parts of phonemes or phonemes. Different types of networks can be used. This module is adaptable and trainable with speech samples of phonemes from a speech corpus.

• *A higher-level fuzzy rule–based system* performs approximate reasoning over fuzzy rules for phoneme, words, sentence, concept, and meaning recognition. The higher level is, in general, a multilayer structure of fuzzy rules which represent different layers of speech and language knowledge.

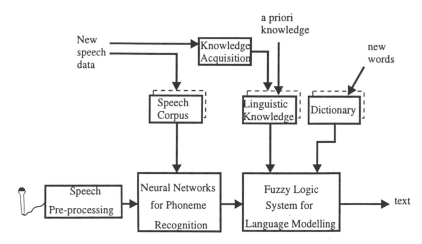

Figure 6.14
A multimodular hybrid system for speech recognition and language understanding.

It can be a simple flat fuzzy rules system or a quite complicated system, depending on the task. For example, the fuzzy system realizes linguistic rules from a set of linguistic knowledge, forms words and matches the recognized words into a pre-defined dictionary.

The following principles are used when building a concrete speech recognition system based on the model of figure 6.14:

• *The principle of hierarchy.* The speech elements are recognized through their natural hierarchy of subunits, units, strings.

• The principle of a *delayed decision.* A lower-level decision is temporarily accepted for further processing, but is subject to correction due to the higher-level knowledge available and the interaction between the levels in the system.

• The principle of the *fuzzy winner.* At each level, not one, but many possible subunits and units are kept for further processing and not just the one winning at that moment.

• The principle of *making use of both data and knowledge* when building a speech recognition system. This principle means also applying both "unconscious," "blind," or "stimulus-reaction" recognition, and "conscious," rule-based or directed, recognition.

• The principle of *adaptability*. A system based on the model is adaptable to new variations of speech, new vocabularies, etc. The adaptability is achieved in three ways: (1) additional training of the neural networks at the lower level with examples of new speech variations; (2) adding or changing fuzzy rules in the higher-level module for representing the new speech characteristics; (3) learning fuzzy rules from new speech data and adding these rules to the already existing ones for higher-level processing.

• The principle of *biological, physiological, and psychological plausibility*. At each level of recognition the system tries to imitate as much as possible what is known about the human's ear, brain, and mind.

Higher-level fuzzy processing can be implemented by using fuzzy inference methods, facilitated in different fuzzy engineering tools; and connectionist systems that process fuzzy rules, an example of such a system being NPS.

The above described model is illustrated by an examplar system for phoneme-based spoken digits recognition in section 6.8.

6.7   Hybrid Systems for Decision Making

Complex decision-making problems very often require considering huge amounts of information distributed among many variables and also different techniques for processing of this information. Hybrid systems are appropriate for solving such problems as it is explained below.

6.7.1   Why Hybrid Systems for Decision Making?

Building decision-making systems, whatever type of knowledge is available, requires:

• Good explanation facilities and preferably presenting the decision rules used

• Dealing with vague, fuzzy information, as well as with crisp information

• Dealing with contradictory knowledge, for example, two experts who predict different trends in the stock market

• Dealing with large databases with a lot of redundant information, or coping with lack of data

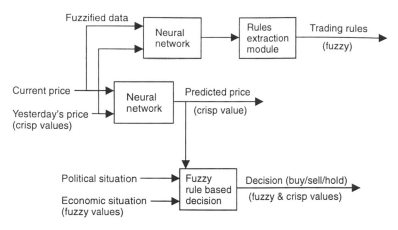

Figure 6.15
A block diagram of a hybrid system for stock market prediction and action recommendation.

Decision making is not usually a one-level process. Just the opposite: it involves different levels of considering the problem, comparing different possible solutions and offering alternatives.

6.7.2   Hybrid Systems for Stock Market Prediction and Decision Making

Stock market index prediction is a good example of a complex AI problem. Figure 6.15 shows a block diagram of a variant of a hybrid system for solving this problem. There are several tasks within the global one: (1) to predict the next value for the index; (2) to predict longer-term values taking into account rules on the political and economic situation; (3) to extract trading rules from the system. A neural network can be used to predict the next value of the index based on the current and the previous-day value of this index. The predicted value from the neural network module can be combined with expert rules on the current political and economic situation in a fuzzy inference module. These two variables are fuzzy by nature and fuzzy values are used as inputs for them. The final decision suggested is produced as a fuzzy one and as a crisp one after defuzzification.

Another branch in the solution diagram leads to extracting fuzzy trading rules that may be used to explain the current behavior of the market. A partial implementation of the above model in FuzzyCOPE is given in appendix I.

6.8   Problems

Part A: Case Example Solutions

1. *Speech recognition: the phoneme recognition task—building a hybrid system for spoken digits recognition.* A small experimental system is presented here as published in (Kasabov et al. 1995) to illustrate the hybrid model in figure 6.14. The experiment is conducted on recognizing 21 speech units—20 phonemes and a silence which take part in the digits words. 21 neural networks are used, each for recognizing segments of each of the spoken phonemes as shown in figure 5.30A. A set of fuzzy rules is applied to two consecutive segments recognized by the neural networks over the time scale, labeled by the label of the corresponding phoneme, in order to decide on the whole unit pronounced. Here, details on the experimental system are given.

   a. Speech data compilation, and preprocessing. Digitized speech is recorded and a fast fourier transform (FFT) is performed over 11.6-ms segments of speech with the use of a Hamming window and with a overlapping between the segments of 50%. Two hundred fifty-six-point FFTs are calculated from the speech, sampled at 22,050 Hz. Mel-scaled cepstrum coefficients are then calculated from the FFTs. Mel-scale transformation is considered to be plausible in the sense in which the inner ear works. Twenty-six coefficients are obtained from each 256-point FFT for this experiment.

   b. Two-layer neural network-module is used at the low-level. To train the 21 neural networks from the first layer, examples of the allophonic realizations of the phonemes were extracted from the speech corpus described in appendix G of a selected group of speakers (see figures 5.30A and 5.33B). The extracted portions were taken from the stable parts of the phonemic realization; therefore each of the segments taken carried substantial information about the realized phoneme. This meant the portions were very short in duration, but informative. Mel-scale cepstrum coefficients were calculated for these portions and used to train the phoneme neural network from the first layer (see section 5.6.3 for more details). The second-layer neural network module is a single neural network that takes three consecutive over time 21-element output vectors

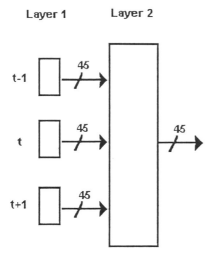

Figure 6.16
The second-layer neural network in the neural network speech recognition module; a general
diagram for all the 45 phonemes in English.

from the first-layer neural networks (the phoneme units) and produces a 21-element output vector of the recognized phonemes in a
three times bigger time-frame as shown in figure 6.16. This network
performs time-alignment and aggregates the already classified phoneme segments over three speech time intervals. The training of the
second-layer network is done with the use of both *real data* as
obtained through the first-layer classification of the training data
from the speech corpus and labeled correctly according to the
desired classes, and *synthetic data*, which are synthetically generated. For example, one rule for generating synthetic training examples is the following: The activation value of the phoneme is 0.8 in
all three time frames (the three 21-element input vectors) and the
rest of the inputs are 0 then the output for the same phoneme is 1.0
while the rest of the output values are 0. We can denote this rule as:
0.8, 0.8, 0.8 → 1.0. Examples of other rules for generating allowed
combinations in the synthetic training data are: 0.6, 0.9, 0.6 → 0.8;
0.6, 0.6, 0.6 → 0.5. For shorter phonemes, e.g., /f/, two consecutive
input values of 0.8 are used in the first rule, rather than three, e.g.,
0.8, 0.8, 0 → 1, etc.

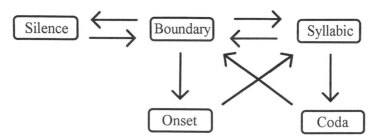

Figure 6.17
Different clusters of rules for recognizing the syllable boundaries and the correct sequences of phonemes in each part of a syllable.

   c. Language modeling block based on fuzzy logic techniques. The module has two submodules:

     i. A fuzzy rule-based system. Fuzzy rules represent the likelihood of a phoneme to happen or not to happen when certain phoneme has preceded it (has been recognized at the previous timeframe). Again, the principle of specialization (modularity) is used here. This block is multimodular, that is, one fuzzy rule-base module is used for each of the phonemes. This allows for easy tuning of the fuzzy rules for a particular phoneme according to the performance of the whole system (Kasabov et al. 1995). There are separate clusters of fuzzy rules for syllables boundary recognition, onset, syllabic and coda, based on the allowed phoneme sequences in the language (see appendix J and also Gimson 1989). The different clusters of rules and their relations are shown in figure 6.17. The fuzzy system submodule takes as inputs the certainty degrees to which two consecutive time-segments belong to different phonemes and produces a certainty degree to which the second phoneme segment is correctly recognized. The fuzzy system works continuously over time as shown in figure 6.18. Three exemplar fuzzy rules are given below:

IF (Onset) AND ($/s/_{t-1}$ is High) AND ($/n/_t$ is High), THEN $/n/_{out}$ is High

IF (Onset) AND ($/s/_{t-1}$ is Medium) AND ($/n/_t$ is Medium), THEN $/n/_{out}$ is Low

IF (Onset) AND ($/n/_t$ is Low), THEN $/n/_{out}$ is Low,

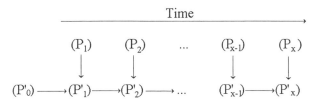

Figure 6.18
The fuzzy system submodule takes as inputs the certainty degrees to which two consecutive time-segments belong to different phonemes as produced in the neural network module and produces a certainty degree to which the second phoneme segment is correctly recognized. The fuzzy system works continuously over time.

where the membership functions shown in figure 6.19 are used. After "filtering" the activation values of the phonemes from the first, speech recognition module, through the fuzzy rules, an output sequence is produced. The output from the fuzzy system for the pronounced word "one" as used in the experiment of figure 5.30 is shown in figure 6.20.

ii. A look-up table that contains the dictionary words (e.g., the digits) to be matched partially by the fuzzy system sequence of phonemes. Many-to-many matchings are allowed; for example, any of the recognized phoneme sequences of $/f//ai//f/$ and $f//ai//v/$ will match the word "five" from the look-up table (figure 6.21). In the look-up table module a level of *system's tolerance* is introduced to define the level of partial match which the system should tolerate. In an extreme case, the level of tolerance can be set high enough that a sequence of $/z//e//ou/$ or $/z//e/$ may match sufficiently the word "zero."

2. *NPS realization of fuzzy rules for phoneme recognition. General and specific fuzzy rules* are articulated for deciding on eight spoken phonemes based on speech segments recognized in a previous module at time moments t and $(t + 1)$. These segments are used as condition elements in the rules, called "input 1" and "input 2." The conclusion in a rule is called "output." The realization of the fuzzy rules is done with the use of NPS. Nine rules represent the expert knowledge. NPS allows for a variable to be used in a rule that reduces the number of the rules when compared with a standard fuzzy inference engine (see the previous case example). The rules written in the syntax of NPS are

a.

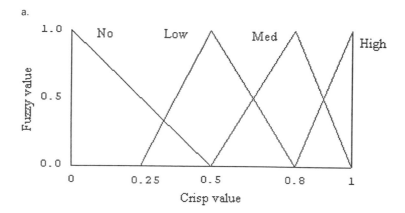

b.

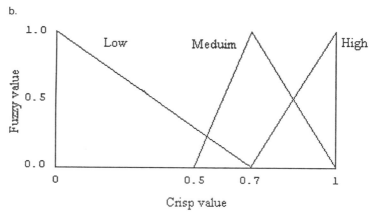

Figure 6.19
Membership functions for the input and output variables of the fuzzy system for language modeling.

given in figure 6.22. The system is tested on continuous speech. The output from an NPS for a pronounced word "one" is shown in figure 6.23. Before displaying the output values, defuzzification was done on the fuzzy values inferred by NPS. The figure shows a clearly recognized sequence of phonemes.

3. *Hybrid system for the Bank Loan case example.* Two variants of a hybrid solution of the Band Loan problem are given below. The first uses a neural network trained to produce the membership function of the variable "decision" when the membership functions for the three fuzzy variables are entered. The final solution is taken after the value

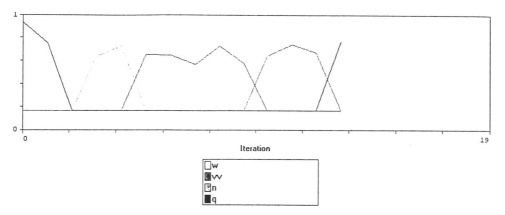

Figure 6.20
After "filtering" the activation values of the phonemes from the first, speech recognition module, through the fuzzy rules, an output sequence is produced. The output from the fuzzy system for the pronounced word "one" as used in the experiment of figure 5.30.

Word	Pronunciation(s)		
"Zero"	zerou	serou	zeərou
"One"	wʌn		
"Two"	tu		
"Three"	θrɪ	θərɪ	
"Four"	fɔ	fɔr	
"Five"	faiv	faif	fai
"Six"	sɪks		
"Seven"	sevɪn	sevən	
"Eight"	eit	ei	
"Nine"	nain	nai	

Figure 6.21
Possible variations in pronunciation of the digit words that the system tolerates.

```
// general rules
Dx     Gx -> Ax (0.3, 0.4, 1, 0.8);
Dx     Hx -> Ax (0.3, 0.4, 1, 0.8);
Ex     Gx -> Ax (0.3, 0.4, 1, 0.8);
Ex     Hx -> Bx (0.3, 0.4, 1, 0.8);
Ex     Ix -> Bx (0.3, 0.4, 1, 0.8);
Fx     Hx -> Bx (0.3,  0.4, 1, 0.8);
Fx     Ix -> Cx (0.3 , 0.4, 1, 0.8);

// specific rules
DB DD -> AD (0.3, 0.4, 1, 0.8);
GB GD -> AD (0.3, 0.4, 1, 0.8)
```

Figure 6.22
Fuzzy rules in the syntax of NPS for the small task of recognizing eight English phonemes, where the following notation is used: for the first letter in a fuzzy proposition: A, output high; B, output medium; C, output low; D, input 1 is high; E, input 1 is medium; F, input 1 is low; G, input 2 is high; H, input 2 is medium; I, input 2 is low; for the second letter in the fuzzy propositions, represented as a variable x, possible values for binding are the following phonemes: A, silence; B, /w/; C, / ∧ /; D, /n/; E, /z/; F, /e/; G, /r/; H, /ou/.

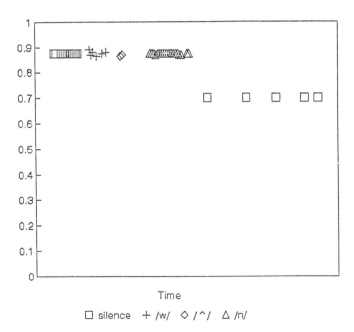

Figure 6.23
Recognized phonemic segments over time for a pronounced word "one" in a hybrid system consisting of eight neural networks for low-level pattern matching and NPS, for aggregating recognized by these neural network segments.

```
(defrule rule1
        (client $?list_in)
    =>
        (recall "Net1" $?list_in $?list_out)
        (assert (decision $?list_out)))

(defrule rule2
        (decision  ?x0 ?x1 ?x2 ?x3 ?x4 ?x5 ?x6 ?x7 ?x8 ?x9 ?x10)
    =>
        (if (and (> ?x9 0.7) (> ?x10 0.8))
            then (printout t " Loan approved ! " crlf)
        else (if (and (> ?x0 0.9) (> ?x1 0.8))
            then (printout t "Loan disapproved ! " crlf)
        else (printout t " Sorry, the system failed to recommend any particular
        decision " crlf))))
```

Figure 6.24
A set of two production rules written in FuzzyCOPE to realize a hybrid decision-making
system for the Bank Loan Decision Problem.

produced by the network is logically analyzed. Figure 6.24 shows a segment of a program written in the syntax of FuzzyCOPE. In another variant of a solution (figure 6.25), two neural networks are used. A neural network "Net2" is trained to make the final solution at a higher level.

4. *Hybrid system for prediction and control of the effluent flow to a sewage plant.* A simplified block diagram of a sewage plant is given in figure 6.26 (see Railton et al. 1995) Incoming flow is pumped to the plant from three pump sites which operate independently based on local conditions. A flow time-series data is explained and graphed in appendix C. Once the flow reaches the plant it is held in an anaerobic tank to allow suspended solids to settle. This tank operates as a storage unit and is limited to 650 cubic meters. Predicting the flow for the next hour or next few hours is crucial for the operation of the whole plant because of the physical and biological constraints of the plant. The flow from the anaerobic tank to the denitrification and nitrification tanks and to the clarifiers is controlled through a penstock gate whose aperture can be controlled. The task here is to control the level in the anaerobic tank based on the external conditions. This task has two subtasks: (1) to control the penstock; (2) to

```
(defrule rule-with-two-neural-networks
        (client $?list_in)
    =>
        (recall "Net1" $?list_in $?list_out)
        (recall  "Net2" $?list_out ?x1 ?x2)
        (if (> ?x1 0.95) then (printout t "Loan approved!" crlf)
        else (if (> ?x2 0.95) then (printout t "Loan disapproved!?")
        else (printout t "No recommendation, sorry"))))
```

Figure 6.25
A production rule written in FuzzyCOPE to realize a hybrid decision-making system for the
Bank Loan Decision Problem that uses two neural networks for implementing two modules
of the solution.

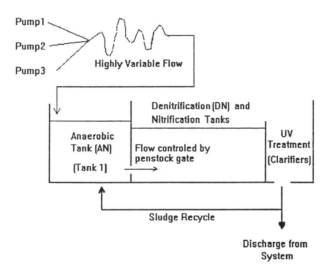

Figure 6.26
A block diagram of a sewage plant. A data set for the sewage water flow is given in appendix
C (part A).

predict the incoming flow to prevent an overflow in the tank. A fuzzy system with two input variables, the level of the sewage in the anaerobic tank and the difference in the level for two time intervals, and one output variable, the penstock aperture, is used in this task (Bailey et al. 1995). For the subtask of prediction a neural network, a fuzzy system or a fuzzy neural network can be used as shown in chapter 7.

Part B: Practical Tasks and Questions

5. Explain the following concepts
   a. Comprehensive AI
   b. Multimodular hybrid system
   c. Hierarchical hybrid system
   d. Recurrent hybrid system
   e. Hybrid connectionist production system
   f. Hybrid connectionist logic programming system
   g. Hybrid connectionist fuzzy production system
   h. ("Pure") connectionist production system (CPS)
   i. Refractoriness in a CPS
   j. Random selection of a rule in a CPS
   k. Selection strategy in a CPS
   l. Production execution cycle in a CPS
   m. Hidden Markov model
   n. Dynamic time-warping method
   o. Time-alignment problem in speech recognition
   p. Speech segments classification into phonemic classes

6. In order to change the criterion for decision-making used at the higher level in the production rules for loan approval (see figure 6.24) to be: approve, if $x10 > 0.8$, or $(x9 > 0.9$ and $x10 > 0.6)$, or $(x8 > 0.8$ and $x9 > 0.8$ and $x10 > 0.7)$, do you need to retrain the neural network?

7. In order to change the criterion for decision-making at the higher production level in the production from figure 6.25, do you need to retrain the neural network "Net2?"

8. Use the general two-level model of figure 6.1. Can you imagine what the two levels of processing may mean in the case of predicting stock index? What about predicting the movement of the ozone hole?

9. In an example in section 6.3, a goal to a hybrid connectionist logic programming diagnostic system is shown. What are the similarities and the differences between the ways a goal is given to a hybrid system and a goal is a given to a PROLOG program (see chapter 2)? What can be expected as answers in the two cases?

10. List the advantages and disadvantages of using hybrid connectionist systems for character recognition.

11. List all the steps to be taken for developing a hybrid, phoneme-based speech recognition system as part of an intelligent human computer interface (see figures 1.20 and 6.14) to a database containing clinical data.

Part C: Project Specification

Topic: Small Hybrid System Development

Create a small hybrid system for solving a chosen problem by following the given steps below.

1. Explain on one page the main characteristics of hybrid systems.

2. For the task chosen from the list below, create a multimodular block diagram of a possible solution to the problem.

3. Choose appropriate techniques for solving each subproblem represented as a module. What alternatives are there for each of them?

4. Create subsystems for solving each of the subproblems. Compile the whole hybrid system.

5. Make experiments with the hybrid system and validate the results.

List of Possible Problems for the Project (See appendix C for some data sets and for a detailed description of some of the problems.)

1. Handwritten digits recognition

2. Bank loan approval decision-making system

3. Mortgage approval (see appendix C)

4. Stock market prediction (see appendix C)

5. Unemployment prediction (see appendix C)

6. Phoneme recognition

7. Spoken words recognition, for example, "on"/"off"; "yes"/"no"; "stop"/ "go."

6.9   Conclusion

This chapter introduces the basic approaches, techniques, and applications of hybrid systems as a beginning to the development of comprehensive AI systems. The hybrid systems presented in the chapter incorporate different connectionist techniques, symbolic AI methods, and methods of fuzzy logic into one system. A hybrid systems environment, FuzzyCOPE, and a connectionist production system, NPS, are introduced and used for solving complex AI problems like speech recognition and stock market prediction.

6.10   Suggested Reading

Many applications of hybrid systems for solving AI problems have been reported in the literature. Further information on the material presented in this chapter and some additional material can be found in the following:

General principles of hybrid systems—Medsker (1995); Sun and Bookman (1994); Takagi (1990); Kasabov (1990, 1993a,b, 1995b); Arbib (1995)

Hybrid connectionist production systems that use CLIPS as a production language—Kasabov (1993a, 1995b); Wang et al. (1993); Rocha et al. (1993)

General hybrid connectionist platforms—Schwinn (1993); Kasabov (1995b); Rocha et al. (1993)

Soft computing—Sanchez (1992); Yamakawa (1994)

Hybrid systems for speech recognition and language analysis—Lange and Dyer (1989); Kasabov (1995a); Morgan and Scofield (1991); Kasabov et al. (1995, 1994)

An overview of currently used hybrid connectionist systems for decision-making—Goonatilake and Khebbal (1994)

Geographic information processing through hybrid connectionist production systems—Kasabov and Trifonov (1993)

Robot planning in a hybrid connectionist system—Morasso et al. (1992)

Hybrid systems for financial forecasting—Deboeck (1994)

Connectionist logic programming systems (see section 6.3)—Kasabov and Petkov (1992); Ding (1992)

Connectionist fuzzy production systems and FuzzyCOPE—Kasabov (1995b)

Neural production system (NPS)—Kasabov and Shishkov (1993)

7   Neural Networks, Fuzzy Systems, and Nonlinear Dynamical Systems. Chaos; Toward New Connectionist and Fuzzy Logic Models

Having discussed the use of neural networks and fuzzy systems as knowledge-engineering methods in previous chapters, this chapter introduces links between chaos theory, neural networks, and fuzzy systems. Connectionist and fuzzy logic models are under constant development along with the improvement of our knowledge on the human brain and the advance of technology. There are several points of interest here:

• What is chaos? The usefulness and the "nastiness" of chaos? How to control chaos?

• Some connectionist and fuzzy logic models manifest chaotic behavior and can predict chaotic processes.

• What new connectionist and fuzzy logic models are emerging?

7.1   Chaos

Here, some basic notions from chaos theory are presented.

7.1.1   What Is Chaos?

If a system seems to behave randomly we call such a system chaotic or say that it demonstrates *chaos*. Two types of chaotic systems are:

1. *Deterministic chaos.* The system's behavior can be approximately or exactly represented by a mathematically or heuristically expressed function; the seemingly unpredictable random behavior is produced by a completely deterministic function; this type of chaos is discussed here and is referred to as "chaos."

2. *Nondeterministic chaos.* The system's behavior is not expressible by a deterministic function and therefore is not at all predictable.

Chaos is a complicated behavior of a *nonlinear dynamical system*. It is also a self-organized process according to some underlying rules.

Nonlinear dynamical systems are those whose next state on the time scale can be expressed by a nonlinear function from its previous time states. Dynamical systems can evolve in continuous or discrete time, and can thus be expressed by the formulas:

$dx(t)/dt = F(x(t))$—continuous time,

$x(n + 1) = F(x(n))$—discrete time,

where x is a variable from the domain space.

Example 1   A chaotic function used to model fish population growth (Gleick 1987) has become very popular:

$$y(n + 1) = \lambda y(n)(1 - y(n))$$

We can represent this function in a slightly modified form as:

$$y(n + 1) = 4gy(n)(1 - y(n))$$

The behavior of this first-order differential equation changes dramatically when the *bifurcation parameter* g is altered. When $g < 0.25$ the output y goes to zero. For $0.25 < g < 0.75$ the output converges to single non-zero value. When g goes beyond 0.75 the output begins to oscillate between two values initially, then between four values, then between eight values, and so on. For $g > 0.89$, the output becomes chaotic.

Example 2   A typical chaotic function is the Mackey-Glass chaotic time series, which is generated from the following delay differential equation:

$$dx(t)/dt = [0.2x(t - D)]/[1 + x^{10}(t - D)] - 0.1x(t),$$

where D is a delay; for $D > 17$ the function shows a chaotic behavior.

Example 3   Another example of a chaotic process is the movement in the value of the stock market (see appendix C). As we can see from figure 1.23 chaos is one possible state of it. The next value of a stock index depends in a nonlinear fashion on its previous values and it usually depends on some other parameters as well. The patterns of the index do not repeat over time exactly, but there are underlying rules which make them repeat approximately.

Example 4   *The Water Flow to a Sewage Plant* case example (see appendix C, figure C.1). Water comes to a sewage plant from three major sources: (1) domestic water; (2) industrial water; and (3) rainwater. For a certain period of the year rain can be assumed to be at a constant level and for simplicity in the experiments it will be ignored. The patterns of water flow are always different. This time series seems to be not random and not

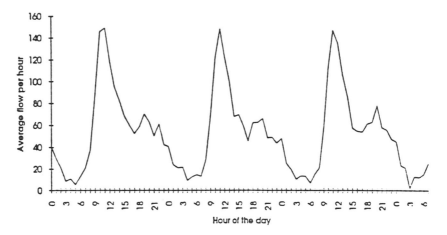

Figure 7.1
Smaller portions from the water flow data show clear patterns of repetition which may be possible to capture in a set of rules.

periodic, but rather chaotic. Figure 7.1 shows three consecutive "patterns" from the water flow data.

There is evidence that parts of the brain, as well as individual neurons, exhibit chaotic behavior. (Freeman 1987; Freeman and Skarda 1985).

The noiselike behavior of chaos includes very important information. Understanding of a chaotic process is a crucial step toward its prediction and control. In order to better understand chaotic behavior, one needs to become familiar with some basic notions that characterize every chaotic process:

• *The phase space of a chaotic process* is the feature space where the process is traced over time. For example, the movement of an inverted pendulum can be traced over time in the two-dimensional space of the two parameters, the angle and the angular velocity. The position of the pendulum at any moment in time can be represented as a point in this space. Traces of points recorded over time are called trajectories. If a process goes periodically through the same points in the phase space at each time moment $(t_0 + n \cdot \Delta t)$, where $n = 1, 2, \ldots$, and Δt as a time interval (period), such a process is periodic, not chaotic. A chaotic process does not repeat the same trajectory pattern over time. Choosing the phase space is very important for understanding any process. For example, if the state space for representing a stock market index comprises two consecutive values $V(t)$ and $V(t + 1)$, where t represents a day, then the process may be seen either as random or chaotic; but if $V(t)$ and $V(t + 1)$ are two averaged values of the index over a year (t represents a year), then the same index may look periodic and stable.

• A chaotic process goes around areas or points of its phase space, but without repeating the same trajectory; such areas, or points, from the phase space are called *chaotic attractors*. One chaotic process may have many attractors in the phase space, many *unstable fixed points*. How to find them to predict chaotic behavior is a crucial question.

• *Sensitivity to initial conditions* is an important characteristic of a chaotic process. A slight difference in the initial values of some parameters that characterize the chaotic process will result in quite different trends in its further development.

• *Stretches and contractions* of a chaotic process may be observed in its phase space. A parameter called the *Lyapunov exponent* provides the average rate of divergence or convergence for a chaotic process. Based on the Lyapunov exponent, another parameter q called predictive power can be calculated for any chaotic process, as $q = 1/L$, where L is the largest Lyapunov exponent. This parameter can be used, for example, to evaluate roughly how many days in the future a stock index can be predicted, based on today's value and on some previous values of the index.

• *Fractal dimension* indicates the complexity of a chaotic system, for example, a low-dimensional attractor (3–4) would suggest that the problem is solvable. A chaotic process has a fractal dimension. Imagine a random process in two-dimensional space (see figure 4.23). The process occupies the whole space. It has two dimensions: $d = 2$, or simply $d2$. Now imagine that a process occupies a small fraction of the whole space, for example, all the points are grouped around the center forming a *chaotic attractor* (see the second square in figure 4.23). This process has a dimension between 1 (the dimension of a point) and 2, say $d1.2$, so it has *fractal dimensions*, or is a *fractal*. Fractal geometry was first described by Benoit Mandelbrot (see McCauley 1994). The dimensions of the space where the fractal lies are called *embedding dimensions*. The fractal dimension of a chaotic process is defined by its attractors. Some tasks that are very useful to perform for a particular chaotic process are finding the fractal dimension of a process, and finding the minimum embedding dimension.

• *Lyapunov exponents* (*LEs*) play an important role in the process of analyzing a chaotic process (chaotic function f). There is one LE for each dimension x in the phase space. The LE λ can be calculated with the use of the formula:

$$\lambda = \lim[(\textstyle\sum_{(i=1,N)} \ln df/dx|_{x_i})/N], \text{ for } N \to \infty$$

where N is the number of points from the trajectory of the function f used over time and N tends to infinity.

A positive LE measures stretching in phase space, that is, how rapidly nearby points diverge from one another. A negative LE measures contractions, that is, how long it takes for a system to reestablish itself after it has been perturbed. Any chaotic system contains at leats one positive LE. The magnitude of this LE reflects the time scale on which the system becomes unpredictable (Wolfe 1985).

So chaotic processes seem random, but they are not. They are not periodic, but they do repeat *almost the same patterns* in their phase space. They are predictable, but only for a short time in the future.

7.1.2   What Is the Difference Between Chaos and Noise?

Noise is any small random signal added to the general function that describes the underlying behavior of a process. For example, recording speech for the task of phoneme recognition in a room where people come and go, telephones ring, etc., adds noise to the speech signal. Noise is a small random ingredient r to a function f (not necessarily nonlinear) $y(x) = f(x) + r$. Having noisy measures $y(x)$ means that the value $f(x)$ can be estimated for any value of the independent variable x, subject to a small error due to the noise.

The above is not true for a chaotic function. There is no formula $y(x)$ that can be used to calculate the value for the dependant variable, say the stock index, for any given value of the independent variable, say a certain day over a period of 100 years, or the value of a parameter such as the interest rate. A chaotic process can be noisy too, if a small ingredient is added to the underlying nonlinear dynamical function.

Adding noise can be useful when doing computer simulations, as it makes them more "realistic." For example, noise added to training examples makes the neural network more robust to variations in data and leads to a better generalization.

7.1.3 Applications of Chaotic Systems

Some systems whose behavior can be described as nonlinear dynamics are:

• Macroeconomic systems, where many factors have to be considered and the state of a system depends in a nonlinear fashion on its previous states

• Financial systems, for example, exchange rates

• Market systems, for example, the stock market, the bond market

• Biological systems, for example, the brain, the heart beat when a heart attack occurs

• Geographic and ecologic systems, for example, the ozone hole movement, and many others.

Some tasks for dealing with chaos are:

• *Chaos prediction*: The goal is to predict the next state of a chaotic process.

• *Chaos suppression*: In this case the chaotic behavior is not desirable, as in the case of a heart attack. The goal is to suppress it and to return the process to its periodic mode.

• *Chaos restoration*: This is the case when the chaotic behavior is desirable. It is the natural behavior of a system. If the behavior of such a system becomes periodic, that is the undesirable mode and the goal is to restore as far as possible the chaotic behavior. There is evidence that epilepsy, for example, is an anomalous periodic behavior of a small part of the brain and its treatment may consist in restoring the previous chaotic behavior (in one way or another, e.g., inputting impulses to the brain). The latter two tasks can be unified under the name of *chaos control*.

There are numerous applications of computer models, including mathematical modeling theory, neural networks, and fuzzy systems, for dealing with chaotic processes. Here, only a few application-oriented systems are listed to give an impression of the variety of chaos applications:

• Chaotic systems identification and signals identification

• Nonlinear systems diagnosis

• Modeling of brain seizures

• Information encryption systems development

- Simulation of biological populations
- Simulation of natural phenomena, like earthquakes, floods, etc.
- Simulation in astronomy
- Control and recovery from epilepsy, recovery from a heart attack
- Turbulence control
- Stock market control
- Energy saving by tracking the chaotic behavior of consumers
- Modeling a congress
- Modeling electrical circuits
- Modeling insect populations
- Modeling chemical and atomic reactors
- Modeling the spread of diseases
- Modeling the solar system

To create information systems for modeling nonlinear dynamic systems and control, special software and hardware are needed. The first chaotic chip was developed by Yamakawa and colleagues (1992b). It consists of three elements: (1) a nonlinear delay element; (2) a linear delay element; and (3) a summation element. Using these elements connected with links including feedback connections, an arbitrary chaotic function describable by a three-segment piecewise linear function can be programmed.

The connection between neural networks and fuzzy systems on the one hand and chaos on the other is twofold: (1) neural networks and fuzzy systems may manifest chaotic behavior under certain conditions; (2) neural networks and fuzzy systems can be used to predict and control chaos. These are discussed in the next two sections, along with some other new models of neural networks and fuzzy systems.

7.2 Fuzzy Systems and Chaos: New Developments in Fuzzy Systems

A set of fuzzy rules can be learned from data that represent either a nonchaotic or a chaotic process. The rules can then be used to model this process and control it. One of the advantages of using fuzzy rules is that they express in a linguistic form the process which may lead to its better understanding.

7.2.1   Fuzzy Systems for Modelling Nonlinear Dynamical Systems

Modeling chaotic time series with the use of fuzzy logic techniques can be achieved by articulating fuzzy rules by experts after observing past data and using their experience, using the rules in a fuzzy inference machine; and by extracting fuzzy rules from data and their consecutive use in a fuzzy inference machine. Both approaches may include refining the rules and choosing an appropriate inference method for better processing. The two approaches are illustrated in case examples below.

Example 1   Predicting water flow to a sewage plant by using rules articulated by experts. Through analyzing smaller portions of the data about the problem [one such portion is shown in figure 7.1] and analyzing the "fuzzy graph" of more data points (figure 7.2A), one can see patterns of repetition which may be captured in a set of fuzzy rules. By analyzing these patterns a set of fuzzy rules, was articulated as shown in figure 7.2B. The fuzzy labels and their membership functions were defined in advance. These rules are now used in a fuzzy inference machine to predict the water flow on test data. Figure 7.3 shows the predicted vs. the real test values. This example demonstrates that a chaotic process can be predicted to a sufficient degree of accuracy subject to the availability of an adequate set of rules. The rules used here are simple fuzzy rules. We can see from figure 7.3 that the above set of rules performs much better than the set of rules extracted through using competitive learning (see figure 5.11B). The reason is simple, here more appropriate features are used, i.e. Time and Previous flow, rather then Time and Day of week.

The two examples on the same data point out at three conclusions: (1) It is very important to use appropriate feature set; (2) human intuition may perform better than an automatic tool; (3) when automatic extraction of rules is performed, tuning may be required to find out the best possible set of rules which approximate the process. This approach is illustrated on the Mackey-Glass chaotic time series (L.-X. Wang 1994). Near-optimal values for the number of fuzzy labels and their membership functions are found experimentally. The following steps describe the experiment:

1. Define the number l of previous values (lags) for the time-series data to be used for predicting k future values; here $l = 9$ and $k = 1$ is used.

2. Define the number of fuzzy discretization intervals and their membership functions; here 29 fuzzy labels are used for each of the 10 input and output values.

a.

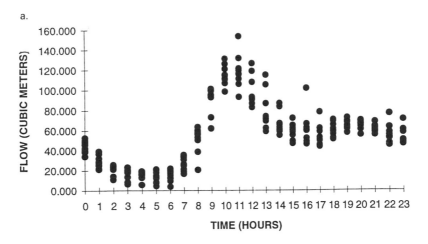

b.
IF   TIME VERY EARLY
         PREVIOUS VERY LOW
THEN NEXT VERY LOW

IF   TIME EARLY
         PREVIOUS LOW
THEN NEXT MEDIUM

IF   TIME MIDDAY
         PREVIOUS MEDIUM
THEN NEXT HIGH

IF   TIME LATE
         PREVIOUS MEDIUM
THEN NEXT LOW

IF   TIME VERY LATE
         PREVIOUS LOW
THEN NEXT LOW

Figure 7.2
(A) The "fuzzy" graph of the flow. (B) Fuzzy rules for the Water Flow to a sewage plant
prediction problem articulated by experts.

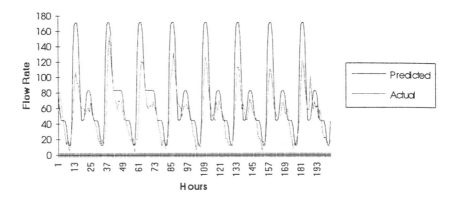

Figure 7.3
Prediction of the water flow on test data done with the intuitive fuzzy rules and a fuzzy
MAX-MIN inference method.

3. Extract fuzzy rules; for this purpose 700 out of 1000 values are used and
the second method from subsection 3.7.3 is applied.

4. Test the generalization ability of the model.

Approximating a function (chaotic or not) from a set of data may be
more difficult than in the example presented above. This is the case when
data contain noise and there are some sections missing from the time
series. A method for extracting fuzzy rules from such data that approximates the real function (without the noise) is presented in Uchino et al.
(1993). Modeling a chaotic time series through a set of fuzzy rules has
several practical applications:

• Having extracted a set of fuzzy rules which model a chaotic process
means that we "store" all the important information about this process in
a small memory space; the rules can be used to restore the functioning of
the process again in the same chaotic manner if it has been disrupted for
some reasons (e.g., a brain seizure or epilepsy).

• If a chaotic behavior is a new, "wrong" phase of a process that is
normally described by a set of fuzzy rules, for example:

IF x_1 is CE and x_2 is CE, then y is CE,

THEN fuzzy rules can be extracted from the new chaotic behavior, for
example:

IF x_1 is $S3$ and x_2, is CE, then y is B.

When the two sets of fuzzy rules are compared, this may give some indication what the reason for the new chaotic phase of the process is and how to bring it back to the old, periodic phase, for example, increase x_1.

Unfortunately, achieving a good generalization over chaotic time-series data by extracting fuzzy rules of the above type may be difficult for the following reasons:

• There is no procedure to define the optimal number of fuzzy quantization intervals and the optimal number of fuzzy labels.

• For a high accuracy of modeling, a huge number of fuzzy rules may be needed.

• If the number of the fuzzy labels and the number of the "lags" used for prediction is too high, and therefore the number of fuzzy rules too large, the whole procedure is slow and inefficient.

A "flat" set of fuzzy rules, as used above, may not be the best choice when modeling a nonlinear function, because a fuzzy rule of this type does not express recursive information, and the chaotic nonlinear functions are recursive. This is one of the reasons for the development of the so-called recurrent fuzzy systems.

7.2.2 Recurrent Fuzzy Systems

Recurrent fuzzy systems consist of recurrent fuzzy rules and fuzzy inference methods. A recurrent fuzzy rule uses in its antecedent one or more previous time-moment values of the output fuzzy variable, for example:

IF $x_1(t)$ is $A1$ AND $x_2(t)$ is $A2$ AND $y(t-1)$ is $B1$, THEN $y(t)$ is B,

where t and $(t-1)$ are two consecutive time moments. This rule can be represented graphically, as shown in figure 7.4.

In general, a fuzzy recurrent rule can be represented as follows:

IF $x_1(t)$ is $A1$ AND $x_2(t)$ is $A2$ AND $\dots x_k(t)$ is Ak AND $y(t-l)$ is $B1$
  AND $y(t-l+1)$ is $B2$ AND $\dots y(t-1)$ is Bl, THEN $y(t)$ is B,

where l consecutive "lags" of previous values of y are used to calculate its next value. A set of recurrent fuzzy rules may include internal fuzzy variables, for example:

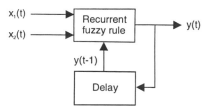

Figure 7.4
A graphical representation of a recurrent fuzzy rule with two inputs and one delay element.

Rule 1: If $x_1(t)$ is $A1$ AND $x_2(t)$ is $A2$ AND $y(t-1)$ is $B1$, THEN $y(t)$ is B

Rule 2: IF $x_1(t)$ is $A3$ AND $y(t-1)$ is $B2$ AND $y(t)$ is $B3$ AND $z(t-1)$ is $C1$, THEN $z(t)$ is C,

where y is an internal variable, the output variable being z.

Fuzzy inference over recurrent fuzzy rules may include fuzzy rule evaluation, based on multiplication of the membership degrees to which new data belong to the membership functions of the antecedent elements, and on the center-of-gravity defuzzification method. The major advantage of using recurrent fuzzy rules is that a small number of such rules can model a complex nonlinear dynamic system. For example, a simple network of several recurrent fuzzy rules can model the Duffing chaotic time-series oscillator (Teodorescu et al. 1994).

7.3   Neural Networks and Chaos: New Developments in Neural Networks

New connectionist models continue to emerge. Some of them have been inspired by chaos theory itself, but more have been inspired by the new discoveries about the cognitive functions of the brain. By presenting only few of them here, one should be aware of the need to continually update this section.

7.3.1   Neural Networks for Modeling Nonlinear Dynamical Systems

Neural networks are universal approximators. The type of the function to be approximated does not have to be known. A nonlinear dynamic function of the form of:

$$x(t+1) = f(x(t), x(t-1), x(t-2), \ldots, x(t-l)),$$

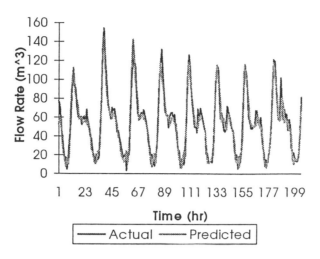

Figure 7.5
Real test data for the (chaotic) Water Flow to a Sewage Plant Prediction Problem and the network predicted by a trained MLP.

can be approximated in a properly set neural network with *l* inputs and one output-subject to enough points in the data set.

Example An MLP network for predicting water flow to a sewage plant (see appendix C). In the previous section some solutions to the Water Flow prediction problem were given based on fuzzy techniques. A better prediction can be achieved if more variables are considered. A statistical analysis on the data produces correlation coefficients between the current flow and the flows at the previous four hours, correspondingly 0.85, 0.59, 0.30, 0.05. An MLP is set with five inputs (the input variables are time in hours; day—workday or holiday; the last three values for the water flow, e.g., three lags) and one output, the value of the water flow in the next hour. Two intermediate layers are used, each having six neurons. After 20,000 epochs of training, the network was tested on the same test data as in the previous section (figure 7.5). The network prediction for one hour ahead is quite good. The absolute mean error over the whole test data is 6.8 cubic meters per hour. Iterative prediction of the flow for several hours ahead can be also done (see figure 7.6).

For the purpose of modeling chaotic functions, a recurrent neural network would perform better than an MLP network, as the feedback connections help to learn time-dependencies over short periods of time. An

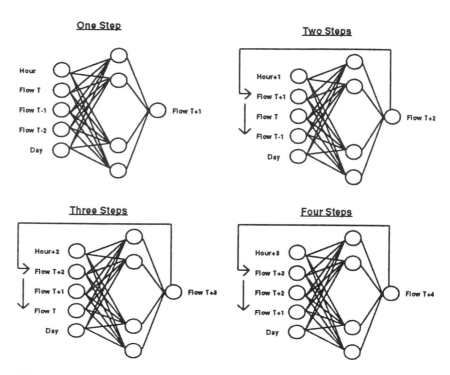

Figure 7.6
Iterative prediction of the water flow for several hours ahead by using the MLP from fig. 7.5.

example of using an MLP and a recurrent network for chaotic function modeling of the SE40 stock index was shown in chapter 5.

Fuzzy neural networks can be successfully used as it is shown in section 7.4 on the water flow data.

Can we expect a failure when using neural networks for predicting chaotic behavior? The answer is yes. A failure of a neural network to learn a nonlinear dynamic function could be due to several factors:

1. An improper neural network architecture, for example, an MLP network trained with the backpropagation algorithm can get "stuck" to a local minimum, when expected to converge to the global minimum.

2. Lack of sufficient training examples, or lack of sufficient time for training. The number of epochs used for training may not be enough for the network to learn the behavior of a system.

3. Training data are characterized by chaotic behavior at a higher dimensionality than the dimension of the input space. We may not have considered some important variables while modeling the process, for example, we might have considered fewer "lags" than necessary.

4. Data are characterized by too difficult a chaotic behavior at a lower dimensional space for the architecture of the network.

In Yamakawa et al. (1992b), the following nonlinear dynamic system has been used for testing the predicting abilities of the neo-fuzzy neuron:

$$y(t + 1) = f1(y(t)) + f2(y(t - 1)) + f3(y(t - 2))$$

$$= 5 \cdot y(t)/(1 + y(t)^2) - 0.5y(t) - 0.5y(t - 1) + 0.5y(t - 2)$$

A feedback from the output to the inputs of the neo-fuzzy neuron is also used. The neo-fuzzy neuron was used successfully for several future time unit predictions. The number of the time units ahead a network can successfully predict depends on how much chaotic the process is. For the water flow prediction this number was three.

7.3.2 Chaotic Neurons

Chaos theory has inspired the development of new connectionist models. A *chaotic neuron* with graded output and exponentially decaying refractoriness has been reported by Aihara et al. (1990). The neuron's output is calculated with the use of the following output function:

$$o(t + 1) = g(u(t) - \alpha \sum_{d=0,t} k^d \cdot r(o(t - d)) - \Theta),$$

where o is the neuron's output value (between 0 and 1); u is the external stimulus; g is the output function; r is a refractory function; α is a scaling parameter; k is a decay parameter; and Θ is the threshold.

Another model of a chaotic neuron has been developed and investigated by Dingle et al. (1993). The neuronal output is calculated as:

$$o(t + 1) = 1 - 4(1 - u)o(t)(1 - o(t)),$$

and $u = \sum w_i x_i$, where x_i are the input signals to the neuron, and w_i are the weights. The behavior of this neuron depends on its net input u. When $u < 0.11$ the neural unit displays chaotic activity; for $0.11 < u < 0.25$ it produces periodic activity, while for $u > 0.25$ it produces a single value which increases with u and becomes 1 when $u \geq 0.75$. This chaotic neuron was used by the authors for creating a self-organizing chaotic map, analogous to the Kohonen SOM. The SOM neural network is chaotic. Chaos introduces a controlled randomness into the self-organizing maps, which, according to the authors, results in an improved ability for clustering.

Further development of the idea of building chaotic neurons and using them for modeling the chaotic behavior of large ensembles of neurons leads to oscillatory neurons and oscillatory neural networks.

7.3.3   Oscillatory Neurons and Oscillatory Neurocomputers

Oscillatory models of different brain functions (memorizing, attention, hearing, etc.) and parts of the brain (visual cortex, olfactory bulbs, etc.) have been around for quite some time (Freeman 1987; Hoppensteadt 1986). It was proved experimentally that oscillations of about 40 to 60 Hz can occur in the visual cortex after application of a stimulus. In some cases, synchronized oscillations can occur between parts of the brain which are not geometrically close to one another. K. von den Malsburg raised the hypothesis that the brain aggregates separate features into an integrated object as a result of correlated and synchronized oscillations of groups of neurons. A short introduction to some oscillatory models and oscillatory neurocomputer architectures follows.

An *oscillator* is an elementary functional unit of an *oscillatory system*. Its functioning is described as *oscillation*, characterized by three parameters: (1) *frequency*, (2) *phase*, and (3) *amplitude*. An oscillatory element can be built up of two neurons (or groups of neurons), one of them being excitatory, and the other inhibitory (figure 7.7). An ensemble of oscillatory neurons can become synchronized. *Synchronization* can be described as the moment when all the oscillatory units in an ensemble stabilize their frequency to a constant value, and stabilize their phase difference to zero:

$$Fk(t) \rightarrow Fconst, \text{ for } t \rightarrow \infty,$$

$$|Pk(t) - P[k+1](t)| \rightarrow 0, \text{ for } t \rightarrow \infty \text{ and every } k = 1, 2, \ldots, n - 1,$$

where $Fk(t)$ is the frequency of the kth oscillator at a time moment t in the ensemble of n oscillators, and $Pk(t)$ is its phase at the same time moment t. Major questions are *when* and *how* can synchronization occur in an oscillatory ensemble?

We can represent information processing as a sequence of collective states of oscillatory units (neurons). Each of them is characterized by its

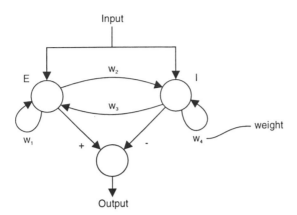

Figure 7.7
An oscillatory unit comprising one excitatory (E) and one inhibitory (I) neuron (or group of neurons).

frequency, phase, and amplitude. This representation is different from the way information is represented as binary vectors in the von Neumann computers. But what kind of operations can be applied over such oscillatory representation? How can operations like "AND," "OR," "multiply," "divide," and so on, be handled? Is it really necessary to use these operations for information processing, or will different ones "serve" better?

A simple oscillatory neural network and an oscillatory computer architecture have been proposed by Inoue and Nagayoshi (1992). An oscillatory neuron is made up of two coupled oscillators, one excitatory, and one inhibitory, as shown in figure 7.8. The output of the unit $o_i(t)$ at a discrete time moment t is expressed in the version of a binary neuron as:

$o_i(t) = 1$, if $\Delta i(t) < \varepsilon$ (synchronized), and 0, otherwise,

and in the version of an analog neuron as

$o_i(t) = 1/(1 + \exp(-z/z0))$, with $z = \varepsilon/\Delta i - 1$.

The following parameters describe the behavior of the neuron:

- An analog parameter $z0$, which is 1 when the neuron is binary
- Difference $\Delta i(t) = |x_i(t) - y_i(t)|$
- Activation values $x_i(t)$ and $y_i(t)$, calculated with the use of the following activation functions:

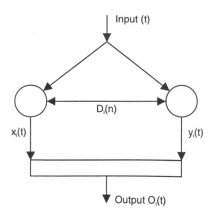

Figure 7.8
The oscillatory neuron of Inoue and Nagayoshi (1992).

$x_i(t + 1) = f(x_i(t)) + D_i(t)(y_i(t + 1) - x_i(t + 1)),$

$y_i(t + 1) = g(y_i(t)) + D_i(x_i(t + 1) - y_i(t + 1)),$

where $D_i(t)$ is the coupling coefficient between the two oscillators in the ith neuron at the time moment t. The functions f and g are chosen to be, respectively,

$f(x) = ax(1 - x); g(x) = by(1 - y),$

where a $(0 < a < 4)$ and b $(0 < b < 4)$ are control parameters. When the coupling coefficient becomes large, the two units are synchronized if $a = b$, and nearly synchronized if $a \approx b$. An asynchronous motion appears if $D_i(t)$ takes certain small values.

In order to build a neural network from the above-described oscillatory neurons, ith and jth neurons are connected to each other with a weight of w_{ij}. The relation between w_{ij} and $D_i(t)$ is expressed by the formulas:

$D_i(t) = DD_i(t)$, if $DD_i(t) > 0$, and 0, otherwise

where $DD_i(t) = \sum_j w_{ij} o_j(t) + I_i - \Theta_i.$

Here I_i is the input stimulus, and Θ_i is the threshold value. All the neurons in such an oscillatory neural network are simultaneously updated, that is, the mode of processing is parallel and synchronous. Such a mode is extremely fast when implemented on parallel-processing hardware.

The oscillatory neural network described above can be used to simulate the standard backpropagation algorithm and Boltzman machine. But it has more advantages when dealing with noisy and chaotic information.

Another development in this area is the so-called globally coupled maps which are networks of chaotic neural elements that are globally coupled (each neuron is coupled with every other). Such a network is shown to have a much bigger capacity as an associative memory and is free of spurious states.

Research in the area of neural dynamic systems has been very productive in the last few years thanks to the work of Walter Freeman, John Taylor, Stephen Grossberg, Kunihiko Kaneko, Harold Szu, and others. The question as to why oscillatory neural networks have not been implemented and applied widely for knowledge engineering is difficult to answer. Some of the reasons may be that the binary logic elements, which today's computers are built of, do not particularly suit the oscillatory models; and there has been no real necessity to develop such models, as the standard neural network models have served very well so far, that is, they have been applied successfully in many areas of science and industry.

There are indications that the coming decades will be devoted to the ultimate goal of understanding how the human brain works. In addition, new information-processing technologies are becoming available, for example, optical-processing technologies, which seem to be suitable for implementing oscillatory information-processing models. Will the oscillatory brainlike models become the new information-processing paradigm? Or will some other more biologically and psychologically plausible models take over?

7.3.4   Other Neural Network Models

Spatiotemporal artificial neural networks represent patterns of activities which have some spatial distribution and appear at certain times. For example, the input signals $x1$, $x2$, and $x3$ appear at the inputs of the neural network in figure 7.9 at different time moments, have different amplitudes, and have different duration in time. In this case, the input space is not three-dimensional, but four-dimensional, where time is included.

Figure 7.10 shows the architecture of a neural network where there are not only weights but time-delay elements as well, both adjustable through training, thus contributing to learning temporal and spatial patterns.

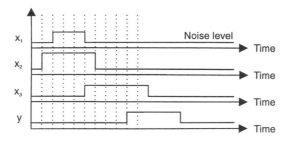

Figure 7.9
A training example can represent a temporal pattern for a certain period of time.

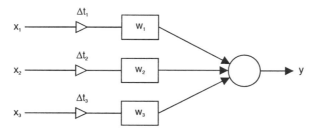

Figure 7.10
A neural network can learn spatiotemporal patterns by adjusting the delay elements and the weights associated with each of the connections.

Using temporal networks becomes useful when artificial neural networks have to cooperate with real biological processes and real neural networks in one system, for example, when implanting artificial neural networks to control heart or brain functions in a human body (Eckmiller et al. 1993).

As pointed out by Kosko (1992) and discussed in chapter 2, a fuzzy set is a point in n-dimensional space. A pattern of activation in the brain can also be viewed as a point in n-dimensional space, where n is the number of neurons whose activation, defines the pattern. We can represent a state of a spatiotemporal object in an n-dimensional space by a spatiotemporal fuzzy pattern. The elements of the space belong to this pattern to certain degrees, and rarely to a degree of 1. The level of activation of a group of neurons can be represented as a fuzzy set which defines the grade to which each neuron contributes to that pattern.

The classic stimulus-reaction paradigm, used in many models of biological neural networks, fails to explain some phenomena observed in the brain, which the hypothesis of the *goal-seeking neuron* tries to explain (Freeman 1991; Kaneko 1989). According to it, the neurons in the brain not only process received information (stimuli) to create patterns. They also seek information (stimuli) with which to confirm already existing patterns or create new ones. The stimulus-reaction mode is a data-driven inductive-type reasoning mode. The goal-seeking mode is rather a backward-chaining reasoning. There are implementations of this theory in the area of neural network hardware.

An interesting connectionist model is the wavelet neuron (Yamakawa 1994), which has wavelets instead of connection weights. Wavelets are spatiotemporal transformations of signals with many applications in knowledge-engineering (see chapter 2).

The goal of achieving in artificial neural networks the functioning abilities of a biological brain has led to experimentation with *biological computers*, that is, computers that use biological substances to process information, along with electronic, optic, and other technologies.

7.3.5   Adaptive Intelligent Information Systems: Adaptation and Forgetting in Fuzzy Neural Networks

Adaptation is a feature of intelligence. Adaptation means ability of a system to change its structure and functionality according to dynamically changing environment for a better reaction. Adaptive intelligent information systems should be able to change their knowledge base during operation. For example, a fuzzy system should be able to change its rules, a neural network should learn new data "on the fly."

Two different ways to make space in a neural network in order to adapt to new data are: (1) to expand the structure if necessary by adding new nodes as new data come; and (2) to make the system forget about old data, thus making space for the new ones.

Forgetting happens when an already trained neural network is further trained with new data without having been rehearsed with the old ones (see chapter 4). This prevents connectionist models from being used as adaptive systems without retraining them with both new and old data. It may be crucial to know how much a trained neural network would forget after having been trained with new data in situations when forgetting is desirable, or in situations where it is not desirable. For example, a neural network that predicts stock market prices should be able to gradually forget the old values two years back and keep only general "rules" for a future trading. On the other hand, some connectionist models are required to adapt quickly to new data without forgetting the old ones. An example of this case is a connectionist system trained on speech corpus data and required to adapt in real time to new speakers. Adaptive control systems should adapt to changes in the process under control. Controlling the level of forgetting and adaptation in a system might be as important as controlling the level of learning and generalization.

There are different ways to introduce forgetting in a neural network structure: (1) use of decay parameter when calculating a next neuronal activation value based on the previous one; (2) decay of connection weights during training; (3) pruning of weak connections; and (4) *zeroing* weak connections, which is discussed below.

The following steps form a general methodology for evaluating the adaptation and forgetting in a connectionist model:

1. A data set is randomly divided into sections (sets) A, B, C, etc.

2. A connectionist model is initialized, trained on set A, and tested for generalization on set B. Corresponding errors E_{train} and E_{gener} are calculated. RMS error may be applicable depending on the type of the data set.

3. The model is further trained on the set B (error $E_{\text{ad.train}}$) and tested on the set A (error E_{forget}). It is also tested on the set C.

4. Coefficients of adaptation CA_d and forgetting CF_r are calculated as follows: $CA_d = E_{\text{gener}}/E_{\text{ad.train}}$); $CF_r = E_{\text{forget}}/E_{\text{train}}$.

5. The above steps from (1) to (4) are repeated on next data sections and average values are calculated.

The following are steps for updating a fuzzy neural network structure FuNN (see figure 4.38 and section 5.3.4) through *zeroing*, in order to make the FuNN structure adaptable to new data and to control the adaptation/forgetting phenomenon: (1) A FuNN architecture is initialized (either randomly or according to an existing set of initial rules). (2) The FuNN is trained with data. (3) Fuzzy rules are extracted from the trained FuNN. for example by using REFuNN algorithm (a threshold is set in advance, e.g., 0.7). (4) The FuNN architecture is then updated according to the extracted fuzzy rules by zeroing the connection weights which are less than the threshold (or their absolute values are less than the threshold if NOTs are used in the extracted fuzzy rules). A new updated FuNN is obtained. (5) The process of further training and updating (zeroing) the FuNN structures and adapted rules extraction continues.

Zeroing small connection weights seems to be biologically plausible in the sense that small synapses which have not been updated for a certain amount of time die out.

7.3.6   Representing Emotions, Consciousness, and Awareness in Artificial Neural Networks and Fuzzy Systems

Recent research in this area conducted by John Taylor and Igor Aleksander moves the area of artificial neural networks to its border with psychology. Can a neural network or an information system be aware of what it really is, of what it can do, of what it knows, and of what its "colleagues," also artificial neural networks, are? Fuzzy systems have been used to model emotions (Yanaru et al. 1994). But can two "emotional" fuzzy systems interact with each other? And, how?

This question will be left open here, as it is too early now to try to give an adequate answer. We must work for the answer, but it should not prevent us from making some speculations. The reader is invited to do so.

7.4   Problems

Part A: A Case Example Solution

1. *Comparative analysis on different techniques for the water flow series prediction* (Kasabov 1996). The water flow time series from figure C.1 was divided into four equal sections, as shown in figure 7.11. The first section was used for rules extraction by using the REFuNN algorithm and human intuition. Five triangular uniformly distributed membership functions were used to fuzzify the two input variables, time (in hours) and current flow, and the output variable, the next flow. The second section was used for training a neural network architecture until a minimum test error was achieved, measured on the third section of the data. The fourth section was used for validation of the different systems. First, an MLP was trained with the backpropagation algorithm and validated. Two types of fuzzy neural networks were also tried, as shown in figure 4.38. The first (FuNN-1), a three-layer network (the layers within the dashed vertical lines), uses membership degrees as inputs and produces membership degrees for the five output labels.

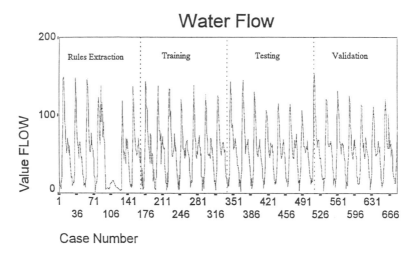

Figure 7.11
The water flow data set is divided into four sections: rules extraction, training, testing, and validation of different models for solving the problem.

After training it for 10,000 epochs until RMS = 0.02 rules were extracted by using the REFuNN algorithm. The strongest five rules are shown in figure 7.12. The second (FuNN-2), a five-layer network, has two inputs and one output as described in section 4.8 in chapter 4. Each of the two architectures was randomly initialized, trained and validated, and separately initialized by inserting the intuitive rules (see figure 7.2) and the extracted rules (figure 7.12), and then trained and tested. NPS (see chapter 6) was also used to implement the REFuNN extracted rules and was validated. The test and validation RMS error for the different systems are shown in table 7.1. The best neural network model in terms of compromise between training time and RMS seems to be the FuNN-2 model initialized with the automatically extracted rules.

Part B: Practical Tasks and Questions

2. Is the following function, used for generating pseudorandom numbers, chaotic:

$$y(t) = a + b \cdot y(t - 1),$$

where a and b are real numbers (constants)? Give an explanation.

3. Is the SIN function a nonlinear chaotic function? Explain.

IF   TIME NOT EARLY
       PREVIOUS NOT LOW
THEN NEXT NOT VERY LOW

IF   TIME VERY EARLY
       PREVIOUS VERY LOW
THEN NEXT NOT MEDIUM

IF   TIME VERY LATE
       PREVIOUS VERY LOW
THEN NEXT NOT MEDIUM

IF   TIME VERY EARLY
       PREVIOUS VERY LOW
THEN NEXT NOT VERY HIGH

IF   TIME LATE
       PREVIOUS LOW
THEN NEXT LOW

Figure 7.12
Five strongest rules extracted by using the REFuNN Algorithm from a fuzzy neural network (see figure 4.38).

Table 7.1
A comparison of different models for solving the Water Flow Prediction Problem (see text)

	Epochs	Test_error	Val_error
NPS	—	0.05	0.09
FuNN-1 Randomly initialized	150	0.0213	0.0196
FuNN-1 Extracted rules used	100	0.0205	0.0185
FuNN-1 Intuitive rules used	70	0.0230	0.0215
FuNN-2 Randomly initialized	950	0.043	0.037
FuNN-2 Extracted rules used	600	0.017	0.018
MLP(2-8-1)	2900	0.005	0.005

4. Give an example of a three-dimensional chaotic function.

5. Explain the following concepts:

    a. Phase space

    b. Attractor

    c. Unstable fixed point

    d. Random process

    e. Nonlinear dynamic process

    f. Chaotic process

    g. Oscillator

    h. Oscillatory neuron

    i. Recurrent fuzzy rule

    j. Recurrent neural network

    k. Coupled oscillators

    l. Chaotic neuron

    m. Neo-fuzzy neuron

    n. Wavelet neuron

    o. Goal-seeking neuron

    p. Spatiotemporal neural network

    q. Biological computer

    r. Frequency, phase, and amplitude of an oscillator

    s. Oscillator synchronization

    t. Sensitivity to initial conditions

    u. Trajectory in a phase space

    v. Lyapunov exponent of a chaotic process

    w. Stretches and contractions of a chaotic process

    x. Chaotic time series

    y. Mackey-Glass chaotic time series

    z. Consciousness and awareness in artificial neural networks

6. Is a deterministic chaos predictable? Why?

7. Is a stock market predictable? When? (see figure 1.23)

8. Draw a diagram of the simple nonlinear function:

$y(t) = 2y^2(t - 1)$,

for values of $t = 0, 1, 2, 3, 4, 5$; $y(0) = 0 \cdot 2$; $y(0) = 0 \cdot 3$.

9. Outline different models to approximate the above function:

a. MLP

b. Recurrent neural network

c. Neo-fuzzy neuron

d. Fuzzy neural network (figure 4.38).

Part C: Project Specification

Topic: Comparative Analysis on Different Techniques for Non-linear Function Prediction

This project aims at comparing different ways to predict time series: fuzzy rules articulated by humans which describe the process; fuzzy rules automatically extracted from data; MLP neural network; recurrent neural network; statistical regression analysis. The following steps define how the project should be done.

1. Collect time-series data which seem to represent chaotic behavior (You may choose one of the problems listed below.) Explain its characteristics if possible. Divide it into a training and a test data set.

2. Articulate, with the help of an expert, fuzzy rules which describe the process. Apply fuzzy inference over the fuzzy rules for the test data. Evaluate the error.

3. Use one of the methods for fuzzy rules extraction from data presented in the book. Apply the set of rules to the prediction task. Evaluate the test error over the test data used in the previous point.

4. Train an MLP feedforward neural network with the backpropagation algorithm using the training data. Evaluate the test error over the test data set.

5. Train a recurrent neural network and evaluate the test error.

6. Apply stepwise linear regression analysis and find an approximation of the goal function. Calculate the test error over the test data set.

7. Make a comparative analysis between the different techniques used for prediction.

List of Problems for the Project

1. Gas consumption prediction (see appendix B)
2. Unemployment prediction (see appendix C)
3. SE40 stock market prediction (see appendices C and I)
4. Water flow to a sewage plant prediction (see appendix C)
5. Beer sales prediction (see appendix C)
6. Fish population prediction
7. Migration of birds (use your own data set)
8. Animal population growth (use your own data set)
9. Plant growth (use your own data set)
10. The *ozone hole* movement (use your own data set)
11. Spread of a fire in a forest (use your own data set)
12. Spread of weeds (use your own data set)

7.5   Conclusion

This chapter is the closing chapter. Chaos, as a concept and as a practical model, was introduced. It was shown that processes that have chaotic behavior can be predicted in a short term by using neural networks and fuzzy systems.

Several new connectionist and fuzzy logic models are discussed. The presentation in this chapter is far from being exhaustive, but it demarcates areas for future development of new models and their applications.

This chapter was also designed to encourage speculation on future possibilities of fuzzy and neurosystems development and applications. In this respect, the reader is asked to speculate freely in answering the following questions:

• How is memory organized in the human brain? How is information stored there? Are artificial neural networks biologically plausible in this respect?

• What are "emotions," "free will," "consciousness?" Do they have a role to play in the future development of models for knowledge-engineering and information processing?

• Which technique would better suit representing "emotions," "free will," and "consciousness"—artificial neural networks, fuzzy logic, genetic algorithms, symbolic AI, or some combination of these?

• Should we continue to build humanlike information-processing systems, that is, systems based on modeling the way the human brain works and the way people solve problems?

• After all, is it really possible to understand how the brain works? Or we can only see the surface? If we ever manage to see further, will it in any way benefit the information technologies?

• Could a machine be more intelligent than a human?

7.6 Suggested Readings

The following are recommended to those wanting to learn more on specific topics:

A general introduction to chaotic systems—Ditto and Pecora (1993); Deboeck (1994); Abarbanel (1993); McCauley (1994)

Neural networks and dynamical systems—Barndorff-Nielsen et al. (1993)

Neuronal models with oscillatory and chaotic behavior—Kaneko (1990), Bulsara (1993); Bulsara et al. (1991)

Use of chaos theory for controlling epilepsy and heart failure—Shiff et al. (1994)

Chaotic models for financial applications—Deboeck (1994); Peters (1991)

Hardware implementation of spatiotemporal neural networks—Eckmiller and Napp-Zinn (1993)

Oscillatory neural networks—Freeman (1987); Borisyuk (1991); Borisyuk and Kirillov (1991, 1992); Hoppensteadt (1986, 1989); Kaneko (1989, 1990)

Wavelets and wavelet neurons—Yamakawa (1994)

Learning fuzzy rules for chaotic function prediction—L.-X. Wang (1994)

Consciousness in real and artificial neural network systems—Aleksander and Morton (1993); Arbib (1995)

Adaptive fuzzy neural networks and systems—Brown and Harris (1994); Wang (1994)

Fuzzy systems for modeling emotions—Yanaru et al. (1994)

Appendixes

The following appendixes give more information on suggested software and data sets for the exercises in the book. They cite previous use, references, and provide *File Transfer Protocol* (*FTP*) addresses and *World Wide Web* (*WWW*) sites from which free copies of software products or data sets can be obtained.

Appendix A   Iris Plants Database

The following database is available free from the University of California, Irvine Repository of Machine Learning Databases and Domain Theories (Murphy and Aha 1992). Some other databases can also be found there. The *FTP* address is: *ics.uci.edu:pub/machine-learning-databases*. The Web page is: *//www.ics.uci.edu/vmlearn/MLRepository.html*.

The following information is provided with the Iris database:

Sources

Creator: R.A. Fisher

Donor: Michael Marshall (MARSHALL%PLU@io.arc.nasa.gov)

Date: July 1988

Past usage

Fisher RA. 1936. The use of multiple measurements in taxonomic problems. *Annals of Eugenics* 7 (pt 2): 179–188.

Duda RO, Hart PE. 1973. *Pattern Classification and Scene Analysis.* New York, John Wiley & Sons.

Dasarathy BV. 1980. Nosing around the neighbourhood: A new system structure and classification rule for recognition in partially exposed environments. *IEEE Transactions on Pattern Analysis and Machine Intelligence* 1, 2: 67–71.

Relevant Information

This is perhaps the best-known database to be found in the pattern recognition literature. Fisher's paper is a classic in the field and is referenced frequently to this day (e.g., see Duda and Hart 1973). The data set contains three classes of 50 instances each, where each class refers to a type of Iris plant. One class is linearly separable from the other two; the latter are not linearly separable from each other.

Number of instances

One hundred fifty (50 in each of three classes)

Number of Attributes

Four numeric, predictive attributes and the class attribute. Attribute information: sepal length, sepal width, petal length, petal width (in centimeters). Classes: Iris Setosa, Iris Versicolor, Iris Virginica.

Missing Attribute Values

None

Summary Statistics

	MIN	MAX	Mean	SD	Class Correlation
Sepal length:	4.3	7.9	5.84	0.83	0.7826
Sepal width:	2.0	4.4	3.05	0.43	−0.4194
Petal length:	1.0	6.9	3.76	1.76	0.9490
Petal width:	0.1	2.5	1.20	0.76	0.9565

Class distribution: 33.3% for each of 3 classes.

The database is also available through anonymous *FTP* from: *eros.otago.ac.nz /pub/programs/ai/data-sets.*

Appendix B   Gas Consumption Database

The following database is published in Gonzales (1992). It contains data on the average monthly gas consumption (in gallons per capita) and the average minimum temperatures (in degrees Celsius) in the city of Hamilton, New Zealand, for the period January 1988 to July 1992.

No.	Month	Gas	Temperature	No.	Month	Gas	Temperature
1.	Jan 88	2.3	12.10	28.	Apr	2.84	10.70
2.	Feb	2.20	15.10	29.	May	5.77	7.30
3.	Mar	2.48	11.10	30.	Jun	7.24	4.80
4.	Apr	4.44	8.20	31.	Jul	8.59	5.10
5.	May	5.89	7.80	32.	Aug	7.05	6.00
6.	Jun	8.07	6.10	33.	Sep	6.44	6.10
7.	Jul	7.79	5.80	34.	Oct	3.78	9.50
8.	Aug	7.32	6.00	35.	Nov	2.68	9.80
9.	Sep	4.92	8.80	36.	Dec	2.04	12.00
10.	Oct	4.35	9.50	37.	Jan 91	2.22	12.70
11.	Nov	3.19	11.60	38.	Feb	2.09	12.60
12.	Dec	1.88	14.00	39.	Mar	2.71	10.10
13.	Jan 89	2.38	15.50	40.	Apr	3.89	8.60
14.	Feb	1.57	12.60	41.	May	5.99	6.20
15.	Mar	2.26	11.00	42.	Jun	7.91	5.30
16.	Apr	3.78	8.60	43.	Jul	8.70	3.00
17.	May	6.33	7.20	44.	Aug	6.29	6.70
18.	Jun	7.46	4.50	45.	Sep	5.16	7.40
19.	Jul	9.73	2.10	46.	Oct	4.18	9.00
20.	Aug	7.98	5.80	47.	Nov	3.17	9.40
21.	Sep	5.05	8.00	48.	Dec	2.02	11.10
22.	Oct	3.82	10.20	49.	Jan 92	2.29	12.70
23.	Nov	3.26	10.40	50.	Feb	2.24	12.60
24.	Dec	2.29	11.00	51.	Mar	3.15	9.20
25.	Jan 90	1.79	14.10	52.	Apr	4.66	6.50
26.	Feb	2.22	14.80	53.	May	6.32	6.10
27.	Mar	2.58	12.70	54.	Jun	8.32	3.60

The database is available through anonymous *FTP* from: *eros.otago.ac.nz/pub/programs /ai/data-sets* and from http: *//divcom.otago.ac.nz:800/COM/INFOSCI/KEL/software.htm.*

Appendix C   Sample Data Sets for Time Series Prediction and Decision-Making

All data sets are available through anonymous FTP. The following data sets are part of a data sets library available through anonymous FTP from: *eros.otago.ac.nz/pub/programs/ai /data-sets*, and from Web page: *//divcom.otago.ac.nz:800/COM/INFOSCI/KEL/software.htm*.

A   Water Flow to a Sewage Plant

The problem is as follows: Given a data set for the water flow (in cubic meters) incoming to a sewage plant and the hour and the day it is recorded for a certain period, to predict the water flow at the next hour, as well as the flow at the next several hours. The data set contains three attributes: "time in hours," "day," and "water flow." Figure C.1 shows graphically part of the data.

B   The SE40 Time-Series Data Set

This is a data set for the stock exchange index SE40 collected daily for a period of several years. Figure C.2 shows graphically part of the data.

C   Beer Sales Data Set

The data set has five attributes: (1) the consecutive time (in months); (2) the month; (3) the maximum average monthly temperature (in degrees Celsius); (4) the minimum average monthly temperature (in degrees Celsius); and (5) the total monthly sale of beer (in gallons) (figure C.3).

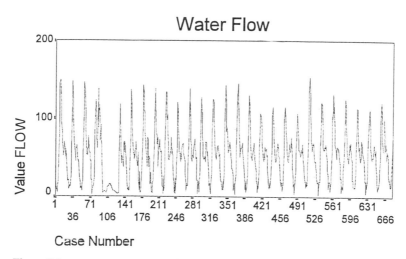

Figure C.1
A graph of the data for the Water Flow to a Sewage Plant Prediction Problem.

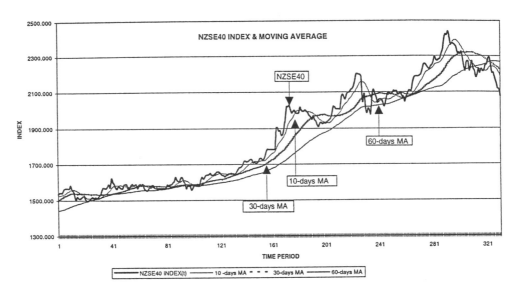

Figure C.2
Stock market SE40 index data collected daily for a period of several years.

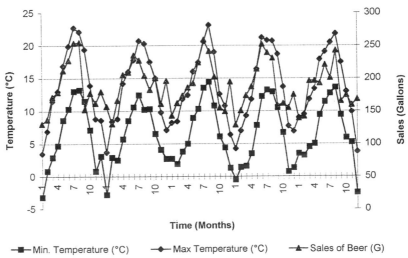

Figure C.3
The beer consumption data. Series 1 is the beer consumption; series 2 the maximum monthly temperatures; series 3 the minimum monthly temperatures.

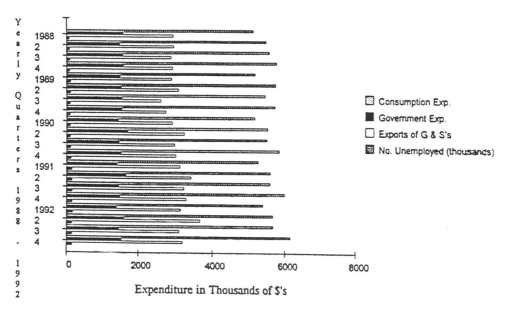

Figure C.4
Bar graphs representing the unemployment rate data set.

D Unemployment Rate Data Set

The data set contains five attributes: (1) time in quarters; (2) quarter; (3) private consumption expenditure; (4) government expenditure; (5) exports of goods and services. Figure C.4 represents the data as a bar graph.

E Mortgage Approval Data Set

This data set has nine attributes: (1) character (0, doubtful; 1, good); (2) total assets; (3) equity; (4) mortgage loan; (5) budget surplus; (6) gross income; (7) debt servicing ratio; (8) term of loan; (9) decision (0, disapprove; 1, approve).

Another group of data sets concerning time-series prediction problems was used in a competition of prediction methods organized by the Santa Fe Institute. These data sets, as well as other time-series data sets on which methods for prediction can be tried, can be accessed free from the *FTP* address: *ftp@santafe.edu*. Experimental results and analysis connectionist and statistical methods for prediction applied over different time-series data sets can be found in Weigend and Gershefeld (1993).

Appendix D CLIPS Commands

CLIPS stands for *C language interpreter of production systems*. It is produced by NASA (Giarratano 1989; Giarratano and Riley 1989) and by *COSMIC* Company, University of

Georgia, Athens. Information about the latest versions of CLIPS can be received from the *Internet e-mail* address: *service@cossack.cosmic.uga.edu.*

The following functions are available in the CLIPS production language.

Math Functions

+	Addition
−	Subtraction
*	Multiplication
/	Division
**	Exponent

Comparison Predicate Functions

=	Numeric equal
!=	Numeric not equal
>	Numeric greater than
<	Numeric less than
⇐	Numeric less than or equal
⇒	Numeric greater than or equal
eq	Non-numeric equal
neq	Non-numeric not equal

Other Predicate Functions

numberp ⟨value⟩   Tests for numeric value
stringp ⟨value⟩   Tests for string value
wordp ⟨value⟩   Tests for word value
integerp ⟨value⟩   Tests for integer value
evenp ⟨value⟩   Tests for even value
oddp ⟨value⟩   Tests for odd value

Flow of Control Functions

if ⟨predicate-function⟩, *then* ⟨actions⟩   Procedural "if" [*else* ⟨actions⟩]
while ⟨predicate-function⟩ [*do*] ⟨actions⟩   Procedural "while"
halt Halts execution

Input/Output (I/O) Commands

read [⟨logical name of a file⟩]   Reads a single field
readline [logical name of a file]   Reads a line of input
printout ⟨logical name⟩ ⟨print information⟩
open ⟨file name⟩ ⟨logical name⟩ [⟨file access⟩]   Opens a file
close [⟨logical name⟩]   Closes a file

Other Useful Functions and Commands

bind ⟨variable⟩⟨value⟩   Binds a variable

system ⟨values⟩   Executes a system command

gensym   Returns unique symbol

Other Math Functions

min, max, log, log10, exp, sqrt, trunc, abs, mod

Trigonometric Functions

cos, sin, tan, sec, csc, cot, acos, asin, atan, asec, etc.

String functions and *conversion functions* are implemented in CLIPS as well

Examples of How to Use Different Functions in Productions

(assert (number =(+ ?n 1))

(bind ?var (read)) ;   Binds the variable var to the input value.

(test (> ?size 20)) ;   A condition element with a constraint about an already introduced variable.

(stack-size ?size&:(> ?size 20)) ;   Constrained field in a condition element

---

Appendix E   Functions of *FuzzyCLIPS* for Dealing with Fuzzy Variables and Fuzzy Inference

An extension of CLIPS called *FuzzyCLIPS* was released in April 1994 by the National Research Council of Canada [NRC Canada 1994]. FuzzyCLIPS is available free via anonymous *FTP* from the following address: *ai.iit.nrc.ca* and via the WWW address: *http://ai.iit.nrc.ca/fuzzy/fuzzy.html*.

FuzzyCLIPS has built-in functions to deal with fuzzy variables and fuzzy inferences, some of them being:

Defining Fuzzy Variables

(*deftemplate* ⟨name⟩
    ⟨from⟩ ⟨to⟩ [⟨unit⟩]
    (⟨list of primary terms⟩)
    [⟨list of modifiers⟩])

Example

(deftemplate temperature
    0 30 Celsius
    ((low (0 1) (5 1) (10 0.5)
    (OK (PI 10 20))
    (high (20 0.5) (25 1) (30 1))

((very sqr)
(quite user_function)))

In the above example one standard membership function PI was defined. Other standard membership functions are "s" and "z" (see chapter 3).

Defining Fuzzy Facts

(*deffacts* ⟨name⟩
(⟨fuzzy fact⟩ [⟨CF⟩]))

Example

(deffacts "dd"
((temperature (z 2 15) CF 0.85)))

Assertion of Fuzzy Facts

(*assert* (temperature (0 1) (5 1) (10 0.2) CF 0.95))

COG Defuzzification

(*moment-defuzzify* ?⟨fact-variable⟩ or ⟨integer value of the fact number⟩)

The fact-variable must be bound first to a fuzzy value whose COG will be calculated and returned after the execution of the above function.

Mean of Maxima Defuzzification

(*maximum-defuzzify* ?⟨fact-variable⟩ or ⟨integer value of the fact number⟩)

Accessing the Universe of a Fuzzy Variable

(*get-u* ?⟨fact-variable⟩)

Accessing a Fuzzy Set

(*get-fs* ?⟨fact-variable⟩)

Accessing the Certainty Factor

(*get-cf* ?⟨fact-variable⟩)

Setting an Evaluation Certainty Factor in a Rule

(*set-CF-evaluation* ⟨value⟩)

This is similar to the "salience" in the ordinary production rules in CLIPS.

Accessing the Rule Evaluation Certainty Factor

(*get-CF-evaluation*)

Appendix F   Data Set for the Soil Classification Case Example

The data have been collected and used by Max Beily. It is available through ftp from: eros.otago.ac.nz/pub/programs/ai/data-sets and from http: //*divcom.otago.ac.nz:800/COM /INFOSCI/KEL/software.htm*. A short description follows:

Attributes

Eight input variables represent the average concentration of the following elements: (1) NH_4^+, (2) NO_3^-, (3) SO_4^{2-}, (4) Ca^{2+}, (5) Mg^{2+}, (6) K^+, (7) Na^+, (8) Cl^- (see table 1.1).

Classes

(1) Egmond YBL, (2) Stratford YBL, (3) Taupo_YBP, (4) Tokomaru YGE, (5) Matapiro YGE, (6) Waikare YBE

Data Set

Contains 12 examples of each class.

Appendix G   University of Otago Speech Data Base

A speech database of New Zealand English containing pronounced digits by 11 male and 10 female speakers of New Zealand origin is available through anonymous ftp from: *eros.otago. ac.nz:/pub/programs/ai/speech* and from the Web page given. Each pronounciation is kept in

Digit	Phonemic representation
zero	zerou
one	wʌn
two	tu
three	θri
four	fɔ
five	faiv
six	sıks
seven	sevın
eight	eit
nine	nain

Figure G.1
Phonemic representation of the digits "zero" to "nine" spoken in English.

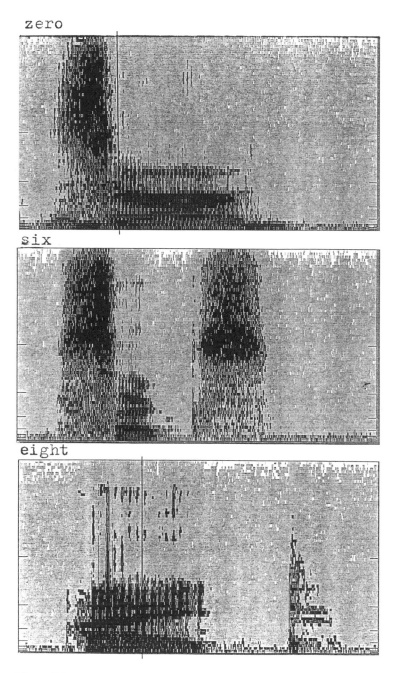

Figure G.2
Samples of speech from the Otago Speech database represented by their spectra.

one file as a wave form (.pcm file) of the speech sample. Segments of these files, which contain realizations of certain phonemes, can be extracted either by using speech software systems available in the public domain or by using a program for automatic segmentation. Such a program, called "segment" and instructions for its use, can also be found in the above given site. Figure G.1 shows the phonemic representation of the spoken digits and figure G.2 shows speech samples from the database. Some of the figures contain lines that indicate a possible starting point to extract a segment. Different transformations can be applied on the extracted segments, for example, FFT, mel-scale cepstrum coefficients, etc. Web page: *//divcom.otago. ac.nz:800/COM/INFOSCI/KEL/speech.htm.*

Appendix H   FuzzyCOPE: Commands and Programming Examples

FuzzyCOPE (*Fuzzy co*nnectionist *p*roduction systems *e*nvironment) is available free through anonymous FTP from: *eros.otago.ac.nz/pub/programs/ai/fuzzy-cope* and from Web page: *//divcom.otago.ac.nz:800/COM/INFOSCI/KEL/fuzzycop.htm.*

Here, some of the functions are given and also some examples of how to use these functions. Full description can be found in the Manual which is also available free.

User Functions

User functions for calling neural networks, fuzzy inference, data transformations, and rules extraction modules:

Functions for Fuzzy Inference

Max-min compositional inference (fidfuzzy) and decompositional inference (dcmpfuzzy):

fidfuzzy (char *rulefile, MF inputs), returns output vector.

Example   (bind $?out (fidfuzzy "a:\\loan.rul" $?in))

dcmpfuzzy (char *rulefile, MF inputs & optional IOtype = 1 (singleton = 0, fuzzy = 1), implication = 0 (Rm = 0, Ra = 1, Rc = 2, ..., R$ = 14), composition = 0 (Max-min = 0, Max-lambda = 1, Max-theta = 2), link = 0 (AND = 0, OR = 1), returns output

Example   (dcmpfuzzy "a:\\loan.rul" $?a 1 2 0 1))

Functions for Neural Networks

Initialize, train and recall MLP and SOM, and also labelling a SOM (labelkoh):

newbp (char *weightsfile, int in, hid, out), returns 1 if ok.

Example   (bind $?status (newbp "a:\\bp.wgt" 4 10 3))

trainbp (char *weightile, *trainfile, int epochs, & optional float alpha = 0.01, eta = 0.03, errSqConv = 0.01. returns int trainingError.

Example   (bind $?error (trainbp "a:\\bp.wgt" "a:\\bpiris.trn" 2000 0.5 0.01 0.05))

recallbp (char *weightsfile, MF inputs), returns MF outputs, or

recallbp (char *weightsfile, *inputfile), returns MF outputs, or

recallbp (char *weightsfile, *inputfile, *outfile), returns 1 if ok.

Examples (bind $?outputset (recallbp "a:\\bp.wgt" inputset))

(bind $?outputset (recallbp "a:\\bp.wgt" "a:\\bpiris.rcl"))
(bind $?status (recallbp "a:\\bp.wgt" "a:\\bpiris.rcl" "a:\\bpiris.out"))
newkoh (char *weightsfile, int inputs, mapsize), returns 1 if ok.

Example (bind $?status (newkoh "a:\\kohiris.wgt" 4 25))

trainkoh (char *weightsfile, *trainfile, *gainterm,int radius,learnPeriod), returns 1 if ok.

Example (bind $?status (trainkoh "a:\\kohiris.wgt" "a:\\kohiris.trn" 0.5 2 300))

labelkoh (char *weightsfile, MF labels), returns MF coordinates, or
labelkoh (char *weightsfile, *labelfile), returns MF coordinates, or
labelkoh (char *weightsfile, *labelfile, *outfile), returns 1 if ok.

Examples (bind $?XYcoords (labelkoh "a:\\kohiris.wgt" $?in))

(bind $?status (labelkoh "a:\\kohirs.wgt" "a:\\kohiris.lbl" "a:\\kohiris.out"))

Functions for Data Conversion and Rules Extraction

Data normalization, fuzzification, rules extraction according the REFuNN method (see chapter 5).

normalize (char *infile, *outFile, & optional int type = 0 (standard = 0, lg10 = 1, lgE = 2)), returns 1 if ok.

Example (bind $?status (normalize "a:\\kohiris.trn" "a:\\nrmIris.trn" 1))

fuzzify (char *infile, *outFile, int number of membership Sets), returns 1 if ok.

Example (bind $?status (fuzzify "a:\\iris.trn" "a:\\fzIris.trn" 3))

extract (char *weightsfile, *rulefile, & optional int method = 0 (no weighting-simple = 0, -using bias = 1 weighted-simple = 2, -using bias = 3), float threshold = 0.05, int IncludeNOTs = 0 (don't = 0), returns 1 if ok.

Example (bind $?status (extract "a:\\bpfuzz.wgt" "a:\\fzIris.rul" 3 1.0 1))

Appendix I   A Hybrid Connectionist Fuzzy Production Rules System

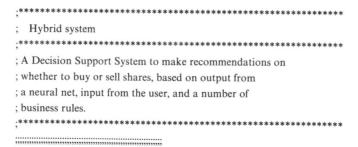

```
;***********************************************************
;   Hybrid system
;***********************************************************
; A Decision Support System to make recommendations on
; whether to buy or sell shares, based on output from
; a neural net, input from the user, and a number of
; business rules.
;***********************************************************
;;;;;;;;;;;;;;;;;;;;;;;;;;;;;;;;;;;;;;;;;;;;;;;;;;;;;;;;;;;
;;;;;;;;;;;;;;;;;;;;;;;;;;;;;;;;;;;;;;;;;;;;;;;;;;;;;;;;;;;
```

```
; defining fuzzy variables and their fuzzy values
;;;;;;;;;;;;;;;;;;;;;;;;;;;;;;;;;;;;;;;;;;;;;;;;;;;;;;;;;;;;;;;
(deftemplate economic_climate ;fuzzy variable
    0 9
    ((bad (z 2 7))      ;Z function
    (good (s 2 7)))     ;S function
    ((very sqr)))       ;modifier very
(deftemplate political_climate ;fuzzy variable
    0 9
    ((bad (z 2 7))
    (good (s 2 7)))
    ((very sqr)))
(deftemplate predicted_value
    0 9
    ((down (z 3 5))
    (same (pi 2 5))     ;Pi function
    (up (s 5 7))))
(deftemplate shares
    0 9
    ((sell (z 3 5))
    (hold (pi 2 5))
    (buy (s 5 7))))
;;;;;;;;;;;;;;;;;;;;;;;;;;;;;;;;;;;;;;;;;;;;;;;;;;;;;
; defining input data for the current run
;;;;;;;;;;;;;;;;;;;;;;;;;;;;;;;;;;;;;;;;;;;;;;;;;;;;;
(deffacts initial
    (current_price 0.3)      ;crisp normalized value
    (yesterdays_price 0.2)       ;crisp normalized value
    (political_climate       ;fuzzy value
    (6 0.5) (7 1) (8 0.5) CF 0.8)
    (economic_climate        ;fuzzy value
    (very good) CF 0.8)
    (start)          ;to start the initial rule)
;;;;;;;;;;;;;;;;;;;;;;;;;;;;;;;;;;;;;;;;;;
;the set of production rules
;;;;;;;;;;;;;;;;;;;;;;;;;;;;;;;;;;;;;;;;;;
(defrule hybrid_system_rule_1
    (declare (CF 0.95))
    ?step1 ← (start)
    (current_price ?current_price)
    (yesterdays_price ?yesterdays_price)
```

```
⇒
; initialize, train and recall a backpropagation neural network:
   (bind $?net_input ?current_price ?yesterdays_price)
   (bind ?m (newbp "stockbp.wgt" 2 6 1))
   (bind ?e (trainbp "stockbp.wgt" "stock2l.trn" 0.5 10000 0.01 0.05))
   (bind ?predicted_price (recallbp "stockbp.wgt" $?net_input))
   (printout t "The predicted price is: " ?predicted_price crlf)
   (retract ?step1)
   (assert (step_2))
   (assert (predicted_price ?predicted_price)))
; A rule which categorizes the predicted value from the neural network
(defrule hybrid_system_step_2_r1
   (declare (CF 0.9))
   ?step2 ← (step_2)
   (current_price ?cp)
   (predicted_price ?pp)
⇒
   (if ( < ?cp ?pp), then
      (assert (predicted_value up))
   else (if ( < (abs ?cp ?pp) 0.1), then
      (assert (predicted_value same))
   else (assert (predicted_value down)))
   (assert (step_3))
   (retract ?step2))
;;;;;;;;;;;;;;;;;;;;;;;;;;;;;;;;;;;;;;;;;;;;;;;;;;;;;;;
; business rules follows, but only one is shown here
;;;;;;;;;;;;;;;;;;;;;;;;;;;;;;;;;;;;;;;;;;;;;;;;;;;;;;;
( defrule hybrid_system_step_3_r1
   (declare (CF 0.9))
   ?step3 ←(step_3)
   (political_climate good)
   (economic_climate good)
   (predicted_value up)
   ⇒
   (assert (shares buy) CF 0.9)
   (assert (end_run))
   (retract ?step3))
;;;;;;;;;;;;;;;;;;;;;;;;;;;;;;;;;;;;;;;;;;;;;;;;;;;;;;;;;;;;;;;;;;;;;;;;
; final rule for printing the results and extracting fuzzy trading rules
;;;;;;;;;;;;;;;;;;;;;;;;;;;;;;;;;;;;;;;;;;;;;;;;;;;;;;;;;;;;;;;;;;;;;;;;
```

```
(defrule final
   (cnd_run)
   ?f ← (shares ?)
⇒
```

;printout the suggested decision as a fuzzy set and as a defuzzified

;(crisp) value

(printout t crlf "THE DECISION OBTAINED BY THE SYSTEM IS:" crlf (get-fs ?f) crlf "with a degree of certainty of:" (get-cf ?f) crlf "On the scale of 0–9 levels, where 0 means definitely sell, 5 means hold, and 9 means definitely buy, the suggested action is" (moment-defuzzify ?f))

; extract fuzzy trading rules through fuzzification of the training data, training a network and
; analyzing the network

(bind ?s (fuzzify "stock2l.trn" "stock2lf.trn" 3)

(bind ?s (newbp "stockbpf.wgt" 6 6 3))

(bind ?s (trainbp "stockbpf.wgt" "stock2lf.trn" 0.5 10000 0.01 0.05))

;extracted fuzzy trading rules will be placed in a file *.rul

(extract "stockbpf.wgt" "stock2lf.rul" 1 1)

Appendix J   The English Phonemes and Their Clusters

This material is offered as a background for some of the speech recognition examples in the book and also the exemplar hybrid system presented in chapter 6. A list of the English vowels with examples of words they appear in is given in figure J.1. Figures J.2 and J.3 give corresponding lists for the diphthongs (the complex vowels that are formed by a connected pronunciation of two elementary vowels) and the consonants.

There are different clusters (sequences) in which phonemes appear in different parts of the English words and English syllables (see Gimson 1989). Knowing these clusters, one can anticipate one phoneme following another and some sequences of phonemes not happening at all in spoken English. This linguistic knowledge has been used and implemented as a multimodular fuzzy system in chapter 6. Figure J.4 shows the allowed phoneme clusters of two consecutive consonants appearing in the beginning part (onset) of a syllable (see figure 6.17). Figure J.5 shows allowed clusters for the coda (the last part of a syllable). The syllabic is a vowel or a vowel cluster. Different combinations of onset, syllabic, and coda are possible (figure 6.17).

Symbol	Example (word)	Example (phonetic)
i	*see*	si
ɪ	s*i*t	sɪt
e	*g*et	get
æ	c*a*t	kæt
ʌ	h*u*t	hʌt
ɜ	b*i*rd	bɜd
ə	b*a*nan*a*	bənanə
a	f*a*ther	faðə
ɒ	h*o*t	hɒt
ɔ	s*o*rt	sɔt
ʊ	p*u*t	pʊt
u	t*oo*	tu

Figure J.1
A list of the English vowels with examples of words they appear in.

Symbol	Example (word)	Example (phonetic)
ei	d*ay*	dei
ou	g*o*	gou
ai	fl*y*	flai
au	c*ow*	kau
ɔi	b*oy*	bɔi
iə	*ear*	iə
ɛə	*air*	ɛə
uə	t*our*	tuə

Figure J.2
A list of the diphthongs in English.

Symbol	Example (word)	Example (phonetic)
p	*p*in	pɪn
b	*b*ay	bei
t	*t*oy	tɔi
d	*d*ie	dai
k	*k*ey	ki
g	*g*et	get
m	*m*e	mi
n	*n*ot	nɒt
ŋ	si*ng*	sɪŋ
f	*f*ive	faiv
v	*v*an	væn
θ	*th*ick	θɪk
ð	*th*en	ðen
r	*r*ing	rɪŋ
h	*h*e	hi
s	*s*ee	si
z	*z*inc	zɪŋk
ʃ	*sh*ip	ʃɪp
ʒ	mea*s*ure	meʒə
tʃ	*ch*in	tʃɪn
dʒ	*j*am	dʒæm
l	*l*ight	lait
j	*y*es	jes
w	*w*in	wɪn

Figure J.3
A list of the consonants in English.

Possible syllable onset clusters.

		First phoneme														
		p	b	f	v	t	d	θ	s	z	ʃ	k	g	h	m	n	l
Second Phoneme	m								✓		?						
	n								✓		✓						
	l	s	✓	✓					✓		?	s	✓				
	r	s	✓	✓		s	✓	✓			✓	s	✓				
	w					✓	✓	✓	✓		?	s	✓				
	j	s	✓	✓	✓	s	✓		✓	✓		s	✓	✓	✓	✓	s
	p								✓								
	t								✓								
	k								✓								

Notes:
✓ indicates that combination is possible.
s indicates that combination is possible, and may be preceded by /s/
? indicates may be acceptable, for example in shmuck, schnapps, shlep, Schweppes

Figure J.4
The allowed phoneme clusters of two consecutive consonants appearing in the beginning part (onset) of a syllable.

		Second Phoneme													
		p	t	tʃ	k	b	d	dʒ	f	θ	s	z	m	n	l
First Phoneme	r	f	f	✓	f	✓	✓	✓	✓	✓	✓	✓	✓	✓	✓
	l	f	f	✓	f	✓	✓	✓	✓	✓	✓	✓	✓	✓	
	m	o								o					
	n		o	o			✓	✓		o	o	✓			
	ŋ				o										
	k		o								o				
	p		o								o				
	d											✓			
	s	o	o		o										

✓ indicates that combination is possible.
o indicates that combination is possible, and may be followed by an obstruent
f indicates that combination is possible, and may be followed by a fricative

Figure J.5
The allowed clusters for the coda (the last part of a syllable).

References

Abarbanel H. 1993. Analysis of observed chaotic data in physical systems. *Reviews of Modern Physics* 65:1331–1392.

Abu-Mustafa YS. 1995. Machines that learn from hints. Scientific American 272(4):64–69.

Abu-Mustafa YS. 1993. A method of learning from hints. In *Proceedings of the Australian Conference on Neural Networks*, 1993, Sydney, Australia, 2–5 February, Sydney University Electrical, pp 37–40.

Aha DW, Kibler D, Albert MK. 1991. Instance-based learning algorithms. *Machine Learning* 6:37–66.

Aihara K, Takake T, Toyoda M. 1990. Chaotic neural networks, Physics Letters A, 144:333–340.

Ajjanagadde V, Shastri L. 1991. Rules and variables in neural networks. *Neural Computing* 3:121–134.

Aleksander I (ed). 1989. *Neural Computing Architectures. The Design of Brain-like Machines*. Cambridge, Mass, MIT Press.

Aleksander I, Morton H. 1990. *An Introduction to Neural Computing*. London, Chapman & Hall.

Aleksander I, Morton H. 1993. *Neurons and Symbols*. London, Chapman & Hall.

Aluja J, Teodorescu H, Gil Lafuente A, et al. 1992. Chaotic fuzzy models in economy. In *Proceedings of the Second International Conference on Fuzzy Logic and Neural Networks*, Iizuka, Japan, July 17–22, 1992, pp 153–155.

Amari S. 1967. Theory of adaptive pattern classifiers. *IEEE Transactions on Electronic Computers* 16:299–307.

Amari S. 1977. Neural theory of association and concept formation. *Biological Cybernetics* 26:175–185.

Amari S. 1985. *Differential-Geometrical Methods in Statistics*. New York, Springer-Verlag.

Amari S. 1989. Characteristics of sparsely encoded associative memory. *Neural Networks* 2:451–457.

Amari S. 1990. Mathematical foundations of neurocomputing. *Proceedings of the IEEE* 78:1143–1163.

Amari S. 1993. Mathematical methods of neurocomputing. In Nielsen O, Jensen J, Kendall W, (eds), *Networks and Chaos—Statistical and Probabilistic Aspects*. London, Chapman & Hall.

Amari S, Arbib M. 1977. Competition and cooperation in neural nets. In Metzer J (ed), *Systems Neuroscience*. New York, Academic Press, pp 119–165.

Amit D. 1989. Modelling brain function: The world of attractor neural networks. Cambridge, England, Cambridge University Press.

Anderson J. 1995. *An Introduction to Neural Networks*. Cambridge, Mass, MIT Press.

Anderson J. 1983b. Cognitive and psychological computations with neural models. *IEEE Transactions on Systems, Man and Cybernetics* 13:799–815.

Anderson J. 1983a. *The Architecture of Cognition*. Cambridge, Mass, Harvard University Press.

Angeniol B, Vakbois F de La C, Le Texier J-Y. 1988. Self organizing feature maps and the travelling salesman problem. In *Actes de Neuro-Nimes*, Nov, Nimes, France.

Aptronix I. 1993. *Fuzzy Logic—From Concepts to Implementation. Technical Report*. Aptronix Inc., San Jose, California.

Anthony M, Biggs N. 1992. *Computational Learning Theory: An Introduction*. Cambridge, England, Cambridge University Press.

Arbib M. 1987. *Brains, Machines and Mathematics*. Berlin, Springer Verlag.

Arbib M (ed). 1995. *The Handbook of Brain Theory and Neural Networks*. MIT Press.

Bailey M, Kasabov N, Cohen T, et al. 1995. Hybrid systems for prediction—A case study of predicting effluent flow to a sewage plant. In Kasabov N and Coghill G (eds), *Proceedings of the Second New Zealand International Conference on Artificial Neural Networks and Expert Systems*, Dunedin, New Zealand, November 20–23, 1995, Los Alamitos, California, IEEE Computer Society Press, pp 261–264.

Bakker P. 1992. Don't care margins help backpropagation learn exceptions. In Adams A, Sterling L (eds), *Proceedings of the Fifth Australasia Joint Conference on AI*. Singapore, World Scientific, pp 139–144.

Bamu E, Haussler D. 1989. What size net gives valid generalization? *Neural Computation* 1:151–160.

Barhen J, Gulati S. 1989. "Chaotic relaxation" in concurrently asynchronous neurodynamics. In *Proceedings of the International Joint Conference on Neural Networks*. Washington DC, June 1989, vol 1. pp 619–626.

Barlett P. 1993. The sample size necessary for learning in multi-layer networks. In *Proceedings of the Fourth Australian Conference on Neural Networks*, Melbourne, Australia, 1–3 February 1993, Sydney University Electrical Engineering, 14–17.

Barnden J, Shrinivas K. 1991. Encoding techniques for complex information structures in connectionist systems. *Connection Science* 3:269–315.

Barndorff-Nielsen O, Jensen J, & Kendall W (eds), 1993. *Networks and Chaos—Statistical and Probabilistic Aspects*. London, Chapman & Hall.

Beale R, Jackson T. 1990. *Neural Computing—Introduction*. Bristol, England, Adam Hilger.

Bezdek J (ed). 1987. *Analysis of Fuzzy Information*, 3 vols. Boca Raton, Fla, CRC Press.

Bezdek J, Pal. S. (ed) 1992. *Fuzzy Models for Pattern Recognition*. New York, IEEE Press.

Binaghi E. 1992. Empirical learning for fuzzy knowledge acquisition. In *Proceedings of the Second International Conference on Fuzzy Logic and Neural Networks*, Iizuka, Japan, July 17–22, 1952, pp 245–251.

Bochereau L, Bourgine P. 1990. Rule extraction and validity domain on a multilayer neural network. In *Proceedings of the International Conference on Neural Networks*, vol. 1. New York, IEEE, pp 97–105.

Bosc P, and Kacprzyk J (eds). 1995. Fuzziness in Database Management Systems. Berlin, Physica-Verlag, c/o Springer-Verlag.

Borisyuk R, Holden A, Kryukov V (eds), 1991. Interacting neural oscillators can imitate selective attention. In *Neurocomputers and Attention. Neurobiology, Synchronization and Chaos*. Manchester, England, Manchester University Press, pp 189–200.

Borisyuk R, Kirillov A. 1992. Bifurcation analysis of neural network model. *Biological Cybernetics* 66:319–325.

Botha E, Barnard E, Casasent D. 1988. Optical neural networks for image analysis: Imaging spectroscopy and production systems. In *Proceedings of the IEEE International Conference on Neural Networks*, vol I, pp 571–576.

Bratko I, Lavrac N (eds). 1987. *Progress in Machine Learning*. New York, Sigma Press.

Brock WA. 1991. Causality, chaos, explanation and prediction in economics and finance. In Casti J, Karlqvist A (eds), *Beyond Belief: Randomness, Prediction, and Explanation in Science*. Boca Raton, Fla, CRC Press, pp 230–279.

Brown M, Harris C. 1994. Neurofuzzy adaptive modelling and control. Prentice Hall Int. (UK) Ltd.

Bulsara A. 1993. Bistability, noise, and information processing in sensory neurons. In Kasabov N (ed), *Artificial Neural Networks and Expert Systems*. Los Alamitos, Calif, IEEE Computer Society Press, pp 11–14.

Bulsara A, Jacobs E, Zhou T, et al. 1991. Stochastic resonance in a single neuron model: Theory and analog simulation. *Journal of Theoretical Biology* 152:531–555.

Burkitt A. 1993. External Stimuli in Biased Attractor Neural Networks. In Leong P, John M (eds), *Proceedings of the Fourth Australian Conference on Neural Networks*. Melbourne, Australia, 1–3 February 1993, Sydney University Electrical Engineering, 30–33.

Carpenter GA, Grossberg S. 1987a. ART 2: Stable self-organization of pattern recognition codes for analog input patterns. *Applied Optics* 26:4919–4930.

Carpenter GA, Grossberg S. 1990. ART3: Hierarchical search using chemical transmitters in self-organizing pattern recognition architectures. *Neural Networks* 3:129–152.

Carpenter GA, Grossberg S. 1987b. A massively parallel architecture for a self-organizing neural pattern recognition machine. *Computer Vision, Graphics, and Image Processing* 37:54–115.

Chakraborty K, Mehrota K, Moham C, et al. 1992.. Forecasting the behaviour of multivariate time series using neural networks. *Neural Networks* 5:961–970.

Chen S-M. 1988. A new approach to handling fuzzy decision making problems. *IEEE Transactions on Systems, Man and Cybernetics* 18:1012–1016.

Churchland P, Sejnowski T. 1992. *The Computational Brain*. Cambridge, Mass, MIT Press.

Clark A. 1989. *Microcognition: Philosophy, Cognitive Science, and Parallel Distributed Processing*. Cambridge, Mass, MIT Press.

Cohen MA, Grossberg S. 1983. Absolute stability of global pattern formation and parallel memory storage by competitive neural networks. *IEEE Transactions on Systems, Man and Cybernetics* 13:815–826.

Cornsweet T. 1970. *Visual Perception*. New York, Academic Press.

Cybenko G. 1989. Approximation by superpositions of a sigmoidal function. *Mathematics of Control, Signals and Systems* 2:303–314.

d'Alche-Buc F, Andres V, Nadal J-P. 1992. Learning fuzzy control rules with a fuzzy neural network. In Aleksander I, Taylor J (eds), *Artificial Neural Networks*, vol 2. Amsterdam, Elsevier Science, pp 715–719.

Davalo E, Naim P. 1991. *Neural Networks*. New York, Macmillan.

Davis L (ed). 1991. *Handbook of Genetic Algorithms*. New York, Van Nostrand Reinhold.

Davis SB, Mermestein P. 1980. Comparison of parametric representations for monosyllabic word recognition in continuously spoken sentences, *IEEE Transactions on Acoustic, Speech and Signal Processing*, vol. 28(4), Aug, pp 357–366.

Dean T, Allen J, Aloimonos Y. 1995. Artificial intelligence, theory and practice. Benjamin/Cummings. Redwood city, California.

de Bollivier M, Gallinari P, Thiria S. 1990. *Cooperation of Neural Nets for Robust Classification*. Université de Paris-Sud, Report 547, Informatiques.

De Garis H. 1989. "COMPO" conceptual clustering with connectionist competitive learning. In *Proceedings of the First IEE International Conference on Artificial Neural Networks*. London, Oct 16–18 1989, pp 226–232.

Deboeck G (ed). 1994. *Trading on the Edge*. Reading, Mass, Addison-Wesley.

Dempster A. 1967. Upper and lower probabilities induced by a multivalued mapping. Annals of Mathematics and Statistics 38:325–339.

Ding L. 1992. A Proposal of Parallel Resolution Inference on Neural Logic Network. In *Proceedings of the 2nd International Conference on Fuzzy Logic & Neural Networks*, Iizuka, Japan, July, 1992, pp 237–240.

Dingle A, Andreae J, Jones R. 1993. The chaotic self-organizing map. In Kasabov N (ed), *Artificial Neural Networks and Expert Systems*. Los Alamitos, Calif, IEEE Computer Society Press, pp 15–18.

Ditto W, Pecora L. 1993. Mastering chaos. *Scientific American* 269 (August): 78–84.

Dolan P, Smolensky P. 1989. Tensor production system: A modular architecture and representation. *Connection Science* 1:53–68.

Doyle J. 1979. A truth maintenance system. *Artificial Intelligence* 12:231–272.

Dubois D, Prade H. 1980. *Fuzzy Sets and Systems: Theory and Applications*. New York, Academic Press.

Dubois D, Prade H. 1985. A review of fuzzy sets and aggregation connectives. *Information Sciences* 36:85–121.

Dubois D, Prade H. 1988. *Possibility Theory. An Approach to Computerized Processing of Uncertainty*. New York, Plenum Press.

Duda R, Hart P. 1973. *Pattern Classification and Scene Analysis*. New York, John Wiley & Sons.

Eaton H, Oliver T. 1992. Learning coefficient dependence on training set size. *Neural Networks* 5:283–288.

Eckmiller R, Napp-Zinn H. 1993. Information processing in biology—Inspired pulse coded neural networks. In *Proceedings of the International Joint Conference on Neural Networks*, Nagoya, Japan, October 25–29, 1993, IEEE, pp 643–648.

Elliot T, Scott P. 1991. Instance-based and generalization-based learning procedures applied to solving integration problems. In Steels L, Smith B (eds), *Proceedings of the British Conference on Artificial Intelligence and Simulation of Behaviour*, London, Springer-Verlag, pp 159–186.

Elman J. 1990. Finding structure in time. *Cognitive Science* 14:179–211.

Feigenbaum M. 1989. *Artificial Intelligence, A Knowledge-Based Approach*. Boston, PWS.

Feldkamp A, Puskorius G, Yuan F, et al. 1992. Architecture and training of a hybrid neural-fuzzy system. In *Proceedings of the Second International Conference on Fuzzy Logic and Neural Networks*, Iizuka, Japan, July 17–22, 1992, pp 131–134.

Fisher DH. 1989. Knowledge acquisition via incremental conceptual clustering, *Machine Learning* 2:139–172

Fisher R. 1936. The use of multiple measurements in taxonomic problems. *Annals of Eugenics* 7 (pt 2):179–188.

Fletcher D, Goss E. 1993. Forecasting with neural networks. An application using bankruptcy data. *Journal of Information and Management* 24:159–167.

Fodor JA, Pylyshyn ZW. 1988. Connectionism and cognitive architecture: A Critical approach. *Cognition* 28:1–73.

Fogel D. 1995. *Evolutionary Computation: Toward a New Philosophy of Machine Intelligence*. IEEE Press, NJ.

Freeman W. 1987. Simulation of chaotic EEG patterns with a dynamic model of the olfactory system. *Biological Cybernetics* 56:139–150.

Freeman W. 1991. The physiology of perception. *Scientific American*, 2:34–41.

Freeman J, Skapura D. 1992. Neural Networks Algorithms, Applications and programming techniques, Addison-Wesley Publ. Comp., Reeding, Massachusetts.

Freeman W, Skarda C. 1985. Spatial EEG patterns, non-linear dynamics and perception: The neo-Sherringtonian view. *Brain Research Reviews* 10:147–175.

Fogelman F, Lamy B, Viennet E. 1993. Multimodular neural network architectures for pattern recognition. Internationl Journal of Pattern Recognition and Artificial Intelligence, 7(4).

Freisleben B. 1995. A neural network that learns to play Five-in-a-Row. In Kasabov N and Coghill G (eds), *Proceedings of the Second New Zealand International two-stream conference on Artificial Neural Networks and Expert Systems ANNES'95*, Dunedin, New Zealand, 20–23 November, 1995, IEEE Computer Society Press, Los Alamitos, 87–90.

Fu Li-Min, 1989. Building expert systems on neural architectures. In *Proceedings of the First IEEE International Conference on Artificial Neural Networks*, 1989, pp 221–225.

Fukushima K. 1993. Neural networks for recognizing connected handwritten characters. In Kasabov N (ed), *Artificial Neural Networks and Expert Systems. Proceedings of the First New Zealand International Conference on Artificial Neural Networks and Expert Systems*. Los Alamitos, Calif, IEEE Computer Society Press, pp 76–78.

Fukushima K, Miyake S, Ito T. 1983. Neocognition: A neural network model for a mechanism of visual pattern recognition. *IEEE Transactions on Systems, Man and Cybernetics* 13:826–834.

Funahashi K. 1989. On the approximate realization of continuous mappings by neural networks. *Neural Networks* 2:183–192.

Furuhashi T, Hasegawa T, Horikawa S, et al. 1993. An adaptive fuzzy controller using fuzzy neural networks. In: *Proceedings of Fifth International Fuzzy Systems Association World Congress, IEEE*, pp 769–772.

Furuhashi T, Nakaoka K, Uchikawa Y. 1994. A new approach to genetic based machine learning and an efficient finding of fuzzy rules. In *Proceedings of the World wisemen/women Workshop*, University of Nagoya, Japan, August 9–10, 1994, pp 114–122.

Fuzzy CLIPS, 1994. *User's Manual.* NRC (National Research Council) Canada.

Gallant S. 1988. Connectionist expert systems. Communications of the Association for Computer Machinery, 31 2., pp 152–169.

Gallant S. 1993. *Neural Network Learning and Expert Systems.* Cambridge, Mass, MIT Press.

Gallinari P, Thinia S, Fogelman-Soulie F. 1988. Multilayer perceptrons and data analysis. In *Proceedings of IEEE International Conference on Neural Networks*, vol 2, July 24–27, 1988, pp 1391–1399.

Geisser S. 1975. The predictive sample Rense method with applications. *Journal of the American Statistical Association* 70:350.

Giacometti A, Amy B, Grumbach A. 1992. Theory and experiments in connectionist AI: A tightly-coupled hybrid system. In Aleksander I, Taylor J (eds), *Artificial Neural Networks 2*, Amsterdam, Elsevier Science, pp 707–710.

Giarratano J. 1989. *CLIPS User's Guide, Artificial Intelligence Section*, vol 2. Lyndon B. Johnson Space Center.

Giarratano J, Riley G. 1989. *Expert Systems.* Boston, PWS.

Gimson A. 1989. An introduction to the pronounciation of English. Edward Arnold London.

Glarkson T, Goarse D, Taylor J. 1992. From wetware to hardware: Reverse engineering using probabilistic RAM's. *Journal of Intelligent Systems* 2:11–30.

Gleick J. 1987. *Chaos: Making a New Science.* New York, Viking Press.

Goldberg D. 1989. *Genetic Algorithms in Search, Optimization and Machine Learning.* Reading, Mass, Addison-Wesley.

Gonzalez L. 1992. *Report on Temperature Effect on Gas Volumes*. Dunedin, New Zealand, Department of Finance and Quantitative Analysis, University of Otago.

Goonatilake S, Campbell J. 1994. Genetic fuzzy hybrid systems for decision making. In *Proceedings of the 1994 IEEE/Nagoya University World Wisemen/women Workshop*, Nagoya, Japan, August 9–10, 1994, pp 143–155.

Goonatilake S, Khebbal S. 1994. *Intelligent Hybrid Systems*. New York, John Wiley & Sons.

Grossberg S. 1969. On learning and energy-entropy dependence in recurrent and non-recurrent signed networks. *Journal of Statistical Physics* 1:319–350.

Grossberg S. 1982. *Studies of Mind and Brain*. Boston, Reidel.

Guida G, Tasso C. 1989. *Topics in Expert Systems Design. Methodologies and Tools*. Amsterdam, North Holland.

Gupta M. 1992. Fuzzy logic and neural networks. In *Proceedings of the Second International Conference on Fuzzy Logic and Neural Networks*, Iizuka, Japan, July 17–22, 1992, pp 157–160.

Gupta M, Sanches E (eds), 1982. *Fuzzy Information and Decision Process*. Amsterdam, North Holland.

Hanser J, Sastry S, Kokotovic P. 1992. Nonlinear control via approximate input-output linearization: The ball and the beam example. *IEEE Transactions on Automatic Control* 37:392–398.

Hart A. 1992. *Knowledge Acquisition for Expert Systems*. New York, McGraw-Hill.

Hartigan J. 1975. *Clustering Algorithms*. New York, John Wiley & Sons.

Hashiyama T, Furuhashi T, Uchikawa Y. 1993. A study on a multi-attribute decision making process using fuzzy neural network. In *Proceedings of the Fifth International Fuzzy Systems Association World Congress*, pp 810–813.

Hayashi Y. 1991. A neural expert system with automated extraction of fuzzy if-then rules and its application to medical diagnosis. In Lippman RP, Moody JE, Touretzky DS (eds), *Advances in Neural Information Processing Systems*, ed 3. San Mateo, Calif, Morgan Kaufmann, pp 578–584.

Hebb D. 1949. *The Organization of Behavior*. New York, John Wiley & Sons.

Hech-Nielsen R. 1987. Counterpropagation networks. Applied Optics 26, 4979–4984.

Hech-Nielsen R. 1988. Applications of counterpropagation networks. Neural Networks 1:131–139.

Hendler J. 1989. On the need for hybrid systems. *Connection Science. Hybrid Connectionist/Symbolic Systems* 1:3.

Hendler J, Dickens L. 1991. Integrating neural network and expert reasoning: An example. In Steels L, Smith B (eds), *Proceedings of the British Society of Artificial Intelligence and Simulation of Behavior Conference*. Springer-Verlag, pp 109–116.

Hertz J, Krogh A, Palmer R. 1991. *Introduction to the Theory of Neural Computation*. Reading, Mass, Addison-Wesley.

Hinton J (ed). 1990. Connectionist Symbol Processing. Cambridge, Massachusetts, MIT Press.

Hirota K. 1984. *Image Pattern Recognition*. Tokyo, McGraw-Hill.

Hirota K. 1995. Fuzzy logic and its hardware realization. In Kasabov N and Coghill G (eds), *Proceedings of the Second New Zealand Intern. Conference on Artificial Neural Networks and Expert Systems ANNES'95*, Dunedin, New Zealand, 20–23 November, 1995, IEEE Comp. Society Press, 102–105.

Holland J. 1992. *Adaptation in Natural and Artificial Systems*. Cambridge, Massachusetts, MIT Press.

Holland J. 1975. Adaptation in Natural and Artificial Systems. The University of Michigan.

Hopfield J, Tank D. 1985. Neural computation of decisions in optimization problems. *Biological Cybernetics* 52:141–152.

Hopfield J, 1982. Neural networks and physical systems with emergent collective computational abilities. *Proceedings of the National Academy of Sciences of the United States of America* 79:2554–2558.

Hopfield J. 1984. Neural networks with graded response have collective computational properties like those of two-state neurons. *Proceedings of the National Academy of Sciences of the United States of America* 81:3088–3092.

Hopfield J, Feindtein D, Palmer R. 1983. Unlearning has a stabilizing effect in collective memories. *Nature* 304:158–159.

Hoppensteadt F. 1986. *An Introduction to the Mathematics of Neurons*. Cambridge, England, Cambridge University Press.

Hoppensteadt F. 1989. Intermittent chaos, self-organization and learning from synchronous synaptyc activity in model neuron networks, *Proceedings of the National Academy of Sciences of the United States of America* 86:2991–2995.

Hoptroff A. 1993. The principles and practice of time series forecasting and business modelling using neural nets. *Neural Computing and Applications* 1:59–66.

Hornick K. 1993. Some new results on neural network approximation. *Neural Networks* 6:1069–1072.

Hornik K. 1991. Approximation capabilities of multilayer feedforward networks. *Neural Networks* 4:251–257.

Hornik K, Stinchcombe M, White H. 1989. Multilayer feedforward networks are universal approximators. *Neural Networks* 2:359–366.

Hoskins JC, Himmelbaum DM. 1990. Fault detection and diagnosing using artificial neural networks. In Mavrovouniotis ML (ed), *Artificial Intelligence in Process Engineering* Orlando, Fla, Academic Press, pp 123–160.

Hruska SI, Kuncicky DC, Lacher RC. 1991. Hybrid learning in expert networks. In *Proceedings of the International Conference on Neural Networks*, vol 2. Piscataway NJ, IEEE Press, pp 117–120.

Inoue M, Nagayoshi A. 1992. Boltzman machine learning in an analog chaos neurocomputer. In *Proceedings of the Second International Conference on Fuzzy Logic and Neural Networks*, Iizuka, Japan, July 17–22, 1992, pp 559–562.

Ishikawa M. 1995. Neural networks approach to rule extraction. In Kasabov N and Goghill G (eds), *Proceedings of the Second New Zealand International Conference on Artificial Neural Networks and Expert Systems*, Dunedin, New Zealand, 20–23 November 1995, IEEE Computer Society Press, Los Alamitos, California, pp 6–9.

Ishikawa M. 1992. A new approach to problem solving by modular structured networks. In *Proceedings of the Second International Conference on Fuzzy Logic and Neural Networks*, Iizuka, Japan, July 17–22, 1992, pp 855–858.

Ishikawa M, Moriyama T. 1995. Prediction of time series by a structural learning of neural networks. *Fuzzy sets and systems*, Special Issue "Hybrid connect. systems".

Isshiki H, Endo H. 1992. Learning expert's knowledge by neural network and deduction of fuzzy rules by Powell's method. In *Proceedings of the Second International Conference on Fuzzy Logic and Neural Networks*. Iizuka, Japan, July 17–22, 1992, pp 95–98.

Jacobs R. 1988. Increased rates of convergence through learning rate adaptation. *Neural Networks* 1:295–307.

Jia J, Chua H. 1993. Market prediction using artificial neural network: A case study for modeling and forecasting deutsche mark exchange rate. In Kasabov N (ed), *Artificial Neural Networks and Expert Systems*. Los Alamitos, Calif, IEEE Computer Society Press, pp 373–377.

Jordan M. 1986. Attractor dynamics and parallelism in a connectionist sequential machine. In *Proceedings of the Eighth Annual Conference of the Cognitive Science Society*. Hillsdale, NJ: Erlbaum, pp 531–546, IEEE, New York.

Jordan M, Jacobs R. 1994. Hierarchical mixtures of experts and the EM algorithm. *Neural Computation* 6:181–214.

Kanal L, Lemmer JF. 1986. *Uncertainty in Artificial Intelligence*. Amsterdam, Elsevier Science.

Kandel A (ed). 1991. *Fuzzy Expert Systems*. Boca Raton, Fla, CRC Press.

Kaneko K. 1989. Pattern dynamics in spatiotemporal chaos. *Physica* 34D:1–41.

Kaneko K. 1990. Clustering, coding, switching, hierarchical ordering, and control in network of chaotic elements. *Physica* 41D:137–172.

Karaivanova M, Kasabov N, Hristov I. 1983. Predicting the scope of effect of anticancer medicines [in Russian]. Experimentalnaya Onkologia 5:51–54.

Kasabov N. 1990. Hybrid connectionist rule based systems. In Jorrand P, Sgurev V (eds), *Artificial Intelligence—Methodology, Systems, Applications*. Amsterdam, North-Holland, pp 227–235.

Kasabov N. 1993a. Hybrid connectionist production systems. *Journal of Systems Engineering* 3:15–21.

Kasabov N. 1993b. Learning fuzzy production rules for approximate reasoning with connectionist production systems. In Gielen S, Kappen B (eds), *Proceedings of the International Conference on Artificial Neural Networks*. New York, Springer-Verlag, pp 337–345.

Kasabov N, 1995a. Building comprehensive AI and the task of speech recognition. In Alspector J, Goodman R and Brown T (eds), *Applications of Neural Networks to Telecommunications 2*, Lawrence Erlbaum Assoc, Publ, Hillsdale, NJ, 178–185.

Kasabov N. 1995b. Hybrid connectionist fuzzy production systems: Toward building comprehensive AI. *Intelligent Automation and Soft Computing* 1(4):351–360.

Kasabov N. 1995c. Learning fuzzy rules and approximate reasoning in fuzzy neural networks and hybrid systems. *Fuzzy Sets and Systems*, special issue "Hybrid conn. systems".

Kasabov N. 1996. Adaptable neuro production systems. *Neurocomputing*, in press.

Kasabov N. 1994. Connectionist fuzzy production systems, *Lecture Notes in Artificial Intelligence*, No. 847, Springer-Verlag, pp 114–128.

Kasabov N, Clarke G. 1995. A template based implementation of connectionist knowledge based systems for classification and learning. In Omidvar O (ed), *Advances in Neural Networks*, vol. 4, Ablex Publ. Company, 137–156.

Kasabov N, Nikovski D. 1992. Prognostic expert systems on a hybrid connectionist environment. In du Boulay B, Sgurev V (eds), *Artificial Intelligence—Methodology, Systems, Applications*. Amsterdam, Elsevier Science, pp 141–148.

Kasabov N, Nikovski D, Peev E. 1993. Speech recognition with Kohonen's self organized neural networks and hybrid systems. In *Proceedings of the First New Zealand International Conference on Artificial Neural Networks and Expert Systems, ANNES'93*. Dunedin, New Zealand, 24–26 November 1993, IEEE Computer Society Press, Los Alamitos, 113–118.

Kasabov N, Peev E. 1994. Phoneme recognition with hierarchical self organized neural networks and fuzzy systems—a case study. In Marinaro M, Morasso P (eds), *Proceedings of the International Conference on Artificial Neural Networks 94*, Italy, Sorento, Springer-Verlag, vol. 2, 201–204.

Kasabov N, Petkov S. 1992. Neural networks and logic programming—A hybrid model and its applicability to building expert systems. In Neumann B (ed), ECAI'92. *10th European Conference on Artificial Intelligence*, Vienna, Austria, New York, John Wiley & Sons, pp 287–288.

Kasabov N, Shishkov S. 1993. A connectionist production system and the use of its partial match for approximate reasoning. *Connection Science* 5:275–305.

Kasabov N, Trifonov R. 1993. Using hybrid connectionist systems for spatial information processing. In *Proceedings of the Fifth Colloquium of the Spatial Information Research Centre*, University of Otago, Dunedin, pp 85–95.

Kasabov N, Sinclair S, Kilgour R, et al. 1995. Intelligent human computer interfaces and the case study of building English-to-Maori talking dictionary. In Kasabov N and Coghill G (eds), *Proceedings of the Second New Zealand International Conference on Artificial Neural Networks and Expert Systems*, Dunedin, New Zealand, November 20–23, 1995, Los Alamitos, CA, IEEE Computer Society Press, pp 294–297.

Kasabov N, Watson C. 1994. Automatic Speech Recognition, Report, Departm. Information Science, University of Otago, Dunedin, New Zealand.

Kasabov N, Watson C, Sinclair S, Kilgour R. 1994. Integrating neural networks and fuzzy systems for speech recognition. In *Proceedings of the Speech Science and Technology Conference SST-94*, Perth, University of South Australia, pp 462–467.

Katayama R, Kajitami Y, Kuwata K, et al. 1993. Self-generating radial basis function as neuro-fuzzy model and its application to nonlinear prediction of chaotic time series. In *Proceedings of the Second IEEE International Conference on Fuzzy Systems*, San Francisco, pp 407–414.

Katoh Y, Yuize Y, Yoneda M, et al. 1992. Gradual rules in a decision support system for foreign exchange trading. In *Proceedings of the Second International Conference on Fuzzy Logic and Neural Networks*, Iizuka, Japan, July 17–22, 1992, pp 625–628.

Kaufman PJ. 1987. *The New Commodity Trading Systems and Methods*. New York, John Wiley & Sons.

Keller J, Chen Z. 1992. Learning in fuzzy neural networks utilising additive hybrid operators. In *Proceedings of the Second International Conference on Fuzzy Logic and Neural Networks*, Iizuka, Japan, July 17–22, 1992, pp 85–87.

Khan E. 1993. NeuFuz: An intelligent combination of fuzzy logic with neural nets. In *Proceedings of the International Joint Conference on Neural Networks*, Nagoya, Japan, October 25–29, 1993, IEEE, 2945–2950.

Kohers G. 1992. The use of modular neural networks on time series forecasting. In *Proceedings of the 23rd Annual Meeting of the Decision Sciences Institute*, San Francisco, Nov 22–24, pp 759–761.

Kohonen T. 1982. Self-organized formation of topologically correct feature maps. Biological Cybernetics, 43:59–69.

Kohonen T. 1988. *Self-Organisation and Associative Memory*, Series in Information Sciences 8, Heidelberg: Springer-Verlag.

Kohonen T. 1990. The self-organizing map. *Proceedings of the IEEE* 78:1464–1497.

Kohonen T. 1993. Physiological interpretation of the self-organising map algorithm *Neural Networks* 6:895–905.

Kolmogorov A. 1957. On the representations of continuous functions of many variables by superpositions of continuous functions of one variable and addition. *Dokladi Academii Nauk USSR* 114:953–956.

Kosko B. 1986. Fuzzy entropy and conditioning. *Information Sciences* 40:165–174.

Kosko B. 1987. *Foundations of Fuzzy Estimation Theory*, PhD thesis, June 1987, Department of Electrical Engineering, University of California at Irvine, Ann Arbor, Mich, University Microfilms International.

Kosko B. 1988a. Feedback stability and unsupervised learning. In *Proceedings of the Second IEEE International Conference on Neural Networks*, July 1988, vol. 1, pp 141–152.

Kosko B. 1988b. Bidirectional associative memories. *IEEE Transactions on Systems, Man and Cybernetics* 18:49–60.

Kosko B. 1990. Unsupervised learning in noise. *IEEE Transactions on Neural Networks* 1:44–57.

Kosko B. 1991. *Neural Networks for Signal Processing*. Englewood Cliffs, NJ, Prentice Hall.

Kosko B. 1992. *Neural Networks and Fuzzy Systems: A Dynamical Approach to Machine Intelligence*. Englewood Cliffs, NJ, Prentice-Hall.

Lam K, Su C. 1992. Inference network for optimization applications. In *Proceedings of the Second International Conference on Fuzzy Logic and Neural Networks*, Iizuka, Japan, July 17–22, 1992, pp 189–192.

Lange T, Dyer M. 1989. High-level inferencing in a connectionist network. *Connection Science* 1:181–217.

Le Cun Y, Boser B, Denker J, Henderson D, Howard R, Hubbard W, and Jackel L. 1990. Handwritten digit recognition with a backpropagation network. In *Advances in Neural Information Processing Systems 2*, Touretzky D (ed), San Mateo, CA: Morgan Kaufmann, pp 396–404.

Lee C, Gauvin J, Pierracini R, et al. 1993. Sub-word based large vocabulary speech recognition. *AT&T Technical Journal*, Sept/Oct, pp 25–36.

Lim M, Rahardja S, Gwee B. 1995. A GA paradigm for learning fuzzy rules. *Fuzzy Sets and Systems*, Special Issue "Hybrid Connectionist Systems".

Lim M, Takefuji Y. 1990. Implementing fuzzy rule-based systems on silicon chips. *IEEE Expert*, February, pp 31–45.

Limkens D, Nie J. 1992. Rule extraction for BNN neural network–based fuzzy control system by self-learning. In Aleksander I, Taylor J (eds), *Artificial Neural Networks*, vol 2. Amsterdam, Elsevier Science, pp 459–466.

Lippman R. 1987. An introduction to computing with neural nets. *IEEE ASSP*, April, pp 4–21.

Lippman R. 1989. Review of neural networks for speech recognititon. *Neural Computation*, 1–38.

Luger G, Stubblefield W. 1989. *Artificial Intelligence and the Design of Expert Systems*. Benjamin/Cummings.

Maclagan M. 1982. An acoustic study of New Zealand vowels. *New Zealand Speech Therapists' Journal* 37:20–26

Mamdani E. 1977. Application of fuzzy logic to approximate reasoning using linguistic synthesis. *IEEE Transactions on Computers* 26:1182–1191.

Maren AJ. 1990. Hybrid and complex networks. In Maren AJ (ed), *Handbook of Neural Computing Applications*, San Diego, Academic Press, pp 203–217.

McCauley JL. 1994. *Chaos, Dynamics and Fractals, an Algorithmic Approach to Deterministic Chaos*. Cambridge, Englewood, Cambridge University Press.

McClelland JL, Rumelhart DE, Hinton GE. 1986. A general framework for PDP. In Rumelhart DE, MacClelland JL, PDP Research Group (eds), *Parallel Distributed Processing: Explorations in the Microstructure of Cognition*, vol. 1: *Foundations*. Cambridge, Mass, MIT Press.

McCulloch WS, Pitts W. 1943. A logical calculus of the ideas immanent in nervous activity. *Bulletin of Mathematical Biophysics* 5:115–133.

McDermott J, Forgy C. 1978. Production system conflict resolution strategies. In Waterman DA, Hayes-Roth F (eds), *Pattern-Directed Inference Systems*. New York, Academic Press, pp 177–199.

McShane J. 1991. *Cognitive Development:An Information Processing Approach*. London, Basil Blackwell.

Medsker L. 1995. Hybrid Intelligent Systems. Boston, Kluwer Academic Publishers.

Metcalfe A. 1994. *Statistics in Engineering–A Practical Approach*. London, Chapman & Hall.

Michaliewicz Z. 1992. *Genetic Algorithms + Data Structures = Evolutionary Programs*. Berlin, Springer-Verlag.

Minsky ML, Papert S. 1969. *Perceptrons: An Introduction to Computational Geometry*. Cambridge, Mass, MIT Press.

Mitchel I, Keller R, Kedar S, et al. 1986. Explanation-based generalization: A unified view. *Machine Learning* 1:1.

Mitra S, Pal S. 1995. Fuzzy multi-layer perception, interencing and rule generation. *IEEE Transactions on Neural Networks* 6(1):51–63.

Mizumoto M, Zimmermann H. 1982. Comparison of fuzzy reasoning methods. *Fuzzy Sets and Systems* 18:253–283.

Moody T, Darken C. 1989. Fast learning in networks of locally tuned processing units. *Neural Computation* 1:281–294.

Morasso P, Vercelli G, Zaccaria R. 1992. Hybrid systems for robot planning. In Aleksander I, Taylor J (eds), *Artificial Neural Networks*, vol 2. Amsterdam, Elsevier Science, pp 691–697.

Morgan D, Scofield C. 1991. *Neural Networks and Speech Processing*. Boston, Kluwer Academic.

Mukaidono M, Yamaoka M. 1992. A learning method of fuzzy inference rules with neural networks and its application. In *Proceedings of the Second International Conference on Fuzzy Logic and Neural Networks*, Iizuka, Japan, July, 1992, pp 185–187.

Murphy P, Aha D. 1992. *VCI Repository of Machine Learning Databases*. Department of Information and Computer Science, University of California, Irvine.

Neapolitan R. 1989. *Probability Reasoning in Expert Systems. Theory and Algorithms*. New York, John Wiley and Sons.

Newell A, Simon HA. 1972. *Human Problem Solving*. Englewood Cliffs, NJ, Prentice Hall.

Nigrin A. 1993. *Neural Networks for Pattern Recognition*. Cambridge, Mass, The MIT Press.

NRC Canada. 1994. *Fuzzy CLIPS. User's Manual*. Ottawa. National Research Council of Canada.

Oja E. 1992. Principle components, minor components and linear neural networks. *Neural Networks* 5:927–935.

Okada H, Watamabe N, Kawamura A, et al. 1992. Knowledge implementation multilayer neural networks with fuzzy logic. In *Proceedings of the Second International Conference on Fuzzy Logic and Neural Networks*, Iizuka, Japan, July 17–22, 1992, pp 99–102.

Owens FJ. 1993. *Signal Processing of Speech*. London, Macmillan.

Ozawa J, Yamada K. 1994. Answering to conceptual queries. Yokohama, International Laboratory for Fuzzy Engineering, TR-5POO8E, Japan.

Pao Y-H. 1989. *Adaptive Pattern Recognition and Neural Networks*. Reading, Mass, Addison-Wesley.

Peng Y, Reggia JA. 1989. A connectionist model for diagnostic problem solving. *IEEE Transactions on Systems, Men and Cybernetics* 19:295-298.

Peters E. 1991. *Chaos and Order in the Capital Markets*. New York, John Wiley & Sons.

Picone J. 1993. Signal modelling techniques in speech recognition. *Proceedings of the IEEE* 81:1215-1247.

Pinker S, Prince A. 1988. On language and connectionism: Analysis of a PDP model of language acquisition. *Cognition* 28:73-193.

Pratt I. 1994. Artificial Intelligence. The Macmillan Press Ltd. London.

Quinlan J. 1986. Induction of decision trees. *Machine Learning* 1:1.

Rabelo LC, Avula XJR. 1991. Intelligent control of a robotic arm using hierarchical neural network systems. In *Proceedings of the IEEE International Conference on Neural Networks*, vol 2, Piscataway, NJ, IEEE Press, pp 359-366.

Rabiner L. 1989. A tutorial on hidden Markov models and selected applications in speech recognition. *Proceedings of the IEEE* 77:257-285.

Railton D, Campbell J, Cohen A, et al. 1995. Innovative waste water treatment at Paraparaumu. In *Proceedings of the New Zealand Waste Water Association Annual Conference*, Auckland, New Zealand, 5-8 September 1995, Auckland, NZ Waste Water Association, pp 1-9.

Ralescu D. 1995. Fuzzy random variables revisited. In *Proceedings of the International Joint Conference of the Fourth IEEE International Conference on Fuzzy Systems and the Second International Fuzzy Engineering Symposium*, Yokohama, Japan, March 20-24, 1995, IEEE, pp 993-1999.

Ralescu A, Hartani R. 1995. Some issues in fuzzy and linguistic modelling. In *Proceedings of the International Joint Conference of the Fourth IEEE International Conference on Fuzzy Systems and the Second International Fuzzy Engineering Symposium*, March 20-24, 1995, IEEE, pp 1903-1910.

Ralston D. 1988. *Principles of AI and ES Development*. New York, McGraw-Hill.

Rao V, Rao H. 1993. *C++, Neural Networks and Fuzzy Logic*. New York, MIS Press.

Ray AK, Misra RB. 1991. A neural network based expert system tool for diagnostic problem solving. *CSI Journal Computer Science and Information* 21:17-25.

Renals S, Rohwer R. 1989. Phoneme classification experiments using radial basis functions. In *Proceedings of International Joint Conference on Neural Networks*, Washington, DC, June 1989, pp 461-467.

Robinson D. 1988. *Artificial Intelligence and Expert Systems Development*. New York, McGraw-Hill.

Rocha P, Khebbal S, Treleaven P. 1993. A framework for hybrid intelligent systems. In Kasabov N (ed), *Artificial Neural Networks and Expert Systems*. Los Alamitos, Calif, IEEE Computer Society Press, pp 206-209.

Rolls E, Treves A. 1993. Neural networks in the brain involved in memory and recall. In *Proceedings of Internatonal Joint Conference on Neural Networks*, Nagoya, Japan, Oct 25-29, 1993, IEEE, pp 9-14.

Romaniuk S, Hall O. 1992. Decision making on creditworthiness, using a fuzzy connectionist model. *Fuzzy Sets and Systems* 48:15-22.

Rosenblatt F. 1958. The perceptron: A probabilistic model for information storage and organization in the Brain. *Psychology Review* 65:386–408.

Rumelhart D, Smolenski P, McClelland J. 1986a. Schemata and sequential thought processes in PDP models. In *Parallel Distributed Processing: Exploration in the Microstructure of Cognition*, vol 1: *Foundations*. Cambridge, Mass, MIT Press, pp 224–250.

Rumelhart DE, Hinton G, Williams R. 1986b. Learning internal representation by error propagation. In Rumelhart DE, McClelland JL, PDP Research Group (eds), *Parallel Distributed Processing: Exploration in the Microstructure of Cognition*, vol. 1: *Foundations*. Cambridge, Mass, MIT Press.

Rumelhart DE, McClelland JL (eds). 1986. *Parallel and Distributed Processing: Exploration in the Microstructure of Cognition*, vol. 1: *Foundations*. Cambridge, Mass, MIT Press.

Sanchez E. 1992. Genetic algorithms, neural networks and fuzzy logic systems. In *Proceedings of the Second International Conference on Fuzzy Logic and Neural Networks*, Iizuka, Japan, July 17–22, 1992, pp 17–19.

Schalkoff R. 1990. *Artificial Intelligence: An Engineering Approach*. New York, McGraw-Hill.

Schoenenburg E. 1990. Stock price prediction using neural networks: A project report. *Neurocomputing* 2:17–27.

Schwefel H, Manner R (eds). 1990. *Parallel Problem Solving from Nature*. Berlin, Springer-Verlag.

Schwin J. 1993. A hybrid approach for knowledge presentation and reasoning. In Kasabov N (ed), *Artificial Neural Networks and Expert Systems*. Los Alamitos, Calif, IEEE Computer Society Press, pp 214–215.

Sejnowski T, and Rosenberg. 1987. Parallel networks that learn to pronounce English text. *Complex Systems* 1:145–168.

Shafer G. 1976. *A Mathematical Theory of Evidence*. Princeton, NJ, Princeton University Press.

Shastri L. 1988. A connectionist approach to knowledge representation and limited inference. *Cognitive Science* 12:331–392.

Shastri L. 1991. Relevance of connectionism to AI: A representation and reasoning perspective. In Barnden J, Pollack J (eds), *Advances in Connectionist and Neural Computation Theory*, vol 1. Norwood, NJ, Ablex.

Shavlik JW, 1994. Combining symbolic and neural learning. *Machine Learning* 14:321–331.

Shiff S, Jerger K, Duong D, et al. 1994. Controlling chaos in the brain. *Nature* 370:615–620.

Simpson P. 1990. *Artificial Neural Systems*. Tarrytown, NY, Pergamon Press.

Smith M. 1993. *Neural Networks for Statistical Modeling*. New York, Van Nostrand Reinhold.

Smolenski P. 1990. Tensor product variable binding and the representation of symbolic structures in connectionist systems. *Artificial Intelligence* 46:159–216.

Steels L. 1989. Connectionist problem solving—An AI perspective. In Pfeifer R, Schreter Z, Fogelman-Soulie F, et al (eds), *Connectionism in Perspective*. Amsterdam, Elsevier Science–North Holland, pp 215–228.

Stillings N, Weisler S, Chase C, et al. 1995. *Cognititve Science, an Introduction*. Cambridge, Mass, MIT Press.

Stolcke A. 1992. *Cluster Program Manual*. Boulder, University of Colorado.

Suddarth S. 1992. Theoretical and practical challenges in chaos computing. In *Proceedings of the Second International Conference on Fuzzy Logic and Neural Networks*, Iizuka, Japan, July 17–22, 1992, pp 977–980.

Sugeno M. 1974. *Theory of Fuzzy Integral and Its Applications*, PhD thesis, Tokyo Institute of Technology, Tokyo.

Sugeno M. 1985. An introductory survey of fuzzy control. *Information Science* 36:59–83.

Sun R, Bookman L (eds). 1994. *Computational Architectures Integrating Neural and Symbolic Processes*. Boston, Kluwer Academic Publishers.

Sun R. 1992. On variable binding in connectionist networks. *Connection Science* 4:93–1124.

Takagi H. 1990. Fusion technology of fuzzy theory and neural networks—Survey and future directions. In *Proceedings of the First International Conference on Fuzzy Logic and Neural Networks*, Iizuka, Japan, July 20–24, pp 13–126.

Takagi T, Sugeno M. 1985. Fuzzy identification of systems and its applications to modelling and control. *IEEE Transactions on Systems, Man and Cybernetics* 15:116–132.

Taylor J, Mannion C (eds). 1989. *New Developments in Neural Computing*. Bristol, England, Adam Hilger.

Teodorescu HT, Yamakawa J, GilAluja A, et al. 1994. Chaos in neuro-fuzzy systems and modelling issues. In *Proceedings of the 1994 IEEE/Nagoya University World Wisemen/women Workshop on Fuzzy Logic, Neural Networks and Genetic Algorithms*, Nagoya University, Nagoya; Japan, August 9–10, 1994, pp 79–92.

Terano T, Kiyoji A, Sugeno M. 1992. *Fuzzy Systems Theory and Its Applications*. London Academic Press.

Thornton C. 1992. *Techniques in Computational Learning, an Introduction*. London, Chapman & Hall.

TIL Shell. 1993. *User Manual*. Irvine, California. Togai Infra Logic, Inc.

Togai M, Watanabe H. 1986. Expert system on a chip: An engine for realtime approximate reasoning. *IEEE Expert Fall*, 1:55–62.

Touretzky D (ed). 1989. *Neural Information Processing Systems*, 3 vols. San Mateo, Calif, Morgan Kaufmann.

Touretzky D, Hinton G. 1988. A distributed connectionist production system. *Cognitive Science* 12:423–1466.

Tsypkin YZ. 1973. *Foundation of the Theory of Learning Systems*. New York, Academic Press.

Uchino E, Yamakawa T, Miki T, et al. 1993. Fuzzy rule-based simple interpolation algorithm for discrete signals. *Fuzzy Sets and Systems* 59:259–270.

Vaga T. 1990. The coherent market hypothesis. *Financial Analysts Journal*, November–December, pp 1–14.

Wang C, Khor E, Tang S. 1993. NCLIPS—A platform for implementing hybrid expert systems. In Kasabov N (ed), *Artificial Neural Networks and Expert Systems*. Los Alamitos, Calif, IEEE Computer Society Press, pp 202–205.

Wang, L-X. 1994. *Adaptive Fuzzy Systems and Control—Design and Stability Analysis*. Englewood Cliffs, NJ, Prentice Hall.

Waterman DA, Hayes-Roth F (eds). 1978. *Pattern-Directed Inference Systems*, New York, Academic Press.

Waibel A, Hanazawa T, Hinton G, et al. 1989a. Phoneme recognititon using time-delay neural networks. *IEEE Transactions on Acoustics, Speech, and Signal Processing*. 37(3):328–339.

Waibel A, Sawai H, Shinano K. 1989b. Modularity and scaling in large phonemic neural networks. *IEEE Transactions on Acoustic, Speech and Signal Processing* 37:1888–1897.

Weigend A, Gershefeld N. 1993. *Time-Series Prediction: Forecasting the Future and Understanding the Past*. Reading, Mass, Addison-Wesley.

Weiss S, Kulikowski C. 1991. *Computer Systems That Learn*. San Mateo, Calif, Morgan Kaufmann.

Werbos P. 1990. Backpropagation through time: What it does and how to do it. *Proceedings of the IEEE* 87:10.

Werbos P. 1992. Neurocontrol: Where it is going and why it is crucial. In Aleksander I, Taylor J (eds), *Artificial Neural Networks*, 2. Amsterdam, Elsevier Science, pp. 61–70.

Whalen T, Schott B. 1985. Alternative logics for approximate reasoning in expert systems: A comparative study. *International Journal of Man-Machine Studies* 22:327–346.

Widrow B, Hoff ME. 1960. Adaptive switching circuits. In 1960 *IRE WESCON Convention Record*. New York 4:96–104.

Wolfe A. 1985. Determining Lyapunov exponents from a time series. *Physica* 16D:285–317.

Yager R, Zadeh L (eds). 1992. *An Introduction to Fuzzy Logic Applications in Intelligent Systems*, Boston, Kluwer Academic.

Yamakawa T. 1989. Stabilization of an inverted pendulum by a high-speed fuzzy logic controller hardware system. *Fuzzy Sets and Systems* 32:161–180.

Yamakawa T. 1990. Pattern recognition hardware system employing a fuzzy neuron. In *Proceedings of the International Conference on Fuzzy Logic and Neural Networks*, Iizuka, Japan, July 1990, pp 943–948.

Yamakawa T. 1993. A fuzzy inference engine in nonlinear analog mode and its application to a fuzzy logic control. *IEEE Transactions on Neural Networks* 4:496–520.

Yamakawa T (ed). 1994. *Proceedings of the Third International Conference on Fuzzy Logic, Neural Networks and Soft Computing*, Iizuka, Japan, Kyushu, Japan, Kyushu Institute of Technology. August 1–8, 1994.

Yamakawa T, Miki T, Uchino E. 1992b. A chaotic chip for analyzing nonlinear discrete dynamical network systems. In *Proceedings of the Second International Conference on Fuzzy Logic and Neural Networks*, Iizuka, Japan, July 17–22, 1992, pp 563–566.

Yamakawa T, Uchino E, Miki F, et al. 1992a. A neo fuzzy neuron and its application to system identification and prediction of the system behaviour. In *Proceedings of the Second International Conference on Fuzzy Logic and Neural Networks*, Iizuka, Japan, July, 1952, pp 477–483.

Yanaru T, Hirota T, Kimura N. 1994. An emotion processing system based on fuzzy inference and its subjective observations. *International Journal of Approximate Reasoning* 10(1):99–122.

Yi H-J, Oh KW. 1992. Neural network–based fuzzy production rule generation and its application to approximate reasoning. In *Proceedings of the Second International Conference of Fuzzy Logic and Neural Networks*. Iizuka, Japan, July 17–22, pp 333–336.

Zadeh L. 1965. Fuzzy sets. *Information and Control* 8:338–353.

Zadeh L. 1968. Probability measures of fuzzy events. *Journal of Mathematical Analysis and Applications* 22:421–427.

Zadeh L. 1971. Similarity relations and fuzzy ordering. *Information Sciences* 3:177–200.

Zadeh L. 1978a. Fuzzy sets as a basis for a theory of possibility. *Fuzzy Sets and Systems* 1:3–28.

Zadeh L. 1978b. PRUF—A meaning representation language for natural language. *International Journal of Man-Machine Studies* 10:395–460.

Zadeh L. 1979. A theory of approximate reasoning. In Hayes, Michie Mikulich (eds), *Machine Intelligence*, vol 9. New York, Elsevier, pp 149–194.

Zadeh L. 1984. Making computers think like people. *IEEE Spectrum*, August, pp 26–32.

Zadeh L. 1985. The role of fuzzy logic in the management of uncertainty in expert systems. In Gupta M, Kandel A, Bandler W, et al (eds), *Approximate Reasoning in Expert Systems*. North Holland.

Zadeh L. 1989. Knowledge representation in fuzzy logic. *IEEE Transactions on Knowledge and Data Engineering* 1:89–98.

Zahedi F. 1993. *Intelligent Systems for Business. Expert Systems with Neural Networks*, Belmont, California, The Wadsworth Publ. Company.

Zahzah E-H, Desadry J, Zehada M. 1992. A fuzzy connectionist approach for a knowledge based image interpretation system. In *Proceedings of the Second International Conference on Fuzzy Logic and Neural Networks*, Iizuka, Japan, July 17–22, 1992, pp 1135–1138.

Zemankova-Leech M, Kandel A. 1984. *Fuzzy Relational Data Bases—A Key to Expert Systems*. Cologne, Verlag TUV Reinland.

Zimmermann H. 1987. *Fuzzy Sets, Decision Making, and Expert Systems*. Boston, Kluwer Academic.

Zurada J. 1992. *Introduction to Artificial Neural Systems*. St Paul, Minn, West.

Glossary

Adaptive intelligent systems Information systems that are able to change their knowledge base and their structural and functional characteristics during operation in a dynamically changing environment for a better reaction.

Adaptive resonance theory (ART) A neural network invented and developed by Carpenter and Grossberg. The network learns to categorize and adopt new patterns ("plasticity") while retaining previously learned patterns ("stability").

Alan Turing's test for artificial intelligence (AI) Definition for AI introduced by the British mathematician and computer scientist Alan Turing. It states approximately that a machine system is considered to possess AI if while communicating with a person behind a "bar," the person cannot recognize whether it is a machine or a human.

α-cut of a fuzzy set Subset of the universe of the fuzzy set consisting of values that belong to the fuzzy set with a membership degree greater (weak cut) or greater or equal to (strong cut) a given value $\alpha \in [0, 1]$.

Apparent error The error calculated on the basis of the reaction of a neural network to the data used for its training. It is usually calculated as a mean square error (MSE) or root MSE (RMS).

Approximate reasoning A process of inferring new facts and achieving conclusions in an intelligent information system when inexact facts and uncertain rules are present.

Artificial neural network Biologically inspired computational model consisting of processing elements (called neurons) and connections between them with coefficients (weights) bound to the connections, which constitute the neuronal structure. Training and recall algorithms are also attached to the structure.

Automatic speech recognition system (ASRS) A computer system which aims at providing enhanced access to machines and information via voice commands (instructions, queries, communication messages).

Backward chaining Goal-driven inference process which starts after a goal is identified. A search for a rule which has this goal in its consequent part is performed, and then data (facts) which satisfy all the conditions for this rule are sought in the database. The process is recursive, that is, a condition in a rule may be a conclusion in another rule (other rules). The process of searching for facts goes backward.

Bidirectional associative memory (BAM) A neural network which has the characteristic of a heteroassociative memory. It can memorize pattern associations of the type $(\mathbf{a}^{(p)}, \mathbf{b}^{(p)})$, where $\mathbf{a}^{(p)}$ is an n-dimensional vector (pattern) and $\mathbf{b}^{(p)}$ is its corresponding m-dimensional pattern. If at least one of the patterns, even corrupted, is given as input, the network eventually produces the two patterns associated during training.

Brain-state-in-a-box network (BSB) An autoassociative network that is a recurrent but not fully connected network, in which a connection from a neuron's output to its input is allowed; the interconnection weights are nonsymmetric in general. The state space of the system is restricted to a hyper-cube ("box"), the edges being the desired states [previously learned patterns].

Catastrophic forgetting Phenomenon representing the ability of a network to forget what it has learned from previous examples, when they are no longer presented to it, but other examples are presented instead.

Center-of-gravity defuzzification method (COG) Method for defuzzification, for example, transforming a membership function B' into a crisp value y' such that y' is the geometrical center of B'. The following formula is used: $y' = \sum \mu_{B'}(v) \cdot v / \sum \mu_{B'}(v)$, where v are all the values from the universe V of the fuzzy variable y.

Chaos   A complicated behavior of a *nonlinear dynamical system* according to some underlying rules.

Chaotic attractor   An area or points from the phase space of a chaotic process where the process often goes through time, but without repeating the same trajectories.

Chaotic neuron   An artificial neuron whose output is calculated with the use of a chaotic output function.

Classification problem   A genetic AI problem which arises when it is necessary to associate an object with some already existing groups, clusters, or classes of objects.

Comprehensive artificial intelligence   The area of integrating ordinary, symbolic AI, neural networks, fuzzy systems, and other AI techniques (genetic algorithms, evolutionary programming chaos, etc.)

Connectionist expert system (CES)   An expert system that has its knowledge represented as a neural network.

Connectionist production system   A connectionist system that implements productions of the form IF C, THEN A, where C is a set of conditions and A is a set of actions.

Control   Process of acquiring information for the current state of an object and emitting control signals to it in order to keep the object in its possible and desired states.

Decision-making systems   AI systems which choose one among many variants as a solution to a particular problem. The solution is then recommended to the user.

Defuzzification   Process of calculating a single output numerical value for a fuzzy output variable on the basis of an inferred membership function for this variable.

Design   Creating objects that satisfy particular requirements following a given set of constraints.

Destructive learning   Technique which destroys the initial neural network architecture, for example, removes connections, for the purpose of better learning.

Diagnosis   Process of finding faults in a system.

Distributed representation   A way of encoding information in a neural network where a concept or a value for a variable is represented by a collective activation of a group of neurons.

Dynamical system   A system which evolves in continuous or discrete time.

Expert system   A computer system for solving difficult problems usually solved by experts; the system can provide a similar expertise to the one provided by experts in a restricted area, for example diagnosis of breast cancer, finding a cheap route for a round-the-world trip, etc.

Expert system shells   Systems which have the architecture of an expert system but are "empty" of knowledge. They are tools which facilitate rapid phototyping of an expert system.

Explanation in expert systems   Tracing, in a contextually comprehensible way, the process of inferring the solution, and reporting it.

Extension principle   A method which defines how to find the membership function of a fuzzy set $f(A)$ in the universe V, where A is a fuzzy set in the universe U and the function $f : U \to V$ is given.

Fast Fourier Transform (FFT)   Special nonlinear transformation applied on (mainly speech) data to transform the signal taken at a small portion of time from the time-scale domain into a vector in the frequency-scale domain.

Feedforward neural network   A neural network in which there are no connections back from output to input neurons.

Feedback neural network   A network in which there are connections from output to input neurons.

Fitness   See **Goodness**.

Forecasting   See **Prediction**.

Forward chaining inference   A inference method of applying all the facts available at a given moment to all the rules in a rule-based system in order to infer all the possible conclusions, and repeating this process until there are no more new facts inferred.

Fractals   Objects which occupy fractions of a standard (integer number of dimensions) space called the *embedding space.*

Frames   Information (knowledge) structures that represent structured information for standard situations. Frames consist of slots (variables) and fillers (values). The slots represent the most typical characteristics of the objects.

Fuzzification   Process of finding the membership degree $\mu_A(x')$ to which input value x' for a fuzzy variable x defined on an universe U belongs to a fuzzy set A defined on the same universe.

Fuzzy ARTMAP   Extension of ART1 neural network models (see Adaptive Resonance Theory) when input nodes represent not "yes/no" features, but fuzzy features instead, for example, a set of features (sweet, fruity, smooth, sharp, sourish) used to categorize different samples of wines based on their taste.

Fuzzy control   In a broad sense, this is application of fuzzy logic to control problems. A fuzzy control system is a fuzzy system applied to solve a control problem.

Fuzzy clustering   Procedure of clustering data into possibly overlapping clusters, such that each of the data examples may belong to each of the clusters to a certain degree, but all its membership degrees sum up to 1.

Fuzzy expert system   An expert system to which methods of fuzzy logic are applied. Fuzzy expert systems may use fuzzy data, fuzzy rules, and fuzzy inference, in addition to the standard ones implemented in the ordinary expert systems.

Fuzzy expert system shell   A tool that facilitates building and experimenting with fuzzy expert systems. It facilitates building the main modules in a fuzzy expert system.

Fuzzy neural network (FNN)   Neural network designed to realize a fuzzy system, consisting of fuzzy rules, fuzzy variables, and fuzzy values defined for them and the fuzzy inference method.

Fuzzy propositions   Propositions which contain fuzzy variables and their fuzzy values. The truth value of a fuzzy proposition "X is A" is given by the membership function μ_A.

Fuzzy query interface   Interface to a standard database which allows the users to use fuzzy terms (values) in their queries, which values are not stored in the database.

Fuzzy relations   A relation which links two fuzzy sets by assigning a number between 0 and 1 to each element of the cross-product U × V of the universes of the two fuzzy sets. It makes it possible to represent vague or ambiguous relationships.

General linear transformation   Transformation $f(\mathbf{x})$ of data vectors x such that f is a linear function of x, for example, $f(x) = 2x + 1$.

Generalization   The ability of an information system to process new, unknown input data in order to obtain the best possible solution, or one close to it.

General nonlinear transformation   Transformation f of data vectors $\mathbf{x}$ where f is a nonlinear function of $\mathbf{x}$, for example, $f(x) = 1/(1 + e^{-x \cdot c})$, where c is a constant.

Genetic algorithms   Algorithms for solving complex combinatorial and organizational problems with many variants, by employing analogy with nature's evolution. The general steps a genetic algorithm cycles through are: generate a new population (crossover) starting at the beginning with initial one; select the best individuals; mutate, if necessary; repeat the same until a satisfactory solution is found according to a goodness (fitness) function.

Goodness criterion   A function which evaluates the appropriation of prospective decisions when solving an AI problem, for example, playing games.

Growing neural network   A neural network which has the ability to start training with a smaller number of nodes, and subject to the error calculated, to increase this number if necessary.

Hamming network   Network which performs the task of pattern association, or pattern classification, based on measuring the Hamming distance, i.e., the number of bits two boolean vectors differ in.

Hebbian learning law   Generic learning principle which states that a synapse connecting two neurons i and j increases its strength w_{ij} if repeatedly the two neurons i and j are simultaneously activated by input stimuli.

Homophones   Words with different spelling and meaning but which sound the same, for example, "to," "too," "two" and "hear," "here."

Hopfield network   Fully connected feedback network which is an autoassociative memory. It is named after its inventor, John Hopfield.

Hybrid connectionist logic programming system   A system which consists of a logic programming language and neural networks.

Hybrid fuzzy connectionist production system   A system which consists of a production rule-based system, neural networks, fuzzy inference machine, and, possibly, some other modules which facilitate communication between the above, for example, rule extraction module, data processing (normalization, fuzzification, etc.).

Hybrid connectionist production system   A system which consists of a production rule-based system and neural networks.

Inference   Process of matching current data from the domain space to the existing knowledge in a knowledge-based information system and inferring new facts until a solution in the solution space is reached.

Information   Collection of structured data. In its broad meaning it includes knowledge as well as simple meaningful data.

Information retrieval   Process of retricving relevant information from a database by using a query language.

Initialization of a neural network   The process of setting the connection weights in a neural network to some initial values before starting the training algorithm.

Interaction (human computer interaction)   Communication between a computer system on the one hand and the environment or the user on the other hand, in order to solve a given problem.

Knowledge   Concise presentation of previous experience which can be interpreted in a system.

Kohonen SOM   A self-organised map neural network invented and developed by Teuvo Kohonen.

Language analysis   A process where a command or enquiry from user given in a restricted natural language is recognized by a computer program from the point of view of the syntax, the semantics, and the concepts of the language used before the command is interpreted in the system.

Leaky integrator   An artificial neuron which has a binary input, a real-value output, and a feedback connection, which keeps the output of the neuron gradually decreasing in value after the input stimulus has been removed from the input.

Learning   Process of obtaining new knowledge.

Learning vector quantization algorithms LVQ1, LVQ2, and LVQ3   A supervised learning algorithm, which is an extension of the Kohonen self-organized network learning algorithm.

Linguistic variable   Variable which takes fuzzy values, for example "speed" takes values of "high," "moderate," and "low."

Local representation in neural networks   A way of encoding information in a neural network in which every concept or a variable is represented by the activation of one neuron.

Lyapunov exponent   A parameter which provides the average rate of divergence or convergence for a chaotic process.

Machine-learning methods   Computer methods for accumulating, changing, and updating knowledge in an AI computer system.

Membership function   Generalized characteristic function which defines the degree to which an object from a universe belongs to a fuzzy set.

Memory capacity   Maximum number m of patterns which can be learned properly in a pattern associator neural network.

Methods for feature extraction   Methods used for transforming raw data from one input domain space into another; a space of features.

Modular system   System consisting of several modules linked together for solving a given problem.

Monitoring   Process of interpretation of continuous input information to an information system, and recommending intervention if appropriate.

Moving averages   One of the theories used mainly for predicting stock market time-series. The theory says that by computing average values over periods of time the volatility of the time series is smoothed and the trends of the market are indicated. This is also a general method for time-series data processing.

Neural network   See **Artificial neural network**.

Noise   Any small random signal that is added to the function which describes the underlying behavior of a process.

Nonlinear dynamical system   A system whose next state on the time scale can be expressed by a nonlinear function from its previous time states.

Normalization   Moving the scale of raw data into a predefined scale, for example $[0, 1]$, or $[-1, 1]$, etc.

Optimization   Finding optimal values for parameters of an object or a system which minimize an objective (cost) function.

Oscillatory neuron   An artificial neuron built up of two elements (or two groups of elements), one of them being excitatory and the other inhibitory. Its functioning is described as *oscillation*, characterized by three parameters: *frequency*; *phase*; *amplitude*.

Overfitting   Phenomenon which indicates that a neural network has approximated, learned, too closely the data examples, which may contain noise in them, so that the network can not generalize well on new examples.

Pattern matching   Matching a feature vector, a pattern, with already existing ones and finding the best match.

Phase space of a chaotic process   The feature space where the process is traced over time.

Phonemes   Linguistic elements which define the smallest speech patterns that have linguistic representation in a langauge.

Planning   Important generic AI problem which is about generating a sequence of actions in order to achieve a given goal when a description of the current situation is available.

Power set of a fuzzy set   Set of all fuzzy subsets of a fuzzy set.

Prediction   Generating information for the possible future development of a process from data about its past and its present development.

Productions   Transformation rules applied to obtaining one sequence of characters from another, usually represented in the form of: IF <conditions>, THEN <actions>.

Production system   A symbolic AI system consisting of three main parts: (1) a list of facts, considered a working memory (the facts being called "working memory elements"); (2) a set of production rules, considered the production memory; (3) an inference engine, which is the reasoning procedure, the control mechanism.

Pruning   Technique based on gradual removing from a neural network the weak connections (which have weights around 0) and the neurons which are connected to them during the training procedure.

Queues   Data structures similar to the stack structure, but here two pointers are used—one for the input and one for the output element of the structure. They are also called FIFO structures (first input, first output).

Recall phase   Phase of using a trained neural network when new data are fed and results are calculated.

Recurrent fuzzy rule   A fuzzy rule that has as condition elements in its antecedent part one or more previous time-moment values of the output fuzzy variable.

Recurrent networks   Networks with feedback connections from neurons in one layer to neurons in a previous layer.

Reinforcement learning, or reward-penalty learning   A neural network training method based on presenting input vector $\mathbf{x}$ and looking at the output vector calculated by the network. If it is considered "good", then a "reward" is given to the network in the sense that the existing connection weights get increased, otherwise the network is "punished"; the connection weights, being considered as "not appropriately set," decrease.

Representation   Process of transforming existing problem knowledge into some known knowledge-engineering schemes in order to process it in a computer program by applying knowledge-engineering methods.

Sensitivity to initial conditions   A characteristic of a chaotic process in which a slight difference in the initial values of some parameters that characterize the chaotic process will result in quite different trends in its further development.

Spatio-temporal artificial neural networks   Artificial neural networks that represent patterns of activities which have some spatial distribution and appear at certain times.

Spurious states of attraction   Patterns in which an associative memory neural network can wrongly converge during a recall process. These patterns are not presented in the set of training examples.

Stability/plasticity dilemma   Ability of the ART neural networks to preserve the balance between retaining previously learned patterns and learning new patterns.

Stack   A collection of ordered elements and two operations which can be performed only over the element that is currently at the "top," that is, "push" an element on top of the stack, and "pop" an element from the stack.

Statistical analysis methods   Methods used for discovering the repetitiveness in data based on probability estimation.

Supervised training algorithm   Training of a neural network when the training examples comprise input vectors $\mathbf{x}$ and the desired output vectors $\mathbf{y}$; training is performed until the neural network "learns" to associate each input vector $\mathbf{x}$ with its corresponding and desired output vector $\mathbf{y}$.

Support of a fuzzy set A   Subset of the universe U, each element of which has a membership degree to A different from zero.

Test error   An error that is calculated when, after having trained a network with a set of training data, another set (test, validation, cross-validation), for which the results are also known, is applied through a recall procedure.

Time alignment   A process where a sequence of vectors recognized over time are aligned to represent a meaningful linguistic unit (phoneme, word).

Time-Delay neural network (TDNN)   Modification of a multilayer perceptron which uses delay elements to feed input data through. The input layer is a shift register with delay elements.

Time-series prediction   Prediction of time-series events.

Training error   See **apparent error**.

Training phase   A procedure of presenting training examples to a neural network and changing the network's connection weights according to a certain learning law.

Tree   Directed graph in which one of the nodes, called *root*, has no incoming arcs, but from which each node in the tree can be reached by exactly one path.

Unsupervised training algorithm   A training procedure in which only input vectors **x** are supplied to a neural network; the network learns some internal features of the whole set of all the input vectors presented to it.

Validation   Process of testing how good the solutions produced by a system are. The solutions are usually compared with the results obtained either by experts or by other systems.

Validation error   See **Test error**.

Variable binding   Substituting variables with possible values in an information system.

Vigilance   Parameter in the ART network which controls the degree of mismatch between the new patterns and the learned (stored) patterns which the system can tolerate.

Wavelets transformation   Nonlinear transformation which can represent slight changes of a signal within a chosen "window" from the time scale.

Index